Praise for *The Texas Rangers:*
Wearing the Cinco Peso, 1821–1900

"A richly detailed and sweeping historical narrative . . . This modern masterpiece does full justice to both the reality and the myth of the Texas Rangers—a great organization of which I was honored to be a part for twenty-seven years."

—H. Joaquin Jackson, Texas Ranger (Ret.),
and author of *One Ranger: A Memoir*

"*The Texas Rangers: Wearing the Cinco Peso, 1821–1900* is a masterpiece of inspired research, an enlightening and compelling saga about this unique American law enforcement institution. Cox writes with authority and candor about this historic and legendary 'band of brothers.'"

—Mike Cochran, award-winning journalist

Also by Mike Cox

Time of the Rangers

Volume II

From 1900 to the Present

Mike Cox

A Tom Doherty Associates Book

NEW YORK

TIME OF THE RANGERS: FROM 1900 TO THE PRESENT

Copyright © 2009 by Mike Cox

A Forge Book
Published by Tom Doherty Associates, LLC
175 Fifth Avenue
New York, NY 10010

www.tor-forge.com

Forge® is a registered trademark of Tom Doherty Associates, LLC.

The Library of Congress has catalogued the hardcover edition as follows:

Cox, Mike, 1948–
    Time of the rangers : Texas Rangers : from 1900 to the present / Mike Cox.—1st ed.
        p. cm.
    ISBN 978-0-7653-1815-2
    1. Texas Rangers—History—20th century. 2. Frontier and pioneer life—Texas.
3. Law enforcement—Texas—History—20th century. 4. Violence—Texas—History—
20th century. 5. Texas—History—1846–1950. 6. Texas—History—1951–. 7. Texas—
Race relations—History—20th century. I. Title.
    F391.C7837   2009
    363.28—dc22
                                                                    2009012870

ISBN 978-0-7653-2525-9 (trade paperback)

First Edition: August 2009
First Trade Paperback Edition: June 2010

0 9 8 7 6 5 4 3 2 1

For all my good friends, old and new

Acknowledgments

Many individuals—librarians, historians, friends—singled out in the acknowl-edgments included in the first volume of this history of the Texas Rangers, *The Texas Rangers: Wearing the Cinco Peso, 1821–1900,* helped with this book as well. To save a tree in their honor, I'll simply offer my thanks to all again.

The people I particularly want to recognize this time are the many readers of Volume One who took time to e-mail, write, or telephone me either to say how much they enjoyed the book or to offer suggestions for this second volume.

Too, though the extent of book reviewing appears to be on the decline as newspapers and magazines constrict in the face of the continuing growth of the Internet, I want to thank those who gave Volume One almost universally favor-able reviews. Professional writers ply their trade for money, but knowing that people like what you write is chocolate fudge on the ice cream.

Also deserving thanks are the independent and chain booksellers in Texas who stocked and became cheerleaders for this history of the Rangers, including my friend Felton Cochran of Cactus Books in San Angelo, bookseller Ron An-derson of Kerrville, who owns Main Street Books in Fredericksburg, Jean Hardy of Front Street Books in Alpine, and Jo Virgil, the community relations manager for one of the Barnes & Noble stores in my hometown of Austin, Texas.

Peace officers usually don't become historians, and vice versa. But an excep-tion is Glenn Willeford of Chihuahua City, Mexico, and Alpine, Texas. After a fifteen-year law enforcement career, Willeford returned to school and earned a master's degree in history from Sul Ross State University in Alpine. The two chapters on the Rangers and the Mexican Revolution benefited greatly from his scrutiny.

Another helpful reader was lay Ranger historian Sloan Rodgers, who also read and commented on Volume One. (Incidentally, in that book I had said Rodgers was a direct descendant of Revolutionary War ranger Robert Rogers. Sloan is related to him, but in a more roundabout way.)

No one can delve into the history of the Rangers and not spend a lot of time at the Texas State Library and Archives in Austin. As with Volume One, archivist Donaly Brice was always happy to help me. Also deserving recognition is John Anderson, the library's go-to person for photographs.

Numerous retired and current Texas Rangers also assisted me as I worked on this book. Retired Ranger captains Lefty Block, Bruce Casteel, Barry Caver, the late Bob Mitchell, Bob Prince, and Grady Sessums provided insight into the modern Rangers, as well as retired Rangers Joe Davis, Joaquin Jackson, Ramiro Martinez, and Al Mitchell. Among Rangers still wearing the *cinco peso,* Dave Duncan, Jess Malone, and others took time to answer questions and fill me in on certain cases and modern Ranger culture.

Tela Mange and Tom Vinger, former colleagues at the Texas Department of Public Safety Public Information Office (full disclosure: I hired them when I ran the office), provided requested information at various times as I worked on completing this second volume.

Finally, my wife, Linda, continued to keep the household running while I focused on this book, periodically reminding me as I fretted about something or another connected to it that I have had the same concerns with all of my books and that things always work out. Indeed, they do.

Contents

Preface

As a kid in the early-to-mid-1950s I seldom missed a weekly episode of the televised exploits of *The Lone Ranger*. To this day, hearing the *William Tell* Overture does not make me think of Switzerland or splitting apples with arrows but of the masked man with silver bullets in his six-shooter who rode with his faithful Indian companion, Tonto, to keep the West safe.

Clayton Moore's character was fictional, of course. But *The Lone Ranger* soon shared the airwaves with a reality-based TV show, *Tales of the Texas Rangers*. When that Saturday morning series had its TV debut (it began as a radio drama) on NBC in 1955, I quickly became a faithful viewer. I also read all the ten-cent Dell comic books produced to accompany the series.

In other words, like most male-born Baby Boomers, my first awareness of the Texas Rangers came via popular culture. That's why as a first-grader I found it particularly exciting when my mother told me that a real Ranger lived just across the street from us. I would not meet him in person until I was grown and his Ranger days had ended, but I remember seeing Ranger Doyle Currington's black state car parked in front of his house, his matching state-furnished horse trailer sitting in his yard ready for quick use. (Because we lived in an Austin suburban neighborhood, the Ranger had to keep his horse stabled elsewhere.)

The first Ranger I ever shook hands with was Jerome Preiss, who served in Company D under Captain A. Y. Allee in the Rio Grande Valley. Skinny, tall, and with a smile that covered his whole face, Preiss dropped by the 1964 Outdoor Writers of America convention in McAllen. My grandfather L. A. Wilke coordinated that year's gathering and had called on his friend Colonel Homer Garrison, director of the Texas Department of Public Safety, to have a Ranger show up to impress all the out-of-staters attending the convention. When Preiss took his horse (which he had brought for the kids to pet) to a nearby car wash to cool it down following his visit with the writers, the story made national news. Governor John Connally also made an appearance at the convention that summer, but I was more impressed by having met a Texas Ranger than getting the autograph of an elected official who had survived an assassination attempt in Dallas the year before.

While most of the post–World War II generation never learned much more about the Rangers than what they saw on those long-ago TV series, while growing up I heard interesting Ranger stories from my granddad. Later, I got to meet quite a few Rangers during the nearly two decades I spent as a newspaper reporter.

Switching to what the media sees as the dark side, in 1985 I got hired as a public information officer by the DPS, which includes the Rangers. For the next fifteen years, as a spokesman for the agency, I worked with the Rangers on many routine and not-so-routine cases, answering media questions and handling interviews about their activities.

About a year before I left the DPS in 2000, I decided to write a detailed modern history of the Rangers, something to replace the old standard, Dr. Walter Prescott Webb's 1935 book, *The Texas Rangers: A Century of Frontier Defense*. The research took much longer than anticipated, but the first volume, *The Texas Rangers: Wearing the Cinco Peso, 1821–1900*, finally hit the bookstores in March 2008.

This second volume picks up where I left off with the first book, at the turn of the twentieth century, and traces the evolution of the modern Rangers from horseback lawmen who eventually adapted to Model Ts to the men and women Rangers of the twenty-first century, their investigative abilities enhanced by an array of high-tech tools their predecessors could never have imagined.

Since my early understanding of the Rangers had been thoroughly influenced by popular culture, I have tried to relate their history in the context of their portrayal in literature and on the big and little screen. Another goal has been to separate reality from legend.

Writing a lengthy narrative history of an institution that still exists is something like shooting at a 70-mile-an-hour mourning dove—hard to do. Just as a dove does not stop flying the moment you pull the trigger, neither have the Rangers stood still. Texas may be a much safer place to live than it was during the time of the Comanches, but crime has not been totally eliminated and never will be. And the Rangers are still on the job, their modern story a moving target.

Since I completed this manuscript initially, the Rangers have increased materially in number, added the first new company since the 1950s, and played a major role in two criminal investigations that gained national news media attention. To make this second volume as inclusive as possible, these new developments and cases have been added to the final chapter of this book.

As I did with the first volume, I have tried to continue to relate the history of the Rangers through storytelling—hoping to neither glorify the force nor shy away from the low points in the organization's history. As a former journalist, I have aimed to keep this book as objective as possible. With apologies to actor-director Clint Eastwood, my modus operandi has been to relate the good, the bad, and the ugly of the Ranger story.

That said, I think the record shows that the Rangers have done far more good than harm over the course of their long history. But there have been some flagrant abuses of authority, blatant political involvement, and failures of leadership or integrity.

Still, thanks to the explosive growth of technology, an ongoing emphasis on professionalism, and a constant awareness of the tradition they must live up to, the Rangers endure as a highly effective arm of their parent organization, the Department of Public Safety. As Stephen F. Austin first envisioned in the early 1820s, the force continues to assist in the "common defense" of Texas, though the foe has changed.

As this book went to press, the DPS faced intense legislative scrutiny, but a consultant's report released by the Public Safety Commission in the fall of 2008 did not propose any significant changes for the Rangers. That's because no matter what the organizational chart shows, Texas still needs well-trained law enforcement officers with statewide authority.

To finish this preface where it started, it's interesting to look at how beginning in 1949 and continuing through the early 1950s Hollywood took the Ranger function beyond the Old West and past the modern day and well into the future with television shows such as *Captain Video and His Video Rangers, Rocky Jones, Space Ranger,* and *Rod Brown of the Rocket Rangers.* In these early science fiction dramas, a futuristic constabulary "ranged" the whole universe, continuing the timeless fight for law and order in the depths of space and on distant planets. The notion that it would take Rangers to tame alien creatures, while only the stuff of fiction, nevertheless shows the lasting mystique of the Texas Rangers. This is the rest of their story.

—MIKE COX
Austin, Texas
December 2008

Time of the Rangers

1

"Heroes of Old"

THE RANGER FORCE, 1900–1910

Sitting in a smoky meeting room of the opulent Oriental Hotel, the former Texas Ranger listened as the mayor's representative welcomed him and his fellow "Heroes of Old" to the thriving city of Dallas.

Four decades earlier, then only twenty years old, British-born Joseph Greaves Booth had helped protect the state from hostile Indians. Now, in the fall of 1900, Booth served as president of the Texas Rangers Association. Standing to address a hundred other men who had ridden for the Lone Star, the successful traveling salesman from Austin—also a veteran of the Confederate Army's Eighth Texas Cavalry regiment—looked out at an assemblage of graybeards who had spent many a night on the ground with only a sweaty saddle for a pillow. Many of them stove up and hard of hearing, on this day the old Rangers crowded a six-story hotel touted as "the most elegant . . . west of the Mississippi," a half-million-dollar redbrick building at Commerce and Akard streets finished with Italian marble and mahogany and capped with an arabesque dome. If they were of a mind to, men who had washed their dusty faces in creeks muddied by the hooves of thirsty horses could soak their aching bones in a Turkish bath, afterward enjoying a good cigar and a jigger or two of whiskey in one of the Oriental's several bars and dining rooms. But their greatest pleasure came in remembering their days as Rangers.

"Comrades, ladies and gentlemen," Booth began, looking toward the official greeter, "in behalf of the Texas Rangers, present and absent, living and dead, I desire to thank you for the welcome accorded us on this occasion. Of the old Texas Rangers but few are left. Time has done for them what the frontier savages failed to do through many years of bloody strife."

Seeing a young man from the *Morning News* scribbling away in the audience, Booth realized he spoke for posterity. He wanted a later generation to better understand the Rangers and what they did for Texas. His fellow old-timers already knew.

"The old Texas Rangers were not marauders or ruffians," he continued. "They were civilized, and in many cases highly educated, pioneers who were engaged in carving out the magnificent state of which we are all so proud, wresting her princely domain from bloodthirsty savages. Many of them were graduates of the best universities, and in intellect and integrity . . . not inferior to the best men left in the states from whence they came."

The Rangers of Booth's youth may not have been ruffians, but their enemies had known them as tenacious fighters. "They were always ready at any hour," Booth went on, "day or night, when warned by a courier to mount and ride to the place of rendezvous, in rain or shine, in the face of the blue norther, or under a blazing sun, and their motto was, 'No sleep until we catch the rascally redskins.'"

When Rangers took up a trail, he said, they armed themselves with "the best weapons the times afforded." For sustenance, they carried a bag of parched meal mixed with brown sugar and spice, strips of jerked meat, and a bottle-gourd of water tied on the horn of their saddle. Once they caught up with Indians, "there was no fighting at long range. Hostilities began whenever the white of the enemy's eye could be seen, and much of it was hand to hand."

Booth listed "a few of the historic names of old Texas Rangers," starting with his old lieutenant Ed Burleson Jr. All these years later, Booth lamented, only a few survived.

Then he said something that must have stuck in the craw of many of the former Rangers, not to mention those still in service to the state: "The necessity that gave birth to these heroic bands has disappeared with the men who composed them. The Texas Rangers of today have different duties to perform, which we believe can be more acceptably performed by the peace officers elected by the people."

Booth did allow that "along the upper Rio Grande a special police force may be required to protect the frontier against Mexican outlaws, but not elsewhere in the state."

No matter what seemed heresy to many, the members of the three-year-old association—an organization first envisioned by the late Ranger captain John Salmon "Rip" Ford—went on to reelect Booth as their leader, accept their historian's resignation, rename themselves the Texas Rangers' Battalion, and set Fort Worth as their next meeting place. Booth adjourned the proceedings and the old Rangers dispersed to mingle in the Oriental's lobbies for the rest of the morning, telling stories of "their adventure during their services on the border." That afternoon, they took the streetcars to the State Fair grounds, "saw the sights and attended the races."[1]

" 'Rangers' Have No Authority . . ."

At the beginning of the twentieth century, many other Texans also questioned a continuing need for the Rangers. Even the force's legal standing had come under attack.

The Rangers' latest problem centered on one of their own—A. L. (Lou) Saxon, a private in Captain William J. McDonald's company. After arresting some fence cutters during a stockman–farmer feud in Hall County the year before, Saxon had been charged with false imprisonment. Further, local citizens petitioned Governor Joseph D. Sayers to withdraw the Rangers from their county, which he did.

Company B moved from the Panhandle to a trouble spot at Athens in East Texas and then on to Orange, a rough lumber town on the Sabine River in the southeast corner of the state. Local officials, unable to cope with a wave of violence fostered by an ugly combination of partisan politics, labor issues, and racism, had petitioned the state for Rangers. In September 1899, the company made twenty-one arrests in Orange and would have effected one more if an offender had not pulled a knife on Private T. L. Fuller. In self-defense the Ranger shot and killed Oscar Poole, son of the Orange County judge. Fuller faced no charge in connection with the

clearly justified homicide, but a grand jury indicted him along with
Ranger Saxon for false imprisonment. Saxon had been accused of using
the barrel of his six-shooter on the heads of two drunks he took into custody. A local prosecutor based his case on his interpretation that the 1874
statute creating the Frontier Battalion, with which Fuller and Saxon
served, only gave officers the power of arrest. Because Fuller and Saxon
ranked as privates, the prosecutor contended that the arrests made by the
Rangers had been illegal. McDonald and his Rangers moved on to their
next assignment, the misdemeanor cases against two of his men lan-
guishing on the docket in Orange. But state officials found the argument
that Ranger privates could not make lawful arrests troubling.

Responding to a request for a formal opinion on the matter, Attorney
General Thomas S. Smith ruled on May 26, 1900, that only the battalion's commissioned officers had full police powers: "Non-commissioned
officers and privates . . . referred to as 'Rangers' have no authority . . . to
execute criminal process or make arrests."[2] At the time, the battalion
consisted of four companies. Suddenly, only four men—the company
captains—had the power to make arrests or serve court papers.

Quickly reacting to the attorney general's letter-of-the-law-versus-
spirit-of-the-law opinion, which in effect put the Rangers out of action,
Adjutant General Thomas Scurry on June 1 reorganized the Rangers into
six companies. Four companies would be made up of a captain, a first lieutenant, a second lieutenant, and three privates. The other two companies
would consist of one first lieutenant, one second lieutenant, and two privates. Each company would have to honorably discharge one private. Arrests had to be made by a commissioned officer, but privates could assist.

In addition, Scurry issued honorable discharges to all special Rangers,
ordering them to return their warrants of authority to his office. "The
governor is much pleased with the efficient service heretofore rendered
by the special rangers, and regrets the necessity of this order," he said.[3]
Within a month, Texas had a hundred fewer men it could call on for law
enforcement assistance.

In an attempt to further improve the force's image, Scurry also
stressed the importance of good conduct on the part of Rangers:

Company commanders will instruct their men to keep within the
bounds of discretion and the law under all circumstances, and

should there be any men now in the service who make unreasonable display of authority or use abusive language to or unnecessarily harsh treatment of those with whom they come in contact in the line of duty, or who are not courageous, discreet, honest or of temperate habits, they will be promptly discharged.

Next, with a stroke of Scurry's pen, six privates appeared on the muster rolls as first lieutenants, with five men upgraded to second lieutenants. The promotions came with one catch: The first lieutenants had to sign an agreement that they were willing to be paid the same as sergeants, $50 a month, and the second lieutenants had to settle for $30 a month, the pay they had drawn as privates. One of the men honored with a new title but no raise was Second Lieutenant (nee Private) Fuller.[4]

Annoying as the Rangers found the circumstances behind the reorganization, the Adjutant General's Department and the rest of the state's government soon faced a much greater problem. On September 8, a powerful hurricane swept over Galveston, the state's largest city. The resulting tidal surge claimed as many as eight thousand lives, the worst natural disaster in the nation's history. Scurry sent most of the state's militia to the devastated island city, but with the Rangers so thinly stretched he assigned only two men to prevent looting.[5]

Captain McDonald, Lieutenant Fuller, and Private Saxon returned to Orange on October 15 for Fuller's trial on the false imprisonment charge. McDonald had argued against going back to Orange, and his concern proved well founded. About 5:30 that afternoon, Saxon sat in a chair at Adams' Barbershop, getting a shave. Fuller stood in the center of the room, washing his face in a basin. As the barber glided his straight razor over Saxon's lathered face, someone appeared at the door of the shop, raised a Winchester rifle, and pulled the trigger. The bullet hit Fuller in the temple and he fell to the floor, his legs kicking involuntarily only a few seconds before he lay still in a spreading pool of blood. Still holding the rifle, the shooter ran to a butcher's shop next door. When local officers arrived a short time later, they arrested Tom Poole, the brother of the man Fuller had killed the year before.[6]

Fuller, with prior experience as a deputy sheriff, had enlisted in the Rangers "with the hope of saving sufficient money to finish his education in the University of Texas, having at that time just completed his freshman year. He was a young man of temperate habits, quiet in his manner and a fearless ranger."[7] Despite a number of witnesses, Poole avoided conviction in the slaying of the Ranger. As Albert Bigelow Paine later explained in his biography of McDonald, "The assassin was made chief deputy sheriff, as a reward, and in due time was himself killed by the city marshal, who, in turn, was killed by the dead man's family."[8]

In the South Texas town of Cotulla on October 24, another of Scurry's new lieutenants, Company E's Will L. Wright, tried to arrest James R. Davenport—an outlaw who had spent five years in prison on a murder conviction—for being drunk and firing a pistol in town. Davenport had been arrested for the same thing several times previously, but this time he resisted, drawing his pistol and shooting at the mild-mannered, bespectacled Ranger. The slug passed harmlessly through Wright's coat. The drunk outlaw did not get a second shot, crumpling to the ground with a .45 round in his chest. A little fire burned on his vest, sparked by the muzzle blast of Wright's six-shooter. This was not the first time Davenport had been shot by a Ranger—he had been wounded when arrested for murder in the 1880s in the Big Bend—but it would be the last time.[9]

Though Lieutenant Wright's attempted arrest of Davenport had been perfectly legal, the law creating the Frontier Battalion clearly needed fixing. At the conclusion of his 1899–1900 report, the adjutant general recommended that the next session of the legislature amend the existing statute so that all Rangers would have clear authority to make arrests. Given that "a number of criminal suits have been brought against privates in the ranger force for false imprisonment," he also requested that lawmakers legalize all arrests made prior to the date of Attorney General Smith's opinion.

"An Oil Geyser"

As Austin hotel, eatery, and saloon owners looked forward to the convening of the twenty-seventh legislature in January 1901, a new era began on a clear, cold morning fourteen miles south of Beaumont, a city of nine thousand near the Texas-Louisiana border. At 10:30 a.m. on the tenth day of the new year the earth shook as a stream of black oil shot into the sky from a drilling rig at a place called Spindletop. It took workers nine days to cap the spewing well, its flow estimated at one hundred thousand barrels a day. "An Oil Geyser" the Beaumont *Enterprise* proclaimed the next morning in large print for the times, adding: "Lubricating Fluid Spurts over 100 Feet into the Air." As with many epochal events, no one yet realized the full significance of what had happened. The "lubricating fluid" blowing out of the well would drive automobiles, airplanes, and a new economy. A second industrial revolution had begun with Texas as the fuel supplier.

As California had discovered during the 1849 gold rush, the prospect of quick riches draws people intent on cashing in, one way or another. Some pursue their fortunes honestly, while others prefer to make their money through illegal means. Texas suddenly had a new law enforcement problem along with a new industry. "In the twinkling of an eye," one observer later wrote, "Beaumont, the slow-moving, sawmill town . . . was converted into a seething, fighting, shouting mob of 15,000 money-mad adventurers." The chief of police, his department overwhelmed, advised citizens to walk in the middle of the streets after dark and "tote your guns . . . in your hands, so everybody can see you're loaded."[10]

While the upper Texas coast boomed on a discovery presaging the state's future, one of the issues facing lawmakers at the beginning of a new legislative session in Austin had to do with an institution rooted in the past, the Rangers.

"This body of men cannot be too highly commended for the manner in which they have discharged the many dangerous and delicate issues incident to their employment," Governor Sayers wrote in his January 10 message to the legislature. "Their services . . . have been invaluable, and may be regarded as an absolute necessity to the State." He urged members to invest rank-and-file Rangers "with such powers of arrest and detention as are conferred upon the officers [in the Frontier Battalion]." The governor warned that failure to "provide properly for the continuance of this force would involve the assumption of a responsibility which no one at all acquainted with prevailing conditions should care to assume."[11]

Four days later, Representative Ferguson Kyle of Hays County filed House Bill 52: "An Act to provide for the organization of a 'ranger force'. . . ." The same day, January 14, Senator William Ward Turney of El Paso introduced a companion bill in the upper chamber. After considerable wrangling over whether Rangers should be required to post

$1,000 bonds as a condition of service, the House approved by voice vote a new Ranger law minus the bonding provision on March 27, 1901. The Senate quickly passed the measure 23–3 and the governor signed the bill on March 29.[12]

The public and the press had long since stopped referring to the Frontier Battalion by its official name. Texans knew the organization as Rangers or often State Rangers. The new act took effect July 9, 1901, and the Frontier Battalion formally became the Ranger Force. The force's slightly amended responsibility now included "suppressing lawlessness and crime throughout the state" as well as its more traditional role of "protecting the frontier against marauding and thieving parties." The law still included the word *frontier*, but for the first time since the early 1870s, the enabling legislation designated the state lawmen as Rangers.[13] However, the language in the "Oath of Service" a new officer had to take before receiving his commission had not changed. It required, among the more traditional items, that Rangers "solemnly swear" that they had "not fought a duel with deadly weapons, nor . . . acted as second in carrying a challenge, or aided, advised, or assisted any person thus offending."

In addition, the new legislation authorized the Rangers four companies of up to twenty men each. The governor had authority to appoint the captains, who in turn selected their own men. As had been the case with the Frontier Battalion, an Austin-based quartermaster with the rank of captain would handle procurement of supplies and other administrative functions. Captains would earn $100 a month, sergeants $50, and privates $40.

Directly addressing the question of Ranger arrest authority, the statute left no ambiguity: "The officers, non-commissioned offers and privates of this force shall be clothed with all the powers of peace officers, and shall aid the regular civil authorities in the execution of the laws. They shall have authority to make arrests, and to execute process in criminal cases. . . ."[14] Not quite a month before the new Ranger law went on the books, in South Texas the Rangers participated in a sensational case demonstrating their continuing relevance.

"Ah, How Many Mounted Rangers . . ."

On the afternoon of June 12, 1901, Karnes County sheriff (and former Ranger) W. T. "Brack" Morris, one of his deputies and a county resident who spoke Spanish, rode in a surrey to the farm of twenty-five-year-old Gregorio Cortez. For several weeks the sheriff had been looking for some men—including Gregorio—suspected of stealing horses in Frio and Atascosa counties. A posse led by the sheriff of that county had followed a set of suspicious wagon and horse tracks into Karnes County, losing their quarry in the vicinity of Cortez's farm, about twelve miles west of Kenedy. Since then, the three stolen horses had been located at a ranch not far from Cortez's place.

Through his interpreter, Morris began questioning Cortez and his older brother Romaldo. Not satisfied with their answers, the sheriff told the translator to inform Gregorio he was under arrest. He asked why.

"For stealing horses," Morris said, the interpreter quickly repeating the sheriff's response in Spanish.

"No one can arrest me," Gregorio blurted in his native tongue.

At that, Romaldo lunged toward the sheriff. Dropping back, Morris pulled his pistol as Gregorio yanked a handgun from under his shirt. Shooting the charging Romaldo in the mouth, the sheriff swung his pistol toward Gregorio and fired again. The lawman missed, but Gregorio snapped off two rounds that hit Morris in his right arm and left shoulder. Enraged, Cortez ran to the downed sheriff and fired a third shot into his gut.

Leaving the sheriff and Romaldo moaning on the ground, Gregorio soon fled eastward on foot. Cornered by a large posse three days later on a ranch in Gonzales County, he shot and killed Sheriff Robert M. Glover, an old friend of Morris's. The landowner, Henry Schnabel, also died in the shoot-out, most likely from a stray shot fired by one of the posse members. Now mounted on a stolen horse, Cortez cut through the brush country to the southwest, heading for the Rio Grande. The manhunt continued another week, the last great horseback pursuit involving the Rangers. In traveling one hundred miles as the crow flies from Karnes County to Webb County, Cortez rode three times that far on a series of stolen horses, his trail winding like a rattlesnake's through the prickly pear, mesquite, cut barbed-wire fences, dry arroyos, and hills. Two sheriffs joining the Rangers and other posse members in the pursuit rode six horses to death in trailing the outlaw.[15]

Officers found Cortez asleep in a vacant ranch house near the border on June 22 and Captain John H. Rogers arrested him without incident. A modest, deeply religious man, the Laredo-based captain dismissed his role in the capture as minor and refused to claim any share of the reward money. "No especial credit is due to me for the capture," the captain told the *San Antonio Express*. "Somebody else would have got him if I hadn't." Convicted of murder, Cortez received a life sentence and a lasting place in South Texas folklore, the story of his long pursuit by the Rangers and other lawmen living on in border country *corridos*.

The balladeers sang:

"Then said Gregorio Cortez / With his pistol in his hand / 'Ah, how many mounted rangers / Against one lone Mexican!' "[16]

The October 1901 issue of *Frank Leslie's Popular Monthly*, a widely read national magazine, further enhanced the Rangers' image with its story by Earl Mayo, "The Texas Rangers: The Most Efficient Police Force in the World." The Rangers, Mayo wrote, had succeeded in driving the Indian, the rustler, and the bad man from Texas. "The success of the Frontier Battalion," he continued,

and the respect in which it is held from the Sabine to the Rio Grande is due partly to the method of its organization, but more to the calibre of its members, to their reckless courage, to their marvelous marksmanship and to the fact that they are not afraid to shoot. Keen of eye, inflexible in the pursuit of duty, and of unfailing nerve, the Ranger's shots seldom fail to find their goal. The laconic entry "killed while resisting arrest" or "killed while attempting to escape" appears often in the records of the Frontier Battalion.

"It is safe to say," Mayo concluded, "that nowhere else in the world can be found a body of men to equal the Rangers for sheer devotion to duty and fighting ability."[17]

In April 1902, not even a year after Rangers formally became Rangers, State Representative John Nance Garner of Uvalde urged abolition of the force. At that, the Seguin *Enterprise* let loose editorially on Garner with both barrels, claiming he "stood with the East Texas element that have been fighting the ranger force for the last twenty years."[18] This represented a turnaround by Garner, who earlier had asked for Ranger help with fence-cutting problems in his district. But by the time the salty lawmaker spoke out against the Rangers, he had a congressional race on his mind. Garner's notion to do away with the force did not go anywhere, but an incident in the Rio Grande Valley less than a month after the future vice president's proposal did nothing to enhance the force's standing with the Mexican-American population along the border.

Ordered to investigate the disappearance of several head of King Ranch cattle, Ranger sergeant A. Y. Baker, accompanied by two privates and a King Ranch cowboy named Jesse Miller, began scouting the adjacent seventeen-thousand-plus-acre El Sauz Ranch, in what was then Cameron County. On May 16, riding up on several unbranded calves tied to mesquite branches, Baker saw a man branding a dogie. The interrupted rustler dropped his red-hot running iron and pulled one of two six-shooters he wore, getting off a quick shot at the sergeant. Just at that moment, Baker's horse raised his head and the bullet entered the animal's left eye instead of the Ranger's chest. Baker fired his rifle at the same time, hitting the gunman in his forehead. The cow thief and Baker's horse both went down.

The Ranger recognized the dead man as Ramon de la Cerda. He came from a large family and had a lot of friends, some prominent in Brownsville. His death, as a Ranger who knew Baker later wrote, led to "a virtual state of war between the Rangers and the border bravos."[19]

The next engagement came about 10:00 p.m. on September 9 as Sergeant Baker, twenty-five-year-old Private Emmett Roebuck, and Miller rode along the Santa Rosalia Road toward their camp about a mile outside Brownsville. With their minds on getting some sleep after a long day, the three men walked their horses straight into an ambush. Hiding in the brush, five men armed with shotguns opened up on the lawmen.

The next morning, lying in a bed at the Miller Hotel with a flesh wound in his left hip from a buckshot round that barely missed his spine,

Baker described the ambush to a Brownsville *Daily Herald* reporter, who wrote:

> Baker and Miller wheeled at once and began firing. . . . Having emp-
> tied their pistols they rode rapidly on toward camp to get their Win-
> chester rifles. In their excitement they had not noticed that Roebuck
> took no part in shooting. . . . He still sat upright on his horse without
> uttering a word, and rode on with them, for about thirty yards, when
> his horse fell behind them. Just as they reached the pasture gate, they
> saw his horse come up riderless. . . . Securing their rifles and sending
> a messenger to town to notify the authorities, they hurried back and
> found poor Roebuck lying in the road, having fallen . . . about 150
> yards from the place where they were ambushed.

Captain J. A. Brooks and two other Rangers, along with Brownsville City Marshal Lawrence Bates (Baker's cousin) and numerous citizens, had rushed to the scene of the attack. The captain did not have much doubt as to the identity of the attackers. He had been warned by letter that a plot existed to kill Baker and Miller. Brooks's informant named Alfredo de la Cerda, the fifteen-year-old brother of the man Baker had killed that spring, as the one making the plan.

The captain asked Marshal Bates to send men to watch the residences of de la Cerda and two other men believed to have been involved in the ambush. Within a short time, de la Cerda and four other suspects occupied cells in the Cameron County jail. "The good citizens were very much enraged on account of the cowardly assassination of Private Roebuck," Brooks later reported, "and there was much talk of lynching the parties in jail, but myself and men felt it our duty to give them protection, and would have given our lives in their defense, although we were fully satisfied we had the parties who were responsible for the assassination of our comrade."[20]

On October 3, Baker ran into Alfredo de la Cerda, who along with the other defendants had been released on bail, at Tomas Fernandez's store near the corner of Thirteenth and Elizabeth streets in Brownsville. Baker later said that de la Cerda seemed to be reaching for a pistol. Others averred the young man had only been trying on a pair of gloves. Whatever the case, the Ranger did not await further developments, killing de la Cerda with his rifle. Some said Baker shot him in the back.[21]

Marcelo Garza Sr., described as "a respected businessman, one of Brownsville's most highly regarded citizens of Mexican descent," testified that de la Cerda had not been armed when Baker confronted him as he sat in the doorway of the store, talking to the owner. Garza said he saw the Ranger "stalking him [de la Cerda] like a wild animal." After killing him, the Ranger fled to a nearby saloon where he joined several of his Ranger colleagues. From there, using a back door, they retreated to the safety of the Fort Brown military reservation. When Captain Brooks arrived, he arrested Baker and charged him with murder.

Baker faced trial for the deaths of both brothers. Jurors concluded that each of the shootings had been in self-defense. Adjutant General Scurry, dispatched to the Valley by the governor to look into the situation, found no evidence that Baker had done anything but defend himself.

The year before, a grand jury had praised the Rangers for their work in the Valley. But to avoid further trouble, Scurry ordered Brooks's company relocated to Alice and moved Captain John R. Hughes in from his longtime duty station in El Paso County. Writing the governor to protest the transfer, District Judge Stanley Welch, who had tried the case, said: "All the ills of the De la Cerda killings have settled themselves, and I believe that with the aid of the Rangers under Captain Brooks, crime can be eliminated from Cameron County. The local officers cannot reach the outlaws."[22]

De la Cerda had been one of three criminals killed in engagements with Rangers from November 1, 1900, to August 31, 1902. During that period, the Rangers made 602 arrests, including 72 for either murder or assault to murder. They rode out on 748 scouts and covered 155,041 miles in their travels, averaging 7,047 miles a month.

"The fact that the rangers are kept on the move has a wonderfully deterrent influence over thieves," Scurry wrote in his 1901–1902 report, "who are unable to keep trace of them and constantly fear being surprised and captured by them." The general continued:

Many of the scouts made by the rangers are in pursuit of fugitives from justice, which requires hard riding, night and day. They are frequently thrown into positions which require good judgment, quick action and undoubted courage. They are frequently required to trail criminals, who are known to be without fear, desperate, and with a knowledge of the country as good as that of the ranger. To the credit of the force it can be said that they never refuse to face a danger when duty requires it. The moral effect of their presence in any disturbed district is well known.[23]

Scurry stepped down as adjutant general in January 1903 following the inauguration of a new governor, Samuel W. T. Lanham. The governor soon appointed someone with more military experience as Scurry's replacement. Born in Missouri but raised in Gainesville, Texas, thirty-one-year-old John Augustus Hulen had risen through the ranks in the state militia, receiving a promotion to brevet lieutenant colonel during the Spanish-American War. He fought Philippine insurrectionists in the jungles of Luzon from 1899 to 1901.[24]

The Spindletop oil boom sputtered for a time, but new discoveries in 1903 northwest of Beaumont in Hardin County proved that production in Southeast Texas would not be an anomaly. Crime also continued to be a serious problem as drilling expanded.

"Murders are becoming so frequent in Beaumont and vicinity they have ceased to excite more than ordinary interest," the Beaumont *Journal* editorialized in May 1903.[25] The city had eighty-one saloons, many with gambling rooms in the back and brothels upstairs.[26] But city and county officials had begun to sober up, realizing an economic windfall did not come without social consequences.

The following December, former governor James S. Hogg and business partner James Swayne of Fort Worth traveled by rail from Beaumont to Houston. Jointly the two men owned a large tract of land in the oil field. As the Southern Pacific train passed through Sour Lake, the men looked out the window at the oil wells and began discussing the growing problem of lawlessness in the area. Across from them sat Edward Arthur Sterling and his twelve-year-old son, William Warren.

"My father," Sterling later recalled,

stated that the local officers were both unwilling and unable to cope with the situation. I have never forgotten Governor Hogg's next statement. . . . Pointing his finger toward the new oil fields, he said in emphatic tones, "There is only one way to stop that lawlessness. If I were still governor, I would have Rangers in Batson before sundown tomorrow." When I get to Houston, I am going to wire Sam Lanham [the governor] and urge him to send them there.[27]

Hogg followed through. On January 20, 1904, he wrote J. S. Cullinan in Beaumont, founder of the Texas Company, to tell him that "the Governor has ordered Capt. Brooks of the Ranger force to go there [to Batson] to cooperate with the local officers. . . . He is a careful, capable officer from whom much good can be expected, in the performance of his duties."[28]

Arriving in Batson by train from South Texas, Brooks quickly came to the conclusion that "bad feeling" existed between local officers and oil-field workers. He informed both elements that he intended to keep the peace, predicting "it will only be a few days before they have it in for me."[29]

Hulen told Brooks to come to Austin to brief the governor on conditions in the new boom town. The captain left for the capital on January 28. After hearing his report, Lanham ordered him back to Batson "to protect life and property." When the captain returned to the boom town on February 7, he had three of his Rangers with him, Sergeant Winfred F. Bates and two privates. This marked the first Ranger deployment to tame an oil boom town.

The state lawmen spent their first night in what passed for a hotel, a hastily constructed structure of uncured pine, more barn than inn. That night, someone shot and killed a man "on his way home" from a hard day's work. The next day the Rangers got a tent, borrowed some cooking gear, and set up camp beneath a stand of pines just outside town. But they did not spend their time idling around a fire drinking coffee.

The night of February 8, one of the local roughs strapped on a pair of six-shooters and "went out to the west side and run some of the women out, fired off his pistol and caused some little stir." Brooks later reported to Hulen that he arrested the man "and I chained him up. There is no way of holding a prisoner here except to chain him with chain and lock. It is very unpleasant for one Ranger to be compelled to police a tough place like this." Hulen replied, "I will order as many Rangers to Batson as you request. I certainly do not want you to jeopardize your life." The captain quickly replied, "I just said it was unpleasant. I didn't ask for help."[30]

Batson did not have a jail or even a building sturdy enough to hold prisoners, so the Rangers continued Brooks's practice of chaining miscreants and felons to trees. Some days as many as a dozen men in varying moods and stages of sobriety sat under trees until they could be transferred to the county jail in Kountze. Eventually the more civic-minded elements got a jail built.

One of the crooks Brooks and his Rangers had to deal with wore a badge. The sheriff's deputy assigned to Batson not only collected a rake-off from the open sale of beer to oil-field workers; he also treated his prisoners cruelly. A big man, the dirty deputy made it known that the Rangers would not be long in town if they stuck their noses into his business. When the deputy started beating up a woman in one of Batson's many joints, the proprietor yelled for the Rangers. Sergeant Bates hoofed it to the bar. The damsel in distress might not have been much of a lady, but Bates saw no call for a peace officer beating her up. The Ranger ordered the deputy to leave her alone. At that, the beefy county lawman reached for his pistol. But before the deputy's pistol cleared leather, the barrel of Bates's .45 crashed down on the bully's head. When the deputy woke up, he found himself chained to a tree.

Newspapers in Beaumont and Houston made much of a 120-pound Ranger whipping a 220-pound deputy. Bates later said the story had been exaggerated. He actually weighed 125 pounds. The bantamweight sergeant clearly had no qualms about dispensing justice as he saw fit. When the Rangers arrested a pimp for roughing up one of his prostitutes, Bates tossed him in jail. That done, the Ranger sergeant had a quiet conversation with the only other prisoner in the lockup at the time, a semiprofessional bare-knuckles boxer with a weakness for booze. If the boxer cared to get in a few practice punches on the pimp, the Ranger whispered, he would see to his early release from jail for good behavior.[31]

Batson's law-abiding residents collected money for a "Card of Thanks" published in the Houston *Post* expressing their appreciation of "the Texas Rangers for their valuable services in maintaining order in Batson and especially to Captain Brooks . . . Before his arrival the town was in a constant turmoil, while now everything is peace and quiet. The bad man full of whiskey with his six-shooter has taken to the woods, but not until the captain has laid down the law." Brooks had a lot of friends in the Valley, where the Brownsville *Daily Herald* reprinted the notice on March 14.

In coping with the situation in Batson as they saw fit, the Rangers established a protocol for town taming that would stand as the standard operating procedure for the next three decades. "Their plan has never been improved upon," a later-generation Ranger who had used the model himself wrote in 1959. "Rangers first go in and handle any corrupt officers found preying on the working men. The next step is to round up the other criminals. Most of these usually depart on the heels of the deposed officials."[32]

Brooks and his men moved in and out of Batson through August 1904. In addition to their pacification efforts in the oil patch, they assisted local officers in Hempstead (a busy railroad town in Waller County and perennial trouble spot nicknamed "Six Shooter Junction") and scouted in Crockett, Dimmit, Kinney, La Salle, Pecos, Val Verde, and Webb counties—a huge expanse of territory. From September 1, 1902—eight days prior to the killing of Private Roebuck in the Valley—through August 31, 1904, Brooks's company traveled 47,834 miles.[33]

Though the days of Indian fighting in Texas were long gone, as were many of the old Rangers who had ridden after war parties, the state treasury in 1906 received $375,418.94 from Congress as repayment for frontier defense expenses incurred by the state from February 28, 1855, and June 21, 1860. Additional claims amounting to $204,476.72 for the cost of frontier defense from June 21, 1860, to March 4, 1861, remained pending.[34] Adjutant General Hulen spent ten pages in his 1906 report explaining this huge infusion of federal money—more than six times the Rangers' annual appropriation—but made no mention of what had been a very touchy situation regarding state–federal relations in Brownsville during the dog days of summer in 1906.[35]

Black troops had been stationed at Fort Brown in July, and as happened elsewhere in similar postings, racial friction developed. Following an incident in which a white woman reported that a black soldier pulled her by her hair, a curfew had been imposed on the fort's soldiers. Around midnight on the day the order took effect, a party of armed men shot up the center of the city, killing one person and wounding a policeman. Spent shells and clips from Springfield rifles pointed to soldiers as the offenders.

Captain McDonald happened to be in Dallas when the incident made the newspapers the following day. Though even the governor and the adjutant general considered the investigation of the incident a federal responsibility, the killing had occurred in the city of Brownsville, not on the military reservation. Fuming at what he perceived to be official inaction, the Ranger reached Brownsville on August 21. After gathering what amounted to little more than hearsay evidence, McDonald called on the fort's commander and demanded to interview the soldiers.

The captain also prevailed on District Judge Welch to issue arrest warrants for thirteen soldiers on charges of conspiracy to commit murder. On August 24, McDonald sent the warrants to Major Charles W. Penrose, but the post commander refused to turn over the troops. When the Ranger learned that the major had orders to ship the soldiers to Oklahoma Territory, McDonald marched to the railroad station and gave his own order: The train intended for the removal of the troops could not leave the city.

Local officials, envisioning mob action or a miniature Civil War between state Rangers and federal soldiers, agreed with the military's desire to get the soldiers out of town as quickly as possible. Judge Welch withdrew the warrants and threatened McDonald with contempt of court if he persisted in trying to arrest the soldiers.

"You are zealous, you are a good officer, and you think you are doing right," attorney and South Texas political boss Jim Wells told McDonald that night, "but if you attempt to interfere with those soldiers . . . this matter will break out anew and we will lose a great many lives here. You must remember our wives and children."[36]

Only a terse telegram from the governor got McDonald to back down: "Consult district judge and sheriff and act under and through them."

At 6:30 a.m. on August 25 the troops entrained for Fort Reno in Oklahoma. The dozen soldiers suspected in the shooting incident would be retained in San Antonio pending further investigation. President Theodore Roosevelt eventually ordered the entire unit dishonorably discharged from the army and the U.S. Senate held hearings on the matter, but the situation died down after the national elections.[37]

"It is possible," an army officer who investigated the incident later ventured, "McDonald might have fought the entire battalion with his four or five rangers were their obedience as blind as his obstinacy."[38] Perpetrators of the Ranger myth seized on the incident as the epitome of courage—a Ranger captain willing to take on a whole army. Others saw it as overt racism, even though at the time most Texans and even most Americans could be termed racists, at least by later definition. Though no less afraid of headlines than of anyone who stood in his way, McDonald had done what he thought right.

The wiry captain never seemed to lack an opinion or be reluctant to share it. The same year McDonald captured the public's attention with his bluster in Brownsville, a former Ranger captain, one of the original Frontier Battalion company leaders, decided to tell his story. Jeff Maltby paid a job printer in Colorado City to publish his recollections, *Captain Jeff, or Frontier Life in Texas with the Texas Rangers*. The softcover book, though self-serving and not well organized, nevertheless shed considerable light on how the early Rangers thought and fought. His posterity assured, two years later Maltby died of old age.[39] Publication of *Captain Jeff* also may have given Captain McDonald a notion to see his own story in print.

Detective Work

While Texans read of Maltby's Indian-fighting adventures, the new Rangers grew more sophisticated in their operations. They still hunted fugitives, corralled cattle rustlers, prevented lynchings, assured order in courts, cleaned up unruly towns, ran off crooked officers, and stood by during labor trouble, but they had begun to solve crimes through detective work.

One of the best examples of a Ranger role in a homicide investigation during this transitional period dated to September 28, 1905. Before dawn that morning, J. F. Conditt left his residence near Edna to work on a rice farm six miles away. That afternoon, seventeen-year-old Monk Gibson—a black teenager who had worked as a hired hand for Conditt— approached Conditt with bad news: His wife, Lora, and two of their children had been murdered. Jackson County officers intercepted the two on the way to the Conditt house and arrested Gibson for the murders. While he had told Conditt his wife and two children had been slain, officers had earlier found the woman and four of her five children slaughtered. Wielding an adz, someone had crushed the woman's skull. Her twelve-year-old daughter had been raped before her killer slashed her throat. Finally, Mrs. Conditt's three sons had been stabbed or beaten to death. Only her infant son survived, and he, too, had been beaten by someone who clearly left him for dead.

Two days after his arrest, Gibson escaped while being transported by two deputies to Hallettsville as a precaution against lynching. As deputies and scores of vengeance-minded vigilantes scoured the county for the suspect, National Guardsmen came to Edna on October 3 to prevent his lynching if apprehended. In addition to two companies of infantry and two troops of cavalry, General Hulen ordered two captains—Hughes and McDonald—and several of their men to the scene. After Gibson's recapture on October 9, the state troops and Rangers kept the suspect under protection until passions cooled. The Rangers also made "a careful investigation . . . of the premises where the murder was committed, and all the information possible regarding the matter obtained."

After studying the bloody crime scene, McDonald did not believe the teenager had acted alone. Local officers thoroughly grilled the youth—at one point the captain interceded to prevent Gibson from torture—but the suspect would not implicate anyone else. The captain arrested and put together a circumstantial case against Felix Powell— the man he suspected to be the other guilty party—but a grand jury would not indict him. The sheriff and most of the community believed that Gibson had acted alone. Powell went free.

A year later, after reinterviewing Powell and numerous others, Mc-Donald succeeded in getting him rearrested after finding traces of blood on his razor-sharp folding knife. The Ranger finally broke the case when he convinced Powell to place his hand on a piece of camphor-smoked paper. Though that print still did not match a bloody handprint found at the crime scene, the Ranger had a sudden inspiration. Giving Powell an object the same size as a folded knife, McDonald asked him to make another impression. "I saw that Felix Powell's hand with a knife in it, would fit the print left on . . . the walls, to a gnat's heel," the Ranger later said. "He [McDonald] deserves the gratitude of the entire public for his detective work," the Victoria *Weekly Advocate* said on December 15, 1906.[40]

"Have you any experience as a detective?" Victoria County Attorney J. V. Vandenberg asked McDonald at Powell's trial.

"I have about twenty years' experience," the captain replied confidently.

Convicted of murder, Powell hanged in Victoria on April 2, 1907. In a retrial, a jury convicted Gibson in Cuero, where the DeWitt County sheriff hanged him June 28, 1908. Captain McDonald attended both executions.[41]

". . . Constantly Ordered Out . . ."

Hardly a day passes without receiving in this department a request for the detail of one or more men on some very important duty that can not be complied with, owing to the very small force we now have [eighteen privates supervised by four sergeants and three captains]," Hulen reported.[42] Reflective of a new management philosophy, the general and his staff tracked Ranger movements with numbered pins stuck in a map at the Adjutant General's Department in the Capitol. Until Hulen took over as adjutant general, the bulk of the force had been concentrated along the border and in West Texas. Hulen, however, stationed Rangers "at different points where they are easily available in case their services are required in any part of the state."[43] Local officials in East and Southeast Texas called for Rangers more than they ever had, Hulen wrote, "and there is every indication of this condition continuing for some time to come."[44]

In August 1906 the San Antonio *Daily Express* published an article about the Rangers that read like a paid advertisement. Hulen clearly knew how to use the press to advance the image and needs of the force. "It is probable," the article concluded, "that an effort will be made to increase the Ranger service to its full quota of men at the next session of the Legislature." Clearly, that effort already had begun.

Captain Hughes's company had been moved to Austin, the newspaper reported, and "is in close touch at all hours of the day and night with the Adjutant General's Office. In case of emergency the members of this company can be sent to any part of the State immediately upon receipt of information that their services are needed."

Since their arrival in the capital, the captain and his men had been busy, Hughes "being constantly ordered out to some scene of trouble or threatened disturbance." The San Antonio newspaper continued: "His fearlessness and ability as an officer is recognized all over the State and his presence or that of any member of his company is of quieting effect whenever there is trouble at any place."

In East Texas, the community of Groveton soon found itself in need of Hughes's celebrated "quieting effect." The former Newton County attorney had complained to the governor about the conduct of the Ranger stationed there. Hughes traveled to Groveton and returned to the capital with the Ranger in tow for a face-to-face visit with the governor. Lanham told the Ranger that he would be reassigned but allowed him to stay in Groveton for a time to take care of his sick wife.[45]

New trouble soon broke out elsewhere. When someone assassinated District Judge Welch in Starr County in November 1906 prior to a hotly contested local election, Jim Wells wired the governor for Rangers. "Be sure and send Captain John R. Hughes and his company if at all possible, but do not think of sending anyone other than Captain Hughes or Captain Brooks. You will understand why it should either be Captain Hughes or Captain Brooks."[46] But the popular Captain Hughes—stern but diplomatic—could not be everywhere.

Governor Lanham sent the blustery Captain McDonald, then stationed at Alice. Soon the governor received a wire that someone had tried to kill the captain and his men as they approached Rio Grande City at a point on the old Military Road known as Casitas. The captain's new automatic rifle jammed after the first shot, but the other Rangers carried more reliable Model 1895 Winchesters. When the shooting stopped, four Mexicans lay dead, one had been wounded, and two nervously stood with their hands up. None of the Rangers sustained any wounds. "Well, I don't guess I missed any of them," McDonald later quipped.[47]

In the shoot-out that followed Welch's assassination, the Rangers had done better with their older lever-action rifles than McDonald had with a state-of-the-art weapon. Hulen did not quibble over weaponry, but he believed the Rangers needed a more up-to-date authorization statute. "The law under which this force is maintained is antiquated, and should be materially revised," he wrote in his annual report for 1906. Hulen also urged that the force be enlarged. "There is enough work, that by all means should be done, to employ from 75 to 100 officers and men continually. . . . The officers should be better paid, more especially the men, and the State should mount and equip them."[48]

The Rangers may have been low paid, but they could still resolve a dangerous situation. In December 1906, Ed Putnam, who had killed two men in the process of stealing and selling a herd of sheep, took a family hostage in their house when Rangers cornered him in Del Rio. The hostages escaped, but Putnam engaged Captain Rogers and two of his men in an hour-long shoot-out. Putnam ran from window to window, firing at the Rangers any time he could. Between them, the fugitive and the Rangers fired some three hundred rounds during the gun battle, which went on for nearly an hour. Rookie Ranger Frank Hamer finally ended the standoff with a rifle bullet to Putnam's heart. Six feet three inches tall, Hamer could roll a tin can with his .45 at one hundred yards and already had a deserved reputation for fearlessness.[49]

Earlier that year, the San Antonio *Daily Express* had published a photograph of four Ranger captains, a Ranger private, and a former Ranger taken at a meeting in Austin. "The accompanying photograph is by many said to represent the most effective 'fighting machine' that was ever thrown into action for the defense of Texas," the caption read. Shown were Brooks, McDonald, Rogers, L. P. Sieker, and [private] T. A. Weed [sic] along with former Ranger Lieutenant John B. Armstrong, men "whose valor and glorious deeds are old in song and story." The cutline writer went on to say: "Every one of them has demonstrated not only his courage, but his remarkable capacity for successfully extricating himself and those for whose protection he fought from menacing situations, in other words, each has proved his heroism and generalship under testing circumstances."[50]

The "fighting machine" soon lost two of its most talented leaders. Brooks—the only tarnish on his image being a reputation as a hard drinker—resigned in November 1906 after twenty-four years of service, followed in January 1907 by McDonald, who after seventeen years with the Rangers took an appointment as state revenue agent. With two of the state's most experienced Ranger commanders gone, the job of maintaining the effectiveness of the Rangers went to James Oscar Newton, a career citizen-soldier who had been in the state militia since 1893. Newly inaugurated governor Thomas M. Campbell promoted the thirty-one-year-old Milam County native from lieutenant colonel to adjutant general on January 23, 1907.[51]

That month, with the legislature in session, a man named Taylor Thompson wrote a long letter to the Houston *Chronicle* suggesting how the state could save $40,000 to $50,000 a year: abolish the "so-called" Rangers. "In the first place," he began,

> the name as applied to the present force is a misnomer; the so-called Rangers of today are merely state police, and are wholly unnecessary to a proper enforcement of the law. In fact, there are probably few sheriffs or other peace officers that would not rejoice to see this state police force done away with. . . . It is a shame that the deathless name won by the old-time Texas Ranger should be borne by mere policemen.

While praising nineteenth-century Rangers such as Jack Hays and Rip Ford, the letter writer said the Rangers of 1907 "do their scouting in railroad trains and on hired or borrowed horses, and their bivouac is made in . . . hotels and boarding houses."

Thompson scored McDonald for patronizing a health resort at Mineral Wells and for his handling of the investigation into the murder of Judge Welch. McDonald added a clipping of Thompson's letter to his scrapbook, but while he must have fumed at Thompson's comments, as his fellow East Texans like to say, he no longer had a dog in the hunt. Thompson continued:

> The dispatches announced next day that the Rangers had been ambushed by Mexicans and fired on, that the Rangers returned the fire, killing four Mexicans and wounding two. Not a Ranger was hurt, though the Mexicans got in the first shot. It transpired later that the Mexicans were drunk, were in a hack returning from a *baile* [dance], and the four men were killed and two wounded while in the hack. I have heard and read of many ambushes and have seen a few, but I never heard of men going out in a hack, while drunk, to ambush anybody. The public knows as much of this "ambush" as it ever will, and many another Mexican who were quiet, inoffensive men,

have looked up to heaven with staring, glassy eyes, down on the lower Rio Grande, about whose death the public never knew anything save that they were killed by Rangers.

When Rangers ventured to Central or East Texas, the letter writer continued, "we have heard of no 'ambushes' and no men have been killed. If any Americans had been done to death somebody would have been held to answer."

Thompson's final word: "Abolish the state police, yclept [named] Rangers, and save the money paid them."[52]

In Groveton on April 26, 1907, former Newton County Attorney R. O. Kinley fired a load of buckshot at Ranger J. D. Dunaway and the incumbent county attorney. The former county attorney died, and the Ranger had six pieces of lead in him. Calling for paper and pencil, the bleeding Ranger scribbled a message to be wired to the adjutant general: "I am shot all to pieces. Everything quiet." The Ranger survived.[53]

Given the strong public sentiment in Groveton, the district judge moved Kinley's trial to Houston on a change-of-venue motion. In town to testify in the case, the beginnings of which went back to when Dunaway served under him, McDonald granted an interview to a reporter for the Houston *Post*. The journalist left the Rice Hotel with a scoop of sorts—the captain would be "writ up" by noted New York writer and war correspondent Jim Creelman in the "August number of one of the leading magazines." The Ranger's story, related during a two-week interview session in New York, would be serialized in the magazine and then published in book form. McDonald said he had been approached many times to tell his story but "would never entertain such a proposition while connected with the ranger service of the state."

The *Post* writer went on to gush that there "is no denying that Captain McDonald is one of the most picturesque characters in the United States, and his experience as a member of the Texas ranger force was one that is probably without a parallel in the . . . history of the country."

The veteran lawman, the writer continued, "can sit down any time and spin a yarn from memory that will make the heart of a New York newspaper man glad and it is said that his scrap books are filled with scores of blood curdling tales of daring reflecting incidents in various sections of the border country in Texas in which he was the principal actor. Some of these stories have received additional embellishments as they are repeated, but the facts are there."[54]

Despite all the controversy involving the Rangers, when the presiding officers of the legislature gaveled the 1907 regular session to an end the force still existed. Lawmakers had, however, cut its appropriation. With the nation's economy still trying to recover from the financial panic of 1906, the drop in funding may not have been totally political, but it only stretched the Rangers thinner. As Adjutant General Newton noted in his 1908 report, "The force should be increased to at least fifty officers and men." He also recommended that Ranger pay be increased:

This would hold the experienced men in the service. The present rate of pay is not sufficient to hold good men without their making personal sacrifices, which they are doing for the love of the service. Several good men have left . . . to accept more lucrative positions in civil life, and most of them have been given these positions because of their records as Rangers. Hardly a man who has been in the service six months has not been offered better paying positions in civil life.[55]

Despite the perennial reluctance on the part of Texas lawmakers to hire more Rangers or provide them better salaries, most Texans still paid them homage orally and in writing. In January 1908, Katie Daffan, president of the Texas Women's Press Association and the Texas division of the United Daughters of the Confederacy, wrapped up a book for Texas grade-school children, *Texas Hero Stories*. Dedicated to her father, the red hardback contained twelve chapters, including "The Rangers on the Plains." Her writing as flowery as a patch of bluebonnets, Daffan offered a general history of the Rangers. But the chapter read more like an adoring tribute to the Ranger, whom she called "nature's nobleman," than history text.

After explaining chivalry and knighthood, Daffan wrote:

Medieval knight-errantry is surpassed by the romantic, picturesque ranger, who is secure in history, song and story, and because of his grasp and performance of duty Texas may challenge all other states in adventure, encounter, personal bravery and sacrifice, and the ranger is one of the chief factors in making our history a classic.[56]

For the benefit of her young readers, Daffan noted that Rangers "are those men who protected the Texas frontier from the Indians and the Mexicans who haunted every stump and tree, and they held, safe and secure, the early Texas homes from bandits and desperadoes . . . [giving] police protection to men, women and children."

Rangers still protected Texans. Twenty-seven-year-old Ranger Homer White suffered a fatal gunshot on February 4, 1908, in Weatherford "while attempting to arrest a man . . . abusing a woman at the railway station."[57]

Daffan went on in her book to set down the Ranger myth for another generation of young Texans:

Free as the unchained winds that sweep the boundless prairie, he was a terror to the incarnate Mexican Devils, a sworn foe to the Indians, who with torch, tomahawk and blood-freezing war whoop terrified helpless women and children; the ranger, characteristic exponent of the Anglo-Saxon race, drove every enemy away from him and established peace and contentment.[58]

Plenty of farm-raised boys and girls may not have known what *exponent* meant, but Daffan had made her point. She and most other Texans viewed Rangers as heroes. Daffan's book got good exposure in Texas, but another book soon gave readers across the nation an opportunity to learn much more about the Rangers.

Though McDonald had talked with Jim Creelman about doing a book on his life, Albert Bigelow Paine, biographer of Mark Twain, ended up taking on the project. Published on March 1, 1909, *Captain Bill McDonald Texas Ranger: A Story of Frontier Reform* appeared first as a serial installment in *Pearson's Magazine*. "Taken as a whole," one newspaper said of Paine's book, "the events recorded . . . constitute a tale as marvelous as any fiction, stirring and intensely interesting from beginning to end. No man can read it without feeling his blood quicken, or without being stimulated to nobler achievement."[59]

Puffery aside, the book would have considerable influence in the perpetuation of Ranger mythology, including the first appearance of what evolved as the prime Ranger anecdote—the "one Ranger, one riot" story. As Paine wrote:

> It is told of him [McDonald] in Dallas how once he came to that city in response to a dispatch for a company of Rangers . . . to put down an impending prize-fight.
>
> "Where are the others?" asked the disappointed Mayor, who met him at the depot.
>
> "Hell! Ain't I enough?" was the response. "There's only one prize-fight!"[60]

The book also credits McDonald as uttering the phrase that became the Ranger creed: "No man in the wrong can stand up against a fellow that's in the right and keeps on a-comin'."[61]

Despite all the positive publicity the Rangers received in the press and popular culture, some still clamored for their dismantling. "Outlaws Wish Texas to Disband Rangers" read the headline of a story in the Los Angeles *Times* on January 10, 1909. A special correspondent from Austin noted that when the legislature convened "an attempt will be made . . . to abolish the military organization known as the Texas Rangers."

The article continued:

> This little body of dare-devil peace officers and gunfighters has incurred the bitter enmity of the people in some localities of the state where . . . the members have had to conduct their operations. In many counties where the sheriff failed to do his duty, the rangers stepped in and enforced the law without fear or favor. The opposition to them and the movement for their abolishment . . . comes mainly from disgruntled sheriffs, it is claimed.

Adjutant General Newton, however, saw the Rangers as an "indispensable adjunct to the State Militia." In his last biennial report, he noted the force had only twenty-seven men but needed at least a hundred Rangers to handle all the requests for assistance the department received. Those twenty-seven Rangers, Newton said, had in the previous year made 1,017 arrests, 458 for felonies. Mostly by rail and horse, Rangers had traveled 277,371 miles in attending to their duties.

". . . WE ARE NOT BLACKGUARDS . . ."

Numbers could not measure moral authority. While not all Rangers attended church every Sunday or abstained from alcohol, men such as Captain Hughes had a strong vision of right and wrong. Once, when someone the Austin correspondent described only as a "tenderfoot" visited Hughes's company at Ysleta, the captain welcomed the man warmly only to boot him from camp when he started using profanity and telling bawdy stories.

"I thought I was welcome," the man protested.

"You were, as long as you used decent language," the captain replied.

"I thought you were Rangers," the visitor continued.

"We are," Hughes answered, "but we are not blackguards."[62]

With Governor Campbell about to leave office after two terms, General Newton stepped down in December 1910. Robert H. Beckham, a Spanish-American War veteran, took over as interim adjutant general on December 15 pending the inauguration of the new governor, Oscar Branch Colquitt.[63]

The vagaries of politics had no impact on fictional rangers. English-born William MacLeod Raine, a former member of the Arizona Rangers (a mounted police force modeled after the Texas Rangers) turned Western yarn spinner, wrote the century's first piece of contemporary Ranger fiction, a novel called *A Texas Ranger*. Published in 1910, the book started out like a Western set in the previous century, but its modern setting became evident by the beginning of the third chapter when Ranger lieutenant Steve Fraser and a fellow traveler ride up on "a telephone-line which stretched across the desert and joined two outposts of civilization." The Ranger "strapped on his climbing spurs" and went up a pole with his "test outfit." Soon, Raine continued, the Ranger "had Moreno on the wire and was in touch with one of his rangers."[64] As the book's jacket copy touted, the story told "how a member of the most dauntless border police force ever known to the world carried law into the mesquite, saved the life of an innocent man after a series of thrilling adventures, followed a fugitive to Wyoming, and then passed through deadly peril to ultimate happiness." (The Ranger got the girl, naturally.) Though Raine set his novel in Texas, the landscape and story details clearly drew inspiration from his experiences in Arizona, where he wrote the book. Still, for some reason he seemed to think it more important to have his book be about the Texas Rangers than the Arizona Rangers. The novel would stay in print for years.

The same year Raine's book came out, the Rangers broke into a new medium—film. The first known motion picture dealing with the Rangers, *Ranger's Bride*, flickered across American theater screens in 1910. The silent film starred Gilbert M. "Bronco Billy" Anderson, the world's first Western star.[65]

With the back-to-back books by Paine and Raine and the expansion of the Western fiction genre to the nascent motion picture industry, the status of the Rangers as an American icon had been further solidified.[66]

2

Los Rinches

REVOLUTION IN MEXICO, 1910–1915

Cecilia Almaguer Rendon never forgot the night the Rangers came to her family's farm outside Brownsville.

Los rinches woke them about 2:30 a.m., dragging her twenty-one-year-old cousin from bed. Wearing only underwear, Encarnacion Garza stood handcuffed in the glare of the Rangers' car headlights as the men searched the house. Whether the lawmen seized anything they considered incriminating Rendon never knew. All she saw them leave with were freshly made tortillas and *pan dulce,* pastries her mother baked, and her barefoot cousin, whom they figured for a bandit.

The men with the big hats and guns drove Garza to a nearby *camposanto* (cemetery), stood him in front of one of the crosses, and shot him. "We heard the [shots]," Rendon recalled. "They left him laying there. . . . Poor cousin . . . , he had fallen right on my grandfather's grave, although the '*rinches*' didn't know that. . . . We just wrapped him in a sheet and a blanket, dug a deep grave, and put him in it."[1]

The decade-long Mexican Revolution filled thousands of graves along the Texas-Mexican border in the early twentieth century. While some Mexican nationals and their sympathizers in Texas violently pursued their cause, most Mexican-Americans, innocents like Rendon and her family, could do nothing more than "pray to God that *'los rinches'* go away."[2]

Texas officials and most citizens—at least the Anglos—saw the situation differently. "The work of the Ranger force from inception of the border troubles up to the time the Federal government had an adequate force to deal with the situation was of the highest order and worthy of the best traditions of the Ranger force," the Adjutant General's Department reported.[3]

When forty-nine-year-old Oscar Branch Colquitt, a Georgia-born newspaperman turned politician, ran for governor in 1910, he told Texans he believed the Rangers—already much smaller in size than reputation—had outlived their usefulness.[4] Despite Colquitt's belief that local officers could handle law enforcement in the state, during the campaign he spent most of his time giving speeches opposing Prohibition, then the hottest issue in local and state politics. While Texas did not need the Rangers, the "wet" candidate argued, it definitely needed lower taxes and less government. But when growing unrest south of the border erupted into violence in the fall of 1910, bullets soon posed a far more serious threat to Texas than "wet" versus "dry" issues or the size of state government.

The trouble on the other side of the Rio Grande had begun during the administration of Colquitt's predecessor, Governor Campbell. Mexican president Porfirio Díaz—a man who had ruled with an iron hand since 1877—allowed a presidential election because it looked democratic, but the eighty-year-old dictator had no intention of leaving office. However, when reform-minded opponent Francisco I. Madero, the intellectual son of a wealthy Coahuila landowner, seemed to be making inroads on the incumbent, the upstart candidate found himself in prison. Bailed out by his family, Madero on October 5, 1910, left San Luis Potosí for Texas, where he began fomenting revolution. From San Antonio he soon issued a proclamation urging the Mexican people to remove Díaz from power.[5]

Anti-Díaz and anti-American demonstrations broke out in Mexico City and elsewhere in the country beginning November 10. The protests came in reaction to news that a Mexican national, Antonio Rodriguez, accused and probably culpable of killing a Texas rancher's wife in Edwards County, had been burned at the stake in Rocksprings on November 3, but the demonstrations also reflected the growing unrest of many Mexican citizens. The following day, much closer to Rocksprings, an angry crowd hurled stones at the U.S. Consulate in Ciudad Porfirio Díaz (later renamed Piedras Negras), across the river from Eagle Pass. "It is not believed that the demonstration has anything to do with the Mexico City outbreak," the Eagle Pass newspaper opined.[6] "All Quiet on the Rio Grande," the Eagle Pass *News-Guide* declared in its next edition. "Recent disturbances in Mexico," the newspaper continued, "have really existed mainly in the minds of sensational newspaper men in both countries."[7]

Even so, outgoing Governor Campbell ordered his Ranger captains to assess the situation on the border. Captain Hughes took the train from El Paso to Marfa, continuing down into the rugged Big Bend on November 26. In Presidio, the captain found nervous Texans arming themselves in anticipation of spillover violence, but nothing had happened yet.[8]

Captain Rogers reached the same conclusion after visiting Laredo. "All was quiet," the Eagle Pass *News-Guide* reported, "and there is no longer any necessity for [the Rangers] to stay on the border. However, they may return to assist in the search for Madero [for violating U.S. neutrality statutes], whom many [believe] to be in Texas."[9]

The crack of rifle fire shattered the uneasy calm December 15, 1910, when Madero's *insurrectos* engaged Díaz's soldiers four miles upriver from Ojinaga, the Mexican town opposite Presidio. Captain Hughes and the county sheriff had watched the maneuvering of Mexican troops from a rooftop on the Texas side. Two days later, with Mexican refugees streaming across the river, the Marfa *New Era* called for more state protection along the border.[10]

Downriver, Eagle Pass *News-Guide* editor Joseph O. Boehmer with obvious relish reprinted a clipping from the November 28 Middleton, New York, *Daily Times Press*. Crediting the information to "a well known citizen who has lately returned from the western borders of Texas," the story said Eagle Pass lay at the center of the revolution. Texans, however, could rest easy as long as the Rangers rode the river:

> That portion of Texas bordering on the Rio Grande . . . is being
> guarded from the invasion of the Mexican revolutionists by the

grandest, bravest body of horsemen ever assembled under the stars and stripes or flag of any country, viz: the Texas rangers. They are in a measure similar to the Pennsylvania constabulary or the mounted police of Canada, all young, alert, brawny, keen-eyed Texans and frontiersmen, quick on the trigger, can shoot from the hip, swing the lasso and are unequaled horsemen, superior in fact to the Cossacks of Russia. They are the brave defenders of the "Lone Star State."

Calling the story "the most magnificent lie about Eagle Pass it has ever been our pleasure to read," Boehmer continued:

Naturally we would like to see one of those magnificent Texas rangers. We have lived here some twenty years and nary a dad-burned Texas ranger have we seen in Eagle Pass yet.[11]

Shortly after Colquitt's January 17, 1911, inauguration, Captain Hughes traveled to Austin to discuss the situation along the upper border with the new governor. After the meeting, the well-respected fifty-six-year-old Ranger told journalists that Texas and the United States would maintain strict neutrality along the border.[12] On February 11, Colquitt issued a three-page proclamation urging "every citizen of Texas in good faith to strictly observe the [U.S.] neutrality laws, and refrain from encouraging, aiding, abetting or participating in any manner in violating either the letter or spirit of same."[13]

Rangers, however, would have to do their part in upholding neutrality with fewer men. Acting on his campaign rhetoric, Colquitt eliminated one of the three Ranger companies, leaving the force with only two authorized captaincies, two sergeants, and nine privates—a total of thirteen Rangers for a state with a population approaching four million. Not only had the Rangers reached an all-time manpower low, but the force lost half its senior leadership with the January 29 resignation of Captain Rogers to accept appointment as a deputy U.S. marshal. The governor demoted the man who had been the third captain, M. E. Bailey, to sergeant and hired former Caldwell County sheriff John J. Sanders as captain of Company B to replace Rogers. About Hughes's age, Sanders stood six-two and had a reputation for no-nonsense law enforcement.

Colquitt completed his Ranger leadership team with the appointment of English-born Henry Hutchings as adjutant general. Like the governor, the forty-five-year-old Hutchings had a newspaper background. In 1890 he had established the Austin *Evening News,* later becoming publisher of the Austin *Statesman.* Joining the state militia soon after moving to Texas from Iowa in 1885, now he commanded Texas's militia as well as its small Ranger force.[14]

A month after the Ranger cutback, the *Texas Magazine* opined that the border situation would "go far toward stemming a movement which has been on foot [sic] for some time to disband the Ranger organization." Those wanting to abolish the Rangers, the magazine continued, centered their case on the fact that with no frontier to protect, "they are now used chiefly to perform the duties that properly belong to the peace officers of the different counties, such as enforcing the local option law, the law against gambling, and in preventing mob violence."

The other side of the argument held that the Rangers remained useful "because they can be sent by the Governor at any time and to any place in the State where the county peace officers, on account of local conditions or influences, or through a spirit of indifference, are known to be lax in enforcing the law." The magazine predicted that "sentimentality and a pride in the many wonderful deeds of valor of the Rangers may defeat the present movement."[15]

Harsh reality also had a lot to do with keeping a Ranger force afield. By March 2, 1911, rebel fighters held Mexican federal forces under siege in Ojinaga. U.S. troops embarked from trains at Marfa and marched to the border to make sure the fighting did not spill over into Texas. At Ciudad Juárez, across from El Paso, rebels attacked the Díaz garrison at 10:30 a.m. on May 8. Errant rifle bullets whizzing across the Rio Grande killed five U.S. citizens and wounded sixteen.

"We are all . . . watching the fight at Juarez," Hughes said in a telegram to Hutchings. "Wish you and all the force could be here to enjoy the Fun." The veteran captain took in the action in his official capacity as the ranking state official in El Paso, but with local retailers doing a brisk business in field glasses, many other residents cheerfully paid a dollar for access to rooftops affording a view across the Rio Grande. "Stay away from the danger zone," the A. D. Foster Company advertised in the city's two daily newspapers, "but See Everything Across the

River Today" by taking advantage of low prices on "field glasses . . . of the finest foreign make." Under the watchful eyes of Hughes and thousands of other El Pasoans, the Battle of Juárez ended two days later with Madero's soldiers in control. The *insurrectos* had killed as many as a hundred federal troops while losing only fifteen of their own in taking the city, which Madero quickly proclaimed Mexico's provisional capital. As Madero struggled to return Juárez to some sense of normalcy, in El Paso the Hotel Taxi Cab and Auto Company offered round-trip tours of the battle-scarred city across the river starting at fifty cents.[16]

Díaz's Ojinaga garrison had held for two months, but during the night of May 10 the federals withdrew for Chihuahua City, farther in the interior. Fifteen days later, faced with similar defeats elsewhere in his country, Díaz resigned and fled to Europe with his wife and former vice president. The crisis seemingly over, U.S. troops returned to their garrisons and Texans along the border felt more at ease.[17]

Even so, the revolution had changed Colquitt's mind about the Rangers. The governor traveled to Hutchinson, Kansas, to discuss border issues with President William Howard Taft on September 26. Touting the usefulness of the force along the Rio Grande, Colquitt made the familiar Texas pitch for federal monetary assistance. As General Hutchings wrote, the "representations . . . to the President as to the value of the services the ranger force could render during the unsettled conditions on the border, so appealed to the President that he agreed to recommend to Congress the reimbursement to the State of the extra expenses involved."[18] Back in Texas, Colquitt called for what Hutchings later termed a "reorganization" of the Rangers. A better word would have been *buildup*, the governor's campaign position made moot by circumstances beyond his control. With the promise of federal money, Colquitt reinstituted a third Ranger company and increased the force to forty-two Rangers.

NEW ENABLING LEGISLATION

A legislative act reconstituting the Rangers became law October 1, 1911. As in previous enabling legislation, the governor retained authority "to organize a force . . . for the purpose of protecting the frontier against marauding or thieving parties, and for the suppression of lawlessness and crime throughout the state." The size of that force was "not to exceed four companies of mounted men, each company to consist of not to exceed one captain, one first sergeant and twenty privates." Captains would be appointed by the governor to two-year terms "unless sooner . . . removed by the Governor."[19]

With the federal money promised by President Taft, Colquitt appointed two more captains on October 5, J. Monroe Fox and William Smith. Of the two, the heavyset, baby-faced Fox, a forty-five-year-old Austin cop, would become the best known.[20]

Under the new Ranger statute, Fox and the other men still had to furnish their horses, but the state would pay "at a fair market value" for any mount killed. The state also would provide "one improved carbine [a .30-caliber Model 1895 Winchester] and pistol at cost, the price of which shall be deducted from the first money due such officer or man." In addition, the state furnished food, forage, camp equipment, and ammunition. The legislation even prescribed each Ranger's daily food allowance:

Twelve ounces of bacon or twenty ounces of beef, twenty ounces of flour or corn meal, two and two-fifths ounces of beans or peas, one and three fifths ounces of rice, three and one-fifth ounces of coffee, three and one-fifth ounces of sugar, one-sixth gill of vinegar or pickles . . . one [ounce] pepper, four and four-fifth ounces of potatoes, sixteen twenty-fifths of an ounce of baking powder.

If Rangers could not eat in camp, the state paid per diem up to $1.50. As for horses, they got twelve pounds of corn or fourteen pounds of hay a day.

Hutchings also published twelve regulations covering the Rangers, four of the rules clearly in response to accumulated criticisms from various citizens, local officials, and legislators. One rule provided that only "courageous, discreet, honest" men "of temperate habits and respectable families" would be hired as Rangers. Another regulation stressed that the force was "not intended to supplant the ordinary constabulary, and its operations will be confined to arrests of persons charged with the commission of felonies and carrying of concealed weapons and to the prevention of breaches of the peace." The new rules forbade political participation by Rangers, further enjoining them to "keep within the bounds of discretion and law under all circumstances." Captains would "promptly discharge any member of his company who may make any unreasonable display of authority, . . . use abusive language," or be "guilty of unnecessarily harsh treatment toward those with whom he comes in contact."[21]

While Hutchings issued orders aimed at making the Rangers more mannerly, Madero faced a much larger problem. He had started the revolution, but his October election as president did not stop it. Two of Madero's key military men, Pascual Orozco and Francisco "Pancho" Villa, had broken with him within days of the Juárez victory. Soon they took up arms not only against Madero but each other as well.[22]

Given the fatalities in El Paso during the Battle of Juárez, Colquitt grew increasingly concerned about the safety of El Paso residents should fighting break out again across the river. Newspaper correspondents sensationalized the situation, adding to public concern. The governor ordered most of the Ranger force to El Paso and dispatched Hutchings to report on conditions firsthand. But when forces loyal to Orozco took control of Juárez on February 27, 1912, only minor fighting occurred. For the next several months the Rangers stayed busy assisting federal authorities in keeping arms from being shipped from Texas into Mexico, participating in large seizures in El Paso and Laredo.[23]

That spring federal forces commanded by General Victoriano Huerta massed for an attack aimed at retaking Juárez. Again Colquitt sent Hutchings to El Paso along with additional Rangers to supplement Hughes's company.

On May 21, a squad of U.S. cavalry and two of Captain Hughes's horseback rangers—Charles R. Moore and Charles H. Webster—shadowed a large rebel force maneuvering near Ysleta on Pirate's Island, the same piece of no-man's-land where Ranger captain Frank Jones had been killed in 1893. The brush-covered spit lay part in Mexico, part in Texas, with no distinct line of demarcation. Seeing that Moore and Webster blocked the road before them, a contingent of more than three dozen *insurrectos* spurred their horses into a charge. The khaki-clad American cavalrymen pulled back cautiously, but Moore and the other Ranger stayed put, ordering the Mexicans to stop.

"This is Texas," Moore warned, his upraised arm signaling the Mexicans to ride no farther. At that, the Mexican commander sent a party to parley with the Rangers. Moore told them he did not care whose cause they supported in Mexico, he would arrest any of them who rode into Texas. The rebel captain, though his force outnumbered the Rangers fifteen-to-one, decided not to push it and ordered his command to turn around. The cavalry lieutenant who witnessed the standoff later called the Rangers "cool, collected men of nerve and good judgment who upheld the Rangers' reputation . . ."[24]

General Huerta recaptured Juárez for Madero on August 16, 1912, but seven months later another attack on the city by rebels seemed imminent. On January 29, 1913, Rangers Moore and Webster, this time accompanied by an El Paso County sheriff's deputy, found six *insurrectos* occupying Texas soil on Pirate's Island. When the rebels fired on the state lawmen, the Rangers shot back. A Mexican carrying a battle flag fell dead from his horse while two of his colleagues suffered wounds. The survivors hastily returned to Mexico. Before he rode off to report the incident, Moore picked up the rebel banner. Back in El Paso, he and Webster posed with the captured flag for a photographer before Hughes forwarded it to the adjutant general.

When Hughes wired the governor to inform him of the confrontation, Colquitt replied: "Keep me advised of the situation and shoot straight if necessary."[25]

Colquitt liked the way Hughes and his men took care of business. "I think the time has come when the State of Texas should not hesitate to deal with these marauding bands of rebels in a way which they will understand," the governor wrote. "I instruct you and your men to keep them off of Texas territory if possible, and if they invade the State let them understand they do so at the risk of their lives."

If the governor had any hope that the worst had passed in Mexico, that ended on February 25, 1913, with the assassination of an arrested President Madero and his vice president, Jose Maria Piño Suarez, during a midnight "transfer" from Lugumberri prison in Mexico's Federal District. The revolution-torn republic soon had its third president in as many years: General Victoriano Huerta, erstwhile chief of the Mexican army.[26]

The United States saw a more peaceful transition of power on March 4 with the inauguration of President Woodrow Wilson. Beginning his second term, Colquitt became even more outspoken about Mexico. Keeping most of the Ranger force on the border, he urged American intervention "not for conquest or territorial gain but to restore order and protect life and property."[27]

Though they stood ready to keep Mexican combatants out of Texas, in April 1913 Hughes and his men warmly welcomed an Ohio dentist-turned-novelist when he arrived to do firsthand research for his next book. When Zane Grey stepped off the Southern Pacific train at El Paso's Union Station, newsboys hawked papers full of stories of violence or rumored violence along the border. But the author of *Riders of the Purple Sage* did not have to depend on the work of journalists for material for his forthcoming novel. From Hughes's Rangers Grey got plenty of insight into life—and death—on the river separating two nations. Former Ranger Joe Sitters told the visiting writer that he considered the border "[almost] as bad an' wild as ever!"

Hughes's company impressed Grey. He dedicated his book *The Lone Star Ranger* to the captain and his men with "the hope that it shall fall to my lot to tell the world the truth about a strange, unique, and misunderstood body of men—the Texas Rangers—who made the great Lone Star State habitable, who never know peaceful rest and sleep . . . who will surely not be forgotten and will some day come into their own."[28]

Despite the continued unrest south of the Rio Grande and Colquitt's saber rattling, some Texans still questioned the necessity of the Rangers. In July, during a special session of the thirty-third legislature, first-term representative W. E. Cox of Ellis County tried unsuccessfully to eliminate the force by cutting its appropriation from the state's budget.[29]

At the national level, Wilson's administration did not recognize the Huerta regime and proceeded with a doctrine labeled "watchful waiting." Sound reasoning lay behind the policy. The various armed factions in Mexico outnumbered the U.S. Army along the border. Military planners believed that if the United States invaded Mexico to restore order, the republic would unite and counterattack. If that happened, Texas cities along the river easily could fall into Mexican hands.[30]

Colquitt, commanding a small Ranger force and 2,812 National Guardsmen, continued to talk tough about not putting up with Mexican transgressions. As resistance to Huerta grew in Mexico and Colquitt continued to posture, the misfortune of one man triggered a three-way confrontation involving the Rangers, Mexico, and federal policy that gained national attention.

CLEMENTE VERGARA

Clemente Vergara ranched in Webb County about forty miles upriver from Laredo near the small Palofox community across the internal boundary from Hidalgo, Mexico. Around 9:00 a.m. on February 12, 1914, someone came to Vergara's house, a small stone structure on a bluff high above the river. The visitor excitedly reported to Vergara's daughter Delores that Mexican soldiers had driven their horses off Isla Grande, a spit of no-man's-land created by a course change of the river that Vergara used for grazing. Looking toward the island, the girl saw no horses. Lifting her gaze to the Mexican side of the river, she observed a party of soldiers driving her father's remuda toward Hidalgo. Delores sent a rider hurrying to Palofox to notify her father, who returned to his ranch and crossed the river in his rowboat. Officials in Hidalgo listened to Vergara's demand that his horses be returned but said they could take no action until the local commander returned.

The next day, as Vergara tended to his chores, someone yelled from across the river that the matter of the horses could now be cleared up if he would come over. As the prow of his boat pushed up on the muddy bank, several armed men appeared. Soon Delores Vergara learned that Mexican *federales* had arrested her father, beaten him, and taken him to the military barracks in Hidalgo.

On Valentine's Day, Vergara's wife and daughter brought him baskets of food and bedding. Mexican authorities could not explain his untreated injuries, but they permitted his family to stay until well into the evening, when Mrs. Vergara and Delores left to spend the night with friends. The next morning, a Mexican soldier returned the food and bedding, telling them Vergara had been taken upriver to Piedras Negras. When Vergara's wife and her daughter called on the *commandante*, his orderly said the officer had left on some urgent matter.

Though the federal authorities had politely seen to the return of Mrs. Vergara's food basket and bedding, they had executed her husband. But two weeks went by before word reached Vergara's family. "Hanging of Texan by Huerta Troops Arouses Border Men," the Austin *Daily Statesman* yelled on February 26.[31]

The Vergara case clearly ran deeper than a dispute over ownership of eleven horses. Vergara had been killed because the federals suspected him of providing rebel forces with mounts and ammunition. Colquitt, however, saw the rancher's death in Mexico not as the relatively unsurprising consequence of interfering in someone else's fight but as an act of banditry. Hoping to take legal action, the governor had an opinion on his desk from Attorney General B. F. Looney that those responsible for Vergara's death could be charged with horse theft in Texas. Assuming it could be proven that the crime had occurred on Texas soil, the offenders could be extradited.

The governor sent a strong telegram to President Wilson demanding federal action in the case. Colquitt also sought permission to send Rangers into Mexico to round up those responsible for Vergara's death: "In view of condition of anarchy, can not [the] State of Texas obtain consent of United States Government to send Rangers across Rio Grande in pursuit of the lawless element of either faction when they cross into Texas and commit crimes?"[32] William Jennings Bryan, Wilson's secretary of state, firmly denied the governor's request. So did the president. By treaty, only federal forces could cross the river in pursuit of marauders, and even then it had to be with the Mexican government's permission.

"I do not want to invade Mexico with military force," Colquitt said in another telegram to Washington. "I asked your consent to allow me to send Texas Rangers, who are peace officers, in pursuit of those who are constantly transgressing our law." To that the secretary of state replied that the federal government saw no difference between the Rangers and any other armed force.

Wilson and Bryan worried that Colquitt and the Rangers would touch off a war. Indeed, the ranking military officer in Texas, General Frederick Funston, wrote Washington from his headquarters at Fort Sam Houston in San Antonio that the Rangers in trying to "aggrandize themselves" could "become a source of international danger."[33] Though Washington remained adamant in refusing permission for Rangers to cross the river, Colquitt could get no answer to his question as to which government of Mexico the United States considered official: Huerta's regime or the rebels now unified under Venustiano Carranza, who opposed him. In fact, the secretary of state never answered Colquitt's question on which of the two men he should deal with.

As correspondence and telegraphic exchanges continued between Austin and Washington and from Austin to Laredo and Mexico, on the night of March 7 Clemente Vergara reappeared on Texas soil. Somehow his body had been exhumed and returned to the Texas side of the river.

Given their prior communications with Colquitt, the president and secretary of state read with great interest the story beneath the March 9 banner headline in the *Washington Post:* "Armed Texas Rangers Boldly Invade Mexico and Bring Back Mutilated Body of Vergara." The Rangers, the newspaper continued, had "determined that for once American manhood should not truckle to Mexican trickery and deceit." With "their carbines as their warrants and their six-shooters as their passports," the Rangers had led ninety men into Mexico to reclaim one dead Texan.

Less sensationally, the San Antonio *Express* reported that only nine men had been involved. While Rangers had been in the "vicinity," the Texas newspaper account continued, the gruesome operation had been carried out by "friends and relatives" of Vergara.

A firm supporter of the public's right to know, Colquitt gave reporters in Austin the wording of a brief telegram he received from Captain Sanders: "Have just returned from Hidalgo, Mexico. Have the body of Clemente Vergara on Texas soil."[34]

Acting almost as if Vergara had been returned to Texas alive, Colquitt boasted: "Give me 100 Texas Rangers and I can do more towards keeping law and order in Texas than 10,000 troops." Then, as if not wanting to be all that insulting to the federal government, the governor added, "Texas Rangers are peace officers and can arrest suspected parties at any time. This the United States troops can not do."[35]

The governor received more than one hundred telegrams from across the nation congratulating him on, as the Austin *Daily Statesman* put it, "the action of the Rangers and Texas in venturing into Mexican territory and securing the body." A telegram from Hagerstown, Maryland, represented the opinion of many:

Hearty congratulations to you and your State for the action of the Rangers. I believe all patriotic Americans are with you in heart and rejoice at the success of your sturdy example. . . . May it ever shine in history when it is placed by the side of our watchful, waiting disgrace.

A flurry of laudatory letters followed the telegrams. "I want you for the next President of the United States," wrote John F. Howard of Silver

Lake Assembly, New York. "Several million people up here feel the same way. I suppose you are a Democrat, but that does not matter at all, even to Republicans. I would vote for you even if you were a Prohibitionist." A woman in Roxbury, Massachusetts, penned: "Bully for you and your Texas Rangers."[36]

A few days later, following numerous exchanges between Washington and Austin and Washington and Mexico, the governor suddenly sought to clarify the meaning of the fifteen-word telegram from Captain Sanders. Despite the brevity and seeming lack of ambiguity in the Ranger's communication to the governor, the Dallas *Morning News* and other Texas newspapers now quoted Colquitt saying that the message had been misinterpreted. Actually, the governor explained, Sanders and his Rangers had come into possession of Vergara's mutilated body (in addition to three gunshot wounds, his fingers on one hand were charred and his skull had been crushed) on the Texas side of the river. As for the telegram, Sanders said he had asked Alonzo B. Garrett, the American consul at Nuevo Laredo, to send the governor the message and that the State Department official had mistakenly used the words "returned from Hidalgo" when Sanders had dictated "returned to Laredo."[37]

A Vergara family member also said Rangers had not participated in the predawn exhumation. The Laredo *Times* pronounced the recovery "the work of ten men, fully armed and determined," who came from the Vergara ranch and Palofox.[38]

While now maintaining that Texas had "not committed an act of aggression against Mexico," Colquitt would not discuss what the Rangers might do in any future emergency along the border. The governor did, however, offer a $1,000 reward for anyone returning Vergara's killers to Texas. In addition, responding to a petition from Cameron County asking for more Rangers, on March 20, 1914, Colquitt sent a telegram to Captain Hughes, currently working out of Raymondville, to "look for every man suitable" to augment Ranger strength in the Valley. "My instructions to him are to get men who can shoot and will shoot when necessary," the governor told an Austin reporter. "As long as the border is overrun with Mexican refugees, the acts of lawlessness will continue. These Mexicans are emboldened by the policy of President Wilson and Secretary of State Bryan."[39]

That summer, the Dallas *Morning News* ran a story tracing the history of the Rangers reprinted in newspapers across the nation. The reporter who wrote the piece had sought out former captain McDonald for comment on the type of men making up the small force. Almost always happy to talk to a newsman, the captain obliged. The way he used to pick Rangers, the captain said, "was to look in a man's eyes . . . I could tell in a minute if he had the right stuff in him. I never got fooled, either." While Rangers had a reputation as fierce fighters, he continued, they were not "a rowdy, reckless set of men." To the contrary, McDonald said, Rangers "are just naturally as peaceful and God-fearing men as you'll find anywhere."[40]

Though the Vergara incident brought national attention to Texas and its Rangers, only one of Vergara's stolen horses ever made it back to Texas and no one ever faced trial in connection with the theft. Nor did the governor pay any reward money for Vergara's killers. The adjutant general's report for January 1, 1913, to December 31, 1914, did not even mention the incident.[41]

No matter Colquitt's high standing among hawkish Texans and Americans, he had served two terms and opted not to seek another two years in office. His successor, Temple lawyer-banker James E. Ferguson, also opposed Prohibition, but that issue quickly became the least of his concerns. Only a few days after his inauguration in January 1915, Ferguson and the Rangers became embroiled in what amounted to a guerrilla war in South Texas and the Big Bend.

3

Los Sediciosos

TROUBLES ON THE BORDER, 1915–1919

♦ ver beer in a saloon that Basillio Ramos Jr. and several associates ran in the Duval County town of San Diego in South Texas, a grand revolutionary vision evolved. On the other side of the Rio Grande, Mexicans had been fighting and dying for five years to eliminate oppression. Why should the equally dominated Mexican-Americans in Texas and elsewhere in the Southwest not arise against an Anglo establishment that saw them as little more than cheap labor for the Anglos' farms and ranches? Other Mexicans had a more active role in fomenting the movement, but the twenty-four-year-old Ramos, a Huerta partisan who had found it expedient to come to Texas when Venustiano Carranza assumed power as Mexico's latest president, would get most of the notoriety for setting forth what came to be known as the Plan of San Diego.

Slipping out of San Diego owing money, Ramos took a chance on returning to Mexico, where he promptly got arrested by the *carrancistas*. Unlike many Huerta supporters, Ramos survived a brief stint in a Monterrey prison and made it back to Texas.

Unluckily for him, Ramos shared his seditious views with one too many people. That led to his January 24, 1915, arrest in McAllen by Hidalgo County sheriff's deputy Tom Mayfield. The lawman found an assortment of papers in Ramos's possession, including an important-looking document in Spanish with eight signatures, including Ramos's.

About the same time Mayfield took Ramos into custody, Zane Grey's latest Western novel, *The Lone Star Ranger*, hit the bookstores. The book had a simple story line: Stalwart Rangers led by reformed outlaw Buck Duane take on bad men and prevail, at the end the hero also winning the heart of a girl. But as readers across the nation enjoyed Grey's latest Western, federal authorities pored over an instrument that portended more violence than any shoot-'em-up novel.

The thousand-word pronouncement taken from Ramos featured fifteen points, the first being: "On the 20th day of February, 1915 . . . we will rise in arms against the Government and Country of the United States proclaiming liberty and independence from Yankee tyranny . . . and at the same time and in the same manner we will proclaim the independence and segregation of the States bordering upon the Mexican Nations." The plotters, in short, envisioned Texas, New Mexico, Arizona, Colorado, and California transformed into a new republic. Clearly Ramos and his fellow signers had no notion of accomplishing their dream through peaceful means: "It is strictly forbidden to hold prisoners, either civilians or soldiers. . . . [T]hey shall be shot immediately without any pretext."[1]

The Hidalgo County sheriff referred the matter to federal authorities, including the U.S. Marshal's Service, the Immigration Service, and the Bureau of Investigation, predecessor of the FBI. A federal grand jury indicted Ramos and the other seven whose names appeared on the seized document for conspiracy to levy war against the United States, but not everyone familiar with it took the plan seriously at first.[2]

Though the Rangers had no hand in the discovery of the Plan of San Diego, they had an active, and controversial, part in dealing with its ramifications. But in doing so, they would no longer be able to rely on their most experienced and effective commander. Sixty years old, Captain Hughes ended his twenty-eight-year Ranger career effective January 31, 1915. Governor Ferguson had not reappointed him.[3]

Two days after Hughes unbuckled his gunbelt, the Associated Press broke the story of Ramos's arrest, but it did not get much play in the newspapers. Upstate, the Austin *Statesman* ran the two-paragraph item on page three. Ramos, the story said, "is held on a charge of plotting against the United States . . . among several races who are extensively represented in Texas, New Mexico and Arizona."[4]

The wire service learned a few more details of the plot on February 8, but not the planned start date. The military along the border quietly went on alert, but February 20 passed peacefully. Unknown to the authorities, a new timetable had been set. Though indicted for sedition, Ramos got out of jail in Brownsville on a reduced bond. He was never heard from again on the U.S. side of the river.

By March, livestock thievery in South Texas reached a level not seen since the 1870s, when Captain Leander McNelly policed the Nueces Strip. Still, no one connected the activities to the Plan of San Diego. On March 5, Captain Sanders, based in Del Rio, met with the new governor and General Hutchings "relative to the cattle thieves who are infesting border counties." The day after the meeting, the Austin *American* reported that the governor favored "adding enough men to the [Ranger] force to drive the thieves out of the state and give the necessary protection to the ranchers and cattle raisers along the border." Within the month, the thirty-fourth legislature appropriated $10,000—enough for ten more Rangers for five months' service—and Ferguson quickly signed the emergency measure into law.[5]

President Wilson and his cabinet had bigger worries than the situation along the border. On May 7, 1915, a German U-boat operating in international waters sank the British passenger liner *Lusitania* in the Atlantic. Many Americans went down with the ship, making eventual American involvement in the European war look likely. Germany, however, hoped to keep the United States preoccupied with affairs in Mexico. As Washington nervously followed developments in Europe, rampant theft of cattle, horses, saddles, and equipment continued in South Texas. As Captain Sanders reported, he found "considerable uneasiness among white people" in the Valley.[6]

Trouble had been breaking out all along the river, not just in South Texas. In the Big Bend on May 23, Company B private Eugene Hulen— younger brother of former adjutant general John A. Hulen—died in withering rifle fire along with ex-Ranger Joe Sitters, one of the tough lawmen who had impressed Grey in El Paso. Mexican bandits under Chico Cano had ambushed them in a desolate mountain pass in Presidio County. Farther upriver, suspected bandits shot Ranger private Robert Lee Burdett to death on June 8, 1915, near Fabens in El Paso County. On the same day, two of Burdett's fellow lawmen killed Anastacio Segura at Pilares, a village in Presidio County. They said he had been a member of the party that ambushed Hulen and Sitters.[7]

As tensions continued to rise, an editorial in the June 1915 issue of *Army & Navy Journal* proposed a novel solution for border protection: federal rangers. The U.S. Army, the author wrote, was too big for the job, the Texas Rangers too small. Under the magazine's plan, the U.S. Rangers would be equally supported by the federal government and the state.[8]

Governor Ferguson had a more practical idea. "Conditions along the Mexican Border continue to grow worse," he said in a June 11 letter to President Wilson. "Marauding bands from Mexico make raids almost daily upon the property of our citizens. . . . If you would advise that you could ask Congress . . . to appropriate Thirty Thousand Dollars for the maintenance of thirty additional Texas Rangers, I feel sure that Congress would make the appropriation with the same alacrity as when President Taft made a similar recommendation." The governor backed his request with a legislative resolution, but Washington took no action on it.[9]

In an irony not immediately recognized, on the 139th anniversary of the signing of the American Declaration of Independence, the campaign to liberate Texas from the United States began. Mexican anarchists and Mexican-American seditionists under Luis de la Rosa—a mustachioed redheaded grocer from Brownsville—struck in the lower Valley thirty miles inside Cameron County, stealing several horses. On July 12, *sediciosos* robbed a store at Lyford, escaping with food and ammunition. The first Anglo fatality in the Valley came five days later, when raiders killed a young ranch hand eighteen miles east of Raymondville. In addition to killing, robbing, and stealing livestock, raiders targeted infrastructure. They burned railroad trestles, snipped telegraph and telephone lines, and vandalized irrigation pump stations.

Having scraped up more emergency state funding, on July 20 Governor Ferguson commissioned Spanish-American War veteran and former Houston police chief Henry Lee Ransom as captain of newly created Company D with authority to enlist seven new Rangers. The governor put nothing on record, but Ferguson later said that he had instructed

Ransom to do whatever it took to stop Mexican incursions in the Valley "if he had to kill every damned man connected with it."[10] Knowing he had the pardoning power of the governor behind him, Ransom traveled to South Texas ready to eliminate every bandit or suspected sympathizer he ran across.[11]

The new captain established camp at Harlingen. To cover the rest of the border, Sanders's Company A left the Valley for its headquarters at Del Rio. Captain Fox's Company B worked out of Marfa in the Big Bend.

By the end of July, Valley citizens had organized a Law and Order League dedicated to the proposition of meting out summary punishment "upon any suspected bandits who may fall into their hands." But so far, Rangers, sheriff's deputies, and posse men had been unable to find any of the raiders. While some of the *sediciosos* wore white hatbands proclaiming "Viva la Independencia de Texas," from the point of view of many Anglos along the border skin color alone indicated sympathy to their anarchist movement. "Firearms discovered in the possession of Mexicans in rural communities of this section is practically equivalent to a death warrant unless that Mexican is well known to Americans as being peaceful," the Associated Press reported from the Valley.[12]

"The whole country is infested with armed men," Cameron County judge W. L. Yates wired Hutchings on August 3. "Hold-ups which have been of nightly occurrence are now happening by day. The bandits in a fight this morning were armed with Mausers [and] act with remarkable facility and organization. . . . Any overt act by the United States Government anywhere in Mexico would this time be ruinous to the Lower Rio Grande Valley."

The judge concluded: "I cannot wire all I know for obvious reasons. Don't give publicity to this."[13]

After reading that communication and other reports, the adjutant general decided to go to the Valley to oversee Ranger operations. He also ordered Captain Fox and his men from West Texas to Brownsville. Hutchings arrived August 6 and soon learned that Mexican riders had struck Sebastian, ten miles above Harlingen, dealing the new Law and Order League an early blow by killing president Alfred L. Austin and his son, Charles. The general led Captain Ransom and four Rangers, augmented by local officers, on a search for the raiders. That night the posse surrounded a house belonging to a family suspected of involvement in the Austin killings. A father and son died in the gunfight that ensued. Though wounded, the dead man's other son managed to escape. When Rangers searched the house again the next morning, they found the surviving son. He got off a shot at Ranger Joe Anders, powder burning his prominent nose, before the Rangers killed him. "Had fight at Paso Real and killed Guzman and his son," Ransom noted in his scout report that month. "Watched house . . . killed boy under bed after he wounded ranger."[14]

Later that day, Ferguson announced that the Ranger force would be augmented by twenty more men. "The ridding of Texas of this lawless element," he told reporters, "is purely a local affair and the state will make quick work of it."[15]

"They Are Damned Bandits"

The same day newspapers published the governor's promise, the "lawless element" made its boldest strike yet. Not that Willacy County sheriff J. C. Adkins and King Ranch manager Caesar Kleberg did not have some advance warning of trouble. Early on August 8, Adkins had called for help after Kleberg reported that riders believed to be Mexican bandits had been seen on the El Sauz Ranch, one of the sprawling ranch's five divisions. That Sunday afternoon, General Hutchings and the men of Captain Fox's company, accompanied by members of a local militia unit, left Brownsville by special train for the ranch's Norias division, sixty-eight miles to the north. At Harlingen they picked up Captain Ransom and his men as well as eight U.S. cavalrymen.

Leaving the soldiers to guard Norias, Hutchings and the two Ranger companies left on horses furnished by the ranch to check a water hole twelve miles to the southeast. Division foreman Tom R. Tate and a couple of cowboys went along as guides. A short time later, three U.S. Customs inspectors (Portus Gay and former Rangers Marcus Hines and Joe "Pinkie" Taylor), Cameron County sheriff's deputy Gordon Hill, and one or two other armed volunteers arrived at Norias on the regular train.

The *sediciosos*, already on their way to attack the ranch subheadquarters, likely heard the Rangers riding through the brush and kept quiet in the thick cover until they passed by less than a half mile from them.

Back at the ranch house, about 6:20 p.m. Hines noticed riders in the distance.

"Well, I see the boys coming back," he said. "They must have missed them bandits."

Then he realized the horsemen—fifty to seventy in number—wore sombreros. They also carried a bloodred flag.

"They are damned bandits," Gay shouted, snapping off a rifle shot in their direction as they swept in a long line toward the ranch house. More for effect than impact at that range, the three-hundred-pound Hines let loose a load of buckshot from the 10-gauge shotgun he carried. As the soldiers scurried into prone positions with their Springfield .30-06s, Gay took charge and shouted to the ranch hands and a few locals who had been playing poker to take cover on the slope of the railroad grade separating the two-story ranch house from the bandits.

"If you can't get a man, get a horse," Gay instructed the men.

Intense fire from the soldiers, the officers, and the civilians eventually forced the Mexicans to pull back and take shelter in a tool house and the railroad section house. Knowing a high Brahma bull–proof fence built to keep livestock off the railroad tracks would stop the raiders if they charged, the defenders withdrew to the white frame house. That marked the beginning of a protracted standoff.

The bandits had not thought to cut the telephone wires, so someone inside the ranch house had called to report the attack. But the badly outnumbered defenders ran low on ammunition. Late in the evening, the raiders made a second desperate charge, but it lost momentum when one of the defenders knocked their leader off his horse. Shouting, "Gringos cabrones!" the attackers finally withdrew about 8:10 p.m. Having found no sign of the raiders at the water hole, the Rangers arrived back at the ranch less than an hour after the raiders fled.

Checking the railroad section house, the Rangers found a dead woman identified as Manuela Flores, the wife of a ranch employee. She had been killed at the outset of the attack after refusing to tell the raiders how many Anglos they faced. The number of Mexicans killed in the fight varied with the telling, but their losses ranged from five to ten men killed outright, mortally wounded or killed as a prisoner after the battle.

One of the wounded raiders, who gave his name as Jose Garcia and said he lived in San Benito, told the Rangers he had been forced to participate in the attack. A report filed by a special correspondent for the Dallas *Morning News* attributed to Garcia that "the plan of the Mexicans contemplates the freeing of a portion of Texas between the Rio Grande and the Nueces River from American rule and the annexation of this territory to Mexico." What became of Garcia after Rangers questioned him was not reported by the newspaper.[16]

Fearing ambush, Hutchings decided not to trail the raiders that night. But Captain Ransom began schooling the defenders on what they should have done. Finally, tiring of hearing how he would have handled it if he had been there, one of the defenders (some accounts say it was "Pinkie" Taylor, another that it was Hines) said in disgust, "Well, Captain, I don't know what else you'd have done. We were here before they came, we were here while they were here, and we're still here."

Bolstered by additional volunteers arriving overnight, Hutchings, the two Ranger companies, soldiers, lawmen, ranch hands, and posse men set out in pursuit of the raiders in the morning. While never catching the main band, they skirmished with a smaller group of suspected raiders on August 12, killing one of them.[17]

Word of the Norias attack reached the vacationing governor at Rockport. Ferguson ordered Hutchings to meet him at the coastal resort as soon as possible to brief him on the border situation. After the meeting, the governor directed the general to get as many more Rangers to the Valley as possible. With Ransom and Fox's companies already on hand, Hutchings ordered Sanders to return to the Valley from Del Rio.

Recruitment proved the least of Hutchings's worries. As news of the Norias raid spread, the Adjutant General's Office received some two hundred applications for Ranger appointments and the letters and telegrams continued to stack up. By August 14 the Dallas *Morning News* reported that the "Ranger force has been recruited to its full quota of fifty men and practically every one of the Rangers is now stationed or en route to the Texas-Mexican border country." The same day, Captain Fox gave a reporter a progress report: "We got another Mexican—but he's dead." Meanwhile, the federal government rushed more soldiers to the Valley, doubling the garrison at Fort Brown.[18]

By automobile and horseback, Rangers crisscrossed Cameron, Hidalgo, Starr, and Willacy counties looking for *sediciosos* or anyone they thought supported their cause. Sheriff's posses, incensed ranch owners

and their hands, and military patrols joined the hunt. Ransom reported
he traveled 1,582 miles during July and more in August.

"As long as the present extreme vigilance is maintained," the Dallas
Morning News reported a week after the Norias attack, "officers do not
believe attempts at reorganization of large bands on the American side
will be undertaken. They think a wholesome lesson has been taught by
the uncompromising character of the Ranger campaign throughout the
valley and realizing no mercy will be shown such offenders, others will
hesitate to embark on a career of organized depredation."

But only ten days later a seditionist *pronunciomento* published
widely in Mexico and Texas urged that all "good Mexicans" take up
arms in the cause against the United States. "Organized depredation"
continued, with September seeing eight confrontations of varying san-
guinity with seditionists and the discovery of numerous Mexican
bodies across the Valley. "The finding of dead bodies of Mexicans has
reached the point where it creates little or no interest," the San Antonio
Express reported September 11.

"Viva Luis de la Rosa!"

On the night of October 18, the *sediciosos* carried out the bloodiest
raid yet, derailing south-bound St. Louis, Brownsville and Mexico Railway passenger train Number 101 near Olmito only six miles north of
Brownsville. Train engineer H. H. Kendall died when the locomotive,
coal tender, and baggage car careened off the tracks at 30 miles an hour.
Escaping steam badly scalded the train's fireman. Those who had not
been hurled to the floor by the force of the derailment soon threw themselves on it or tried to run as bullets began splintering through both
sides of the two passenger cars.

Shouting, "Viva Carranza!" and, "Viva Luis de la Rosa!" four Mexicans with rifles rushed into the leaning-but-still-upright smoking car.
Inside were state quarantine officer Dr. Edgar S. McCain, Brownsville
district attorney John Kleiber, former Ranger Harry Wallis, three soldiers on their way back to Fort Brown, a traveling salesman, and a Mexican family. As Kleiber lay on the floor he saw one of the masked raiders
shoot a uniformed cavalryman lying right across the aisle from him in
the face. Blood from the wounded soldier soon drenched the district

attorney, who pretended to be mortally wounded when a raider poked him with his rifle barrel and ordered him to hand over his money. The DA did as told, also giving up his gold watch fob and his shoes. Then he played dead to avoid being shot.

McCain and Wallis had bolted for the water closet at the end of the car. The doctor made it to the washroom unharmed, but Wallis caught a rifle slug in the shoulder while another round cut off two of his fingers. Both men made it into the toilet, Wallis managing to lock the door. But a locked door did not stop bullets. The former Ranger embraced the smelly floor, but McCain had opted to stand on the commode. A bullet slammed into his stomach, leaving him mortally wounded.

When the attackers finally galloped away, the train's engineer and one of the soldiers lay dead. The doctor died from his wound later that night.

By daybreak, Rangers under Captain Ransom, sheriff's deputies, soldiers from Fort Brown, and armed vigilantes scoured the brush between Olmito and the Rio Grande looking for the raiders. Having rounded up four suspects, the Rangers marched the Mexicans into the mesquite and shot them. Ransom also wanted to execute two more men arrested by Cameron County sheriff W. T. Vann, but the sheriff protected his prisoners and took them to jail.[19]

The attack made national news. That suspects had been summarily executed was common knowledge. "Rumors of more execution of Mexicans suspected of being implicated in the wrecking and robbing of the St. Louis, Brownsville & Mexico passenger train Monday night were current in Brownsville today," the New York *Times* reported on October 21. "There was no confirmation from any source."

Local newspapers were quick to name the man suspected of masterminding the attack.

"The leader of the marauders was identified by two reputable persons of the Brownsville section as Louis [*sic*] de Rosa, noted as the leader of the 'The Texas Revolution' under the notorious 'Plan of San Diego,'" the Lyford *Courant* reported on October 22. "This deed serves to warn the authorities that there must be no relaxation of the vigilant patrol of the border so long as there is no strong government on the other side of the river."

In November, General Funston complained for a second time to Governor Ferguson of Ransom's heavy-handedness. Ferguson responded

that he feared the allegations against Ransom were "in part true" and
that he had instructed the adjutant general to deal decisively with the situation. That prompted Hutchings to issue an order to all the Ranger captains to prevent illegal executions and to report all casualties along with
the names of witnesses for verification purposes.[20]

However, most Anglos in the Valley liked the Rangers' shoot-first attitude. When Captain Sanders and twelve of his men rode into town one
day in November to pick up supplies, the Kingsville *Record* observed:

> What a sight for sore eyes they were! It's no wonder Mexican bandits
> tremble in terror at the word [*Rangers*]. Strong, determined men they
> are, with courage and daring written on their faces, dead shots, tire-
> less on the trail, cunning as cunning is judge on the border paths, true
> Texas Rangers of the old school, . . . a mighty army within them-
> selves, the State's best gift to her people.

Reprinting the article, the Alice *News* added that Sanders and his
Rangers "are a fine lot of gentlemen and Alice is proud to have them as
citizens."[21]

President Wilson had swallowed bitter medicine and recognized Carranza's presidency on October 19, the day after the attack at Olmito.
That, Wilson hoped, would gain some level of cooperation from the Mexican government in keeping raiders out of Texas. On November 23, Governor Ferguson and General Hutchings traveled to Laredo to meet with
Carranza and returned to Austin with a promise that the Mexican leader
would do more to prevent *sediciosos* from raiding into Texas. Washington did not like a Texas official dealing with a head of state, but the face-
to-face visit—coupled with Wilson's recognition—stopped the raids, if
not the plotting. Valley residents, though still wary of additional attacks,
slowly relaxed. But hundreds of people, mostly Mexicans, had died along
the lower Rio Grande. For years after the last raid, skeletons with .45-
caliber holes in their skulls continued to turn up in the brush.[22]

BLOODSHED IN THE BIG BEND

While conditions in South Texas had improved, in far West Texas the
situation worsened. Mexican federal troops fighting for "First Chief"

Venustiano Carranza had recaptured Juarez on December 20, 1915, with Villa now hiding in the Sierra Madre mountains with no official capacity. Though he still saw himself as a revolutionary, others began to call him a bandit. Chafing at Washington's recognition of Carranza's government, Villa began targeting American interests in Chihuahua. In one incident on January 10, 1916, Villistas (General Villa was not himself present) stopped a train five miles west of Santa Ysabel and executed eighteen American mining engineers en route from El Paso to the mines at Cusihuiriachi with the specific permission of the Carranza government. In the days following near riots resulted in El Paso. Even so, the Wilson government refused to intervene.

Two months later, on March 9, 1916, a force of nearly five hundred Villistas attacked Columbus, New Mexico, killing seventeen Americans. U.S. troops stationed there fought back, killing more than a hundred of the raiders who had lingered to set fire to the town.

The United States had been invaded. President Wilson chose to respond militarily, ordering General John J. "Blackjack" Pershing to organize a punitive expedition of 10,500 soldiers to enter Mexico and get Villa.[23]

The next Villista raid hit Texas. Near midnight on May 5 (the Mexican holiday of Cinco de Mayo commemorating the Mexican defeat of the French at Puebla in 1867) seventy-five Mexican bandits struck the Brewster County settlement of Glenn Spring, located in the rugged foothills of the Chisos Mountains. The community's mostly Mexican residents provided labor for a *candelilla* wax factory and customers enough for one general store owned by O. G. Compton. A squad of nine troopers from the Fourteenth Cavalry had been posted there to protect the place, living in tents and doing their cooking in a grass-roofed adobe building. When the attack came, seven of the nine soldiers fortified themselves in the adobe. Seeing they could not make it, the other two cavalrymen sprinted for the cover of some nearby rocks.

"[The Mexicans] opened fire on the adobe house and I went and got my rifle and counted my cartridges," Compton later recalled. "I had only a hundred. Sitting at the window [of his house], I waited for them to attack."

As the raiders and cavalrymen exchanged gunfire, Compton's three children—an eight-year-old girl and two boys, four and six—woke up frightened by all the commotion. Compton picked up his daughter and ran out the back door to leave her in the care of an older Mexican man who did their laundry. The store owner started back to get his boys and deliver them, but "the Mexicans were too thick and I could not shoot my way through them. I emptied my gun, but they crowded me and I had to head away to the creek and slip behind a rock."

The attackers torched the roof of the adobe occupied by the cavalry-men, forcing them out. Three troopers fell dead to a wave of bandit bullets while the other four—three of them burned—ran to hide in the darkness.

After finally gaining control of the place, the attackers sacked Compton's store and started loading their booty on packhorses. When it got light enough to see, Compton and a badly burned soldier slipped close enough to find that the raiders had not yet left. They hurriedly pulled back and stayed in hiding until later in the day. When they fi-nally came back to Glenn Spring, Compton learned his four-year-old son had caught a stray bullet during the firefight and his body already had been removed to Marathon. Until the two men showed up, every-one thought they had been taken prisoner by the bandits.[24]

On their way back to Mexico the morning of May 6, the raiders robbed another American-owned store in Boquillas, a village on the north side of the Rio Grande, twelve miles from Glenn Spring. Crossing the river after kidnapping the store owner and his clerk, they also struck the Boquillas del Carmen mine office in Coahuila.

Earlier that day, not yet aware of the surprise attack on Glenn Spring, the secretary of war wrote Governor Ferguson that "a near cri-sis . . . seems to have passed." But four days later, with a contingent of U.S. troops already in Mexico on the trail of the Glenn Spring raiders, the federal government mobilized the National Guard for duty in the Big Bend and elsewhere on the border.[25] In Austin, the governor soon announced that the Ranger force would be increased on an emergency basis by another fifty men.[26] With General Pershing and thousands of soldiers on Villa's trail deep in Mexico and President Carranza demand-ing that U.S. troops leave his country, a second U.S.–Mexican war looked likely.

Tracy H. Lewis, a New York *Morning Telegraph* reporter, came to the border to cover the impending hostilities but soon found himself a "warless war correspondent." Returning to New York in August, he self-published in book form the newspaper stories he had filed from El Paso, including a piece he called "Getting the Range of the Texas Ranger."

Lewis's story offered a balanced portrayal of the Rangers, shedding light on their dark side as well as their more traditional heroic image. "Have you ever seen a bunch of chickens scatter when a belligerent rooster stalks into their midst?" the journalist began. "You know then the appearance of a group of Mexicans in any of the border towns when a Texas ranger looms above the horizon." To support that, Lewis repeated a story he had heard concerning a brief encounter between a pair of Rangers and two Mexicans: "We met two Mexicans on the road," the Rangers supposedly reported to their captain, "but did not have time to bury them."[27]

Cultural disdain existed on both sides. "When he has to kill an armed Mexican," folklorist Americo Paredes later wrote,

> the Ranger tries to catch him asleep, or he shoots the Mexican in the back. . . . If it weren't for the American soldiers, the Rangers wouldn't dare come to the Border. The Ranger always runs and hides behind the soldier when the real trouble starts.[28]

Lewis quoted an anonymous El Pasoan who characterized the Rangers as "the most cold-blooded bunch of persons in the world." The unnamed critic added: "They have no regard for human life whatever, and it's because of this that Mexicans are in such deadly fear of them." The reporter's informant said Rangers rarely attempted to disarm arrested Mexicans, allowing them every chance to make a break for it. "They might try to start something if we leave their arms on them," the anonymous source attributed to an equally anonymous Ranger, "and a dead Mexican is always a lot less trouble than a live one."[29]

The New York journalist rounded out his article with a more favorable view of the Rangers:

> One will find just as many persons . . . who have only the highest praise for the rangers and the work they do, and I am inclined to number myself among them. . . . There are no better trail finders nor handier men with their guns in the South. At a hundred yards or

more a man is invariably dead if a ranger judges his life a burden on the community.[30]

The American public had a hardy appetite for stories about the Rangers. While Lewis wrote of them from a journalist's perspective, a San Saba–born cowboy turned silent movie star who had ridden with Captain Ransom cheerfully schooled a Los Angeles *Times* reporter on life as a Ranger. Though George W. "Buck" Connor spent only one month in Ransom's Company D before resigning, the thirty-six-year-old Texan had an eye for detail. While having nothing negative to say about the Rangers, neither did he attempt to gloss over that they had killed many a Mexican on the border.

"During the Brownsville raids," he told the newspaper, "the work of the Rangers was most effective. Even today when one rides through the Brownsville country—the 'land of lone crosses'—and sees those crosses that mark the graves of raiders, and of murderers and other outlaws, he is passing over Texas soil made sacred by that fearless, fighting band, the Texas Rangers." Whether he had a hand in adding to the number of crosses in the Valley while serving with Ransom Connor did not say.

Dressed up with nine photographs, "How Shoot-to-Kill Rangers Keep Order on the Border" appeared in the widely read California daily on March 25, 1917. The piece began:

> With border raids recurring, German spy plots hatching and not a little of the nation's attention focused along the Rio Grande, Buck Connor . . . hove into town yesterday with a tribute to his former comrades who are doing no small part of the work of making the north bank of the borderline river habitable for United States citizens and safe from the gentry who would embroil us with Mexico and Japan.

In eighteen fat first-person paragraphs, Connor offered the best-known description of Ranger life during the bandit era—a period not covered in any known memoirs—including the enlistment process, camp life, culture, equipment, and tactics.

"When going out on a scouting trip you will not ride gallantly down the street with a show of your artillery," Connor told the unnamed compiler of the story. "You will all ride the length of two horses apart, with your eyes not on pretty girls but on the male element. If you are a real ranger, when you stop to investigate a place you won't run up to the house to see or hear all that's happening, but stick to your distance and keep even a keener eye on things in general."[31]

Less than a month after Connor walked into the Los Angeles *Times* newsroom, America entered the European war. That summer, when roughly a hundred soldiers of the all-black Third Battalion, Twenty-fourth Infantry—only recently arrived from Columbus, New Mexico—marched on downtown Houston from their bivouac near Camp Logan to extract revenge for the beating of one of their comrades by a white policeman, rioting broke out the night of August 23. When the free-for-all erupted, former adjutant general Hulen, back in federal service to organize the Thirty-sixth Infantry Division, happened to be in Houston. He telephoned the Governor's Mansion to seek a martial-law declaration from Ferguson but at first could not get through to the governor. Facing removal from office over issues not related to the border, Ferguson had closeted himself with several advisors to discuss strategy, and whoever answered the telephone would not interrupt the meeting. Around midnight, after Hulen finally got the chance to apprise him of the situation, Ferguson—in one of his last official acts—declared a state of emergency and imposed martial law in Houston. This marked the first time the chief executive had used this power since the adoption of the state's 1876 constitution.[32] With almost all of the Rangers concentrated on the border, order had to be restored by local authorities, the National Guard, and military police. Sixteen whites, including five police officers, died outright or suffered mortal wounds in the mêlée.

The next day, the state senate found Ferguson guilty on ten of twenty-one articles of impeachment. He resigned, turning the Governor's Mansion over to Lieutenant Governor William P. Hobby, a Houston newspaperman. On September 29, putting his own people in place, the new governor appointed James A. Harley adjutant general. The thirty-four-year-old attorney and former state senator from Seguin had served as a major with the Thirty-sixth Infantry Division.[33]

On Christmas Day 1917, Mexican raiders struck again in the Big Bend. This time more than forty horsemen attacked the remote Lucas C. Brite Ranch, a 125,000-acre spread thirty miles southwest of Marfa.

The ranch headquarters amounted to a small community, including a store called the Busy Bee, an attached post office, the adobe residence of ranch foreman Van Neill's family, and several other structures. Brite and his family had gone to Marfa for the holiday, but Neill and his wife planned to host a Christmas dinner and had invited numerous guests. Already on hand for the event was Neill's father, former Ranger Sam H. Neill, and his wife.

Up early drinking coffee, about 7:30 a.m. the elder Neill saw a party of armed horsemen riding hard toward the ranch enclave. When they started shooting and shouting, "*Mueren los gringos* [death to the Americans]!" he got his Winchester and started shooting back. His son joined him in the shooting as the old Ranger dropped one rider from his saddle.

The raiders seized a young Mexican ranch hand who had been attending to the morning milking and sent him to tell the Neills to surrender. Though Sam Neill had been wounded, the two men answered the order with more rifle fire. Next the Mexicans sent the boy scurrying to the house of postmaster and store owner Pierre Guyon to demand that he relinquish his keys or die. Guyon chose to do as told, which stopped the shooting as the raiders concentrated on looting the Busy Bee and post office. When the mail wagon arrived from downriver, the bandits stopped their work long enough to kill the two Mexican passengers. Driver Mickey Welch also died, but not as quickly. Annoyed by his incessant cursing, the bandits strung him up from the ceiling of the store and cut his throat. As one of several guests who had begun to show up for lunch fled to notify authorities, the bandits loaded their loot and rode off toward Mexico. "It was the tightest place I was ever in," Sam Neill later said of the raid.[34]

While the military, civilian posses, and several of his Ranger colleagues pursued the Brite Ranch raiders, downstream at Eagle Pass forty-three-year-old Ranger captain Kinlock Faulkner Cunningham learned on December 29 that 160 head of goats had been stolen from the Indio Ranch, eighteen miles above town. No one found the news surprising. Most of the livestock on the Mexican side of the river had been moved into the interior of the war-torn country. That made meat scarce and expensive in northern Mexico. With word of yet another foray onto Texas soil by Mexican thieves, Cunningham notified the U.S. military at Fort

Duncan and left with his Rangers for the Indio Ranch. The captain had been appointed by Governor Hobby only nineteen days earlier.

The next day, with most of the American army facing Germans in France, Captain Cunningham and his Company M Rangers, along with three detachments of the Fourteenth Cavalry and a machine-gun squad, crossed the Rio Grande on the trail of goat thieves. Counting soldiers, Rangers, and several interested Texans who volunteered their services, 150 armed Americans proceeded to the Mexican village of San Jose, about a mile from the river. Outside the residence of the Mexican river guard, the Rangers discovered a cow bearing the Indio brand. Several freshly killed goats hung from trees to bleed out. Had the Americans not interrupted the village's preparations for its New Year's celebration, the meat—buried under coals for slow cooking—soon would have been transformed into *cabrito*. Despite the evidence of recent activity in the village, the Rangers could find only a couple of Mexican men and one woman to question about the provenance of the meat. When rifle fire opened up from the brush, the Americans realized where everyone had gone. Though the soldiers and Rangers found themselves in a cross fire, training and firepower soon made up for that. The contest became even more one-sided when the army's machine gun opened up. Within three hours, the Rangers and soldiers had returned to Texas with the surviving stolen goats. The New Year began with seventeen funerals in Piedras Negras and three at San Jose.[35]

Despite an insufficient legislative appropriation, Governor Hobby had considerably expanded the Ranger force because of the war. With 165 men divided into twelve companies, A through M, the state had not had so many Rangers in the field since the Civil War. Seven companies operated along the border with headquarters at Ysleta, Del Rio, Eagle Pass, Laredo, and Edinburg, with two companies covering the Big Bend, one at Marfa and one at Marathon. The only interior companies were at Sweetwater, in West Texas, and Austin.[36]

In addition to the regular companies, the thirty-fifth legislature soon created a domestic intelligence apparatus. House Bill 15, known as the "Hobby Loyalty Act," empowered the adjutant general to organize a Loyalty Ranger Force of "three picked men from each county." Those commissioned as unpaid special Rangers under the new law would "act as a secret service department for the State" and report to newly commissioned Ranger captain William Hanson, a former U.S. marshal who more recently had lost extensive real estate holdings in Mexico to confiscation by the *carrancistas*.

A Loyalty Ranger's commission had validity only in the Ranger's county of residence, where the Rangers were to work "in harmony, at all times," with local officers to ferret out "disloyal occurrences" and forward statements of witnesses to Austin. "You are not expected to make arrests, but are supposed to work under cover as much as possible, and in a secret capacity," Harley concluded in his general order outlining their duties.[37]

Not all of these newly minted Rangers and special Rangers stood as stalwart upholders of the law. In Marfa, where the army had established a large post in 1914, the Rangers did not have a good reputation with the soldiers. Working in pairs, some of the Rangers supplemented their income by shaking down freshly paid cavalry troopers out on the town, offering $20 cash to pay their fines for them rather than take them to jail.[38]

PORVENIR

The small village of Porvenir lay on the Texas side of the river across from the Mexican village of Pilares, about thirty miles upriver from Candelaria in one of the most isolated parts of Presidio County. Porvenir's residents, fewer than 150, supported themselves by farming or herding goats. But area ranchers, believing that some in Porvenir augmented their income through banditry, talked Captain Fox into "rounding up" the community.

In late January, the captain dispatched eight of his men to meet up with rancher John Pool and other cattlemen for a raid on Porvenir. Fox placed forty-three-year-old Bud Weaver in command of the squad.[39]

Striking in the dead of night, the Rangers and their civilian guides rode into Porvenir looking for those responsible for the Brite Ranch raid. They rousted thirty-one women, children, and old men from their beds and gathered them in the center of the small village. The search netted only one old 10-gauge shotgun and two rifles, but an assortment of new shoes, Crystal White soap, and Barlow pocketknives also turned up— property reported stolen from the Busy Bee store. The Rangers arrested three men and took them back to their camp for questioning, releasing them two days later.

On January 28, Weaver's detachment—accompanied by Pool, his brother Buck, Raymond Fitzgerald, and Tom Snider—rode into an army subpost at the Evetts Ranch manned by Captain Henry H. Anderson and a squad of the Fourteenth Cavalry. Weaver handed Anderson a set of orders from Colonel George T. Langhorne in Marfa instructing him to cooperate with the Rangers, who the captain noticed seemed to have been drinking. The captain called Langhorne to express his concerns, only to be told to abide by his orders. The main thing Weaver wanted, he explained, was for the soldiers to surround Porvenir while he and his men looked for more weapons and suspected raiders.

The state-federal contingent reached Porvenir about midnight. The soldiers set up a perimeter around the town while the Rangers and the four cattlemen searched each of the pole-and-adobe jacales that made up the village. Assembling all but the oldest male residents, the Rangers marched the men about a quarter mile from town. Weaver told Anderson he intended to question the men and no longer needed any assistance.

Robert Keil, one of the soldiers on hand that night, later recalled that he and his fellow troopers had just made it back to their horses, about three hundred yards away, when they heard the loud voices of men followed by a woman's voice and then a woman's scream.

"For perhaps ten seconds we couldn't hear anything," Keil recalled, "and then it seemed that every woman down there screamed at the same time. It was an awful thing to hear in the dead of night. We could also hear what sounded like praying, and, of course, the small children were screaming with fright. Then we heard shots, rapid shots, echoing and blending in the dark."

The cavalrymen rushed back and found what Keil called "a mass of bodies" at the foot of a bluff, "the most hellish sight that any of us had ever witnessed." He continued: "The bodies lay in every conceivable position, including one that seemed to be sitting against the rock wall. . . . A hospital corpsman . . . went over the bodies, but not a breath of life was left in a single one. The professionals had done their work well."[40]

Fifteen men and boys ranging in age from seventy-two to sixteen had been summarily executed by the Rangers. All the bodies bore multiple gunshot wounds, some of the victims nearly eviscerated.[41]

Though his monthly report failed to note the incident, Fox later tried to write the massacre off as an unfortunate accident. He said the Mexican males had been "carried out to the edge of town" so the Rangers could identify them. As his men tried to get their names, the captain continued, "some of their comrades" began shooting at the Rangers from the darkness. That, he said, caused the Rangers' horses to scatter, leaving his men afoot. "They [the Rangers] immediately lay down returning fire on all moving objects in front."

At first the military also tried to cover up what happened at Porvenir, even though it said that no soldiers had taken part in the killings. But slowly, like a spreading bloodstain, word of the atrocity made it beyond the Big Bend, thanks largely to the efforts of Porvenir schoolmaster Harry Warren and J. J. Kilpatrick, Candelaria farmer, store owner, and justice of the peace. The Mexican government conducted a court of inquiry in Ojinaga and forwarded its findings to Washington and Austin. The army sent in a special inspector who succeeded in putting together the true story and at the state level the adjutant general ordered Captain Hanson to investigate. Grand jurors in Presidio County later heard testimony concerning the incident but returned no indictments.[42]

Likely in reprisal for the Porvenir executions, Mexican raiders crossed the river on March 25 and attacked the ranch of Edwin W. Neville in northern Presidio County. They killed his son, Glenn, and murdered their Mexican housekeeper in front of her three children. The following day, U.S. Cavalry troopers who had taken the bandits' trail attacked Pilares, Mexico, killing thirty-three suspected raiders and wounding eight. In addition to a substantial cache of weapons and ammunition, including German-made rifles, the soldiers found evidence linking residents of the village to both the Neville and Brite ranch raids. The soldiers torched the village and returned to Texas barely ahead of a larger contingent of Mexican cavalry.[43]

Harley ordered Fox to Austin on May 16 to discuss what had happened at Porvenir. Less than two weeks later, as outrage in some quarters continued to build, the adjutant general summoned Fox to a second meeting on May 27. Four days later, Fox sent Harley a letter of resignation, "as I don't feel that I am getting a fair deal."[44] On June 4, 1918, the adjutant general ordered Company B disbanded and fired five of its men. (Three other Rangers who had been involved in the massacre had already resigned.) Seven other Company B Rangers got transfers to Company D under Captain Jerry Gray, a 1917 Ferguson appointee.[45]

For the most part, the state and federal investigation into the Porvenir incident played out behind the scenes. Vigorously campaigning for election to a full term as governor, Hobby did not make a public issue of what he and Harley had done. Fox, however, made sure the Marfa newspaper got a copy of a letter he wrote the governor on June 11, a communication that would have amounted to insubordination had he still been a Ranger:

> Why do you not come clean and say that this is purely politics just to gain some Mexican votes? The five men you have discharged are good men and were the best of officers. . . . We have stood guard to prevent Mexican bandits from murdering the ranchmen, the women and children along this border while you slept on your feather bed of ease, and then to have my men discharged is too much for me. . . . You may consider this my resignation.[46]

Harley replied to Fox in the governor's behalf on July 3 in an open letter published in newspapers across the state. A thorough investigation, Harley wrote, had revealed that

> fifteen Mexicans were killed while in the custody of your men after they had been arrested. . . . You know as all peace officers should know that every man whether he be white or black, yellow or brown, has the constitutional right to a trial by jury, and that no organized band operating under the laws of this state has the right to constitute itself judge and jury and executioner. . . . We are fighting a world war now to overthrow ruthless autocracy and do not propose to tolerate it here at home.[47]

Seeking to squelch any further criticism such as voiced by Fox, Harley on September 24 issued a three-part order that "officers and men of the Texas Ranger Force will refrain from criticism of each other" in regard to either private or official acts. "If occasion arises calling for complaint by one commanding officer . . . against another, or if there is a difference of opinion between members of the Texas Ranger Force, such complaint or grievance should be referred to the Adjutant General . . . for equitable and satisfactory adjustment."[48]

Harley's biennial report for 1917–1918 included an overview of the problems the Rangers had faced along the border. Thousands of draft dodgers—"slackers"—had fled to Mexico, many of them stealing from the Texas side of the river or providing information to bandits. In addition, the revolution had depleted Mexico to the extent that "there is a ready market for all that can be stolen on the Texas side and smuggled into Mexico."

While the Rangers "have prevented much lawlessness, there is much work still to be done," the report continued. "Our Ranger Force is inadequate in number to protect our people notwithstanding the fact that they are working day and night. . . . If it was not for the Ranger service people could not live in security within 100 miles of the border. This country is developing wonderfully and the people demand better protection."[49]

Not all the problems confronting the Rangers occurred along the border. In July 1918, Rangers John Dudley White and Walter I. Rowe arrived in San Augustine County in deep East Texas at the request of Sheriff R. L. Watts to help track down a group of deserters and draft evaders hiding out somewhere in the piney woods covering the county. About 10:00 p.m. on July 11, the two Rangers, the sheriff, several deputies, and a National Guard sergeant descended on the farmhouse of Bose Williams, father of one of the deserters. Not finding the two men they sought, the officers decided to stay at the house, located about seven miles from White City, to see if the pair showed up later. About three o'clock on the morning of July 12, as White and Rowe sat on the front porch, two men approached the front gate and began blasting away at the two Rangers. Though mortally wounded by a round from a Winchester rifle, White raised up on his elbow and emptied his six-shooter in the direction of his attackers before he died. Ranger Rowe suffered two rifle wounds but would survive.

Learning of the shooting later that afternoon, General Harley ordered fifteen additional Rangers to San Augustine and said he would send a squadron of cavalry to assist them if it proved necessary. Four days later, Captain Hanson wired the general to report that Rangers had arrested three army deserters and eight draft resisters deep in the Big

Thicket near Brookeland in Sabine County. Two of the deserters, Privates Samuel H. Williams and Daniel H. Evans, would be taken to Camp Travis at San Antonio to face court-martial for the murder of Ranger White, Hanson said.[50]

As the war in Europe wound down, so had the worst of the trouble along the border. By late summer of 1918, the Adjutant General's Department began disbanding Ranger companies as the military pulled back to its permanent posts, abandoning numerous camps and outposts it had set up from the Big Bend to Brownsville. Though gunfire along the river had lessened, many lives had been lost. The long-standing friction between the two principal cultures who populated the border had been rubbed as raw as the back of a poorly cinched packhorse.[51]

4

Jose Canales Takes On the Rangers

Reorganizing the Rangers, 1919

Adjutant General Harley did not try to deny Ranger excesses during the bandit troubles, but he did seek to put them into perspective:

> In handling the Ranger Force during my incumbency there necessarily have been some unpleasant features. Perhaps at times things that seemed to us right and proper did not meet the approbation of everyone, but . . . I have earnestly endeavored to establish a policy that was both humane and just to all concerned and at the same time uphold the dignity of the law and the honor of this great State.[1]

Some Texans, however, thought the Rangers could do a better job of upholding that dignity. In fact, State Representative Jose Tomas Canales—a distant relative of Juan Cortina and a cousin of Catarino Garza's widow—had come to regard the Rangers as neither humane nor just, especially in the performance of their duties along the border. The lawmaker's opinion represented a significant change in attitude. Well-to-do and well-educated, the forty-one-year-old Brownsville lawyer had been around Rangers most of his life. As a boy and young man, he had seen his father welcome the state officers to the family ranch, La Cabra. "They stayed there," Canales recalled, "came there at all hours, got our horses, got meals there, and they got our services." Indeed, he added, men like retired captains Hughes and Rogers were "some of the noblest men I know."

But in Canales's view, the Rangers had lost significant moral and ethical ground since the beginning of the bandit troubles in 1915. Many of the lawmen, he believed, rated little better than the criminals the state paid them to apprehend. Too many Mexicans had ended up dead or missing after reportedly trying to escape from Ranger custody. Canales even became convinced that Rangers had abused one of his family members, their apparent intent to goad the man into giving them an excuse to kill him. (The relative in question, whom the Rangers suspected of warning off a mescal smuggler they had been lying in wait for, probably did get cussed out, but no facts ever surfaced to prove actual mistreatment.) Canales's criticism of the incident did net the lawmaker a provable example of Ranger excess: Sergeant Frank Hamer, who had been involved in the incident with Canales's relative, confronted Canales in downtown Brownsville and told the legislator that he would get hurt if he kept up his anti-Ranger talk. Disingenuously, Hamer had not minded repeating the warning in front of a witness. Canales took the threat seriously, reporting it to Cameron County sheriff Vann. No fan of the Rangers or Hamer, Vann suggested that Canales "take a double-barreled shot-gun . . . and kill that man. . . . No jury would ever convict you. . . ." Canales also wrote Governor Hobby, calling the Rangers stationed in Brownsville a "gang of ruffians." The governor, wiring Canales that he would look into it, referred the matter to General Harley.[2]

Harley soon wrote Canales to express his regret over the alleged threat and, while assuring the lawmaker he would investigate it, intimated in so many words that it might all be a matter of miscommunication. Canales fired back a letter assuring the general that Hamer's threat had not been in the least ambiguous. In response, Harley wired Canales on December 23, 1918, that the sergeant had been ordered not to threaten Canales. In fact, the adjutant general said, Hamer had been told to protect the representative. Not trusting Hamer or his boss, Captain Hanson, Canales wrote Congressman John Nance Garner asking for federal intervention in getting the Rangers—"American Bandits"—removed from the Valley. Garner forwarded the letter to the White House, which in turn passed it to the War Department.

A military intelligence officer stationed in Brownsville received orders to look into the matter. His findings moved back up the chain of command to Washington, where a report prepared by the army's adjutant general put the matter into perspective: The Rangers had "served a very useful purpose in suppressing lawlessness in the State and along the border, and while it is true that their methods are not always in conformity with strict judicial procedure, they are never-the-less effective" and should not be withdrawn from South Texas. The general added: "The complaint of Mr. Canales appears to have been inspired to some extent by personal animosity and political differences."[3]

The South Texas lawmaker could definitely be contentious. Traveling by rail with Captain Hanson from Brownsville to Austin on October 14, 1918, Canales lit into the captain over an incident eight days earlier near Rio Grande City. In trying to arrest a slacker, Ranger John J. Edds shot him when he tried to grab Edds's Winchester away from him. As it turned out, Edds had been trying to run in the wrong man. Even so, Hanson viewed the killing as a matter of self-defense. But Canales did not and he wanted justice. Their argument grew so heated that the legislator got off the train at its next stop.[4]

Not two months later, Hamer had threatened the South Texas representative. If Hamer had believed his size and demeanor could intimidate Canales, he calculated wrong. The incident made the lawmaker more determined than ever to straighten out the Rangers. Canales decided to take on the Rangers legislatively. When the thirty-sixth legislature convened in January 1919, the Valley lawmaker introduced House Bill 5, an act reducing the size of the force to twenty-four men. To assure a higher quality of officer, Canales's bill required that recruits have at least two years' law enforcement experience and a conviction-free past. The measure also would require Rangers to post a significant bond to assure professional behavior. For privates the bond would be $5,000, with captains having to put up three times that amount. Beyond seeking to raise Ranger standards, the bill provided that Rangers deliver anyone they arrested to a county sheriff. That official, a county judge, or county commissioners could release a Ranger's prisoner if the person arrested had been mistreated. And if local officials wanted the Rangers removed from their county they would have to leave within ten days or lose their law enforcement status in that county. Finally, the Canales bill allowed for the filing of civil lawsuits against Rangers.[5]

Canales quickly realized his legislation had no chance of passage as written. Governor Hobby made his attitude toward the Rangers plain in a written message to the people of Texas, published January 18 in the state's major newspapers:

> In my opinion this force has never rendered more efficient service to the state and to the federal government since its organization than during the war with Germany, when German propaganda was being spread over the country.
>
> The regular rangers, the loyalty secret service department and the special rangers have worked in unison with the city and county officials to keep down disloyalty, apprehend deserters, alleviate unsettled conditions along the border and contribute their efforts toward the successful prosecution of the war.[6]

Beyond law enforcement, the governor also had used the Rangers to oversee the electoral process in South Texas. From the perspective of Hobby's political rivals, *oversee* meant "control," though in reality both factions practiced election fraud to some extent. No matter, the political establishment needed the Rangers. Hobby and his adjutant general did not mind weeding out rogue Rangers, but they would not hamstring the entire force. Since the political importance of the Rangers to Hobby could not be argued on the record, supporters fell back on tradition. A representative from West Texas declared the Rangers one of the three "great monuments to Texas history," the other two being the Alamo and the Battle of San Jacinto.[7]

Though Canales and a few Anglo Populist colleagues argued hard for HB 5 on second reading, the measure did not make it to engrossment, the final step before a vote. Texas's major dailies covered the debate in detail, but the big headlines concerned Canales's assertion that his life had been threatened by Hamer, who despite Harley's assurances seemed to be shadowing Canales wherever he went in Austin.

"You don't know what is going on down there," Canales said on the

House floor, referring to conditions in the Valley. "You might as well send me home feet first as to kill this bill, for within six months you will read in the papers that Canales, a Mexican violator of the law, was killed in a fight with the rangers." The lawmaker then went public with Hamer's threat, noting that he still remained on the force.[8]

The next day, the South Texas lawmaker made some progress. While he did not get his bill any further along, Canales succeeded in pushing through a resolution requesting that the Adjutant General's Department hand over its 1917–1918 Ranger records to the chief clerk of the House. If he could not reform the Rangers on the basis of his bill alone, the Brownsville representative would engineer a legislative investigation to publicly prove the abuses he knew had occurred along the border.

Three days later, Harley wrote Speaker of the House R. E. Thomason agreeing to provide the requested information. But he asked that Canales's resolution, which called only for an investigation into allegations of Ranger misconduct, be expanded into a "full and complete investigation" of the Rangers "and all its activities with reference to its conduct and efficiency, the good that it does, and the forces of evil that it must necessarily encounter."

Clearly, the Hobby administration had decided to frame the issue as "keep or abolish the Rangers" rather than one aimed at reform.

Representative Barry Miller of Dallas, the leading opponent to Canales's efforts, stood waving telegrams from supporters of the Rangers. A House colleague read a wire from Brownsville mayor Albert Brown reporting that a mass meeting of citizens had voted "the unanimous opinion . . . that many statements made by Mr. Canales on the floor . . . were gross exaggerations if not absolute misrepresentations, and reflect an unwarranted stigma on the ranger force." The Brownsville men wanted no further action on Canales's bill until a delegation of Valley citizens could get to Austin to express their views on the Rangers.

Later that day, the House passed Concurrent Resolution 20, a measure creating a seven-member investigating committee. Four members would be from the House, three from the Senate. Canales's bill, with various friendly and unfriendly amendments, went back to the Military Affairs Committee.[9]

"I do not want to destroy the Ranger force," Canales had declared during the debate on his resolution seeking records from the adjutant general, "but to regulate [it]. . . . I want to get high-minded men and would increase their pay to that end."[10]

Though Harley favored a general investigation, many of his men did not. Ranger partisans—both in and out of the service—focused on Canales as the prime mover in the investigation. But the Brownsville lawyer, who also had served as Cameron County's school superinten-dent, would not sit either as the chair or vice chair of the investigative committee. Those jobs went to Representative William H. Bledsoe of Lubbock (who replaced the first chair, Representative Leonard E. Tilson) and Senator Paul D. Page of Bastrop County.[11]

Even before the swearing in of the first witness, Harley had quietly begun cleaning up the Ranger companies still extant. On January 5, Captain Sanders and one of his men went on suspension "pending result of Legislative Investigation Committee." Nine days later, all special Rangers received honorable discharges.[12]

Three Rangers, including Sergeant Hamer, got orders to place them-selves at the service of the committee "for the purpose of summoning and serving witnesses in the twenty-third Senatorial District."[13] The hearings began on January 30 with statements from Harley and Canales. The adjutant general asked the committee to look into eleven issues ranging from the purpose of the Ranger force, including its duties and scope of work, to Canales's charge that a Ranger had vowed to kill him. Senator Page accepted Harley's list and instructed Canales to submit his charges in writing as well.[14]

Harley brought in Dallas attorney Robert E. Lee Knight to represent the Adjutant General's Department, and the Texas and Southwestern Cattle Raisers Association—always closely allied to the Rangers— furnished lawyer Dayton Moses to assist in defending the force's inter-ests.

When the committee began hearing witnesses January 31, the initial appearances amounted more to testimonials than testimony. Assuring those present that the legislature had no intent of abolishing the Rangers, Bledsoe said he wanted testimony on specific incidents, not blanket endorsements of the Rangers. Canales did succeed in getting some damning testimony on the record. Much of it, however, consti-tuted hearsay.

The hearing even brought to light a couple of examples of linguistic evolution. The word *evaporate* took on new meaning in describing the sudden disappearance of Mexicans in Ranger custody. Sometimes those "evaporated" prisoners had been taken by Captain Ransom. In those instances, *Ransomized* developed as a synonym describing the same mysterious phenomenon. As the Austin *American* explained, " 'Evaporate' and 'Ransomize' are two expressions that may be new to many of the people of Texas, but the Ranger hearing in progress . . . is getting in touch with those two phrases right along."[15]

Dozens of people, including several Ranger captains, received subpoenas to appear before the committee. Austin's hotels, particularly the venerable Driskill, filled with other Rangers ostensibly having business in the capital city. One of those was thirty-six-year-old Private Bert C. Veale. He had enlisted in Company C the previous October 24 and had seen service on the border with Captain J. L. Anders.

With so many Rangers in town, Austin should have been the safest city in Texas during the hearings. But the adjutant general soon had to cope with a public image disaster. As Canales proceeded with his argument that many Rangers tended to see themselves as above the law, a group of Rangers proved that some of them indeed did.

On the afternoon of February 7, four Rangers—Veale, Headquarters Company sergeant W. E. Mayberry, and two captains—set out in Veale's touring car for a ride in the country. Armed with their pistols and a couple of bottles of whiskey, Veale and the other Rangers drove across the Congress Avenue bridge and out toward Barton Springs, a scenic area southwest of the Capitol.

Along the way, the Rangers did some practice shooting at fence posts, their ammunition supply diminishing along with their liquor. Sick drunk, Company M captain K. F. Cunningham—the ranking Ranger in the 1917 raid on San Jose, Mexico—vomited on the running board of the car. Captain Harry M. Johnson, Ranger quartermaster, pleaded with Veale to return to town, but the Ranger had more recreation in mind: matching silver dollars. Not wanting to confront a fellow captain, Johnson sat in the car while Veale and Cunningham flipped coins.

Johnson happened to be looking in the opposite direction from the two Rangers when he heard Veale cursing, followed by: "We'll settle it right now!"

"I turned and saw Veale pulling his gun," Johnson later testified. "I got out of the car and attempted to get between Cunningham and Veale. Before I could get to Veale, who had already drawn, he fired twice. Captain Cunningham then pulled his gun."

Johnson ran in front of Veale, yelling, "Men, don't do that!"

Grabbing Mayberry, Veale held him from behind, snapping off a third shot at Cunningham. His ears ringing from the muzzle blast of the .45, Mayberry backed away as Cunningham circled him, aiming at Veale. The sergeant realized Cunningham wanted to avoid shooting him but intended to open up on Veale.

As Mayberry put distance between himself and the two combatants, the other private and the captain blasted away at each other until Veale crumpled on the dirt road. Mayberry ran to the prostrate Ranger, finding him already dead. Looking up, Mayberry saw Cunningham behind a cedar tree.

"I called to him and asked if he was hurt," Mayberry said. "He replied that he was shot, but did not think he was seriously hurt."

The three drunk Rangers walked to a nearby house and asked to use a telephone. When the occupant said he did not have one, they hailed a passing car and got a ride downtown. Mayberry and Johnson helped the bleeding Cunningham into the Driskill and asked the front desk to call a doctor and the sheriff. Travis County sheriff George Matthews arrived at the hotel to find that the Ranger captain had a bullet hole in his hat, a flesh wound in his neck, and a bruise on his abdomen. Cunningham's gold watch had saved him from a gut shot.

A sketchy account of the incident—"Texas Rangers Have Shoot Fest with 2 Casuals"—appeared on page one of the Austin *American* the next morning. The story noted that Cunningham had already been fired and Captain Johnson and Sergeant Mayberry placed on suspension. In addition to losing his job, Cunningham faced a murder charge. Rather than jail him, Sheriff Matthews let the captain spend the night at his house. Later in the day on Saturday, three of the Ranger's friends posted his $1,000 bond.[16]

The governor had Harley issue an order stating that effective 8:00 p.m. that day, "all Rangers who are in attendance upon the Legislative Ingestigation [sic] are ordered to unarm themselves during their stay in Austin."[17]

Meanwhile, the reduction in force continued. Harley suspended Company G captain Charles Stevens along with Captain Anders and two privates on February 11 "pending results of the Investigation Committee of the Legislature." Two days later, Hobby fired Captain Johnson and Sergeant Mayberry over their role in the Austin shooting. Anders got his job back later that month, but Captain Sanders, who had escaped the first round of the governor's Ranger housekeeping, learned that he would not be reappointed. Company K captain W. L. Wright got orders to take over Sanders's territory and men.[18]

Testimony before the legislative committee concluded on February 13, with eighty witnesses having been heard. A committee report recommending a reorganization of the Rangers went to the full House on February 19. The same day, Harley sent letters to all the Loyalty Rangers asking them to return their commissions.[19]

On March 10, Harley disbanded Companies A, L, and M "due to the fact that the war time emergency for Border protection no longer exists." The adjutant general transferred some of the affected Rangers to other companies and reduced others in rank. In addition, some Rangers received honorable discharges. "All men who are eligible and have honorable discharges may file applications for reinstatement when the Ranger Force is reorganized next September under the new reorganization plan," Harley said in the order.[20]

Despite all the turmoil, the Rangers still did their traditional work. Captain Ransom had been dispatched to the booming Eastland County oil town of Ranger in January. The same day Harley disbanded the three companies, Sergeant Sam McKenzie and Private Lee Saulsbury got orders to take the next train to Burkburnett to "give protection to Inspectors M.L. Portwood and Joe Jayne, of the State Food & Drug Department, in the discharge of their duty."[21]

The housecleaning through attrition continued on March 19 with the disbanding of Company E captain W. L. Barler, his sergeant, and five privates, who all received honorable discharges. Captain Wright had to reduce his company to one sergeant and eleven privates. In addition, Sergeant McKenzie got his honorable discharge papers, as did one of the privates in Headquarters Company.[22]

The joint investigative committee's report filled two thousand pages in three volumes. Testimony implicated Rangers in twenty deaths stemming from three incidents. In addition, the report alleged numerous cases of drunkenness, assault, and torture. The most damning incident detailed in the report occurred following the October 1915 train attack north of Brownsville. The sheriff had arrested two suspects, the Rangers four.

"I had made my preparations to take my prisoners back to town to jail when Ransom came to me," Cameron County sheriff Vann testified.

" 'What are you going to do with your prisoners?' he asked.

"I told him I was coming back to town with them.

"He asked, 'Are you going to kill them?'

"I said no, they are prisoners and I shall take them to jail.

"He said, 'You haven't got the guts to kill them.'

"I said I didn't see it would take much guts to kill unarmed Mexicans and he said, 'Well, that's what I am going to do with mine.' "

Vann said he took his prisoners to Brownsville.

"When I returned Ransom had taken his men out about three-quarters of a mile and shot them."[23]

The committee report concluded: "From its inception, the policies of the Ranger force have been the same, and these are now accepted as traditional, 'Get your man and keep no records except of final results.' " As one witness said, "We cannot get along without the Rangers but we want character with it."[24]

While the report did admit "gross violation of both civil and criminal laws" on the part of some Rangers, Harley saw the report as a vindication of the force. Indeed, the report noted that the adjutant general deserved "the commendation of the Senate and House for the able, efficient, impartial, and fearless manner in which he has discharged the duties placed upon him as the head of the Ranger Force."[25]

A substitute to Canales's HB 5, much less of a bill than Canales had hoped for, passed 95–5 in the lower chamber on March 8. After adding amendments concurred on by the House, the Senate approved the bill 27–1 on March 17. Governor Hobby signed the measure on March 31.

The new law reduced the Rangers to four companies of fifteen privates, a sergeant, and a captain. An additional headquarters company of six men would be supervised by a senior captain, the first use of that term since John Salmon "Rip" Ford had the title in 1858. The force would continue to have a quartermaster, but he no longer had to worry about furnishing foodstuff for the companies. The new act provided $30 a month per man for subsistence "when at their station" and up to $3 a day actual expenses when on duty elsewhere. Rangers still had to furnish their own horses, but the act authorized payment of $50 a month for "repairs and upkeep" when "any company of said force furnishes motor transportation without expense to the State." Rangers also could be reimbursed for actual railroad expenses when traveling on duty. Railroad passes, a problem for years, would no longer be used. While the authorized strength of the Rangers was somewhat smaller than it had been, the act gave the governor authority "to increase the force to meet extraordinary conditions."[26]

Beyond the new law, the Canales hearings had another effect, one that proved longer reaching. His interest in the Rangers already piqued by the extensive newspaper coverage of the various border incidents, the revelations that came out of the legislature convinced Walter Prescott Webb he should change horses in midstream on his master's thesis. Finding that no one had ever written a general history of the Rangers, Webb talked with Dr. Eugene Barker, head of the University of Texas's history department. Barker said yes, he could change his topic to the history of the Rangers.[27]

As Webb began delving into the Rangers' past, Harley continued to define the postwar force. A letter concerning fornication gave the general an opportunity to share his views with one of his captains.

Captain Gray in Marfa had forwarded Harley a request from Pecos County sheriff D. S. Barker, a former Ranger, asking for Ranger help in rounding up fornicators. "While this department is emphatically opposed to illicit intercourse between men and women and does not mean to countenance it in any way," Harley responded on June 30, 1919, "there is too much illicit intercourse in the State of Texas and too few Rangers for us to undertake to eliminate this social evil through the Ranger Force." The general went on to say that Gray could use his own judgment in regard to "this particular instance" but added: "I must impress upon you as upon all other captains that you may in turn impress upon other peace officers of the State that the Ranger Force has a larger and a more important duty to perform than that of chasing the phantom passion of the human race."

The general continued:

> In the future Rangers will not be used to do the work of local officers, only . . . to assist them when matters get beyond their [local officers'] control, or in sections of the State where wholesale violations of the law are notoriously known to exist and cannot be successfully coped with by local authorities. Always remember the Ranger Force is a higher and more important arm of the police power of the State than the local officers and that they are not to do the little things that local officers should do.[28]

The new Ranger law became effective July 1. While the 1911 Ranger law required men hired as Rangers to be of "good moral character," the new law required prospective Rangers to furnish "satisfactory evidence thereof." Too, the governor would do all the hiring, not the individual captains. In addition to being sober and of sound judgment, Rangers had to be citizens of the United States. Preference "shall always be given to discharged soldiers holding certificates of honorable discharge from the United States Army." Should any Rangers not live up to these statutory standards, the act further provided that "it shall be the duty of any citizen who knows of any . . . misconduct or violation of the law on the part of any member of the ranger force to at once notify the Adjutant General in writing of [such] misconduct." If a complaint were made, the act stipulated, the adjutant general would have the right to conduct an investigation through a local magistrate. That magistrate would receive a $3 fee from the state for subpoenaing witnesses and having testimony reduced to writing by a stenographer. The stenographer would be paid fifteen cents per hundred words of testimony. The adjutant general then could "take such action thereon as the facts make necessary." For the first time in Ranger history, a formal means of handling citizen complaints was in place.

Harley had his captains distribute to all Rangers copies of a fourteen-page booklet outlining the new set of rules and regulations. The document's preamble made the state's new attitude toward its Rangers pretty plain:

> The Texas Ranger Force was created by a special Act of the Legislature for the purpose of protecting all good citizens against depredation upon their property and their rights. A Ranger who is appointed under this law is a creature of the law, and any authority he may have, or any power he may exercise, is given and received by virtue of the law under which he operates. All officers of the law are creatures of it and a creature cannot become bigger than a creator and whenever an officer undertakes to set himself up as superior to the law or superior to the citizens, whose servant he is, his usefulness as an officer ceases.[29]

In July, the newly reconstituted Rangers got a chance to protect "all good citizens against depredation" when a newspaper story triggered a race riot in the East Texas city of Longview. Copies of a black-owned newspaper published in Chicago "in which appeared a scurrilous item concerning a white woman of Gregg County, Texas" circulated in Longview. When "a number of young white men" went to the black section of town looking for the man distributing the newspaper, "a fight [took] place between the negroes and the whites, shots being exchanged and several of the white men being slightly wounded." Several black houses went up in flames and "the situation became very tense."[30] With local officers no longer able to maintain order, Harley ordered Austin-based quartermaster and captain Roy W. Aldrich and six other Rangers to Longview on July 11. Skinny, tall, and politically savvy, Aldrich had been a Ranger since 1915. Three more Rangers joined Aldrich over the next several days, along with National Guard troops following a martial law declaration by Governor Hobby on July 13. The show of force and "merited" arrests calmed the situation, enabling the governor to lift martial law on July 18.[31]

Adjutant General Harley stepped down as of September 30, 1919, leaving as his legacy—with some help from Canales—a more professional Ranger service. Ignoring the abuses that had occurred on his watch, Harley praised the Rangers in his final report to the governor:

The Ranger Force, as it exists today, is composed of high class, experienced, and efficient men. They have responded to every call and obeyed every order issued to them as befits a high class peace officer, and I cannot too strongly commend these efficient officers for the valuable service they have rendered this State.[32]

Disappointed that he had not been able to do more to reform the Rangers, Canales opted not to seek reelection in 1920, primarily because of animosity from other legislators. Despite several threats, no Ranger ever laid a hand on him, but his political career had evaporated as surely as any "Ransomized" Mexican.

5

"An Asset to Any Law Abiding Community"

THE 1920S

Not even two years after the end of the war that President Woodrow Wilson believed made the world safe for democracy, constitutional safeguards in the south began to fade in the flickering light of burning crosses. In secret ceremonies across Texas, hundreds and then thousands of men took a chilling oath:

> Sirs: Have you assumed without mental reservation your Oath of Allegiance to the Invisible Empire? Mortal man cannot assume a more binding oath; character and courage alone will enable you to keep it. Always remember that to keep this oath means to you honor, happiness and life; but to violate it means Disgrace, Dishonor and Death.[1]

In Houston on October 9, 1920, the annual parade of the United Confederate Veterans had a new feature: white-hooded Ku Klux Klan members marching and on horseback. That night, the Sam Houston Klan Number 1 gained the distinction of getting Texas's first KKK charter. Klan organizers had been in the Bayou City since September, recruiting one hundred men "of notable standing" to help fix everything they saw as wrong with a rapidly urbanizing Texas. George B. Kimbro, Texas's king kleagle, soon began a vigorous statewide membership campaign. Meanwhile, a Houston manufacturer of overalls altered his product line, enjoying a brisk sale of cotton Klan robes at $1.50 each.[2]

Earlier that year, at the nation's busiest cotton port, labor strife disrupted life in Galveston nearly as much as a hurricane. And the Rangers soon stood in the eye of the storm. The problem began March 19, 1920, when sixteen hundred dockworkers belonging to the International Longshoremen's Association coastwise locals in Galveston joined a week-old nationwide walkout over wage parity with deep-sea locals. Instead of sixty cents an hour, the mostly black Caribbean longshoremen who loaded and unloaded coastwise vessels wanted eighty cents an hour, the same pay other longshoremen, predominantly white, earned for handling freight carried by oceangoing ships. When the Mallory steamship line tried to bring in nonunion workers on May 10, scattered violence peppered with gunfire broke out along the docks in the island city.

Pro-union Galveston officials supported the strike, but they did not want violence. Responding to a May 13 request for Ranger assistance, Adjutant General W. D. Cope sent his headquarters troubleshooter, Captain Aldrich, and three Rangers to investigate conditions. Aldrich soon reported various violent acts by "strikers and their sympathizers" and asked for more Rangers to snuff a "smoldering powder keg." Responding to appeals from the business community and open-shop advocates, Governor Hobby sent Cope to Galveston to assess the situation. Based on Cope's findings, and with the strike threatening to leave a record cotton crop stacked at the wharves as well as "hundreds of tons of merchandise . . . consigned to merchants in all parts of Texas," Hobby declared martial law along the waterfront effective June 7 and dispatched Brigadier General Jacob F. Wolters and a thousand troops. Three days later, with National Guardsmen in campaign hats manning dockside machine-gun emplacements and horseshoes clicking on pavement as cavalry patrolled the city, strikebreakers loaded the first freighter with cotton and rice.[3]

What began as a move by the governor to reopen the nation's second-busiest port expanded into a general cleanup of the wide-open island city, a place offering conventioneers, maritime workers, and soldiers stationed at Fort Crockett convenient access to bootleg booze, gambling, and houses of prostitution amid swaying palms and fragrant oleanders. Under the Volstead Act, manufacturing or selling alcoholic beverages had been a federal crime since 12:01 a.m. January 16, 1920. Constitutional Prohibition having an adverse impact on the city's economy, Galveston's law enforcement agencies had not gone overboard in enforcing the new law. But smuggled liquor made striking longshoremen even more a threat to the scabs working for the shippers. Realizing that, the Rangers and guardsmen cracked down, seizing a considerable amount of contraband liquor.

Frustrated by unenthusiastic local cooperation, Hobby expanded the scope of his martial law declaration, suspending the police chief and all members of his department effective 3:30 p.m. July 15. The governor also relieved the uncooperative city administration of any law enforcement authority. General Wolters announced that "all vagrants must be apprehended and put to work, that all gambling and immoral houses must be closed and the illegal manufacture, sale, and importation of intoxicating liquor must be stopped."

After meeting with a Galveston citizen's committee on September 18, the governor agreed to end martial law as soon as possible and hand law enforcement responsibility to the Rangers. Within days, twenty-four mounted Rangers from as far away as the Big Bend patrolled the city.[4]

Hobby placed Captain Joe B. Brooks in command of the Rangers on the island, ordering him to "assume control and authority over the Police Department, and all peace officers, both regular and special, in the City of Galveston" effective midnight September 30. The governor told Brooks to "enforce the laws of the State without partiality and keep open those arteries of trade . . . essential to the prosperity and uninterrupted conduct of business in Texas." In doing so, Hobby expected the captain to "avoid entanglements and the slightest alignment with any faction or element or organization between home issues or controversies that have arisen with respect to the situation at hand."[5]

With so many Rangers in Galveston, Sergeant C. J. Blackwell got promoted to captain on October 1 and placed in command of Austin-based Emergency Company Number 1. A Ranger company had never before been given a numeric designation or formally called an emergency company. Hobby's authority to raise the company came under Article 6561 of the new Ranger statute, which provided that "in cases of emergency . . . the Governor shall have the authority to increase the force to meet extraordinary conditions."

The same day Blackwell became a captain, twenty-nine-year-old Manuel Trazazas Gonzaullas, an impeccable dresser who could shoot almost as straight as the starched creases in his trousers, received his Ranger commission in Austin. Born in Spain to naturalized American citizens, Gonzaullas grew up in El Paso. The stories he heard and read about Captain Hughes inspired Gonzaullas to join the Rangers, the beginning of a career that would last longer than Hughes's. Almost immediately after becoming a Ranger, Gonzaullas left for Wichita County with Captain Aldrich to help pacify things in the still-rowdy oil-field boomtown of Burkburnett. An independent sort, in less than two months the young Ranger had already shot and wounded a Prohibition violator in Eastland County and earned a nickname that would stick for the rest of his life: Lone Wolf.[6]

Hobby lifted martial law in Galveston on October 7, leaving the Gulf city solely to the Rangers. Throughout the fall, Rangers kept the peace, their efforts ranging from investigating felonies to issuing misdemeanor citations to speeders, the first-ever traffic law enforcement by state officers. By December 1920, the strike broken, the union longshoremen had gone back to work. Rangers, in turn, began returning to their previous stations across the state. Mayor H. O. Sappington told reporters he hated to see the state lawmen leave. "The rangers are an asset to any law abiding community and we all want them to stay with us," he said. Despite the circumstances that had made Brooks their de facto boss, the members of the Galveston police force presented the Ranger captain with a diamond stickpin before he left the island.[7] During their four-month stay on the island, Rangers had made 1,510 arrests. But the Ranger effort to save Galveston from vice proved no more enduring than a child's sand castle on the beach.

In Galveston, the Rangers had functioned as police officers. Earlier that year, Hobby had used the Rangers to assert the state's sovereignty. For years, Texas and Oklahoma had been arguing over what constituted their true boundary—the center of the Red River or its south bank. The dispute actually predated both states, going back to 1819, when Spain and the United States had entered into a treaty establishing the border between Spanish territory and the young American republic. But as production in the rich Burkburnett oil field expanded north into the river's floodplain, a 480-acre tract known as the Burk Divide field suddenly had an estimated value of $100,000,000. Lawsuits started piling up in both state and federal courthouses like so many past-due bills. "The millions of dollars involved in any decision rendered forecast a great legal battle when the suit comes to trial," the Associated Press reported from Washington on January 10, 1920.

The battle of briefs soon verged on a battle of bullets as claimants on both sides of the issue—and the river—argued that the Burk Divide oil wells belonged to them. District courts in both states placed the contested real estate under receivers pending resolution of the conflicting claims. Concurring with the state attorney general's position that the wells south of the Red River's centerline belonged to Texas, Hobby sent Adjutant General Cope to assess the situation in Wichita County. Cope quickly realized that violence could erupt at any moment. Armed guards working for the Burk Divide Oil Company, supported by Tillman County, Oklahoma, sheriff's deputies, stood ready to enforce signs that warned: "This is Tillman County Land—Keep Off!"

On January 20, reporters in Fort Worth saw fifteen heavily armed Rangers newly arrived from South Texas boarding a train for Wichita Falls. "Rangers Prepare for Action," the Austin *Statesman* declared in large type across its front page the following day. Word in the oil patch had it that Hobby intended to use the Rangers to seize the disputed wells. Newspapers fanned the flames. While the Rangers waited out a winter storm in the comfort of the St. James Hotel, the stakeholders in the controversy alternately blustered and negotiated. When the weather improved, a contingent of twenty-five Rangers left by automobile for the disputed field at 11:45 a.m. on January 24. Arriving a couple of hours later, they pitched tents on a bluff overlooking the oil wells in question. Across from the Rangers, well within rifle range, some fifty armed Oklahomans had their own camp.

Though newspapers used the words *civil war* in reporting on the situation, the attorneys general of each state agreed that Texas would hold the field until the matter could be resolved in federal court. After the Rangers and Oklahoma law enforcement officers succeeded in peacefully disarming civilian hotheads on both sides, General Cope returned to Austin on January 28. Just in case, he left behind a detachment of Rangers.[8]

In one of numerous lawsuits filed in state court, attorney Jesse B. Root did not overburden his petition with legal jargon in saying what he thought about the Texas Rangers' role in the issue:

There appears to have been a studied effort upon the part of persons that wrote affidavits to leave the impression that the Burk Divide guards were outlaws and bandits and that the Texas Rangers were merely religious missionaries sent to that wild region to open and conduct Bible classes.

But, the lawsuit continued,

it is known by 20,000 persons in Tillman County in Oklahoma and in Wichita County in Texas that the Texas Rangers successfully carried out a *coup d'etat* . . . by suddenly rushing into the bed of Red River armed with rifles and revolvers and overpowering the Burk Divide guards, seized the property. The Rangers were in boot[s] and big hats. There were twenty Rangers; five went to each well.[9]

The matter dragged on in the courts for another seven years, but the Ranger role in the dispute had ended.[10]

The episode ended the Ranger career of Company A captain Charles Stevens, who had refused Hobby's order to move into the contested field. Asserting that he would "not be a lawbreaker simply to protect private claimants," Stevens resigned his commission effective February 3. Hobby, in turn, disbanded Stevens's entire company.[11]

A Ranger's Son Becomes Governor

After three years in office, Hobby decided not to seek a second full term. The new governor would be Pat Neff, who defeated former U.S. senator Joseph Weldon Bailey in a runoff election in August 1920.[12]

Neff, a fifty-year-old lawyer from Waco whose father had ridden as a Ranger, took the oath of office on January 18, 1921. In one of his first official acts, the Baptist governor—a former McLennan County district attorney—asked for the resignation of any Ranger who drank or gambled. "It was made plain . . . that neither drinking nor gambling would for a moment be tolerated, and that [Rangers] must be law abiding citizens . . . ," Neff later wrote. "I could see nothing incompatible in a man being both a Ranger and a gentleman."[13]

Two days after his inauguration, Neff appointed Amarillo drugstore owner Thomas Dickson Barton, a veteran of the Spanish-American War and the world war, as adjutant general. The politically ambitious Barton took on the job with vigor, joining Rangers on raids and soon becoming the most hands-on adjutant general since Mabry. Some believed that Barton's enthusiasm for law and order stemmed from his support of the Klan, if not secret membership.[14] Whatever Barton's motivation, with Texas once again living up to its national reputation as a wild and woolly place, he stayed busy.

"Texas," Neff recalled, "was being swept by the greatest crime wave in her history. Cold, cruel, calculating crime was organized . . . one of the established industries of the State."[15] Not that law-abiding folks took the situation in stride. Texas reported more lynchings in 1920 than any other state.

TEQUILEROS

Prohibition had a lot to do with the upsurge in crime. Available for $2 to $3 a gallon in Mexico, liquor could be sold in Texas for $3 to $10 a quart. "This proves a very lucrative business for the lawless element," the Adjutant General's Department said in its 1917–1918 report, two years before national Prohibition. "The magnitude of this traffic is inconceivable. During the last few months two Rangers and custom guard[s] have lost their lives assisting the local and Federal officers to capture the outlaws."[16]

Rangers killed *tequileros* as well. Fifty-three-year-old Captain Will Wright's company, responsible for 350 miles of border from Brownsville to Laredo, had eight gunfights with smugglers in 1921. A report sent to Austin on September 19 shed light on the company's activities, results, and attitude:

Captain [Wright] and I are going to Cotulla today as court convenes there. We landed a bunch of horseback smugglers on the tenth. You ought to have been along. One of them thought he would learn us how to shoot, so I naturalized him (made an American citizen out of him, you know).

On November 17, 1921, Wright and his Rangers ran into armed smugglers sixty miles south of Hebbronville. Chasing them five miles, the Rangers captured three men and eleven horses. The next day, forty-five miles east of Laredo, the Rangers engaged a twenty-man party, taking three prisoners and collecting eighteen horses. Then, on November 22, 1921, Wright and his men battled sixteen smugglers fifteen miles northwest of Realitos on the Barronena Ranch in Duval County. Wright's Rangers wounded some of the Mexicans, but all the *tequileros* escaped into the brush. Still, the Rangers seized three thousand quarts of liquor and thirty-seven horses. On top of that, the smugglers left behind two freshly cooked goats, which the Rangers converted to state use.[17] College-educated J. Frank Dobie, a South Texas cattleman's son just beginning a lifelong interest in Texas folklore, had been riding with the Rangers when they jumped the smugglers. "I've never enjoyed two days so much in my life," he wrote his wife, Bertha, shortly after the firefight. Wright, meanwhile, apologized to headquarters for letting some of the smugglers get away. "I am very sorry," the captain wrote, "but they will have something to remember from the Rangers." By year's end, the Rangers had captured ninety-five head of horses and confiscated or destroyed ten thousand quarts of liquor.[18]

Most Rangers did not share Dobie's enthusiasm for their new Prohibition-related duties. "Apprehending violators of the eighteenth amendment was always a distasteful duty to the Rangers," one longtime Ranger recalled. "They were never interested in the cargoes of pack trains, as such. Other serious factors were involved in the movement of this illicit liquor." *Tequileros* rode into Texas well armed, "[constituting] an armed invasion of the United States." Most of these horsebackers would readily shoot any officer trying to arrest them and take their inventory. The horses and pack animals of the smugglers also brought ticks into Texas, a major problem for cattle raisers.[19]

Crime in the oil patch also continued to keep the Rangers busy. On

February 11, 1921, Captain Aldrich left Austin by train for Cisco, where he met three Rangers who came in from Breckenridge. With the Eastland County attorney, the four Rangers drove to the boomtown of Ranger to visit the Commercial Hotel. As the adjutant general later reported: "This resort was conducted with about as much secrecy as a grocery store, and could not possibly have been operated in so open a manner without the knowledge of the local peace officers." Sending two men to cover the back fire escape, Aldrich took the front door with Ranger W. L. Lesueur. On the third floor, they barged in on a gambling operation.

"We were fortunate in capturing and holding ninety men, while some ten or fifteen escaped," Aldrich reported. Sorting through the crowd, the Rangers determined only three men "were not habitués of such resorts" and released them. The others would have gone to jail, but proprietor Alfred "Kid" Jordan and business partner Cleve Barnes assured a justice of the peace that they would cover the men's bail and fines. Aldrich left the seized gaming paraphernalia in the custody of the JP, to "dispose of . . . as the law directs." True to their word, Jordan and Barnes paid the $20.70 fine for each of the eighty-seven gamblers arrested. Perhaps proving that when people do good things, good things happen to them, a jury later found Barnes not guilty of operating a gaming place. Correctly reading the tea leaves that they had no hope of getting any prosecution, the Rangers pulled out of the town named in their honor on April 1. In fact, they all but vacated the oil patch, leaving only a few men in Wichita Falls.[20]

Rangers had better results in dealing with the destruction of county-owned livestock dipping vats by cattle raisers who did not take to the notion of the government telling them they had to treat their herds for ticks. That spring, parties unknown dynamited several dozen vats in Cass, Bowie, Gregg, Milam, Red River, Shelby, and Titus counties. "Since the State force was sent into the trouble zone," a federal livestock inspector reported on June 1, "not a vat has been destroyed and the majority of those blown up during the past three years have been rebuilt." The Rangers "went about their work in the characteristic Ranger way," he continued. "They didn't spend any time in arguing, but went right after the disaffected ones, and the result has been that we have been able not only to rebuild the destroyed vats but to construct a number of new ones, and the infected cattle are being brought in and dipped as ordered."[21]

Many Texans had finally awakened to the dangerously infectious nature of the KKK. By July 1921, some eighty floggings had occurred in the state. But the Klan's kidnapping at Tenaha of a young woman suspected of bigamy outraged law-abiding Texans. Hooded men stripped her to the waist, beating her with a wet rope before applying tar and feathers. The incident in the small Shelby County community brought national media attention and marked the turning point in public opinion toward the Klan in Texas.[22]

Despite Neff's tough talk about crime, the thirty-seventh legislature reduced Ranger funding by $50,000 effective September 1. Barton had to issue honorable discharges to one sergeant and twelve privates, decreasing the size of the Ranger force to fifty men—down from eighty-seven only two years earlier. Company A took the hardest hit, losing five men. Captain Tom Hickman, a Ranger since 1919 and now commander of Fort Worth–based Company B, had to let go four Rangers. Company C captain Aaron W. Cunningham resigned in disgust, but Hickman, a rodeo cowboy with a big smile, would go on to have a significant role in shaping the twentieth-century Rangers.[23]

The border had settled considerably since the teens, but it remained a likely trouble spot for the Rangers. On Christmas night 1921, a holiday celebration at a small community on the Rio Grande in Presidio County led to the line-of-duty death of Ranger B. J. Buchanon. Forty-eight hours later, on Marfa Chamber of Commerce stationery Captain Gray wrote a two-page letter to Adjutant General Barton providing the details:

> On the knight of Dec 25 the Mexicans was having a Dance at Polvo in the Army camp. About 12 oclock two strange Mexicans came into the Dance Hall. Buchanon ask several Mexicans who they was. None seemed to know. So Buchanon went to them ask who they was and what their business was. They replied that it was none of His Dam business. Buchanon hit one of them in the face. Then the two Mexicans pulled there guns, also Buchanon. Buchanon shot first but missed his man. Then they both began to shott Buchanon. He was shot in the right Shoulder the first shot. So he was unable to use his gun any more. We trailed them into Mexico and up the River about one half mile then they crossed back to this side. . . . Looks like they was sent there to do what they did . . . Yours to command, Capt Jerry Gray.[24]

Gray and his men never found Buchanon's killers. "Fear still stalks the river," H. W. Schutze wrote in a letter to the editor published in a Marfa newspaper. "Foul murder lurks there and there is no protection. Bandits across the border are a menace to all."[25] Since the beginning of the Mexican Revolution eleven years earlier, nine Rangers had died violently along the Rio Grande.

No matter the dicey state of affairs along the upper Rio Grande, one of the department's most respected captains got transferred from his border post. Frank Hamer, captain of Company C in Del Rio, got orders to relocate in Austin effective January 1, 1922, to take over supervision of Headquarters Company.[26]

MEXIA

Less than a week after beginning his new assignment in Austin, Hamer helped coordinate a major crackdown in another oil boom town. Mexia, forty-one miles east of Waco in Limestone County, had grown from a quiet county seat of twenty-five hundred to a city of thirty thousand with the suddenness of a well blowout.[27] "The easy money to be earned in the oil fields attracted thousands of honest people who came with their families, hoping to improve their circumstances, but it also attracted a great band of criminals of every type from the desperado to the common vagrant," the adjutant general reported. Before long conditions in Mexia had deteriorated to "a state of lawlessness that amounted to anarchy."[28]

On January 7, Adjutant General Barton, with Assistant Attorney General Clifford Stone to handle the legal paperwork, led two Ranger companies under captains Hamer and Hickman on a raid of the two most notorious joints in the area, The Winter Garden, four miles from Mexia off the Teague highway, and the Chicken Farm, near the community of Wortham. The fifteen Rangers—armed with scatterguns and some of the new .45-caliber Thompson Model 1921 submachine guns—confiscated gambling devices and bootleg whiskey and made numerous arrests.

The Chicken Farm, the Rangers noted, did a thriving business only two hundred yards from the residence of a Limestone County sheriff's deputy. A check of county deed records showed that the deputy had sold the four-acre tract where the "farm" now stood for $750 an acre, though he had prudently retained mineral rights. "I do not know what was going on in this building after it opened," the deputy later claimed in an affidavit.

After crashing the joint at gunpoint, the Rangers could be more specific. In addition to gambling paraphernalia and whiskey, they found some unusual architecture for a restaurant and cabaret: a small room, one of its walls lined with a series of portholes, that afforded a view of the interior and front portion of the establishment. When the Rangers burst in, men armed with rifles sat on the stools atop an elevated platform in the room. In the back, Rangers noted a trapdoor clearly intended for rapid egress from the building. Rangers also discovered a trapdoor sufficient for the disposal of bootleg liquor, if necessary.

Not satisfied with the low level of cooperation from local prosecutors and law enforcement officials, on January 11 Governor Neff declared martial law in portions of Freestone and Limestone counties effective the following day. A contingent of National Guardsmen from the Fifty-sixth Cavalry Brigade and 141st Infantry descended on Mexia. The same day, roughly three thousand residents apparently realized they had important business elsewhere and quickly left town.[29]

Two days after the state takeover, fire broke out downtown. As flames threatened the business district, a mob estimated as large as fifteen thousand formed. Guardsmen dispersed the crowd while Rangers patrolled the back alleys to prevent looting. With Mexia's jail not nearly large enough to handle all those arrested, the state troops transported prisoners to nearby county seats. For the first time in Ranger history, their prisoners got photographed and fingerprinted. The state had no such forensic expertise but called on the Houston Police Department, which sent its expert in the Bertillon fingerprint identification system.

In the first known use of an airplane in Texas for law enforcement purposes, the state employed aerial photography to locate illicit stills hidden along the Trinity River in eastern Freestone County. Armed with that evidence, Neff expanded his martial law declaration on February 2 to include all of the county.

During the cleanup, Rangers and soldiers made 602 arrests and captured twenty-seven stills. They destroyed 2,270 gallons of liquor and 213 barrels of corn mash. Rangers also seized $4,000 worth of narcotics and turned the drugs over to federal officers. In addition to drying up the supply of alcohol and other drugs, Rangers recovered fifty-three stolen automobiles and seized thirteen other vehicles for federal forfeiture because bootleggers used them.

The activities of the Rangers and guardsmen, Wolters wrote, "resulted in a general civic awakening in Mexia." Residents held mass meetings aimed at retaking control of their city. The county attorney's office, the sheriff's department, and the police force were reorganized. On Wolters's recommendation, the governor lifted martial law on March 1. Most of the troops had left the day before. From salaries to stationery, the forty-seven-day operation cost the state $14,793.07.[30]

"It has been for years the common belief that soldiers and Rangers could not work together harmoniously," Wolters wrote. "Whatever foundation there may have been for this general belief, and whatever may have been the actual experience in the past . . . it is with pride that I report that no finer spirit of harmonious co-operation between men charged with the performance of difficult and unpleasant duties could possibly have prevailed."

The men under Hamer and Hickman, the general reported, had "proved themselves to be gentlemen in the broadest sense of that often misused term. Courageous and impersonal in the performance of duty, they exemplified on every occasion the highest ideals and the best traditions of the Ranger Force that constitutes so great a part of the glorious history of Texas." As for the law-abiding people who stayed in Limestone County after the state takeover, for years a running joke held, "It took the Rangers, the National Guard, and a fire to clean Mexia up!"[31]

The Rangers had made a dent in lawlessness in one oil boom town, but despite growing opposition, the Klan continued to fester. With more than a hundred chapters, the Klan had an estimated seventy-five to ninety thousand members in Texas. Many prosecutors, judges, police chiefs, sheriffs, and journalists donned white hoods. In the opinion of those opposed to the Klan's terrorism, even Governor Neff seemed soft on the hooded order. His only counsel to the Rangers concerning the Klan was to monitor KKK activities, not stop them or try to identify those involved in illegal activity.[32]

To former Frontier Battalion Ranger James B. Gillett, the state of affairs in Texas during the Neff administration made the days of his service seem practically tranquil by comparison. But he still had an interesting story to tell. In February Gillett published a book that would become a Texas classic, *Six Years with the Texas Rangers*. The old Ranger sent copies to a number of friends, including former captain John H. Rogers. The captain, who had spent a much longer time than Gillett as a Ranger, liked what he read. "Your book is different from most . . . in that it is written in modesty, and relates truths, whether they be favorable or unfavorable, in given cases," Rogers said in a thank-you letter to the new author. Then Rogers offered an opinion about the Rangers in general: "In the main the success of this historic old force is simply wonderful and I have but little doubt it has been the most successful small force of peace officers that the world has ever known, and accomplished more bringing about a state of civilization in Texas, and especially the frontier."[33] Gillett peddled his memoir for $2.50 postage paid, but the book broke into the national mainstream in 1925 with a new edition from Yale University Press. Publication of this edition, edited and with an introduction by Milo M. Quaife, marked the first scholarly recognition of the Rangers.

The Anti-Klan League found the contemporary Rangers more interesting than their nineteenth-century predecessors. The organization demanded that Neff provide the names of any KKK members in the Rangers or Texas National Guard. The governor said he would have Barton look into the matter. On June 17, 1922, the adjutant general reported that he had "personally or by written inquiries" interviewed "the Captains of the companies, all Rangers and members of the Adjutant General's Department, and have failed to find any who are members of the Ku Klux Klan."[34]

"We Damn Near Ran the Trains . . ."

Satisfied that the Rangers harbored no Klan members, Neff soon handed the force another major task. This time the trouble arose in Denison, the state's rail gateway. The North Texas town had the largest freight yards south of Chicago. Roughly four hundred thousand railroad workers nationwide walked off the job on July 1, 1922, over a pay dispute. In Texas, some fourteen hundred railroad workers belonging to six Federated Shop Craft Union locals joined the strike, paralyzing the Denison yards of the Texas and Pacific as well as the Missouri, Kansas and Texas Railroad. The strike looked to be getting out of hand on the night of July 11, when idle railroad men kidnapped twenty-four strike-breakers "in the presence of county, precinct, and city officers" and took them north to the Red River bridge. After beating them, the strikers banished the scabs to Oklahoma. In addition, strikers met all incoming trains to "take charge" of any new employees coming in. At least a hundred imported workers had already been flogged.

On July 15, Neff ordered his adjutant general and Captain Hickman to Denison to assess the situation. The governor followed that up by traveling there "in disguise" for a firsthand look. Convinced that conditions there had not been exaggerated and likely would worsen, on July 23—one day after he won the Democratic primary in his bid for a second term—Neff ordered the entire available Ranger force to Grayson County. The Rangers, "booted and spurred, broad-brimmed hats pulled low over bronzed faces, side arms peeping from under coats," set up camp in Forest Park, not far from the MK&T shops.

Neff had forty-four Rangers on the scene, leaving only three Rangers to cover the rest of the state, but railroad officials said it would take hundreds more "properly armed and trained" men to keep the peace. Worried about the strike's effect on the nation's commerce, the federal government agreed with the railroad. A none-too-veiled threat that one thousand federal troops from Fort Sam Houston in San Antonio would be sent to Denison if Neff took no further action resulted in the governor reluctantly declaring martial law in Denison on July 24. Soon 473 National Guard troops converged on the community to keep the peace. In addition to the Rangers already on hand, as had been done during the labor troubles in Galveston Barton raised a contingent of emergency Rangers. "While of necessity these emergency Rangers had to be quickly enlisted, the class of men chosen was of high quality, taken as a whole," the adjutant general reported. "Out of the total number employed, some 450 at the high point, but a small percentage proved unworthy, and these were at once discharged when their unfitness became apparent."[35] The various railroad companies crippled by the strike gladly covered all the costs connected to these emergency rangers.

Though the Denison effort got most of the public attention, Neff used the open-port law—an act passed during his predecessor's administration that prohibited any action hindering free trade in the state—to justify sending Rangers to other important railroad centers across the state, including Amarillo, Big Spring, Cleburne, Dalhart, Gainesville, Marshall, Palestine, Texline, Tyler, and Waco. The governor also posted Rangers in Baird, Childress, Fort Worth, Kingsville, Longview, Lufkin, Quanah, Sherman, Smithville, Stamford, and Texarkana—all significant rail points. Leaving Hickman in Denison, Barton dispatched Captain Hamer to Amarillo, Captain Roy Nichols to Marshall, and Captain Wright to Cleburne. Rangers stood guard at roundhouses and patrolled tracks to prevent sabotage. As one Ranger later put it, "We damn near ran the trains and everything else."[36]

Neff continued military control in Denison until October 22, when the emergency Rangers returned to civilian life and the regular Rangers moved on. Some three hundred arrests had been made, mostly for assault or vagrancy, but sympathetic local juries found few defendants guilty. Even so, Neff later wrote, the state occupation "brought order out of chaos and respect out of threatened violence."[37]

In his 1921–1922 biennial report, Adjutant General Barton said Texas needed twice as many Rangers as it had. "Even with that strength," he wrote, "it will not be possible for the Ranger Force to answer all the urgent calls which are made upon it." Indeed, Neff's use of Rangers to keep the railroads running had left most of Texas virtually unprotected at the state level for most of 1922.[38]

"The Bootlegger Must Go . . ."

Neff said on January 12, 1923, in one of his eight legislative messages that Texas had averaged three murders a day in 1922. Declaring that law enforcement remained "the burning question" in Texas, the governor promised to "revivify, rehabilitate, and re-electrify" the state's criminal statutes, particularly those involving Prohibition. "The bootlegger must go," the governor said.[39]

Despite state and federal efforts, finding a drink in Texas posed no great difficulty, particularly in the state's largest city. With a population exceeding two hundred thousand in addition to a large military presence, San Antonio warmly embraced its soldier boys as well as other visitors with money in their pockets. Bristling at the Alamo City's flagrant disregard for the Prohibition law, the governor dispatched Rangers to shut down the party. On July 24, Barton, Captain Hamer, and three

Rangers raided a joint called the Pastime Club, arresting twenty-six people. Then they hit other, smaller clubs, making more arrests under the Prohibition statute.

Bexar County district attorney D. A. McAskill pronounced the Ranger operation "splendid work," but San Antonio Fire and Police Commissioner Phil Wright dismissed the raids as "merely a repetition of what the police do virtually ever night." Mayor John W. Tobin and Chamber of Commerce president Claude V. Birkhead spoke more frankly: Their city had "no need of state Rangers."[40]

The governor saw it differently. Neff authorized an emergency Ranger command designated as Company E and appointed San Antonio resident and former U.S. Secret Service agent B. C. Baldwin as captain. Baldwin's charge: Stop bootlegging and gambling. The new captain established his headquarters in an old two-story house at 331 Garden Street, south of the Alamo. He had a telephone installed, kept a desk sergeant on hand to take calls, and in effect ran a separate police department. Men whose predecessors in the service had fought Indians, outlaws, and border bandits had been transformed by a staunch Baptist governor into vice cops. The urban Rangers divided their time between raids and "skylarking."[41]

As Neff later explained,

San Antonio is a fine place to live in the year around, owing to its climate . . . [and] a great many tourists, good and semi-good, are usually in the city. It also has a large foreign population. This combination . . . helps to make it a rather fertile place for violations of the law. To aid in the enforcement of the State laws, I decided to station a squad of [Rangers] there. No one asked me to do so. Vigorous opposition met the announcement of my decision.[42]

While scouting the border for bootleggers and shutting down speakeasies and gambling dens preoccupied the Ranger force, the Ku Klux Klan continued to take the law into its own hands despite declining public support. On August 15, 1923, men in white robes adorned with blood-red crosses flogged and then tarred and feathered a reputed booze peddler in Amarillo, the adjutant general's hometown. Another group of Klansmen at Iowa Park in Wichita County flogged a suspected lawbreaker.

The next day, passionately anti-Klan lieutenant governor T. W. Davidson, acting governor with Neff out of state, dispatched Captain Hamer to Amarillo to investigate the Klan's activities there. Two days later, Davidson ordered Rangers to Port Arthur, Texarkana, and Wichita Falls to investigate other acts of Klan brutality. Back in Texas on August 19, Neff said he would continue using the Rangers to suppress Klan actions. The Rangers had no difficulty in gathering enough evidence for the filing of charges against suspected Klan members, but only in Amarillo, where the several defendants included the sheriff, did prosecutors succeed in getting a conviction. A Potter County jury sentenced the local Klan leader to two years in prison, but another jury acquitted the sheriff and four other Klan members.[43]

Along the border, Captain Wright and his men continued to ride the Rio Grande looking for bootleggers. Late that summer, a rookie named William A. (Bill) Dial joined Wright's company. Dial's commission noted his age as twenty-one, but in truth, the new Ranger's birth certificate recorded that he had come into the world on February 7, 1903. Not wanting to lie about being shy of his legal majority, before showing up to be sworn in as a Ranger Dial had scribbled the number "21" on a scrap of paper and placed it in one of his boots. When asked his age with his right hand raised, Dial truthfully replied, "I stand over twenty-one."[44]

With the Klan, Prohibition, and politics dominating newspaper headlines that year, country publisher J. Marvin Hunter believed a market existed for stories of earlier days, a time when the Comanche moon posed a greater threat to Texas than moonshine. In October 1923 Hunter brought out the first issue of *Frontier Times*, a pulp magazine offering nonfiction stories of the Old West. The first issue featured an article on Captain Jack Hays, the legendary Republic of Texas–era Ranger leader. Stories on the "Old Guard," as Hunter sometimes referred to the Rangers, appeared frequently in the magazine, further adding to the Ranger mystique.

In Ranger-occupied San Antonio, that mystique wore thin. When Rangers raided the exclusive University Club, they found Mayor Tobin (who had been sheriff of Bexar County 1900–1908 and again 1910–1923) among those sitting at a table covered with playing cards. Arrested for gambling despite his protest that he and his associates had only gathered for a friendly game of bridge while following play-by-play wire reports of the World Series, the mayor posted a $50 bond in justice court.

If the mayor could be charged with a crime, so could the Rangers. As Captain Baldwin reported to headquarters:

> The writer and six of his men have been "prosecuted" in the local courts by the district and county attorneys, with two convictions, no defense being offered by us. We paid a fine in one case and the governor issued a pardon in the other conviction.[45]

One of Baldwin's men soon faced a more serious legal problem. When an informant called the Ranger station to report a man moving a supply of bootleg whiskey into his place of business, Ranger Y. H. Taylor went to the location, a small downtown grocery on Soledad Street. Hiding behind an abandoned automobile in an adjoining vacant lot, the Ranger saw a man removing bottles of whiskey from beneath a pile of lumber. "I'm a Ranger," Taylor commanded as he stepped into view. "Give me that whiskey. You're under arrest." At that, the man swung at Taylor with a bottle. In the ensuing struggle, Taylor cracked the man's head with his .45. When the Ranger hit him a second time, the semiautomatic discharged into the man's left temple. Leaving the bleeding bootlegger on the ground where he fell, Taylor walked inside the store and called headquarters to report the shooting. He then left the scene, returning to the Ranger office before city police arrived.

"Local Grocer Killed," the *Express* reported the next morning, "Ranger Fires Bullet into Brain of Soledad Street Business Man . . . Says It Was Accident . . . Was Beating Merchant on Head, He Claims, When Gun Fired."[46]

Captain Baldwin told reporters and the police that the shooting had indeed been an accident, the safety of the Ranger's pistol having slipped with the second blow to the suspect's head. But to the public it looked like heavy-handedness on the Ranger's part. So that the matter could be resolved in court, Baldwin took Taylor into custody and filed on him for murder the following morning. Soon free on $2,500 bond, the Ranger resumed his duties.[47]

Meanwhile, the Klan, its members holding the majority of the seats in both houses of the legislature, took aim at the Governor's Mansion. The New York *Times* noted that seventy-five thousand Klansmen had gathered recently in Dallas, the state's Klan headquarters. That city and Fort Worth, the newspaper said, "are completely dominated by the masked knights."[48]

That summer six candidates—two of them pro-Klan and one an official Klan candidate—vied for votes in the Democratic primary in a time when winning the Democratic nomination amounted to victory in the general election. Neff had decided not to run for reelection, leaving Lieutenant Governor Davidson to face five other candidates, including Miriam A. "Ma" Ferguson, wife of impeached governor James Ferguson. "Farmer Jim," a polished political speaker, stumped the state for his wife. Running against the Ferguson name would be tough enough, but the lieutenant governor also had to contend with a candidate who shared his last name, Lynch Davidson, a Dallas lumberman. Another candidate, Klan-backed Felix D. Robertson, a Dallas County criminal district judge, wanted Texans to know "there is one District Judge in Texas who does not jump every time some big Jew or Catholic yells 'frog.'" Adjutant General Barton and former state senator V. A. Collins of Dallas rounded out the field.[49]

By this time, if Barton had ever been a Klan member, the man in charge of the Rangers no longer belonged to the invisible empire. One contemporary writer asserted the adjutant general had "quit the Klan cold." Had Barton not done so, the writer continued, "no doubt, he . . . would have been banished." No one in the Klan would have tried to impose the order's death penalty, because "he was the head of the Texas Rangers and the brave men who had been guilty of whipping women did not care, in the least, about punishing Mr. Barton." Even so, the general got only eighteen thousand votes. A runoff would pit Mrs. Ferguson against Robertson, the Klan candidate.[50]

"THE ENTIRE RANGER FORCE IS ILLEGALLY ORGANIZED. . . ."

Litigation could be as effective an instrument of change as the ballot box. On August 1, 1924, seventy-four-year-old John E. Elgin of San Antonio—an old Indian fighter who had pushed stock up the cattle trails before the railroads came to Texas—sued Neff and other state officials, seeking an injunction against the Rangers. On page one, the San Antonio *Express* summarized Elgin's contention:

> The entire Ranger force is illegally organized and the statutes creating the State police are in direct violation of the Texas Constitution, according to a petition for injunction filed in 57th District Court. Elgin asks that Gov. Pat Neff, Comptroller Lon A. Smith, Treasurer C. V. Terrell and Adjutant General Thomas D. Barton be restrained from taking actions which would recognize the rangers as State officers, and Capt. B. C. Baldwin and all other rangers . . . be restrained from posing as peace officers.[51]

In the petition, Elgin's lawyers asserted that the 1901 law creating the Rangers, as amended in 1919, violated six sections of the Bill of Rights and five articles of the state constitution. In addition, the petition claimed, the Ranger law stood "in derogation of some 24 or 25 constitutional rights" of the plaintiff "and the rest of the people of Texas." The lawsuit also asked that the governor be restrained from "employing spies, stool pigeons, informers or detectives, or issuing orders to them."

Though not mentioning the San Antonio situation directly, the Reverend Atticus Webb of Dallas, superintendent of the Anti-Saloon League, clearly had it in mind when he wrote:

> When the state constabulary comes into a county that fails to maintain law and order the criminals are the first to react. They organize their forces to secure the expression of protest from officials and respected citizens. . . . The good citizenry must not be deceived. The fight on the state constabulary is simply the criminals fighting back.[52]

The following day, after reading the twenty-two-page petition, which alleged that the Rangers in Bexar County operated "in direct opposition to the wishes of the people and the regularly elected officers," Judge R. B. Minor refused to grant a temporary injunction and set for October 20 a hearing on the merits of the case.[53] Though some San Antonio residents considered the Rangers a burr under their saddle, the day after the district judge's action they filled the chilled water–cooled Royal Theater for the Sunday afternoon opening of Western star Tom

Mix's latest silent movie, a screen adaptation of Zane Grey's *The Lone Star Ranger*.

In an interview with the San Antonio *Light,* Elgin said he had filed the lawsuit because county officials had not done so. "The whole ranger system and Governor Neff's ideas of executive functions are at variance with the genius of our American institutions," he said. "Governor Edmund J. Davis sought to govern Texas by the same method Pat Neff has adopted," he continued, recalling Reconstruction. "It set the state aflame. A great taxpayers' convention was called to protest against its illegality."[54]

Neither Elgin's lawsuit nor the upcoming change in administration in Austin intimidated Captain Baldwin. Five days after the lawsuit's filing, the San Antonio–based Rangers seized 335 bottles of beer and a "complete beer making outfit," taking one prisoner to jail for violation of the federal Prohibition act. The same day, Rangers arrested five men for vagrancy at a gambling house on North St. Mary's Street. On August 8, Baldwin's men destroyed one thousand gallons of still-warm mash in a raid on a barn on the banks of the San Antonio River near Eads Avenue. That fall, the captain expanded his role as San Antonio's moral arbiter by banning the screening of movie footage showing the Jack Dempsey–Louis Firpo boxing match.[55]

In the August 23, 1924, runoff, "Ma" Ferguson beat Robertson by 97,732 votes in a gubernatorial election that saw the largest turnout in state history up to that point. She would face a Republican candidate in November, but that posed virtually no threat to her election.[56]

"There is going to be a big change under the new Governor," Captain Aldrich wrote after Mrs. Ferguson's election that fall, "but nobody knows just what it will be."[57]

The governor-elect had nothing to do with the first big change. On January 15, 1925, Judge Minor held that the Ranger statute violated three articles of the state constitution. He enjoined the state comptroller, the state treasurer, the adjutant general, Ranger Quartermaster Aldrich, Captain Baldwin, and even Southwestern Bell Telephone Company from dispersing any state funds to pay for Ranger salaries or operations. Hoping to keep the Rangers funded at least on the short term, Assistant Attorney General W. A. Wheeler requested suspension of Minor's injunction until the matter could be ruled on in the Fourth Court of Civil Appeals. Wheeler argued that without a Ranger force, the state's

Mexican border "is at the mercy of marauding bands, aliens, and smugglers." Most of the Ranger force served on the border, he continued, and would have to remain inactive unless Minor suspended his writ. Two days later, declaring that he no longer had jurisdiction because the state had announced it would appeal the case, Minor denied the state's motion. That, for all practical purposes, put the Rangers out of operation.[58]

D. B. Chaplin, Elgin's attorney, felt confident his case would hold up. "If the higher courts uphold Judge Minor," Chaplin said, "and I believe they will, hereafter Texas governors will be the state's chief executives and that only. They will be governors and not dictators."[59]

Most Texas newspapers supported the Rangers. "Few forces of law and order in all history have served so admirably," the Fort Worth *Star-Telegram* editorialized.[60] After hearing about the injunction, Western writer Owen P. White, who grew up in El Paso and knew many of the old-time Rangers, wrote the Ranger's obituary for the New York *Times*. "The Texas Ranger is no more," he began. "He has passed away, not in a blaze of glory, with his boots on and wrapped in a wreath of his own six-shooter smoke, but merely because a court has declared him to be unconstitutional and useless." With the court decision, the Rangers had taken a figurative bullet, but White's judgment that they were dead proved premature. Still, in lamenting their demise he put into perspective the importance of the Rangers:

> Let us be thankful that it has taken the courts of Texas a long, long time to find out that the Rangers are illegal. . . . What a difference it would have made—how disastrous would have been the effect, not only upon the romantic traditions of Texas, but upon the life and happiness of the people as well, if such a decision had been handed down, say, in 1875 instead of 1925.[61]

In one of the Rangers' darker hours, White understood what made them different from other lawmen with guns and what would sustain them organizationally: tradition. "The men, all of them, live up to the traditions of their force and are proud of their connection with it. And they should be," he wrote.[62]

Neff left office five days after the ruling by the San Antonio trial court. During his four years as governor, Neff later wrote, no lynching or "demonstration of mob violence" occurred "when a Ranger was on the ground." He had kept the Rangers in almost constant use. He wrote:

> They were called upon on an average of once a month . . . to protect prisoners who were being tried, and to prevent mob violence. Almost every day demands of some kind were made for them. We could not begin to respond to all calls.

The former governor soon published his memoir, *The Battles of Peace*. Seeking to justify his order sending Rangers to San Antonio, he wrote: "When the people of any place enter a vituperative protest against the presence of the Rangers, it is rather conclusive proof that . . . they are needed. San Antonio proved no exception." Rangers shut down forty-one gambling houses "operating in the main part of the city, besides many smaller ones in more secluded spots." In addition, thirty-three pool halls were closed and several "notorious cock [fighting] pits, which for months had operated unopposed by the [local] officers, were done away with." A grand jury returned twenty-seven felony indictments for operating gambling houses. Three hundred and sixteen guilty pleas or convictions were obtained, "mostly in the Federal Court." Numerous indictments were handed down in state court, Neff continued, but "for some reason, no prosecutions resulted." Twenty whiskey-manufacturing cases were presented to the Bexar County prosecutor, but no convictions resulted. Never mentioning the Bexar County lawsuit, the former governor concluded: "It is my conviction that I made no mistake when . . . I sent the Rangers to the Alamo City to assist in enforcing, not the laws of San Antonio, but the laws of Texas."[63]

As in the case of San Antonio, Neff often had sent Rangers without invitation. On occasion, they arrived undercover as "secret servicemen." Neff said he sometimes read newspaper editorials taking him to task for not providing Rangers "when in reality . . . they had been there for days." During his administration, the Rangers made more than five thousand arrests, destroyed more than five hundred stills, and recovered more than five hundred head of stolen livestock.[64]

With the Rangers hobbled like a bulldogged steer, on January 22, 1925, fifteen armed Mexicans rode into Texas, looting ranches north of Laredo. Eleven days later, on February 2, a gang of car thieves shot a Fort

Worth police officer and fled to Denton, where local officers surrounded two of them inside a house. Taking the position that he still had a duty to deploy Rangers during emergencies, newly appointed adjutant general Mark McGee had ordered Captain Wright on January 31 to "take all necessary steps to protect life and property" in his area and later told Captain Hickman to do the same in Denton County.

Wright and his Company D Rangers soon ran the border raiders back across the Rio Grande and Hickman talked the two fugitives in Denton, Wilbur Martin and Yancy Story, into giving up. "Even though Tom Hickman was constrained by a court injunction," the Dallas *Morning News* observed, the words " 'Texas Ranger' clothed him with a power and dignity that caused the men to surrender."[65]

The Rangers under fire in the courts, a history professor at the University of Texas in Austin galloped to their rescue, hoping to cut off Ranger critics at the pass by seeking redress in the court of public opinion, a venue where perception had more muzzle velocity than a .30-30. Walter Prescott Webb had begun researching the history of the Rangers in 1919. He had written his doctoral dissertation on the Rangers and had in mind using his academic work as the foundation for a book. Toward that end, the summer before he had taken a trip along the border with Captain Aldrich and one-armed Ranger Arch Miller from below Laredo all the way to El Paso. The Rangers even gave the professor a Ranger commission so he could carry a pistol on the tour. Webb listened to their stories, saw them in action, and made friends. He shared pinto beans and tortillas with them in camp and, in a figurative sense, remained in their camp even after returning to Austin.[66]

Writing a favorable article on the Rangers for the Dallas *Morning News*, Webb argued that Texas's border with Mexico remained unsafe. He pulled no punches in trying to evoke an emotional reaction from his readers:

Alarming reports are coming in [from the border] all the time, but the "interior" is safe. There is no danger that our little girls will grope about leaving bloody handprints on our cottage floors and walls. Therefore we go into court and get judicial opinions that the law that prevents such things is unconstitutional, that the Texas rangers are illegal and can not operate in Texas. We do this only after the force has been operating for fifty years, after the rangers have faced every danger that has confronted the state, after they have made the state a fairly safe place—on the interior—in which to live.[67]

A few days later, the new Ferguson regime decided that while Texas might still need the Rangers, it did not need as many. One month after the wife of Texas's only impeached governor took office, Adjutant General McGee announced the reduction of the force from fifty-one to twenty-eight men. "The cut follows the administration's policy of retrenchment and reduces the ranger payroll about $2,500 a month," the Associated Press reported.[68]

In addition to slashing the force nearly in half, the new adjutant general announced a policy vastly different from Neff's: Rangers no longer would be sent unless requested by that county's officials "except in unusual cases where the adjutant general and the governor believe the situation demands that the initiative be taken." San Antonio would be abandoned by the Rangers, with most of the remaining state lawmen sent to the border, McGee said.[69]

Six Rangers had been let go in Presidio County, which suited folks in neighboring Brewster County just fine. At the end of its term, a grand jury reported to the judge who had impaneled it:

> We respectfully request that you transmit to her Excellency the Governor of Texas, Mrs. Miriam A. Ferguson, the unanimous recommendation of this body that in the future when Rangers are stationed in Brewster County, if any be so stationed—and we do not think any are needed—that they be instructed and cautioned in the authority which they have and in the powers that may be lawfully exercised by them.[70]

The Rangers also came under legislative attack. In an effort led by Senator Alvin Wirtz of Seguin, with strong support from colleague and south Texas political boss Archer Parr of Duval County, the upper chamber passed a bill reducing the size of the force. As presiding officer of the Senate, Lieutenant Governor Barry Miller of Dallas broke a 14–14 tie to defeat the measure. Wirtz, again working with Parr, also tried to prohibit expenditure of state funds for a Ranger force stationed anywhere but Travis County, unless a county sheriff or commissioner's court requested a Ranger presence, but that effort failed as well.[71]

In an opinion issued February 25, Judge William Seat Fly, chief justice of the San Antonio–based Fourth Court of Civil Appeals, took the Ranger constitutionality argument advanced in the district court's action apart piece by piece. Fly's opinion contained twelve findings, the most significant ones being that Rangers did not usurp the powers of county sheriffs, that the law creating the Rangers did not grant the governor another office by putting Ranger forces under his command, and, finally, that "construction placed upon laws for many years by past officers and Legislatures should have great weight with courts weighing constitutionality of act, and should be sufficient to resolve doubt in favor of validity [of the Rangers]."[72]

The chief justice's ruling supported the constitutionality of the Rangers, but the judge clearly believed Neff's San Antonio undertaking had been over the top. Fly denounced the quartering of Rangers "on unoffending communities to establish a system of espionage on its citizens and spend their time in arresting crap throwers, chicken fighters and petty offenders against the Volstead or Dean laws."

Fly continued:

This court does not seek to extenuate or defend any criminal, tyrannous or unlawful acts that have been committed by members or units of the ranger force, especially in the last two years, but condemns all such acts as well as the acts of those in the background who have aided and abetted such violations of the law. No one who loves liberty and believes in the supremacy of law can sustain such assaults on our liberty.[73]

"We suppose the San Antonio judge has made himself solid with his constituents," one newspaper said of Judge Minor after learning that the appeals court had lifted the injunction against the Rangers. "The rangers have a way of enforcing law that is not at all popular down Alamo City way."[74]

The Rangers sat back in the saddle, but three veteran captains did not like the new governor's policy that the force would only be used in response to requests from local officials. Captains Gray, Hamer, and

Wright all resigned (though the adjutant general immediately reenlisted Hamer as a private who would work directly for him). Wright, who tended to see good and bad in black and white only, wrote General McGee that with the Rangers "curtailed as to number and liberty of action" they could "be but figureheads." Texas, the captain continued, needed a "non-political and independent force."[75]

Elgin's lawyers, meanwhile, took their case to the state supreme court, which on May 13 upheld the appeals court. The Austin *American* applauded the high court's action, noting "there is just as much need for the Rangers today as in former years." But while endorsing the court's decision, *American* editorial writer DeWitt Reddick grabbed the Rangers' figurative bridle long enough to offer a friendly word of warning:

> Their methods of justice smack of the flavor of years ago. Their code is stern. If they are sent to bring a man to justice, they set out to bring him in, with too little regard for local or municipal laws or for the dignity of local police forces. Their methods jar on some who think they are too high-handed in their dealings. They should remember that today they are but one of a number of agencies working toward the same end, the prevention of crime and the capture of criminals. Cooperation with these other agencies is necessary to maintain harmony.

With this "added touch of professional courtesy," Reddick continued, "the state ranger force will be able for many a day to live up to the compliment paid to it in the statement made recently by an officer of the Royal Canadian mounted police, who said: 'The only police force in the world to whom the R.N.W.M.P. takes off its hat is the Texas rangers.' "[76]

On July 15, the governor moved Captain Hickman from Fort Worth to Austin to run Headquarters Company. Three companies, A, B, and D, got orders for border duty, with Company C under Captain Nichols retained in Marshall to keep fighting bootleggers. The force spent the rest of the year primarily enforcing Prohibition, though Rangers solved a high-profile murder case in Erath County and prevented a triple lynching in East Texas.[77]

Cowboy humorist Will Rogers visited the Fergusons at the Governor's Mansion in Austin on February 16, 1926, and left with an honorary Ranger commission. Issued by Adjutant General Dallas J. Matthews, who had replaced McGee, the commission made the forty-six-year-old Oklahoman an uncompensated private "for the period of two years, unless sooner discharged by proper authority." The Dallas *Morning News* reported the entertainer's appointment the following day, noting the man with the big smile had been appointed as a Ranger "for protection while in the State."[78]

Under the Ferguson administration, at least in the opinion of those opposed to the governor's politics, Rogers needed that protection in Texas. "The Texas Rangers," one decidedly anti-Ferguson Texan wrote, "are for the present resting on their arms because of the political situation which has developed in the great commonwealth. . . . There is no lack of work for the men to do, but they are handicapped by the local political attitude which pledged the governor to dispense with the use of Rangers as far as possible."[79]

Other states had high crime rates as well. With mobsters blazing away at each other in Chicago, a Dallas *Morning News* editorial offered Windy City officials a solution: "What Chicago really needs, but hasn't the capacity to avail itself of, is a corps of three hundred Texas Rangers armed with six-guns and authority to bring the known outlaws in dead or alive." The newspaper went on to demonstrate that mainstream Texas still appreciated the Rangers:

> The Texas Rangers do not prevent outlawry in Texas. But the answer to that is that they do when they are given the authority to do so. Some of our squeamish citizens oppose the Rangers, not that the latter are ineffective, but that they are too effective. In no case has a Texas Ranger surrendered to the lawless in lieu of asserting the majesty of the law.

Historian Webb, augmenting his modest state teaching salary, had been writing gushingly positive articles about the Rangers for *The State Trooper*, a law enforcement magazine published in Detroit. "The Rangers will be restored to their former authority," he predicted. "They are without doubt the strongest force for law and order that has ever existed in the state."[80]

The Rangers were not entirely handcuffed during Mrs. Ferguson's term. Shortly after the May 20, 1926, disappearance of Dr. J. A. Ramsey, a popular physician with a practice in the South Texas community of Mathis, the Rangers began working with the San Patricio County sheriff and other officers to find him. Rangers tracked a suspect to Mexico, succeeded in getting him returned to Texas, and convinced him to lead them to the doctor's body. They found Ramsey in a shallow grave, one arm protruding stiffly above the dirt. Unraveling the case took more than three months, but eventually the Rangers charged the suspect who had returned from Mexico and another man with murder. Webb, the Rangers' self-appointed press agent, admitted in one of his *State Trooper* articles that the service did not deserve all the credit in solving the murder but noted that "their hands were seen all along the line. They gathered up the threads of evidence, pieced them together and followed the criminals from place to place across the state."[81]

In a runoff election on August 23, five days before the Rangers and San Antonio police made the final arrest in the Ramsey case, Texas voters picked redheaded attorney general Dan Moody over a second term for Mrs. Ferguson by a quarter-million votes. Moody had made a reputation prosecuting the Klan in Williamson County and would soon reenergize the Rangers.[82]

THE HICKMAN METHOD

A couple of weeks after the election, while investigating a Dallas County bank holdup, Captain Hickman learned the Red River National Bank in Clarksville might be next on the robbers' list. The Ranger drove to Clarksville and enlisted the assistance of Stewart Stanley, who only recently had left the Rangers. On September 8, 1926, the two men staked out the bank, sitting nonchalantly in Hickman's car. When two middle-aged men entered the financial institution, Hickman paid little attention. But moments later a man with a mask over his face emerged from the bank, grabbed two little girls who had just walked up, and pulled them inside. The captain quickly repositioned his car and, as he later told reporters, "prepared to meet the men as they came out."

When they did so, Hickman saw that one of them carried a suitcase. Relieved that the men had not thought of using the young girls as hostages, Hickman watched them walk toward a nearby parked car. As soon as they stepped off the busy sidewalk, Hickman and Stanley jumped from their car, leveled rifles at the pair, and ordered them to drop the bag and put up their hands. Instead, one of the robbers fired at the captain. As Hickman and Stanley opened up on the pair, town constable B. Q. Ivy, along with Stanley's father, rushed to the scene and joined in the short-lived gunfight. One of Hickman's first assignments as a Ranger had been teaching marksmanship. Within moments, both robbers lay dead on the street. When the Ranger and local officers checked the suitcase they found it held $33,135, including $3,000 in silver.

The others in Hickman's informal posse also fired on the robbers, but the Company B captain got the credit for the killings. In addition to considerable publicity and a laudatory state senate resolution, Hickman netted $2,300 in reward money—an amount nearly equal to his annual salary—for the two dead robbers. "I commend and endorse the Hickman method of preventing bank robberies," the Bexar County district attorney said in a wire to the Red River County sheriff's office. The *Houston Post Dispatch* concurred: "A few incidents like the one in Clarksville will do much to discourage this form of outlawry in Texas."[83]

"Law and Order Have Been Restored . . ."

Moody took office on January 17, 1927. Five days later, he appointed Robert Lamar Robertson adjutant general. "Governor Dan Moody is now executive of Texas," Webb wrote in another article for *The State Trooper*. "Law and order have been restored . . . and the Texas Rangers are active in restoring it."[84]

Two weeks after his inauguration, Moody proved he intended to stand by his campaign promises to battle government corruption. The opportunity came from an unlikely source: an honest lobbyist. Representing the state's optometry association, Willis W. Chamberlain wanted to kill a bill imposing a $50 annual fee on eye examiners. Approaching Representative H. H. Moore of the Delta County community of Cooper, Chamberlain got a rude brush-off. But with a wink, Moore suggested that Chamberlain take the matter up with his colleague Representative F. A. Dale of Bonham. When Chamberlain invited Dale to dinner, the Fannin County lawmaker said his calendar appeared clear, assuming Chamberlain intended to pick up the tab. That evening, Chamberlain pleaded his association's case. Dale, however, did not find the merits of the issue particularly interesting. He said supporters of the bill already had committed $750 to get the measure out of committee and placed on the House calendar.

"That is a mighty hard deal for us," Chamberlain said, trying to smother his disgust at the not at all subtle tone of the conversation. Dale only got plainer: For $1,000, the bill would languish in committee "until the cows came home."

Chamberlain said he would be back in touch and signaled their waiter for the check. But instead of going to his association for the money, he reported the shakedown effort to House Speaker Robert L. Bobbitt. The speaker, in turn, contacted Moody, who ordered the Rangers to look into the matter. Hamer, now back to work as a captain, and Hickman met with Chamberlain and told him to go ahead with the payoff.

The following night, Chamberlain and Dale visited Moore at his hotel room. Continuing his deep-pocket posturing, the lobbyist called room service and ordered three chicken dinners. After a convivial meal, Dale led the lobbyist to a dark alley behind the hotel where he accepted a wad of marked bills. As Dale walked off, a big man seemingly appeared from nowhere and buttonholed the startled state representative.

"I have information that you have recently accepted a bribe," Hamer said.

Hamer left Dale with Hickman and went to talk with Moore. The Bonham lawmaker denied the payoff scheme, but Hamer felt he had enough evidence to make a case against both legislators. Within a week, a House committee voted unanimously to recommend expelling the two members. The speaker urged his fellow legislators to move quickly "to show the people of Texas we are not a bunch of bribe takers and bootleggers." The House voted to boot both men.[85]

BOOMING BORGER

More than five hundred miles from Austin, an oil boom in the Panhandle began scattering money like a tornado ripping through a bank. In Hutchinson County, northeast of Amarillo, a place called Borger had grown into a city of forty thousand–plus inside three months. By April, local conditions bordering on anarchy, Moody ordered captains Hamer and Hickman, along with eight privates, to restore order.

"Borger and nearby towns have been running wide open," the Associated Press reported on April 8, 1927, the day after the Rangers arrived. "Many persons have been killed including several officers and two or three women. Daylight robberies, hold-ups, explosions, bootlegging and vices . . . have continued practically unabated." The adjutant general later summarized the Ranger operation in 120 words:

> A thorough-going clean-up was put underway. The liquor traffic was broken up, many stills being seized and destroyed, and several thousand gallons of whiskey being captured and poured out. Two hundred and three gambling slot machines were seized and destroyed. Numerous gambling resorts were placed under surveillance and forced to clean up, and in a period of twenty-four hours it is assumed that no less than twelve hundred prostitutes left the town of Borger. As the result of a demand on the part of the citizens of Borger for administration of the law, the Mayor, City Commissioners, Chief of Police, and practically all of the Police Force of Borger resigned and were replaced by citizens pledged to enforce the laws.[86]

Though pleased with the results in Borger, Moody thought the Rangers needed a little housekeeping. On April 30, Adjutant General Roberts notified nine Rangers, including some officers, that they would be honorably discharged in a general reorganization, effective May 15. Twelve men got transfers, including the captains who had survived the makeover.[87] Will Wright went back on the state payroll as captain of Company A at Marfa; Company B, stationed at Del Rio, became Company C, with veteran Ranger John H. Rogers returning to state service as commander. The bullet-scarred captain, now sixty-four, had left the force in 1913 for an appointment as U.S. marshal. W. W. "Bill" Sterling, who had first served in the Rangers in 1915, transferred from the Del Rio company to run Laredo-based Company D, and Hamer went from Laredo to Austin, to once again assume command of Headquarters Company.[88]

Moody had made the staffing adjustments he wanted, but the legislature had some ideas as well. Senator J. W. Reid of Canyon favored increasing the size of the force from thirty to fifty men, and Adjutant General Robertson said he needed double the amount of his department's previous appropriation.

"One Ranger is a potent power for good and the Legislature should provide a sufficiently large mobile force that can be sent to points in the state as needed and without delay," the Panhandle senator said. "The Rangers are crime deterrents and we should have an ample supply."[89]

Senator Parr had a different vision of the Rangers. The Duval County kingpin, trying again to curtail the service, introduced another bill that would keep the Rangers corralled in Austin unless requested by a county sheriff or a petition of one hundred or more citizens of a county.[90] The legislature went on to concentrate most of its energy on defeating just about anything Moody wanted passed. The governor and the lawmakers had at least agreed that the Parr bill deserved the death it got. When the special session ended, the Rangers had neither lost nor gained significantly.

Not long after the legislature adjourned, one old-time Ranger expressed his sentiments that it would be fitting to have a monument to the Rangers standing in view of future state lawmakers and the general citizenry. At the annual reunion of the Ex-Rangers Association that July, C. C. Thompson of Colorado City proposed a Ranger monument on the Capitol grounds. "It should stand as a guiding light to the youth of this land that they might know that the brave men who made up this frontier army were of sterling worth and are entitled to the respect and admiration of the world," Thompson told the ex-Rangers assembled near Captain Dan Roberts's old Frontier Battalion camp at Menard. "It is unnecessary to guard the frontier with musket and powder horn but we must hold sacred the heritage that is ours," he continued. Though a committee had come up with four possible methods for funding the statue (private donations, donations from the schoolchildren of the state, the sale of emblems, and legislative appropriation), Thompson said he believed that state money should fund the monument. "The State of Texas owes her existence in a great measure to the Texas Ranger of frontier times," he said. "Civilization and industry followed in his foot-path. Without him we would today be far behind the progress of which we boast." After Thompson's talk, the old Indian fighters and outlaw hunters cussed and discussed the proposal. One old Ranger summed up the prevalent feeling:

I am opposed to the Texas Rangers raising a fund to erect a monument of this kind; I am opposed to the Texas Ex-Rangers' Association raising a fund to lobby for an appropriation by the legislature to build a monument to the Texas Ranger. If posterity does not appreciate what the Texas Rangers did for Texas to the extent of building a memorial to our achievement, then we should let the matter die.[91]

Supporters of a Ranger monument for Austin would have had a hard time collecting donations in Borger. A mass meeting of the Panhandle boomtown's business and professional community on July 21 ended with a vote that the Rangers should be removed. The locals charged that some Rangers had thrown in with the bootleggers and those involved in graft. No one ever proved corruption on the part of the Rangers in Borger, but Ranger Jack DeGraffenried had been charged with shooting Hutchinson County deputy sheriff W. H. Bates. Locals also found it galling that one of the invading Rangers had said Borger would not be such a problem if it had more native Texans as residents.

"Has the State closed the doors of its citizenship to all who were not born in the Lone Star State?" the Borger *Daily Herald* asked on July 21. "Cannot a great and growing Empire like the Panhandle draw some of its ever-increasing population from neighboring states, and offer them the protection of government and the ordinary privileges of citizenship? . . . Borger resents the insinuation that it is a foreign city transplanted on Texas soil."[92] The Rangers soon left Borger. But they would be back.

Having kept up with news accounts of Ranger town takeovers and the legal and legislative challenges mounted by those who did not support a strong state law enforcement body, writer Eugene Cunningham understood that the Rangers had done more than make Texas safe from Indians and outlaws. In a piece published by the New York *Herald-Tribune*, Cunningham wrote: "Wherever one turns . . . the ex-Ranger is found. He has sat in the Governor's chair; he controls the activities of great railroads and financial institutions; he is the prosperous farmer, the cowman, master of hundreds of thousands of acres, and he is poet and novelist as well."[93]

SANTA CLAUS HAD A GUN

Captain Hickman waited at the Missouri, Kansas, and Texas depot in Austin on December 23, 1927, about to board the "Katy Flyer" for Fort

Worth when a messenger from the governor's office found him. Some-one in a Santa Claus suit along with three other men had just robbed the First National Bank at Cisco, an oil field town in Eastland County. Po-lice Chief G. E. "Bit" Bedford and one of his officers had been mortally wounded in the wild shootout that followed the holdup. The robbers, police and numerous outraged citizens had fired an estimated one hun-dred rounds. One of the bandits, Louis Davis, had been gravely wounded and left behind by his colleagues when they tried unsuccessfully to change getaway cars. The gunman also accidentally left behind their haul, $12,400 in cash and $150,000 in bonds they had not had time to discover were nonnegotiable.

Reaching Fort Worth that night, Hickman hurried to the Tarrant County Jail, where the moribund Davis had been taken by a Cisco fu-neral home to save him from a lynch mob. The captain tried to get the dying man to name his accomplices, but he was too far gone to talk. Opt-ing not to wait for the next train and realizing that driving the one hundred miles of dirt road from Fort Worth to Cisco would keep him from getting any rest before starting on the trail of the robbers, Hick-man prevailed on the driver of the hearse, which was still parked out-side the jail, to take him to Cisco. Arriving on the scene five hours later, Hickman assumed leadership of one of the largest manhunts in Texas history. However, the captain and Sergeant "Lone Wolf" Gonzaullas fur-nished a bit more than expertise in criminal detection: Each Ranger ar-rived armed with a Thompson submachine gun in addition to his other weaponry.

On December 27, four days after the robbery, Eastland County law-men confronted the three suspects at a crossing of the Brazos River near the South Bend community as they tried to slip back into Cisco in a stolen car on the theory that no one would look for them there. In the gunfight that followed, deputies wounded and captured Marshall Ratliff, the twenty-four-year-old gunman who had worn the Santa Claus suit. The other two men, also wounded, abandoned their car and es-caped into the rugged cedar brakes along the river.

With roughly 150 officers in cars, on horseback and on foot unable to find the last two suspects, Hickman wired Fort Worth for an airplane. (Newspaper accounts of the manhunt do not reflect who furnished the plane.) The pilot flew to Graham, where Gonzaullas awaited him. The

Ranger went up in the canvas-winged biplane on December 28 and again the next day, but the two robbers continued to elude the local and state officers. Gonzaullas's two days of reconnaissance flights marked the first time in Texas history a Ranger had taken to the air to assistant in a manhunt.

A week after the robbery—wounded, hungry, and cold—Henry Helms and Robert Hill practically captured themselves by showing up in Graham and asking someone for directions. In releasing names of the two men to the press, Hickman was quick to point out that Helms, an ex-convict, had been pardoned by former Governor Miriam Ferguson. While the arrests concluded any direct Ranger involvement in the case, Ratliff ended up getting lynched in Eastland not quite two years later after killing a jailer in an escape attempt. Helms eventually went to the electric chair for the murder of the police chief while Hill, only nineteen at the time of the robbery, got a life prison sentence. He later won a pardon, changed his name, and became a respected citizen.

For the rest of his career, Hickman kept the .45 semiautomatic Helms had used in the robbery, a gift from the sheriff of Eastland County.[94]

Captain Hamer soon injected himself into a situation that read like something from a cheap novel. During the previous three years, forty-three banks had been robbed in Texas. By comparison, only twenty-four robberies had been reported in the eight years prior to 1924. After noting fifteen bank robberies during the first nine months of 1927, the Texas Bankers Association decided to place a bounty on bank robbers. Each of the more than fifteen hundred banks in Texas displayed this sign:

$5,000 **REWARD**
DEAD BANK ROBBERS WANTED
$5,000 **Cash Will Be Paid for Each Bank Robber**
Killed While Robbing a Texas Bank

The reward also covered any yegg killed during a night burglary. The association set no restrictions on how near the bank a crook had to be killed. A person could collect on a bank robber killed "in the banking house, as the robber or robbers leave the bank, as they climb into their car, ten or twenty miles down the road as they flee, or while resisting a posse giving chase."

Bank robbers taken alive had no cash value, however. "They rarely are identified, more rarely convicted, and most rarely kept in the penitentiary when sent there—all of which operations are troublesome and costly." As president W. M. Massie put it, his association had resolved "to make bank robbery unhealthy in Texas."[95]

Since November 1927, three robbers had been killed and two others wounded, one critically. While the association's program clearly had made bank robbing a more dangerous undertaking, it created business opportunities for others. Hamer, noting the sudden upsurge of supposed bank robbers shot in the dead of night, became suspicious. Looking into the circumstances of several cases in West Texas, he came to realize that local officers had framed hapless drunks as bank robbers, to be killed in the act. But the captain could not get any interest in prosecuting the cases or cooperation from the bankers association in changing its rules to prevent fraud.

In one of the earliest instances of strategic use of the press by the Rangers, on March 12 Hamer distributed a written statement to statehouse reporters in Austin exposing how corrupt local law enforcement officers had been staging bank robberies to collect the standing reward. Calling it a "perfect murder machine," the captain said, "I haven't any brief for bank robbers to be shot down by reward seekers." Though he was more accustomed to solving problems with a bearlike slap to someone's face, or a well-aimed bullet, Hamer's media campaign worked. After some resistance, the association modified its reward policy and the "murder machine" became inoperable.[96]

As the Rangers continued to ride herd over Texas lawbreakers, West Texas congressman C. B. Hudspeth introduced an amendment to a 1927 pension act granting a modest consideration to "certain soldiers who served in the Indian wars from 1817 to 1898." His amendment would bring incapacitated ex–Texas Rangers under the law, entitling them to receive monthly pensions of from $20 to $50, depending on their age. Widows would receive $30 a month.[97]

At the end of fiscal 1928, the adjutant general reported the strength of the Rangers had varied from thirty to thirty-three men. Each of the five companies had a captain, a sergeant, and from three to four privates. The Rangers had operated on an appropriation of $76,750 during the first year of the biennium, $83,500 the second year. The state still provided more money for forage and horseshoeing than for automobile upkeep (in fiscal 1927, $4,250 for horses and mules to $3,000 for motor vehicle maintenance). But money expended for transportation by railroad outweighed the allocations for both horses and cars. The Rangers paid $2,000 in rent and $1,000 for ammunition.[98]

Though he kept his headquarters in West Texas at Fort Stockton with one man stationed on the border at Presidio, Captain Wright and most of his Rangers spent a lot of their time in the oil patch. Sitting in his room at the Miller Hotel in the new town of Wink, the captain scratched out a letter to Adjutant General Robertson on hotel stationery. Wright had been attending court in Kermit and felt a good grand jury had been impaneled. "You will find inclosed [sic] a clipping from the New York *World*. You might show it to the Governor it might please him. With personal Regards, yours to command, W.L. Wright."

Wink, the *World* reported, had been "so tough that toughness was a civic virtue. . . . Some of the more public spirited citizens often said most of their fellow-townsmen were so hard they would have had to wear clothes while bathing to keep from scratching the bathtub, except they had no bathtubs. . . . Now, however, the Texas Rangers are there with some businesslike clean-up orders from Gov. Dan Moody." The article went on to say that since the arrival of four Rangers—"computed to be enough to clean up four towns"—Wink "has been decimated as if by a great cataclysm."[99]

While a Ranger might make his nightly rounds through a sand-swept oil-field boomtown on the back of a horse, more and more Texans did their traveling in automobiles and trucks. As the decade neared its close, the state had almost nineteen thousand miles of highways, more than half paved. That traffic began causing new problems: Speeding and drunk driving claimed in a single year more lives in traffic accidents than Texas ever lost to Indians or outlaws. In an act providing new traffic regulations, the forty-first legislature authorized the state highway department to create a fifty-man state highway patrol to enforce laws pertaining to traffic and vehicles on public roadways. The legislation included in the new patrol's responsibilities the Highway Department's original charge of regulating truck sizes and weight, a function that had been handled by nonuniformed license and weight inspectors.[100]

In June 1929, during the second called session of the forty-first legislature, Senator Wirtz again sought to reduce the Rangers from thirty-six to thirty men. Using Rangers to enforce Prohibition, he argued, amounted to interference in county government. Local law enforcement officers had done a commendable job, the anti-Prohibitionist senator said. Ironically, Wirtz did not even drink.[101] Representative John C. White of Borger, his constituents still rankled over the 1927 state takeover, tried to get the Ranger appropriation reduced from $118,000 to $82,950, which would cut the force to sixteen men. "How much would that save the bootleggers of Texas?" Representative B. J. Forbes of Weatherford, a minister, asked during the debate over the proposed measures. "What are the Rangers for?" countered Representative M. E. O'Neill of Collin County. "To hunt outlaws or to hunt bootleggers?"[102]

As Rangers continued to employ nineteenth-century methodologies in trailing bootleggers on the border, police in Detroit found that their new radio system—the nation's first—enabled them to catch more criminals. Soon crime-ridden Chicago also established radio communication for its police department. The law enforcement community had begun to understand the importance of new technology, but modernization would be slow paced in Texas. For Rangers, communication continued to be by telegraph, telephone, or mail. If a Ranger needed a fingerprint identification to make a case or a photograph of a suspect, he had to rely on a city police department or county sheriff with that capability.

When someone shot forty-nine-year-old Mason County sheriff Allen T. Murry to death on a rural road in his county on February 28, 1929, Captain Hamer and another Ranger rushed from Austin to assist local officers in the search for Murry's killer. To provide other law enforcement agencies and the citizenry a description of a vehicle believed used by the sheriff's assailants, the local officers prevailed on San Antonio radio station WOAI to broadcast the information as a public service. When officers arrested one suspect and later a second, the state could provide no forensic assistance in developing the case. Instead, a Sutton County deputy with forensic training drove one hundred miles to Mason to fingerprint and photograph the suspects. Each suspect had a pistol in his possession when taken into custody, one of which had belonged to the slain sheriff. While that made a strong circumstantial case, the deputy from Sonora lifted prints from the weapon and compared them against the ridges and whorls on the fingerprint cards of the two jailed men. One of the prints on the sheriff's pistol came from the right thumb of Offilio Herrera, one of the men in custody. Convicted of murder, Herrera died later that year in the electric chair.[103]

Though the legislature did nothing to help the Rangers acquire their own forensic experts and equipment, lawmakers did approve a $94,600 budget that included a pay increase effective September 1, 1929. Captains would earn $225 monthly, sergeants $175, and privates $150. After two years' continuous service, Rangers would be entitled to a 5 percent raise and 5 percent for each additional year, not to exceed 20 percent. The "violation or breach of such rules and regulations for the governing of the Ranger Force" would result in forfeiture of the pay increase and longevity pay.[104]

The Rangers' reputation for toughness continued to be the force's most effective weapon. The September 13 assassination in Hutchinson County of forty-three-year-old district attorney John A. Holmes—shot five times in front of his wife and mother-in-law by someone hiding in the bushes outside Holmes's residence—precipitated another state takeover in Borger. On September 28, Governor Moody declared martial law there. His proclamation, effective at 3:00 p.m. the following day, suspended from office Borger's mayor, police chief, his officers and the county sheriff for as long as martial law remained in effect. Fourteen Rangers and a National Guard contingent of eighty-four troops under Brigadier General Wolters quickly took control of the city, arrests beginning as soon as the Rangers and guardsmen stepped off the train. Wolters sent a detachment to City Hall to disarm the local officers. Another detachment drove to the county seat at Stinnett, eleven miles north of Borger, to shut down the sheriff's office.

As they had done two years before, Rangers and guardsmen raided the joints and rounded up miscreants and felons. The adjutant general's provost marshal fined those arrested for misdemeanors, while felony cases went to a grand jury for consideration. Wolters also convened a military court of inquiry made up of two guard colonels and one major as well as the county judge, county attorney, and newly appointed district attorney to "investigate all matters pertaining to crime and law enforcement in Hutchinson County." The court interviewed a hundred witnesses, reducing their testimony to a thousand-page document handed over to the grand jury. The report "clearly established the existence of a criminal ring in Borger and Hutchinson County, involving many persons and Peace Officers."[105]

The sheriff tendered his resignation October 14. Three days later, Ranger private C. O. Moore, given a one-year leave of absence, took over as sheriff. Borger's city commission did its part by hiring Albert Mace as the new police chief. A well-respected town tamer, Mace had been chief of Mexia's police department.

With Wolters satisfied that local government once again rested "in the hands of competent and trustworthy persons," the guardsmen left Borger on October 18. Rangers stayed until the new sheriff and police chief had their departments reorganized and functioning. In addition to those fined or jailed, "many other undesirable persons were invited to leave Hutchinson County and State of Texas and to return to the places from which they came. These invitations were accepted and complied with."[106] The governor lifted martial law October 29, but two Rangers remained in Borger for months.

The Rangers in the 1920s had proven adept at calming rowdy oil towns, busting bootleggers, and exterminating bank robbers,[107] but the overall quality of the force pivoted on politics. An honest governor kept the Rangers clean. A governor with his—or her—own agenda used the Rangers to their own purpose, as the diverse administrations of Neff, Ferguson, and Moody had readily demonstrated.

"It is to be regretted that the Texas Ranger force must come under the influence of varying . . . administrations and should have to exist under the shadow of political vagaries," the Fort Worth *Record* editorialized near the end of the decade. "The force is entitled to a better fate. It is one institution that should have been strictly 'civil service' ever since its first organization back in the youth of the Republic of the Lone Star. It has served Texas, and Texas should serve it to better advantage than that of making it a battledore of factional antagonisms."[108]

6

Crime Outrides the Rangers

LAST YEARS UNDER THE ADJUTANT GENERAL, 1930—1934

Pistols drawn, Captain Frank Hamer and two of his Rangers faced the crowd inside the Grayson County courthouse.

"The Negro is upstairs," Hamer said, "and there he stays."

"We're coming up to get him!" someone yelled.

"Well, if you feel lucky," the captain answered, "come on up. But if you start up the steps, there'll be a lot of funerals in Sherman tomorrow."

One of the men felt lucky. When he and a few others stepped toward the Rangers, Hamer and his men bounced the barrels of their .45s off several heads. The crowd fell back and the Rangers pushed the men outside. The state officers had won round one.

The Sherman trouble began with the sexual assault of a white farmer's wife on May 3, 1930. By day's end, Sheriff Arthur Vaughn had a suspect in custody, forty-one-year-old George Hughes—a black man. As word of the incident spread, unfounded rumors that the victim had been mutilated fueled growing unrest.

On Monday, May 5, a group of citizens, their mood ugly, gathered outside the county courthouse. They left without incident, but the next morning District Judge R. M. Carter telephoned Governor Moody and asked for two Rangers. Hoping to stave off mob action by moving the case quickly through the criminal justice system, the judge set Hughes's examining trial for Thursday. Even so, on Tuesday night a crowd again developed on the square. This time deputies had to fire several shots into the air to disperse it.

When Hughes pled guilty at the Thursday arraignment, Judge Carter ordered a trial before the court the following day. He also contacted the governor again, requesting two additional Rangers. To the judge's relief, Moody told him that Hamer, Sergeant J. B. Wheatley, and Privates J. W. Aldrich (Captain Roy Aldrich's brother) and J. E. McCoy had already left Austin by train for Sherman.[1]

In an overflowing courtroom, Carter called the case at nine o'clock that Friday morning, May 9. Outside the brick courthouse, a crowd grew. Bumper-to-bumper traffic jammed the roads leading into town. Later that morning, with the first witness on the stand, Hamer began hearing "murmurings" outside. The captain and the other Rangers descended the stairs to find that a contingent of angry citizens had entered the courthouse, intent on seizing the defendant and administering their own justice.

Thirty minutes after Hamer's funeral threat, the mob charged the courthouse a second time. Again the Rangers and local officers repelled them. Tear gas and more pistol whipping repulsed a third assault. The fourth wave came at 2:30 that afternoon. By then, as a precaution, the defendant had been locked inside a large walk-in vault inside the county clerk's office. This time, Hamer fired a shotgun into the crowd, but he had the scattergun loaded with bird shot and aimed low. Several of their leaders peppered with pellets, the crowd again withdrew.

On its fifth attempt to reach Hughes, the mob tried a different tactic: Someone tossed a can of gasoline into a basement window. Flames spreading rapidly through the seventy-one-year-old courthouse, Hamer desperately tried to locate someone who knew the combination to the safe so Hughes could be removed. Finding no one who could open the vault, Hamer realized if he and his men did not immediately leave the courthouse they would die. The captain ordered the Rangers to get out, the prisoner still trapped in the vault. Fire soon enveloped the building, the mob holding back the firemen and even cutting their hoses.

Hughes died, from either the heat or lack of oxygen. But the mob, estimated at four thousand strong, remained unconvinced. Later that evening, rioters cut their way into the safe with a looted blowtorch. Finding that Hughes had indeed died, they threw his body from the gutted building. The rest of the mob carried it away, using a chain to hang the remains from a cottonwood tree. Then they gathered furniture from a looted store and set a fire beneath the body.

Several hundred National Guard troops with fixed bayonets and additional Rangers under Captain Tom Hickman finally gained control of Sherman later that night.

"Sherman has been disgraced," a Houston newspaper lamented the next day.

> All Texas hangs her head in shame. . . . The only encouraging thing in this terrible story, is the fact that Frank Hamer, brave Ranger captain, and his handful of men, repulsed the mob for hours and stood faithfully at their posts of duty until the courthouse was burning over their heads. All honor to them.[2]

Adjutant General Robert Robertson included an account of the riot in his department's biennial report. "The situation encountered at Sherman was as trying as any peacetime situation which the National Guard of this State has faced," he wrote. Four hundred and sixty-seven guardsmen and eleven Rangers had finally restored order, but not before "a number of buildings" in the black section of the city had been destroyed.[3] One of eight guardsmen injured in suppressing the riot, Dallas lawyer and world war veteran Captain Albert Sidney Johnson, in a few years would play a crucial role in determining the future of the Rangers.

A follow-up investigation by the Rangers led to the indictment of fourteen of sixty-five persons arrested on various charges ranging from attempted murder to riot. Of those, only two persons drew convictions, each receiving a two-year prison sentence for arson and riot.[4]

The Rangers confronting the mob in Sherman had learned their jobs the traditional way—through experience. But Texas was changing. Five months prior to the racially motivated riot in North Texas, the state's first law enforcement training school had begun at Camp Mabry, the state-owned National Guard facility on the northwestern edge of Austin. The graduates were not Rangers, but some of them eventually would be.

To protect Texas's growing network of paved roadways and bridges, the state highway department in 1927 had hired twenty nonuniformed, noncommissioned inspectors to enforce licensing and vehicle weight regulations. Two years later, a bill to expand the License and Weight Division died on the calendar of the forty-first legislature. But during a second called session, lawmakers passed a different measure, Senate Bill 11, transforming the License and Weight Division into a traffic police force effective September 1, 1929. Officers would wear gray uniforms with bow ties and patrol the highways on motorcycles.[5]

Bespectacled Louis G. Phares, supervisor of the original License and Weight Division, got the job as head of the new state highway patrol. A Dallas native, Phares had begun his law enforcement career as a Dallas County sheriff's deputy. He also had served for a time as a Ranger, taking part in one of the Borger cleanups shortly before landing the Highway Department job.[6]

Five lieutenants from the old Inspection Division—with assistance from the Attorney General's Office, the state health department, and selected Rangers—schooled the Highway Patrol recruits. This first training class had been selected from a pool of more than fourteen hundred candidates. "At the end of seven weeks intensive training, during which time not a single disorder, cross word or fight occurred among the men," the Highway Department's biennial report declared, "[the new patrolmen] were assigned to their various stations through the State."

Prowling the highways in pairs, the motorcycle officers had made 3,503 arrests, including 406 drunk-driving cases, by August 31, 1930. In addition to enforcing traffic laws, Highway Patrolmen lived up to their new motto of "Courtesy, Service and Protection" by changing tires for women drivers, helping stranded motorists with minor repairs, and directing traffic at county fairs.[7]

The nascent state highway patrol and the Rangers soon confronted a major new challenge—the state's biggest-ever oil boom. Unlike Spindletop three decades earlier, this new bonanza started slowly. It began October 3, 1930, when Columbus Marion "Dad" Joiner brought in the Daisy Bradford Number 3 in Rusk County. But full realization that an important new field had been discovered did not sink in until December 27 when a twenty-two-thousand-barrel-a-day gusher shot heavenward on the Lou Della Crim Farm in Gregg County, nine miles from Joiner's well. The East Texas field eventually covered six hundred square miles in four counties, one of the world's largest oil fields.

As had happened before elsewhere, speculators, land men, drillers, roughnecks, roustabouts, muleskinners, bootleggers, con men, hijackers, gamblers, pimps, prostitutes, and others hoping to make easy money descended on small communities in the area. Kilgore became the epicenter, growing from a population of only a few hundred to ten thousand in a matter of weeks.[8]

While the new oil field boomed, a man who soon would use the Rangers to support a critical aspect of its development took the oath of office as governor on January 20, 1931. Oilman Ross Sterling, having defeated another gubernatorial bid by "Ma" Ferguson and easily besting his token Republic opponent, had received many recommendations as to whom he should select as adjutant general. The man he picked had not been among those touted for the job—South Texas Ranger captain W. W. "Bill" Sterling.

The governor's connection to the young, tall big-eared Ranger had to do with a mule. As the governor later told the story, while working in the Dayton old fields in 1914 he had seen a teamster mercilessly beating his mules. Just then a stranger walked up. "If you hit those mules another lick with that whip," the man said, "I'll knock your block off." The teamster eased up on the mules and the future governor walked up to congratulate the Good Samaritan for intervening in behalf of the work animals. To Sterling's surprise, the man introduced himself as Sterling—Edward Arthur Sterling. They talked family long enough to conclude they were not related, but their chance meeting marked the beginning of a friendship that eventually extended to the man's son, Ranger Bill Sterling.[9]

Only eight days after Governor Sterling assumed office, Gregg County sheriff Martin Hays requested state assistance in coping with lawlessness attendant to the new East Texas field. Captain Hickman sent three Rangers to the Kilgore area to assist local officers, arrest or run off crooked officers, and do the same with oil-field trash. Busy as that kept the Rangers, public discussion of their overall relevancy arose again.[10]

When *Frontier Times* editor J. Marvin Hunter published an excerpt from James Gillett's Ranger memoir that winter, he prefaced the reprint with a thinly veiled editorial. Noting it had been suggested that the legislature merge the Rangers with the new state highway patrol and "the armed representatives of the state game, fish and oyster commission who guard the coast fisheries and the hunting areas of the state against poachers," Hunter opined, "the picturesque identity of the rangers will probably be lost." Even so, he continued, Rangering had changed:

> Instead of being in the saddle perhaps 18 hours out of 24 for weeks and months on end, as was done in the early days, the rangers now sit around their comfortable headquarters in Austin and other modern towns, swapping stories and waiting for an alarm to be turned in of a bank holdup or some other equally commonplace affair, whereupon they get into their automobiles and speed to the scene over paved highways.[11]

"Where There Is Oil, There Is Hell . . ."

One of those paved highways led Ranger Gonzaullas and a colleague to Kilgore on February 2, 1931. "Crime may expect no quarter," the "Lone Wolf" announced to reporters when he and Private J. P. Huddleston hit town. "Gambling houses, slot machines, whiskey rings, and dope peddlers might as well save the trouble of opening, because they will not be tolerated in any degree. Drifters and transients have their choice of three things: engaging in a legitimate business, getting out of town, or going to jail!"[12]

Gonzaullas again resorted to an extraconstitutional technique that had worked in pacifying oil towns the previous decade: checking hands. The Ranger figured a man with rough, dirty hands was hardworking and honest. A man having smooth, clean hands more likely made his living, as Gonzaullas later explained, as "a pimp or gambler or thug or some other kind of outlaw."[13]

Caught either smooth-handed or red-handed in the commission of a crime, prisoners ended up chained to trees on "trotlines" in the time-honored method of temporary incarceration perfected nearly thirty years earlier by Gonzaullas's predecessors following Spindletop. To protect his prisoners from the weather, Gonzaullas soon took over Kilgore's old First Baptist Church, which had been replaced with a larger house of worship. Prisoners got one meal a day and a tin can passed from man to man served as their urinal. Jailers used the church's former pulpit for fingerprinting new arrivals.[14]

"Where there is oil, there is hell," one newspaper sighed. Law-abiding citizens meeting in Kilgore's high school on April 1 passed a resolution thanking "the governor . . . the adjutant general and others who have sent and kept the Texas Rangers among us for vigilant service to this section." The document also promised local cooperation "in the promotion of their service and in every effort for the general civic and social welfare of this oil territory."[15]

While Gonzaullas and other Rangers policed the boisterous East Texas oil patch that spring, in Austin members of the forty-second legislature struggled to adopt a state budget. Despite the deepening Depression and decreasing tax revenue, lawmakers expanded the state highway patrol to 120 officers, including Chief Phares, five captains, five lieutenants, five sergeants, and 104 privates. The Rangers, still under the Adjutant General's Department, received funding allowing up to fifty positions.[16]

Legislators took no action on a Ranger–Highway Patrol merger, but with passage of House Concurrent Resolution 58 on May 18, 1931, they created a joint committee to look into the function and cost of state government. Meeting initially on June 10, the Joint Legislative Committee on Organization and Economy soon hired a Chicago-based consulting firm, Griffenhagen and Associates, to assess the state's government and recommend spending reductions.[17]

Three hundred miles from Austin, the oil boom in the pines continued apace—and sometimes violently. Newly assigned to Gladewater, fifteen miles from Kilgore, forty-eight-year-old Ranger Dan L. McDuffie happened to be at the police station on the night of July 7 when a caller reported a drunk blazing away with a rifle along Main Street. Police Chief W. A. Dial, a former Ranger who had served on the border with Captain Wright a decade earlier, drove McDuffie and two of his officers to the scene. They arrived to find fifty-five-year-old Jeff Johnson, a former jailer Dial had fired for sexual impropriety with female prisoners and chronic drinking, staggering around with a .30-.30. Before the officers could get out of the car, Johnson fired at his former boss. The bullet blew out the windshield in front of the chief, struck the car's steering column, and ricocheted into McDuffie's left leg. Dial leaned out of the car with his rifle and pumped seven rounds into Johnson, dropping him dead in his tracks. The wounded Ranger's femoral artery spurting blood, he exsanguinated before reaching a hospital in Longview.[18]

"War" with Oklahoma

Ten days after McDuffie's death, the Rangers got tangled in another legal dispute with Oklahoma, this time over a bridge. Near midnight on July 17, the officers of Texas's Fifty-sixth Cavalry Brigade and their wives danced atop the roof garden of the Baker Hotel, a resort property in Mineral Wells. The brigade had descended on Mineral Wells, sixty miles west of Fort Worth, for its annual maneuvers at Camp Wolters. Among those waltzing under the stars were Adjutant General Sterling and his wife. Also sashaying across the dance floor were Captain Hickman and his wife, down from Fort Worth. Shortly before midnight, a bellboy made his way through the crowd and told Sterling he had an urgent telephone call from the governor. Governor Sterling told him to be at the new Red River bridge north of Denison by dawn.

A joint project between the Texas Highway Department and its Oklahoma counterpart, the recently completed span stood adjacent to an old privately owned toll bridge. Since travelers would be able to cross the new bridge for free, the owners of the seventy-five-cent-per-vehicle toll bridge had worked out a compensation agreement with the Texas Highway Commission. But with the new bridge about to open and no money having changed hands, the toll bridge owners got an injunction in federal court to keep the free bridge closed until the matter could be resolved.

Oklahoma governor William H. "Alfalfa Bill" Murray wanted the new bridge open, arguing that the injunction bound Texas, not Oklahoma. When Murray ordered his highway department to take down a barricade erected on the Texas side of the bridge, Governor Sterling called his adjutant general to see to it that the next barricade that went up stayed up.

Sterling and Hickman left Mineral Wells almost immediately after the governor called, stopping in Fort Worth only long enough to pick up another couple of Company B Rangers. When the sun came up, the adjutant general and three Rangers stood near the Texas side of the bridge. "This time," Sterling later recalled, "the bridge stayed closed."

Learning of the situation, reporters from Fort Worth and Dallas hurried to the scene. The fourth estate quickly exaggerated a matter of civil litigation into impending civil war between Texas and Oklahoma. The press got plenty of help from Oklahoma's colorful governor. After hearing that the Rangers had replaced the road closure sign, Murray had his state's highway department bulldoze the pavement leading to the bridge. Then he declared martial law and called out National Guard troops.

That allowed General Sterling, never one to disappoint reporters, to invoke the old "one riot, one Ranger" line even though he had three Rangers up against thirty-two Oklahoma National Guardsmen. Before leaving the situation in the hands of Captain Hickman and his men, Sterling obligingly posed defiantly in front of the disputed bridge, rifle in hand. The photograph of the tall Texan made *Life* magazine and appeared in other publications around the world.

While lawyers and lawmakers dealt with the bridge dispute in other venues, Hickman and his Rangers amused the press and bystanders with shooting exhibitions, Ranger Bob Goss cutting playing cards in half with .45 slugs while holding his six-shooter upside down. "Bob is just a new man we are breaking in as a Ranger," Hickman clowned. For his part, the captain hit eighteen out of twenty matches shooting from the hip at fifty feet.

On July 25, two days after Texas's legislature passed a bill allowing the bridge company to sue the state for compensation, the Rangers removed the barricades from the new bridge and left. A judge permanently dissolved the injunction on August 6 and the Oklahoma troops withdrew.[19]

HOT OIL

The "war" with Oklahoma had been a legal dispute rewritten as comic opera by the press. Texas had a much more serious issue within its own borders—overproduction in the East Texas field. The governor, worried about runaway drilling in the rich new field, had called the legislature into special session on July 14 to come up with a law giving teeth to a provision of the state constitution declaring the "conservation and development of all the natural resources" of Texas to be "public rights and duties."[20] Stretching his constitutional authority as thin as the paper it was printed on, Sterling on August 16 declared martial law in Gregg, Rusk, Smith, and Upshur counties, proclaiming that certain producers were "in a state of insurrection against conservation laws [and] . . . in open rebellion against the efforts of the constituted civil authorities."

In reality, the problem had more to do with economics than potential violence. While crude oil prices had continued to sink as the Depression worsened, dropping below a dime a barrel, the flow from more than sixteen hundred wells in East Texas approached a million barrels a day— one-third of the nation's total production. Forgetting the fundamental economic principle of supply and demand, producers ignored the Texas Railroad Commission's efforts to cap production. The big oil companies saw the situation building toward financial disaster, and Governor Sterling, a former oilman himself, agreed. Meanwhile, independent operators continued to pump crude.[21]

"Some of my enemies warned that when I signed the martial law order, I signed the death warrant for my second term," Sterling later recalled. "Reelection was the least of my worries at that point."[22]

The day after Sterling's martial law declaration, twelve hundred National Guard troops of the Fifty-sixth Brigade—fresh from their summer maneuvers—and ten Rangers (plus four Rangers already on hand) set about shutting down the oil field.[23] Without violence and within twenty hours, the state controlled the field. With cavalry on patrol, the state allowed production to resume September 2. The Railroad Commission set a per-well limit, but that proved nearly impossible to enforce. Producers simply drilled more wells or openly ignored the order, pumping what came to be called hot oil. A month after the commission action, production substantially exceeded the maximum allowed.[24]

After several independent operators won a federal injunction against the state proration orders, Sterling ordered the state troops, with the Rangers as peacekeepers, to regulate the flow of the wells.[25] Captain Hickman assigned one Ranger per twenty-man cavalry troop to patrol the field, looking for illegal pumping. The Rangers handled any arrests that needed to be made.

In addition to enforcing well production limits, the state officers continued to roust bootleggers, gamblers, and prostitutes. "Beer joints, tourist camps and dance halls on the highways near here were visited Saturday night by rangers," the Associated Press reported on August 30, 1931. "Ranger Capt. Tom Hickman . . . ordered dance halls to close at midnight on Saturday. His men arrested 21 suspicious characters, ordering some of them to leave the county Sunday, and confiscated liquor at several places."[26]

Later that year, still in Kilgore, Gonzaullas investigated an armed robbery at a movie theater. Checking nearby boardinghouses, the Ranger located a man matching the description of the gunman. Searching his room, the Ranger found an assortment of pistols, ammunition, and holsters, including a law enforcement style Sam Browne belt. The Ranger also discovered a large amount of cash and a stash of jewelry hidden in a toilet tank. The robber had wrapped the valuables in a handkerchief in which two evenly spaced eyeholes had been cut. Finished tossing the room, Gonzaullas took the suspect and another man who had been in the room to the scene of the crime. The box office cashier identified one of the men as the robber, but based on the items Gonzaullas had found in the room, he locked up both men.

When Gonzaullas checked the men's car, he found a Louisiana Highway Police badge. The next day the Ranger learned that the badge belonged to an officer recently robbed by two men who had descended on his parked patrol car. The hijackers had taken the patrolman's badge, gun, Sam Browne belt, and car, leaving him on the side of the road. By the time Gonzaullas and local officers completed their investigation, the two men arrested in Kilgore had been linked to a string of robberies in Texas and Louisiana as well as a rape and an aggravated assault.

The case made headlines in Shreveport, where a local automobile dealer later expressed his appreciation to the Rangers by giving Gonzaullas the keys to a brand-new Chrysler, complete with armor plating, bullet-resistant windshields, and a swivel-mounted machine gun in the front passenger's seat. The car salesman's generosity also netted the kind of publicity that could not be bought—unless one factored in the wholesale cost of a 1932 eight-cylinder customized coupe. Gonzaullas, a sharp dresser, obligingly posed for photographs standing next to the shiny new car, which he put to good use in Kilgore.[27]

A three-judge federal panel held on February 18, 1932, that the governor could not assume the functions delegated legislatively to the Railroad Commission, in effect negating Sterling's use of martial law in the oil field to enforce proration.[28] National Guard troops went home to their families, but the oil field continued to keep the Rangers busy.

Governor Sterling's stand on proration, which eventually did make its way through the courts and become an effective conservation tool, cost him his job. He had figured as much. Mrs. Ferguson ran for a second term and defeated Sterling in an August 27, 1932, runoff by only 3,798 ballots. A different set of numbers told another story: the votes cast exceeded the number of poll-tax receipts. Illegal voting in East Texas, where Sterling had few admirers and the Fergusons many friends, made the difference. Sterling later said that if he had used the Rangers to prevent voter fraud—a campaign his adjutant general had started before the governor ordered him to stop—he would have remained in the Governor's Mansion.[29] Though Mrs. Ferguson would face a Republican challenge in the fall general election, her primary victory in overwhelmingly Democratic Texas meant she would be governor again.

Three days after that summer's runoff, former Ranger captains J. A. Brooks and John R. Hughes dropped by the Capitol to visit the adjutant general. Sterling suggested they go see Captain Dan Roberts, the old Indian fighter, and have a group photograph taken. Captain Hamer joined them. The resulting image spanned fifty-seven years of Ranger history, from 1875, when Roberts's Company D scouted the West Texas frontier for Indians, to the era of the Thompson submachine gun. It is the last known photograph of Roberts, who died only a few years later.[30]

While Sterling helped preserve the Ranger legacy by arranging for that photograph, he also had a vision of the service's future. Well aware that he would soon be out of office, the adjutant general recommended in his 1932 biennial report that "the Ranger Service be taken out of the hands of the Adjutant General . . . [who] in almost every case is a military man and has no conception of the duties of a Ranger. He is constantly called upon to make decisions for the Rangers, and his training does not fit him to handle the problems of the Rangers." Continuing his brief, Sterling observed that the "military organization of the State has now grown to such an extent that the Adjutant General should devote his entire time to the military."

Obviously writing for posterity, the general continued:

It is freely admitted that the Ranger Service today is in the highest state of efficiency in the history of Texas, and that the present group of Rangers is the finest body of peace officers ever assembled. I have endeavored to carry on the Ranger Service in a manner that would make every honest Texan proud of the famous Texas Rangers.[31]

MA FERGUSON RETURNS

When Mrs. Ferguson prevailed as expected in the November general election, many of Sterling's Rangers resigned, including Senior Captain Hamer.

Despite Hamer's resignation, and the general political turmoil, the Rangers continued to function. At 11:15 a.m. on November 8, two gunmen robbed the Carmine State Bank in Fayette County, escaping with $1,400. By 1:30 p.m., as the La Grange *Journal* reported, "two State Rangers, coming from Austin, appeared . . . and took up the trail." Identified as Raymond Hamilton and Gene O'Dare, the two robbers managed to elude the Rangers but they still found it expedient to leave Texas. The duo skipped out to Bay City, Michigan, where state police arrested them on December 6. Eight days later, they sat behind bars in Texas, awaiting trial.[32]

Though their senior captain had wanted nothing to do with a governor named Ferguson, Captain Hickman and Sergeant Gonzaullas opted not to resign. On January 17, 1933, they handled an assignment they must have found personally distasteful: escorting Mrs. Ferguson to the platform on the south side of the Capitol to be sworn in as governor.

The next day, in one of her first official acts, Governor Ferguson named sixty-nine-year-old Henry Hutchings, the man who had served in the same capacity from 1911 to 1917, as General Sterling's successor. The new governor then fired both Rangers who had stood by during her inauguration and forty-two of their colleagues—the entire force. Charitably, the discharges later appeared on the record as honorable.[33] What happened next surprised a lot of former Rangers who thought they had seen everything: Hamer's fifty-year-old older brother, Dennis Estill Hamer, who went by Estill, got the job as captain of Headquarters Company. Estill Hamer's willingness to work for a Ferguson nearly brought the former captain and the new captain to blows.[34]

Estill Hamer's Headquarters Company had one sergeant and three privates. Company A, under Jefferson Eagle Vaughan in Marfa, had four privates; Harry T. Odneal's Company B, headquartered in Fort Worth, had

four privates; E. H. Hammond's Company C, Houston, had four privates;
Captain James R. Robbins's Company D, based in Falfurrias, had five
men. Four other Rangers worked out of Austin, though not technically
part of Headquarters Company. Roy Aldrich, fired by General Sterling
when he took control of the Rangers, got rehired as quartermaster.[35]

As the Fergusons continued their political pogrom, the forty-third
legislature had before it the result of the efficiency study commissioned
in 1931. The thirteen-volume, two-thousand-plus-page report reviewed
all aspects of the state's fiscal and administrative agencies. Titled *The
Government of the State of Texas,* the weighty document came to be
called the Griffenhagen Report. Though the study said the state could
save up to $6 million a year without reducing services, the legislature
took no action on the consulting firm's recommendations. Some of the
report's proposals would not have been right for Texas, but Part 3, covering state law enforcement, endorsed and expanded on General Sterling's
recommendation that the Rangers be separated from the Adjutant General's Department and joined with the Highway Patrol. Noting the costs
associated with Governor Sterling's use of the National Guard in the
East Texas oil field, the report said state troops should only be called out
in the event of rioting or a major disaster. Sterling's martial law declaration in East Texas, the study continued, "cost not less than five times as
much as would have been necessary to handle the situation as well or
better by a properly organized State police force." The report even suggested a name for such an agency: the Department of Public Safety.[36]

With the nation still mired in an economic—and to some extent
psychological—depression, a fictional Texas Ranger rode to the rescue
of the public mood. On January 30, 1933, the first episode of a radio series called *The Lone Ranger* aired on WXYZ in Detroit. Scripted by Fran
Striker, a prolific writer originally from Buffalo, New York, the show
rapidly grew in popularity. Soon the finale of the *William Tell* Overture
"Cavalry Charge," became more familiar as the Lone Ranger theme music than as a classical composition. With the program broadcast nationwide three nights a week, almost anyone in America could recite the
serial's opening:

A fiery horse with the speed of light, a cloud of dust, and a hearty, "Hi
Yo, Silver!" It's the Lone Ranger. With his faithful Indian companion,

Tonto, the daring and resourceful masked rider of the plains led the fight for law and order in the early West. Return with us now to those thrilling days of yesteryear. The Lone Ranger rides again!

Played by a succession of deep-voiced radio talents, the new hero embodied traits of Robin Hood and Zorro. But instead of using longbow or rapier to right wrongs, the Lone Ranger, the sole survivor of a Ranger company ambushed by outlaws, carried six-shooters loaded with silver bullets. His sidekick, Tonto, was portrayed as a Potawatomi (a tribe first known in Michigan that never lived in Texas) who had saved his life.[37] No matter to what extent the Texas Rangers inspired Striker, public awareness of the legendary Texas lawmen was good for the radio show, and vice versa.

The real Rangers certainly did not carry silver bullets. The Depression made the state's never lavish funding even more tight. Adjutant General Hutchings issued an order noting that the state attorney general had ruled that the $30 a month allowed for subsistence "is not a part of Ranger pay, but merely . . . the rate for subsistence while at home station." A week later, another order said that because of "limited funds for auto up-keep, the several company commanders will see that railroad transportation is used whenever possible."[38]

Though political realities coupled with a that's-how-we've-always-done-it attitude quickly relegated the Griffenhagen Report to a shelf in the Legislative Reference Library, the state's lawmakers did do some cost-cutting. They slashed Ranger salaries, ended longevity pay, reduced travel budgets, and shrank the service to thirty-two positions from thirty-nine. In all, the Ranger budget took nearly a 47 percent hit, dropping from $156,160 for the fiscal year ending on August 31, 1933, to $82,765 for each year of the coming biennium.[39]

While the legislature reduced the Ranger appropriation, the State Board of Education put a little money in one old Ranger's pocket: It adopted the children's version of Gillett's *Six Years with the Texas Rangers*—a book already being used in schools on the East Coast and in the Midwest—as a sixth-grade reader for Texas schoolchildren. In guaranteeing the sale of another thirty thousand copies of Gillett's book, the board's action exposed a new generation of Texans to the history of the Rangers.[40]

The state did not have enough tax revenue to pay for very many full-time Rangers, but the governor and her husband found appointing non-salaried special Rangers a good investment in political capital. During her administration, Ferguson would name 2,344 special Rangers.

General Hutchings on June 23 set forth the Ferguson philosophy of state law enforcement in another general order: "The Sheriffs of the various Counties are their chief enforcement officers. All members of the Ranger Force will act in cooperation with them on their requests." Should other county or district officers feel they needed Rangers, the order continued, they were to "act through the Sheriffs." In "exceptional cases" they could appeal directly to the governor, "stating why the request does not come through the Sheriff." If local authorities did not want Rangers in their jurisdiction, all they needed to do was ask the governor to remove them. Curiously, the next two numbered points in Hutchings's order dealt with gambling. The Rangers, the order continued, were "maintained to meet major activities and will not initiate independent raids on slot machines and other minor activities that should be handled by the Sheriffs or subordinate officers." Even more strangely, the fourth point stipulated: "If such raids are made in cooperation with the Sheriffs then such raids will be made impartially on all makes of such machines."[41]

In only a few months under Governor Ferguson, the Ranger service had less money, reduced authority, and fewer men, most of them political appointments with little or no experience and of questionable character. The caliber of at least one new Ranger soon became apparent in Austin, where recently commissioned private W. S. Byars resorted to his six-shooter to resolve an argument with his neighbors, Mr. and Mrs. J. R. Munro. The July 3 difficulty stemmed from access to their garages, which faced the same alley. The Ranger shot and killed Munro and wounded his wife. Austin police arrested Byars and charged him with murder and assault with intent to murder.[42]

Texans had no tolerance for murder, but drinking was another matter. One minute after midnight on September 15, 1933, national Prohibition ended. The Rangers would no longer be bogged down trying to keep illegal alcohol out of Texas, a task that had proven impossible. Few of them lamented the law's demise.[43]

Governor Ferguson's politicizing of the Rangers made the good old days seem all the more attractive for many Texans. Former Frontier Battalion Ranger George B. Black, commander of the three-hundred-member Texas Ex-Rangers Association, mailed a recruitment circular that fall to all the former Rangers he could identify. More than two hundred men of what Hunter in his *Frontier Times* referred to as "the Old Guard" received the flyer. "If you will join our association," Black wrote

> you will find a great deal of pleasure in meeting old friends you had nearly forgotten. This satisfaction will more than offset the annual dues of $1.00. Besides, you must remember that both Congress and the State Legislature will listen to an organization of this kind when we ask for some recognition. They have done so in the past, and only recently I appealed to Congress in behalf of a ranger's widow and received everything I asked for.[44]

"I Hated to Bust a Cap on a Woman"

In the winter of 1934, a new generation of Rangers proved unequal to a new generation of outlaws. On a foggy winter morning at the state's Eastham Farm in the Trinity River bottom near the East Texas community of Weldon, a Dallas hood named Clyde Barrow Jr. sprang his bank-robbing friend Raymond Hamilton and three other inmates out of prison. An auburn-haired woman from Dallas named Bonnie Parker came along for the ride. It did not take prison officials long to learn how the couple pulled off the spectacular January 16 escape. The day before they had hidden a pair of .45 semiautomatics beneath a culvert near the prison farm's wood yard. As the convicts marched to work in the field that day, Hamilton and inmate Joe Palmer grabbed the pistols. In the shooting that followed, they mortally wounded a guard. The two armed inmates and two other prisoners ran to Barrow's waiting car. Guards blazed away as the vehicle screeched off, but the car quickly disappeared.

Two brothers estranged by politics—Ranger captain Estill Hamer and former captain Frank Hamer—would lead the search for the young outlaws, soon known across the Southwest simply as Bonnie and Clyde.

"We know practically all the places in which Barrow has hidden since things got so hot for him," Captain Estill Hamer told a reporter.

"Through the cooperation of officers in Texas, Oklahoma, Colorado, Kansas, Missouri, Arkansas, Louisiana, Nebraska and Ohio and other states, we have an organization which will make sure that he will not remain one place for long."[45]

With no public fanfare, Frank Hamer joined the effort on February 10, when prison director Lee Simmons hired him to track down the killers of the prison guard. Through informants, Hamer began learning everything he could about the outlaws, from the type of cigarettes they smoked to the brand of whiskey they favored. The outlaws revealed their preference in weaponry on February 19, when they pulled off a nighttime burglary at the National Guard armory in the West Texas oil-field town of Ranger. Entering the public building with little difficulty, the gang collected Browning automatic rifles (BARs), Colt .45 semiautomatic pistols, and a lot of ammunition.[46]

On February 27, the Barrow bunch robbed the Henry Bank in the Dallas County community of Lancaster, escaping with more than $4,000. Unknown to the officers looking for them, Hamilton and his girlfriend parted company with the notorious couple, albeit on friendly terms.

The search for the outlaws soon grew even more intense. On Easter Sunday, April 1, Barrow and running buddy Henry Methvin—with Parker sitting in their car—gunned down two Highway Patrolmen, H. D. Murphy and E. B. Wheeler. The double killing happened near Grapevine in Denton County, north of Dallas. The following day, a Fort Worth police fingerprint expert identified a latent print found on a whiskey bottle left at the scene as Barrow's.

Eight days later, when Frank Hamer telephoned Highway Patrol Chief Phares to give him the plate number and description of the outlaw couple's latest car, Phares told the former Ranger captain he wanted another man on the case. While the prison system would pay their salaries, Phares said he would cover their expenses through the Highway Patrol's budget. "I asked for B. M. Gault," Hamer recalled. Gault had served as a Ranger private under Hamer until losing his job when Ferguson took office. The former Ranger joined Hamer in Dallas on April 14. The day before, in Joplin, Missouri, the Barrow gang had killed a police detective and a constable in a wild shoot-out. "This man [Barrow] is dangerous," the Joplin Police Department understated in the wanted poster it soon circulated.[47]

The Dallas *Morning News* on May 4 published a letter from Evans Smith of Kemp, a small East Texas community in Henderson County. To capture Bonnie and Clyde, Smith said, "the state must have a Ranger force that is adequately mobilized and armed. . . . Arm these men with the criminals' own weapon, the machine gun, and give them orders to get their prisoner dead or alive, and we will find that Texas crime will take a very decided drop." Smith then recommended about what the Griffenhagen Report had proposed:

A closer banding together of the law enforcing bodies of Texas: the establishment of a central office at some strategic point where criminal records, fingerprints and other material of a like nature could be used by all forces, and where a competent corps of specialists in this work could help any sheriff, police chief or officer. . . . Let the people of Texas rise up and call for a united effort on the part of the governor, the county judges, the county sheriffs, and themselves, to do away with this dark spot that is being formed on the white pages of Texas history.

The criminal element in Texas took more advantage of improved transportation, communication, and technology than law enforcement did. Dallas Prohibitionist Atticus Webb had recognized the problem ten years earlier:

Railroads, automobiles and airplanes with the assistance of telephones and wireless communication are rapidly obliterating county and state lines. The failure to recognize this fact is responsible for much inefficiency in the enforcement of law. These modern conditions . . . make more necessary the use of the state constabulary.[48]

Though poor law enforcement communication made it easier for Bonnie and Clyde to avoid apprehension, another form of communication led to the couple's downfall. Having learned the rural location where Barrow came to pick up mail left for him by a supportive acquaintance, Hamer, Gault, two Dallas County sheriff's deputies, and two Louisiana officers waited by the side of Highway 154 near Arcadia, Louisiana, until the outlaw couple showed up at their "post office" in Barrow's new Ford V-8.

When the six officers stepped from their hiding place and Hamer yelled for the couple to "stick 'em up," the young pair reached instead for their weapons. Before the outlaws had time to shoot, the officers opened up on them, firing a withering 167 rounds in a matter of seconds.

Later that day—May 23, 1934—someone stole a blood-splattered copy of the June issue of *True Romances,* a pulp magazine favored by Parker, from the couple's bullet-riddled automobile. A rifle slug had ripped through ninety-six pages before coming to a rest against the word *LAW* boldly printed in an advertisement. As a United Press writer hyped, "The eloquent muteness of an inscrutable fate was indelibly written by a bullet."[49]

The press credited the dead outlaws with far more holdups than they actually pulled, but the Barrow gang had been responsible for twelve homicides. Two former Rangers—though they had help from other officers—had blown the couple away, but the Ranger force supervised by Hamer's brother, despite the application of a considerable amount of man-hours, had never been able to find them. However, two Ferguson Rangers, Jim Shown and W. R. Todd, later rounded up five people believed to have aided Barrow during his time on the run.

"Sure I can tell you how it happened," Hamer told a reporter. "We just shot the hell out of 'em." Not one to wax on about his role in the case, he chose his words as carefully as he aimed a rifle. "I hated to bust a cap on a woman," the former Ranger said shortly after the shooting, "especially when she was sitting down. However, if it wouldn't have been her, it would have been us."

"Hamer-Gault Hero Day Is Set," the Austin *Statesman* proclaimed in a banner headline the day after the killings. The story said Travis County sheriff Lee O. Allen planned a big appreciation dinner even though "the silent Frank Hamer and the modest Manny Gault may not want any celebration in their honor."[50] Indeed, the two lawmen did not desire any hoopla. The testimonial dinner never materialized.

"TEXAS IS ONE OF THE MOST CRIMINAL STATES IN THE UNION"

Even with Bonnie and Clyde dead, crime in Texas fueled a heated gubernatorial campaign that summer. "Texas is one of the most criminal states in the Union," Southern Methodist University faculty member Karl Everett Ashburn wrote in *Southwest Review*, the school's prestigious literary quarterly. "In 1933 it ranked sixth in the number of crimes committed per capita." Justice Department figures showed that only Nevada, Arizona, Washington, Oregon, and South Carolina, in that order, outranked Texas in crimes per 1 million population. "The City of Dallas, like other cities of Texas, has become the headquarters of gangs of outlaws who rob and plunder the surrounding territory," Ashburn continued.

The teacher urged creation of "an adequate, highly trained, and well-equipped state police force" divided into "four or five police districts." Officers should be hired "on the basis of competitive examinations under the direction of a Civil Service Board." Under Ashburn's model, the chief would be selected from those officers by the governor. Like federal judges, all officers on the force would hold their jobs for life, "subject to good behavior." Every state, Ashburn went on, should have such a law enforcement agency. To coordinate law enforcement activities, he continued, a National Police Board needed to be set up in Washington.[51]

That an academician should advocate a near-fascist approach to national law enforcement showed the seriousness which with Texans viewed crime. Newspapers, crime-busting radio heroes, newsreels, J. Edgar Hoover, and his G-men in snap-brim hats had the law-abiding people of the nation ready for all-out war on crime. The home state of the late Bonnie and Clyde stood on the front line.

Today magazine sent writer Edgar Sisson to Texas in the summer of 1934 to look into why crime seemed to have outridden the Rangers. He summed it up in two words: Jim Ferguson. "Not the Fergusons as a pair, but Jim Ferguson himself is responsible for making a political football of the Rangers," Sisson wrote. "Until his first term, now quite a distance in the past, no governor ever laid a political interfering finger upon the Rangers."

While that was overbroad, the best that could be said of Mrs. Ferguson's second term was that it was not as scandal ridden as her first. Still, she pardoned hundreds of prisoners, a system that began to be called the Texas Open Door. Some of the special Rangers she commissioned turned out to be recently released convicts. "The smashing of the Rangers for political reasons and the widespread misuse of the parole and pardon

power are the two greatest obstacles to stamping out crime in Texas,"
Sisson went on. "The power of the ballot is often overestimated, but in
this case the people of Texas can correct these evils—both chargeable to
gubernatorial laxity. . . . The choice, whether crime shall march on in
Texas, is squarely up to the people."[52]

The crime problem was not unique to Texas. The previous summer,
during hearings conducted by a U.S. Senate subcommittee, a prison
warden urged that Congress make all major crimes federal offenses. He
also recommended that the president declare a modified martial law
until a constitutional amendment eliminating state lines could be rati-
fied. While Congress did not go that far, it did pass a series of crime bills
in the spring of 1934. One of those new laws made bank robbery a federal crime. In a statement that raised goose bumps in Texas and other
solid states' rights areas, Assistant U.S. Attorney General J. B. Keenan
warned that if law enforcement across the country did not improve, the
federal government would assume responsibility.[53]

As the public and its government nervously discussed the future of
law enforcement in the Depression-ravaged nation, two Texans—a history professor and a newspaper reporter—spent a lot of their time
looking backward. With a book in mind, University of Texas faculty
member Walter Prescott Webb had been collecting information about
the Rangers for fourteen years. But the necessity of supporting his family, and while he was at it writing a groundbreaking book called *The
Great Plains*, had prevented him from making steady progress on his
planned history of the Rangers. In 1933, however, he had decided to
complete his book in time for the upcoming one hundredth anniversary
of Texas independence. Webb finished the book in 1934 and mailed the
manuscript to the venerable Boston publishing house of Houghton and
Mifflin. But Claude L. Douglas, a reporter for the Fort Worth *Press*, beat
Webb to the draw with the publication of his book *The Gentlemen in
the White Hats: Dramatic Episodes in the History of the Texas Rangers*.
Douglas did write in his introduction that his book should not be considered an "attempt to tell a full and detailed story of the Ranger service."
Instead, he continued, "I shall be content to present this narrative from
the background of certain personalities as they pertain to the epoch of
Texas history in which they moved."[54] Even so, in a readable if not always accurate way, Douglas's book was the first to trace the history of

the Rangers from Jack Hays through Hamer and Gault's eradication of Bonnie and Clyde.

On July 18, 1934, General Hutchings further codified the Ferguson administration's view of the role of the Rangers: "The fundamental duty [of the service] . . . is to put the power of the State behind the various sheriffs on their request when resistance is made to the due course of the law." A Ranger could "initiate investigations independent of sheriffs only on such rare cases as shall first be specifically authorized by the Governor." The general's order also muzzled the Rangers in another way, forbidding them to grant interviews to reporters or make public presentations on matters related to the force unless they had gubernatorial approval.[55]

Rangers in South Texas concentrated their efforts on gambling—engaging in it, not stamping it out. Hitting one operation in Friotown, forty-eight-year-old Captain Robbins seized all the cash, furnishings, and the structure itself. Ordering the owner to leave town, the Ranger moved in to run the place himself. Meanwhile, Company D Rangers raided competitors not paying for protection. The captain's entrepreneurial roll of the dice came up snake eyes later that summer with his arrest by Bexar County authorities on August 9, 1934, in San Antonio for theft and embezzlement.[56]

While the former captain of Company D awaited trial, another former captain completed the last-minute preparations for a trip across the Midwest and into the Northeast to visit and assess state police agencies. After Governor Ferguson booted him from the Rangers, Tom Hickman had gone to work as a special investigator for the state comptroller's office, working in North Texas out of Fort Worth. In August 1934 he took an extended leave of absence to make the fact-finding trip with his wife. How Hickman could afford to do that on a state salary or whether someone picked up the tab went unreported the following December when the Dallas Morning News began a seven-part series by Hickman in which he evaluated the various law enforcement agencies he visited on his three-month, ten-state tour.[57] No matter how the former captain's tour came about, it would play a part in changing Texas law enforcement.

"A Great Unstrapping of Six-shooter Belts . . ."

THE DEPARTMENT OF PUBLIC SAFETY, 1935–1939

On August 26, 1934, six days after Tom Hickman left on his cross-country trip, two-term attorney general James V. Allred of Wichita Falls narrowly won the Democratic gubernatorial primary. A former district attorney and dedicated New Dealer, the thirty-six-year-old Allred had promised during his campaign that if elected he would see to the creation of a new state law enforcement agency.

Allred's nomination being tantamount to election in an overwhelmingly Democratic state, most of the Ferguson Rangers—both fully commissioned and special Rangers—realized their time was about up. The Democratic Committee, meeting in convention that September in Galveston, added a plank to the party's platform that Texas should have a modernized state police force. With a special session under way, the state senate got on board and passed a resolution September 25 creating a crime-investigating committee charged with issuing a report for the next regular session.[1]

Appearing in early December, Hickman's Dallas *Morning News* articles (dictated to his wife while they were on the road, though likely touched up by someone on the newspaper's staff) weighed the pros and cons of the various police agencies he had visited and made the case that modern Rangers needed training, better equipment, and improved communication and forensic capabilities to continue to live up to their venerable reputation. Appearing in one of Texas's oldest and most-respected newspapers, Hickman's series would help set the agenda for the next legislative session.[2]

On January 23, 1935, the newly inaugurated governor ordered his recently appointed adjutant general, former state American Legion commander Carl Nesbitt of Mineola, to revoke all special Ranger commissions signed by Ferguson. The general had been shocked to discover that commissions had been issued by Mrs. Ferguson to nightclub bouncers, gambling house security personnel, dog- and horse-racing track guards, and even singer Kate Smith. Others holding commissions included a barber, a chamber of commerce manager, a dentist, a painter, a retail liquor distributor, a rock mason, an undertaker, and a wrestling referee.[3] Nesbitt asked Texas's sheriffs to collect the credentials. "The sheriffs were 'tickled pink' to co-operate," a Dallas newspaper noted. "There followed a great unstrapping of six-shooter belts all the way from Brownsville to the Panhandle, and from El Paso to Texarkana." During the Ferguson interim, the newspaper continued, "Texans watched all this political maneuvering with the feeling that the old world-famous force of he-man caliber was degenerating from a body of super-fighting men into an ordinary police outfit."[4] Of the thirty-two Rangers on the state payroll when Allred took office, only three kept their jobs. Captain Estill Hamer was not among them.[5]

Nesbitt quickly rehired Hickman to once again command Company B. "Hard-Riding and Straight-Shooting Tom Hickman Back," the Austin *American* proclaimed on January 24. Hickman came to Austin to pick up his new captain's commission and quickly left for Buffalo, a small town in Leon County about halfway between Dallas and Houston, to investigate a bank robbery. Less than a week later, Nesbitt got a telegram from Wynnewood, Oklahoma. Hickman had two suspects in custody, a confession, and part of the cash taken in the holdup. "Texans looked over the morning newspapers and smiled," the Dallas *Dispatch* reported. "Captain Hickman's report sounded like old times. The . . . Rangers were back in the saddle."[6]

During his campaign, Allred had asked attorney Albert Sidney Johnson, who as a National Guard officer had been injured by a flying brick during the 1930 Sherman riot, to begin work on a bill creating a new state law enforcement agency. Johnson agreed to take on the job, later admitting he did so only as a personal favor for his friend the governor. Before drafting the proposed measure, Johnson studied four state police forces: Illinois, Michigan, New York, and Pennsylvania. He also had the benefit of material collected by his longtime friend Hickman, including the annual reports of the state police agencies he had visited, copies of their organic statutes, and other reference materials.[7]

Senator John W. E. H. Beck, a doctor from DeKalb, introduced Johnson's measure as Senate Bill 146 on January 24, 1935.[8] The Senate's Investigating Committee on Crime issued its report on February 2, recommending that "it would be for the best interest of all the people of Texas to create a State Department of Safety, to be known as the Department of Public Safety."[9]

Most of Texas's movers and shakers agreed with the Senate committee's findings. "There was a time," wrote University of Texas Bureau of Municipal Research staffer Paul E. Fidler in *Texas Municipalities*,

> when one could boast with pride and conviction that one Ranger was sufficient to quell one riot, but our sister states must wonder whether such a reputation is merited when notorious criminals can roam the vast area of the state, robbing, killing and kidnapping as they go for months on end without being apprehended.

Fidler added that he did not fault the Rangers individually. "It's the change of the times," he wrote. "Ranger methods are no longer suited to fighting modern crime."[10] The state needed "a central bureau to fight crime."

But with the right personnel, old-style Ranger methods could still work. One of Allred's new Ranger captains was another old friend, forty-eight-year-old James W. McCormick, a tough former Ranger and one-time Wichita Falls police chief. In the 1920s, McCormick had earned repute for his ability to restore order in rowdy oil boom towns. Like many Rangers of his era, the blue-eyed, 170-pound lawman did not mind using a six-shooter for clubbing or killing—whichever a situation seemed to require. The governor told McCormick, who through various enlistments had eight years' experience as a Ranger, to head for the tall pines of San Augustine in deep East Texas, one of the state's oldest towns.[11]

In the final days of the Ferguson administration, on December 22 two men had died (two others suffered mortal wounds) when fisticuffs turned to shooting on a crowded street in front of the W. R. Thomas hardware store in downtown San Augustine. In one of his last official acts, Senior Captain Estill Hamer responded to a request for help from the local sheriff and sent a captain and three Rangers to town on January 5, 1935. Underexperienced and lame ducks as well, they had little effect in getting at the root of the real problem—two well-embedded gangs specializing in everything from hog theft to robbery to murder.[12]

Bringing new Rangers Leo Bishop and Dan Hines with him, Mc-Cormick went to work in classic blustery Ranger fashion. Walking around town with two pistols on his hips and occasionally a third revolver hanging from a shoulder holster (plus a fourth handgun stuffed in his pocket), the captain guaranteed the townspeople they need not worry about reprisal if they came forward with information on the criminal activities taking place in the county. The Rangers soon began taking statements and collecting evidence that would lead to multiple grand jury indictments followed by convictions. By March 22 McCormick and his men had made so much progress toward taming the town that local citizens threw a street dance in their honor.[13]

Back in Austin, State Representative Alfred Petsch of Fredericksburg, a forty-eight-year-old Democrat in one of Texas's few Republican enclaves, sponsored the governor's bill in the House. The DPS bill had passed the Senate with only one dissenting vote, but after moving out of the House Committee on State Affairs on February 22, it bogged down. Behind the scenes the Highway Department, and even some in the Adjutant General's Department, worked against the proposed merger. One at a time, the House member from the Texas Hill Country succeeded in fighting off, albeit by narrow margins, various floor amendments that would have kept the Rangers under the Adjutant General's Department and the Highway Patrol under the Highway Department.[14]

Even as the legislature pondered the future of the Rangers, the force kept busy. In one five-day period beginning April 10, five Rangers raided a bar in the capital city where liquor was being sold illegally, and in

Corpus Christi three Rangers looked into allegations of election irregularities. A Ranger arrested an accused killer in Kilgore and a district judge in Webb County telegraphed the adjutant general asking for Rangers to calm striking onion field workers. The activity did not go unnoticed in the legislature, where Representative J. W. Hunt Jr. of Comb said Governor Allred's Rangers "had done more in three months than any other force had done in 12 months."[15]

A compromise Highway Patrol–Ranger merger bill crafted by a conference committee finally passed the Senate by a 29–1 vote on May 3. Four days later, the DPS measure gained final approval in the House, 83–44.[16] Texas would have a new state law enforcement agency, but since the bill did not receive a two-thirds vote in the House, it would not go into effect until ninety days after the session. Under the new law, the Highway Patrol would be increased to 140 men (plus a chief and five inspectors), with its officers having full law enforcement authority. Previously they had only been empowered to enforce misdemeanor traffic laws. The Rangers would be reduced to a headquarters company and two mounted companies, but the legislation had specific language keeping the force alive. A pleased Allred signed the bill shortly after it reached his desk and began considering his appointments to the three-member commission that would oversee the new department's operations.[17]

Adjutant General Nesbitt on May 14 named Hickman as captain of Headquarters Company in Austin, handing the captaincy of Company B over to Fred McDaniel. Sergeant Sid Kelso, with no funding for him to be made captain, would lead Company A in Houston. Captain McCormick would continue his station in San Augustine as commander of Company C while William W. McMurrey would run Company D from Hebbronville.[18]

"Times Have Changed . . ."

Times have changed and so have law enforcement requirements in Texas," the *Christian Science Monitor* noted. "In recent years cities have become the crime centers, and while rangers were often able to adjust their traditional rough-and-ready methods to new problems, they were in many instances duplicating the efforts of other authorities.

Moreover, on occasion such duplication caused turmoil." Local officials did not always request or appreciate the dispatching of Rangers to their city, the article noted. Using Rangers to referee hot local elections "has at times been construed as political on the part of the directing state administration." The newspaper concluded:

> Looking backward, Texas realizes the need of the most modern co-ordinated law enforcement organization, but yields due credit to the rangers for having helped to make safe for habitation wide expanses of the old Southwest. Like the Northwest Mounties in tradition, the Texas rangers nearly always "got their man" when on the trail of an outlaw.[19]

Texas sheriffs read about the new law enforcement agency with some nervousness, concerned much of their authority would be usurped by the new law enforcement agency. Longtime Ranger supporter J. Marvin Hunter also viewed the new DPS warily. "We hope that under the new arrangement the efficiency of the Ranger force will not be crippled, for there is not an organization anywhere in the world that can compare, in point of loyalty, courage, efficiency, and tact, with the Texas Rangers," he wrote in his *Frontier Times*.[20] Former Ranger Gillett, while not mentioning the upcoming reorganization, told a West Texas newspaper that the Rangers' focus had changed over the years. "In my time," he said, "we didn't go around looking for saloons and gambling halls. We were after big game—rustlers, murderers, cattle thieves and Indians. Of course, it is no reflection on the Rangers themselves. Now, as then, the Rangers do as they are told. It is just a change of the times."[21]

Gathering in Dallas, the Public Safety Commission convened for the first time on Sunday August 11, 1935, the day after the DPS law became effective. Sworn in as members were George W. Cottingham, editor of the Houston *Chronicle*; Ernest R. Goens, former Smith County district attorney; and Johnson, who was elected chairman. The commission then named Hickman as senior captain of the Rangers. At its next meeting later that month, the commission appointed Phares, the fifty-five-year-old chief of the Highway Patrol, the department's acting director effective September 1. With an appropriation of $455,346, Phares began organizing a new law enforcement agency.[22]

Despite concern that the new DPS would usurp the power of county officers, the September issue of the Sheriff's Association magazine congratulated Phares on his appointment. "It is a laudable promotion, well deserved," the magazine said. "Faced with a task not greatly different from that which faced him when he took over direction of the infant Highway Patrol, Mr. Phares has much responsibility. . . . There is much to do, and comparatively little with which to do it. . . . The Association membership wishes him continued success."[23] Elsewhere in the edition an article praised the new agency as the "initial step toward modernization of Texas' war on modern crime. . . . The rangers . . . have been designated the state's 'G-Men,' or detective agency; the highway patrol . . . as the field force." Some Texas newspapers began referring to the state officers as S-men, but the term did not last.

Phares picked one of his Highway Patrol captains, Homer Garrison Jr., a big, affable man from East Texas, to help him run the DPS. Named assistant director on September 15, Garrison had been on the state payroll since 1929, when he started out as an inspector with the license and weight arm of the Highway Department. He joined the new Highway Patrol a year later and rose steadily through the ranks.[24]

The acting director rounded out his top-level job selections by hiring former Ranger "Lone Wolf" Gonzaullas away from the Gregg County District Attorney's Office to head the department's Bureau of Intelligence, which would include a crime lab. Gonzaullas had been working as chief investigator since losing his Ranger job in the Ferguson purge.[25] Rangers and Highway Patrolmen already working for the state automatically became members of the new agency, but on a six-month probationary basis. "Undesirable officers will be weeded out during the probationary period and all replacements will be required to pass a rigid civil service examination," the Sheriff's Association magazine told its readers. "Both new and old officers must go through a special training school, stressing the most modern methods of combating crime [and] promotions will be on merit, alone."[26]

RANGERS OR S-MEN?

Phares moved quickly to professionalize the Rangers, on September 19 issuing DPS General Order Number 1. It required the agency's thirty-six

Rangers to mail weekly written reports to headquarters "each Saturday night" showing their daily activities, contacts, and miles traveled "by air, on horseback, by rail, by bus, in car with others and in your personal car." Phares later amended the order, instructing field Rangers to submit their required reports to their captains.[27]

"When we build a good department, you will all probably consider this the day that it got started," Chairman Johnson said in opening the commission's October 6 meeting. "We plan to be one force, one Department of Public Safety. I do not wish you to get the idea that we are going to do away with the Highway Patrol or the Rangers. . . . The Ranger Force is the finest thing in the world. . . . However, in the last few years they have suffered terribly . . . through politics."[28]

Five days after that meeting, longshoremen went on strike, shutting down Texas's ports. With violence between union members and scabs appearing imminent in Corpus Christi, the city council asked Governor Allred for Rangers. A couple of days later, five Rangers arrived. One was A. Y. Allee, thirty, a pre-Ferguson Ranger who had gone back into the service after Allred's election. Allee and the other Rangers guarded a convoy of provisions needed for strikebreakers and assisted local police in escorting replacement workers to the docks.

The Rangers belonged to a new agency, but they had the same old philosophy in keeping the peace. "The Rangers who came into Corpus Christi to deal with the strike were always profane when addressing any group of strikers," striker Gilbert Mers recalled. "I couldn't say about the force as a whole, that strike marking my only observation of them."[29]

After a strikebreaker got hurt during the first week of November, a car stopped in front of the strike headquarters. Ranger Allee ordered the men standing outside to come around to his side of the vehicle. "I've got a message that I want you to hear and deliver," the Ranger said. "Listen careful. We know who's masterminding this violence. It's that sonofabitch Gilbert Mers. You tell that sonofabitch that we know what he's up to. And you tell him for me: The next act of violence that occurs in . . . Corpus Christi, I'm coming after him, and I'm going to lay him on a cold slab. You tell the sonofabitch that." Mers got the message.[30]

While Rangers on the coast kept an eye on the strikers, the new governor pressed for a crackdown on illegal gambling. Most Rangers saw the enforcement of misdemeanor gambling statutes as the duty of local law enforcement, and Senior Captain Hickman was no different. With direct orders from the governor, the captain reluctantly organized a raid on the Top o' the Hill Terrace, a nightclub in Tarrant County between Fort Worth and Dallas. Hickman knew the place well, later admitting that while off duty he had taken his movie friend Tom Mix there one time. Equally aware that Tarrant County would not prosecute any gambling cases the Rangers made there, in an October 31 meeting with Allred and Phares the captain was not shy in saying so. But orders being orders, Hickman planned a raid on the North Texas club.[31]

In an unmarked state car with phony license plates, Hickman drove from Austin to Fort Worth with three DPS employees—Highway Patrolman E. M. Wells, the patrolman's wife, and Doris Wheeler, widow of the motorcycle patrolman killed by the Barrow gang. Wells, dressed in civilian attire, would accompany the two women to the Top o' the Hill, get inside the well-guarded joint, and engage in gambling with $100 personally donated by the governor. That, Allred and Phares believed, would be sufficient to ice a solid case against the club's owner.

The next day, November 2, Hickman insisted that the three operatives use his car, not the vehicle they had driven to Fort Worth in. That night, the trio tried unsuccessfully to talk their way inside the club. The bouncer at the gate, they later asserted, seemed to have known something was up, paying particular attention to the plates on Hickman's car. Hickman and Captain McDaniel raided the club later that night, but they found no gaming. The captain later said he had "felt like a monkey" inside the club, which had been packed with some of Fort Worth's most prominent citizens, including some friends of the governor's. As soon as the Rangers left, a couple of witnesses later reported, the gambling resumed.

On November 6, the Rangers returned. Summoned from San Augustine, Captain McCormick led the raid this time. During a rainstorm, he and Sid Kelso (recently demoted to private and reassigned from Houston to Austin) snuck up the rocky prominence that gave the Top o' the Hill club its name and climbed through the back windows. Finding gambling under way in an underground room, the Rangers arrested owner Fred Browning along with four employees and seized all the gaming equipment they found. The raid made big headlines, but less than two weeks later a Tarrant County grand jury no-billed the five defendants.

The next day, Phares called Hickman on the carpet over the botched first raid, calling it a "water haul." Meeting in the new art deco Highway Department building across from the Capitol, the Public Safety Commission questioned the three unsuccessful operatives before interviewing the senior captain. After Hickman left the room, as the commission minutes related, "the Commission and Director Phares discussed at some length Captain Hickman's past activities and the Top of the Hill Terrace raid. It was unanimously decided . . . that Captain Hickman was not suited for the place of Senior Captain of the Texas Rangers and that he be advised that the Commission would like to have his resignation by December 1st."[32]

Following the meeting, Hickman met privately with Johnson, who as an old friend urged him to step down as requested. Hearing that, the captain got up and walked to the door. Turning, he told the chairman he was not about to quit.

"I have no intention of resigning," the Associated Press quoted Hickman a few days later. But the "booty, ruddy-faced" Hickman would not further discuss the matter. Neither would Governor Allred or Phares. The DPS acting director did say he had taken the action with the "advice and consent of the commission," pointing out that all department employees had been on six months' probation. Discussing the situation in a three-way long-distance telephone call on November 12, the commission members agreed to fire Hickman since he had refused to step down voluntarily. His replacement as senior captain would be two-gun Captain McCormick, who would be transferred from East Texas to Austin. Hoping for intervention from his friends in the legislature, the nearly fifty-year-old Hickman left on a deer-hunting trip.[33]

Phares, meanwhile, intended to adhere to the governor's wishes and keep the pressure up on gamblers. But true to the "Courtesy, Service and Protection" slogan he had originated for the Highway Patrol, he wanted the Rangers to go about it in a more civilized way. Rather than visualizing Rangers crashing into a gambling operation wearing their traditional cowboy hats and six-shooters, Phares saw them as plainclothes S-men, their pistols in concealed shoulder holsters. It could be, the director continued, the DPS would use women carrying a handgun-in-handbag to penetrate gambling establishments. He even flirted with the idea of having Rangers don dresses, hose, wigs, and makeup to gain entry to clubs.

The Associated Press picked up on the Ranger versus S-men di-
chotomy in a story published in most of the state's newspapers on
December 31, 1935: "Texas rangers, some booted and spurred on horses,
with well oiled six guns in their holsters and aided by comrades in
speedy automobiles, are again in pursuit of cattle rustlers in the vast
ranch country while other colleagues have donned 'boiled shirts' in the
state's war on gambling in and near the larger cities."

The story said that while Captain McMurrey and his men hunted
cattle thieves in West Texas other Rangers "had resorted to dress suits
to gain entrance in suspected gambling establishments at Houston during the busy holiday season and have adopted a sit-it-out plan to stop
gambling." Rather than burst in as in days of old, Rangers would "simply sit and observe the proceedings, ready to seize any gambling paraphernalia which may appear." Though the journalist who filed the report
did not quote McCormick directly, the article noted that the new senior
captain said he did not think dressing Rangers as women would be necessary. Behind the scenes, however, McCormick did not like the notion
one bit. Nor did he and his men take to the media's use of "S-men" to
describe Rangers.[34]

On New Year's Eve weekend, a tuxedo-clad Phares commanded a
squad of penguin-suited Rangers, plainclothes Highway Patrolmen,
and freshly hired female pistol packers who fanned out over Houston
hoping to make gambling cases at places like The Grove, The Rendezvous, and The Top Hat. With word of the effort having spread, the
S-men (and S-women) found no gambling. However, their presence at
least prevented any gambling on the nights they "sat it out" at the
nightclubs.[35]

"The gaming houses are proving a prime source of crime in Texas,"
Phares said in a speech to the Austin Technical Club on January 10.
"Any argument that they are patronized only by persons financially
able to bear the losses incident to gaming can't stand the test of true
experience." A reporter covering Phares's speech for the Austin
Statesman described the acting director's demeanor that night as
"fiery." Allred had ordered the gambling crackdown, but Phares clearly
believed that attacking vice would make Texas a safer place to live and
work.[36]

Publicly, even Captain McCormick towed the company line. "With the help of local officers and others who want to see the laws enforced," the Ranger commander told the Austin newspaper, "we believe we have the big gamblers on the run in Texas."[37]

Looking through the not always translucent windowpane to the past, historian Walter Webb had a traditional view of the Rangers. He followed these developments with keen interest. His book *The Texas Rangers: A Century of Frontier Defense* had reached the nation's bookstores. "This book is a Texas history," the New York *Herald-Tribune* opined. Admitting he had "profoundly enjoyed" the book, reviewer Lewis Gannet did note that Webb's "passionate border patriotism . . . sometimes seems to blur the perspectives." Texan Stanley Walker picked up on that in his review in the New York *Times*: He said he found the published result of Webb's long research on the Rangers "thoroughly satisfying" if "a bit on the patriotic side."[38]

"At last the Texas Rangers have got what was coming to them," editor Hunter wrote in his *Frontier Times* after reading Webb's book "kiver to kiver." The "lavishly illustrated" book, Hunter continued, "contains 584 pages of the best written history of the greatest body of fighting men ever assembled in America, and Professor Webb gives the record of these intrepid guardians of the peace in a most thrilling and entertaining manner."[39]

Some traditionally minded Texans, including Hunter and Webb, continued to worry that the new DPS would mean the end of the Rangers. Phares's public comments, coupled with his demonstrated use of Highway Patrolmen for criminal law enforcement, added to their unease. "It is safe to say that as time goes on," Webb had added at the end of his book, "the functions of the un-uniformed Texas Rangers will gradually slip away."[40]

Indeed, though he had once been a Ranger, Phares showed he held little allegiance to the Rangers as they had operated before the merger. Still, Chairman Johnson thought he had done a good job and deserved to be named director of the DPS. When the Public Safety Commission met on April 7, 1936, and moved to remove the word *acting* from Phares's job title, Commissioner D. D. Baker of Seguin voted no.

The Sheriff's Association of Texas had been circulating a petition to the commission urging the appointment of one of their own, Bee County sheriff J. B. Arnold, to head the new agency. While the petition had not been received, the president of the association had wired the commission that it was on its way and asked that no action be taken on naming a director until the document arrived. Though not acquainted with Arnold, the newly appointed Baker (he had replaced Commissioner Goens, who had resigned in October) knew the DPS had to have the cooperation of Texas's 254 sheriffs to succeed. Baker urged that the commission wait until August to appoint a new director, leaving Phares in his acting capacity. When his fellow commissioners went ahead and finalized Phares's appointment, Baker resigned in irritation. McCormick, no fan of Phares's, also threatened to quit.[41]

The Sheriff's Association, which met in San Antonio starting April 9 for its annual convention, continued to fuss about Phares's appointment. Particularly vocal was Bexar County sheriff Albert West, who argued that Phares had not gone out of his way to cooperate with the state's sheriffs. Commission chairman Johnson countered that West had been the only Texas sheriff to protest Phares's promotion.

"On the other hand," Johnson said, "there are 95 sheriffs who send the safety department fingerprints of criminals daily and 147 other sheriffs constantly were telephoning the department for assistance and cooperation in its work." To West's charges that the Rangers had been paying undue attention to gambling enforcement in San Antonio, the chairman countered that "conditions in San Antonio are worse than in any other large city in the state."

Johnson went on to say that Phares was "a splendid officer and is doing good work." McCormick, meanwhile, had cooled off and decided to stay with the department.[42]

Only one month later, at its next meeting on May 9, the commission reversed itself. It accepted Phares's requested resignation as director and returned him to his old job as commander of the Highway Patrol. But the public safety panel did not give the director's job to Sheriff Arnold or any of his colleagues in county law enforcement. The new head of the DPS would be world war veteran Horace H. Carmichael, who as a National Guard major had worked with the Rangers during the Borger cleanup in the late 1920s. Now a lieutenant colonel in the Guard, the forty-eight-year-old Carmichael had served as assistant adjutant general under Governors Moody and Sterling. After Allred's inauguration, he had reappointed Carmichael to that number two post.

Carmichael quickly sought to reassure Texans that the DPS did not intend to put the Rangers to pasture. "Anyone who thinks the Rangers are on their way out is mistaken," he said. "They are entering a new era."[43]

The new director soon called the field Ranger captains to Austin and ordered them to cooperate with local officers in enforcing the state's gambling laws, still an obsession of Governor Allred's. The big difference was that Rangers would be expected to work in concert with sheriffs if at all possible. "I told the captains that I wanted the anti-gambling laws enforced, but I wanted them first to co-operate with local officers . . . if possible," Carmichael told the Sheriff's Association. "I further told them that if they didn't have enough men we would get some more. . . . No particular spots have been singled out, but the law should be enforced over all the state. We hope to get the co-operation of local officers, but if we don't, we are prepared to act alone."[44]

Meanwhile, old-timers like Hunter continued to fret about the Rangers. "Last year the Texas Legislature practically closed the career of the Texas Rangers," he wrote in *Frontier Times*. "While the law creating the Department of Public Safety does not actually abolish the name of the force, it reduces the number of companies."[45]

The DPS was only ten months old, but Texas was getting ready to celebrate a century of independence from Mexico. With long-leaf yellow pine logs trucked in from Gladewater, a $25,000 rustic two-story cabin that would house historic relics pertaining to the Texas Rangers went up at the State Fair grounds in Dallas, site of the Texas Centennial Exposition. With the Highway Patrol and the Rangers temporarily working out of an abandoned fire station, the log cabin also would become the new headquarters for Company B. When the celebration began on June 6, 1936, twenty-five horseback Rangers rode in the opening day parade through the skyscraper-made canyons of downtown out to the fairgrounds.[46] Throughout the exposition—which brought visitors from across the nation—Rangers escorted dignitaries and celebrities (including President Franklin D. Roosevelt), posed for photographs, and assisted in security. Numerous members of the former Ranger association also came to the exposition and used the log cabin as their gathering place.

Hoping to capitalize on all the Texas centennial publicity, a publishing house in New York brought out the first issue of a new pulp Western magazine, *Texas Rangers*. With an action-filled color cover of a white-hatted Ranger holding a blazing six-shooter, each issue of the ninety-eight-page monthly contained a novelette featuring Ranger Jim Hatfield and his horse, Goldy, as well as four formulaic short stories with a Ranger as the protagonist. Almost immediately successful, the magazine further popularized the Rangers.[47]

Four days after the start of the centennial exposition, the fifty-eighth annual convention of the Sheriff's Association of Texas got under way in the Grand Ball Room of Waco's Roosevelt Hotel. Representing Colonel Carmichael, who had gone to West Point to see his son graduated from the Military Academy, assistant director Garrison assured the county lawmen that the DPS would "run no competition to sheriffs, but is rather to aid them through its rangers, highway patrol, department of identification and records, and its department of criminal intelligence."[48]

The Public Safety Commission, however, continued to have trouble getting the right people in the right jobs at the new agency. On June 23, the commission relieved McCormick of duty as senior captain and relocated him to Wichita Falls to head the Ranger company based there. Five days later, back from New York, Carmichael announced he had assumed the duties of senior Ranger captain in addition to his responsibilities as director. "The transfer was at the request of Captain McCormick," Carmichael said of the latest shakeup. He continued:

> The Rangers and the Department of Public Safety are functioning harmoniously. We are re-districting the state for Ranger assignments and for reasons of efficiency have placed Company E at Wichita Falls. Of course, Rangers will be sent anywhere needed, regardless of their headquarters.[49]

Despite all the politics attendant to the birth of the new DPS, the Ranger mystique fared just fine. That August Dallas hosted the world premiere of the King Vidor movie *The Texas Rangers*, ostensibly based on Webb's new book. In truth, the author had, in consideration of $7,800, signed a movie option renouncing "everything except the fact that [I] had written the book." Webb did not even get an invitation to the first showing. When director Vidor arrived in Big D for the film's premier, his first official stop was the Ranger cabin at the State Fair grounds, where 8,000 people watched as he unveiled a bronze statue of a Texas Ranger—his gift to the people of Texas.[50] Merely another Hollywood oater, the movie did net a lot of attention for Texas and the Rangers. The Dallas *Morning News* published an editorial applauding the fact that the Rangers had been given "a high place of honor at the Texas Centennial." While laudatory of the Rangers' past, the editorial reserved judgment on the force's future. "Like the State, the Rangers face their second hundred years. Their record will be what they make it. A good start will be to follow the admonition of [the] chairman of the Public Safety Commission, which is 'no politics.' "[51]

FBI director J. Edgar Hoover came to Dallas in October to visit the Centennial Exposition. The top G-man posed for a photograph being fingerprinted at the Ranger cabin.[52] While the DPS took Hoover's photograph, for a modest fee one of the corporate exhibitors set up at the fair snapped official-looking photographs of boys and girls interested in obtaining Junior Texas Rangers credentials.

Not all the publicity received by Texas and its Rangers during the Centennial year was favorable, particularly the news coverage of a situation that developed in South Texas. Fifty-seven-year-old Luther Blanton and his twenty-four-year-old son, John, lived with their families in a small cottage just outside the famous King Ranch. On November 18, after working on their beet crop, father and son put away their hoes and Luther got his shotgun and a pocketful of shells, hoping to bag a few ducks on the lagoon about five hundred yards from their farm. Few things were more traditional in Texas than a man going hunting to put meat on his family's table, but the lagoon lay on the sprawling South Texas ranch run by the heirs of Richard C. King. Though fence climbing was only a misdemeanor, the King Ranch took it seriously, especially if it involved hunting. No one ever saw the two farmers again. The Rangers, welcome guests on the King Ranch since Captain McNelly's time, never found the missing men or established what had become of them.[53]

Despite their lack of success on the Blanton disappearance, the Rangers broke several other major cases thanks to the department's new crime lab at Camp Mabry. Rangers helped Haskell County sheriff Giles Kemp solve the murder of a seventy-eight-year-old woman found beaten to death in her residence. Two men were convicted, one of them receiving the first death sentence ever assessed in that West Texas county. In another case, evidence submitted by Rangers to the crime lab proved an apparent suicide in Eastland County to be a murder, the killer having dug up the body of his victim and suspended it from a tree to make it look like the man had hanged himself.

The department cited both of these cases in its first annual report, a document clearly written to put the best light on the agency's first year. Gonzaullas's nascent Bureau of Intelligence and Scientific Crime Detection Laboratory had completed 140 of 142 cases by August 31, more than a third homicides. Though the report named the victims in the highlighted cases, none of the Rangers or crime laboratory personnel involved were singled out. The commission wanted the Rangers seen not as men with towering reputations but as part of the DPS.

"In presenting this plain account of the work of the Department of Public Safety, the members of the Commission do so with a keen appreciation of the cooperation shown the Department by local law enforcement agencies," the report said. "The record is not alone that of the Department, but that of every sheriff, constable, chief of police, justice of the peace, county and district attorney in the State. Without the cooperation of these local officers, the Department is useless to the state."

But the fledgling agency did not want to go without at least some recognition: "And it might be said that many times the work of these officers would prove unavailing were not the Department able to assist them."[54]

Colonel Carmichael and Gonzaullas left Austin in January 1937 on a two-month tour of police crime laboratories in the Northeast and Canada to familiarize themselves on the state of the art in forensics.[55] Gonzaullas, who as a federal Prohibition agent had received training in fingerprinting, also sent scores of letters to corporations and assorted researchers seeking data and journal articles to expand the scientific resources of the new department.[56]

As Gonzaullas and the DPS director continued their efforts to modernize the Rangers, writers of Western fiction kept as busy in perpetuating the Ranger legend, particularly the one Ranger, one riot myth. In the foreword of his second novel, *It's Hell to Be a Ranger*, Caddo Cameron had Captain Henry Clay Houston reading a telegram from the manager of a large ranch. "Old Satan is runnin' wild on this here range, and the Good Lord has done took to the tall timber. Send a army," the message read. "So he sent Badger Coe and Blizzard Wilson," Cameron wrote. By Cameron's arithmetic, if one Ranger could handle one riot, two Rangers ought to equal one army. Three hundred and five pages later, Badger and Blizzard had done the work of an army, but it had not been easy. "It's hell to be a Ranger!" Blizzard muttered as he rode off into the sunset at the end of the novel.[57]

Texas could be tough on its sheriffs, too. On March 10, 1937, someone shot and killed Marion County sheriff J. A. Brown in Jefferson, an old riverboat town in deep East Texas. Houston-based Captain H. B. Purvis and two of his Rangers, Leo Bishop and Bob Goss, spearheaded the investigation. Six days later, after questioning dozens of people, the Rangers had a suspect in custody. The next day, March 17, Charlie Brooks—a man the sheriff had arrested earlier that month for allegedly stealing $1.40 from a woman in a bar—confessed to the murder and told the Rangers where he had tossed the 12-gauge shotgun used in the killing. The Rangers' quick work in the case went a long way toward easing any lingering hard feelings the state's county lawmen had about the creation of a new state police agency.[58]

The day after the Rangers wrapped up the investigation of Sheriff Brown's murder, a shop teacher at the New London School in Rusk County flipped the switch on a sanding machine, igniting an undetected natural gas leak. The March 18 explosion destroyed the three-story brick school, burying 298 students and teachers in the debris. As Ranger Goss reported, "Under orders of Capt. Purvis and Col. . . . Carmichael assisted Rusk Co. Sheriff's department in the enforcement of law and order at the London school disaster until martial law was declared. Miles traveled in personal car. 42." After two days in New London, Goss and Purvis returned to Jefferson to transport a prisoner to the city jail in Kilgore. When he typed out his weekly report on March 21, Goss showed 617 miles traveled.[59]

The public continued to be fascinated with Texas's modernization of an Old West institution. Western writer Westmoreland Gray—author of pulp stories such as "G-man Jones"—interviewed Colonel Carmichael and got him to agree to let his name appear as the writer of an article for

Best Western Action Stories called "We Rangers: Lawmen of the Frontier, 1937 model." Carmichael said the Rangers of 1937 featured the best elements of the old and new. "In the past," he wrote, "no one looked closely into rough justice. Today the Ranger must not only get his man, but he must bring him in."[60]

That fall on the other side of the state, two hundred El Paso area residents gathered on November 14, 1937, in Ysleta for the unveiling of a twelve-hundred-pound gray granite state historical marker honoring Captain Frank Jones, killed by Mexican outlaws along the Rio Grande forty-four years before. On hand was one of the Rangers who took part in the gunfight that claimed his young captain's life, Ed Bryant. Also there was the man promoted as Jones's replacement, a still-spry John R. Hughes. Before pulling a Texas flag from the marker, County Judge S. J. Isaacs, a member of the El Paso County Centennial Committee, sought to put the Ranger force into perspective. "Had it not been for the Rangers," the judge said, "Texas might have been what some choose to call it—a lawless state. It took men like this man we're here today to honor to make the state safe for law-abiding citizens."[61]

The press did not record what the old Rangers gathered at Ysleta thought of the removal of the Ranger force from the Adjutant General's Department, but the DPS had made considerable progress in a short time. Still, Colonel Carmichael and the commission believed the department could be improved with yet another management change. On April 1, 1938, the commission relieved Phares as Highway Patrol chief, a function that would be taken over at least temporarily by Assistant Director Garrison. In a twenty-two-page written statement distributed to the press, Phares argued that his firing was political. Despite that effort, he did not get his job back.[62]

HOMER GARRISON

The next major change in DPS leadership did not come as the result of a personnel action. On September 24, 1938, the fifty-one-year-old Carmichael died of a heart attack behind the wheel of his car in South Austin, the vehicle crashing into a service station. Three days later, the commission promoted thirty-seven-year-old Garrison as Carmichael's successor, the third director in as many years.

"I always knew Homer would someday assume great responsibilities," his mother told the hometown Lufkin *Daily News* after learning of her son's appointment. "He was always so dependable as a boy, always so steady and helpful to me." The Lufkin newspaper went on to characterize the new colonel as likable, smart, honest, and hardworking.[63]

Although having a three-member commission as a buffer between the governor and the DPS kept the Rangers more insulated from politics than they had been as a component of the Adjutant General's Department, changes in administration still had an impact. When Governor Allred opted not to seek a third term, thirteen men filed as candidates in the Democratic primary. Only four had sufficient qualifications to lead the nation's fifth most populated state, but none of them got elected. The man who did get the job, W. Lee O'Daniel, had made his name as a radio flour salesman.[64]

Voters in the November 8 general election also repealed a portion of the 1876 constitution requiring state officeholders to swear they had never fought a duel—at least not with a deadly weapon. "Pappy" O'Daniel was no duelist, but on July 12, 1939, he shot the Rangers' budget full of holes. Two captains, one private, and five investigators lost their jobs. O'Daniel even cut from the DPS appropriation $760 earmarked for Ranger ammunition. Overall, the DPS lost funding for 20 percent of its personnel—amounting to 133 positions—as of September 1, the beginning of the state's new fiscal year. Garrison would hold on to some jobs through transfers or reductions in rank, but as the commission said in a written statement released to employees and the press, "the choice of the personnel to be dropped will be a difficult one."[65]

With the slash of a pen, a governor could lessen the amount of money a state agency had to spend, but that did not affect the Rangers' workload. In fiscal 1938–1939 the Rangers investigated 187 homicides and 370 cattle-rustling cases. In addition, they worked more than five hundred burglary and theft cases and confiscated $95,000 in gambling paraphernalia.[66]

Despite the drastic budget cut, the Public Safety Commission said in its statement that "active law enforcement and criminal investigation" would "go on in its entirety, and we have found a willingness on the part of chiefs and employees to knuckle under and do everything possible. There are no hours among our field men. They will work day and night . . . and the criminal element . . . need not take encouragement from the reduction in our forces."[67]

At decade's end, though in the midst of a budget crisis, the new DPS and the Rangers had begun to stabilize under an energetic, politically astute director who would be around for a long time.

8

"The Name of the Texas Rangers Has Been Carried to the Battlefields of the World"

THE 1940S

When Ranger quartermaster R. W. Aldrich got his mail that fall morning in 1939, it contained a postcard sent from Pecos on October 14: "I am headed for Austin. . . . Will leave here when I eat all the good things the good women of Pecos are feeding me. Capt. John R. Hughes. The old Ranger."

Though he had some family in Austin, Hughes spent most of his time in El Paso, his longtime duty station. The gray-bearded former captain enjoyed celebrity status in his adopted hometown, serving as parade marshal during the annual Sun Bowl Festival, and, as his postcard indicated, never had trouble making a meal off folks who liked to hear his stories of the old horseback Ranger days. Gone from the Rangers for nearly a quarter of a century, he stayed in touch with his younger successors. Aldrich had joined the Rangers in 1915, the year Hughes left.[1]

Visiting the capital city at least once a year, Hughes always drove his shiny Ford to Ranger headquarters at Camp Mabry. Wearing his dress black Stetson, on December 13, 1940, he showed up to receive from Colonel Garrison one of five certificates for valor awarded nationally that year to peace officers in recognition of a lifetime of service.[2]

During another visit the following September, after Aldrich and

Hughes caught up on how their lives had been going since the last time they had talked, Aldrich filled Hughes in on assorted cases the Rangers had been handling. Saying he had something he wanted to show him, Aldrich took Hughes to a nearby small white frame building recently constructed in front of the Ranger horse stables. Painted in black above the door of the twelve-by-twelve foot structure were the words "KTXA Texas State Police."

Cobbled together with loaned or donated equipment, the DPS's first radio facility had recently begun broadcasting. Ever alert to publicity opportunities, Aldrich arranged for a DPS crime lab photographer to get some shots of Hughes sitting at the microphone in the shiplap radio shack. For the first time in the force's history, the Rangers had the ability to transmit law enforcement information via radio. But Rangers in the field could not yet talk to headquarters or communicate with each other. The department having no funding for two-way radios, the Rangers had to make do with receiver sets only in their cars. With 500 watts of power on a frequency of 1,658 kilohertz, the base station's signal barely covered Travis County, but the radio amounted to a vast improvement over Hughes's day.[3]

During this Camp Mabry visit, Hughes obligingly posed next to a Highway Patrol motorcycle, another innovation since his days of state service. He also climbed up on a horse, something he could still do with ease. The photograph of the former captain admiring the state-of-the-art DPS equipment appeared in newspapers across the state.

Most Texas editors did not mind running a canned photograph of an old Ranger, but the worsening political turmoil in Europe grabbed most of the headlines. Two years earlier, after reading newspaper reports of Germany's September 1, 1939, invasion of Poland, Frank Hamer had fired off a letter to the king of England offering the services of forty-nine former Rangers to deal with the Nazis. Four days later, Hamer received a telegram from Buckingham Palace advising him to check with the British Embassy in Washington. When the federal government got wind of Hamer's offer, President Franklin Roosevelt wrote the Texas governor to remind him of the United States' position of neutrality. Hamer's Nazi-fighting idea went no further.[4]

As war spread in Europe, Colonel Garrison had made some administrative changes affecting the Rangers. On January 5, 1940, he issued a general order placing all Rangers under his direct supervision, effectively doing away with the senior captain function. Five weeks later, following a lengthy meeting of the Public Safety Commission, Garrison announced several additional organizational and personnel changes. "Lone Wolf" Gonzaullas, at his request, would transfer back to the Rangers as captain of Company B in Dallas, effective February 26. Ranger captain Royal Phillips, who had been stationed at Dallas, would take over management of the Bureau of Intelligence that Gonzaullas had put together. The Crime Detection Laboratory, previously a part of the Bureau of Intelligence, would be placed under the Bureau of Identification and Records.[5]

Three hundred and twenty miles south of the DPS headquarters, a young Brownsville newspaperman with an interest in folklore and music completed *George Washington Gomez*, a manuscript he had been working on for four years. Americo Paredes set his novel in the Rio Grande Valley during the Mexican Revolution. Though presented as fiction, the novel had an authentic feel. Paredes's father had ridden for a time with Catarino Garza in the early 1890s. The author, as a youngster, had listened on summer nights as his father and other old men smoked cornhusk cigarettes and talked "in low, gentle voices about violent things." The first paragraph of the novel clearly showed how many Mexican-Americans viewed the Rangers, *los rinches*, even a quarter century after the last bandit raid in South Texas:

> Along the edge of the chaparral wound the road, and down the road four Texas Rangers were riding. . . . One was a middle-aged man with a John Brown beard; two were sour-looking hardcases in their thirties; the fourth was a boy in his teens, with more dust than a beard upon his face. At first sight one might have taken them for cutthroats. And one might have not been wrong.[6]

A book starting like that had a hard time finding a publisher in 1940. Paredes never offered a reason in print, but his manuscript would lie dormant for decades as the sentiments it reflected smoldered among Mexican-Americans in South Texas like one of his father's discarded cigarettes.

Those Mexican-Americans could vote, provided they could afford to pay the poll tax, but in 1940 politics in Texas remained all white and all Democrat. On July 23, 1940, Governor O'Daniel won the Democratic nomination for a second term.[7]

During his campaign, at practically every stump speech, O'Daniel had bashed the DPS, complaining that as governor he had no real control over the law enforcement agency or its Rangers. Often he would ask for a show of hands from anyone in the audience who had ever heard of the Public Safety Commission, the panel vested with authority to oversee the law enforcement agency. Most of the time, no one raised a hand. Later that summer, the governor asked state attorney general Gerald Mann for an opinion on the constitutionality of the act giving the Public Safety Commission and the DPS—but not the governor—authority over the Rangers. As one newspaper summed up Mann's September 6, 1940, written opinion, "O'Daniel Can't Boss Rangers, Mann Rules / Governor Must Use Moral Suasion to Enforce Laws." Not two weeks later, the attorney general reversed himself, apologizing that in his opinion he had overlooked a section of the 1935 law creating the DPS that held the governor did, in the event of "a public disaster, riot or insurrection, or the formation of a dangerous resistance to the enforcement of the law . . . have the authority to assume command of and direct the activities and functions of the [Public Safety Commission] and of the [DPS] during the existence of such an emergency or necessity."[8]

Garrison had a good political instinct, which basically amounted to trying to get along with anyone in public office while keeping his agency as apolitical as possible. He realized the only way to cope with O'Daniel was essentially to grin and bear it. But as a new legislative session approached, the Texas press suddenly had a lot of positive things to say about the Rangers.

"Old Glory Still Clings to the Texas Ranger," read one newspaper headline. The story beneath went on to define the 1941 Ranger:

He's a strange combination of the old and the new . . . with the glory of the old still clinging to him and shining out with the glory of modern achievement in his line of work. He has of necessity, clung to the traditions and methods of a vanishing age, yet at the same time, he is a modern-day scientific criminal investigator, fully schooled in the utilization of ballistics, chemistry, finger-printing, and all the other scientific devices through which up-to-date law enforcement agencies bring criminals to justice.

The article also pointed out that Ranger investigations had decreased "because of reductions in . . . personnel and travel."[9]

A couple of months later, the Austin *American-Statesman* ran what amounted to an editorial under Garrison's byline tracing the evolution of the Rangers from frontier fighters to criminal investigators. Someone on Garrison's staff more likely wrote the piece, probably Aldrich. Either way, a public relations effort clearly had begun.[10]

No matter the favorable press coverage generated by the DPS, on May 28, 1941, Governor O'Daniel sent a message to both houses of the legislature asking that the Rangers be moved back to the Adjutant General's Department. But a House bill that would make that recommendation a matter of law never made it out of committee.[11] To Garrison's relief, O'Daniel soon left office to become a U.S. senator.

"Stop Texas Rangers"

That summer, with the status quo of the Rangers assured for at least another two years, rising meat prices brought back to the table an old law enforcement problem: cattle rustling. Like the Rangers, cattle thieves took advantage of new technology. The practice of horseback rustlers' driving off someone else's stock had faded, replaced by growing use of cattle trucks to get stolen beeves to a distant market in a hurry. With a steer bringing $100, Texas cattlemen suffered unusually heavy losses.[12]

Garrison tasked Ranger sergeant Ernest Best, a leather-skinned West Texan with thirty years' experience as a law officer, to take on the problem. Best attacked it three ways: he sent horseback Rangers into the field to check cow camps for stolen stock, staged a series of roadblocks on major highways, and set up a systematic way of checking livestock auction rings and other sales points. To assist its sister agency in operating the roadblocks, the state highway department manufactured portable reflective signs for the DPS that read: "Stop Texas Rangers."

"Livestock being transported in trucks was checked carefully for marks and brands," *The Cattleman* magazine reported. "When a driver was found who did not have the proper papers showing the ownership, description and destination of the livestock, he was advised of the law which requires such papers and informed that strict compliance with this law would be expected in the future."

Shortly after they began manning the roadblocks, Rangers halted a vehicle driven by a Stetson-wearing, pipe-smoking rancher from Kimble County—Coke Stevenson, the new governor. Having more than a casual interest in livestock theft, the governor parked his car on the side of the road and spent a few hours watching the Rangers at work. He left impressed with what he had seen.[13]

Garrison declared the Rangers' antirustling program a success and said it would be expanded across the state. "Of course the biggest handicap is the lack of a comprehensive branding law," he said, "but we are not going to cry about that. I believe the Rangers and the sheriffs of Texas, working together on this problem, can accomplish a great deal toward quelling livestock thefts."[14]

The director liked the way Sergeant Best handled the crackdown on cattle thieves. Effective September 1, 1941, Garrison promoted Best to captain. The DPS's new budget provided six additional positions, increasing the service to forty-five Rangers and five criminal investigators divided into four field companies and a headquarters company. All of the new Rangers had respectable résumés—two had served as county sheriffs, one had been a chief deputy sheriff for thirteen years, one had nine years' experience as a deputy constable and deputy sheriff in Bexar County, one had been an inspector for the Texas and Southwestern Cattle Raisers Association, and one had been a Highway Patrolman since 1937.[15]

The increase in personnel piqued the interest of the Dallas *Morning News*. Capitol correspondent Felix McKnight wrote a four-part series on the DPS, with one installment featuring the Rangers. "The Texas Ranger is still the same," McKnight wrote. "The equipment has just changed."

McKnight alluded to former governor O'Daniel's recent effort to move the Rangers from the DPS back to the Adjutant General's Department. "Periodically," McKnight continued, "politicians around Austin start a feeble movement to have the ranger force abolished. It never gets off home base. To Texans, it is almost a subversive movement."

Like the FBI's J. Edgar Hoover, the forty-one-year-old Garrison had become the face and voice of the agency he had headed for three years. Polite, politic, and personable and with a clear vision of how the DPS and its Rangers should operate, Garrison had many admirers across the state and nation. The Rangers respected him greatly, and though he expected a lot of them, he returned the favor.

"Never shall the tradition of the ranger force be equalized," Garrison told journalist McKnight. "The ranger force will ever go forward— never retreat. . . . The prestige of the ranger force is just as great as it was 100 years ago. In those days a ranger was a feared man. He still is. Just ask the border folks. One or two rangers can still stop a mob by their very presence."[16]

In the field, Garrison's Ranger captains sang from the same sheet of music.

"The Rangers are better trained, better equipped, better paid and better qualified than ever before," Captain Gonzaullas told a Rotary Club in Waxahachie, "and they do a better job by reason of these things."[17]

While Garrison and his Rangers worked not too subtly to spread the word of their value to Texas taxpayers, the fictional Texas Rangers stood as tall as ever in American popular culture. With war sweeping across Europe, the men in big white hats reassured a nervous nation that Adolf Hitler and his panzer divisions could be stopped. "By power of brain and brawn," Western novelist Tex Holt said in the final paragraph of his *Texas Terror,* "by never-failing courage and the cool steel of a man's heart, Lee Armstrong had saved Texas and between the forces of evil who sought to ruin the great country, his guns interposed, ever ready to uphold the law of the Lone Star State." From Hollywood, Prescott Pictures, Inc., wrote the DPS asking if the words *The Texas Rangers* could be used in a planned motion picture serial. At its October 25, 1941, meeting the Public Safety Commission told Garrison the panel had no objection to Hollywood using the name "if the script was presented to this department for approval."[18]

One of the Rangers who had worked with Captain Best on the cattle-rustling crackdown, W. E. (Dub) Naylor, had started his law enforcement career as one of Garrison's Highway Patrolmen before the creation of the DPS. He and his fellow Rangers soon would be confronting a different set of problems, with Naylor blazing a new trail.

PROTECTING THE HOME FRONT

Though a fair number of Texans had never heard of Pearl Harbor prior to December 7, 1941, the Japanese attack on the U.S. Navy base there forced the nation into war. The Hawaiian Islands lay nearly twenty-four hundred miles from San Francisco, but with its Pacific Fleet severely impaired, the military feared the Japanese might attack the West Coast or land on the less-protected shores of Mexico. A thrust into Mexico likely would lead to Texas.

With that possibility in mind, in January 1942 Adjutant General J. Watt Page commissioned former Ranger Jack Moore of Alpine in far West Texas to raise a mounted battalion of not less than one hundred men up to the age of sixty-five to serve in the Texas Defense Guard, an organization authorized by legislation in 1941 to protect the state in the event the government federalized the National Guard.[19] Moore, who had served in the Rangers for seven months in 1916, told a reporter that his organization would be patterned after the Frontier Battalion of the 1870s. "If the need arises, my battalion will be in service along the Rio Grande," Moore told the Houston *Post*. "I hope to get permission for the men to wear cowboy boots and hats instead of regulation uniforms."[20]

Not even global war could stop Texas bravado or razzing from other states. When newspapers that summer carried a story about the Texas Defense Guard training in guerrilla warfare against the possibility of foreign invasion, the St. Louis *Post-Dispatch* found the news puzzling. "What has become of the Lone Star State's former implicit faith in the ability of the Texas Rangers to take on all comers and whip the world if necessary?" the Missouri newspaper asked in an editorial. The writer then went on to tell the shopworn one riot, one Ranger tale.

"Texas is taking no chances," the Wichita Falls *Times* responded. The piece continued:

The defense plan calls for one ranger to deal with each division of the invader, with the guerrilla organization prepared to go into action when the number of divisions exceeds that of the rangers. The 1,000 guerrillas are to take care of the excess. Texas realizes that if the Japs do come, they'll do so in a big way. There are 30 rangers, or enough to handle 30 divisions. The guerrillas will go into action if the Japanese send more than that number.[21]

The nation also worried about Fifth Columnists. On February 27 in Galveston, Rangers from Houston joined FBI agents, city police, and Galveston County sheriff's deputies in searching seventy-two residences for Germans, Italians, or Japanese. The team rounded up forty-four persons and seized shortwave radio sets, photographic equipment, firearms, and ten pounds of gunpowder. The officers also found an aerial photograph of a Texas carbon black plant, several maps of the Galveston port and other harbors, and a Very gun for shooting flares. After questioning by U.S. District Attorney Douglas W. McGregor and three of his assistants, all but six Italians, four Germans, and one Japanese were released. Those eleven aliens were turned over to immigration authorities.[22]

Early in the war, the federal government also scrambled to set up a civil defense system. That led to a new assignment for Ranger Naylor: He would travel the state showing war preparedness films, the subjects ranging from airplane silhouette identification to how to cope with a gas attack, to local law enforcement agencies, schools, and civic groups. The Rangers had played a role in training other Texas peace officers before, but in reaching out to the citizenry Naylor became the first Ranger to engage in a public information campaign. The Ranger crisscrossed the state in a marked car, preparing Texans for the possibility of foreign attack. In the vehicle's trunk, in addition to standard Ranger equipment, he toted a movie projector and an assortment of metal film cans. "The dream of every Patrolman," the *DPS News* paraphrased Naylor, "is to have a car equipped like his. . . . The nightmare of everyone is to have a job like his."

The Ranger had been in Fort Worth lecturing on gasses, the DPS newsletter continued. "We may all find the use of gas masks and detection of certain gasses to be necessary in home defense and many of us probably will have experience with gas on the FRONT. Naylor is doing fine work. Keep it up, sir."[23]

True to tradition, one Ranger had been tasked with one big job. Realistically, Garrison and Governor Stevenson knew everyone had a stake in getting Texas ready for the uncertainties that lay ahead. The state had a five-step defense plan: Industrial and public works would be protected by private guards, backed by local law enforcement if necessary. If local officers could not handle a situation, the DPS and the Rangers would step in. Should a situation get beyond their abilities, Governor Stevenson, through his adjutant general, would call out the newly created Texas Defense Guard. If the state still needed help, the governor would request U.S. military intervention.[24]

By early spring, the governor believed the situation in Texas was pretty well in hand. "I am convinced from all I have seen that Texas is right at the top in the co-operative war effort and in defense work," he said on March 24. "There is no complacency in this state."[25]

As the Rangers continued their readiness efforts on the home front, George Sessions Perry, a promising young writer from Rockdale, Texas, made his own preparations. He soon would be leaving for Africa to cover the war for *The New Yorker*. But before then, he signed copies of his new book from New York's venerable publishing house of McGraw-Hill, *Texas: A World in Itself*. Early in his book, Perry codified for a national reading audience the prevailing Texas view of the Rangers. In discussing how Texas's three biggest cities had no Chicago-style gangsters, he wrote:

> If an indiscreet soul branches out into the realm of physical violence, as did the Chicago racketeers, it is not well for him to take up a permanent abode in Texas. . . . The city policeman may . . . roll over accommodatingly, and play dead. But half of the country sheriffs will be hungry for the sight of him; so will two-thirds of the highway police, and all of the Texas Rangers. . . . Their pride, their belief in the legend that they are the gutsiest men on earth, has become involved. And with unerring certainty, they'll cut him down.[26]

Texas had seen its Sam Basses and Bonnie and Clydes, Perry continued, but "our outlaw gunmen have all had the same history: they lived on the go and were killed on the wing."[27]

About the time Perry's book came out, eighty-two-year-old H. H. Halsell of Fort Worth, a man who had known Indian-fighting Rangers, privately published a novel called *Ranger*. Though his book did not get the national attention that Perry's work enjoyed, Halsell's effort reinforced a powerful myth. He wrote: "Rangers are selected out of the very highest type of Western cowboys. They know no fear. They are not only gallant and fearless, but they are the most expert horsemen and finest shots . . . ever known in the West."[28]

The Ranger mystique had long since spread beyond the continental boundaries of the United States. The Associated Press reported on August 20, 1942: "Many French officials and some diplomats were excited today by mistaken reports that 'Texas Rangers' had landed in Dieppe with Allied commandoes." In reality, three units of the British Second Canadian Division had been put ashore at the seaport in occupied France, some hundred miles northwest of Paris. A report from London incorrectly had American army rangers participating in the action. But the operation, nothing more than a test probe, involved only British forces. Earlier, the newspapers had leaked news that the U.S. Army planned to organize ranger units patterned after the British commandos, which apparently contributed to the confusion. Even so, faster than a panzer division, the rumor swept through Europe that Texas Rangers neared the Rhineland. Adolf Hitler's propaganda minister, Dr. Joseph Goebbels, had to get on the radio to deny the reports. He assured nervous citizens of the Third Reich that the invasion had been easily repulsed and no Texas Rangers had been involved.[29]

"How do you guys like the publicity you got in the news recently?" the department's employee newsletter, the *DPS News*, asked. "Those people in Vichy thought it was Texas Rangers who made the raid on Dieppe. On second thought, we bet they wish to Hell it had been."[30]

Not to be outdone by the army, the U.S. Marine Corps organized its own special unit, a Texas-raised battalion the Corps intended to name in honor of the Rangers. "The men in that outfit will probably be so tough that they'll be afraid to sleep by themselves," Garrison wrote in his "Colonel's Corner" column in the *DPS News*. "Any man who can take enough to become a full-fledged Marine just has to be a fighting demon. When Marines come from Texas—as one-third of them do—they're fightin' fools both by nature and by training. And when you hang the name 'Texas Rangers' on a bunch of those lads, there just won't be any stopping them."[31]

In Dallas on September 19, Captain Gonzaullas and three of his Rangers watched the induction of more than 150 marine recruits into the newly created Texas Ranger Company. "We are indeed proud . . . to know

that the United States Marine Corps, which we consider one of the greatest fighting organizations in the world, should so honor us by choosing to
designate a unit of their organization as the Texas Ranger Company of the
U.S. Marines," Gonzaullas said at a ceremony the night before.

Ranger Naylor, meanwhile, continued to receive training in areas he
could in turn teach to others. He and several other DPS officers attended a commando school for the Texas Defense Guard at Camp
Bullis, near San Antonio. A lieutenant colonel in the British army
showed Naylor and the others how to make "Molotov cocktails" and
fight a guerrilla war in Texas if necessary.[32]

Before the war, the DPS had about six hundred employees, about
half of them peace officers. By the fall of 1942, the department had 189
men and women on military leave. While most of the drain on DPS
manpower had been from the Highway Patrol, veteran Ranger Pete
Crawford announced plans to resign and join the military. Most of the
Rangers, generally older men, stayed with the state.

The military on both sides of the Atlantic had come to realize the
power of the word *ranger,* and so had Garrison. In a live statewide radio
hookup on October 1, 1942, the DPS director swore in two million
Texas schoolchildren as Junior Texas Rangers. Their job would be to
collect scrap metal for the war effort.[33]

RIDING THE RIVER

While Ranger Naylor continued traveling Texas teaching air-raid war-
dens how to recognize enemy aircraft, the six Rangers of San Angelo–
based Company E saddled up to protect Texas the old-fashioned way.
Captain Best ordered the men of his company to meet him at a ranch
outside San Angelo where the owner graciously kept a string of horses
for Ranger use. The men loaded horses into their black state-issued
trailers and caravanned to Alpine in Brewster County. There they met
Ranger Leo Bishop and bought provisions for a week or more in camp
along the Rio Grande.

Early on November 15, the Rangers left Alpine for a point about
sixty-five miles upriver from Presidio, "the roughest stretch of country
along the Mexican Border and the farthest outpost from civilization."

After establishing a base camp, Best divided his men into teams of two and sent them on scouts up and down the river. Four U.S. Customs officers also participated in the effort. After traveling the river ten or twelve miles, the riders cut back through the rugged mountains to the east and returned to camp.

The Rangers and federal officers found no spies or saboteurs or even any evidence of suspicious river crossings, though Ranger Zeno Smith roped a wandering mule with a Mexican brand on its flank. The horseback scout did result in a couple of shooting incidents. As the *DPS News* later reported tongue-in-check, a deer inadvertently strayed into the field of fire as the Rangers worked in some rifle practice. That accident apparently did not conflict with a memorandum credited to Best that "ammunition must be used for killing Japs. If through mistake a deer is killed, it must be no bigger than a Jap." The second shooting came as the men broke camp. When a Ranger tossed some trash on the fire, he accidentally included an unspent cartridge. The round exploded, sending a bullet zinging past the ear of one of the men.[34]

The San Angelo *Standard-Times* did not know the Company E Rangers had managed to do a little deer hunting on state time but later informed its readers: "Findings of the [river] survey were not divulged by Capt. Best, nor can he reveal other new activities thrown upon his staff by the war."[35]

Enemy aliens for the most part posed only a theoretical problem for the Rangers, but the war greatly increased the service's workload. The *DPS News* described the situation in East Texas:

> We have 500,000 soldiers in the vicinity, a powder plant at Texarkana, a shell loading plant at Texarkana, a steel mill at Daingerfield, a TNT plant at Marshall, and now to climax it, we are going to have an Army Camp at Tyler on the East Side with an Air Force Training School in the West. Ah, but we love our work.[36]

The influx of soldiers and pilots-in-training along with the booming wartime economy sent the Texas crime rate into the wild blue yonder. The petroleum refineries along the coast and every plant involved in war production presented an ongoing security concern for all Texas peace officers, including the Rangers. The state lawmen continued to cope with more traditional problems as well.

"Most of our time is taken up running down cattle thefts," Lubbock-based Captain Manny Gault—Frank Hamer's right-hand man during the pursuit of Bonnie and Clyde—reported from the South Plains, "and we have recovered lots of stolen cattle." In addition to dealing with rustlers, Gault continued, "it seems that people like to rob our banks out here. I don't know whether it is the wide open spaces or whether they think we are easy. But whatever the case is, they cause us lots of worry and in most instances we cause them a little trouble, too."[37]

Cattle theft and bank robbery constituted serious crimes, but in October 1942 Rangers in Central Texas confronted a case involving any parents' worst nightmare—the disappearance of a child. When eight-year-old Lucy Rivers Maynard did not show up after school, her worried mother, wife of the Bastrop County judge, called the sheriff's office. By nightfall, the Rangers and the Highway Patrol had joined the search for the missing girl.

The next morning, the child still unaccounted for, Garrison sent Assistant Director Fred Hickman to take charge of the investigation. That afternoon, a Highway Patrolman found the third-grader, bleeding and unconscious, in a ravine off a dirt road north of Bastrop. Scattered nearby lay her books and the satchel she had been carrying home from school when someone attacked her, apparently bent on sexual assault.

As doctors fought to save Lucy's life, troopers sealed off the scene so Rangers and DPS crime lab personnel could comb it for evidence. The search revealed a set of tire tracks obviously made by a heavy vehicle with deep treads. When Rangers located two witnesses who had seen a military vehicle in the area the day before, the focus of the investigation shifted to Camp Swift, a huge army installation east of Bastrop.

Working with military authorities, Rangers learned the tracks at the crime scene matched a military carryall. Though the post's motor pool had hundreds of vehicles, the fleet included only three of the carryalls in question. The military soon found that one of the trucks had been checked out to Private George S. Knapp at the time of the girl's disappearance. When military police discovered bloody clothing in the soldier's footlocker, they started looking for Knapp.

But Knapp, they soon learned, had gone AWOL. When someone reported a car stolen off the post, the DPS issued a statewide bulletin for officers to be on the lookout for Knapp and the car the agency believed he had stolen. Late that night, an Austin police officer stopped the car and arrested the soldier.

Rangers and MPs transferred Knapp to the Camp Swift stockade, where at 1:00 a.m. a military investigator began questioning him. Three hours later, the investigator gave up, asking Assistant Director Hickman to take over. Hickman, a Ranger and a trooper, then went in the room with Knapp. A short time later, Hickman emerged to say that the officers needed a stenographer to take down the soldier's confession.

Based on evidence developed by the Rangers and the DPS's forensic experts, coupled with the soldier's confession, the military tried Knapp for murder. The following March, the army hanged him.[38]

A year after Pearl Harbor, Garrison tried to put things into perspective in his "Colonel's Corner" column in the departmental newsletter:

With few exceptions, we of the Department of Public Safety have not only changed our way of living but our way of working. While we have continued to lose men at a rate four times greater than the rate of replacement, one new job after another has been heaped upon our shoulders. Being "snowed under" has become an everyday situation.

The next year would not be any easier, Garrison continued. "All of us will sacrifice more and yet more," he wrote. "The military forces, the Federal Government, and other agencies will find more things for us to do. Only God and perhaps Mr. [Paul V.] McNutt [chairman of the War Manpower Commission] knows where we're going to get the manpower to do these jobs with. But as long as there's one man left, our banner will keep flying."[39]

"Lone Wolf" Gonzaullas was one of those men still on the job. No stay-behind-the-desk supervisor, in the winter of 1943 he joined his men in an intense manhunt for a four-time prison escapee named Robert Lacy. Doing a life sentence for the 1937 murder of a traveling salesman in Dallas, Lacy had escaped from the Retrieve prison unit with fellow inmate Cleo Anderson on January 21. Five days later, having learned from an informant that the wanted men were headed for Gladewater, the captain set a trap for them. Joined by Upshur County sheriff Gordon

Anderson, Gregg County sheriff Lonnie Smith, three deputies, a constable, and an investigator from the Gregg County District Attorney's Office, Gonzaullas and Rangers R. L. Badgett and Dick Oldham waited for the men to show up. At 8:45 p.m. the officers spotted the car the pair had stolen when they escaped. Blocking the vehicle with their cars, the officers yelled for the men to surrender. Instead, the convicts opted to shoot it out and began firing at the lawmen.

The officers opened up on the car with rifles and pistols, killing Lacy immediately. When Andrews slumped down in the vehicle, they thought he was dead as well. Approaching the bullet-riddled vehicle's front passenger door with his pistol in his left hand, the captain used his right hand to open it. At his side stood Sheriff Anderson.

"Look out, Cap. I think he's playing possum," Anderson yelled.

The Ranger instinctively ducked just as Andrews fired point-blank at him, the bullet ripping through Gonzaullas's tweed suit coat and grazing his shoulder. At the same instant, still holding his revolver in his left hand, Gonzaullas emptied it into the gunman. Five bullets slammed into the convict, leaving the captain covered with blood and brain matter.[40]

As Gonzaullus had been the latest to demonstrate, a Ranger could be deadly serious when necessary. But the Ranger culture also valued hardy senses of humor, especially when it came to intramural prank playing.

The ringing of his telephone awakened Victoria-based Ranger M. W. (Willie) Williamson at 2:00 a.m. one day in the spring of 1943. The Ranger quickly recognized the voice of the early-morning caller as that of a crook he had handled before: Ollie York. Sent to prison for life, York had escaped. Ranger Williamson and his colleagues had been turning over every rock in Texas to find him.

But York had called the Ranger to taunt him, not to surrender. Thinking fast, Williamson tried to drag the conversation out while his wife went next door to another telephone to get the operator to put a trace on the call. As the Ranger continued to stall for time by engaging the convict in small talk, York said, "Well . . . looks like the cops coming, guess I'd better get out of here."

Deducing that York must be calling from the town's only all-night gas station, the Ranger pulled on his clothes, strapped on his pistol, and rushed to make the arrest. When he screeched to the scene in his state car, the pump jockey greeted him with a smile.

"Dub Naylor and L. H. Purvis said to tell you hello," the service station attendant said.

Unknown to Williamson, the two Rangers had picked up York in Corpus Christi. When they stopped for gas in Victoria on their way to Huntsville, the captured con had obligingly helped them play a joke on Williamson. Someone wrote the incident up in the next edition of the *DPS News*, but whatever Williamson did by way of payback went unreported.[41]

No humor could be found in what happened in Beaumont that summer. On June 15, 1943, when workers at the Pennsylvania Shipyard learned that the wife of one of their coworkers had allegedly been raped by a black man that afternoon, some three thousand blue-collar workers with decidedly red necks left the yard and converged on the police station. After police informed the mob that the woman had not been able to identify her attacker, the workers headed toward the black area of the city to settle the matter themselves. In the riot that followed, the rampaging ship workers torched several buildings and forcibly entered one hundred black homes. Two people—one black and one white—died in the mêlée. The following day, Acting Governor A. M. Aikin, a senator from the North Texas town of Paris, declared martial law for Beaumont. Texas State Guard troops, Rangers, and Highway Patrolmen quickly took control of the city. Military control continued until June 20, with Rangers and other officers making three hundred arrests.[42]

For the first time in several years, Garrison summoned all six Ranger captains to Austin on August 5 for an emergency powwow on the growing incidence of war-bred crime.

"So many officers have gone into armed forces that Texas law enforcement as a whole is very short on manpower," Garrison said after the meeting. "The Rangers already have their hands full assisting local officers. The crime situation is growing steadily worse, and will reach a peak after the war. That is what we are trying to prepare for—we are digging in for a storm of major crime."[43]

Wartime conditions in Texas were stormy enough, with Rangers spending much of their time on manhunts. With a shortage of guards, Texas prisons had 255 escapes during the 1942–1944 biennium. In addition, 142 German prisoners of war succeeded in breaking out of various POW camps across the state. Another 262 U.S. military prisoners, soldiers being held in disciplinary barracks, escaped. A complimentary letter Garrison received from R. C. Suran, Special Agent in Charge of the FBI's San Antonio office, summarized one case: Ranger captain Fred Olson and Rangers Norman Dixon, Dub Naylor, Joe Thompson, and Trueman Stone, along with three Highway Patrolmen and two radio operators, had participated in the capture of two German POWs who escaped from Camp Swift on May 25, 1944. "The cooperation and assistance that they rendered in this matter was invaluable," Suran wrote.[44]

The Rangers contributed to the war effort on the home front, but the Ranger as American icon figured in both theaters of the conflict. After escorting a bombing raid over Nazi-occupied France, Lieutenant Colonel Jack S. Jenkins of Levelland, Texas, posed for a photograph standing next to his P-38 fighter, an aircraft he had named *Texas Ranger*. In England, a B-24 crew named their bomber after the Rangers. Two companies of marines had decided their nickname would be the "Texas Rangers," and the U.S. Army had started calling its commandos "Rangers."

"The name of the Texas Rangers has been carried to the battlefields of the world," the DPS's Biennial Report for 1942–1944 proclaimed.[45]

Texans certainly saw the Rangers as equal to any task. A member of the legislature tried to use them as pawns in the stormy political controversy following the January 1945 firing of University of Texas president Homer Rainey, a man the school's board of regents considered too liberal to be entrusted with the education of Texas college kids. As a slap against anti-Rainey regent D. F. Strickland, an attorney who represented Texas motion picture operators and owners, State Representative Rae Mandette filed a bill that would have put the Rangers in the movie censorship business. Her bill called for the establishment of thirty-one movie censorship boards around the state, each board having at least three women members. The Rangers would be given authority to close any theater that continued to show a censored movie.[46] The measure died in committee.

While the legislature took no action on the suggestion that the Rangers get into the business of arbitrating public taste, the DPS responded quickly to any perceived slight in the press. When *Frontier Times* publisher J. Marvin Hunter observed that the Rangers had practically lost their identity with the creation of the DPS a decade before,

Captain Aldrich shot the Bandera-based magazine a quick letter to set the matter straight.

"I enlisted in the Ranger Force more than 30 years ago, and can truthfully say that there has never been a greater demand for its services than at the present time," Aldrich wrote, "excepting during the bandit trouble on the border in 1915 and 1916. . . . I assure you that there are as many, in fact more, murder cases, robberies, and other major crimes to be handled now as in earlier times, and our present day Rangers are doing the job in the traditional way." In the magazine's July issue, Hunter said his comment had been a "grave error" and published a portion of Aldrich's letter. Even before he had Garrison to back him up, the well-read old Ranger had been a fierce protector of the Ranger image.[47]

With hurricane-force winds battering Texas's middle coast in September 1946, raincoated Ranger Naylor, still the force's unofficial PR man, stood in water halfway to his boot tops to give Texans a "gust-by-gust" account of the hurricane via radio. "His words were received at Corpus Christi, piped by telephone to San Antonio and there received by WOAI," Garrison said in a letter to *Texas Week* magazine, correcting an earlier report in the magazine "that Aransas County was cut off from the outside world . . . during the hurricane."[48]

"The Hair Is Rising on My Neck . . ."

The beginning of a series of murders that would terrify Texarkana and result in an entire company of Rangers being sent to that Northeast Texas city did not get a lot of news media attention. On the night of February 22, 1946, a tall masked man with a pistol slipped up on a young couple parked along a lovers' lane on the edge of town. The gunman knocked the man unconscious with blows from his pistol and then sexually molested the woman. Though the man suffered a skull fracture and the woman was left emotionally traumatized, they at least survived the incident.

A month later, another couple fared much worse. On March 24, a passing motorist drove up on a parked car just south of the location of the first attack. When he saw a man slumped over inside the car, he hurried off to call police. The location being outside the city limits, a Bowie County sheriff's deputy hurried to the scene. He found twenty-nine-year-old Richard Griffin and seventeen-year-old Polly Ann Moore shot to death inside the car.

The next day, Ranger Jim Geer came to Texarkana to assist the sheriff's department in the investigation. Geer and another Ranger arriving a short time later followed more than two hundred leads but got nowhere.

The killer struck again April 14. Officers found seventeen-year-old Paul Martin first, lying in a ditch in Spring Lake Park. When officers determined the victim's identity and learned he had been with a date when last seen, a search party soon combed the park. A few hours later, someone found Betty Jo Booker behind a tree. She had been raped and shot to death.

As soon as he learned of the latest double murder, Captain Gonzaullas headed for Texarkana to take charge of the investigation. He ordered every man in Company B to join him. In addition to the Rangers, four technicians from the DPS crime lab in Austin were sent in, along with a contingent of Highway Patrolmen in four patrol cars newly equipped with two-way radios.

"The people in Texarkana and vicinity [are] all scared to death," Highway Patrol Chief W. J. Elliott said in a memo to Garrison.

As the state officers descended on Texarkana, so did reporters from around the state and nation. "I have arrived in Texarkana, the home of the Phantom Slayer," one reporter hyperventilated in his published report. "I am quartered at the Grim Hotel, and the hair is rising on my neck." The reporter's sensationalism aside, the people of Texarkana lived in terror. Nothing like this had ever happened in their city.

Three weeks later, the killer struck again, this time in Arkansas, about ten miles from Texarkana. On the night of May 3, farmer Virgil Starks got a bullet in the back of the head as he sat in his living room listening to the radio. Someone firing through a window from outside hit Kate Starks twice, then tried to get inside the residence. Though wounded, the terrified woman ran out the front door to a neighbor's house. The killer, officers later found, entered the house through the back door as she fled. For some reason, he had decided not to pursue her.

"Murder Rocks City Again: Farmer Slain, Wife Wounded," the next day's *Texarkana Gazette* screamed in big type. This time, the killer had used a .22. The earlier victims had been shot with a .32, but since that fact had been reported by the media, investigators believed the killer had discarded the gun. Some officers doubted a connection between the Starks case and the other murders attributed to the Phantom, but the homicide stayed on the list.

Several nights after the Starks murder, *Gazette* editor J. Q. Mahaffey talked with Chief Max Tackett at the Texarkana, Arkansas, police station when someone living near the Starks residence called to report seeing a light inside the house. Thinking that for some reason the killer had returned, Tackett and several of his officers rushed to the scene. The chief let Mahaffey tag along.

When the police cars skidded to a stop outside the house, the chief—pistol in hand—hopped out of his vehicle. The officers surrounded the house, Tackett yelling for the people inside to come out.

"*Life* magazine!" a woman's voice yelled. "Lone Wolf Gonzaullas," a man said authoritatively.

When the local officers holstered their pistols, Captain Gonzaullas and an attractive photographer for *Life* cautiously emerged. Gonzaullas explained to the chief that he had been showing the woman the crime scene.

At that, the police chief turned to the young newspaperman and said loud enough for all to hear, "Mahaffey, you can quote me as saying that the Phantom murders will never be solved until Texarkana gets rid of the big-city press and the Texas Rangers!"

By October 1946, with no new cases, Gonzaullas quietly ordered his men to return to their own areas. He further directed them to keep their departure a secret for fear that the killer would strike again if he knew the Rangers had left Texarkana. Gonzaullas had tried everything from using Rangers in parked cars as decoys to questioning known sex offenders. Despite an intense investigation that built a thick case file, the identity of the killer remained his secret.[49]

That November, a twenty-two-year-old photographer for the Houston *Post* found that some Rangers—unlike Captain Gonzaullas—did not like having their picture taken. When the *Post*'s Caroline Valenta snapped a shot of veteran Captain Hardy Purvis walking out of the grand jury room in the Harris County courthouse, two Rangers quickly flanked her as Purvis grabbed her Speed Graffic, pulled out the film, and then politely offered to buy her a cup of coffee. She declined, and the following day the *Post* ran an indignant story about the incident.

Whether the crusty captain, who favored one leg because of a gun-fight earlier in his career, had been truly camera shy or merely annoyed at the *Post* is a matter of conjecture. The *Post* had a habit of chiding Rangers for their occasional gambling arrests, which the newspaper referred to as "poor man's raids." The "big hat boys," the newspaper inferred, picked only on the players, not the operators.[50]

Gambling raised concern in Dallas, as well. During the war, a well-defined portion of the city had run virtually wide open to accommodate the many military men stationed in North Texas. Envisioning postwar Dallas as a growth market for vice, a Chicago gambling syndicate had big plans for Big D. But with district attorney–elect Will Wilson vowing to clean up the city, the out-of-state players realized they needed the deck stacked in their favor to do business in Dallas. A thirty-seven-year-old convicted murderer from the Windy City who hit town in 1940 after his release by pardon from prison in Kansas approached newly elected sheriff Steve Gutherie with a bribe offer on November 1. Gutherie, a thirty-three-year-old former GI, pretended to play along, asking for another meeting and more information. He then contacted Colonel Garrison in Austin as well as the Dallas police to report the bribery attempt. Working with local detectives and a couple of former FBI agents hired as DA investigators by Wilson, the Rangers began what turned out to be a forty-five-day effort to make cases against all the Chicago-connected players. A Company B Ranger hiding under the sheriff-elect's house recorded a subsequent high-stakes offer of a monthly protection fee. On the basis of that recording and other evidence, a team of Dallas officers and Rangers rounded up three men on charges of bribery and conspiracy.[51]

During the war, the DPS and the Rangers prepared for a home-front emergency that never came. But all the planning and training proved valuable on April 16, 1947, when the ammonium nitrate–laden French freighter SS *Grandcamp* exploded at the dock in Texas City in Galveston County. The blast disintegrated the ship and ignited nearby refineries and chemical plants. With a huge cloud of black smoke billowing into the air, a portion of the city looked like it had been hit with an atomic bomb. Hundreds lying dead or injured, the DPS rushed Highway Patrolmen, Rangers, and a portable radio station to assist in the stricken city.

Austin-based rookie Clint Peoples, a former Montgomery County sheriff's deputy, sped to the scene of the explosion a few hours later. The assignment came close to being the Ranger's last. A second fertilizer-laden freighter, the *High Flyer*, exploded at 1:10 a.m. on April 17 as Peoples and others searched for victims in the wreckage of a school. "It felt as though my head was caving in. . . . I was dazed and fell against a wall," the Ranger recalled. When he recovered sufficiently, Peoples made his way outside. Debris continued to fall; a piece of steel from the ship shot by Peoples's head and buried itself twelve feet in the ground only three feet from where he stood.[52] Peoples and the other Rangers on hand assisted the department's forensic experts in identifying victims. Of 405 bodies taken to a morgue the DPS set up at nearby Camp Wallace, a World War II army base, department personnel identified 86 percent. Counting 113 people listed as missing, the final death toll came to 581. Texas City had been the worst disaster in the state since the 1900 Galveston hurricane.[53]

Captain Hughes had stayed spry longer than many men, but by the spring of 1947 the old Ranger's health had failed. "I did not expect to live to the age that I am now," he had told a reporter a few years earlier. Recalling his days along the border, he said, "I expected to be killed." A few years before, Hughes had decided to permanently relocate from El Paso to Austin, where he could stay with relatives. He still talked occasionally with his old friend Aldrich, but now he had more bad days than good days. On June 3, with the same decisiveness that had made him a great captain, Hughes picked up the pearl-handled .45 revolver that had helped to keep him alive during his twenty-eight years as a Ranger and walked out the back door of his relative's house. Ninety-two years old and sick, he calmly put the six-shooter against his head and pulled the trigger. Garrison and many of the Rangers attended the captain's funeral and later stood by as workers lowered his coffin into a grave at the State Cemetery east of the Capitol.[54]

With the beginning of a new fiscal year, the authorized strength of the Ranger service increased to fifty-one effective September 1, 1947, the first expansion in six years and only the second in the history of the DPS.[55]

One of those new Rangers, fresh from six years in the Highway Patrol, soon proved his mettle. Assigned to Alpine, Arthur T. Hill arrested a ranch foreman on a warrant obtained by his recently transferred predecessor, Ranger Joe Bridge. Drunk before noon, the owner of the ranch showed up at the Brewster County courthouse to demand his employee's release, nosily pointing out that no Ranger could come on his property without his permission. Hill heard him out, then told him he was under arrest for public intoxication. At that, the ranchman took a swing at the short, stocky Ranger. In fewer words than his .45 semiautomatic held bullets, Hill later related, "After that he didn't fare too well." The Big Bend cattleman ended up in jail along with his foreman.[56]

Garrison, already an old hand at public relations, often saw to it that a strategic message went into his agency's biennial reports. Clearly he wanted an increase in the DPS appropriation from the next session of the legislature:

> The nature of the Ranger's work has changed greatly since that orig-
> inal band took up the job of guarding settlers from Indian raids. To-
> day's Ranger must cope with frustrated men who have gone "mad
> dog" on society. . . . To combat these social menaces it is essential
> that they have the most useful and modern equipment, including all
> modes of transportation which should be at their disposal to enable
> them to "fight fire with fire." . . . A Ranger is fully cognizant of the
> responsibility he has shouldered, and he is vulnerable to defeat only
> when he isn't given public support and physical material he must
> have, to function effectively.[57]

The colonel also wanted a new headquarters in Austin. "Due to the overcrowded conditions and existing fire hazards at our Headquarters at Camp Mabry, it is respectfully requested that consideration be given to providing adequate quarters for this Department," he wrote in his letter of transmittal to Governor Beauford Jester and the members of the legislature.[58]

"I Should Like to Do a Series of Stories . . ."

The pile of mail Garrison's secretary carried into his office on June 17, 1948, contained a letter from the governor forwarding a chatty letter from Stacy Keach, a producer with RKO Radio Pictures, Inc., in New York. Only seven years before, Keach had been a lecturer at Texas State College for Women in Denton. While in Texas, he had married a Texas woman.

After explaining all that and saying he would like to make a movie or movies in Texas, he got to the point: "I should like to do a series of stories, with a central character as a symbol of the Texas Rangers." Keach noted that "some successful radio shows have been based on the actual case histories taken from the files of the FBI. . . . These shows have brought added honor and glory to these Governmental agencies." He could do the same thing for the Texas Rangers, the producer wrote.

The letter marked the beginning of a relationship that would give Garrison a chance to continue to mold the image of the Rangers. The director became deeply involved in Hollywood's portrayal of the Rangers, eventually doing something a lawsuit could have quickly ended—virtually licensing use of the words *Texas Rangers.*

By August, after a face-to-face visit with the DPS director, Keach had Garrison talked into giving him exclusive rights to "make a series of motion pictures based on official records of the Texas Rangers and with the official sanction and approval of the Texas Rangers." As soon as Paramount Pictures got wind of the deal, the company protested that it had the rights to the words *Texas Rangers* by virtue of its adaptation of Walter Prescott Webb's 1935 Ranger history.

Keach called Garrison and asked if he would write Paramount in his behalf on "Texas Ranger letterhead." He then sent a draft of a letter for Garrison to send to the studio. The colonel obliged on August 11, using Keach's letter almost word for word:

> I trust you do not have in mind to attempt to control our use of a
> name which we originated and have been using for 125 years. I have
> been advised by the Attorney General of Texas that we can go into
> Federal court and establish our ownership of that name despite the
> many copyrights which are held on it.

While Keach had "put his cards on the table and is trying to present the Texas Rangers in an interesting and dramatic, and at the same time truthful, light," Garrison reminded Paramount that its 1936 movie "portrayed two holdup men as becoming Rangers." The director continued:

> We were even more incensed recently when another studio came to
> us for free research and then went directly contrary to written prom-

ises, portraying the State Police of the Reconstruction Days as if they were one and the same with the Rangers, when in truth the Rangers were resurrected after a temporary eclipse in order to straighten out the rotten situation that was allowed to exist under the regime of the Carpetbagger Governor Davis and his Black and Tan State Police.

If "further provocation" occurred, Garrison said, the DPS would take legal action "to keep this organization from being further libeled."

A couple of weeks later, Garrison formalized his agreement with Keach. The letter of agreement granted Keach "authority to proceed with plans for the production of a series of motion pictures based upon official records of the Texas Rangers, with the official sanction and endorsement of the Texas Rangers, and with permission to use the name of the Texas Rangers in the titles or billing of the picture."[59] The approval could be withdrawn if the DPS director or the Public Safety Commission concluded that "the dramatizations were being presented in such a manner as to reflect discredit upon the organization."

Keach said he hoped to begin filming in Texas by October and planned to use as many real Rangers as possible in the project. "I think we could assure you that Captain Gonzaullas and I and seven or eight Rangers would be available to be used in this picture," Garrison wrote.

Garrison had given Keach copies of several case reports. The first screenplay, he wrote, would contain elements of six true cases plus "anecdotes which I received from several of your Rangers."[60]

By November, Keach had the screenplay completed. The Public Safety Commission reviewed the script, The Texas Ranger Story, and unanimously approved it on November 11. "You may be assured of our full and complete cooperation to you in this enterprise," Garrison wrote.[61]

Keach reported on March 9 progress in getting financial backing for the film. Meanwhile the Rangers showed up for a two-nation movie premiere in Brownsville of South of St. Louis, a Western starring Joel McCrea and Alexis Smith. Garrison had Captain Allee and five of his Rangers on hand for the Brownsville screening. When the movie had its debut in Austin, Garrison took McCrea and Smith to meet the governor and then had lunch with them.[62]

Most of Garrison's duties as director of the DPS were a lot tougher than dealing with Hollywood. On March 14, Inez Martin of Texarkana, the mother of one of the young men killed in the Phantom murder case, wrote the colonel a letter reflecting the continuing anguish over her loss:

> I clung to hopes for some time, that the Rangers and the city police might bring the slayers to admit or surrender, but I have no hopes now of either doing anything. I have . . . some hints, that I want to give to some one who would be interested in showing who did the double slaying at the time Paul was murdered. I don't put any faith in the city police or Rangers. Can you suggest some help?

Garrison replied immediately:

> You may be assured that this Department, through Captain Gonza-ullas and the Rangers under his command, have spent many days and traveled thousands of miles in this investigation. We will continue to do so until the culprit is brought to justice. I can assure you that the Texas Rangers is one of the most outstanding law enforcement organizations in the world today and we will never quit the investigation of a case until it is finally solved.[63]

The DPS director, meanwhile, received an education in moviemaking, at least in the difficulty of getting a film into production. The screenplay had been rewritten and renamed *Lone Star*, Keach wrote on April 6. "The story treatment in this particular script seems to me to be far superior to the treatment that we were using in the previous one," Garrison replied, sounding more like a producer than the director of a state law enforcement agency.[64]

Though still hoping for a feature film, Keach had begun thinking about a possible TV series based on true Ranger stories. Late that April, he sent Garrison a couple of scripts. Keach said he had showed the first story outline to a friend at an advertising agency. "He thinks we have done an excellent job with the story and said if you gave me the Television rights, he felt that he might be able to get a sponsor for us."[65]

The Public Safety Commission and Garrison had begun to lose patience. While admitting that the scripts looked "pretty good," the colonel reminded Keach that he could not give approval without the blessing of the commission. "Frankly, it is going to be difficult to get the approval of these scripts before something definite is established about the production of the 'main picture.'" The commission, he continued, had been "a little bit disappointed because we have not gotten any faster action."[66]

By July Garrison and the commission had seen and okayed the movie script, but the project continued to languish for lack of funding. With a similar lack of movement on the contemplated TV series, Keach concentrated on developing scripts for a radio show on the Rangers.[67]

While Keach worried about getting money for his Ranger screen-play, Garrison became increasingly concerned with organized crime, particularly keeping the Mafia out of Texas. In the booming postwar economy, Texas had attracted the mob's attention, but Garrison intended to see to it that Italian organized crime never gained a foothold in the Lone Star State.[68] The Ranger reputation, underscored by the handling of a high-profile case in Houston, had as much to do with discouraging the mob as actual police work.

A red rosebud pinned to the lapel of his expensive suit, on July 15, 1949, sixty-five-year-old Carlos Villone drove from the restaurant he owned toward his mansion on Chocolate Bayou Road. About 10:00 p.m., a dark sedan pulled up to his Cadillac. A blast of buckshot from a 12-gauge shotgun blew out the rear window of the car, striking Villone in the back of the head. Houston police officers later found the restaurateur's bloody dentures on the floorboard of his car.

Villone was no innocent citizen on his way home after a night on the town—in the journalistic style of the times, reporters dubbed him a "police character." His record went back more than a decade, to when he and Sam Maceo, Galveston's gambling king, had been tried in federal court in 1938 for selling narcotics. Villone had beaten that rap, as well as an assault charge stemming from a shooting the same year. A Harris County jury had handed Villone a ninety-nine-year sentence in 1941 for murder, but he only served four years before receiving a pardon in 1946. Since his release from prison, he had been operating an Italian restaurant, running a horse-racing book, and planning to open a Galveston-style casino in Houston.

Houston-based Ranger John Klevenhagen, a tall former Bexar County sheriff's deputy hired in 1941, worked with Harris County investigators in trying to find why Villone's luck had finally run out. On October 15, Klevenhagen and Harris County sheriff C. V. (Buster) Kern arrested thirty-one-year-old Diego Carlino, a war veteran and Houston grocer. Dodging reporters and photographers, the law enforcement team already dubbed by the local media as "The Gold Dust Twins" took their suspect to a jail at Texas City for interrogation. When they returned to Houston with their prisoner, the two officers displayed a typewritten confession from Carlino. Villone's killing had been a contract hit, they said. The Mafia had wanted a piece of Villone's planned new casino. Villone had opted to go it alone, a fatal decision. Carlino hired one of Texas's best-known defense attorneys, Percy Foreman. The story would stay in the news for the next three years.[69]

For years, when the need arose, Rangers had taken to the air in machines belonging to other agencies.[70] In 1946, Joe Thompson, a Ranger stationed at Waco, had purchased a World War II surplus Vultee BT-13 Valiant with his own money. He occasionally used the aircraft on state business, buying his own gasoline. For the next three years, the Rangers and other DPS officers periodically flew in privately owned small planes when necessary. Finally, in September 1949 the DPS received funding to buy its own plane, a single-engine Ryan Navion. Max Westerman, promoted from the Highway Patrol, got the job as the department's first pilot, going on the payroll as a Ranger. One of the department's young communications specialists, Jim Boutwell, became his copilot.[71]

Westerman soon added to the Ranger legend by making the first aerial traffic stop in the service's history. Assisting in the search for a suspected arsonist, the young pilot spotted the wanted firebug's fleeing vehicle. Banking, the flying Ranger brought his plane in for a steep landing on the highway—directly in front of the speeding vehicle. The surprised suspect barely had time to stop before Westerman jumped out of the cockpit with his pistol pointing at the wanted man.[72]

The airplane cost only a pittance compared to the money Garrison wanted for a new DPS headquarters. The department had run out of space at Camp Mabry. A new, larger building elsewhere in Austin, Garrison felt, would complete the separation from the Adjutant General's Department begun fourteen years earlier. Beyond that, the colonel realized that having a new facility would further the efficiency of the DPS and the Rangers in a postwar era that promised to be challenging.[73]

9

Garrison's Rangers

THE 1950S

Watching the big clock next to the red "On Air" light, veteran Western actor Joel McCrea read a few final lines into the studio microphone at the conclusion of another episode of *Tales of the Texas Rangers.*

"From the days when they are reputed to have 'filed scalps instead of reports' to the present time the Texas Rangers have exhibited a graphic display of courage and ability in combating the forces of inequity and crime," McCrea began.

He continued:

Whether the occasion has demanded painstaking trail cutting in pursuit of cattle rustlers, bank robbers and murderers or beating the draw of a "gun slinger," the Rangers have consistently been there "fastest with the mostest." Today, as yesterday, the Texas Rangers are the same group of relentless, hard-riding, straight-shooting men that struck terror to the hearts of the badmen of the Southwest. . . . Perhaps no greater tribute can be paid to the Texas Rangers as an organization than the fact that their various activities have enshrouded them in a natural halo of glory and legend based upon fact but generously interspersed with myth. That the legends are principally fact, however, is attested to by the multitude of criminals who have been meted the full measure of justice at the hands of the Texas Rangers.[1]

The show debuted April 19, 1950, with a pilot episode carried on the National Broadcasting Company network.[2] Like *Dragnet*, the radio drama took listeners through a real case, the action concluding with a postscript reporting the criminal's conviction and sentence. In Austin a week later, the Public Safety Commission granted the producer exclusive radio and TV rights "to present stories of the Texas Rangers based upon the official records."[3]

"Murder Money," the first regularly scheduled episode, aired at 8:30 p.m. Eastern Time July 8. Keach's program replaced the venerable quiz show *Truth or Consequences*. Sponsor General Mills hoped to move more Wheaties off the shelf, but the new show also sold the crime-busting Rangers to a jittery, communism-fearing nation. The boxed cereal would keep a growing boy healthy, and the Rangers would keep him, the state of Texas, and even the nation safe. Keach already had a tan suit—the unofficial Ranger uniform—made for McCrea, who began appearing at grocery stores to promote the show, Wheaties, and the Rangers.[4]

Not long after *Tales of the Texas Rangers* hit the airwaves, Company B sergeant Jay Banks and Captain Gonzaullas drove from Dallas to Wichita Falls. Wichita, as the locals called it, had quieted down since the oil boom days, but production throughout West Texas continued to be active, and good money could be made—legally and illegally.

That's what attracted Mickey Cohen, a sawed-off but impeccably dressed West Coast mobster whose interest in branching out to the Lone Star State had come to the attention of the DPS. On August 30, Cohen and two associates flew from Los Angeles to Odessa, where they visited a local oilman and heavy-betting Las Vegas gambler. From Odessa, they paid someone to drive them to Wichita Falls, where they checked into the downtown Kemp Hotel. After a brief strategy session, Banks, Gonzaullas and Captain Richard R. "Bob" Crowder, who had driven in from Company C headquarters in Lubbock, left to pay a 3:00 a.m. social call on the Mafioso from California. The two Rangers got a key from the front desk of Cohen's hotel and rousted the gangster from his room, sans warrant. They booked Cohen and his associates into the Wichita County Jail for the night and then went to get a little sleep.

"I have a beautiful wife . . . but she spends a lot of money," Cohen told a reporter as he and one of his traveling companions posed glumly for a newspaper photographer, the short out-of-staters bookended by the six-foot-three Crowder and the five-foot-ten Gonzaullas. "I came to Texas to see about an oil deal."

Banks later recalled:

We went out to his hotel . . . and knocked on his door. A voice said, "Come back later." About that time, the door came off its hinges. For an insignificant little cuss, I never saw a person traveling with so many clothes. We took him by car to the Fort Worth Airport, where we had a plane waiting. He was putting up a fuss, threatening to sue. I went on the plane with him and convinced him that going back to Los Angeles was the best thing for him to do.[5]

Cohen's traveling companions also got a free ride to Fort Worth. At El Paso Cohen tried to sneak off his west-bound flight, but local officers, contacted by the Rangers, saw that he got back on board after they took the compulsive hand washer to jail for fingerprinting and a mug shot. Back in Los Angeles, Cohen claimed he had been roughed up by the Rangers. He intended to seek remedy in the courts, he blustered. But he never did. Nor did he ever return to Texas.

"I did have to emphasize my message with a little physical persuasion," Banks later said. "Maybe if you studied what I did, it kind of crowded the law a little bit. But it was effective."[6]

The extrajudicial expulsion of underworld figures made an interesting column item for Los Angeles *Mirror* radio-TV editor Hal Humphrey. "When two Texas Rangers recently flushed little Mickey Cohen out of the Lone Star State," Humphrey wrote, "one newspaper reader was heard to remark: 'Why, I didn't know they had Texas Rangers anymore.'" If Cohen and "this uninformed reader had bothered to tune their radios to NBC-KHI's 'Tales of the Texas Rangers,'" Humphrey continued, "they would have discovered the Rangers still are very much a going concern, and Cohen might have saved his plane fare."[7]

Cohen's bum's rush from Texas demonstrated the extent of Garrison's iron-fisted control, a J. Edgar Hoover–like power. The colonel's exercise of that power ranged from handpicking new Rangers to dealing harshly with crooks. Not only did he run the Rangers, but he also carefully controlled their image, generally having the final word on virtually everything about them that got on the air or in print. Any time Keach got wind that someone else had a Ranger project in mind, he turned to Garrison for help. Eventually the colonel must have realized that he had been a bit too cooperative in backing Keach and admitted he could not really restrict the use of the words *Texas Rangers*. Garrison wrote:

> The Department does not care to enter into any kind of controversy with reference to the production of a picture, radio or television [*sic*] with anybody over the use of the name "Texas Rangers." We do not feel that we have full authority to grant exclusive permission for the use of this name and particularly if such reproductions are from the actual files.[8]

Less than a week later, reviewing the script for "The Broken Spur," the fourth episode of the radio show, Garrison wrote:

> Page 23. Where Ben tells Pearson to put 'em up and says "I'll take your hardware," that won't go. It's O.K. to have Pearson throw up his hands and keep him covered and get away, but under no circumstances would the Ranger deliver his gun. He would go down in a gun fight before he would hand his gun to anyone.[9]

Garrison wired Keach approval for each script. Occasionally the colonel followed with a letter containing suggestions: "I thought the Script was good," he wrote on October 24, "however, I was just wondering if we are not killing too many people in each story. In the last one . . . we killed the jailer and the negro porter, when I thought one would have done just as well."[10] Critiquing an episode called "Blind Justice," Garrison had five suggestions, ranging from his opinion that the sheriff in the show should talk "more like a Texan and less like a hillbilly" to reminding Keach that Rangers did not wear uniforms.[11] Not only did the colonel help Keach in his official capacity, but Keach paid the director's wife, Mary Nell, to provide Ranger-related tidbits for use at the end of the show.[12]

Thanks to radio and the monthly pulp Western magazines, which still spit out action-packed Ranger stories like so many .45 slugs, the words *Texas Rangers* had as much name recognition in the early 1950s as Harry Truman or Douglas MacArthur. As Americans worried about their sons and daughters in Korea and Russia's development of its own atomic bomb, the fictional Rangers continued a simpler fight against bad guys far easier to corral than communists. The January 1951 issue of Better Publications' *Texas Rangers* featured "Gun Paradise," a novel-ette by Jackson Cole. The story centered on Texas Ranger Jim Hatfield and his horse, Goldy. According to the pulp story's subhead, "Avenging Texas Ranger Colts Bark When a Scheming Land-grabber Turns Elysia into a Hotbed of Oppression!"[13]

Hoping to do its part in forestalling the spread of communism, on February 21, 1951, the fifty-second legislature passed a law requiring all communists in Texas to register with the DPS. Not registering could net an offender ten years in prison and a $10,000 fine. Governor Allan Shivers signed the bill into law six days later, saying he hoped it would give the state the ability to arrest "those who would overthrow the government by force." No one came forward to register as a communist, and no one made any arrests under the new law. "The word Communist, at least in the Texas usage," San Angelo newspaper publisher Houston Harte opined, "has come to mean practically anybody the rest of us don't like—a regrettable perversion of the old-fashioned son-of-a-bitch."[14]

Texas seemed to be holding its own against communists and gangsters, but organized gambling still worried the law enforcement community. State attorney general Price Daniel knew from federal tax records that Texas had more than ten thousand illegal slot machines in operation. On March 19, 1951, Texas's district attorneys gathered in Austin to talk about the problem. To stimulate discussion, Daniel gave the prosecutors the name and address of everyone who had paid taxes on a slot machine the previous year.

"Within a week let's have them gone and out," he told the prosecutors.

Working with local officers where they could, Rangers rounded up the usual one-armed suspects. Also suddenly indignant about slot machines, the legislature passed a law prohibiting their manufacturing, ownership, leasing, or storage.[15]

"I Won Out in All My Fights"

With the real Rangers pressing on with yet another politically driven crackdown on misdemeanor gaming, in California Keach sweated whether NBC would gamble on a second season for *Tales of the Texas Rangers*. He believed the show would be back on the air by September 7, albeit with less money going to the producer and staff. But even as he produced radio scripts for a new season, Keach hoped to transform the show into a TV series. "There is considerable interest in television," he wrote Garrison. The colonel replied: "Within the past few weeks, I have received several letters from people over the country demanding that I make the National Broadcasting Company put this show back on the air because, according to their letters, it is the best show anywhere. I am sure that you might agree!"

Garrison also filled Keach in on a big party being planned for July 10, 1951, in honor of Captain Gonzaullas's retirement. A number of newspapers and magazines had contacted him asking "to write [Gonzaullas's] life story, but he has informed them that this cannot be done because he now has an agent. He has even requested that . . . I not give out anything on him until I clear with him. That guy is not dumb!"[16]

Henderson County sheriff Jess Sweeten, an old friend of Gonzaullas's and the DPS, hosted the farewell event at the Koon Kreek Club near Athens in the tall pine of East Texas. Garrison and the rest of the department's brass, most of the Rangers, and scores of peace officers from across the state gathered to honor the retiring captain. The queen of England had not conferred knighthood on the old Ranger, but in a figurative sense, a Texas knight neared the end of his time at the round table. He would keep his modern-day Excalibur—a set of gold and silver inlaid Colts presented him by grateful citizens—but Gonzaullas told a reporter that he had given away 580 firearms he had taken from criminals over the years, along with hundreds of knives and blackjacks. The gift Colts, he continued, soon would hang over his mantel. The pistols bore an inscription evocative of the days of knighthood bold: "Never draw me without cause, nor shield me with dishonor." Gonzaullas spoke quietly in answer to a reporter's question about the handguns. "I've tried to follow that code," he said. "I won out in all my fights." Just how many of those fights had ended in someone's death he would not say, admitting only to "several."[17]

Beyond marksmanship, the snappy-dressing captain had been the bridge between the old and new Rangers. Gonzaullas had begun his career well before the creation of the DPS and had seen the agency from infancy to early maturity, playing a major role in the modernization of the Rangers. Inside the DPS, he had gone from being called Lone Wolf to Pappy.[18]

"As he stood there in the July sunshine, tall, lithe, and agile as a man half his age, he didn't dwell on his deeds which have become Texas legend even in his lifetime," one author wrote of Gonzaullas a few years later. "Like John Hughes, from whom he had learned so much, he let his career speak for itself. After thirty years as a Texas Ranger, he shook a lot of hands, ate a lot of barbecue, and said goodbye."[19] Gonzaullas's retirement even made *Newsweek*. The article noted that the captain had been a consultant for the NBC radio series on the Rangers and would do the same for an upcoming TV version "armed with a two-foot stack of scrapbooks instead of his .44s."[20]

As Keach continued his efforts to get *Tales of the Texas Rangers* on television, Garrison obligingly fended off others interested in capitalizing on the Rangers, even if he could not legally control the use of the words *Texas Rangers*. To one producer contemplating a TV series, Garrison explained the rationale behind the DPS's exclusive agreement with Keach:

> This agreement was necessary because of the growing tendency on the part of theatrical producers to use the name "Texas Rangers" indiscriminately, indiscreetly, and without our sanction and approval. It is a reflection on the Texas Ranger organization when writers and producers, having no knowledge of the history, background and development of this organization and of the character and integrity of the men who have distinguished themselves in this outstanding service, portray the characters and actions of our personnel in a wholly irresponsible, unbelievable, and highly fictionalized manner.[21]

Garrison kept up a steady correspondence with Keach, but he had much more serious matters on his mind that summer. For more than a year, parties unknown had been sporadically dynamiting black-owned houses in previously all-white portions of South Dallas. So far, no one had been hurt in any of the blasts. In July, with no arrests in any of the fifteen bombings despite a $1,000 reward, the Dallas city council requested that the Rangers assist in the investigation.

"The Rangers are in," Captain Crowder (who had just moved to Dallas to replace Gonzaullas) told a newspaper reporter after emerging from a City Hall meeting with the police chief on July 6.

Dallas *Morning News* columnist Lynn Landrum put the situation into perspective:

> Halting the bombings is one of the most serious issues ever to face the people of Dallas. Involved in it are interests and passions which move men to risk and to violence. Murder and riot are almost certain to come of it, if the bombing continues. No matter what a man's feelings are about the crumbling of segregation in Dallas, every man in Dallas, black or white, is going to lose something if the bombing breaks over into war of race against race.[22]

Five days after the Rangers entered the investigation, an explosion rocked a South Dallas neighborhood at 8:15 p.m. on July 11. The blast destroyed the back of a new house built specifically for sale to blacks. "It had been hoped that the calling in of state and federal enforcement agencies would stop the bombing of Negro homes," the Dallas *Morning News* lamented. "This hope seems to have been blown up along with one more Negro home."[23] But someone in Dallas thought the bombings had gone too far. That person called the police and gave them a name. The tip went straight from the officer who received it to Police Chief Carl Hanson, who immediately contacted Captain Crowder. The man named by the informant lived in the area where the bombings had been occurring and had a rap sheet showing arrests for bootlegging. The Rangers put the man under surveillance. Ten days later, on July 23, the Ranger heading the investigation, Sergeant Banks, thought he had enough probable cause to arrest the suspect and another man. Banks and Dallas police arrested forty-two-year-old Claude Thomas Wright of Dallas and his sixty-one-year-old half brother, Arthur Eugene Young, a farmer who lived near Greenville in Hunt County.

Banks took the lead in interrogating the two men, who at first denied any knowledge of the bombings. The Rangers transferred Young, who had diabetes, to Parkland Hospital for treatment. Following his release from the hospital and after questioning at the Rangers' log cabin company headquarters on the State Fair grounds, he confessed that he had been with Wright when he placed bombs at two locations. Banks took Wright to DPS headquarters in Austin for a polygraph examination the next day. Back in Dallas late that night, Wright led Rangers to a spot south of the city where he had hidden a dynamite bomb he had intended to use on another black-owned house. The Rangers filed on both men for arson by explosives, a felony carrying a possible sentence of from two to twenty years.

"These definitely are not the leaders of these bombings," Crowder told reporters. "We intend to keep investigating until we find the person planning the bombings."[24]

But with those arrests, the Rangers, working with Dallas police investigators and the city fire marshal's office, developed enough information to unravel the case. By the third week of September, a special grand jury had handed down thirteen indictments in the bombings, which had ended with the blast on July 11.[25]

As the investigation into the racial bombings wound down in Dallas, Keach and a film crew came to Texas to shoot footage for a TV pilot. Gonzaullas, a man who had faced killers at gunpoint, got too nervous to complete a scheduled role in the film.[26] Keach shipped Garrison a 16mm print of the pilot for him to show to the Rangers. "We saw the television pilot film the other day and everybody agreed it was the best thing of its kind they had ever seen," Garrison wrote.[27]

Out in West Texas, folks in San Angelo did not have to rely on Hollywood for entertainment in February 1952. A murder trial moved to Tom Green County from Houston supplied plenty of theatrics. In defending accused mob figure Diego Carlino, flamboyant Houston attorney Percy Foreman tried the character—and patience—of Harris County sheriff Buster Kern and his best friend, Ranger John Klevenhagen. Moments after the jury acquitted Carlino in the shotgun killing of nightclub owner and gambler Vincent Vallone, Kern and Klevenhagen confronted Foreman in a hallway outside the courtroom. Fists flew. Kern later admitted to throwing one punch, but Foreman claimed he had been hit four times. Klevenhagen had no comment.

Later that night, both officers pled guilty to simple assault, a misde-meanor. When City Court Judge Jimmy Keene assessed their fine at $5 each, several men who had been in the courtroom, including other offi-cers, quickly collected the money for both lawmen.[28]

Despite its rapid progress through the legal system—from offense to payment of fines in less than three hours—the assault of Foreman made bigger news than the not-guilty verdict in the murder trial. The chair-man of the Texas State Bar's grievance committee said the incident would cost the Ranger his job. Garrison said he had received no com-plaint and could take no action without one, though he did promise an investigation if that occurred. If Garrison ever took any action against Klevenhagen, it did not interrupt the progress of his career. Four years later, Garrison promoted him to captain of Company A.

The real Rangers stayed far busier than their Hollywood counterparts. During the biennium ending August 31, 1952, the fifty-one Rangers trav-eled two million miles by car, plane, and horseback in handling 11,567 criminal investigations leading to 909 felony arrests and 1,355 misde-meanor cases. In doing all this, the Rangers wrote 2,111 reports, inter-viewed 51,993 people, and took 3,014 sworn statements. This took them 154,000 regular hours and 57,000 hours of what the 1952 annual re-port called night duty. Ranger investigative work led to the assessment of four death sentences and 2,764 years of prison time.

"The versatility of the Texas Rangers is reflected in the diversity of the assignments in which they have engaged," the DPS reported to the legislature. "Running the gamut from cattle rustling and burglary to the investigation of bank robberies, they have encompassed the field of law enforcement in establishing and manning road-blocks, engaging in man hunts, seeking escaped prisoners, diving for drowning victims, search-ing for missing persons and lost children, and rendering reports on parole violators." Rangers also assisted the legislature's Crime Investigating Committee "in that body's successful efforts to ferret out crime inter-ests within Texas."[29]

"Drive-In," the ninety-sixth and final episode of the radio version of *Tales of the Texas Rangers*, aired on September 14, 1952.[30] At the height of its popularity, the show enjoyed a 10.8 Nielsen and Trendex rating. That meant an estimated seven million persons heard the show each week.

Company H Rangers *under Captain Frank Johnson at Harlingen in 1904.* (Author's collection)

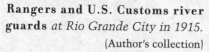

Rangers and U.S. Customs river guards *at Rio Grande City in 1915.* (Author's collection)

Bodies of Mexican raiders *killed during the 1915 attack on Norias in South Texas.* (Author's collection)

Four Rangers sent to prevent violence in Galveston *during a long-shoreman's strike in 1920 displaying their weapons aboard a ship with cargo to be unloaded.* (Author's collection)

Rangers standing with confiscated stills and prisoners *during the 1922 cleanup of the oil boomtown of Mexia.* (Author's collection)

Oil boomtowns across Texas *saw Rangers on horseback and in automobiles.* (Author's collection)

Captain Will Wright, *kneeling second from left, and his Rangers scoured the South Texas brush country for bootleggers in the 1920s.* (Author's collection)

Surrounded by people and cars, a horseback Ranger *keeping order in Borger.* (Author's collection)

Captain Tom Hickman, his son, and wife *posing on an ocean liner on their way to a rodeo performance in England.* (Author's collection)

Rangers in camp near Stamford *during that West Texas town's annual Cowboy Reunion around 1930. Second from left is Company B Ranger Stuart Stanley; far right is Captain Tom Hickman.* (Nita Stewart Haley Library, Midland, Texas)

Rangers making arrest *in Kilgore.* (Author's collection, photo courtesy of Ken Wilson, Dripping Springs, Texas)

The entire Ranger force lines up on the east side of the state capitol in Austin *shortly after the election of Governor Ross Sterling, second from left in front row. Left of the governor is Adjutant General W. W. "Bill" Sterling, no relation to the governor. At far right is Liz Sterling, identified as "Sweetheart" of the Rangers.* (DPS photo)

WANTED FOR MURDER
JOPLIN, MISSOURI

F.P.C.29 - MO. 9
26 U 00 6

CLYDE CHAMPION BARROW, age 24, 5'7",130#,hair dark brown and wavy,eyes hazel,light complexion,home West Dallas,Texas. This man killed Detective Harry McGinnis and Constable J.W. Harryman in this city,April 13, 1933.

BONNIE PARKER CLYDE BARROW   CLYDE BARROW

This man is dangerous and is known to have committed the following murders: Howard Hall, Sherman, Texas; J.N.Bucher,Hillsboro, Texas; a deputy sheriff at Atoka, Okla; deputy sheriff at West Dallas, Texas; also a man at Belden, Texas.

     The above photos are kodaks taken by Barrow and his companions in various poses,and we believe they are better for identification than regular police pictures.

     Wire or write any information to the

                    Police Department.

Former Rangers Frank Hamer and Manny Gault *helped track down Bonnie Parker and Clyde Barrow in 1934.* (Author's collection)

Captain Frank Hamer. (DPS photo)

Rangers presenting a set of six-guns to Governor James V. Allred, *who had pushed for the merger of the Highway Patrol and Rangers.*
(DPS photo)

Unidentified Ranger taking time to pet a dog *in front of his car and horse trailer at the Company B headquarters on the State Fair grounds in Dallas in this late 1930s photograph.*
(DPS photo)

Early-day Ranger Captain John R. Hughes, *seated, checking out the DPS's new radio system in the early 1940s at Camp Mabry in Austin.*
(DPS photo)

Company C Rangers headquartered in Lubbock. *Captain Manny Gault partici-pated in gun battle with the outlaw couple Bonnie and Clyde six years earlier.* (DPS photo)

Rangers standing around a campfire *near their modern-day chuck wagon, 1941.* (West Texas Collection, Angelo State University)

Company E Rangers *on scout in the Big Bend in 1942.* (West Texas Collection, Angelo State University)

The DPS got its first airplane in 1949. *Sitting in the cockpit was Ranger-pilot Max Westbrook.* (DPS photo)

Company B Captain M.T. "Lone Wolf" Gonzaullas *visiting with Superintendent M.F.E. Anthony of the Royal Canadian Mounted Police.* (DPS photo)

During the 1950s the Rangers acquired a military-surplus armored vehicle *for touchy situations. Ranger in hatch aiming a Thompson submachine gun.* (DPS photo)

Texas Ranger Frank Probst *posing with confiscated slot machines typical of those seized during the 1957 Galveston cleanup.* (DPS photo)

On a visit to Texas, actor James Arness, *better known as Marshal Dillon of Gunsmoke fame, posing with Texas's top cop at the time, DPS Colonel Homer Garrison, Jr.* (DPS photo)

Ranger Captain Jay Banks *stood as the model for this statue by sculptor Waldine Tauch not long before getting fired in 1960.* (L. A. Wilke photo, author's collection)

DPS acquired its first helicopters in the late 1960s *but Rangers sometimes still needed horses to do their job.* (DPS photo)

Rangers displaying the array of weapons and equipment *at their disposal in the early 1970s.* (DPS photo)

Following the death of Colonel Homer Garrison, Jr., *in 1968, Wilson E. Speir became DPS director.* (DPS photo)

Senior Captain Clint
Peoples *displaying a pair
of Texas Ranger commemo-
rative BB guns produced as
part of the Rangers' 150th
anniversary celebration
in 1973.* (L. A. Wilke photo,
author's collection)

Bill Wilson *became senior
Ranger captain following
Clint Peoples's retirement.*
(L. A. Wilke photo, author's
collection)

Rangers and state
prosecutors *standing in
front of their temporary
Duval County head-
quarters during their
investigation into the
dealings of political boss
George Parr.* (DPS photo)

Rangers Joe B. Davis and R. G. Wilson *inspecting the brand on a calf.* (DPS photo)

Five Company E Rangers *on the Iron Mountain Ranch in far West Texas in 1976.*
(Nita Stewart Haley Library, Midland, Texas)

Funeral procession in 1978 for Bobby Paul Dougherty, *first Ranger killed in the line of duty since 1931.* Inset, *official DPS photo of Ranger Dougherty.* (DPS photos)

Fort Fisher in Waco *is headquarters of Ranger Company F and home of the Texas Ranger Hall of Fame and Museum.* (L. A. Wilke photo, author's collection)

Former FBI deputy director James B. Adams *became head of the DPS in 1980.* (DPS photo)

Lee Roy Young *became the first African-American Texas Ranger in 1988.* (DPS photo)

Senior Captain H. R. "Lefty" Block *posing with visiting British police inspector J. Stephens from Kent.* (DPS photo)

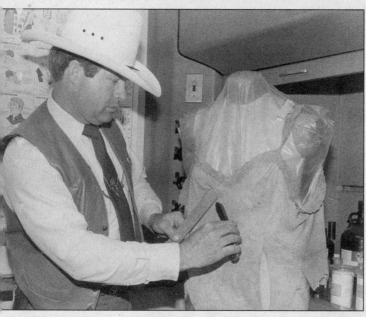

In the DPS crime
lab Texas Ranger
Ron Stewart
*examining clothing
worn by a stabbing
victim.* (DPS photo)

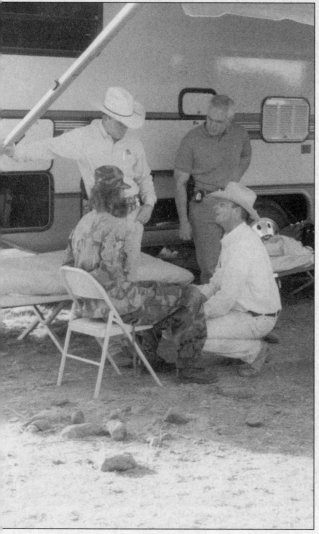

Colonel Dudley M. Thomas
*headed the DPS from 1996
to 2000.* (DPS photo)

**Rangers in 1997 peacefully
ended a confrontation** *with
a Republic of Texas separatist
group in Jeff Davis County.*
(Author's collection)

THE COMANCHE · TEXAS RANGERS
PEACE POW WOW
LAWTON, OKLAHOMA · JUNE 07, 2005

For over half a bloody century the Lords of the Plains and the Texas Rangers battled each other for control of Texas. On the 130th anniversary of the cessation of hostilities, they came together in peace as eternal friends.

Shelton Smith, Chairman FTRF; Hon. Thomas Blackstar, Honored Comanche Elder and Medicine Man; Hon. Wallace Coffey, Chairman, The Comanche Nation; Legendary Texas Ranger Joaquin Jackson.

Attempt to execute a symbolic peace traffic *between the Rangers and Comanches failed in 2005. From left, Shelton Smith, former Texas Ranger Foundation board chairman; Thomas Blackstar, Comanche elder and medicine man; Wallace Coffey, Comanche National chairman; and retired Ranger Joaquin Jackson.* (Photo courtesy of Shelton Smith)

Ranger in far west Texas *oversees a nighttime search for a murder victim's body.* (DPS photo)

While the Rangers faded from the nation's airways, in the more traditional medium of the printed page they still sat tall in the saddle of popular American culture. With the Christmas shopping season approaching, parents of children who had enjoyed the radio show could buy a copy of Allyn Allen's just-released *The Real Book About the Texas Rangers*. Part of a newly launched line of nonfiction books for young readers from Random House in New York, the Ranger title and other *Real Books* soon filled the shelves of school libraries across the country. Allen concluded:

> The Rangers today are certainly different from the Rangers of earlier years, as different as our present is from Texas revolutionary times, or from the days of the great cattle drives. The Rangers are no longer so independent. They work according to established rules as do other law enforcement bodies. But they still bear proudly and well the name of Texas Rangers.[31]

By December, more than a year after finishing the television pilot, Keach still struggled for a sponsor. Public Safety Commissioner Sam Aldridge wrote Garrison that "the radio program has tended to make better public support of the Texas Rangers and I see no reason why the televising of the program would do otherwise." Keach had offered 5 percent of the net profits of his planned TV series to be placed in a benevolent fund for the Rangers and their families.[32] The three commissioners voted to approve a two-year extension of Keach's exclusive agreement with the DPS.

Three hundred and seventeen TV stations beamed their signal in 208 American cities by May 1953, reaching an estimated 27.4 million TV sets. Despite the burgeoning new market and the demonstrated success of the radio show, Keach's TV series still lacked a sponsor or distributor. Even so, Keach and his writers polished scripts in expectation of a sale. Anheuser-Busch showed some interest, but Garrison nixed that. "It would not be a good policy, particularly in the State of Texas, for a Ranger program to be sponsored by a beer manufacturer," Garrison wrote. "I am sorry, my friend, but there would be no way that this could be done."[33]

The DPS left its home of eighteen years in 1953 and moved from Camp Mabry to its $1.3 million new headquarters on an 84.12-acre tract at 5805 Lamar Boulevard on the northern outskirts of Austin. The two-story white limestone building had one hundred thousand square feet of floor space. The fifty-first legislature had authorized construction of the new facility in 1949 by using "all funds remaining in the Operators and Chauffeurs License Fund" at the end of the following three fiscal years.[34]

The same year the Rangers got new office space, the first issue of *True West* magazine rolled off the press. Published in Austin by Joe Small, a University of Texas graduate and World War II veteran, *True West* quickly gained a national circulation. Small had published an outdoor magazine before the war and took up where he had left off when he got out of the military, but in 1953, with encouragement from Webb and writer J. Frank Dobie, he decided to try something new. The young publisher took J. Marvin Hunter's successful *Frontier Times* formula—publishing real stories about the Old West—and improved on it with livelier writing, illustrations, and a flashy cover. The idea worked. With the specter of nuclear war looming like an approaching thunderstorm, Americans flocked to the West—in their minds. Like Hunter, whose *Frontier Times* Small soon bought, the young publisher would be hard-pressed to turn down a story about the Texas Rangers. Many old Rangers, including the retired Frank Hamer, became subscribers.[35]

Not everyone in Texas appreciated the Ranger heritage. Charles J. Lieck Jr., a young state representative from San Antonio, introduced a bill during the fifty-fourth legislature to abolish the service on the grounds that Rangers violated the law while enforcing it. Rangers made arrests, Lieck said, "with or without warrants," had slapped defense attorneys, and obtained confessions by beating suspects: "They go swaggering around wearing pistols and beating hell out of people."

Maury Maverick Jr., another House member from San Antonio, introduced a tongue-in-cheek resolution naming Lieck an honorary Ranger. Dubbing him "Tex" Lieck, twenty-three of the House's 150 members signed the resolution. Lieck's bill to do away with the Rangers, one member said, had "as much chance as a snowball in San Antonio."[36]

Texans were not ready for something as radical as doing away with the Rangers, but within the service a change almost as profound had come. The handgun that helped forge the Rangers' reputation—the six-shot .45-caliber Peacemaker favored by Rangers since the mid-1870s—

slowly was being replaced by Colt Model 1911 .45 semiautomatics (with a seven-round magazine) or double-action Smith & Wesson revolvers chambered for harder-hitting .357 Magnum rounds.

Sixty-nine-year-old Bob Coffee, stationed at Sierra Blanca in far West Texas, had the distinction of being the last Ranger to hang up his day-to-day six-shooter in favor of a more modern firearm. In South Texas, Captain A. Y. Allee had long since taken to carrying a semiautomatic, but he still holstered a Peacemaker any time he worked brush country on horseback.

"All this isn't generally known throughout the nation," writer Hart Stilwell said in the new *True West* magazine, "and, strangely, there is a reason. The American people flatly insist that the Peacemaker lives on. And the Texas Rangers are perfectly willing to keep the tradition alive."[37]

"Harsh Words Flew"

Allee may or may not have cared about perpetuating the six-shooter tradition, but he gladly would have killed off another sort of tradition in South Texas: the patron system. Anglo political bosses still controlled the predominantly Hispanic counties along the border, but none as ruthlessly as the Parr machine. Since the turn of the century, someone named Parr had held undisputed political control of Duval County, a sparsely populated rectangle on the map an hour's drive west of Corpus Christi. Senator Archer Parr, no supporter of the Rangers, had died in 1942. His son, George, took over the county after his father's death. In 1948, Parr had been the man behind the curtain in Lyndon Johnson's controversial election to the U.S. Senate by a margin of only eighty-seven votes, a come-from-behind victory over Coke Stevenson brought about by Parr's discovery of 202 uncounted votes in Precinct 13 in Jim Wells County.

Though powerful enough to change history, Parr, like tyrants before him, could not stave off revolution on the part of a freedom-hungry citizenry. In 1949, political opposition began to develop as young Mexican-American war veterans in South Texas decided that if they could defeat oppression abroad, they could do it at home. They called themselves the Freedom Party. Even some Anglos, especially in nearby Alice, turned against Parr and his "Old Party."

Opposing Parr could be life threatening. A Jim Wells County sheriff's deputy, a man loyal to Parr, shot to death journalist and radio commentator W. H. Mason on July 29, 1949, in Alice. Despite the sheriff's allegiance to Parr, with investigative assistance from the Rangers the deputy ended up with a ninety-nine-year prison sentence for killing the fifty-one-year-old journalist.

Two years later, the Parr machine again resorted to murder. On September 8, 1952, someone shot and killed twenty-two-year-old Jacob (Buddy) Floyd Jr. outside his home in Alice. Captain Allee and his Rangers soon found that the young man had been killed by mistake. The real target had been the victim's father, Jake, a political enemy of Parr. Rangers traced a .38 pistol found in a trash can near the scene of the crime to Mario (El Turko) Sapet, a San Antonio bar owner and former Duval County sheriff's deputy. Though the triggerman had escaped to Mexico, the Rangers filed on Sapet for conspiracy to murder. Tried in North Texas on a change of venue, he got a ninety-nine-year prison sentence.[38]

Despite the prospect of more violence to anyone Parr perceived as a threat, political resistance continued to grow. On January 16, 1954, Parr and some of his pistoleros showed up at a political rally in San Diego. The Duke, who had held office first as county judge and next as sheriff, pulled a pistol on Manuel Marroquin, a writer for an anti-Parr Spanish-language newspaper. If Parr figured to intimidate Marroquin and other members of the opposition Freedom Party, it backfired. With help from the Rangers, Marroquin filed on Parr for possession of a prohibited weapon. Parr claimed Marroquin had been mistaken. What he had in his hands that day had been a pair of binoculars, not a gun, he said.

When the misdemeanor firearm case came up on the docket in Jim Wells County, Parr stayed in San Diego, sending his attorney to the courthouse. The county attorney demanded that Parr be present in court, and the judge ordered Rangers Joe H. Bridge and Walter Russell to bring him to Alice. Before leaving for San Diego, Bridge telephoned Archer Parr, the current Duval County sheriff and Parr's nephew. The Ranger told Parr to have his uncle come to his office. Parr said he would do that, but instead, the two Parrs drove to Alice, leaving the Rangers cooling their heels in San Diego.

By the time the two Rangers got back to Alice, Parr had already been fingerprinted and photographed. Spitting mad, when Bridge saw the two

Parrs talking with Captain Allee outside the courtroom, he confronted Archer Parr. As the New York *Times* described it, "harsh words flew" between the Parrs, Bridge, and his captain. "A brief scuffle ensued that ended in only a few bruises," the New York daily reported.[39] Caro Brown, a reporter for the Alice *Echo*, witnessed the January 18, 1954, incident and could be more specific:

> Faster than we could keep up with it, Bridge struck the younger Parr, knocking the latter's glasses to the floor. George Parr jumped forward at that, and immediately Allee grabbed him, at the same time disarming the sheriff [Archer], who had reached for his gun.
>
> [George] Parr's ear received an open tear when it was twisted by the Ranger captain, who also hit Parr with his fist before sticking his gun in his ribs.
>
> At that point I stepped into the middle, begging "Cap, please don't, please don't."
>
> Repeatedly the Ranger captain told George Parr:
>
> "I've had all I'm going to take of you and the way you've been handling things."

Parr later told reporters that Brown saved his life, one of the more truthful statements he ever made.[40]

"Parrs, Rangers Trade Punches," the Austin *Statesman* reported in a page one, four-column Associated Press report that afternoon. The following morning, Allee had five Rangers patrolling Alice, "keeping rein on tempers that flared into an explosive brawl with political kingpin George B. Parr."[41] Though the district attorney declined to file charges, a Jim Wells County grand jury saw the incident as assault with intent to murder and handed down indictments against the two Rangers.

The Dallas *Morning News* seemed not at all offended that a Ranger captain had slugged a citizen of the state inside a courthouse. "In a county like Duval," the newspaper said on its editorial page, "it takes courage to defy a powerful political boss and to laugh off threats of violence. But there the new Freedom party has been holding open meetings, with Texas Rangers as guards, and appears to be gaining some strength. It aims to make Duval a county in which voters mark their ballots independently and in which votes are counted honestly."[42]

A judge dismissed the complaint against Ranger Bridge in late March but not the charge against Allee. With Allee's assault with intent to murder case about to go before a jury, on April 20 Parr magnanimously asked the district judge to drop the matter "for the good of the community." Afterward, with photographers clamoring for a shot, Allee refused to shake Parr's hand. "I just don't like George Parr or nothing about him," the captain told reporters. "He's a dangerous man who would do anything under the sun, and I don't treat a tiger like I do a rabbit. I'm not sorry I hit Mr. Parr."[43]

Riot at Rusk

Texas had more than one tiger. A year later, on Saturday, April 16, 1955, Assistant Supervisor Clyde White accompanied Dr. L. D. Hancock as he made his morning rounds in the maximum-security unit of the Rusk State Hospital. One hundred and twenty miles from Dallas in northeast Texas, the facility held twenty-five hundred inmates, including six hundred considered criminally insane. Hearing that someone had been hurt in a fight, White and the doctor hurried toward the building containing Ward Seven.

True enough, someone had been injured, but the two men walked into a trap. Six-foot-two, 220-pound inmate Ben Riley and several others had severely beaten an attendant they particularly disliked. When two other guards tried to intervene, the inmates overpowered them. Taking their keys, the inmates—armed with baseball bats, broom handles, broken pieces of furniture, ice picks, and scissors—rushed downstairs to Ward Six. When White and Hancock arrived, Riley and the others took them hostage, beating both of them.

Riley ordered the doctor to telephone hospital superintendent Dr. Charles Castner and ask him to report to Ward Six. When Castner entered the ward about five minutes later, he found his medical colleague seriously injured, suffering from stab wounds and a concussion. Insisting that Hancock be removed for emergency treatment, Castner agreed to stay in his place. The inmate allowed Hancock and several guards to leave, but he and eighty other inmates had control of the building and three hostages. The ringleader demanded to talk to a newspaper reporter.

When Emmett Whitehead, the twenty-seven-year-old editor of the

Rusk *Cherokeean*, reached the hospital, Riley began listing instances of inmate abuse at the hands of trusties known by the inmates as "floor bouncers." For someone adjudged criminally insane, the bare-chested, cigar-chewing inmate proceeded to rationally enumerate a set of concerns and demands: better counseling, organized exercise time, no more inmate beatings, and privileges equal to those granted white inmates. Further, Riley wanted a hearing with state officials. If police officers came into the building or if he and his fellow inmates did not get what they wanted, he contended, they would kill Dr. Castner, White, and attendant Bill Curtis. Riley felt he had nothing to lose. "There's nothing these sons-a-bitches can do to us, 'cause we're already crazy," he said.

After his photographer took pictures of inmates showing scars they said came from mistreatment in the hospital, Whitehead left to print an extra edition of his weekly newspaper. His story described what had happened so far and quoted Riley on his concerns about conditions at the state facility.[44]

In Dallas, just back from lunch, Captain Crowder got a telephone call from Garrison notifying him of the situation at Rusk and offering that he "ought to get down there." The captain told the colonel he would be on his way and ordered three of his men to head in the same direction. Ninety minutes later, Crowder and his new Oldsmobile rolled into Rusk.

As soon as he reached the hospital, Crowder learned that Riley wanted to talk to a Ranger "if he represented the government." Before agreeing to meet with the inmate, Crowder set ground rules over the telephone. "I want to tell you one thing," he began. "I'm not coming in unarmed because you've already got three people . . . as hostages and I don't want to be the fourth one—and I'm not going to be. . . . If something goes amiss, I know who's going to fall first."

Next Crowder questioned the local newspaper editor and hospital employees to learn as much as he could about conditions inside the inmate-controlled building. At 3:10 p.m., the tall, two-hundred-pound Ranger captain walked through the electrically operated gate toward the two units under inmate control. When the captain reached the entrance, Riley emerged, a pair of scissors stuck under the belt holding up his khaki pants.

For the next twenty minutes, the two talked. Crowder calmly pointed out that Riley had made a bad mistake and that if anything happened to the hostages "it's just going to be worse for you." Riley, in turn, restated the inmates' grievances. The captain listened quietly. When Riley asked again for a hearing, the Ranger said, "OK, I'll see that you get a hearing."

Crowder then told Riley to drop his weapons and to have the other inmates come out and do the same. "I want the superintendent and the two attendants down here unharmed," he added.

Riley threw down his ice pick and scissors and yelled for the others to follow suit. As Crowder stood by, his two .45s still holstered, all the inmates emerged from the unit and put down their weapons. Finally, the three hostages appeared, uninjured.[45]

In entering the hospital the Ranger captain had been brave but not foolhardy. Crowder had posted Highway Patrolman Jim Ray with a scoped rifle only about fifty yards from Riley. As the Ranger talked with the riot leader, the uniformed officer had the crosshairs lined up on Riley's heart. If the inmate had moved toward the captain, the patrolman would have squeezed the trigger.

Though Crowder had faced Riley without body armor, the Rusk incident convinced Garrison that the Rangers could use better protection in armed standoffs. The DPS in May purchased an army surplus M-8 light armored vehicle for the Rangers. The department's auto shop painted the turreted vehicle white and installed a two-way radio.[46]

It had taken Keach years of work, but on September 22, 1955, the first episode of *Tales of the Texas Rangers* aired on TV stations in sixty-four markets. "The Texas Rangers are among the best known heroes in American history," Screen Gems, Inc., asserted in a promotional booklet. "Their 120 years of active duty is symbolic of the highest courage and greatest devotion that any law enforcement body could claim." Playing to the anticommunist sentiments of the times, the booklet pointed out that the show offered "healthy, human heroes fostering constructive social attitudes for every viewer to emulate and to identify with your product." But *Tales of the Texas Rangers* aired without the popular Joel McCrea. Six-foot four-inch Willard Parker got the part of Jace Pearson, with his sidekick played by Harry Lauter.[47]

Tales of the Texas Rangers could not claim to be the only TV show with the word *Ranger* in its title. The Lone Ranger, that stalwart crime-fighting masked man, and his "faithful Indian companion Tonto" had a huge weekly following of radio listeners and, since 1949, TV watchers. Counting readers of Lone Ranger books and comics, an estimated ninety million people followed the adventures of the man Tonto called Kemo Sabe. In the *Congressional Record*, U.S. senator Price Daniel of Texas said that the Lone Ranger played a major role "in keeping alive in the minds of people, both in the United States and abroad, the traditions and ideals of the Texas Ranger organization and its work in maintaining law and order."[48]

Thanks to news coverage of events like the Rusk riot and fictional exploits portrayed on *Tales of the Texas Rangers* and *The Lone Ranger*, the DPS had no difficulty recruiting new Rangers. But answering letters from would-be Rangers did take up some time at headquarters. The Rangers passed along one letter addressed to "The Texes Rangers, Texes," for publication in the department's newsletter, the *DPS Chaparral*: "Dear Sir—I don't know how two starte this letter. But I would like a job down there. Me? I am out of a job and can't fine one. . . . I can milk cows, farm work, and woolen mill work." The thirty-one-year-old author, who said that he stood six feet one inch tall and weighed 186 pounds, continued:

> The job I would like is Borderman Gaurde. All I know about the West is whate I read about in books. I don't have too much money to get there on, but I will get there if you could help me. And I know the Ranger's are nice people I rode a horse three times . . . If I don't here from you in one week I am acomming out there.

The *Chaparral* editor graciously omitted the correspondent's name and state.[49]

Children frequently wrote the department. A Boy Scout from Trenton, New Jersey, sent a letter saying he had completed his scrapbook thanks to a brochure the DPS had sent him on the history of the Rangers and would be getting his first merit badge. From Philadelphia another boy wrote:

> How are the Rangers? Have you caught any outlaws lately? . . . My friend said that he could push a Ranger down but I do not believe

him. Are there such a thing as Texas Rangers girls? . . . Your Ranger
Pal, Bruce.

Not all the letters came from out of state. A boy in Mountain Home,
Texas, sent this letter:

> I would like to join the Texas Rangers. I am ten years old but I can
> shoot straight, ride hard, drive, and don't get scared easy. I know I
> am kind of young to join up but I know L.H. Purvis [the Ranger then
> stationed in Kerrville] real good. He could teach me what to do to
> become a Ranger.[50]

Americans young or old seemingly could not get enough of the
Texas Rangers. In the realm of Ranger fiction, a new hand thrust his
boots in the stirrups in 1956—Walt Slade, "The Greatest of the Texas
Rangers." Created by writer Bradford Scott, Slade and his "great black
horse," Shadow, made their debut in *Texas Terror,* a 127-page paperback
original brought out by Pyramid Books in New York. Lieutenant and
"aceman of the Texas Rangers," Slade could "outdraw, outshoot, and
outwit any drygulcher who plots evil in the wide-open West."

While Slade's exploits appealed to mature readers, another New
York publisher released a Ranger book for younger teens, *Ten Tall Tex-
ans: Tales of the Texas Rangers.* Author Lee McGiffin grew up in Indiana, but she met and married a Texan, while working as a newspaper
columnist in Buffalo, New York, and later moved to Texas. Her book
had chapters on all the usual suspects in Ranger lore: Noah Smithwick,
Big Foot Wallace, Jack Hays, Samuel Walker, John B. Armstrong, Jim
Gillett, Lee Hall, John R. Hughes, Bill McDonald, and M. T. "Lone
Wolf" Gonzaullas. Offering a new generation of young readers all the old
Ranger clichés, from "one riot, one Ranger" to "No man in the wrong
can stand up against a feller that's in the right and keeps on a-comin'!"
McGiffin made up one of her own:

"When the need arises," McGiffin wrote, "the Texas Rangers are
quick witted, fast drawing, and hard hitting. A century or more ago, the
Rangers lived and fought by a simple code: 'Be sure you are right, then
go ahead, even if it means losing your life.' "[51]

Garrison knew his Rangers did not always do right and certainly enjoyed no invincibility, but as their place in American popular culture continued to grow, most Texans and many others worldwide sure thought they did. The DPS director had no formal education in communication theory or public relations, but just like Hoover at the FBI, Garrison understood the power of image. Public perception did not stop bullets, but it gave a peace officer an extra edge and helped out when the legislature considered his department's latest budget proposal. Nor did it hurt when it came to what the DPS called sack dragging.

That spring, the Lone Star Boat Company of Grand Prairie donated a twenty-one-foot cabin cruiser and trailer to the Rangers. The DPS did buy two thirty-horsepower outboard motors, fitting the boat out with a two-way radio and spotlights. The department also purchased diving equipment and trained some Rangers in its use. The craft would be used by the Rangers on the Highland Lakes in Central Texas and elsewhere in recovering bodies and evidence. The Rangers now had an airplane, a tank, and a fast boat in addition to cars and horse trailers.[52] As Ranger prestige continued to grow, some internal jealousy at the DPS occasionally manifested itself. "We are proud of the Rangers and all that 'Special Equipment' they are getting," someone from the San Angelo Highway Patrol office said in his news report to the DPS's employee publication. "But we do wonder about the Highway Patrol. Do you think we could catch a speeder in a Tank? And that 'Errol Flynn' looking boat, we do believe we could use it out in San Angelo in our high water details." (At the time, Texas broiled in the midst of its worst drought in modern history.)[53]

On July 7, 1956, Houston-based Ranger Klevenhagen coordinated the search for a mentally deranged man who had shot a deputy sheriff in Somerville. When prison bloodhounds tracked the man down, he started shooting at officers. Reaching the spot, Klevenhagen kicked the sides of his horse and galloped toward the brush with his reins in one hand, his cocked .45 in the other, and a shotgun in his saddle scabbard.

"This is Texas Ranger Johnny Klevenhagen," he shouted as he reined his horse. "Come out with your hands up and you won't be harmed." At that, the man emerged from his hiding place. As instructed, he had his hands raised, but each one held a pistol. Without a word, his arms dropped and he started shooting at the horseback Ranger. A bullet buzzed by Klevenhagen's ear, and his horse started circling and pitching in fear. The two men blazed away at each other only fifteen feet apart, but both missed as Klevenhagen's terrified horse continued to buck. The Ranger finally managed to get out of the saddle and shoulder his 12-gauge, putting two loads of 000 buckshot into the gunman. Later Klevenhagen handled his report of the incident in twenty-six words:

> Searched on foot, horseback, and in cars. After 75 hours, located subject in Yegua Creek bottom. Subject resisted and fired on Ranger Klevenhagen. Subject was killed.[54]

Rangers would continue to use horses as necessary, but the case marked the last time in the service's long history that a Ranger engaged in a horseback gun battle. Another ending came a few weeks later. It did not get as much publicity as Klevenhagen's mounted charge, but on July 25 a 104-year-old man named Noah Armstrong died in Coleman, Texas. According to state pension records, he had been the last living veteran of the Frontier Battalion.[55]

Alert and active nearly to the end of his long life, the old Indian fighter had lived to see the beginning of the end of racial segregation in Texas. Those who followed Armstrong into the Ranger service, men such as Klevenhagen, still could use a gun to permanently close the case file on a suspected felon, but in the 1950s the service faced some far more complicated issues. In investigating the Dallas residential bombings, the Rangers had helped to head off the possibility of racially motivated violence. That indirectly improved the climate for peaceful desegregation efforts in Texas's second-largest city. Five years later, though Governor Allan Shivers had been reluctant at first to send them in, the Rangers kept the peace during the state's first school desegregation crisis.

"THIS NEGRO TRIED TO ENTER A WHITE SCHOOL . . . "

Seventeen miles from Fort Worth, the Mansfield school district had fewer than eight hundred students—only sixty of them black. Even so, it had a "separate but equal" elementary school just for blacks. The town's black teenagers had to take a bus to Fort Worth and walk twenty blocks to a black high school. The National Association for the Advancement of Colored People filed a federal lawsuit in October 1955 on behalf of three black teens seeking integration of the Mansfield high school. U.S. District Judge Joseph E. Estes of Fort Worth agreed with the school district's argument that it needed more time to bring about desegregation and refused to order the high school's integration. But the NAACP appealed Estes's ruling to the Fifth Circuit Court of Appeals in New Orleans. The justices ordered the school desegregated and remanded the case to Judge Estes's supervision. The school board said it would comply with the order, but Mansfield's white residents opted to resist. School officials began receiving anonymous threatening telephone calls in the middle of the night. Burning crosses appeared in yards in the predominantly black part of town two nights in a row.

With the first day of school less than a week away, on August 28, 1956, someone stuffed straw into a set of men's khaki work clothes, made a face and hands they painted black, splashed on red paint, and suspended it from a wire at the intersection of Main and Broad streets. A sign attached to the effigy read: "This Negro Tried To Enter A White School, wouldn't this be a horrible way to die." A passerby notified the Tarrant County Sheriff's Office, which sent a deputy to take it down.

Forty-eight hours later, with tensions continuing to build, the NAACP sent a telegram to Governor Shivers urging him to send law enforcement officers to Mansfield "to assure that law and order will be maintained and that these students will be protected in their right to attend Mansfield High School." Garrison also received a copy of the telegram. The NAACP attorney followed his wire with a telephone call to the DPS director, who said he would not send officers unless he got a request for assistance from the sheriff.

Apparently in response to news media coverage of growing unrest in the small town, the governor issued a statement on the morning of August 31 reiterating what Garrison had said: No state officers would go to Mansfield unless requested by the Tarrant County sheriff, and no request had been received. "I am certainly not inclined to move state officers into Mansfield at the call of a lawyer affiliated with the [NAACP], whose premature and unwise efforts have created this unfortunate situation at Mansfield," the governor said.

Throughout the morning, the mood in Mansfield continued to worsen. Stores closed. Local residents stopped motorists outside town to prevent the arrival of "outsiders." Now three effigies hung downtown, along with more racist signs. Residents ran two TV cameramen from the Dallas–Fort Worth area out of town. As reports from the scene continued to sound more ominous and with word that the mayor, police chief, and other community leaders had left town for the Labor Day weekend, Shivers changed his mind and ordered Rangers to Mansfield "to cooperate with local authorities in preserving peace." The governor announced that he had asked Garrison "to instruct his men to arrest anyone, white or colored, whose actions are such as to represent a threat to the peace at Mansfield."

Sergeant Banks and Ranger Ernest Daniel arrived from Dallas and spent several hours in Mansfield that day but left when the situation seemed to have cooled down.

Shivers could have instructed the Rangers to enforce the federal order, but he did not. Instead, the governor suggested that the school transfer from the district any "scholastic, white or colored, whose attendance or attempts to attend Mansfield High School would reasonably be calculated to incite violence." Though Shivers had chosen his words carefully, stressing that he had taken his action in the interest of preventing violence, he had virtually assured the maintenance of the status quo for the time being. In his view, the matter needed to be resolved in the U.S. Supreme Court.

Six Rangers stood by at Mansfield High School on September 4 for the first day of classes, with three other Rangers working undercover in the crowd. None of the three black students named in the lawsuit tried to register, and the day passed without violence. All agreed that the Ranger presence had a soothing effect, but the governor had done nothing to advance the cause of civil rights.

Again the ranking Ranger at the scene, Banks blamed "agitators" for the trouble, not local residents. As he later wrote:

The Rangers announced that they were strictly neutral, as far as the point at issue was concerned, but they intended to restore order and enforce the law. Anyone on either side who interfered or violated the law would be arrested. . . . The black school children who had intended to try and enroll . . . never showed up and by the second day the trouble appeared to be over.[56]

In Little Rock, which within a year would see regular army troops sent in by President Dwight D. Eisenhower to enforce desegregation, a columnist for the *Arkansas Gazette* had fun with the Mansfield story.

"Well I see by the news dispatches from down Texas way that the Texans have dragged out that old cactus-covered boast of 'one riot, one Ranger,'" wrote Ernie Deane, an expatriate Texan. "The incident that revived this Texanism occurred at Mansfield when a Ranger shouldered his way through a crowd of angry segregationists . . . the fact that five more Rangers and other armed officers were at hand nearby was sort of minimized in the report from Texas that I saw in my favorite newspaper."

Deane said he did not intend to disparage the Rangers: "They have put a halter on trouble on more than one occasion when nobody else seemed able to do so, or willing to try," but "this 'one riot, one Ranger' thing is mostly just another product of that remarkable brand of state pride that oozes out of the average Texan like sweat from the brow of a *bracero* in a cotton patch in August."[57]

Since the days when Captain McNelly pursued cattle thieves in South Texas on horses furnished by the King Ranch, most ranchers welcomed Rangers onto their land. The famous 6666 Ranch near Gutherie hosted the Rangers of Lubbock's Company C for a company meeting on October 3, 1956. At Snake-den Tank, as the DPS employee newsletter reported, "every one did a little fishing and a lot of eating."[58] The other Ranger companies had similar meetings, mixing business and socialization, at various locations across the state, usually on ranches.

Rangers liked to get together, but they did not have time to do it often. The average Ranger spent seventy-four hours and thirty minutes a week on the job, with no overtime pay. Even in remote parts of the state such as Sierra Blanca, Ranger J. S. Nance handled 166 criminal cases in 1956, including four homicides, two bank holdups, a kidnapping, several armed robberies, and sixty-eight burglaries. Ranger J. A. Sikes investigated eighty-one cases, logging 2,055 daylight working hours, 821 night hours, and 200 hours scouting the Rio Grande.[59]

In January 1957, Tom Hickman, fired from the Rangers in 1935, became the first former Ranger ever appointed to the three-member Public Safety Commission. The gray-haired Hickman, who still believed his dismissal from the newly created DPS had been political, found the honor singularly satisfying.[60]

Four months later, in the new commissioner's old North Texas stomping grounds, an Oklahoma ex-con on the FBI's Ten Most Wanted list busied himself preparing for the caper of his career, what he figured for a $500,000 heist. Gene Paul Norris planned to hit the Carswell Air Force Base branch of the Fort Worth National Bank on the day the military payroll arrived. Known as the "smiling killer," Norris obtained a drawing of the bank's layout from a shady contact who had done time with the former manager of the bank, a man in for embezzlement. Not only that, Norris had the name and address of the cashier, Elizabeth Barles.

Norris, a professional criminal with a rap sheet going back into the 1930s, and his accomplice, William C. "Silent Bill" Humphrey, would go to the woman's house and take her and her twelve-year-old son hostage. With her bank keys and vehicle, which had a sticker on its windshield that would get them past the Air Policemen at the Carswell gate, Norris would gain entry to the bank. Next they would waylay the armored car couriers when they showed up with the base payroll. With the couriers hog-tied and relieved of their money, Norris and Humphrey would return to Mrs. Barles's house and pick up their getaway car. Before leaving, Norris would kill the woman and her son so as to leave no witnesses.

A convicted hit man suspected of forty or more murders, Norris had the cunning, nerve, and weaponry to pull off the robbery. He just failed to consider the possibility of an FBI telephone tap, which allowed law enforcement officers to learn the cold-blooded details of his scheme. Knowing Norris would be casing the bank employee's house and the bank before the planned April 30, 1957, robbery, Banks—recently promoted to captain—and Ranger Klevenhagen (who considered Norris a suspect in a Houston double homicide) staked out the woman's house in an unmarked car. Fort Worth police chief Cato Hightower, Tarrant County sheriff Harlan Wright, and other officers waited with the two Rangers.

Humphrey at the wheel, the two crooks drove by the bank on April 29 on a practice run. Spotting the officers, Humphrey stomped the accelerator of his souped-up Chevrolet, breaking through a roadblock. With Captain Banks in the lead, the officers chased the pair out the Jacksboro Highway at speeds reaching 115 miles an hour. When Norris started firing at the Rangers and other officers, they shot back. Twenty-one miles later, Humphrey turned onto a muddy back road three miles east of Springtown in Parker County. The car slid out of control and crashed into two trees at the edge of a creek.

The two crooks bailed out and started running, shooting at the officers as they ran. Another state car driven by Ranger sergeant Arthur Hill, with new Ranger Jim Ray riding shotgun, reached the scene moments later. The two Rangers jumped out of the vehicle and joined the firefight. As he tried to cross the creek Humphrey took twenty-three rounds, but Norris kept moving.

"He's getting away! Give me a shotgun," Klevenhagen yelled to Ranger Ray. The Ranger tossed Klevenhagen his scattergun. "Just as my shotgun reached Klevenhagen, we heard Norris give out a scream like a banshee, and then came a full burst from Jay's M-3," Ray later recalled.

The pathologist who did the autopsy on Norris counted twenty-eight bullet holes in his body, the wounds ranging from his ankles to his head. Even allowing for sensationalist newspaper coverage, Norris ranked as Texas's worst outlaw since the Clyde Barrow–Raymond Hamilton days nearly a quarter century earlier and on par with the prior century's John Wesley Hardin.[61]

Not every case the Rangers worked ended as spectacularly as the shoot-out with Norris and Humphrey. In West Texas that May, Rangers Gene Graves and John Wood spent ten days in Borden and Gaines counties during an oil-field strike. They prevented any injuries, and only minor damage to private property occurred. "Texas Rangers and Texas sheriffs have brought glory and honor to the Lone Star State many times over the years," the Odessa *American* editorialized on May 22. The newspaper continued:

Such was the case in this area recently when Rangers and local law enforcement men from Gaines and other counties stood up to be counted. The issue was an attempt of union men to threaten and intimidate and show such physical destruction . . . that they could scare some men into joining the drilling crews' union or force some contractors into shutting down their rigs. It is a sorry commentary on our country today that there are laws and lawmakers and law enforcement men who bow down to union violence and the union practice of scaring men and companies alike. But it is good to know that the Permian Basin has men who will stand up for what is right and decent.

CASHIERING GALVESTON

The Rangers had never been held in as high regard in Galveston, where gambling still ran wide open despite periodic attempts over the years to shut it down. Earlier in the year, Garrison had gotten a call from Will Wilson, the newly sworn state attorney general. As Dallas district attorney, Wilson had run professional gamblers out of Big D. Stumping the state, he had promised to do the same statewide—starting with "The Free State of Galveston." Now Wilson wanted help from the Rangers in cashiering for good Texas's illegal but long-tolerated version of Las Vegas.

Wilson hired Galveston County lawyer and former FBI agent James P. Simpson as a special assistant attorney general to serve as his point man. He also compensated a couple of trusted local men as undercover operatives to gather enough probable cause for search warrants. With their wives they visited the Turf Athletic Club and the swank Balinese Room, a popular establishment on Seawall Boulevard extending on a pier over the Gulf of Mexico. The couples dined, danced, and placed a few small bets. The men reported back to Simpson and Wilson with details—the security, the practice drills for when a raid occurred, and the hidden room at the end of the Balinese's six-hundred-foot pier used to stash the illegal gambling devices. The operatives made the rounds of Galveston's other clubs as well, compiling a long list of places to shutter in one sweeping operation.

Despite occasional crackdowns, Galveston had been a safe harbor for gambling practically since its founding. Since the 1920s the island city's entertainment and gaming industry had been controlled by Italian barbers-turned-bootleggers Salvatore "Sam" and Rosario "Rose" Maceo. They opened what would become the Balinese Room in 1923 as a restaurant called the Chop Suey. Following an extensive remodeling and expansion in 1942, the place had been renamed the Balinese. Over the years, the Maceos, who controlled Galveston politically, had managed to turn most previous Ranger raids into part of the club's entertainment. When Rangers periodically hit the place, the house band struck up "The Eyes of Texas" and the patrons gleefully sang along. By the time the lawmen reached the gaming room at the end of the pier, the evidence had been hidden or splashed into the Gulf. By 1957 both Maceos had died, but their nephews Anthony J. and Victor J. Fertitta continued to operate the family businesses.

Operating in tight secrecy, Garrison, Wilson, and Simpson planned a raid on the Balinese and other Galveston gambling joints. On June 6, 1957, under cover of darkness a caravan of Rangers, Highway Patrol troopers, and personnel from the Attorney General's Office pulled onto the Gulf Freeway from a rendezvous point in Houston for the forty-five-minute drive to Galveston. Garrison rode in the lead car. But when the lawmen reached the Balinese, they found the parking lot deserted, the doors locked, the rooms dark and silent. The raid had been carefully choreographed and should have worked. But with numerous public officials on the pad, the Maceo heirs and associates had better odds. Someone had tipped off the Fertittas.

Though Wilson refused to believe it, Simpson suspected a Ranger might have been the source of the leak. "We had every reason to believe," the Galveston County lawyer later wrote, "that the Rangers were paid off. John Klevenhagen . . . was always openly hostile to me. Our actions were shutting off the flow of bribes and posed a threat to the corrupt status quo." Klevenhagen in turn suspected someone in the Attorney General's Office or the Galveston judicial system.

The Galveston operators had won the first hand, but on June 10 Wilson's minions sought injunctions in district court against forty-seven gambling joints, houses of prostitution, and saloons as places of "habitual public nuisance." Seventy-two hours later, Ranger Klevenhagen led raids on two places whose owners had ignored the order. "This is the key that fits all slot machines and opens all doors," the Ranger told journalists as he hefted a ten-pound sledgehammer.

Though the antigambling campaign got most of the news media attention, the Wilson-Ranger effort also brought an end to Galveston's famed Post Office Street red-light district. During one raid, Rangers had about forty prostitutes lined up on the well-known street.

The attorney general later recalled a conversation between a tall Ranger and a petite, well-groomed prostitute:

"What's a nice-looking little lady like you doing in a place like this?" the Ranger inquired with fatherly concern.

"That's exactly what I keep asking myself," she responded. "In Alaska, I was making $25 an hour. In Galveston, I'm making only $10."

On June 15, the Rangers and other officers struck a final, decisive blow against Galveston gaming. With information from someone willing to snitch against the Maceo family machine, Klevenhagen coordinated a raid on old Fort Travis. Built in 1896 on Bolivar Peninsula across the bay from Galveston, the coastal artillery installation had been abandoned after World War II. Instead of giant shells capable of sinking a ship miles at sea, its old concrete bunkers held Galveston's stockpile of gaming equipment. In a nearby long-boarded barrack the officers found other gambling paraphernalia. When Klevenhagen completed his report, he listed 350 slot machines, 150 pinball machines, and assorted roulette wheels and card tables as having been destroyed. The total estimated value came to $350,000.

"The raid hit the jackpot for the state of Texas," the Ranger told a reporter. With transporting gambling machines across state lines recently having become a federal crime, it would be hard for the Maceo interests to replace the destroyed inventory. The Rangers hit a few more places over the next couple of days, but for all practical purposes, the gambling era in Galveston had come to an end.[62]

In September, following the retirement of longtime Company A captain Hardy Purvis, Garrison promoted Klevenhagen as his replacement. The same month, Reader's Digest hit the newsstands with a laudatory four-page story condensed from an article in Argosy by Karl Detzer. The piece began with a version of the shopworn "one riot, one Ranger" legend first published nearly a half century earlier by Captain Bill McDonald's biographer. That story, Detzer wrote, "illustrates not only the awesome respect with which Texans regard their Rangers but also the supreme self-confidence of this small company of big men who help uphold the law and subdue the lawless in the Lone Star State." Noting that only fifty-one Rangers covered a state eight hundred miles wide, the author went on: "That is enough. If they are not the best police in the world, as Texans claim, they surely rank near the top."[63] Indeed, the Rangers had become more effective—and powerful—than ever before in their history.

In exchange for state, national, and even international adulation, Rangers willingly accepted the hard work, long hours, and low pay. Existing in a workaholic culture, they got by on nicotine, caffeine, adrenaline, and the calories from an occasional quick meal. No one left the Rangers unless they retired or died. Only in his midforties, the chain-smoking, ulcer-suffering Captain Klevenhagen would be dead of a heart attack in little more than a year.[64] Despite the job expectations that had to be met, Garrison always had a list of names of other officers who wanted to be Rangers. As the *Reader's Digest* article pointed out, "There is no immediate prospect of enlargement of the force." Asked if the Rangers could use more men, Captain Crowder replied, "Well, there are times when we might use two or three more."

Based on recommendations submitted to the legislature by the Texas Research League, the DPS beginning on September 1, 1957, underwent the most extensive reorganization in its twenty-two-year history. The commission divided the department into six regional commands, each headed by a Highway Patrol major. All DPS officers in a region, including Rangers, would report to the major. These regional commanders answered to Assistant Director Joe Fletcher and, ultimately, Garrison. "This new framework within our ranks will serve to more closely coordinate our varying activities and will produce greater efficiency in state police functions," Garrison explained in the summer edition of the *DPS Chaparral*. For the first time since the creation of the agency, Rangers would not be under the direct command of the colonel. In addition, the reorganization relocated three Ranger captains—Allee, Gully Cowsert, and Clint Peoples. Allee had to move to Corpus Christi from Carrizo Springs, Cowsert got uprooted from Junction to Midland, and Peoples got sent from Austin to Waco to convert the old Headquarters Company into a newly designated Company F. Two Ranger sergeants and ten privates also got new stations, though two of the privates had just been promoted from the Highway Patrol.

Rangers did not like the idea of reporting to someone in uniform and neither did quite a few legislators, most law enforcement officials, and the news media. The matter came to a head that winter, when Major Walter J. Elliott in Waco told Captain Peoples that he intended to assign Rangers to patrol the highways in marked cars during the Operation Motorcide campaign, an enhanced enforcement effort coupled with a public information endeavor intended to reduce traffic fatalities during a holiday period. "Chief, I like you very much," Peoples later said he told the major, "but as long as there is breath in my body I'll not assign a Ranger to a patrol car to work traffic."[65]

That winter, after considerable behind-the-scenes politicking on the part of Peoples, the Public Safety Commission reversed its position on Ranger captains reporting to regional commanders. Garrison sent a message over the department's teletype system saying that effective January 1, 1958, "Ranger Captains and those under their command will be responsible to the director." The regional command structure remained, but the relative autonomy of the Rangers would stand. Peoples said Garrison later admitted to him the temporary placing of Rangers under uniformed command had been "one bad mistake."[66]

The Rangers' traditional chain of command secure, another Texas institution, the University of Texas, published a book by Americo Paredes detailing how many of the state's Mexicans viewed the Rangers. The author, a UT professor who specialized in the folklore of the border, had started with the intention of studying *corridos* or Mexican folk songs. The project evolved into a book on Gregorio Cortez, the fugitive trailed by Rangers and other officers across South Texas more than a half century before.

But *"With His Pistol in His Hand"*—a title taken from the *corrido* about Cortez—amounted to more than good storytelling. The book called into question the validity of the Ranger myth. Paredes wrote:

> If all the books written about the Rangers were put one on top of the other, the resulting pile would be almost as tall as some of the tales that they contain. The Rangers have been pictured as fearless, almost super-human breeds of men, capable of incredible feats. . . . Evildoers, especially Mexican ones, were said to quail at the mere mention of the name.[67]

The folklorist went on to list the English translation of sayings and anecdotes demonstrating what many border Mexicans thought of the men they called the *rinches*. The Mexican beliefs Paredes set forth ranged from the view that Rangers always carried a rusty pistol to toss on the ground next to a just-killed Mexican to support a claim of self-defense to a suspicion that Rangers always exaggerated the number of men they killed in the line of duty, especially Mexicans.

"I do not claim for these little tidbits the documented authenticity that Ranger historians claim for their stories," Paredes wrote. "What we have here," he continued, "is frankly partisan and exaggerated without a doubt, but it does throw some light on Mexican attitudes toward the Ranger which many Texans may scarcely suspect. And it may be that these attitudes are not without some basis in fact." Paredes concluded:

> The Rangers and those who imitated their methods undoubtedly exacerbated the cultural conflict on the Border rather than allayed it. . . . Terror cowed the more inoffensive Mexican, but it also added to the roll of bandits and raiders many high-spirited individuals who would have otherwise remained peaceful and useful citizens.[68]

Tobacco-chewing Ranger Zeno Smith proved false the component of the Hollywood-nurtured Ranger myth that only the good guys wore white hats. He only wore black hats. The San Antonio–based Ranger, who would have been much more comfortable kicking in the door at a gambling joint, traveled to Washington to testify before Arkansas senator John McClellan's racketeering committee on November 17, 1958. The committee heard excerpts from a tape Smith had made three years before allegedly of Buck (Curly) Owens of Odessa and Raymond C. Shafer, business agent for Teamsters Local 657 in San Antonio, discussing how Owens stole dynamite to bomb nonunion trucks.

"The West still is wild and wooly, thanks to the Teamsters Union," wrote the Washington *Evening Star* reporter who covered the hearing. "It's not that President James R. Hoffa has set up an endowment to preserve quaint customs. Rough stuff is just incidental to the business of unionizing reluctant truckers in Texas."[69]

The journalist concluded: "A few little atmospheric touches at the hearing salvaged some of the flavor of the old West. Mr. Owens, for example, drawled almost unintelligibly. . . . Zeno Smith . . . who said he talked Mr. Owens into reforming, did even better. . . . He wore fancy-tooled boots and kept his badge pinned to his shirt—under the jacket of a drab business suit."

The D.C. news media had fun with its "Ranger Smith goes to

Washington" story, but Smith received several letters of commendation from senators for his work on the case.[70]

Stealing History

In doing their work, the Rangers occasionally cut the back trail of their own past. That happened on a sticky summer Sunday in the East Texas town of Huntsville, headquarters of the Texas prison system and the final home of Sam Houston, who died there in 1863. The renowned Texan's home had been restored during the Texas Centennial. Nearby, again in the 1930s, the state had constructed a museum to tell Houston's story to future generations of Texans.

Around 4:00 a.m. on June 28, 1959, two burglars broke into the red-brick museum. Uninterested in the pocket change donated by visitors the previous day, the thieves had come to steal a part of Texas's past. After the break-in's discovery, an inventory revealed that thirty-one antique firearms, including five guns that had belonged to Houston, could not be accounted for. Among the missing firearms were the general's personal pistols, their butt plates engraved: "General Sam Houston from Samuel Colt."

Certain that whoever had stolen the artifacts had long since left town, the Huntsville police chief and the Walker County sheriff requested help from local Ranger Mart Jones. Jones, in turn, asked Captain Eddie Oliver in Houston—Klevenhagen's successor—for assistance. The captain dispatched Ranger Ed Gooding to lend a hand in the investigation.

The Rangers agreed with the local officers that the burglary did not have the earmarks of any local crook. The thieves obviously knew they had no chance of turning any profit from their crime anywhere around Huntsville. The Rangers put together a detailed list of the missing firearms with the help of an elderly gunsmith in Dallas who had done work on the weapons, and distributed it to gun dealers across the Southwest.

Two antique dealers in Dallas recalled having been approached by two young men trying to sell old guns. Luckily, one of the dealers had jotted down the plate number of the car the men left in just in case. After learning of the burglary in Huntsville, the dealer contacted Company B's Captain Banks. Checking the registration, Banks found that the owner of the vehicle had an address in Mesquite, a Dallas suburb. The car owner turned out to be a preacher who told Banks that his twenty-two-year-old son drove the car in question. The last time the preacher saw his son, he said, the son said he intended to visit an aunt in Dallas. The aunt told the Ranger that her nephew and a friend had gone to visit his grandmother in Daingerfield.

Banks passed that information along to the sheriff of Morris County, who arrested the two young men on July 1. They quickly owned up to having stolen the guns and told the sheriff where the historic weapons could be found. The sheriff then handed the matter back to the Rangers, notifying Red Arnold in Mount Pleasant. Arnold called Gooding, who went from Houston to Huntsville to pick up Ranger Jones. From there they drove to Mount Pleasant, where Arnold had the young men in the county jail. The pair led the Rangers to a spot along the Sulphur River and showed them where they had hidden the stolen firearms.[71]

About the time Rangers saved Sam Houston's guns for posterity, former adjutant general W. W. Sterling, now in his late sixties, sat in an air-conditioned office in South Texas putting the finishing touches on his memoir. The owners of the McGill Ranch had graciously offered Sterling space in their mission-style headquarters, a building in downtown Alice somewhat reminiscent of the Alamo.

"Second only to the Alamo," Sterling wrote in his preface, "the Texas Ranger is the best known symbol of the Lone Star State."

Though the tall, lanky Sterling perfectly fit the Ranger image, one thing separated him from most Rangers of his generation—a college education. He spent two years in the corps at Texas A&M University and earned more college credit in Oklahoma. He never graduated, but he liked to read and could wrangle words on paper almost as well as he could work cattle astride a good horse.

His intent had not been to write a history of the Rangers, he explained, but a "Ranger's eye view of the Service" aimed at dealing "with aspects that cannot be fathomed by hearsay or research." He would put on paper "some of the interesting incidents that have happened during my lifetime, plus others recounted to me by actual participants in those stirring events." In addition to telling stories, Sterling saw his book as "a commander's consideration of the organization, which includes administrative and political phases." Still sore at the Fergusons after nearly three decades, the former adjutant general said he also intended to warn "of the sinister influences that destroy [the Ranger's] usefulness."[72]

Privately published, the 524-page book could have used a crisper edit and lacked an index, but though he exaggerated some things and glossed over others, the old Ranger did as good a job as anyone had ever done in capturing the essence of the Rangers. Sterling wrote:

> Take two men of equal size and arm them with identical weapons. Call one . . . a deputy sheriff and the other a Ranger. Send each . . . out to stop a mob or quell a riot. The crowd will resist the deputy, but will submit to the authority of the Ranger. There is . . . something in the name "Ranger" that makes the wildest cowboy become com-pletely dedicated to his duty the moment he takes the oath of office. He needs no blowing of bugles or flying of flags to make him carry on. He might be out in the chaparral far away from doctors or ambu-lances and if wounded he would probably, as one old Ranger put it, "lie out there and sour." Nobody would know but he and God, yet he will not flinch or shirk his responsibility.
>
> Any Ranger commander who fails to make full use of these tra-ditions is throwing away a large portion of his efficiency, for with-out an esprit de corps and a heart, the Service becomes a souless [sic] robot.[73]

No higher-ranking former Ranger had ever told his story in detail. The book is not without some subtle self-aggrandizement and is shot through with personal opinion, but *Trails and Trials of the Texas Rangers* made a significant contribution to Ranger history. "Bill has lived the life so many have tried unsuccessfully to write about," R. Henderson Shuffler said in reviewing the book for the Houston *Chroni-cle*. "When he tells it you can see at a glance you have come upon the genuine article." The back of the book's dust jacket said: "General Ster-ling will continue writing . . . stories of Rangers, cattlemen, and the border people." Death, unfortunately, cut short those plans. He died in Corpus Christi the day before his sixty-ninth birthday, only a few months after his book came out.[74]

As the decade ended, Garrison and his fifty-two Rangers (the legislature had just given him one more Ranger slot) stood at the height of their power in Texas, the cumulative effect of their mystique, their accepted reputation for toughness, and their usually successful results on high-profile cases. The days of mysterious mass graves along the border and tough-love town taming had ended, but the Rangers wielded near absolute authority, especially along the Rio Grande and in rural areas across the state. Since the days of the Frontier Battalion, they had been able to get away with bending the law while enforcing it. Big-city police chiefs and the sheriffs of the larger counties had considerable clout themselves, but even they called on the Rangers when they needed help.

Early in the decade, when a state representative had deigned to suggest that the Rangers should be relegated to the history books, no one took him seriously. In the 1960s, attitudes changed.

10

Feet of Clay

To San Antonio sculptress Waldine Tauch—and just about anyone else who saw him—Company B captain Jay Banks personified the Texas Rangers. Tauch chose the six-foot four-inch Dallas-based captain as the model for a larger-than-life bronze of a Texas Ranger she had been retained by the Dallas Historical Commission to produce as a piece of public art. Banks spent two weeks at Tauch's San Antonio studio while the well-known Texas artist, a protégé of Texas sculptor Pompeo Coppini, took his measurements, photographed him, and did some preliminary clay work. To help her assure authenticity, the captain loaned Tauch one of his hats, a spare pair of boots, and an ornately tooled double-rig leather holster with guns.

Colonel Garrison had been happy to oblige the request for Banks's time, provided that the Ranger depicted in the statue not have his hand on his pistol. Ever conscious of image, the DPS director wanted the bronze to demonstrate a Ranger's willingness to let a criminal draw first. At a cost of $15,683, Tauch completed the work in 1958.

"He is exactly my idea of what a Ranger ought to look like," the sixty-four-year-old artist said of Banks. "It's hard work," the captain told a reporter after completing his unusual assignment, "but it did me some good, posing for the statue. Until I did, I always thought models were sissies."[1]

Garrison certainly did not think that, but the DPS director had become convinced that the popular captain had feet of clay. On March 2, 1960, Texas Independence Day, the Ranger so recently immortalized in bronze resigned. Garrison had allowed him that option in lieu of being fired. Given Banks's popularity, the forced resignation touched off a brief controversy similar to the tiff over Tom Hickman's dismissal as senior Ranger captain a quarter century earlier. Ironically, Banks lost his job over the same thing that had cost Hickman his status as senior captain: an allegation that he looked the other way on gambling in Tarrant County. Despite headlines of a possible legislative investigation, the forty-seven-year-old Banks did not get his job back.

Under Garrison, Rangers could get by with excesses like running an organized-crime figure out of the state or slapping an annoying defense attorney but not with breaking Garrison's standards. When Banks hinted to a reporter that his resignation had to do with a difference in opinion over policy, Garrison issued a statement to set the record straight: "There has been no squabble and there has been no difference on any policy matter. Banks' dismissal was ordered solely because of his failure to carry out specified orders." Those orders, the director said, had been to close "certain gambling establishments . . . operating in the Fort Worth area."[2]

"Modern-day Texas Rangers zealously protect the hard-won reputation of decades," an article in the Sunday newspaper supplement *Family Weekly* explained not long after Banks's departure. As an example, the article cited a case in the 1950s where an unnamed Ranger went to Brazil after a murderer wanted in Dallas. The South American nation had no extradition treaty with the United States, but the Brazilian government agreed to cooperate in this particular instance. Authorities declared the Texas fugitive an undesirable alien and ordered him expelled. A Ranger had arrived via ship to arrest the man when Brazilian authorities took him on board. The prisoner, however, made friends with a crew member who released him at the next port of call. When the Ranger reported the escape to Austin, Garrison wired back: "Don't come back unless he's with you." The Ranger prevailed on local military police for assistance and accompanied them into the jungle in search of the man. The next communication to Austin from the Ranger read: "Apprehension made. Returning with prisoner."

The older Garrison got, the more outspoken he became about the Rangers.

"Just tell anybody who thinks the Rangers are dead to come down here and start something—we'll give them a lively reception," the DPS director told the *Family Weekly* writer.[3]

In February 1961, irony compounded irony. Fired from the Rangers in 1935, Tom Hickman became chairman of the Public Safety Commission. "Captain Tom Hickman is a living symbol of law enforcement in Texas," commission member C. T. McLaughlin of Snyder said after nominating Hickman as chairman. "His colorful career as a peace officer covers a span of more than fifty years during which Texas has seen some of its most turbulent periods. We consider him one of the outstanding Texas Rangers of all time."

The old Ranger turned seventy-five on February 21, an occasion celebrated by his many friends with a big barbecue at his Cooke County ranch outside Gainesville in North Texas. As the festivities wound down, Hickman told a reporter, "The Rangers of today are better than those of my day. They are better trained and better equipped."

Still tall and square-shouldered, but sporting a white goatee that made him look a little like Buffalo Bill, Hickman reflected on his Ranger days. "We operated on a shoestring," he called. "The state didn't even furnish us a car." Asked if he felt Texas still needed a Ranger service, Hickman replied, "As long as there are men who break the law, there is a need for officers like the Texas Rangers to uphold it."[4]

On April 30 Dallas civic leaders gathered in the lobby of Love Field, Dallas's busy airport, for the dedication of the statue the deposed Banks had modeled for. A gift of wealthy restaurateur Earle Wyatt and his wife to the City of Dallas, the bronze stood eight feet two inches on a three-foot-nine-inch-high red granite pedestal. Engraved beneath the statue were the words: "Texas Ranger of 1960 One Riot–One Ranger." In a short written statement prepared for the news media, Garrison said, " 'One Riot–One Ranger' is one of those almost legendary utterances which is so deeply rooted in the tradition of the Texas Rangers that its origin is difficult to trace." After reciting the Bill McDonald story, the director continued, "Whether or not this was the real origin . . . does not matter. It is fully in keeping with the creed of the Texas Rangers not only of yesteryear, but of today." Garrison made no mention of Captain Banks, who had been hired by the West Texas city of Big Spring as its police chief.[5]

In addition to his J. Edgar Hoover–like control over the Rangers, Garrison still got just about anything he wanted from the legislature. When the next budget went into effect September 1, 1961, the DPS had money to increase the size of the Ranger force to sixty-two men. The colonel swore in ten new Rangers on October 8, the largest expansion of the service since the merger of the Rangers and the Highway Patrol in 1935.[6]

When a new man made Ranger, Garrison delivered a short, standard speech along with the Ranger badge. The colonel would say that he and Texas expected a lot of a Ranger. The hours would be long and the work often solitary. Each Ranger had a tradition more powerful than a .45 to uphold. A Ranger showing weakness could destroy the effectiveness of the entire service. Failure to uphold that tradition meant giving up the badge.[7]

"You Don't Back out of Situations."

That winter, a veteran Ranger, not one of the new men, in Garrison's judgment failed to measure up. The precipitating incident began shortly before 3:00 p.m. on January 17, 1962.

Talking on the telephone, W. B. Walt, vice president of the First National Bank of Cushing, looked up in surprise when one of his customers walked unannounced into Walt's office just before the regular closing time. The woman looked terrified and he quickly realized why: a man stood behind her with a pistol in his hand. The gunman motioned for Walt to finish his conversation.

"Get the money. I want all of it," the man said when Walt got off the phone.

Marching the banker and the customer into the lobby, the gunman ordered Mrs. J. S. Avery, the cashier, to pull down the shades, a standard practice at closing time. Next he demanded all the money in the vault and the teller drawers. With a pillowcase full of cash, he herded everyone into the vault and swung the heavy metal door shut. Luckily for Walt and the others, the robber could not get the door locked.

As soon as the bank president thought the robber had left, he opened the vault and telephoned the Nacogdoches County Sheriff's Department.

Hearing of the holdup, Ranger Tully Seay of San Augustine hit the road in search of the robber. On State Highway 21 about twelve miles west of town the Ranger spotted a car similar to the one witnesses had seen speeding away from the bank after the robbery.

Seay, a Ranger for twelve years, turned his unmarked state car around, caught up with the vehicle, and forced it off the road. As the slim fifty-five-year-old Ranger walked toward the car, not knowing for sure if he had stopped the right vehicle, the driver jumped out and pointed a pistol at him. Seay's weapon still rested in its hand-carved leather holster. When the robber told Seay to hand over his sidearm, the Ranger complied.

Ordering Seay into the front seat, he drove off, steering with his right hand and keeping the pistol trained on the Ranger with his left. Seay smelled liquor on the man's breath. The bank robber sped through the piney woods of East Texas. At the small community of Broaddus he stopped and bought gas. The Ranger made no effort to escape or reveal his status as a hostage. He did do plenty of talking, hoping he could convince the robber to give up.

The car's tank full, the robber drove through Woodville and Kountze before reaching Beaumont, 126 miles and four hours from the scene of the robbery. The man behind the wheel kept his gun pointed at the Ranger throughout the drive, but he let Seay keep talking. By the time they hit the outskirts of Beaumont, Seay had persuaded the robber he at least needed to let him go.

Stopping on the freeway near the DPS's Beaumont office, the robber released the Ranger. After removing the cartridges, the robber even gave Seay his revolver back. At 7:45 p.m., Seay showed up at the DPS building. He went straight to the radio room to put out a detailed description of the robber and his vehicle.

Less than an hour later, at 8:47 p.m., officers took the thirty-six-year-old robber into custody at a roadblock in Chambers County. They found the $31,699 he had taken from the bank still in the pillowcase.

News accounts of the bank robbery and kidnapping said Ranger Seay appeared calm after his ordeal but noted that the Ranger refused to allow his photograph to be taken. Despite his outer composure, Seay must have realized that in opting to stay alive, even though he had talked his way out of a tight fix, he had committed career suicide.

The media played the story straight, not overemphasizing the capture of the hapless Ranger. Still, the embarrassment to the Rangers appeared on page one of every major newspaper: an experienced Texas Ranger had been kidnapped by a drunk bank robber. Two days after the robbery-kidnapping, in addition to a state armed robbery charge Marcus E. Carter of Houston faced two counts in U.S. District Court, bank robbery and kidnapping.[8]

Seay's humiliation at the hands of a bank robber disgusted Garrison, but the colonel felt somewhat better on January 22 when Rangers elsewhere in the state arrested James Hugh Leggett, a thirty-three-year-old ex-con with a record dating back to 1947. In a three-page press release issued two days later, the DPS said the Ranger investigation leading to Leggett's arrest would solve more than two hundred burglaries in seventy-five counties, "one of the most extensive burglary and safecracking operations in modern-day Texas history." Businesses victimized by the gang over a two-year period included "automobile dealers, feed stores, packing plants, milk companies, lumber yards, grocery stores, office buildings, lending establishments, and beauty colleges." Though DPS public information officer Bill Carter wrote it, a quote attributed to Garrison reflected the department's sensitivity to the egos of other law enforcement officers:

> This is another typical example of the efficiency of our system of local and state law enforcement—a case where officers at every level of government worked hand in hand in a coordinated effort to protect the people of Texas against organized lawlessness. This massive burglary and safe-cracking operation could not have been broken up without the splendid cooperation of all officers at all levels.

Though politic, Garrison had little tolerance for failure. On January 31, the colonel fired Ranger Seay for losing his weapon to a bank robber. The Associated Press carried the story statewide. "A Ranger never retreats," Garrison had once said. "If it is necessary to die in his tracks, a Ranger dies in his tracks. People know that, and consequently, he seldom has to die in his tracks."[9] In Garrison's eyes, by letting the bank robber get the best of him Seay had retreated, discrediting Garrison's carefully cultivated Ranger image. Throughout the 1950s, his philosophy had paid off well. Now the people of Texas realized Rangers were merely human, not infallible.

"There's an unwritten code in the Rangers," Garrison later told a reporter. "You don't back out of situations. If you do, you're through."[10]

Shameful as Garrison found the Seay incident, the story did not stay alive long. Texas reporters had plenty of other things to write about, particularly beginning in February, when the Rangers again became involved in the East Texas oil field following the discovery of a new form of criminal enterprise.

The problem became evident during a murder trial in Henderson. Though J. D. Matthews, an undercover investigator for Houston-based Humble Oil Company, admitted he had shot and killed a man, he claimed it happened accidentally during a drunken fight. The jury agreed and found Matthews not guilty, but testimony in the case had exposed the nature of his work, probing the theft of oil through slant drilling. With Rangers as escorts, inspectors from the state railroad commission began testing wells. Before the investigation ended, all but two of the Rangers had done duty in East Texas. Before the state intervention, as many as three hundred illegal slant-hole wells had been siphoning crude from its rightful owners.

"We checked any and every well the investigators wanted to check," Ranger Glenn Elliott recalled, "all without any serious trouble. . . . The final result: We pretty well stopped slant-holing."[11]

It had not been solely a Ranger effort, however. A federal grand jury returned 109 indictments against two defendants alleging transportation of hot oil and filing false statements. In addition, the state attorney general's office filed dozens of civil suits in connection with the slant-hole scandal. The agency also handed evidence its investigators had collected to district attorneys in Upshur, Wood, Rusk, and Gregg counties. By December 11, 1962, a total of 358 criminal indictments had been returned against sixty-two persons.[12]

Reflective of the pro-American, anticommunist times, in June a Dallas Ford dealer bought an ad in the Dallas *Morning News* using the Rangers for advertising and political purposes. The final paragraph of the eight-paragraph ad read: "No people could have lived with such a glorious tradition without some of the character of the Ranger having rubbed off on them. That may be why the Texan today is an individual, 'a man standing alone between a society and its enemies.' "[13]

That October, the Rangers got new badges, "the tradition-steeped Mexican silver badges worn by their predecessors in frontier days." As Garrison explained in a news release issued by the department, the new badge was a "replica of the badge which old-time rangers carved out of Mexican silver pieces when Texas became a state and their duties changed from military to law enforcement." Not all Rangers wore such badges in the early days, but photographic evidence dating to the 1880s shows that some Frontier Battalion men pinned what came to be called the star-in-a-wheel to their chests. As a memorial to his late father, Captain Hardy B. Purvis, Ranger Hardy L. Purvis and his mother donated to the DPS a supply of Mexican *cinco peso* coins made of .900 pure Cuauhtemoc silver. The gift also included the cost of having the coins cut and stamped into a star-in-a-wheel badge for each of the sixty-two Rangers.[14]

Early the following year, 1963, Stan Redding, longtime police reporter for the Houston *Chronicle,* wrote a lengthy article on the modern Rangers. The story offered significant insight on Garrison's role in shaping the service. "People are always asking me what a Ranger is like," the colonel told Redding. The director went on:

> They mostly have a notion that he's a big-hatted, belted and spurred fellow wading through a cloud of pistol smoke with a gun in each hand. You know what I tell them? I tell them the truth. The Texas Ranger is a family man, a good neighbor, humble, kindly and conscientious. He's a man of integrity, fearless and courageous. He's tough when the occasion demands, able to handle any situation and never retreat. He sits tall in the saddle and casts a long shadow. I know, I raise 'em.

Redding went on to assure readers that Garrison had not been facetious in saying he raised Rangers: "Most of the 62 members of the famed law enforcement group are drawn from the state highway patrol, of which Garrison was a member when it was organized in 1930, and which he has directed since 1938." Garrison, then in his early sixties, knew he would not be director of the DPS and chief of the Texas Rangers forever. But after running the agency for a quarter century, longer than anyone else, he believed the character type he had developed would endure. "Put him under a microscope," Garrison said of his Rangers:

> and he's the same breed of man that served with McCulloch. And he's the same breed of man that will wear the Ranger badge 20 years, 30 years, 100 years from now. The equipment will change, of course. No one can foresee the change in weapons, the technical advances in criminal detection, the change in means of transportation, even clothing styles. But one thing is certain. The individual will be the same.[15]

Ranger captains could make recommendations, but Garrison handpicked the men who would serve as Rangers and, as he had done with Seay and Banks, either fired or requested a resignation of anyone who did not fit his definition of a Texas Ranger. It did not happen often.

A month after Redding's profile on the Rangers, a New York publishing house brought out a paperback original that looked like a factual history of the Rangers, *The Texas Rangers: A Concise History of the Most Colorful Law Enforcement Group in the Frontier West*. While it used correct dates and names, the book's dialogue came from the imagination of a longtime pulp Western writer in Pennsylvania, Joseph Chadwick. His book clearly tracked Webb's history, with an epilogue that would have done for a DPS recruitment brochure: "The force is no longer made up of flamboyant characters and colorful personalities," he wrote. Still, "The Rangers of today are probably every bit as heroic as Jack Hays, L.N.[sic] McNelly, Bill McDonald, Jim Gillett, and scores of others who made Ranger history and helped shape Texas' destiny with blazing guns. But they go about performing their duties in a quiet, disciplined way. And almost certainly they are as efficient as the now legendary figures who preceded them."[16]

CRYSTAL CITY

Chadwick's observation that the Rangers no longer had "flamboyant characters and colorful personalities" did not ring true, however. Cigar-chewing Captain A. Y. Allee, still running Company D in South Texas, had a face someone said looked like a baked potato. Those who knew him well said that look also fit his personality, soft on the inside, tough on the outside. Law-abiding South Texans respected him, the Rangers in his company revered him, and most lawbreakers either feared him or learned to. But as the civil rights movement gathered momentum across the nation, Mexican-Americans beginning to clamor for social, economic, and political equality saw Allee as a living symbol of the old order they wanted to tear down.

The first challenge came with a drive to get Mexican-Americans registered to vote. The effort grew into an ugly, nationally publicized situation that marked the beginning of the end of the Rangers' iron rule in South Texas. It happened in Crystal City, a town 116 miles southwest of San Antonio in the middle of the state's Winter Garden agricultural area. With 80 percent of the U.S. spinach crop grown nearby, the local chamber of commerce touted the Zavala County seat as the Spinach Capital of Texas. A ten-foot statue of Popeye, the cartoon character who drew his strength from a quickly opened can of the iron-rich vegetable, had stood in front of City Hall since 1937. But the Texas Rangers had been around much longer, and in Crystal City, in the eyes of the Anglo power structure, they stood a lot taller than Popeye.

Del Monte operated a large canning plant in the city and its workforce, almost entirely Mexican-American, carried union cards. In 1962, Teamster's Union organizers and members of the San Antonio–based Political Association of Spanish-speaking Organizations (PASO) began working to get Mexican-Americans in Crystal City to pay their $1.75 poll tax. Having some success in their voter registration campaign despite the best efforts of county officials, in February 1963 twenty-three Mexican-American residents organized a group they called the Citizens Committee for Better Government. The committee decided to try for a full takeover of Crystal City's government—they would run five candidates for city council. Still facing resistance from Anglo county officials, and threats that the Texas Rangers would be monitoring the collection of the tax, the voter registration drive continued through the early spring of 1963.

Captain Allee, headquartered in nearby Carrizo Springs, began spending more and more of his time in Crystal City, where his cousin, Tom Allee, served as a county commissioner. "In effect," PASO activist

Henry Munoz later recalled, "Allee put the town under martial law. If there was a traffic violation, Allee wrote the ticket. An unofficial curfew was established and Mexican-Americans walking alone at night were subject to verbal and physical abuse as well as to arrest on a variety of false charges."[17]

Jose Angel Gutierrez, a 1962 graduate of Crystal City High School who would go on to found the La Raza Unida Party, claimed Allee once slapped him so hard it knocked him down. "I fell down and he kicked me once," he later recalled. "That was all I was willing to take, so I ran back to my house."[18]

On Election Day, with Rangers patrolling the town to prevent violence, 97 percent of the now predominantly Mexican-American electorate marked a ballot. Following the final vote tally late that night, all five of the Mexican-American candidates had won election. The ballot box coup got international news media attention.[19]

At the first council meeting after the election, a reporter for the Laredo newspaper saw Sheriff C. L. Sweeten push newly elected mayor Juan Cornejo. The sheriff, Allee, and several Rangers attended the next meeting, on April 29. While reporters made no mention of Sweeten's conduct at this meeting, they reported that Allee carried the only key to the council chamber. Further, the captain held himself as the arbiter of the new council's actions.

"Wait a minute," Cornejo said at one point. "I'm the mayor and this is the city council. We decide this."

Biting down on his cigar, Allee ordered the mayor to sit down and shut up.

When Cornejo refused, the Ranger latched on to his lapel, pulled him into a side room, and shut the door. Sheriff Sweeten, Tom Allee, and City Manager James Dill also went into the room. Cornejo later alleged that the captain had slapped him and slammed him into the wall several times.

"You little Mexican son-of-a-bitch, don't you talk to me like that," Cornejo claimed the Ranger roared. "I'm the law around here." Later that night, someone telephoned Albert Fuentes, PASO state executive director, in San Antonio. Fuentes chartered an airplane to fly Cornejo to San Antonio the next morning. "I didn't want Cornejo killed, and that's where it was headed," he recalled.

The city manager told the San Antonio *Express* that Allee "didn't lay a hand" on Cornejo. Tom Allee said his Ranger cousin told the new mayor "in words he could understand" that he did not appreciate earlier comments Cornejo had made about him in the newspapers. The captain had a three-word comment: "He's a liar."[20] To *Express* journalist Sam Kendrick, Allee later offered:

> Hell, I didn't whip the mayor, it's just politics and I guess somebody put him up to accusing me of roughing him up. Sure we get a little rough sometimes, but if I'd banged Cornejo's head against the wall you wouldn't have seen him flying off to the papers right afterwards. He wouldn't have been able to.[21]

State attorney general Waggoner Carr had asked Garrison to look into Cornejo's allegations of heavy-handedness on the part of the sheriff and Allee. "No complaints have been made to me," Garrison said, virtually the same language he had used eleven years earlier when another of his Rangers had been fined for punching a defense attorney in a courthouse. "The only thing we are doing is keeping the peace. I know the peace has been kept."[22]

On May 6, a Houston labor attorney filed a federal lawsuit against Allee in the mayor's behalf seeking $15,000 in damages and a restraining order.

"We are in a state of fear and intimidation," Cornejo said in a telegram to Governor John Connally. "We need help."

From the governor's perspective, the Rangers were helping. "The Texas Rangers were sent to Crystal City for the sole purpose of maintaining law and order and to prevent violence," Connally responded. "Apparently their efforts have been successful . . . and they will remain as long as the situation warrants. Every effort will be made to insure that the elected officials may perform their duties. I urge your cooperation."[23]

Cornejo's lawsuit eventually got tossed out of court. The Zavala County commissioners court passed a resolution supporting Allee and his men as peacekeepers, and an eight-member delegation traveled to Austin to meet with Colonel Garrison to voice their support for the Rangers.

Though two members of the new Mexican-American council would be removed from office as unqualified because they did not own property, the other three, including Cornejo, served out their terms. But political in-fighting by the activists, coupled with continuing pressure from the Anglo establishment, kept the takeover from having much real effect. Even so, the day of the Rangers' unquestioned authority in South Texas had ended.[23]

The rise of Los Cinco Canidatos, as they came to be called, reigned as the biggest news story in Texas until November 22, when ex-marine Lee Harvey Oswald shot and killed President John F. Kennedy and wounded Governor Connally in downtown Dallas. The Rangers, however, played only a bit part in the investigation of the biggest murder case in Texas history.

On that Friday, Rangers Red Arnold and Glenn Elliott happened to be in Dallas with a couple of burglary suspects they needed to run on the polygraph. When one of the men confessed, the two Rangers took their prisoners to a restaurant about a mile from the DPS regional headquarters in Garland. As they ate lunch, word spread among the customers that the president had been shot. The two Rangers paid their check and raced back to the DPS office with their prisoners. They walked inside to find every telephone ringing. Arnold grabbed one phone, Elliott another, and they immediately recognized the person on the line as Colonel Garrison.

"I want to know what's going on in Dallas," the director said. "Keep this line open until I find out."

Elliott told the colonel that his sergeant and another Ranger were on their way to the Dallas Police Department to see if they could be of assistance. Two other Rangers, Bob Badgett and Ernest Daniels, had gone to Parkland Hospital to augment the wounded Governor Connally's security detail. Arnold and Elliott locked their prisoners in a small room and handled the telephones, relaying information to headquarters in Austin as it came in. Dallas homicide detectives, led by Captain Will Fritz, handled the bulk of the investigation, though the Rangers assisted in providing security throughout Governor Connally's hospital stay.[24]

The following spring, as older men do, Garrison began to think about his legacy, one thoroughly entwined with the overall Ranger legacy. On April 15, 1964, the colonel announced his acceptance of an offer by the Waco Chamber of Commerce to construct a $125,000 building on the Brazos River for use as a Ranger company headquarters and museum. Waco insurance man Jimmie LeBlond led the effort to raise the money. When completed, the building would be deeded to the City of Waco and be operated by the city's Parks and Recreation Department.[25] Though LeBlond had a big hand in the effort to build the Ranger headquarters and museum, Waco businessman, former mayor, and history buff Roger Conger also played a key part. Captain Peoples, stationed in Waco since the DPS reorganization in 1957, helped as well. Conger, the one most familiar with Republic of Texas–era Ranger activities in what would become Waco, came up with the idea of calling the contemplated facility Fort Fisher. That had been the name of the early-day Ranger post. The plans had been set out in a book published the year before, *A Proposal for the Construction of a Replica of Fort Fisher.*[26]

As Garrison and Peoples worked with Waco civic leaders to establish a Ranger museum, writers of Western fiction had begun to professionalize the straight-shooting mythical Ranger, anachronistically applying some of the well-publicized standards established by the DPS to old-time Rangers. Readers of Wade Everett's July 1964 paperback original, *Texas Ranger*, probably did not notice the historical inaccuracies, but they ruined the book for anyone who knew anything about the Rangers. In the book, for example, when Jim Temple decides to quit his job as a deputy sheriff and join the frontier-era Rangers, he is given a two-hour test "on Texas geography and the applicant's knowledge of cattle, horses, brands, homestead laws, laws of arrest and seizure, firearms, customs regulations."[27] Nothing like that had ever been required of a man aspiring to be a Ranger until the creation of the DPS. When Temple is picked as a Ranger, his captain tells him and two other recruits: "A Ranger, by reputation, rides like a Comanche, shoots like a Kentuckian and fears no man or beast. And I'll have no man in my company tarnish that tradition." Garrison's Rangers, a group of men that he and most other Texans believed to be smart, fearless, incorruptible, and bulletproof, had re-created an image even the mythical Rangers would have trouble living up to.

With the Ranger paperback for sale at practically every drugstore and newsstand in the country, in Texas a three-part series in the Houston *Post* raised for the first time since the early 1950s the perennial question of Ranger viability. "Though the Texas Rangers once worked

independently," reporter Douglas Freelander wrote in his first installment, "there are virtually no cases today that they have solved without
the help of other law enforcement agencies. And this raises a question:
Could the cases . . . have been solved without their help? And if they
could have been, are the Rangers really necessary, or are they simply a
holdover from an earlier day when they worked as free and unhampered
lawmen?"[28]

Training certainly separated the Rangers of the 1960s from their "free
and unhampered" predecessors. All six Ranger companies completed an
in-service training session at DPS headquarters in Austin on November
15, the first time in more than two decades that the entire service had
assembled in one place. They took a two-day course on recent U.S.
Supreme Court decisions dealing with evidence and criminal procedure.
Rangers also got an update on criminal modus operandi and did some
shooting on the DPS firing range.[29]

The Rangers had never had a uniform, at least not in the sense of a
shirt with shiny brass buttons and matching trousers with striped legs
like Highway Patrol troopers and most other police officers wore, but in
the 1940s and '50s Rangers wore khakis a lot and always seemed to favor tan. Officially, Rangers had only to wear good boots, a nice hat, and
whatever they needed to in between. But Ranger style changed for a
while when Ranger Frank Kemp noticed that East Texas oilmen favored
tan suits that seemed to stay fresh looking no matter the humidity.

Kemp went to a clothing store to get one for himself. He learned that
the Western-cut suit, called the Mesquite for its durability, belonged
to the product line of a company in Fort Worth. Advertisements
claimed the suit, a blend of 65 percent polyester fiber and 35 percent
combed cotton, still looked new after twenty-five dry cleanings.

Other Rangers followed Kemp's lead and soon word reached Garrison, still a hands-on manager, that several of the Rangers sported Texas-
made suits. The colonel liked his Rangers to always look like they had
just stepped out of a clothing store, so he contacted the manufacturer to
see if he could supply suits for all sixty-two Rangers. The company became the supplier for the Rangers and in the fall of 1964 reaped a publicity bonanza when the Dupont Company's magazine did a story on
the new Ranger fashion.[30]

In 1965 the University of Texas Press reissued Webb's thirty-year-old history of the Rangers. The reprint's new dust jacket reproduced a painting by El Paso artist Tom Lea, *Ranger Escort West of the Pecos*. Other than a ghost-written foreword by President Lyndon B. Johnson, the book contained nothing new on the Rangers. Webb had planned to revise his book, but that possibility died with him in a car crash in Hays County in March 1963. In reissuing the 1935 book, UT Press even let stand Webb's ending, in which he predicted that the Rangers would not survive the creation of the DPS. "At the time," Garrison recalled, "I told Dr. Webb the rangers would never be overshadowed and as long as there was a Texas, there would be Texas Rangers. . . . He just wouldn't believe me then. As the years passed, I always brought the subject up and asked if he [had] seen the death of the Rangers yet." Webb had visited him in 1959 and admitted his mistake, Garrison said. The well-respected historian told the director he intended to republish his book "and bring the Ranger story up to date." But with Webb dead, "The story of the modern-day rangers will have to be told by someone else," UT Press assistant director Eddie Weems told the Dallas *Morning News*.[31]

A major new component of that story would be the impact of the burgeoning civil rights movement, which gained considerable momentum with President Johnson's election in 1964 and Congress's passage of the Civil Rights Act. Labor trouble in the state also shaped the Rangers in the second half of the decade. Beginning in 1966, the two issues merged into a Stetson-sized headache and public relations problem for the Rangers.

"Viva la Huelga"

After the bandit troubles died out in the Rio Grande Valley, that part of Texas had settled into an easygoing way of life among the palm trees. The economy depended on agriculture and a growing tourism industry. Assuming no late freeze ruined the grapefruit crop, citrus growers ran profitable businesses in the subtropical southern tip of the state. Cheap labor drove the system. For forty-five cents an hour, Anglo landowners could hire Latino workers to handle the backbreaking job of picking their crops: vegetables, melons, citrus. With Mexico right across the Rio Grande, growers in the Valley had no shortage of willing labor, even at such low wages.

Then organizers with the AFL-CIO's United Farm Workers came to the Valley. If the field hands would join the union, the union men told the farmworkers, they would earn more money. The farmworkers began to unionize, a move viewed by landowners as a direct threat to their bottom line. Others saw it as one more step in the communist conspiracy to take over the world.

Organized by Eugene Nelson into the Independent Workers Association, Mexican-American farm workers in the Rio Grande Valley struck eight major citrus growers on June 1, 1966. Their principal demand: an hourly wage of $1.25. Seven days later, the IWA voted to join Cesar Chavez's National Farm Workers Association. The same day, the Starr County Sheriff's Department took Nelson into custody near the international bridge at Roma as he tried to talk Mexican National farmworkers into refusing to work. Nelson was released four hours later with no charges having been filed against him, but distrust and ill will grew far faster than a good grapefruit crop.[32]

In the rocky Texas Hill County, a man who grew cattle and exotic wildlife had another form of organization on his mind. Rancher Charles Schreiner III—everyone called him Charlie Three—owned a fifty-thousand-acre ranch near Mountain Home called the Y.O. His grandfather, a man who had ridden as a Ranger, had founded the ranch in 1880. Under Charlie Three's stewardship, the ranch had become one of the nation's most popular hunting resorts. But it remained a working ranch, and Schreiner had one of the largest Longhorn herds anywhere. He formed an association to promote the return of the fabled breed, and he had in mind a publicity scheme that would be both fun and a good marketing tool—a trail drive to Kansas.

Schreiner had inherited his grandfather's guns and Ranger commission and eventually began collecting guns once owned by other Rangers, along with Ranger memorabilia. In a way, Schreiner collected Rangers themselves. He always welcomed them on his ranch, individually or for company meetings. The year before, he had thrown a party for the Outdoor Writers of Texas, also inviting Governor Connally and Colonel Garrison, who showed up with an ornately engraved .45 on each hip. Ostensibly to protect the governor but mainly to visit with the newspaper and magazine writers and eat barbecue, a lot of Rangers also came to the ranch.

When Schreiner came up with the idea of driving one hundred Long-horns from San Antonio to Dodge City, Kansas, retracing a trail drive his grandfather had undertaken, he asked the Rangers for help with security. Two Rangers, Kerrville-based Ed Gooding and Dudley White, Jr. of Midland, landed the assignment. Other than taking care of some kids tossing firecrackers in the Longhorns' pen in San Antonio, handling security proved not much of a chore. Both Rangers got to do plenty of horseback work, however, pushing the herd.

The two Rangers took part in the drive with the department's blessing, though when they reached the Red River they had to leave their state cars behind and start using vacation time. Gooding stayed with the herd all the way to Kansas.[33]

While Schreiner commemorated the past and made headlines with a modern-day trail drive, the organizers of the Valley farmworkers staged their own publicity-generating procession. Starting on July 4, to chants of "Viva la huelga [Long live the strike!]," a hundred striking farmworkers and two thousand supporters began a march across the Valley. Along the way, some of them decided to keep going until they got to Austin, more than three hundred miles to the north. Aided by sympathetic labor organizations and various religious groups, the Huelgistas moved toward the capital in the heat of summer.

With news organizations covering the marchers' progress, Governor Connally, Lieutenant Governor Ben Barnes, and Attorney General Carr felt enough political heat to drive forty-five miles from Austin to meet the procession in New Braunfels on August 31. The governor made it clear he would not have met with the marchers when they arrived in Austin on Labor Day and would not call a special session of the legislature to consider including farmworkers in the state's minimum-wage law. The marchers went on to Austin for a noisy but peaceful rally outside the Capitol. The DPS monitored the marchers as they moved up from the Valley, but no one got arrested.[34]

Though Captain Allee kept him abreast of developments in the Valley, Colonel Garrison continued to devote some of his attention to the Ranger museum project. A few days after the marchers broke up and returned to South Texas, the DPS put out a press release appealing to "public-spirited Texans" for donations of artifacts for the planned museum.

"We are attempting to preserve for posterity . . . a top-flight collection of Ranger mementoes to symbolize the glorious tradition of the oldest police force on the North American continent with statewide jurisdiction," Garrison said. The release continued:

> We feel that this museum can provide an invaluable service for the State of Texas by commemorating for present and future generations the historic bravery of the Texas Rangers in preserving law and order and protecting the people of Texas from frontier days through the space age.[35]

On September 1, the DPS and the Rangers finally joined most of the rest of the world in moving to a five-day workweek. The Sheriff's Association of Texas magazine noted that Garrison said in making the change that "it is believed that the six-day week, inconsistent with work periods in almost all competitive businesses and industries, was a major deterrent to young men, particularly those with families, who would otherwise apply for jobs in the uniformed services." The department had 125 vacancies and would not start another training class until January 3, he said.[36]

While the Rangers now technically only had to work five days a week, the farmworkers continued their strike, still holding out for better wages. Later that fall, someone set fire to a Missouri Pacific railroad trestle in Starr County. The railroad and Starr County officials requested assistance from the Rangers, who arrested several strikers on November 9. The movement continued through the winter with occasional arrests, but the real trouble still lay ahead.

By May 1967, a record melon crop neared harvest. Melons being highly perishable, they had to be picked and on their way to market within a four- to six-week window. Understanding this, union leaders realized they had the leverage they needed to gain the concessions they had been seeking for more than a year. Rather than give in, farm operators began hiring Mexican Nationals to get in the crop. The union countered that if the "foreign strike breakers" could not be talked out of their work, its members would take steps to see that the melons did not get out of the Valley.

On May 11, Colonel Garrison telephoned Allee and told him to go to the Valley "to see what was going on."[37] Two days later, in Laredo, at a meeting of the Mexican American Joint Conference, activist Albert Pena, a county commissioner from San Antonio, offered a resolution criticizing the Rangers for their rough handling of picketers and union organizers in Starr County. The Rangers, the resolution said, provided "comic relief for the rest of the nation in their cowboy boots, large hats, and larger pistols." The situation continued to deteriorate over the next three weeks, with Rangers arresting strikers and allegedly using excessive force.

The most serious incident came May 26 when Rangers arrested a dozen picketers near the railroad right of way outside Mission. When a train approached under the watchful eyes of the Rangers, Reverend Ed Krueger lifted his camera and took a couple of pictures of the lawmen guarding the freight train. The minister had come to the Valley at the behest of the Texas Council of Churches.

"Krueger, you've been wanting to get arrested for a long time," the cleric later said Captain Allee told him. "I'm sick and tired of you."[38]

As the captain grabbed Krueger by his shirt, Mrs. Krueger snapped a picture of that. Seeing that, Ranger Jack Van Cleve moved in and arrested her, seizing her camera.[39]

When the state senate convened the following Monday, May 29, Senator Joe Bernal of San Antonio offered a resolution proposing a committee investigation of the Rangers' role in the Valley strike. The resolution going nowhere, Bernal decided to go to the Valley and take a San Antonio TV crew along with him. While the senator talked with a justice of the peace in Rio Grande City, Captain Allee arrived. As Bernal later recalled, the forty-five-minute meeting "began with polite fencing and degenerated into a shouting match" that concluded when the Ranger captain stormed off "in a blaze of anger."[40]

The following day, the senator and the captain met again, this time in Mission, where Allee's men had arrested more picketers. Their conversation even less cordial than before, at one point the captain said, "I never thought I'd live to see the day some senator would come down here" and become involved in a law enforcement situation. Bernal told Allee "he'd stick to being senator and Allee should stick to being a Ranger," at which the captain told Bernal "not to tell him what to stick to."[41] Not long after the broadcast of that confrontation, Garrison summoned the captain to Austin for a private talk. But as soon as he returned, Allee made headlines again.

Though in sympathy with the strikers, Reverend Krueger did not have a criminal background. Twenty-nine-year-old Magdaleno Dimas, arrested by Rangers the same day as the minister, did have a record. A member of the United Farm Workers Organizing Committee, Dimas had a rap sheet that showed arrests and convictions dating back to 1954, the most serious charge being murder without malice and assault to murder in Wilson County. He had spent three years in prison on that conviction and had done another year in the Starr County jail for aggravated assault. Though his arrest on May 26 had been on misdemeanor charges of secondary picketing and unlawful assembly, five days later Dimas brandished a rifle during a brief confrontation with a foreman for one of the large farms.[42]

Allee did not view an ex-con with a firearm as a healthy combination, especially during an already-volatile strike. On June 1, the captain and Ranger Tol Dawson arrested Dimas and Benito Rodriguez for allegedly displaying a deadly weapon and disturbing the peace. In the process, Dimas sustained a split scalp and a concussion. His reputation among most Anglo Texans unsullied by the Crystal City trouble four years earlier, Allee maintained he had used only "necessary force" in making the arrests. Colonel Garrison backed him up, issuing a statement the next day denying a pro-labor allegation of police brutality well displayed in the morning newspapers. Such claims, the DPS director said, amounted to a "common defense . . . of a professional criminal and agitator. The very simple answer to those critics of the Texas Rangers is this: if they will only obey the law, no Texas Ranger has or ever will molest them."[43]

Responding to a complaint letter from Senator Bernal, Governor Connally also defended the Rangers even as seven of Bernal's Senate colleagues labeled the Rangers "partisan police on the side of management." Liberal U.S. senator Ralph Yarborough of Texas also criticized the "misuse" of the Rangers in breaking a strike. "What would you think of the FBI if we had them patrolling a watermelon patch in a labor dispute?" the senator asked.

Newsweek devoted a two-page story to the situation, the focus being the tarnishing of the Ranger image:

To generations of Americans, the five-pointed star of the Texas Rangers glinted only upon the chest of a true paladin. Pure of heart and clear of eye, the Ranger seemed cast in the heroic mold of a hard-riding, straight-shooting peacekeeper welcomed by all decent law-abiding citizens west and east of the Pecos.

But, the news magazine continued, something new had been added to the myth: cries of "Ranger brutes!" "Down with Ranger storm troopers," and "Rangers go home!"

"Texas' finest," the *Newsweek* story went on, had even been accused of pushing little girls around. "No matter how splendid their legend, the Rangers suddenly had a bigger-than-life image problem on their hands."[44]

In the short term, the controversy wound down with the conclusion of the summer harvest in the Valley. From a legal perspective, following two days of testimony, on June 28 state district judge C. W. Laughlin signed a temporary injunction barring all picketing at La Casita Farms, one of the Valley's largest growers. Though stymied in state court, the farmworkers filed a federal class action suit against Allee and the Rangers.[45] The Rangers had weathered criticism before, but it seldom had been this strong.

"The history of the Texas Rangers has always been filled with minority people who for devious reasons have tried to abolish the Rangers," Garrison told a reporter. "I'm as confident as I sit in this chair that as long as there is a state of Texas there will be a Texas Ranger force— because the people of this state believe in law and order, right and justice." He viewed the charges of Ranger brutality to Valley farmworkers as "totally false and unfounded."[46]

Garrison may have been confident that the Rangers would survive this latest controversy, but he and other old-time lawmen grew increasingly exasperated over federal court decisions they saw as handcuffing their law enforcement powers. Pointing to the Fifth Amendment's protection against someone being "compelled in a criminal case to be a witness against himself," Chief Justice Earl Warren had written an opinion in 1966 in *Miranda v. Arizona* that profoundly changed the way the Rangers and other peace officers did their business. Warren held that persons in police custody had to be warned of their constitutional rights before they could be questioned. The warning, a process that soon came to be known as "Mirandizing," got so much publicity it crossed over into general public awareness.

"You have the right to remain silent," Rangers and other officers had to inform suspects. "Anything you say can and will be used against you in a court of law. You have the right to an attorney. If you cannot afford an attorney, one will be appointed for you."

Failure to warn a suspect of those rights could result in an otherwise solid case being tossed out by the court. Rangers of the old school found the court decision and other Supreme Court rulings they perceived as favorable to the criminal element particularly galling. Though the agency's general orders barred Rangers and other DPS officers from active participation in politics, few—if any—of the old-timers saw any problem with billboards in the Valley reading: "Impeach Earl Warren."[47]

For Garrison, the good old days grew increasingly fond in his memory. On December 12, 1967, the gaunt-faced DPS director, who had undergone radiation treatment for lung cancer that summer, turned the first spadeful of dirt and spoke at the groundbreaking ceremonies at Fort Fisher in Waco. The City of Waco had succeeded in putting together a funding package based largely on a matching federal Urban Renewal grant. After the outdoor ceremonies, a crowd of some four hundred honored Garrison during a luncheon at nearby Baylor University. Governor Connally gave the keynote address. Two honorary Rangers also attended the event, actor Chill Wills and *Gunsmoke* star James Arness.[48]

Though the Valley farmworkers' strike overshadowed the Rangers' other law enforcement activities that year, Rangers had investigated 3,163 cases leading to 1,227 felony arrests. Of one hundred homicides investigated, 84 percent of the cases were listed as developed, with 49 cited as completed (prosecuted).[49]

The Ranger service still had only sixty-two men, but the DPS had continued to grow overall. Now it had some thirty-four hundred employees. Knowing he could not be as much of a hands-on administrator as he had been, Garrison realized he needed to make some changes to the department's organizational chart. All the uniformed services would report to a new chief of traffic law enforcement who would answer to the director and assistant director. The nonuniformed services, including narcotics, intelligence, motor vehicle theft, and the Rangers, would be under the overall command of a new chief of criminal law enforcement.[50]

But Garrison would not get to see how well the new uniform-plainclothes bifurcation would work. He died at M. D. Anderson Hospital in Houston on May 7, 1968. He had been there since April 12 steadily losing his battle with cancer. Sixty-six years old, he had been DPS director for nearly thirty years.

Garrison's funeral two days later—attended by more than one thousand—did not take place at a church but in the lower-level auditorium of the DPS, the agency he had helped to build. "This was his pulpit, his secular church," Methodist bishop Kenneth W. Pope said, "and no one who knew him failed to realize he had a pretty good Gospel." The department suspended all but emergency activities that day, and Governor Connally ordered the state's flag flown at half staff. Following the 10:00 a.m. services, a DPS honor guard stood by at Garrison's burial in the State Cemetery.[51]

A young Ranger named Joaquin Jackson, one of the last Rangers who got his silver star pinned on the first time by Garrison, attended the funeral. "Garrison saved the Texas Rangers," Jackson later said. "He kept the Rangers from being overshadowed by the Highway Patrol and fading away like Webb had predicted."[52]

The Public Safety Commission quickly named fifty-one-year-old Assistant Director Wilson E. (Pat) Speir as the agency's acting director. Four months later, on September 16, 1968, they made it permanent. Speir had given up teaching to take a job in the Highway Patrol in 1941. After three years of military service during World War II, he returned to the DPS and rose steadily through the ranks, becoming the agency's number two administrator on June 1, 1962.[53] After Garrison became ill, Speir had handled much of the day-to-day aspects of running the agency. Garrison left Speir a well-run, generally highly regarded department, but his legacy as director also included the continuing friction between the Rangers and the Mexican-American community in South Texas.

Having drawn six million visitors to Texas, HemisFair—Texas's first international fair—ended its six-month run in San Antonio on October 6. Slum houses and historic structures alike had been cleared southeast of the Alamo to make way for the fairgrounds, a ninety-two-acre showplace dominated by the 750-foot Tower of the Americas.[54] If the new landmark symbolized modern Texas, so did an unprecedented proceeding in the city two months later.

In the Chapel Auditorium of Our Lady of the Lake College, the U.S. Commission on Civil Rights held public hearings on the role of the Rangers in the Valley fruit pickers strike. Ignoring the booing and name-calling, on Saturday, December 14, 1968, Captain Allee, flanked by his attorney and Colonel Speir, walked up on the auditorium's stage to take the witness stand. Allee even waved to the five hundred or so spectators but told the chairwoman, Mrs. Frankie M. Freeman, that he would not testify unless she quieted the protesters.

Despite reports that someone might try to assassinate him, Allee came to the hearing without his .45. Others in law enforcement had taken the rumors more seriously. Eight uniformed city police officers and ten plainclothes detectives stood by in the auditorium. Five of Allee's Rangers and their wives also sat in the audience.

The commissioners walked Allee through his role in the labor dispute and then began pressing him on specific allegations of excessive force, particularly the charges made by Reverend Krueger.

"I never hit Reverend Krueger one time and I never slapped him," Allee said. Nor had Rangers placed the cleric and another person dangerously near a passing train. "I'll be glad to take a lie detector test on that any time."

One of his men arrested Mrs. Krueger, the captain continued, because the Ranger thought she intended to hit Allee with her camera. When most of the audience reacted to that, Allee said, "I appreciate the spectators."[55]

In his testimony, Speir said, "It is not the policy of the Texas Rangers to repress law-abiding citizens of any national extraction or ethnic group. But we have no apology to make for enforcing the law."[56]

As Allee left the hearing, reporters crowded around the captain for a comment. "I don't have anything to say about the commission," Allee said. "They belong up in Washington and we belong in Texas."[57]

Texas had no shortage of its own problems that year. In East Texas, far from Allee's territory along the border, his colleagues faced another difficult labor issue. Twenty-five hundred members of the United Steelworkers of America union struck at the Lone Star Steel plant south of Daingerfield in Morris County on October 16, 1968. At least two Rangers, sometimes more, remained on hand throughout the 210-day walkout, a labor dispute marred by vandalism, assaults, dynamiting, and one murder.[58]

Though tensions ran high around the steel plant in East Texas as Rangers tried to keep strikers and strikebreakers apart, a more upbeat mood prevailed at the October 25, 1968, dedication of the new Texas Ranger Museum and Company F headquarters in Waco. Festivities had begun the night before with a law enforcement stag party at the Ridgewood Country Club. On hand were all six Ranger captains, the new colonel, representatives of all the federal law enforcement agencies, and the commander of the Mexican federal district police.

The following day, the opening ceremonies included the unveiling of a Ranger statue in the lobby of the museum. Paid for with money raised by friends of the late Colonel Garrison, the bronze had been cast from a sculpture by Bob Sumners of Glen Rose. The artist had carved on the base of the statue seven words Garrison had liked to use to describe the Rangers: "They are men who cannot be stampeded." In addition to the statue, the museum unveiled an oil of Garrison astride a horse, a piece of art commissioned by his friends and former colleagues "as a token of their love and affection for this great man."[59]

Three thousand people showed up for the dedication of the new museum, but it had become increasingly evident that not every Texan revered the Rangers or even those who had told their story. A young novelist named Larry McMurtry pulled his literary Winchester from the scabbard that year and cut loose on the late Dr. Webb and his book on the Rangers. "It is a flawed book," McMurtry said of *The Texas Rangers*, "but by no means uninteresting. . . . The flaw in the book is a flaw of attitude. Webb admired the Rangers inordinately, and as a consequence the book mixes homage with history in a manner one can only think sloppy. His own facts about the Rangers contradict again and again his characterization of them as 'quiet, deliberate, gentle' men."[60]

Captain Allee, for one, could not always be described as "quiet" or "gentle," though no one could argue his deliberateness. On April 3, 1969, the captain and his Ranger son, A. Y. Allee Jr., along with Rangers Dawson and Jackson, prevented ten prisoners from a breakout attempt at the Dimmit County Jail in Carrizo Springs. "It was all over in 30 or 40 minutes," Allee said later. "I just don't see how in the world some innocent person kept from getting shot. I thank God they didn't." Despite dozens of shots, only one prisoner sustained a minor wound.

Jackson, stationed in Uvalde, had made it to the jail in twenty-nine minutes. Ranger Dawson rushed to the scene from Del Rio. When Jackson arrived, he found his captain blasting away at the jail and the prisoners, who had armed themselves with guns kept in the sheriff's office beneath the lockup. Clouds of tear gas hung around the jail. "Cap had used up all the gas he had," Jackson said.

Now, with three Rangers backing him up, Allee shouted to the prisoners that they had until the count of ten to surrender. "One," he began. "Two . . . three . . . four." Then he started shooting.

"Captain, you didn't get to ten," Jackson pointed out. "Them sonuvbitches can't count," the captain snorted. When they got inside the jail, Allee shoved Jackson and Dawson aside as they headed up the stairs to get at the prisoners. As he ascended, Allee fired a World War II–era machine gun, the rounds ricocheting off the bars and barely missing the Rangers. When the shooting stopped, the smell of cordite hung in the air, but the prisoners had been corralled with no one getting hurt.[61]

Back in East Texas, the Lone Star Steel strike finally ended on May 11, 1969. The two Rangers most actively involved during the violent labor dispute had been Bob Mitchell, then stationed at Tyler, and Glenn Elliott, based in Longview. Both men had worked many days virtually around the clock. "Who won?" Elliott later pondered. "I have no idea, and I could not care less. That was not my job, nor should it have been. I do know two losers. One was the people of Texas. . . . The other was a young widow who had to raise two small children without their father."[62]

On June 21, 1969, a longtime Ranger gained promotion to the relatively new position of chief of criminal law enforcement. A Ranger since 1957, Jim Ray transferred from Lubbock, where he had been captain of Company C, to Austin. Now he and Joe E. Milner, chief of traffic law enforcement, ranked among the DPS's top four administrators.[63]

One of Chief Ray's first jobs was to deal with the loss of practically a whole company's worth of veteran rangers. Eight men with a total of 261 years' service retired on July 24, 1969, the largest number of mandatory retirements (due to age) in the history of the Rangers up to that time. At a retirement ceremony in Waco, Colonel Speir used the occasion to defend the service. His prepared remarks clearly reflect the

DPS's sensitivity to recent Ranger criticism. "Yet there are some who attack the Rangers," he said after praising the retirees for their outstanding records. Speir continued:

> Some of these critics allege that the Rangers are overzealous. Others say that they fail to do enough. There has always been a penalty attached to leadership, whether it be in the field of science, invention, business or law enforcement; whether it be a great idea, a great work of art, a product of service. Widespread recognition from the world at large is almost invariably accompanied by fierce attempts on the part of a jealous few to suppress, depreciate or destroy.[64]

Near the end of the following month, Speir swore in eight new Rangers to replace the retirees, including thirty-one-year-old Arturo Rodriquez Jr., the first Mexican-American Ranger since the creation of the DPS. A high school graduate and Marine Corps veteran, Rodriguez had worked for the Uvalde County Sheriff's Department and Uvalde police before joining the DPS as a Highway Patrolman in February 1967.

"It's too late," civil rights activist Dr. Hector Garcia said in reaction to Rodriguez's appointment. "As far as I'm concerned the Rangers deserve to be retired and serve only for ceremonial functions."

Rodriguez insisted that he got the job because Captain Allee gave him a good recommendation, not because of his ethnicity. "I wouldn't take it [the promotion to Ranger] if it was that way," he said. A friend of the new Ranger, a Del Rio man, told Los Angeles *Times* reporter Nicholas C. Chriss that Rodriguez had "drifted away from the people." Even worse, the "friend" continued, "He's been brainwashed by the Rangers. He's become too much law-and-order conscious. I think the people should have some say in law and order and the rangers don't believe this."

Chriss interviewed Allee by telephone. The crusty captain denied that Rodriguez's appointment had anything to do with his race. Allee said he just had never had a strong Mexican-American applicant before. "Besides," he continued, "I don't see any Japanese here. I don't see any Chinamen. We can't hire every doggone breed there is in the United States."

In Austin, Lieutenant Colonel Leo Gossett, the assistant DPS director, admitted Rodriguez had an unusual background for a Ranger. The new Ranger had only five and a half years' law enforcement experience, much less than the average new Ranger. But Gossett said the department needed Spanish-speaking personnel in South Texas.[65]

On September 6, Terrell County sheriff Bill Cooksey of Sanderson wrote a blistering letter to Colonel Speir complaining that politics, not qualifications, had entered into the Ranger selection process. Cooksey had served twelve years as a Highway Patrolman before being elected sheriff in 1961. One of sixty men interviewed on July 31 for eight positions to be filled on August 29, he had not been selected. The San Angelo *Standard-Times* turned the issue into a banner story on September 21.[66]

Senator Bernal said on September 20 that he would like to introduce legislation to abolish the Rangers but added, "I know such a bill wouldn't have a chance." Bernal at least would have the vote of one Senate colleague, A. R. "Babe" Schwartz. The Galveston Democrat, a member of the committee that looked into the Ranger handling of the Valley strike, said that to minorities "the Rangers mean oppression and force—boots and pot bellies and billy clubs." That image, he added, "is justified."

Asked by reporters for a response to the anti-Ranger remarks, Governor Preston Smith, Connally's successor, articulated the opinion of most Texans: "Texas without the Rangers would be like Texas without the Alamo."[67]

With only one month left in a decade that had already seen momentous change, the Rangers underwent another major command adjustment. At the request of Public Safety Commission Chairman Clifton W. Cassidy, the legislature had reconstituted the old title of senior captain effective September 1. All the field captains would report to whoever got the job. That person, in turn, would answer to Criminal Law Enforcement Chief Ray. Named to fill the new position effective November 1, 1969, was Company F captain Peoples, who would transfer from Waco to Austin.[68]

Like Hickman and Gonzaullas before him, Peoples never minded seeing his name in print. He soon claimed to be the first senior captain since John Salmon "RIP" Ford, but anyone bothering to look at the record would have realized he was only the first since 1937.

11

"Do the Needful"

Two days before Captain A. Y. Allee's sixty-fifth birthday, more than three hundred friends, colleagues, and family members gathered in Carrizo Springs to wish him well as he neared the end of his thirty-nine-year career in the Rangers.

Before a knife sank into the Texas-shaped chocolate cake, Colonel Speir presented Allee with the Ranger equivalent of a gold watch—a gold captain's badge. The badge and a commission signed by the Public Safety Commission represented his continuing authority as a special Texas Ranger. His law enforcement power no longer would be as broad as it had been, but he could still carry a gun and make arrests. The DPS, the director said, might well be calling on him for help.

"You won't have to call very loud for me to come running," the captain replied. But if no assignment seemed in the offing, he said he intended to "hunt and fish and by God let these women come out and bait my hook."

That drew laughter, but then his tone changed. His bushy eyebrows, as white as the carnation on his lapel, moved closer together as he looked into the crowd. Admitting that at first he had not taken particularly well to the notion of retirement, with the September 30, 1970, date nearly at hand he said, "I have no regrets whatsoever. . . . I would do the whole thing all over again."

Then he said something that would seem strange coming from a peace officer if someone did not know of Allee's controversial record: "In forty-four years [his total law enforcement career] I have never been convicted of anything or lost any lawsuit."[1]

Former Crystal City mayor Juan Cornejo agreed that Allee had never been convicted of anything or hit with a civil judgment and never would. "I know," he said. "I sued him myself." Referring to his allegation that Allee roughed him up after his election in 1963, Cornejo continued, "[He] came up to me and started pushing me around. Just like that. I hauled him into court but in the end it didn't do any good. The judge ruled there were no witnesses."[2]

Speir and Senior Captain Clint Peoples took the remarks of Ranger detractors in stride. "This criticism doesn't bother us one iota," Peoples told the New York *Times* a few months before Allee's retirement. "We're not on either side . . . we're only interested in people not getting hurt or their property destroyed."[3]

But as Cornejo's comments reflected, not everyone stood on the Rangers' side.

"The Rangers are a symbol of plutocracy, a symbol of Feudalism," said Roy Evans of the Texas AFL-CIO. "It's not just the Mexican-Americans, they've also intimidated a hell of a lot of Anglos. That's what they were set up for, to protect the ranchers."[4]

THE MOVEMENT

To some older Rangers, it seemed as if the America—and the Texas— they knew had unraveled. When President Richard M. Nixon sent troops into Cambodia, an apparent expansion of an already unpopular war in Vietnam, the nation saw a surge in protest demonstrations. On May 4, National Guard troops sent to Kent State University in Ohio opened fire, killing four students. As news of that tragedy spread, the nation seemed on the brink of revolution. The morning after Kent State, May 5, thousands of University of Texas students rallied on campus before marching toward the Capitol. Fearing a riot, the DPS ordered extra Rangers and Highway Patrol troopers to Austin. Peoples told his men,

"If any of those long-haired hippies get inside the Capitol, it better be over dead men."[5]

Despite the Ranger chief's unrealistic injunction, the protesters did get inside the state house, smashing some of the ornate building's antique glass doors. Contrary to the old "one riot, one Ranger" myth, it took tear gas and help from Austin police to get the antiwar protesters out of the big red granite building. No one fired any shots and no one died, but seventeen people suffered minor injuries.[6]

The Capitol takeover attempt and another demonstration three days later in which twenty-five thousand protesters marched in downtown Austin symbolized the times. The civil rights movement of the previous decade had been absorbed into the antiwar movement to become a general, if left-leaning, unrest. A growing drug culture and the women's liberation movement added to the mix. Americans burned their draft cards, their bras, and their flag in a polarization of society that the older, more conservative establishment generally perceived as only slightly less dangerous than the debate over slavery and states' rights more than a century before. Icons from the Capitol to the Texas Rangers, representative of what the New Left called the Establishment, came under attack figuratively and sometimes literally in a movement that had come to be called just that, the Movement. "In short," activist Susan Torian Olan recalled, "we believed we were on the eve of full-scale revolution."[7] So did many in local, state, and federal law enforcement. In their view, the Movement amounted to nothing less than a communist-inspired takeover attempt.

Nearly half the Ranger service gathered in Austin on May 22, 1971, to provide security during the dedication of the $18.6 million LBJ Library built on the University of Texas campus to house the papers of former president Johnson. President Nixon, Vice President Spiro Agnew, and numerous members of Congress had come to the Texas capital for the festivities. As war protesters massed at 26th and Red River streets while the speech making went on nearby, Rangers lined up across Red River to keep them from getting any closer to the library. Rangers ducked and dodged as long-haired protesters hurled human excrement and urine-filled bags in their direction.

"Boys, just do the needful," Company E captain Jim Riddell of Midland had told the Rangers from West Texas he had allotted to the library dedication in Austin. That one-sentence instruction gave the Rangers a lot of latitude. Among themselves they began picking targets in the event the protesters charged en masse, but the rowdy crowd the state lawmen faced eventually moved to another area with their signs and chants. By the end of the day, twenty-seven arrests had been made, mostly by Austin police, but the protests at the new presidential library did not get out of hand.[8]

WORKING THE BORDER

One of the Rangers ordered to Austin that day much preferred his home territory, the border town of Del Rio and environs. Ranger Grady Sessums had been in Maverick County as a Highway Patrol trooper since 1963, making Ranger six years later. Unlike his early-twentieth-century predecessors, in the 1970s Sessums and other border Rangers enjoyed a good relationship with officials across the river in Mexico.

Periodically, when a U.S. citizen ran afoul of the law in Mexico, Sessums received a cordial telephone call from the police chief in neighboring Ciudad Acuna. "I have someone I would like you to meet," the chief would tell Sessums. Not removing his badge or gun, the Ranger would drive his state car over the international bridge and park in front of police headquarters. Two beefy officers emerged to guard the DPS vehicle while Sessums went in to talk with their boss. On a bench inside the police station Sessums would find someone in handcuffs with a bruised and swollen face. The chief would inform Sessums that he believed the man might be wanted in the United States. Once he had the man's name and other identifiers, Sessums would step outside and use his radio to check with the DPS dispatcher in Del Rio to see if the person had any outstanding warrants. If that was the case, which it often was, Sessums would give the police chief a box or two of .38 Special ammunition, shake his hand, and offer to provide the prisoner a ride back to Texas. Usually, the person was more than eager to return to the constitutional protections available on the American side of the river. Once back in Texas, Sessums would tell the person he was under arrest for an outstanding felony warrant and contact the issuing jurisdiction to let them know their suspect was in custody. None of that technique—from driving a state car into another country to giving away ammunition—was officially sanctioned by the DPS, but every Ranger from El Paso to Brownsville conducted his business like that back then. As Sessums later recalled, the Rangers got a lot of fugitives back in the United States by working cooperatively with Mexican authorities, even if it took some creativity to get the job done.[9]

In far West Texas, Midland-based Ranger Al Mitchell, a 1970 direct appointment from the New Mexico State Police, held a felony warrant for a doctor who had been illegally prescribing controlled substances. He also was suspected of having killed his wife. Mitchell got information that the physician had fled to Mexico. Calling colleague Clayton McKinney in Alpine, Mitchell asked his fellow Ranger if he had any contacts in Mexico. McKinney told Mitchell to get a hundred-dollar bill and some .45 ammunition and meet him in Alpine. From there, they went to Ojinaga, Mexico, to meet with the Mexican military commander for that part of the border.

"I told him who we were looking for, why we wanted him, and where he was rumored to be," Mitchell recalled. "The general described a grove of cottonwood trees at a certain point on the river and said that in one week we would find the suspect handcuffed to that tree. But then he politely said he could offer another option. 'Perhaps you don't ever want to hear of him again.' "

Mitchell assured the general that he wanted the suspect alive, not dead. A week later, Mitchell and McKinney showed up at the designated location. The fugitive was not there, but the general was. Apologetically he explained that the doctor had fled to Central America.

"Only two things could have happened," the former Ranger said. "Either the general went ahead and had him shot and thrown into a ditch somewhere or the doctor paid more money than I could. Either way, he was never heard from again."[10]

Working in a more populated part of the state, Ranger Ed Gooding, then stationed at Temple in Bell County, found the antiwar movement bewildering. He and a good many of his colleagues had seen action in World War II. "This was what we fought and died for?" Gooding later recalled. He continued:

Ah, for the good old days . . . when I started as a Ranger. What I wouldn't have given for my trusty axe-handle! Unfortunately, the

Rangers had become civilized and we couldn't do that any more. The only thing we could do was stand aside and watch.[11]

Even though most Ranger applicants knew they stood as good a chance of babysitting antiwar protesters as investigating a homicide, when the service's authorized strength increased by two positions effective September 1, 1971, the department had no trouble getting two more men willing to pin on the *cinco peso*. Texas now had eighty-two Rangers. The Rangers also had more stringent hiring standards. No longer could a captain simply sign on a man because he thought he would make a good Ranger. For the first time ever, Ranger applicants had to take a written test and appear before an interview board chaired by the senior captain.[12]

Eighteen months earlier, the Texas State Advisory Committee to the U.S. Commission on Civil Rights had issued a fifty-one-page report making fifty-two recommendations in the areas of education, administration of justice, employment, economic security and welfare and food programs. Of eleven recommendations set forth under the administration of justice category, the final one was that the Rangers be abolished because the force "intimidated" and "repressed" racial minorities. Reacting to the March 9, 1970, report, U.S. Representative Henry B. Gonzalez of San Antonio said it contained "nothing new." Citing the study's $800,000 cost, the congressman added, "Citizens can carefully evaluate the report for what it is . . . faulty and mediocre . . . produced by a prejudiced, preconditioned and highly biased membership."[13]

Colonel Speir supported the Rangers, but he and the senior captain could see some areas needing improvement. With Allee's retirement, the DPS decided to move the headquarters of Company D, which covered thirteen South Texas counties, from Carrizo Springs to San Antonio, effective October 1. Meeting with the company's twelve Rangers at the DPS office in San Antonio, Peoples told them, "We're attempting to do everything we can to better the operations of the Ranger service." The senior captain expanded on his philosophy in an interview with a San Antonio *News* reporter:

We plan to change the image of the Ranger service from a bad image, if there is any, to one that is exceptionally good. . . . We don't think our image is down, but we want to show that the liberals are wrong. . . . To abolish the Rangers would be like . . . tearing down the Alamo. We don't enforce the law on a personal basis and we want it crystal clear that we are not opposed to the Mexican-American people.[14]

A new law allowing the Public Safety Commission to appoint retired DPS officers as special Rangers had also gone into effect. Peoples had worked quietly with friends in the legislature—state employees could not legally lobby—to have all retired Rangers entitled to the commission, but the bill as passed included all honorably retired DPS officers.[15]

Senate Bill 709, another legislative measure passed in 1971, created a Texas Ranger Commemorative Commission to coordinate a 150th birthday celebration for the Rangers. The law authorized the commission to have a medal struck and to oversee the production of commemorative rifles and pistols, as well as other memorabilia focusing on Ranger history. Royalties from the sales of these items would go toward an expansion of the Fort Fisher museum in Waco. The ten-member commission, made up of five persons appointed by the lieutenant governor and five named by the House speaker, would in turn appoint seventy-five members to an advisory board to help plan the 1973 celebration. Peoples got appointed chairman of the new commission, with Waco historian and former mayor Roger Conger as secretary.[16]

Huron Ted Walters

The man in charge of the Rangers began spending a fair amount of state time raising money for a museum and planning a party, but the men in the field continued in their traditional roles. That fall in North Texas, a Company B Ranger made big headlines. It started about 10 p.m. on October 13 when Euless police sergeant Bill Harvell stopped a slow-moving vehicle in a business-industrial area, thinking its driver might be about to pull a burglary. As Harvell walked toward the car, the man behind the wheel emerged with a pistol. Ducking for cover, the sergeant fired toward the gunman, who about the same time opened up on him. Harvell pulled the trigger four more times, but the suspect managed to get back in his vehicle and speed off. After a short pursuit, the fleeing gunman stopped and a woman jumped from the car and ran. The shooter got off three more rounds in Harvell's direction and the officer returned an equal number of shots before the gunman hit the gas again. Soon abandoning his vehicle, the gunman disappeared in the dark into a field.

Returning to take the woman into custody, Harvell learned her trigger-happy companion was fifty-eight-year-old Huron Ted Walters—a career criminal with a rap sheet dating back to the Bonnie and Clyde days. Indeed, shortly before Harvell spotted him, she said, Walters had pulled an armed robbery and shot a store clerk. She said that in addition to a pistol, Walters had a 12-gauge sawed-off shotgun and two boxes of shells.

By this time, Ranger sergeant Lester Robertson and privates Tom Arnold and Howard Alfred were en route to assist local officers in an extensive manhunt. After searching for most of the night, at 4:00 a.m. on October 14 the Ranger sergeant and one of the privates decided to head home. But Arnold opted to keep looking along with the day shift officers then coming on duty.

Walters had succeeded in eluding the officers by making it to a residence in Bedford where he spent the night in a boat kept in the garage. When Hoyt Houston, his wife, Mary, and their five-year-old daughter, Jana, walked into their garage about 7:30 a.m., Walters confronted them with his shotgun and ordered them into their car. Sitting in the backseat holding the shotgun on Houston's head, Walters forced Mrs. Houston to drive. The couple's oldest daughter, still in her room getting dressed, heard the commotion and escaped next door. The neighbor called police, and a dispatcher quickly broadcast a description of the stolen vehicle, a 1969 Mercury, and the fact that Walters now had three hostages.

Ranger Arnold soon spotted the car and, joined by local officers, pursued it toward Grapevine. When Mrs. Houston turned onto State Highway 114 in the direction of the Southlake community, Arnold and a Euless police unit forced her off the road and other officers soon boxed the car in. But the officers could not approach the sedan because Walters still had the 12-gauge against Houston's head. The Ranger used his car's public-address system to try to talk Walters into surrendering, but he did not reply.

Using his car door to support his 30.06 rifle, Arnold laid the scope's crosshairs on Walter's head and waited for him to make a wrong move. That happened when Walters briefly raised the shotgun to look in the direction of a couple of officers slowly approaching on foot. Arnold squeezed the trigger, and the back windshield of the Houston vehicle turned into a giant spiderweb as the high-powered bullet penetrated the glass. When the Houston family bolted from the car, Arnold ran toward it clutching his .45. Seeing that Walters's finger still remained inside the shotgun's trigger guard, the Ranger fired four shots into the gunman's torso. His pistol still cocked, Arnold leaned in for a closer look and saw that his rifle shot had killed the gunman.[17]

A Ranger taking out an armed kidnapper with a single well-placed shot to the brain represented what most Texans continued to think the service existed to provide—solutions to tough problems. But a class action lawsuit making its way through the federal judicial system eventually stripped the Rangers of some of their legal authority. A three-judge federal panel met in Brownsville June 26, 1972, to hear arguments in the five-year-old *Medrano v. Allee* suit. The judges found that the 1967 Ranger presence in Starr County had been meant to break the fruit pickers' strike. The judges declared as unconstitutional five state statutes—two civil and three criminal—that had been used against union organizers and strikers. The state attorney general's office, which represents the state in lawsuits filed against it, appealed the decision to the U.S. Supreme Court.[18]

Abolish the Rangers?

The lawsuit stemming from the Valley labor strife, and other criticism of the Rangers, gave liberal politicians plenty of ammunition. In 1972, the Rangers became the bull's-eye in a wild gubernatorial primary campaign between two Democrats, conservative South Texas rancher Dolph Briscoe and Frances (Sissy) Farenthold. The liberal Farenthold, the state's first female gubernatorial candidate in forty years, advocated liberalizing marijuana laws and abolishing the Rangers. "I think the Texas Rangers are a festering sore," Farenthold said at a meeting of the American GI Forum in San Angelo. "I am in favor of disarming them or disassembling them."[19]

No matter that some Texans proposed doing away with the Rangers, the cachet of the words *Texas Rangers* had not lost any ground nationally. When owner Bob Short moved the Washington Senators from the

District of Columbia to Arlington, a fast-growing city between Dallas and Fort Worth, he renamed the baseball team the Texas Rangers.

The baseball Rangers had a terrible first season, but Briscoe handily won the nomination over Farenthold in the Democratic primary. His victory, however, did not end the debate on the usefulness of the Rangers.

On May 26, 1972, the NBC News show *Chronolog* aired a profile on the Rangers featuring interviews with Allee and another retired Ranger, Dudley White Jr. "Over the years," correspondent Tom Petit said, "they have had a reputation as being tough and controversial, often knee-deep in the intricacies of Texas politics." Petit described the Rangers as "a close-knit group of backward-looking men who glorify their own history."[20]

That September the Dallas bureau of United Press International distributed another version of the perennial "who are the Rangers?" feature story on the Rangers. When the wire service asked about the recent federal court decision on the Rangers' role in the fruit pickers' strike, Senior Captain Peoples had no comment other than to say, "We have more requests from Mexican-American officials in the Valley than we can fill. This bad picture is painted by politicians. We believe in enforcing the law as it is written on the books. We believe in rehabilitation. But at the same time we don't believe the law should be bent in favor of anyone." The service's two Mexican-American Rangers, the captain continued, had made "fine, efficient officers."[21]

None of the touchy issues came up in October when Peoples flew to New York City to tape an appearance on CBS's popular game show *To Tell the Truth*. When three serious-looking men in business suits took their places on the set, moderator Garry Moore told the four celebrity panelists that one of the guests wore the senior captain's badge of the famed Texas Rangers. The chief of Amtrak's New York baggage department and a waiter who worked in one of the city's popular restaurants were the two impostors.

Peoples and the other two guests read a short statement from one of the show's writers:

I, Clint Peoples, am proud to state that I am the Senior Captain of the renowned Texas Rangers. Originally a vigilante group of concerned citizens, the Texas Rangers are actually older than the state of Texas itself. For 50 to 60 years there was a continuous war to the death between the Texas Rangers and the Comanche and Apache tribes and it was the Rangers who drove the Mexicans back across the Rio Grande. To put it simply, the Ranger force held a place somewhere between that of an army and a police force. Today, as a law enforcement branch of the Texas Department of Public Safety, the Rangers' job is still to protect life and property in the Lone Star State.

After the three contenders answered a series of questions from the panelists, the Amtrak employee got two votes as the real Ranger captain, with the waiter and Peoples each receiving one vote, Peoples's coming from panelist Peggy Cass. Though taped on October 31, 1972, the show did not air for nearly a year, finally being broadcast on October 5, 1973.[22]

"I have never seen this show," the captain later recalled, "but I understand it has been shown and reshown throughout the United States on many occasions and still is being shown throughout the nation. I was delighted to have been chosen to appear on this program to represent law enforcement in our state and nation."[23]

The producers of To Tell the Truth bought into the traditional image of the Rangers, but as NBC had recently demonstrated, the news operations of the national TV networks did not mind criticizing the force. For the most part, Texas reporters and broadcasters perpetuated the status quo. Longtime Austin radio-TV personality Cactus Pryor, described as former president Johnson's "Clown Prince," weighed in on Austin's KTBC Radio—owned by the Johnson family—with a favorable commentary on the Rangers in January 1973.[24]

By spring, collectors of Ranger memorabilia signed checks for commemorative items ranging from Daisy BB guns designed to look like Colt thumb-busters and Winchester rifles to a set of medals depicting famous Ranger captains. Winchester Arms produced 150 special Model 94 carbines with sixteen-inch barrels and hand-checkered walnut stocks for $1,000 each and 4,850 Model 94s with twenty-inch barrels for $135. For the sidearm enthusiast, Smith & Wesson brought out a special edition combat .357 Magnum revolver and custom-designed bowie knife that sold for $250. The deluxe custom-engraved set went for $1,000. A limited-edition bronze of two Rangers astride horses by artist Melvin Warren topped the commemorative offerings at $2,000.

"Experts in the field of collecting Texana lore say that any historical material related to Texas continues to grow noticeably in value by the year," a commemorative commission press release hyped. "Persons who purchase any of the materials issued in observance of the Texas Ranger Anniversary will not only be aiding that celebration and the construction of the permanent Ranger Hall of Fame, but also will be making a good investment."[25]

In June, Peoples and six of his Rangers flew to Lake Tahoe, Nevada, to assist with security during the National Governors Conference. The year before, even more Rangers had been present when the meeting had been in Houston. Back in Austin on June 11, Peoples sent a memo to Colonel Speir with a copy of a resolution passed by the fifty governors praising the Rangers on the occasion of their sesquicentennial. "I was especially pleased about this for many reasons," Peoples wrote his boss, "number one, this was the only resolution that passed . . . without any opposition." Continuing to pile it on, Peoples concluded:

> May I say in a personal vein that I was highly honored myself to be
> able to have a part of being associated with these fine gentlemen. I
> spoke personally with many of the Governors and they stated that
> they knew of no resolution that gave them more pleasure in having
> a part in supporting. I would like to express my most sincere appre-
> ciation to you, Colonel [Leo] Gossett, and Chief [Jim] Ray, for mak-
> ing it possible for us to attend.[26]

Later that summer, eighty-one of the state's eighty-two Rangers converged on Waco for the August 4 Ranger sesquicentennial event. More than two thousand persons gathered at midafternoon on a hot summer day for the groundbreaking ceremony for the Texas Ranger Hall of Fame. Smiling for the cameras, Governor Briscoe, Colonel Speir, and Captain Peoples thrust a gold-plated, engraved shovel into a lose pile of rich Brazos River soil to mark the beginning of a $1 million addition to Fort Fisher. Actor Chill Wills got in his own dig after Colonel Speir and Peoples presented the governor with one of the commemorative .30-.30 rifles.

"Be careful spraying that Winchester around," Wills drawled in mock warning to the governor. "Sissy Farenthold might be in the audience."[27] The defeated gubernatorial candidate had not been on the guest list, but Governor Briscoe did take a figurative shot at Farenthold's suggestion that the Rangers be abolished.

The Texas Ranger Hall of Fame, the governor said, would be "more than just a monument to the past. It will preserve the heritage of a great and loyal law enforcement agency, but it will also serve as a hall of progress. For the Texas Rangers have reached a milestone with their 150th anniversary, not a marker at the end of the road."[28]

The festivities continued that night, with many of those present for the earlier event attending a banquet in the new Waco Civic Center. Western star Clint Walker, a big man who fit the Ranger stereotype as easily as a .45 slipped into a finely crafted leather holster, served as master of ceremonies. As the program pointed out, old-time Rangers often had to get by on beef jerky, but those in attendance that night enjoyed a thick Texas steak and all the trimmings.

Not all the media coverage of the Ranger birthday celebration turned out favorably. Chet Flippo wrote a piece for the *Texas Observer*, later reprinted in *Rolling Stone*, offering a different take on the Waco proceedings. He pointed out that the commemorative commission had hired a public relations firm to "shine up the Rangers' badges," a campaign that even featured a country western song written by Tom T. Hall and sung by Johnny Rodriguez called "They Done Took It Up." The PR firm also coordinated the production of a color film about the Rangers, *A Certain Kind of Man*, narrated by Slim Pickens. Using Captain McDonald's "No man in the wrong can stand up against a man in the right" line as a transition, Flippo noted:

These days in Texas . . . it's sometimes hard to tell who's in the wrong and who's in the right. State officials are indicted left and right for offenses ranging from bribery and perjury to stamp theft. Policemen are indicted for murder. The governor runs off to close a whorehouse while a madman in Houston is burying boys in a boathouse and a heroin war rages, unchecked, from San Antonio to the border. . . . The Rangers' reason for existence now, it would seem, is as a prop for the saggin' Texas mystique.[29]

But Hollywood seemed ever fascinated by that mystique, sagging or not. When a producer from Los Angeles approached Peoples about a TV

series on the modern Rangers, the senior captain enthusiastically offered his support. He could provide access to Ranger offense reports and
provide technical expertise. All he needed, he said, was a finder's fee and
a contract providing him $500 a week.

Speir knew that Peoples had been talking to someone in Hollywood,
but he did not know the details. On the surface of it, however, he had
concerns about the propriety of the relationship between the senior captain and the producers. Speir ordered Chief Ray to look into the matter.
Peoples's boss traveled to California and met with two men who had
been dealing with the senior captain. Though Ray could not pin down
whether Peoples had intended to collect money from the producers
while still a state employee or had merely been planning to feather his
eventual retirement, Peoples had no final authority over any Ranger records, which were government documents.

Ray delivered the results of his investigation, which included a transcript of a taped interview with the producers Peoples had been dealing
with, to Speir on November 21, 1973. While there is no record of any
disciplinary action having been taken, on January 31, 1974, Peoples notified Speir of his planned retirement effective May 15, though his last
day in the office would be March 31. The senior captain had 240 hours
of unused annual leave. Rather than be paid a lump sum for that time,
he opted to "burn" it and stay on the state payroll but out of the office
until May 15. That left Peoples's assistant, Captain William D. "Bill"
Wilson, in an acting senior captain capacity, but without any additional
compensation. The two men had never been close. Having to do his
boss's job with no extra pay did nothing to improve Wilson's opinion of
him. Meanwhile, Peoples received an appointment as United States
Marshal for the Northern District of Texas.[30]

As soon as Peoples went off the payroll, Speir promoted Wilson as
the new senior captain. Captain James "Skippy" Rundell came to DPS
headquarters as the Rangers' new number two. Not as articulate as Peoples but much blunter, Wilson would talk to reporters if he had to, but
unlike his predecessor, he did not enjoy the public limelight. He and
many of the Rangers thought the recently retired senior captain had
done too much showboating. To their thinking, Peoples's media interviews and public appearances constituted a major breach of the Rangers'

unwritten code that the lawmen should be low key. Catching crooks, in their view, outranked headlines or building museums.

Five days after Wilson took over as senior captain, the U.S. Supreme Court issued its ruling in *Medrano v. Allee*, upholding the federal district court decision that the Rangers had relied on unconstitutional statutes in their strikebreaking efforts. Justice William O. Douglas read the majority opinion: "In this blunderbuss effort the police not only relied on statutes the District Court found constitutionally deficient, but concurrently exercised their authority under valid laws in an unconstitutional manner. . . . Because of the intimidation by State authorities . . . their leaders and organizers were placed in fear of exercising their constitutionally protected rights of free expression, assembly, and association." For all practical purposes, the days of Rangers as strikebreakers had ended.[31]

FRED GOMEZ CARRASCO

That summer, the Rangers got a chance to demonstrate that Supreme Court decisions aside, they continued to be an effective component of the state's criminal justice system. Shortly after noon on July 24, 1974, three inmates walked into the third-floor prison library at the Walls Unit in Huntsville, the state's oldest correctional facility. No one paid any attention, because during the lunch hour prisoners not under disciplinary sanction had free access to the library.

Fred Gomez Carrasco, Rudy Dominguez, and Ignacio Cuevas sat down at separate tables and started reading. An inmate in for rape sat at another table, writing a letter of complaint to Texas Department of Corrections Director W. J. Estelle. The inmate said, "Hi!" to Carrasco, but his fellow inmate did not seem to be in a talkative mood.

When the 1:00 p.m. whistle sounded, the inmate found out why. Carrasco and the other two inmates pulled pistols from their waistbands and began waving them over their heads. Just to make sure everyone inside the library or within earshot got the point, Carrasco fired a couple of .357 Magnum rounds into the ceiling. Two prison guards running toward the disturbance retreated as more bullets aimed through the double doors of the library scattered shards of glass and chips of concrete.

Ranger Wesley Styles, stationed in Huntsville, got word of the takeover at 1:45 p.m. He made it to the prison within ten minutes, going straight to the office of Warden Hal Husband. A short time later, Styles called his supervisor in Houston, Company A captain J. F. (Pete) Rogers, to report a grim situation. Three convicts armed with revolvers and ammunition somehow smuggled inside had rounded up eighty-one hostages—seventy inmates and eleven civilian prison employees. The thirty-four-year-old Carrasco, a notorious former heroin dealer from San Antonio serving a life sentence for trying to kill a police officer in Nueces County, led the takeover.[32] Rogers told Styles that he and Sergeant Johnny Krumnow would be on their way to the prison immediately.

Carrasco believed he could get out of prison, cross the Rio Grande, and continue his narcotics business in Mexico. The hostages represented a means to that end, human currency to get what he wanted. He realized, however, that he could not just walk out of prison with his prisoners. He needed some equipment to make it easier. First, he demanded handcuffs for the hostages and a TV set so he could see the coverage of his takeover. Receiving fifteen sets of handcuffs and a television, he released sixty-six inmates. That left him with the eleven civilians and four inmates.

An hour after Carrasco's takeover, Father Joseph O'Brien, the prison chaplain, walked inside, hoping to talk the inmates into giving up before anyone got hurt. Instead of giving up, Carrasco told the priest he wanted him to deliver to prison officials a list of supplies he wanted, including six M-16 assault rifles, five extra magazines for the rifles, one hundred rounds of ammunition, protective vests, combat helmets, and three walkie-talkies on the same frequency.

By 3:00 p.m., Estelle reached Huntsville from San Antonio, where he had been giving a speech to a civic club when he got word of the takeover. He left immediately for a quick trip back to the prison to take control of the situation.

Responding to the crisis, the DPS sent scores of Highway Patrol troopers and dozens of rangers to Huntsville. To assist Captain Rogers, Company B's Captain G. W. Burks came down from Dallas. The FBI already had a man on the scene. Agent Robert Wiatt had been interviewing an inmate in connection with one of his cases when Carrasco seized the hostages.

The prison standoff dragged on for the next eleven days. Carrasco made various demands and threats, even pretending to have killed a hostage, as Estelle, with input from the Rangers and FBI agent Wiatt, made minor concessions while stalling for time. The drug kingpin clearly relished the national media attention he received and seemed to sincerely believe he could use his hostages to bargain his way to freedom.

While the talking continued, each side developed plans. The state actually had two scenarios in mind, based on one absolute: The inmates could not go anywhere, no matter what. The first plan worked out by Estelle, his staff, the Rangers, and Wiatt involved what would happen if Carrasco and the other two inmates started killing hostages. Explosives had been placed against the back wall of the library. If shooting broke out inside the library, Rangers would make a dynamic entrance. Even with the explosives, they knew they could not get to Carrasco's stronghold quickly. The casualty rate would be high. The second, preferable plan involved trying to get Carrasco outside the library. In the open, it would be easier to take the three inmates down. That option also came with a better chance of survival for the hostages.

About 6:00 p.m. on August 2, Carrasco released Linda Woodward to set forth his final demand. He and his fellow inmates would leave the library inside a movable shield they had constructed of portable chalkboards and pegboard with heavy law books as armor. Their hostages would be handcuffed to them, she said. They would proceed down a concrete ramp leading from the library to the prison yard, where Carrasco expected an armored car to be waiting.

Early the next morning, Estelle, the Ranger captains, Wiatt, and the other members of the crisis command team met to develop a plan. When Carrasco's shield reached midway on the ramp, an assault team would attack. The simple but challenging goal: save the hostages and capture the three would-be escapees. A smaller team made up of corrections officers would train a fire hose on the shield to knock it over and keep the inmates from shooting.[33]

Rogers and Burks discussed whether to use assault rifles or shotguns and rejected both. Rifles would be unwieldy for close-in fighting, and shotguns did not have the knockdown power they wanted. The two captains opted to go with the weapon that had helped establish the Ranger reputation, the .45 pistol. Both men and most of the other Rangers had long since switched from revolvers to semiautomatics, of course. Each captain would have a pair of pistols, each weapon holding eight steel-jacketed bullets.

The ground rules went unspoken. Rangers and other members of the team would not shoot unless they believed one of the prisoners intended to harm a hostage. They understood that some of the civilians might end up in a hospital or worse, but of all the options they had considered, the plan they stood ready to execute seemed the most likely to work.

Estelle looked on as the two captains silently strapped on their .45s. The prison director marveled at their obvious courage, later reflecting, "When you go into conflict with men like that, whether people believe it or not, courage is as contagious as fear."[34]

Ruben Montemayor, Carrasco's San Antonio attorney, had volunteered to assist prison officials in trying to bring a peaceful resolution to the standoff. At 4:00 p.m., he got Carrasco on the telephone and told him the prison had decided to let him have the getaway vehicle he wanted. The armored car, equipped with two-way radio and mobile phone, would be parked adjacent to the ramp by 7:00 p.m.

The thirteen-member assault team took position in the abandoned dining hall at 6:00 p.m. They found the floor crawling with maggots born in the rotting food left behind eleven days before. Unable to talk or smoke, the team waited in the heat, enduring the terrible stench. When the armored car arrived on schedule from Houston, Carrasco sent one of the inmate hostages out to drive the vehicle to make sure it had not been booby-trapped. Satisfied with the inmate's report, Carrasco ordered him to begin carrying out the women's purses and other items he wanted in the armored car.

Finally, at 9:27 p.m. the ponderous, bizarre-looking reverse Trojan Horse emerged from the bullet-shattered double doors of the library. Inside, each inmate had one of the women hostages handcuffed to his left arm. Offering a silent prayer, an unhandcuffed Father O'Brien walked backward inside the vehicle, serving as "brakeman." The inmates handcuffed the remaining hostages to a rope looped around the outside of the shield.

The Rangers watched as the shield, its wheels squeaking eerily, slowly moved down the ramp. It made the first turn and headed toward the second, where the attack team would make its move. When the convicts and their hostages arrived at that point, the two Ranger captains, the FBI agent, and DPS intelligence agent Winston Padgett rushed out the dining hall door with their handguns leveled at the shield.

"Police officers!" Rogers shouted. "Surrender!"

His command unanswered, the captain yelled, "Hit it with the hoses." As three streams of high-pressure water played against the shield, Rogers and the other officers heard muffled shots from inside.

"It's gone bad," Padgett yelled. "They're shooting the hostages."

Rogers saw a pinpoint of light an instant before a hollow-point .357 slug slammed into his protective vest. Feeling like a mule had just kicked him in the chest, the captain hurtled backward from the impact of the high-velocity round. A bullet also hit Burks's vest, knocking him down. Agent Wiatt lay momentarily unconscious on the concrete, his ceramic vest having stopped two bullets.

The other officers dragged the three temporarily incapacitated lawmen toward cover. Though stunned, Burks knew he had to get up. "You still have a job to do," he thought. "Get up and do it."[35]

As other members of the assault team began firing at the still-upright shield, the two Ranger captains and the FBI agent had recovered sufficiently to rejoin the fight. Behind a four-foot brick wall, the rescue team crouched only a few feet from Carrasco's mobile fortress, but they could not see it or get to it.

"Every time we exposed ourselves, we would draw gunfire," Burks later said. "But they didn't have to expose themselves to fire at us."

Corrections officer Lieutenant Willard Stewart, having completed his task of locking the armored car so none of the convicts could get inside, braved the gunfire to run up to the shield and use his pocketknife to cut the rope holding the outside hostages. As soon as the terrified prison employees could pull loose from the shield, they ran down the ramp to get out of the line of fire. At the same time, one of the fire hoses burst and the pressure in the other lines dropped to practically nothing.

With the Rangers and other officers continuing their fire toward the shield, the prison guards tried to get the hoses working again. When the water pressure returned, the powerful streams again splashed against the shield. Using the water as cover, Ranger sergeant Krumnow and a couple of the other officers thrust an aluminum ladder against the vehicle, finally toppling it. At that, the officers heard two more muffled gunshots, followed by silence. They rushed to the overturned shield.

"Show me your hands! Show me your hands" Burks yelled at the seven people lying in blood on the wet concrete ramp. With all the gore, water, and confusion, the captain and the other officers could not readily distinguish between hostage and inmate, but Burks did not want to risk that one of the convicts might still have a gun.

Father O'Brien, badly wounded but still alive, had fallen on Dominguez and could feel the convict's gun in his back.

"Shoot!" the priest yelled. "He's got a gun!"

At that, Padgett put two bullets in the convict's head as Wiatt added a third.

The shooting had lasted twenty-two minutes, an eternity in a gunfight. Carrasco's hostage, forty-six-year-old Elizabeth Beseda, had been shot once in the heart. Forty-three-year-old Julia Standley, mother of five, had been shot three times. Both lay dead. Carrasco had shot himself in the head, and Padgett and Wiatt had finished off Dominguez. Cuevas had fainted but had not been hit.[36]

"This is one of the meanest days that anyone has ever spent in public service," Estelle said as he opened a press conference at 11:15 that night. "The results of this, under the circumstances, are the very best I'm convinced, we could hope for, considering the people that held our people hostage."[37]

The longest prison siege in American penal history had ended, but not the follow-up investigation into how the inmates got the firearms used in their escape attempt. During the next several months, the Rangers handled that and also put together a capital murder case against Cuevas.

The Dukedom of Duval

When tall, slow-talking John M. Wood—a Ranger since 1949—took over as captain of Company D with the retirement of Allee, he inherited more than supervisory responsibility for all the Rangers in South Texas. Allee's old nemesis, George Parr, had not retired. He still reigned as the boss of Duval County, political patron to his allies, vicious enemy to anyone who chose not to go along with him. By 1963, all of Parr's federal convictions and state charges from the 1950s had unraveled through reversals or dismissals. Of 656 counts against Parr or his associates, none had survived.

Since Parr controlled the judiciary in his county, only the federal criminal justice system posed a threat. In the spring of 1972, a routine Internal Revenue Service audit of an Austin architect's income tax return revealed some interesting bookkeeping in Duval County. Granted immunity from prosecution over irregularities in his return, the architect agreed to talk about kickbacks he made to the Parr machine. By May, the IRS, working with the U.S. Attorney's Office, had an extensive investigation under way. Eleven months later, on April 6, 1973, a federal grand jury in San Antonio indicted Parr on eight counts of income tax evasion and filing false returns. When U.S. District Judge Adrian Spears released him on $50,000 personal recognizance bond, Parr thought he could beat the federal government again. But the climate had changed, one of the reasons being the marital troubles of Parr's heir apparent, his nephew Archer Parr. When Archer's fourth wife filed for divorce on June 25, she soon began cooperating in the investigation into the Parr empire, referred to by the news media as the Dukedom of Duval.[38]

Found guilty March 19, 1974, of all eight counts of income tax evasion, George Parr received a five-year prison sentence and $14,000 fine. As had been done in the 1950s, his lawyers appealed his conviction and the Duke remained free on bond (though the amount had been raised to $75,000) pending the outcome of that effort. The federal court system, however, indicated no sympathy for his position. On March 24, the Fifth U.S. Circuit Court of Appeals affirmed his conviction. Parr intended to take the case to the Supreme Court, but in the meantime federal prosecutors filed a motion to get a court order remanding him to jail in lieu of bond. After he returned to Duval County following a hearing in Corpus Christi on March 31, he disappeared.

Ranger Gene Powell coordinated an extensive search that ended the following morning when an early-spring South Texas fog burned off. A DPS helicopter spotted Parr's Chrysler parked near a windmill on the highest point of his Los Horcones Ranch south of Benavides. When Powell and other officers reached the scene, they found the seventy-four-year-old Duke of Duval dead behind the steering wheel of his vehicle. Parr had chosen to end his story with a .45 bullet to the brain.

With Parr dead and Archer facing prison time, a state task force directed by Attorney General John Hill went on, as one writer put in appropriate metaphor, "to fumigate the befouled den of Duval County once and for all."[39] Captain Wood and Rangers Powell, Ray Martinez, and Rudy Rodriguez, working with DPS Criminal Intelligence Service agents, developed criminal cases against county officials, school board members, and private citizens who had been cogs in the Parr machine.

"Every time we found something in the records that looked funny," Assistant Attorney General John Blanton recalled, "we found five or six more people stealing." Not that records could be found all that easily. When an indicted former Benavides School District employee finally decided to cooperate with the Rangers, he led them to more than two hundred pounds of official papers dating back to 1968 that had been hidden between the ceiling and roof of the Benavides ISD office.[40] Rangers also unearthed diesel-soaked, partially burned school records.[41]

The task force spent nearly two years in Duval County. Their investigation led to 105 indictments against thirty-seven persons, twenty-nine of them convicted. "The Rangers' assistance in gathering evidence was invaluable," federal prosecutor John E. Clark wrote.[42]

The Ranger role in the Duval County cleanup involved taking scores of statements from witnesses, locating and then poring over county records, writing reports, and serving court orders—not shooting. But Ranger firepower still could make a difference in a dangerous situation.

Starting about 3:00 a.m. on June 15, 1975, the dispatcher at the Camp County Sheriff's Department began getting telephone calls from citizens reporting a couple of armed men stopping cars on U.S. 271 three miles south of the Northeast Texas community of Pittsburg. When night watchman Harold Attaway reached the scene, the two gunmen easily got the drop on him. The men also captured the second officer to arrive, Pittsburg police officer Loyd Penshorn.

As the pair ordered Penshorn to take off his clothes, Attaway managed to escape and call for help. The two men then began beating Penshorn with his own pistol and a heavy belt buckle.

When Sheriff Lyndon Morgan and Constable Don Tubbs arrived, they, too, became captives. Then Ranger R. M. "Red" Arnold got there, slipping up behind the two men and the three disarmed officers. When Arnold yelled for them to drop their guns, the two brothers whirled and leveled their weapons at the Ranger. At that, the Ranger started shooting, dropping both men. Andy West died a short time later at a Pittsburg hospital. An ambulance rushed his older brother to Tyler, where he eventually recovered from his wounds.

The day after the shooting, Austin *American-Statesman* editor Sam Wood wrote a page one "Mini View" editorial on the incident.

"I have always had a deep respect for the Texas Rangers," Wood wrote. He continued:

And I have never lost that respect even though some people in recent years have worked hard at giving the Rangers a bad name.... Just when people are saying there is no such thing anymore as "one mob, one ranger," Ranger R.M. "Red" Arnold steps in near Pittsburg Tuesday after two young gunmen had corralled an assortment of peace officers on the highway.... A lot of do-gooders will now be turning their wrath upon Ranger Arnold because apparently the two gunmen . . . did not return his fire. Had Ranger Arnold waited a split second to see if the gunmen intended to squeeze their trigger fingers, the newspaper account most likely would have been about another peace officer killed in the line of duty.[43]

One Ranger could still resolve a touchy situation, but the service needed more manpower to cope with the state's crime rate. Effective September 1, 1975, the Ranger force gained six new men, raising its strength to ninety-four. The year before, another six positions had been added.[44]

"The Texas Ranger has always been the man who went in and did his job without fanfare," U.S. Marshal Peoples said as Waco civic leaders completed their planning for the dedication of the Ranger Hall of Fame in Waco. "There is no mark on the name of the Texas Rangers. They are truly the untouchables."[45]

In Waco at noon on February 7, Governor Briscoe, U.S. senators Lloyd Bentsen and John Tower, and DPS director Speir cut a foot-wide red, white, and blue ribbon with a pair of gold-plated scissors at the main entrance to the $750,000 addition to the museum. Comedian Danny Thomas, a second-generation Lebanese actor and a friend of Peoples, held one end of the ribbon, Senior Captain Wilson the other.

Eighty-five-year-old "Lone Wolf" Gonzaullas, one of twenty Rangers in the first class of inductees to the new hall of fame, joined other spectators in their applause.

"This is a wonderful day for all of us, young ones and old ones like me," he said. "We are proud that the people of Texas are proud enough of us to make this all possible. I go back to those days with the horses, and when I left the Rangers they had the crime labs and all the modern equipment."

The old Ranger did not mind saying for the record that he did not find all aspects of modern law enforcement to his liking.

"Times have changed, some for the best," he continued. "But that Texas Ranger of today has to stop a guy and turn him up and kiss his bottom before he even asks a damned question."[46]

A retired Ranger could still get away with saying something like that in public, but not the current generation. The Rangers clearly had become more sensitive to concerns that they were a lily-white organization dedicated to maintaining the status quo in Texas. As director of the DPS, Speir demonstrated he had as little tolerance for Ranger wrongdoing as Colonel Garrison. Fifty-two-year-old Bob Elder of Houston, a six-year Ranger veteran, lost his job on September 2, 1976, for making racial slurs when arrested for public intoxication by police in Brownsville. The Ranger had been on vacation, but the way Speir saw it, being off the state clock did not give Elder license to get drunk and talk insensitively to fellow officers. Three months later, Elder died of what Houston police called an accidental gunshot wound.[47]

In Medina County, further demonstrating that old attitudes had faded, Rangers investigated the shooting death of twenty-nine-year-old Richard Morales while in the custody of the Castroville city marshal, Frank Hayes. The Rangers' efforts led to Hayes's conviction for aggravated assault and later on a federal charge of violating the prisoner's civil rights.[48]

A decade after his bitter criticism of the Rangers, former state senator Joe Bernal told the Dallas *Times-Herald*, "I see a better future for the Rangers. They have hired some Mexican-Americans. Some of the older men, the racists, have retired."[49]

No DPS-era Ranger had ever been killed in a gunfight and the people of Texas, if not the agency itself, had begun to think of the men who wore the *cinco peso* as essentially bulletproof. In fact, a Texas Ranger had not been shot to death in the line of duty since 1931. But that forty-seven-year aura of invincibility ended in the winter of 1978 near the small community of Argyle in Denton County. Ranger Bobby Paul Dougherty took a .38-caliber bullet in the head during a drug raid. Doctors at a Fort Worth hospital pronounced the forty-one-year-old Ranger dead at 1:15 a.m. on February 21.

The Ranger's death stunned his colleagues, the DPS, and the state.

"I have the same feeling right now that I had the day in this same house 60 years ago when my mama was told Daddy had been ambushed," retired Ranger Dudley White Jr.—whose Ranger father had been killed in the line of duty in 1918—told the Associated Press the day after Dougherty's death. "I feel I've lost a brother."

White said the day he learned his father had been killed by a draft dodger in San Augustine County was the day he decided he would become a Ranger. Referring to the death of Ranger Dougherty, White said it could have happened to him "or any other Ranger who has served this state. God has been with us. All I can do now is weep for this fallen officer and pray for his soul."

Two days after the deadly North Texas drug raid, Dougherty's funeral showed not only the high regard in which his colleagues held him but also the status of the Rangers as a Texas icon. More than twenty-two hundred persons attended Dougherty's funeral services at the First Baptist Church of Lakeside in Tarrant County. Behind his Texas flag–draped casket at the front of the sanctuary stood a floral representation of a Ranger badge. The Reverend Jesse Leonard used the badge to describe the slain Ranger's character: The five points of the star stood for family, friends, his faith, the future, and the fruits of his life.[50]

In September, Captain N. W. (Dub) Clark left the Rangers to become the first commander of the DPS's newly created Internal Affairs Unit. A twenty-eight-year DPS veteran, Clark had been a Ranger since February 1, 1962. Under study for several years, the Internal Affairs Unit would report to the agency's director. The department's in-house newsletter, the *DPS Chaparral*, noted that "the DPS Director said the unit will in no way reduce the authority of line commanders to supervise their own people, but it will provide the means for an independent review."[51]

When Company D's Captain Wood retired, Sergeant Jack O. Dean gained promotion as of November 1, 1978, to fill his former boss's figurative boots. Dean had been wearing the gold captain's badge not quite seven months when a gunman assassinated U.S. District Judge John H. Wood in the driveway of his San Antonio town house as he headed to work the morning of May 29, 1979. From concealment someone had shot the sixty-three-year-old judge in the back with a high-powered rifle. Wood's killing, referred to in FBI documents as "Major Case 21" and "WOODMUR," set off the largest investigation to that point in the Justice Department's history.

Captain Dean and three Rangers responded to the scene of the shooting, along with DPS narcotics and intelligence agents, and offered state assistance. But as federal agents rushed to the Alamo City from Washington and elsewhere, the FBI soon said that while it would welcome any information the Rangers might develop, neither the state officers nor San Antonio police detective would be involved in the investigation.

In early June, Dean got an anonymous call that Charles Harrelson had been in town the day the judge was gunned down. Dean knew the forty-year-old Harrelson, a career criminal who grew up in Huntsville. While stationed in the Rio Grande Valley early in his Ranger career, Dean had handled Harrelson as the defendant in the 1968 contract killing of grain dealer Sam Degelia in Edinburg. Defense attorney Percy Foreman had managed to get a hung jury in Harrelson's first trial, but when tried again in 1974, he was convicted and assessed a fifteen-year prison sentence. But through earning good time, he had already been released from prison. The Ranger captain duly passed the information (as well as mug shots and Harrelson's criminal history) on to FBI deputy director James O. Ingram, who had come to San Antonio to spearhead the federal investigation. While appreciative, Ingram told Dean the bureau would take it from there.

The FBI had already focused on Jamiel "Jimmy" Chagra, an El Paso drug dealer facing trial in Wood's court. While it did seem likely that Chagra or his family had conspired to have the judge killed, the tip that came to Dean is what brought Harrelson into the investigation that culminated in his murder conviction and life imprisonment.[52]

With a series of child murders in Atlanta making national head-lines, newly elected state representative Lanell Cofer, a Dallas Demo-crat, proposed that spring during the sixty-fifth legislature that Rangers be dispatched to Georgia to help solve the crimes. Governor Bill Clements, the first Republican to occupy the Governor's Mansion since Reconstruction, said he could not send Rangers outside Texas without an invitation and that none had been extended.[53] Cofer's suggestion, though not practical, showed how most Texans continued to feel about the Rangers, despite periodic controversy and calls for their dismantling.

Occasionally, however, the Rangers demonstrated human frailty. Placing a "call upon the Senate," a legislative procedure in which law-makers can be compelled to make a quorum, Lieutenant Governor Bill Hobby on May 21, 1979, ordered the Rangers to locate twelve missing senators. The Democratic lawmakers had staged a boycott to protest a Hobby-backed presidential primary bill. When the Rangers proved un-able to find the so-called Killer Bees (named after Africanized bees, heading north into Texas at this time) Hobby called it "ludicrous." He added: "Here there are twelve state senators they are charged with ar-resting and they can't find them."[54]

Nine of the dozen Democrats never even left Austin, hiding in a small apartment rented by one of the senators' administrative assis-tants. One of the legislative fugitives, Harris County senator Gene Jones, declared he could no longer stand the claustrophobic conditions in their one-bedroom hideout and returned to his home in Houston. The Rangers got word of his departure, and two Company A Rangers showed up at his address the next morning.

When a man emerged from the house and picked up a newspaper, the Rangers confronted him. Comparing him to a faxed photo of the missing lawmaker, one of the Rangers asked the man if his name was Jones. When he answered yes, the Rangers took him into custody and drove him to Brenham, where a DPS helicopter picked him up for a flight to Austin. Unfortunately for the Rangers, they had not asked Jones for his first name. The man they hustled to the Capitol was Clayton D. Jones, the senator's brother. The sought-after senator, seeing the Rangers, had slipped over his backyard fence and escaped.[55]

The highly publicized political maneuver and the Rangers' lack of success in finding the "fugitive" legislators moved Senator Bill Meier of Euless to doggerel. Assuming that most Texans knew that *S.O.* on vehicle tags stood for "state official," Meir wrote:

> *The Texas Rangers hunt for them;*
> *Bill Hobby issues pleas,*
> *And says that on their license plates,*
> *It shows they're S.O. Bees.*

On December 31, 1979, after capping his law enforcement career as president of the International Association of Chiefs of Police, Colonel Speir retired as DPS's fourth director. Leadership in the agency, and in the Rangers, changed with retirements, deaths, and promotions, but in the Rangers the philosophy behind that leadership had become institutionalized, as much a part of a Ranger's getup as his *cinco peso* badge, his .45, his boots, or his hat. After his retirement, Ranger Gooding summed up the Ranger style of leadership in his assessment of Bob Mitchell, "the best captain I ever worked for."

Gooding remembered that Mitchell, who had become captain of Waco-based Company F in 1974 at forty, gave any new Ranger who came to his company a short, simple speech:

> You're a Texas Ranger now. By definition, that means you are the best of the best, and I expect you to act like it. Take care of your area and don't call me with every little nit-picking thing that comes along. Just handle it. But if you do need me, I'll be right there.[56]

12

"Ranger Speed"

THE 1980S

Eleven days into the new year—1985—the Rangers of Company F sat around a conference table in a boardroom overlooking the Brazos River at Fort Fisher in Waco. They would be spending most of the day exchanging information, discussing cases, and getting a rundown on assorted managerial issues from their captain, Bob Mitchell. After the company meeting, badges and guns removed and on their own time they had plans for supper, socializing, and, among those who partook, a little whiskey drinking.

Still sipping coffee on this Friday morning, the captain and the other Rangers noted the absence of one of their colleagues, but no one knew why. Ranger Bill Gunn, stationed in Johnson County at Cleburne, a town between Waco and Fort Worth, had not shown up or called in. Mitchell, no micromanager, knew the Ranger would not be late without reason—car trouble or some other urgent matter. The captain began the meeting about nine o'clock without Gunn, introducing former prison director Jim Estelle for a few remarks. When Estelle left, Mitchell's secretary stuck her head in the door to tell him he had a telephone call from Gunn. Excusing himself, Mitchell left to take the call in his office.

When the captain came back into the room, the Rangers could tell by the look on his face that something had happened. Gunn had a child abduction case working and needed help. A thirteen-year-old girl from Alvarado had been forced from her brother's vehicle on their way to school that morning. She had not been seen since. If Gunn had called the day before, Mitchell might have gone, along with another Ranger from Waco. But with the whole company in one place anyway, he decided to cancel the meeting and send everyone.

The Rangers rendezvoused about noon at a fried-chicken place in Alvarado. They wolfed down a quick lunch and then reconvened at a command post that had been set up in a nearby bank. At the bank, Sheriff John Boggs briefed Mitchell and his men: About 7:40 that morning, seventeen-year-old Mark McNeil had been driving his little sister, Amy, and their fourteen-year-old cousin to school. About a mile and a half outside of Alvarado, not far from the McNeils' rural house, a gray car pulled off a gravel side road and began following the Jeep driven by McNeil. When the car sped up, Mark McNeil thought the driver intended to pass him. Instead, the car pulled even with his Jeep and began bumping into the vehicle.

Forced off the road, McNeil did not have time to open his door before a man stuck a sawed-off shotgun in his face. Another man armed with a pistol came around to the other side of the Jeep and grabbed Amy, dragging the screaming seventh-grader into the gray car. Warning McNeil not to call the police, the two men sped off with the blond junior high cheerleader.

About 10:00 a.m., as Mitchell and his men drove toward Alvarado at what the captain liked to call "Ranger speed," Don McNeil, one of the directors of Alvarado State Bank, got a telephone call from one of his daughter's captors. A male voice said he would be calling again about noon. Meanwhile, McNeil should be getting $100,000 in cash together if he ever wanted to see his daughter alive again.

The next call did not come when promised, but at 1:00 p.m. the phone rang in the McNeil home. When McNeil answered, he heard his daughter's voice. She sounded scared but said she was okay. It being a bitterly cold day, McNeil asked if she was warm. "Yes," she said. When McNeil asked if she knew where she was, she said, "No," and the line went dead.

A telephone tap had been installed on McNeil's line, but the conversation had not lasted long enough for it to be traced. The tap did indicate the call had come from the Dallas–Fort Worth area. A couple of minutes after the call from Amy, one of the kidnappers called back. He said to expect another call. The Rangers spent the night at the command post in the bank, sleeping on the floor, but for most of them not very long or well.

On Saturday, the pace picked up. The kidnappers called periodically throughout the day, but the most substantive call came about 5:00 p.m. One of his daughter's captors, the one who had been doing most of the talking, told McNeil to drive to a certain telephone booth in East Dallas for additional instructions about where to drop off the money. In that call, the kidnapper told McNeil to drive to another pay phone in Tyler, a hundred miles east of Dallas. At that phone booth, the kidnapper gave McNeil directions to a closed service station on the edge of Mount Pleasant, in Titus County.

Driving his black Cadillac, McNeil headed for Mount Pleasant with the cash to get his daughter back. Mitchell and his Rangers, several Johnson County sheriff's deputies, and two FBI agents followed discreetly. A DPS helicopter and one of the department's fixed-wing aircraft provided aerial surveillance.

Ranger John Aycock of Temple rushed ahead to the drop point. There he and Mount Pleasant–based Ranger Brantly Foster concealed themselves where they had a view of the telephone booth the kidnappers had selected for the exchange to occur. Lying on the cold ground with high-powered rifles and binoculars, the two Rangers watched for any suspicious activity.

At midnight, a car passed slowly by the service station but did not stop. The Rangers had a hunch the vehicle contained the kidnappers and their young victim, but they opted not to follow it for fear of scaring them away from the planned exchange. About 4:00 a.m., the same car returned. Again, the person behind the wheel drove slowly by the station. This time the car pulled onto Interstate 30, speeding up. Now nearly certain that the car contained the crooks and their hostage, one of the Rangers—using his handheld radio—relayed a description of the vehicle to the other officers. Checking the vehicle's registration, the Rangers learned it had been reported stolen in Arlington, east of Fort Worth, earlier that night.

Rangers Joe Wiley and Jimmy Ray spotted the 1983 Buick a short time later in Mount Pleasant and decided to stop it. As Wiley and Ray got near the car, traveling at more than 100 miles an hour, the Rangers started seeing flashes of orange.

"They're shooting at us," Wiley radioed.

Still parked near the drop point, Mitchell keyed his microphone. "Are you sure?" he radioed.

"I'd sure welcome a second opinion," Wiley replied, bullets pinging into the front of his car. The two Rangers had their pistols out about to start shooting when one of the gunmen held Amy up so that she could be seen. The lawmen held their fire. But the shots from the kidnappers had punctured their vehicle's radiator. With steam billowing from under the hood of their state car, Rangers Wiley and Ray had to drop out of the chase.

The captain realized the Rangers had no hope of getting Amy back the easy way. Now the Rangers had to stop that car and get her out of it before her captors could hurt or kill her. Passing Ranger Wiley's disabled vehicle, the other officers quickly gained on the suspects. In twenty minutes, the high-speed pursuit covered three counties, Titus, Franklin, and Hopkins. The chase ended when the fleeing vehicle slowed and then rolled to a stop in front of a house in the small town of Saltillo. The kidnappers had run out of gas and luck at the same time.

Rangers John Dendy[1] and Howard "Slick" Alford, accompanied by Johnson County sheriff's deputy D. J. Maulder, reached the scene first. As the Ranger unit skidded to a stop, two of the kidnappers got out of their car, took cover behind a van parked outside the house, and started shooting at the officers. The Rangers shot back, laying down a withering fire of .223 slugs from their Ruger Mini-14 rifles. Within moments, the other officers arrived and joined the firefight.

Bullets flying, Rangers Dendy and Alford, both in their mid-fifties, ran toward the Buick they had been chasing. Looking inside, Dendy could see two females and two males. Covering them with his .45, the Ranger ordered the occupants not to move, but one of the females jumped from the car and ran toward Alford.

"She asked me if I was a policeman, and I said, 'Yes,'" the Ranger later recounted. "I asked her if she was Amy, and she said, 'Yes.' Amy and I were awful glad to see each other."

Alford wrapped his arms around the teenager and ran with her back toward his car. The two gunmen down with what proved to be minor gunshot wounds, the Rangers arrested the suspects and called for an ambulance.

McNeil, who had been in Mitchell's car during the chase, ran to his daughter and took her in his arms. "Daddy, I love you," she said as the two literally danced for joy in the middle of the road in front of the house. "It was something like I never experienced before," Alford said later. "I don't know which is the greatest thing in the world, to see your own child born, get your first look at him, or see something like this."

The Rangers and other officers involved in the case had not slept since learning of the kidnapping. Now that the teenager had been recovered and the kidnap suspects booked into jail, Dendy and the others sank into exhaustion. "All he [Dendy] wanted to do was brush his teeth," DPS public information officer Larry Todd told reporters later that Sunday. That night, when a reporter called Dendy's home, Vinita, the Ranger's wife, said her husband had gone to bed. "He was just doing his job," she told the journalist, "but I'm very proud of him and relieved with him. We're just happy the little girl is safe."

"God bless him," the teenager's weary father said of Dendy. "He and everyone else who worked on the case were just remarkable."

The FBI had worked hard, too, but the agents involved refused to talk with reporters even though media outlets in the Dallas–Fort Worth area had agreed to withhold any mention of the kidnapping until the victim had been recovered. The news story, focusing on the Rangers as heroes and glossing over the role of the Johnson County deputy and the federal agents, played big in Texas and across the nation.[2]

"They may be the most fantastic organization in the world," Don McNeil said of the Rangers. "When you've got a situation like this, they move in and they move in to stay. . . . They are there until the problem is solved."[3]

When Mitchell got back to Waco, Governor Mark White called him. The governor thanked him for the good work and asked if the Rangers needed anything to do their job better. Yes, Mitchell offered, Rangers need better radios. Not long after that, the captain got word that the Rangers' radio equipment would be upgraded.[4]

Though Mitchell had not minded asking the governor for something he felt the Rangers needed, the man in charge of the Rangers and the rest of the DPS was James B. Adams. A Texan who had risen to the number two spot at the FBI during a twenty-seven-year career with the agency, Adams had been appointed by Governor White's predecessor, Dallas oilman Bill Clements. Clements, who had run a huge drilling company and served as deputy secretary of defense during the Nixon presidency, took a chief executive officer approach as governor.[5] The new governor had broken DPS tradition by bringing in a director from the outside, appointing Adams effective January 1, 1980, following Colonel Speir's retirement. The fact that Adams had spent a long career in the bureau also galled some of the DPS's powers that could have been, men who did not think quite as highly of the agency as the late J. Edgar Hoover had or Adams did.

But Adams had been on the job for five years by the time of the Ranger rescue of the Alvarado teenager, and the DPS had adjusted to the change. The same day the Rangers shot it out with the kidnappers in North Texas, the state's newspapers carried an Associated Press story announcing the retirement of Senior Captain Bill Wilson. After eleven years as head of the Rangers, he would be hanging up his gun effective January 31, 1985. Fifty-five years old, he could have stayed longer, but the former UT football star faced a new contest, this time with cancer. In remission following surgery and chemotherapy for lung cancer, the captain wanted more time with his family.

Throughout his thirty-two-year law enforcement career, Wilson had been a strict disciplinarian. He expected his Rangers to work hard and keep up a good appearance. "No hair on the collar, no hair on the face," Wilson said of the Rangers. The captain had one other rule: "No love triangles. A man that's happy at home is happy in his job."[6]

Retirements and the occasional forced resignation of ranking personnel had always been factors of change for the DPS—and any organization for that matter—but Colonel Adams had signed off on a policy that in time would permanently alter the composition of the Rangers. The new director ended the long-standing DPS practice of direct appointment of law enforcement officers from other agencies as Rangers. The new policy stipulated that a Ranger applicant must have at least eight years of law enforcement experience, including four years with the DPS. While Adams realized that the Rangers had some good personnel seasoned by other jurisdictions, he believed the new policy would further depoliticize the Ranger appointment process.

Bob Steele, a private in Company D stationed in San Antonio, viewed Adams's action with more than detached interest. His colleagues called him, a native New Yorker, the Yankee Ranger. Twenty years earlier, Steele had been one of New York's finest, walking a beat and adroitly twirling his nightstick in the doubled-breasted blue coat made famous in scores of movies and TV shows. A streetwise big-city cop, he had a dream that lay far beyond the Hudson River: He wanted to be a Texas Ranger. He read all the books he could find on the Rangers, collected Ranger memorabilia, and talked to his fellow cops in the Big Apple about how badly he wanted to wear a Ranger's silver star, the *cinco peso*.

After a decade on the job, including criminal investigation and undercover work, Steele left New York for Texas in 1970. With his background, he easily hired on with the DPS. Even so, he went through the training academy like any other khaki-clad cadet. Ten years later, by then with twenty years of law enforcement experience, he applied with 107 other men for five openings in the Rangers. He got the job, having earned the second-highest score in the written examination. "I'm part of the Rangers' affirmative action program," the White Plains, New York, native liked to joke.[7]

Adams's rule change had come too late to have interfered with Steele's dream of becoming a Ranger, but he and many of the old-timers realized it would affect the service radically as time went on. No longer would a longtime sheriff with an impressive record or a big-city cop with extensive investigative experience be able to go straight into the Rangers. Unless some future director reversed Adams's change, they realized that the day would come when every Ranger would be a graduate of the DPS training academy.

While Adams continued making the improvements he believed the DPS needed, the San Antonio *Light* took a look at the Rangers, including the impact the past continued to have on the service's present. "Modern day Texas Rangers feel the weight of their tradition," wrote reporter Gordon Dillow. The journalist quoted the soon-to-retire Senior Captain Wilson: "The men and myself have a tradition to uphold and I'm not going to—and the men aren't going to—let that tradition down." Not that the plain-spoken captain embraced every aspect of Ranger tradition. "I don't have any damn use for a horse," he once told a reporter. "It's not a requirement that you own a horse. Some Rangers don't like to ride them and I for one don't."[8]

Whether Rangers were horse lovers or not, Ranger attitudes—aided by some key retirements and federal court decisions—had temporized. But the Rangers still reflected old Texas: They had only four Hispanics. No blacks or women yet wore the silver star. No blacks had been promoted into the service because none had qualified yet, Captain Wilson told the newspaper. "Eventually, they say, that will change," Dillow wrote. As to not having any female Rangers, Dillow went on, "Senior Ranger officers decline to discuss what one of them called 'that can of worms.'" Though still just a rookie, Yankee Ranger Steele had some thoughts about what lay ahead: "The future is up to us. We can keep the Rangers as great as they've always been, by doing the best damn job we can do. The Rangers have been handed to us in good shape, and it's up to us to hand it to whoever follows in as good or better shape."[9]

Not long after Wilson and Steele fielded the San Antonio reporter's tough questions about the Rangers, a minor controversy involving the Rangers' image broke out in Dallas. After the opening of the new Dallas–Fort Worth Airport in 1974, the twelve-foot-tall *One Riot–One Ranger* statue had been moved from the lobby of Love Field, where it had stood since the early 1960s, to a not-too-busy corner in Union Station. But Mrs. Earle Wyatt, who with her late husband had donated the statue to the City of Dallas, complained to the city's parks department that its location in the old train station did not give it enough visibility.[10] After considerable discussion, the statue went back to Love Field.

While Mrs. Wyatt worried about the location of the statue, the Rangers had their own problem: oil-field theft. Ever since Spindletop spouted crude in 1901, the oil industry had affected the Rangers in one way or another. A market had always existed for stolen oil-field equipment, but rising costs had brought an increase in the theft of crude oil. The legislature had passed a law in the spring of 1981 making it a second-degree felony to steal oil or natural gas or oil-field equipment, no matter its value. Another bill required used-equipment dealers to keep records of all transactions.

Six Texas oil and gas associations had opened a hot line on July 1 that year to accept collect calls on oil theft information. Suddenly, one out of five Ranger cases involved property crime in the oil patch. Gene Wright, heading an oil-field task force for the Texas Independent Producers & Royalty Owners Association, estimated thefts amounted to $50 million a year. "It's so dang big and hard to get to, I don't think anybody really knows how big it is," he told the Dallas *Morning News*.

That September, as concealed Rangers and FBI agents watched, three suspected thieves accepted delivery of stolen oil-field equipment. The state and federal officers followed them to Oklahoma, where they committed two thefts at oil wells. When the thieves returned to Texas, the Rangers arrested them and recovered the stolen property. Free on bond, one of the defendants soon got caught in the act again during another ranger oil well surveillance operation in Freestone County. By the time the Rangers wrapped up their investigation they had linked the gang to several million dollars in oil-field thefts.[11]

In running down oil-field thieves, Rangers had to cope with a relatively new crime, but reverence for their past continued. The Former Texas Rangers Association, a nonprofit organization tracing its roots to the Ex Rangers Association active from the 1920s to the early 1950s, began having reunions again in the early 1970s. They gathered on the first Sunday of every May at the Pioneers, Trail Drivers, and Texas Rangers Building adjacent to the Witte Museum in San Antonio. At the May 1, 1983, reunion, members of the association—former Rangers or Ranger descendants—dedicated a statue in front of the museum. The large bronze depicted a Frontier Battalion–era Ranger leading a pack mule across rough ground.

A few of the old-timers on hand for the unveiling, including Lee Trimble, had served in the Rangers along the border during the first two decades of the twentieth century and knew firsthand the importance of a good mule. One of the Rangers there that day was Joe B. Davis, then stationed at Kerrville, a Hill Country town west of San Antonio on Interstate 10. A fourteen-year Ranger veteran, Davis and eleven other Rangers had recently undergone hypnosis training, an investigative technique used to get better information from witnesses.

Before traveling to headquarters for the weeklong school, all Davis had known about hypnosis was what he had seen on television. "I guess

I had the same ideas as most people—that it was some kind of trick," he told a reporter. "But I got over that as soon as our training started." By the summer of 1983, Davis had hypnotized more than seventy-five witnesses in investigations ranging from theft to sexual assault to homicide. "Anything we get under hypnosis has to be corroborated with other evidence," he said. "But we can get some leads when we wouldn't have anything else to go on."[12]

Hypnosis had become an important new tool for the Rangers, but in Wichita Falls on May 19, 1983, Company C Ranger William R. Gerth Jr. fell back on a much more fundamental Ranger skill—good shooting. While in his state vehicle that evening, Gerth heard a city police department broadcast that a federal fugitive wanted for the robbery of a Wichita Falls savings and loan had been seen driving on Sisk Road. Checking the area, the Ranger found a parked pickup truck matching the description of the suspect's vehicle. Then he noticed a man walking toward it. As Gerth radioed for a marked DPS unit as a backup, the man got in the pickup and drove off, Gerth following in his unmarked car. When the Highway Patrol car arrived, the trooper turned on his unit's overhead lights to stop the truck. In response, the driver of the truck floorboarded his vehicle.

The Ranger and the trooper, soon joined by a Wichita Falls police officer, chased the suspect west on Southwest Parkway. Suddenly the pickup truck skidded into a curb and stopped. The driver bolted from the cab and began shooting at the trooper with an automatic rifle. The withering fire blew out the glass in the trooper's car, leaving him lacerated on his face and arms, pinned inside, and unable to return his attacker's fire. When the Ranger saw the gunman closing in to kill the outgunned trooper, he fired a 12-gauge shotgun blast at the gunman. The load caught the man in his chest, spinning him around, but to Gerth's surprise, he pointed his rifle toward him and fired on his way to the ground. The shots went wild, but the man got up and ran toward the passenger side of his truck, still clutching his rifle. Gerth fired two rounds from his .45, knocking him down again. Seeing that the man had gotten up on his knees, Gerth fired two more shots, aiming under the truck. Unable to see the gunman's hands, the Ranger fired a final and fatal shot, hitting the man in his head. When Gerth and other officers moved in, they found why it had taken so many shots to bring the man down—he had been wearing body armor. In addition to the rifle he had been firing, he had a knife and a pistol in his pickup.

The Ranger later received the Public Safety Commission's first Medal of Valor "in recognition of the gallant manner in which he risked his own life to preserve that of a fellow law enforcement officer."[13]

"Yes, Sir. I Have About a Hundred of Them."

Barely a month after the Wichita Falls shoot-out, the Rangers became involved in a case that would generate national and international news media interest and eventually controversy. Just before 5:00 p.m. on June 21, 1983, two Montague County sheriff's deputies escorted a one-eyed murder suspect from his jail cell to the nearby county courthouse for arraignment before District Judge Frank Douthitt. Inside the second-floor courtroom, the judge began what he assumed would be a brief, routine proceeding. The jurist was correct only in that it would not take long.

Douthitt asked forty-six-year-old Henry Lee Lucas if he had read the grand jury indictment accusing him of the murder of Kate Rich, an eighty-two-year-old woman who had disappeared on September 16, 1982.

"I didn't read it, but I know I'm guilty of it," Lucas said.

The judge then asked Lucas if he had an attorney.

"I don't even care if I have one," the defendant replied.

Douthitt requested that District Attorney Jack McGaughey read the murder indictment as well as a second indictment for being a felon in possession of a firearm. When the prosecutor finished, Douthitt asked Lucas if he understood the seriousness of the murder charge filed against him.

"Yes, sir," he said. "I have about a hundred of them."

As reporters scribbled that claim down in their notebooks, Douthitt concluded the hearing and deputies quickly returned Lucas to his cell.

By midmorning the following day, TV station helicopters swarmed over the small county seat like so many metal dragonflies. Lucas's statement in open court marked the public beginning of another episode that would trigger an extended controversy for the Rangers.

Stationed in Decatur, north of Fort Worth, Company C Ranger Phil Ryan had been investigating an oil-field theft case and looking into a series of tractor thefts when he first heard from Montague County sheriff W. A. Conway that the elderly Mrs. Rich had disappeared. When Conway learned that Lucas had been working for Mrs. Rich as a handyman, the sheriff checked to see if the chain-smoking drifter had a criminal history. Conway found that Lucas, who had been living at a religious commune near the small community of Ringgold since May 1982, had an extensive rap sheet. One of the crimes on his record got everyone's attention: the murder of his mother, a 1960 offense for which he had served ten years in Michigan. Shortly after his release from prison, he had been arrested and convicted for trying to kidnap two teenage girls. He did five years for that, then migrated south to Jacksonville, Florida, where he met Ottis Toole, a pyromaniac transvestite. Built like a linebacker, Toole had the intelligence of a fourth-grader. The two began traveling the nation's interstate highways in junker cars, killing, as they later bragged, for sex, money, or just the fun of it. Along on many of the trips, and eventually all of the time, was Toole's fifteen-year-old niece, a runaway teenager named Becky Powell.

Lucas's background and the fact that he was the last person seen with Mrs. Rich certainly made him a suspect, but the investigators had no body or any physical evidence connecting him with her disappearance. Working together, the Ranger and the sheriff discovered that Mrs. Rich was not the only acquaintance of Lucas's who was missing. Toole's young niece, whom Lucas claimed as his common-law wife, also had disappeared. Lucas told Ryan and Conway that Becky had returned to her family in Florida, and the officers had been unable to prove otherwise. From the fall of 1982 through the spring of 1983, Lucas drifted in and out of the county, continuing his travels. Ryan and Conway questioned him every time he came back, but still they had nothing.

Even though they could not connect Lucas to either of the two North Texas disappearances, after obtaining statements that Lucas had been seen at the commune with a pistol the officers got Lucas indicted for being a felon in possession of a firearm. On June 11, 1983, they arrested him for that offense and booked him into the Montague County jail.

Two days later, Lucas sent word that he wanted to talk with the two investigators. When they arrived, Lucas confessed that he not only had killed Mrs. Rich but also had slain the missing Becky Powell. He had stabbed Becky to death on August 24, 1982, he said. He had killed Mrs. Rich on September 16.

Lucas led Ryan and other officers to a field in Denton County where he said he had killed Becky and dismembered her body. The officers soon found human remains at the location. Back in Montague County, they recovered charred bones from a wood-burning cookstove Lucas had used to heat the converted chicken coop he had lived in with Becky. Lucas told Ryan he had tried to dispose of the elderly woman's body by cutting it up and burning the pieces in the stove.

All this happened prior to Lucas's admission in district court that he had killed many other women, something he had already told investigators. After hearing of Lucas's claim, Williamson County sheriff Jim Boutwell drove from his office in Georgetown, thirty miles north of Austin, to Montague to talk with the self-proclaimed serial killer about an unsolved murder in his county. On June 22, Lucas confessed to Boutwell that he had killed a hitchhiker in Williamson County three years before. Her body, nude except for a pair of orange socks, had been found in a culvert beneath Interstate 35 on Halloween night in 1979.

Following Lucas's conviction in the two North Texas homicides, in November Boutwell took Lucas to Williamson County, where a grand jury had indicted him for capital murder in the death of the still-unidentified young woman who had come to be called Orange Socks. By the time the chain-smoking ex-convict settled into his solitary cell in the old limestone jail in Georgetown, he had been charged with ten homicides. In addition, based on his voluntary admissions, various other jurisdictions considered him a suspect in 150 other murders from Florida to California. Sheriff Boutwell found himself inundated with telephone calls and teletypes from law enforcement officers across the nation wanting to talk with Lucas about unsolved homicides in their areas. Not having a large enough staff to handle the call load, Boutwell contacted DPS director Adams and asked for help.

Ranger Sergeant Bob Prince, second-in-command of Company F in Waco, soon arrived in Georgetown. Prince began organizing a task force to coordinate the growing number of requests from various law enforcement agencies to interview Lucas. Assisting him would be Ranger Clayton Smith, also stationed in Waco.[14]

"The first day there I had over seventy long distance telephone calls to return," Prince later recalled. "Our role was not an investigative role. Our role was a coordinative role. We scheduled the appointments of agencies and press people wanting to talk with Lucas."[15] As the task force's workload continued to increase, W. A. "Bob" Werner, the DPS's assistant chief of the Criminal Law Enforcement Division, became the ranking member of the team. A half-time secretary assisted with telephone calls and correspondence.[16]

In coordinating the Lucas case, the Rangers had undertaken something of unprecedented scale in state law enforcement. At the same time, Adams approved a plan that would relieve them of one of their traditional roles. That August, the director ordered the creation of a Special Weapons And Tactics (SWAT) team, a unit that would take over a function long handled by the Rangers. For nearly fifty years, the DPS-era Rangers had been the ones called to handle barricaded gunmen and other risky situations. But Colonel Adams wanted a more diversified unit to handle high-risk tactical operations such as "anti-sniper actions, barricaded suspect neutralization, hostage rescue, counter-terrorist activities, apprehension of extremely dangerous individuals, and limited dignitary protection." Those selected for membership on the new team soon began an intensive training regimen.[17]

On March 12, 1984, jury selection began in Lucas's trial on the Orange Socks case. His defense attorneys had succeeded in getting the proceedings moved to San Angelo from Williamson County on a change of venue. Testimony got under way on April 2. Eleven days later, on Friday the thirteenth, the jury found Lucas guilty of capital murder. Five days later, in the punishment phase of the trial, the jury took only forty minutes to decide on the death penalty.

Normally, someone facing capital punishment would have been transferred straight to Death Row pending the long appeal process. But like Scheherazade, the Arabian woman who had to keep telling a fascinating story to the king every night to avoid having her head chopped off, Lucas kept confessing to other murders, claiming in one media interview to have killed as many as six hundred people. So that he could be more easily available to the task force and other investigators, Lucas remained in the Williamson County lockup.[18]

Though Prince repeatedly said that the Rangers never believed Lucas killed as many victims as he claimed, some people, both in the news media and in the law enforcement community, had begun to wonder if Lucas had merely been stringing law enforcement along just to stay off Death Row.

As the task force continued its work, the leadership of the Rangers changed with the retirement of Senior Captain Wilson. Captain H. R. "Lefty" Block, who had been assistant Ranger commander under Wilson since August 1981, took over as senior captain on February 1, 1985.[19] Popular with his men, Block had a reputation as a hardworking Ranger with a lot of successful investigations to his credit. The forty-nine-year-old captain had not been in his new office long before the Lucas case began looking to some more like an instance of serial lying than serial murder.

The April 14, 1985, edition of the Dallas *Times-Herald* carried a long copyrighted story on page one: "Henry Lee Lucas: Mass Murderer or Massive Hoax?" The Sunday story and four sidebar articles made a case that Lucas could not have been responsible for as many murders as he claimed. The Ranger-led task force, the stories asserted, had "ignored or failed to pursue leads that would have proven the deceit of his confessions." The newspaper published four more Lucas stories the following day, including one headlined "Lucas Gets Death on His Word Only."[20]

After poring over all the articles, Colonel Adams decided to meet the allegations head-on. "I am satisfied that he killed a substantial number of people," Adams said at an April 16 press conference at DPS headquarters. The director labeled Lucas's claims that he had only killed three people—his mother, Mrs. Rich, and Becky Powell—as "ludicrous."

The colonel went on to say that 189 homicides had been listed as "cleared" by the various law enforcement agencies that had sent officers to talk to Lucas, but that the Ranger task force had merely been serving as a clearinghouse, not an investigative entity. Any connection between Lucas and a particular murder, Adams stressed, had been reached by other law enforcement agencies, not the Rangers. "I am satisfied that the task force operated within its charter," he said.[21]

Two days before the first Dallas *Times-Herald* story broke, Lucas had been removed from the Williamson County jail on a bench warrant issued by a McLennan County district judge. A grand jury in Waco had begun an investigation into the validity of three confessions Lucas had made to homicides in that Central Texas county. District Attorney Vic Feazell asked for assistance from state attorney general Jim Mattox in investigating Lucas's claims. While in the McLennan County jail, on April 23 Lucas told a reporter that he had never killed anyone except his mother, not even Mrs. Rich or the teenage girl he had taken from Florida to Texas. He had decided to tell the truth, he said, because of his recent religious conversion.[22]

On April 24, Sergeant Prince completed a six-page, single-spaced interoffice memorandum to the new senior captain. Prince went through the background of the Lucas case and listed the task force's four major objectives: coordinating law enforcement interviews with the defendant, conducting preliminary interviews with Lucas for other agencies on case reports mailed to the task force, building a travel log showing the movements of Lucas and Toole, and listing and summarizing cases confirmed by an investigator as committed by Lucas or Toole.

To that point, 976 officers representing 584 law enforcement agencies across the United States and Canada had interviewed Lucas, Prince reported. More than three thousand unsolved homicide cases had been discussed with the prisoner. "According to records compiled," the sergeant wrote, "it is believed Lucas has been involved in 190 murders either by himself or with a partner. It is believed Toole alone was involved in twenty-seven homicides making the total homicides 217.

"During the operation of the Task Force," Prince continued, "members have not fed information to Lucas and are not aware of any officer who purposely fed information in order to get a confession to clear a case."

The sergeant noted that all data compiled and distributed by the Rangers bore this disclaimer: "Much of this information was obtained through interviews conducted with Lucas and/or Toole by various officers and agencies, and the data listed is based upon the officers' response. Although it is felt that this information is confirmed, this Department cannot guarantee the correctness of the information listed. . . . This document . . . contains neither recommendations nor conclusions of this Department."

Prince reported the task force had spent approximately eleven thousand man-hours up to that time. In addition, $11,500 had been spent in expenses, $1,050 in postage, and $30,791 for the use of DPS aircraft to transport Lucas for interviews by local officers. On many of those trips, Prince said, Lucas had led officers to crime scenes only the killer would know how to find.[23]

Five days after Prince turned in his memo, Lucas did another media interview. Again he reversed himself. This time he told radio evangelist Bob Larson, "I killed the people. . . . The truth is I killed 360 people." That was enough for a district judge in Waco, who barred any further media interviews of Lucas. The suspect's lawyer also said there would be no additional interviews of his client by law enforcement officers without an attorney present. Two years after he blurted out in open court that he had about "a hundred" victims, Lucas was transferred to the Texas Department of Corrections' Walls Unit in Huntsville to await execution.[24]

As the Rangers continued to take heat over their handling of the Lucas case, a work of fiction centering on the adventures of two colorful ex-Rangers of the nineteenth century—Woodrow Call and Augustus (Gus) McCrae—soon captured the imagination of the American reading public. Published in June 1985, Larry McMurtry's 843-page novel, *Lonesome Dove*, quickly became a bestseller. Like the Rangers, *Lonesome Dove* had an interesting history. The novel traced back to a screenplay written by McMurtry in 1971 for Peter Bogdanovich, whose well-acclaimed black-and-white adaptation of McMurtry's novel *The Last Picture Show* had done well at the box office. For the *Lonesome Dove* movie, McMurtry and Bogdanovich envisioned John Wayne as Call, Jimmy Stewart as McCrae, and Henry Fonda as a Ranger-turned-outlaw named Jake Spoon. Stewart and Fonda showed some interest in the project, but not the Duke, who did not like the script's end-of-the-West theme. As often is the case with movie deals, the screenplay ended up on the shelf.

When he decided to transform the screenplay into a novel, McMurtry freely admitted he had set out with malice aforethought to kill a myth. "I'm a critic of the myth of the cowboys," he said. "I don't feel that it's a myth that pertains . . . the myth of the clean-living cowboy devoted to agrarian pursuits and the rural way of life."

Indeed, McMurtry's cowboys cum rangers, particularly Gus McCrae, did not fit the mold. McCrae was the first fictional onetime wearer of the *cinco peso* to openly express an interest in sex. Before Mc-Murtry, fictional Rangers might occasionally kiss a pretty girl or even marry her and settle down on her father's ranch, but they never talked of "poking" whores. Another character, Spoon, was a likable rake whom Call and McCrae nevertheless ended up hanging.

Like its lead characters, *Lonesome Dove* had its flaws: The book dragged on for at least a hundred pages before the action became compelling; it contained enough anachronisms, conflicts in geography, or chronological errors to annoy realists; it had too many subplots and too many coincidences and ran too long. But even the novel's critics agreed McMurtry had written a fine story, and the reading public loved it.[25] On the New York *Times* Best Seller List for twenty weeks, McMurtry's novel did what a Western had not done in decades—it moved into the American mainstream, rising to the level of literature. *Lonesome Dove* also further assured the standing of the Texas Rangers as an American icon. The *Odyssey*-like novel received the 1985 Spur Award from the Western Writers of America and the Texas Institute of Letters' Jesse Jones Award for Best Fictional Book and went on to win the Pulitzer Prize for fiction.

Focusing on its own story, on August 9, 1985, the DPS celebrated its fiftieth anniversary with an open house at its sprawling Austin headquarters. The Texas National Guard's Forty-ninth Armored Division Band kicked off the proceedings, followed with introductions by Lieutenant Colonel Gossett and a welcome from Colonel Adams. "In the highest traditions of service to the public," Adams told employees and guests, "we have witnessed the evolution of state-level law enforcement services from the frontier days to the advanced technology age, confident that the Department of Public Safety occupies a special place in the history of the Lone Star State." McAllen attorney Ruben Cardenas, chairman of the Public Safety Commission, introduced Governor White, who gave the keynote address. Following the governor, Mrs. Mary Nell Garrison, widow of the DPS's longtime director, provided a brief history of the agency.

During the noon hour, DPS employees and visitors enjoyed a catered barbecue lunch. The daylong program culminated months of planning by a nineteen-member committee chaired by Maurice Beckham, head of the department's Inspection and Planning Section. In addition to organizing the celebration, Beckham and his committee licensed a variety of commemorative items, ranging from a painting depicting a Ranger on horseback in front of the DPS main building to twelve hundred gold-inlaid .45-caliber Colt semiautomatics that sold for $500 each.[26]

The DPS and the Rangers had observed a major mile marker in their history, but their work went on. Earlier that summer, state senator John Montford of Lubbock, a prosecutor before his election to the legislature, pointed out something that had always set the Rangers apart: "They knew no hours and never punched a clock. They were with you all the way . . . solid as a rock."[27]

But the Rangers were going to have to start watching their hours. Significantly amended by Congress in 1974, the federal Fair Labor Standards Act made it mandatory that workers (supervisors exempted) receive overtime pay for putting in more than forty hours a week. Two years later, the U.S. Supreme Court had ruled that "traditional functions" of states could not fall under federal regulation. That made FLSA requirements strictly optional for state and local governments. In February 1985, however, the high court held 5–4 in *Garcia v. San Antonio Metropolitan Transit Authority* that FLSA requirements could be applied to state and local governments. As a state agency, the DPS would have to comply with the federal law in regard to overtime. In effect, something the Rangers had been doing since long before the FLSA existed—working with little regard to normal hours—would have to stop. The long-term impact on the DPS would be enormous, in both overtime costs and lost man-hours. A year before the landmark decision, all DPS officers, including the Rangers, had put in 290,169 overtime hours. If they were paid at time-and-a-half, that would have cost the agency $6 million. With nothing in the budget for the coming fiscal year to handle overtime, the Rangers and other DPS services would have to hold open vacant positions to save enough money to handle necessary overtime.[28]

Subject to call any time of the day or night, the members of the DPS's first SWAT team would be getting some of that overtime. Each of the team's eleven members, none of them a Ranger, had received 356 hours of specialized training. Led by a Highway Patrol lieutenant, the team included a narcotics sergeant, two narcotics agents, and seven Highway Patrol troopers.[29] Declared operational on December 9, 1985, the new team would not put the Rangers entirely out of the business of confronting dangerous offenders, but its creation represented a major departure from a tradition long predating the creation of the DPS.

Early in 1986, the attorney general's office released a sixty-page report on its investigation of the handling of the Lucas case. Though the report concluded that investigators had uncovered "no evidence to prove that any members of law enforcement in Texas deliberately tried to bring about this scheme of deception," the investigators concluded that they had "found information that would lead us to believe that some officials 'cleared cases' just to get them off the books."[30] In response, the Public Safety Commission issued a statement on January 30 that it had found no evidence of any wrongdoing on the part of the Rangers and that no disciplinary action was deemed necessary.[31]

U.S. Representative Henry B. Gonzalez of San Antonio certainly had nothing bad to say about the Rangers. When President Ronald Reagan asked Congress for $100 million to help the Contras overthrow the dictatorial government of Nicaragua, he warned that terrorists had a base "just two days drive from Harlingen." In response, the South Texas congressman pointed out that the Confederate Air Force—a collection of flying World War II–vintage museum pieces—had its headquarters in Harlingen. Beyond that, he quipped, "We have the Texas Rangers. You know, 'one riot, one ranger.' . . . I do not share the President's fears."[32]

While the Reagan administration continued to rattle sabers for Central America, set construction began in El Paso for *Extreme Prejudice,* a movie starring Nick Nolte as a third-generation Texas Ranger who breaks up a drug ring run by an old friend. To learn the mannerisms of modern Rangers, Nolte spent time in Uvalde with Ranger Joaquin Jackson, a Ranger since 1967. Nolte was not the first entertainer to get some coaching from the tall Ranger. After arresting a young singer named Johnny Rodriquez for goat theft, Jackson had set up an audition for him. Rodriquez went on to become one of the first Mexican-American country-western singers to break into the mainstream. The day after meeting with Jackson in South Texas, Nolte came to the DPS headquarters in Austin for a briefing on Ranger history and culture. The visit caused considerable commotion as female state employees clamored for the actor's autograph.[33]

Rangers familiar with their history knew that in 1906 the legendary Captain Bill McDonald had gone to Colorado County to prevent further bloodshed in a local feud. Eighty years later, the Rangers briefly became the focus of another feud involving parties in the same county. The first affair involved guns, the second only words. The issue revolved around an aluminum historical marker and four paragraphs of raised-letter text. The word war began when James G. and Mary E. Hopkins did the research and provided the money for a historical marker about the origin of the Rangers. When the Texas Historical Commission approved the placing of the marker on the courthouse square in Columbus, the seat of Colorado County, some folks in nearby Austin County took public exception. In their opinion, the new marker would give the public the impression that the Rangers originated in Colorado County. Not so, the Austin County partisans maintained. They believed the marker should go up in San Felipe, a nearby ghost town in their county—twenty-five miles from Columbus. That's where *empresario* Stephen F. Austin had lived when he first envisioned Rangers for his colony. "To say the least, we're a little miffed," Wayne Schavrda told the *Houston Chronicle*. "It's sad, because those people not familiar with Texas history will accept anything etched in stone with the state seal as being fact." San Felipe city secretary Kay Taylor agreed: "They're making a connection with Columbus that isn't there." "We did not say [Columbus] was the birthplace of the Texas Rangers," said Frances Rickhard, head of the Historical Commission's research and marker program. "It happens to be in Colorado County because Colorado County paid for the marker," he continued. "It's just a general topical marker for the area." Despite page one newspaper coverage of the short-lived controversy, the county dedicated the marker as scheduled on May 17.

The counties had sparred over perception, not reality. When Austin proposed hiring ten Rangers to protect his colony neither Austin nor Colorado County existed as a political subdivision. Company A captain Dan North, invited to be a guest speaker at the dedication of the marker, demonstrated the political adroitness it takes to be a Ranger. "I dare say you can make a case for both towns," North said. "Don't get the Rangers in the middle of it, because we don't know."[34]

Captain North's Rangers did get in the middle of the investigation into a crime that occurred on Christmas Eve 1986 at Houston's Intercontinental Airport. A passenger named Clayton Moore (better known as the Lone Ranger) and his wife, Connie, checked their baggage and boarded a flight for California after a promotional appearance in the Houston area. Back on the West Coast, when the couple claimed their luggage they discovered that someone had stolen one of their bags. Whoever took the bag now possessed Moore's two pearl-handled six-shooters, the weapons that had seen him through 169 TV episodes. Holstered in a hand-tooled leather belt with thirty-six bullets (made of aluminum, not silver), the pistols were more than firearms; they were a Ranger icon. Working with Houston police, Rangers soon put together a case against an airline baggage handler who had flipped the chrome-plated .45s for $400 at a Houston pawnshop. The handguns eventually ended up with a Beaumont coin dealer, an ex-con who planned to offer them to collectors for $10,000. But when he learned that the pistols not only belonged to the Lone Ranger, but the real Texas Rangers were looking for them, he turned them over to his attorney. The lawyer, in turn, notified authorities and returned the pistols to Moore.[35]

Two years almost to the day after the Amy McNeil case, many of the same Rangers who had been involved in the young cheerleader's rescue worked together on another kidnapping. This time, the results would be decidedly different.

KIDNAPPING AT HORSESHOE BAY

When Ranger Johnny Waldrip's telephone rang at 3:15 p.m. on January 14, 1987, for once he was actually in his office in the Llano County courthouse. Like most Rangers, Waldrip preferred to be on the move as opposed to behind his desk, but paperwork had to be done and this was one of the days he picked to get caught up. The caller was a county constable whose precinct included a high-end lake resort near Marble Falls called Horseshoe Bay. The secretary of Bill Whitehead, one of the community's well-to-do home owners, had gotten a telephone call from Denise Johnson, employed by the Whiteheads as a maid. Johnson said she had been kidnapped and that "they" had placed a bomb in the Whitehead residence.

Waldrip and Llano County chief deputy Rod Decker drove to Horseshoe Bay. When they arrived at the Whitehead house, they found that local officers and the Horseshoe Bay security service had already checked the house for a possible bomb. Nothing had been found, but Waldrip ordered another search.

Satisfied there was no bomb, Waldrip talked to the secretary who had spoken with the maid. She relayed a bizarre conversation. The twenty-two-year-old Johnson had called her shortly before 2:00 p.m. "Amy, I think I'm being kidnapped," she said calmly. "And I think they put a bomb in the house." The secretary asked her what was going on, and she repeated: "I think I'm being kidnapped. Call the police." Johnson said she was in the house across the street and then hung up.

The Ranger and other officers checked the house immediately across from the Whitehead residence, not finding any signs of an intruder. They searched the house next door as well, but it showed no indication of forced entry.

Waldrip loaned the Whiteheads a tape recorder to connect to their telephone in case Johnson called again. He then began to talk to people who knew the young woman. A week later, Waldrip knew a lot about Denise Johnson. But one thing he still did not know was where she was. No signs of foul play had turned up, but the fact that one of the shopping bags she had returned with was in the garage indicated she might have been unloading her car when for whatever reason she suddenly left. A check of her apartment showed none of her clothing or personal belongings missing. Subpoenaed financial records revealed no activity on her account since her disappearance. Given those sinister findings, Waldrip organized a search of the lakeshore by the Texas Parks and Wildlife Department and Lower Colorado River Authority officers. That effort netted nothing.

At 4:30 a.m. on January 22, a week and a day since Johnson had been reported missing, Whitehead called Waldrip at home, waking him up. He said someone had taken their two-year-old daughter, Kara-Leigh, from their house while they slept. The Ranger notified Captain Bob Mitchell in Waco and the FBI before rushing to Horseshoe Bay.

When Waldrip reached the Whitehead residence, he learned someone had called them about 4:00 a.m. Mrs. Whitehead had answered the phone. "Put Bill on the phone," the caller said. When she asked who he was, he repeated, "Put Bill on the phone." Mrs. Whitehead handed her husband the telephone and went to their kitchen to get the tape recorder that Ranger Waldrip had left with them. On her way to the kitchen, she saw the rear sliding glass door was open. She immediately went upstairs to their children's room and discovered that their baby was gone.

"If you don't want the same thing to happen to your daughter that happened to your maid, you had better listen to me," the caller told Whitehead. "Here are the rules. Number one, no cops. Number two, I want thirty thousand dollars in twenty-dollar bills. Number three, don't let your little boy go to school." He added, "I made hamburger out of your maid, and I'll make hamburger out of your little girl."

Whitehead asked the man if he had his daughter.

"Yes," he said. Young and cocky, the caller talked like a cowboy.

"What about my housekeeper? Did you kill her?"

"Yes, I killed her . . . I'm impervious to killing," he said. "You have twenty-four hours to get the money together or I'll kill your daughter."

When the man hung up, Whitehead called the sheriff's department and then Ranger Waldrip. After Captain Mitchell and most of the other Rangers in Company F arrived that morning, they settled on a tentative plan: When the kidnapper told Whitehead where to drop the money, two Rangers would be hiding in the back of his car, hoping for a chance to rescue the girl and arrest her captor.

At 2:20 that afternoon, the kidnapper called again. He asked for Whitehead, who Mrs. Whitehead said had gone to the bank to get the money. The kidnapper may have thought that was good news, but his call had been a stupid mistake. The FBI had a tracing device on the line and quickly determined that whoever the kidnapper was, he was in the unoccupied vacation home right across the street from the Whitehead residence.

Seven hours later, at 9:20 p.m., the kidnapper called again. He wanted the car Whitehead would deliver the money in to have a full tank of gas. Ten minutes later the kidnapper called and told Whitehead to drive his car into the driveway of the house across from his. Whitehead should have the money in the vehicle and leave the lights on, motor running, and door open. After doing all that, he was supposed to walk away.

Whitehead's Mercedes being too small to accommodate hidden Rangers, District Attorney Sam Oatman had agreed to furnish his personal vehicle, a new Lincoln. The Rangers had taken the backseat out, and two volunteers, Johnny Aycock and Stan Guffey, lay hidden in the back when Whitehead drove the car to the house. As ordered, Whitehead quickly ran from the scene.

As Rangers and FBI agents looked on from various points of concealment, a man came out of the house with a little girl. He placed the child in the front seat and threw the briefcase containing the money into the backseat. The officers watching the driveway could not tell exactly what happened next, but they saw the orange muzzle blasts of handguns and heard the shots. When Guffey rose and identified himself as a Ranger, the kidnapper cursed and fired one shot from a .44 Magnum revolver. Though the bullet hit him in the head, Guffey instinctively squeezed the trigger of his pistol, the shot going wild. Aycock managed to get the little girl into the backseat with him, at virtually the same time firing his 9mm semiautomatic at the gunman, the nine rounds slamming into his body literally blowing him out of his shoes.

In a matter of moments, the kidnapper lay dead and a Ranger was dying, but Kara-Leigh Whitehead had been rescued unharmed. A short time later, Rangers found the body of the missing housekeeper in the boathouse behind the residence the kidnapper had used as his base of operations.

Rangers located the man's driver license and identified him as Brent Albert Beeler, twenty-three. A recent parolee already wanted for violating the terms of that parole, Beeler had been arrested at various times for fraud, forgery, and possession of dangerous drugs. Investigators later learned that Beeler had once worked for the man who owned the residence next door to the house he had broken into.[36]

Four days later, more than 750 people attended Guffey's funeral in Brady, his hometown. "Stan is not the first Texas Ranger to give his life for the people of Texas; and, sadly, he's not likely to be the last," Colonel Adams said in delivering the Ranger's eulogy. "His death will remind the people of this state why they should be extremely proud we have a service like the Texas Rangers." Calling it "as applicable today as it was then," Adams concluded his remarks with a stanza from a poem written ninety years earlier by a Ranger stationed in far West Texas:

> *He may not win the laurels,*
> *Nor trumpet tongue of fame,*
> *But beauty smiles upon him,*

And ranchmen bless his name.
Then here's to the Texas Ranger,
Past, present, and to come,
Our safety from the savage,
The guardian of our home.[37]

That spring, Colonel Adams decided to retire. Assistant Director Leo E. Gossett, passed over when Governor Clements brought in Adams, took over as director of the department on June 1, 1987. The new colonel soon had to deal with his first public relations crisis as the state's top cop. It involved the Rangers, or at least one man's aspirations to become a Ranger.

In July Highway Patrol trooper Michael Scott, an African-American stationed in Houston, learned he had not been chosen for a Ranger opening for which he had applied. On July 17, State Representative Ron Wilson of Houston released a letter he had written to Gossett. "It was a complete and total shock to learn that over the 160-year history of the Texas Rangers, there has never been a black ranger. In this day and time I find this to be an affront to the black law enforcement officers and to those who aspire to become law enforcement officers. Personally, I find it to be unacceptable." The legislator said he wanted to discuss with Gossett "what steps are presently being taken by the department to better assist the black officers in attaining their goals." When the two met, Gossett explained to the lawmaker that other applicants, including the Ranger who got the job, had scored higher in the selection process. Scott stayed in the Highway Patrol.[38]

Later that summer, Senior Captain Block delivered the keynote speech at the August 22 dedication of a state historical marker for the Center Point Cemetery in eastern Kerr County, the final resting place of thirty-two frontier-era Rangers. "The thirty-two . . . Texas Rangers who lie here don't have much in common," the captain said. "They didn't look alike, they went on to do different things after they left the Rangers, and they had different joys and different sorrows in life. But they were Texas Rangers and that did give them something in common, then and now." Block quoted from a book written by one of the men buried there, A. J. Sowell: "A genuine Texas Ranger will endure cold, hunger and fatigue, almost without a murmur, and will stand by a

friend and comrade in the hour of danger, and divide anything he has
got, from a blanket to his last crumb of tobacco." At the conclusion of
the ceremony, the past and the present converged as a squad of horseback modern-day Rangers loped into the cemetery and circled the
graves of their predecessors.[39]

It received no notice in the news media, but among the many laws
going into effect on September 1, 1987, as passed earlier that year by the
seventieth legislature, was an eleven-word amendment to Chapter 147,
Section 411.015 of the Texas Government Code, the statute which relates to the organization of the DPS. The new language read: "The division relating to the Texas Rangers may not be abolished."

That fall, actor Robert Duvall came to Texas to ready himself for his
upcoming role as Gus McCrae in the planned TV version of *Lonesome
Dove*. On September 30, he visited the American Hat Company in
Houston to look at Ranger-style headgear. As the fifty-five-year-old
screen star tried on various cowboy hats upstairs, two young Rangers
happened to show up, also interested in new hats. "Duval met the
Rangers and was impressed," Houston *Post* editor and columnist Lynn
Ashby wrote. "He began asking questions about their work and the
agency. The Rangers thought it would be neat if they had their picture
taken with him. Duval thought it was even better that he had his picture made with them."[40]

After running the DPS for only a year, Gossett announced his retirement effective July 31, 1988. Assistant Director Joe Milner, who had
spent twenty years as chief of traffic law enforcement before becoming
assistant director, would succeed him as the agency's head. Just before he
stepped down, however, Gossett made history, approving the promotion
of the twentieth century's first black Ranger. "There's a certain mystique about the Texas Rangers," Gossett told a reporter. "It's a highly
sought-after job in the department, and many people have to apply many
times—most do—before they're successful."[41]

The outgoing director had the data to back that up. A year earlier,
the department's personnel bureau had prepared Gossett a memorandum with the names of eleven Rangers who had tried from three to ten
times to become a Ranger before succeeding. Average number of attempts by those eleven Rangers was 5.6.[42]

"I feel pretty good," forty-one year-old Lee Roy Young Jr. said after learning that he and three other DPS officers had made the cut. "It's been an ambition of mine for many years." A native of Del Rio and a descendant of a Seminole Indian scout who had settled in Brackettville, Young had been with the DPS for nearly fifteen years. He was working in San Antonio as an investigator with the department's Criminal Intelligence Service when he got the word that he would be promoted.

Gary Bledsoe, president of the Austin chapter of the NAACP, said he was happy for Young but disappointed for Trooper Scott, who still had not been promoted. "He [Scott] really is the person who brought all this to bear." Bledsoe went on to suggest that in the wake of criticism from the NAACP and others, the DPS would "start promoting a few people [of color] because we have to, but we're going to promote people who don't complain or stand up for their rights, people who play by the rules of the game."[43]

Young, however, said he thought the department had a fair promotional system. He had tried three times before to be promoted to Ranger before finally succeeding.[44] Stationed in Garland, a suburb of Dallas, after three months on the job Young told an Associated Press writer that he looked forward to the point when all the publicity surrounding his promotion would end. He liked his new job, he said, and already had been involved in a variety of investigations ranging from forgery to murder.[45]

The only African-American associated with the ex-Rangers of *Lonesome Dove* was a likable character named Joshua Deets, played by Danny Glover. In both the novel and TV miniseries, when the chips are down the trusted scout proves he could be just as effective as any Ranger. Based on a four-hundred-page script by Texan Bill Wittliff, the four-part, eight-hour *Lonesome Dove* miniseries premiered on February 5, 1989, making more money for CBS and getting better reviews than anything any of the big three TV networks had tried since *Roots* in 1977. The first episode enjoyed a rating of 25.2 in the nation's seventeen largest markets, drawing 37 percent of all viewers that Sunday night. Dallas *Morning News* columnist Kent Biffle called the series "the Gone With the Wind of the American west."[46]

A month after *Lonesome Dove* captivated the nation and nearly four years after allegations surfaced that accused serial killer Henry Lee Lucas had confessed to murders he had not committed, the state's highest criminal appeals court upheld the drifter's conviction in the Orange Socks case. The Texas Court of Criminal Appeals' March 22 ruling kept Lucas on Death Row, still occasionally granting media interviews in which he continued to claim he had only been stringing the Rangers along.[47]

On April 27, 1989, President George Herbert Walker Bush came to Austin to address a joint session of the state legislature, the first time a U.S. president had been accorded such an honor in Texas. But Governor Clements, back in office after defeating Mark White, presented the president with something he considered even more special—a gold star-in-wheel badge and an honorary captaincy in the Texas Rangers.[48]

13

"Last Bastion of the Good-Old-Boy System . . ."

THE 1990s

With the United States still pursuing a diplomatic solution to the crisis ignited by Iraq's August 1990 invasion of Kuwait, a San Antonio man figured President Bush needed to know something about the Rangers. In a letter published by the San Antonio *Express-News,* the man suggested that the president had "never learned the mystique, or else forgot the maxim of the Texas Rangers." Attributing the apocryphal expression to Major John B. Jones of the Frontier Battalion, the writer spelled it out for the president: "1. Never carry a gun unless you know how to use it. 2. Never draw your gun unless you intend to use it. 3. Never use your gun except to shoot to kill. It's just possible this policy could eliminate national terrorism."[1]

If a copy of the letter ever made it to the White House, it went unnoticed. The president was too busy getting the nation ready for war to have given it any thought. The 1991 Gulf War lasted only forty-two days. But in Texas the Rangers stood on the verge of a five-year identity crisis during which their culture would be publicly examined and finally reshaped.

James R. Wilson later joked that when he became DPS director on September 1, 1991, following the retirement of Colonel Milner, he thought much of his time would be spent shaking hands at law enforcement fish fries and retirement parties. He shook plenty of hands during his front-office tenure, but he also had to deal with one of the most controversial periods in the Rangers' history. Tall, white-haired, and reserved, Wilson had been assistant director of the agency since 1988. He had joined the DPS in 1963, working in uniform only long enough to be promoted into the department's Criminal Intelligence Service, where as a savvy investigator he steadily rose through the ranks. At night he attended law school, eventually earning a law degree. But his résumé included more than academic achievements: A dead shot, he earned numerous pistol championships. Like his predecessors, the new colonel had never worn the Ranger *cinco peso*, but more than any director since Homer Garrison, he would play a big part in changing the Rangers.

The decade's first major change involving the Rangers caught even the DPS administration by surprise. In a behind-the-scenes legislative maneuver, state lawmakers elevated the status of the Ranger service by making it a separate DPS division. This statutory redrawing of the agency's organizational chart made little difference to the general public, the average Texan being about as likely to think baseball as law enforcement when hearing or reading the words *Texas Rangers*. But the move meant more pay and more power for the senior Ranger captain, who by legislative fiat had become a division chief on equal footing with his former boss, the chief of criminal law enforcement. Both positions reported directly to the colonel or his assistant.[2]

The Associated Press later identified Captain Maurice Cook, second-in-command of the Rangers and heir apparent for the top job, as having quietly used his political connections to orchestrate that structural change. When Senior Captain Block decided to retire effective June 30, 1992, Wilson promoted Cook as Block's successor.[3] A big man with wrists so large he often had to leave his shirtsleeves unbuttoned, Cook grew up in La Porte in Galveston County. At seventeen he dropped out of high school, joined the air force, and got training as a military policeman, a job he liked and decided to pursue as a civilian. After a tour in Vietnam he left the service and applied for admission to the DPS training academy, graduating as a Highway Patrol trooper in 1967. He went on to serve as a criminal intelligence agent and motor vehicle theft investigator before becoming a Ranger in 1973. Going to school while off

duty and taking correspondence courses, Cook acquired a bachelor's degree and then a master's in political science. The new head of the
Rangers, a driven man who worked long hours and almost never took
vacation time, would be another important figure in the coming crisis.[4]

That August, Wilson called all Ranger captains and lieutenants to
Austin for a meeting. His message would have been considered heresy
only a short time before: Actively begin recruiting women and minorities into the Rangers. Texas had come a long way. For one thing, it had a
female governor, Democrat Ann Richards, the first woman to hold the
office since Miriam Ferguson. Beyond that, the legislature's powerful
House Appropriations Committee included several minorities and
women. Only a short time before Wilson's meeting with the Ranger
brass, he and Cook had been read the riot act during a committee hearing on the DPS's budget request. As Representative Pete Gallego of
Alpine later recalled, "We raked them over the coals. The low number
of minorities just stuck out like a sore thumb." Representative Karyne
Conley of San Antonio later amplified on that:

> You hate to write policy through appropriations, but that's the only
> way you get people's attention. The Rangers are the last bastion of
> the good-old-boy system. We sent them a message that their ranks
> would have to be reflective of the state as a whole.[5]

The new governor demonstrated her interest in the Rangers that fall,
when she accepted an invitation to pose for the first group photograph
of all Rangers taken since 1971. She also had the distinction of being
the first governor ever invited to be in such a photo. Taken in front of
the Capitol on October 21, 1992, the photo showed the white-haired
governor—wearing a black blouse and fuchsia jacket—standing among
ninety-four white-shirted, stern-faced men in Western hats. The Dallas
Morning News shot its own picture of the assembled Rangers, running a
cropped color image on page one the following morning under a caption
that read: "Richards gets in Rangers' roundup." Within the year, some
old-timers in the Rangers would be carping that the governor had gotten
into their business as well as their photograph.[6]

Company A lieutenant Robert Madeira, like the other Rangers, believed in following orders. Back in Houston after attending the meeting

where Wilson instructed the Rangers to start looking for women and minorities, the lieutenant asked thirty-two-year-old Highway Patrol trooper Cheryl Steadman to come by his office. Steadman later recalled that the lieutenant said he hated to see women join the Rangers, but that if they had to have one, "he wanted to get someone like me." The lieutenant also asked Steadman, who worked in the Houston region's warrant office, if her family would mind her being called out after hours to handle an investigation. Madeira later admitted he might have said those things, but he also insisted that he had made a genuine effort to recruit Steadman. Whatever Madeira said, the two meetings—one in Austin, one in Houston—had set the stage for major controversy.[7]

Closed-door meetings were nothing new in the state bureaucracy, but developing technology gave the Rangers new ammunition in fighting crime. In 1993, the DPS Crime Laboratory obtained the equipment and technical expertise to begin DNA profiling. This state-of-the-art forensic tool enabled the identification of people and bodies through comparison of DNA profiles contained in biological evidence, such as blood, saliva, or semen. The crime lab began building a database of DNA profiles from inmate blood samples submitted by the Texas Department of Criminal Justice. In time, this database would be as important as the department's fingerprint records.[8]

MAYHEM AT MOUNT CARMEL

On any given Sunday morning in Waco, home of the largest Baptist university in the nation, Baylor, a lot of the city's residents are sitting in church. That was where Company F captain Bob Prince could be found on the morning of February 28, 1993. As he listened to the sermon, he noticed a fellow church member, Waco-based FBI agent Bob Seale, leaving the pew with his pager in hand. Moments later, the agent walked briskly back into the sanctuary and motioned to Prince. Outside, Seale told Prince a Texas National Guard helicopter had been shot down and numerous federal Bureau of Alcohol, Tobacco and Firearms agents killed and wounded while attempting to serve a search warrant at David Koresh's Branch Davidian ranch ten miles east of town.

Prince already knew the backstory. The day before, the Waco *Tribune-Herald* had published the first installment of a seven-part series on

Vernon Wayne Howell, soon to be far better known as Koresh, a long-haired zealot who considered himself the Messiah returned, and his fellow Davidians, a cultlike spin-off from the Seventh-day Adventist Church, based near Mount Carmel in rural McLennan County. While religious practice is constitutionally protected by the First Amendment, the ATF had reason to believe that Koresh had stocked his two-story wooden compound with a cache of illegal automatic weapons and thousands of rounds of ammunition. Too, the state's agency charged with enforcing child welfare statutes had concerns about the treatment of the Davidians' children. Worried that the newspaper would tip their hand, ATF officials had decided to stage its raid that Sunday morning.

But when seventy-plus agents in blue fatigues marked with the yellow letters *ATF* emerged from cattle trailers pulled up in front of the compound at 9:45 that morning, Koresh and his "Mighty Men" had opened fire on the federal officers.

Back in Waco, Prince whispered to his wife that he had to leave immediately and drove home to get his state car. From there, he sped to Mount Carmel. He arrived to find chaos. Koresh had agreed to a cease-fire so the dead and wounded could be removed. Though the report of the downed helicopter had proven unfounded, the ATF had lost four agents killed and sixteen wounded while killing five of the Davidians in a pitched gun battle.

Prince had known the ATF had an investigation under way and planned a raid, but the agency had declined his offer of state assistance. Now he and other Rangers who had arrived did what they could by way of support. About 4:30 p.m. a second shoot-out erupted when a Davidian showed up at the entrance to the compound and pointed a pistol at ATF agents manning the perimeter. The Rangers did not participate in the confrontation, which left another Davidian dead.

Killing a federal agent is a federal offense, but any homicide in Texas is also a state crime. The following day, after consulting with Senior Captain Cook and Colonel Wilson, Prince offered to assist the FBI and the Justice Department in the investigation of the slayings. But he told them that his agency did not have the manpower to conduct the investigation solely. The day after that, the ATF's second-in-command, having flown in from Washington, insisted that the Rangers handle all of the investigation because of their credibility. Prince firmly but politely said no.

Not settling for that, the Washington official asked who the top man at the DPS was. When Prince told him he asked the captain to get Wilson on the phone. After talking to the colonel privately in an adjoining room at the Fort Fisher Ranger headquarters, the ATF official returned and told Prince that Wilson wanted to talk with him. When Prince got on the line, Wilson said, "Captain Prince, do it all, whatever manpower it takes."

Prince and other Company F Rangers worked the case for about three weeks before Cook called in Company B captain David Byrnes from Dallas to take over the investigation. Prince had earlier told Cook he planned on retiring later that year and did not want to spend years after that getting subpoenaed as a witness for the state concerning the events at Mount Carmel.

With an army of FBI agents surrounding the compound and negotiations under way with Koresh, the situation at Mount Carmel settled into a tense standoff. Rangers took statements from ATF agents and the Davidians who left or fled from the compound, but they could do little more in developing a criminal case until they could work the crime scene.

Unknown to the hundreds of reporters who had descended on Waco from all over the world to cover the standoff, Koresh told Houston attorney Dick DeGuerin, who had injected himself into the negotiations as Koresh's lawyer, that he would surrender peacefully—but only to the Texas Rangers. DeGuerin passed that information on to Cook, who in turn consulted the FBI. The agency said no. If Koresh surrendered, it would be to the FBI.

Hundreds of hours of phone conversations and intensive psychological warfare (around-the-clock bright lights and blaring annoying sounds) having failed to dislodge Koresh and his followers, the FBI got approval from U.S. Attorney General Janet Reno to use heavy military equipment from nearby Fort Hood—tanklike M728 combat engineering vehicles and M3 Bradley armored vehicles—and clouds of CS gas to end the siege.

The final assault began the morning of April 19, the fifty-second day of the standoff. As soon as FBI-driven military vehicles began punching holes in the walls of Koresh's wooden fortress and injecting the eye-burning gas, the Davidians began firing at the vehicles and any agent they spotted. At high noon, flames could be seen licking from the structure. Aided by a strong north wind, fire soon engulfed the entire building. Only a handful of its occupants escaped the conflagration.

The ruins of the compound still smoldered when the Justice Department asked the Rangers to take control of the crime scene and proceed with a state investigation. Now the Rangers had not only the deaths of the four ATF agents to investigate but also the violent demise of most of those who had remained in the compound, seventy-six men, women, and children—including Koresh.

Captain Byrnes coordinated the protracted effort, while Prince oversaw the day-to-day activities of his own company. Thirty-five Rangers, more than a third of the service, would work the crime scene along with DPS crime lab technicians and FBI forensic personnel. Over the next several weeks, in the most extensive criminal investigation to that point in their history, Rangers presided over the photographing and removal of charred bodies while collecting and cataloging some two thousand pieces of evidence ranging from three hundred fire-blackened firearms to buckets of fired bullets. The evidentiary items gathered at the crime scene weighed twelve tons. So that the evidence could more easily be used in federal court, the Rangers had been issued U.S. marshal deputations to assure proper chain of custody.

By the end of May, most of the Rangers pulled in from across the state had returned to their normal duties, but the criminal case that became generically known simply as "Waco" would involve the Rangers for years to come.[9]

Three days after the Branch Davidian compound burned along with most of the people inside it, commercial television offered a violent, if fictional, alternative to the seemingly endless video replays of the fire and the killing of the four federal agents at the beginning of the siege.

"One Riot, One Ranger," the first episode of a new series, aired April 21 on the CBS television network. *Walker, Texas Ranger* starred a bearded, black-hatted Chuck Norris as Ranger Cordell Walker, a contemporary Ranger stationed in Dallas–Fort Worth. Clarence Gilyard played Ranger James Trivette, Walker's rookie sidekick.

Show scripts had Walker as the rugged traditionalist while Trivette, a black former professional football player from Baltimore, represented the new breed of lawman. Prone to philosophizing, Trivette tended to rely on logic and high-tech crime-solving techniques. While Walker would sooner chase a bad guy on horseback, Trivette favored cars or helicopters. But neither Ranger minded resorting to more-than-necessary force, with Walker working over villains with his karate and Trivette blasting them with his semiautomatic.

Noble Willingham played C. D. Parker, a former Ranger forced to retire after taking a bad guy's bullet in his knee. Parker, referred to in the show as C.D., ran a country-western bar where Walker and his pals liked to hang out when off duty. More important to moving stories along, C.D. served as Walker's mentor and sounding board. Sheree J. Wilson rounded out the cast as Alex Cahill, an assistant district attorney who liked Walker, though not always his way of doing things.

The show, Norris's first TV series, had been in development since the spring of 1992. The Oklahoma-born actor had been aware of the dramatic potential of the Rangers for even longer, having played a modern Ranger in the 1983 movie *Lone Wolf McQuade*. With Norris and his brother Aaron as executive producers of *Walker*, their company shot episodes at various locations around the Metroplex and at the Studios of Las Colinas, a flashy development in Irving.

"In a time when heroes are scarce," the show's promotional material boasted, "truth and justice ring through Norris' character and contribute to his believability." That might have helped some fans, but the show amounted more to a televised comic book than realistic drama. Even with former Rangers Weldon Lucas and Phil Ryan getting paid as consultants for the series, the Rangers portrayed in the show came off far more glamorous—and violent—than their real-world counterparts. Still, the show enjoyed a large audience and would continue for 203 episodes over nine seasons before the final drama aired on May 19, 2001.[10]

Lieutenant Madiera, one of the thirty-plus Rangers involved in the investigation at the former Branch Davidian compound, had not had much time to watch television during that grueling special assignment. Back to his normal duties in Houston that June, he learned that his talk with Steadman had paid off. The trooper had applied to the Rangers and done well enough on the written examination to be interviewed by the five-member board that would pick the best of the candidates. Thirty-nine-year-old Marrie Reynolds Garcia, a Driver License Division trooper stationed in San Antonio, also scored high on the knowledge test.[11]

"The 170-year-old tradition of the elite, legendary, all-male outfit is about to be shattered," conservative Austin radio and TV talk show host Jack Chambers lamented after learning that two female DPS troopers had made the nine-person short list for promotion to Ranger. "Not surprisingly, feminists are elated about the Texas Rangers. . . . Well, I say it's about time that we stop putting women in men's boots. Rangers are men, and the Rangerettes are a drill team in Kilgore."[12]

Both women made the cut. Effective August 1, 1993, Texas had its first two female Rangers. Assigned to Company A, Steadman got to stay in Houston. Garcia left San Antonio for Garland, where she would be the newest Ranger in Company B.[13] The DPS tried to play it low key, but the feminization of the Rangers, which now had an authorized strength of ninety-nine, captured the public's attention. Most veteran Rangers could not believe the day had come when a woman could wear the *cinco peso* and several, including twenty-seven-year-veteran Joaquin Jackson—the last of the Garrison-Allee–era rangers—retired before that day arrived.

Robert Draper, a young writer for *Texas Monthly*, began doing research that fall for a cover story on the new look of the Rangers. Wilson and Cook refused to be interviewed for the magazine piece, but numerous retired Rangers and others with opinions did not share their reluctance. With ample grousing on the part of old-timers, and sagging with Ranger dirty laundry, the story ran in the February 1994 issue of the widely read magazine. Imposed over a striking sepia image of the recently retired and recently mustachioed Jackson holding a cut-down lever-action Winchester, a few words on the cover told the whole story: "The Myth of the Texas Rangers: A Proud, Hidebound Institution Confronts a World of High-Tech Law Enforcement and Political Correctness."[14] After reading the article, Dallas *Morning News* state editor Donnis Baggett urged Texans to "ride to the rescue of the Rangers." He wrote:

> There's no question the Rangers have sprouted some ugly warts in their 170-year history—particularly in South Texas, where they were as hard on civil rights as on horseflesh. And there's no doubt they've balked at social change, such as accepting minorities and women.
>
> These are failings, to be sure, and the Rangers needed to address them. But let's not toss the baby with the bath water. The New

Texas needs its Rangers every bit as much as the old. It would be a shame to turn them into just another law enforcement agency.[15]

Copies of the *Texas Monthly* issue featuring the Rangers still lay on coffee tables and in barbershops across the state on March 15 when the Rangers of Captain W. D. Vickers's Company A gathered for their annual company meeting. Vickers had invited the senior captain and a few retired Rangers to eat dinner and spend the night at a privately owned, two-bedroom hunting lodge in the tall timber of the Big Thicket near Spurger in Tyler County. New Ranger Cheryl Steadman tried to be one of the boys at the meeting, but some of the boys did things that made her uncomfortable, like drinking, gambling, telling off-color stories, and using the bathroom without shutting the door. One Ranger, she later said, read a bawdy poem about the sexual prowess of a former Ranger. In addition, she later asserted, she had to do "woman's work," including peeling potatoes, making the salad for their supper, and cleaning up after the meal. Refusing to be the only woman spending the night in the crowded cabin, Steadman drove to Beaumont to stay with a female trooper, Dana Wickland. Steadman arrived at her friend's house in tears, almost immediately asking to use the trooper's telephone to call her husband, a DPS trooper.[16]

Back on the job the following Monday, Steadman quickly realized her standing had changed. As the weeks went by, she found being one of the two first women Rangers more and more difficult. Her Ranger career, she later said, "went to hell in a handbasket" after she declined to spend the night at the East Texas cabin. She received only routine assignments, and when she went to Austin for additional training, she said, male officers ridiculed her because she wore a dress instead of pants and shirt. Then, on May 11, she received the worst written performance evaluation of her DPS career.[17]

As one female Ranger grew increasingly unhappy in her new job, another woman in the DPS had her eye on the *cinco peso*. In fact, Lisa Shepherd, a Highway Patrol trooper stationed in Corpus Christi, had taken the Ranger exam along with Steadman and Garcia in 1992. Shepherd had done well, but she also had taken the Criminal Intelligence Service promotional test and had opted for a job as an investigator in that service. A year later, she took the Ranger exam again, made another good score, and got an interview but no job offer. However, in May 1994, after taking the test a third time and doing well in the oral interview, the thirty-three-year-old investigator and forensic artist got a telephone call from Captain Cook. She had been chosen as a Ranger. Though a vacancy existed in Beeville, only seventy-five miles from her home on the middle coast, the captain told Shepherd that she would be assigned to Company D headquarters in San Antonio. Faced with a move she felt would be both demeaning and personally disruptive, she declined the job offer.[18]

Those in the DPS or Ranger command structure knew to be careful with their public remarks if asked about the breaking of the Ranger gender barrier, but no one could control things people said among themselves. On May 1, 1994, two off-duty Rangers had what they assumed to be a private telephone conversation between friends about Highway Patrol trooper Christine Nix, a black female about to be promoted to Ranger sergeant. But a baby monitor in one Ranger's house picked up the conversation from his cordless telephone. Next door, Charles Davilla happened to be using his cordless telephone when the conversation suddenly intruded on his. Disturbed by racial slurs and raw language he heard, including the use of the words *nigger* and *bitch*, Davilla began tape-recording the conversation. Asserting that one Ranger said Nix—married to a white man—would be a disgrace to the Rangers, and that he also made disparaging remarks about Hispanics, Davilla brought his tape recording forward to the DPS.[19]

Steadman, meanwhile, had all she could take. She traveled to Austin to meet with Colonel Wilson on August 4, 1994—a year and a day after the DPS director had handed her a Ranger commission. Complaining about her treatment in the Rangers, she asked for a transfer. Wilson listened to her concerns, said he would order an Internal Affairs investigation into her allegations, and approved her request, moving her to the Motor Vehicle Theft Service effective August 8. When Captain Vickers learned what she had done, Steadman later said, he took her photograph off the wall at company headquarters and tore it up. Steadman's departure made Sergeant Garcia and Sergeant Nix, assigned to Company F in Waco since June 1, the only two female Rangers.[20]

The two male Rangers caught by an electronic fluke in the embarrassing conversation about Nix had been on suspension with pay since

June 24 pending an Internal Affairs investigation. Allowed to return to duty on November 2, they had been placed on six months' probation because their conversation had been paid for with a state-issued telephone credit card and they had discussed creating "a hostile work environment." Ironically, by the time the investigation ended, a new federal law made it illegal to intercept wireless telephone conversations.[21]

In May 1995, Steadman and Shepherd filed civil rights complaints against the Rangers with the Texas Commission on Human Rights. "I want to emphasize," Shepherd told the Associated Press on May 23, "that the problem I experienced with the Rangers was exclusively with the Ranger leadership at the highest level and not a reflection on the Rangers as a whole." In her complaint, Shepherd accused Senior Captain Cook of a "calculated effort . . . to force me to either work in a demeaning and diminished capacity or decline the position, which I eventually did."[22]

"We have tried very hard to recruit qualified females who would feel comfortable in the Ranger service," said Houston attorney Ronald Krist, a Richards appointee who had been chairman of the Public Safety Commission when the first women Rangers got their silver stars. "It pains me enormously that it didn't work out with Cheryl," Krist continued. Referring to Steadman, he said, "The last thing we wanted was to have her fail. We were ridiculed by former Rangers who didn't want women in." Sergeants Garcia and Nix, he continued, "have adapted quite well" as Rangers. "We will continue and hope to progress," he said. "We are not going to be discouraged by one bad experience."[23]

Appearing on ABC's *Good Morning America*, Krist discussed the Ranger company meeting that had upset Steadman:

The Rangers are not a rowdy bunch. There wasn't a bunch of drinking. There was a penny-ante poker game, and that will probably continue. All of the rookie Rangers, including Cheryl, pitched in and did various chores at the retreat. It wasn't just her. She wasn't asked to do any more than other rookie Rangers, according to our investigators.[24]

The Associated Press obtained a portion of Steadman's twenty-three-page written complaint to the state human rights agency, breaking the story May 27. "I was ridiculed in front of my peers for being a female and wanting to wear a dress occasionally," she said in her complaint. "I was denied the opportunity to work high-profile crimes when male co-workers with the same amount of experience as myself were being allowed and encouraged." Citing one particular homicide, Steadman said a supervisor told her, "We don't want you to cut your teeth on something that serious." Referring to being criticized for wearing a dress at the DPS training academy, Steadman said in her complaint: "I was forced to wear gender restrictive clothing and abide by traditions (not policies) that were male dominant in origin with NO consideration for females." She said Cook told her to wear a tie, jacket, Western hat, and boots just like her male colleagues, to "be a part of the tradition." She continued, "I was constantly being reminded that I was too sensitive . . . too ladylike . . . and too feminine whenever I had an adverse reaction to the treatment I received."[25]

Two weeks after a two-hundred-page DPS Internal Affairs report on Steadman's allegations made it to Colonel Wilson's desk on May 19, the Associated Press somehow got a copy. While the report found that comments by some of Steadman's supervisors gave credence "to some of Steadman's perceptions," it concluded that her complaint contained "inaccuracies and half stories and information that is plainly not true."[26] The report continued: "While there was some drinking and some harsh language, there is no evidence to show anyone was drunk or anyone harassed Steadman. . . . There is no evidence Steadman was treated inappropriately."

Commenting on the controversy on June 14, former governor Richards said:

Any time that any of us enter into a sphere that has previously been all male there is going to be a period of time in which you have to make an adjustment on both sides. Systems and a fashion of doing things are not going to change overnight simply because there is the presence of a woman there. I think there are certain accommodations that you have to make.

Of the selection of two female Rangers during her administration, Richards said, "I was delighted and pleased . . . and it occurred without me pushing to make it occur. I think the whole Department of Public

Safety has worked very hard to integrate both females and people of other races into the ranks, and I am real proud of the job they did."[27] Women filling jobs they have never had before, the former governor continued, would not be "as easy as turning a pancake."

To put the issue into perspective, Dallas *Morning News* reporter Christy Hoppe sought the opinion of three experts on women in the workplace. Noting that most organizations had been hiring women for nontraditional positions since the 1960s, Austin-based consultant Sylvia Stern, a former IBM executive, told Hoppe that Steadman had gone "into a culture that was well developed—a wall of brotherhood. Both parties were unprepared." Steadman's part in that came in failing to understand the importance of the existing Ranger culture. "If you want to assimilate into a culture," Stern said, "you play the game. If you want to maintain your identity, that's good, but you're going to have to find a job somewhere else."

Ellen Bravo, executive director of 9to5, National Association of Working Women, agreed that more thought should have been given to such a momentous cultural change: "The Rangers took no proactive measures. It's like assuming you can make a cultural change like this in your organization without any problem—and, of course, you can't. . . ."

A third outside perspective on the issue came from Barbara Childress, police chief for the Dallas suburb of Richland Hills and chairwoman of the Texas Commission on Law Enforcement Standards and Education. "When you're trying to change a culture of 170 years, it's not going to change overnight and there will be some problems. . . . Both sides have to work on the changes." Steadman told Hoppe: "I wish I'd never gone over to the Rangers."[28]

Meeting July 11, 1995, in the same auditorium where Steadman had been promoted to the Rangers, the Public Safety Commission considered her discrimination allegations in an unprecedented board of inquiry. Steadman and her attorney, along with Shepherd, sat in the auditorium as the hearing began. Asked if she wanted to testify, the former Ranger declined. A short time later, as Rangers in Company A testified that her complaints had been "petty" and characterized her as an insecure, disgruntled employee who had not been able to cut it as a Ranger, she quietly walked out of the room. Asked by the commission if she thought she worked in a hostile environment, Sergeant Marrie

Garcia answered, "Never. I love this job. It is the greatest thing I ever did." Sergeant Nix said, "I'm a black woman wearing western wear for the first time. But I've been in the military, so uniforms are not a problem." She continued, "I won't tell you that coming into the Rangers is easy," but added the standards should not be lowered for women.

Following the five-hour hearing, during which ten Rangers and one former Ranger testified, the commission adjourned into executive session at 3:20 p.m. When they reconvened in a virtually empty auditorium at 5:09 p.m., the commissioners issued a short written statement:

> The Public Safety Commission finds from the evidence presented and the affidavits submitted that a female law enforcement officer possessing normal sensitivities should have been able to cope with the conduct exhibited by the Rangers at the . . . meeting. Additionally, the commission finds that a female law enforcement officer of ordinary sensitivities should have been able to cope with the treatment she received as a Ranger during the course of her involvement with the Ranger Service.

The statement continued that "although the Rangers were inexperienced in the management of female Rangers, they were not guilty of any insensitivity toward, harassment of or discrimination against Cheryl Steadman."[29]

The Austin *American-Statesman* played its account of the meeting on page one the following morning. In the same edition, columnist Janet Wilson wrote:

> What was disconcerting about Tuesday's board of inquiry was that most of the discussion was about issues that had nothing to do with [Steadman's] charges of sexual harassment. Instead, she was painted as "too ladylike" in one breath and a whiney complainer in the other, someone who was insecure and overwhelmed by her job and had no "graceful" way out.[30]

The commission had exonerated the Rangers, but negative publicity continued. Having obtained under the Texas Open Records Act documents concerning the DPS investigation into the May 1994 taped telephone conversation of the two Rangers who had made comments about Sergeant Nix, the Associated Press and the Dallas *Morning News* broke the story on July 13.[31] Asked for her reaction to the investigation and subsequent disciplinary action against two of her fellow Rangers, Sergeant Nix told the Associated Press that she felt the matter had been properly handled and that the Rangers as an organization did not discriminate. "You just have to deal with people as they come along," she philosophized. "I stand by my statement that since I joined the Rangers, I have not had any problem—and didn't have any problem prior to making Ranger." She said she had not had occasion to work with one of the Rangers, but that as to the other, "[he] and I work just fine together."[32] The two disciplined Rangers declined comment, but their attorney said her clients' privacy had been violated. "It wasn't as if they were on the courthouse steps preaching," said Linda Bertram Zeman. "This was a private conversation between two best friends. No matter what's said, they have a right to express their opinions privately."[33]

Reacting to the news, Governor George W. Bush defended the Rangers as an institution but said he would not put up with any "racism or sexism or discrimination, and I know that most Rangers feel that way." Referring to the silver-haired woman he had recently defeated at the polls, Bush went on: "I thought Governor Richards put it best when she talked about the long tradition of the Rangers and that it takes a while any time a culture is asked to change." The governor told the Associated Press that he did not think the racial and sexual discrimination allegations had tarnished the Ranger star. "I know that the good far outweighs the bad with the Texas Rangers, that by far the majority of Rangers are good and decent people who care about the security and safety of Texas."[34]

DPS management soon winced at even more adverse news concerning the Rangers. As Bush made his comments in Austin, a grand jury in Houston indicted Company A Ranger Marcus Hilton for aggravated assault. The indictment alleged that Hilton had assaulted and threatened to kill a uniformed DPS trooper on June 27 inside the DPS's regional headquarters in Houston. In front of witnesses, Hilton had confronted the trooper, pulled his pistol, and accused him of having an affair with his wife. The Ranger had been placed on suspension with pay until an internal DPS investigation could be completed. Ultimately he was acquitted of any wrongdoing.[35]

Clay Robison, Houston *Chronicle* capitol bureau chief, did not mention the Harris County grand jury's recent action but offered some opinions on the Rangers in a column published the following day: "The testimony against Steadman went unchallenged and, at times, seemed to be encouraged by leading questions from panel members. . . . The Public Safety Commission put Steadman on trial last week, but the Rangers also are on trial in the court of public opinion." While the hearing had "cast doubt on Steadman's ability to be the kind of hard-nosed investigator a Ranger is supposed to be," the journalist continued, "the Steadman case—and subsequent revelations that two male Rangers were disciplined for allegedly making racial and sexual slurs against another female Ranger, who is black—indicate that some attitudes still needed changing. The Rangers can justifiably take pride in being elite. They have no business being exclusive."[36]

Austin *American-Statesman* political columnist Dave McNeely had a similar view: "As much as I admire and appreciate those in law enforcement, the male Texas Rangers should realize that females are part of the deal now. They should treat women members as they would want their wife, mother, sister or daughter treated."[37]

In December, Steadman and Shepherd filed a federal sexual harassment lawsuit against Captain Cook and the Rangers. Shepherd also alleged that Cook had violated her First Amendment rights, blackballing her because he considered her a "women's libber."[38] The same month, recently retired Ranger sergeant Ron Stewart fired a verbal load of buckshot at his former boss. "We [the Rangers] are divided as never before," said the fifty-year-old Stewart, the son of a Baptist preacher, "and I put the blame squarely on the present senior captain. . . . There is a failing at the top to maintain respect."[39]

Under Cook's direction, the Rangers had handled a tough job in gathering evidence from the ashes of the Branch Davidian compound outside of Waco. But the worst wave of bad publicity the Rangers had received since the farmworkers strike in the 1960s also had swept over the Rangers on Cook's watch. Mike Cochran, a veteran AP staffer and award-winning reporter, learned from sources on February 7, 1996, that the senior captain planned to retire. Declining to discuss personnel matters, the DPS would not confirm the report. However, Public Commission Chairman James B. Francis told Cochran that Cook did intend to retire, though he did not know when.[40]

Cook's decision to start collecting his pension had not been made voluntarily, Cochran reported two days later. The controversial Ranger chief had been given an "ultimatum" to retire or be fired, Cochran wrote, citing two anonymous sources. One, described as "a high level state government source," said the Ranger captain "was told he could retire, resign, transfer or they'd fire him." The second source, someone with "intimate knowledge of the Ranger crisis," said, "The director told him he could find another job or accept a position lower than where he is now. Or he would start the process to fire his (expletive)." Commission chairman Francis denied the report of a forced ouster. "Believe me, that is not true," he said. Travis County sheriff Terry Keel, a Republican running for a House seat in the state legislature, did not mind being quoted by name. "We've had an excellent working relation with everyone at the DPS and everyone at the Rangers except him," the sheriff said of Cook. "Cook has caused unbelievable problems. . . . He is a blight on law enforcement."[41]

In June, Cook sued the AP over the story concerning the events leading up to his departure from the Rangers. He also sued the Amarillo *Globe-News*, the Houston *Chronicle*, Travis County sheriff Keel, and Houston attorney John Phillips. In his petition, Cook alleged libel that inflicted emotional distress. The following month, Cook turned in the paperwork to retire effective August 31.[42]

Cook's retirement brought the promotion of Captain Bruce Casteel, who had been second-in-command of the Rangers, to senior captain effective September 1, 1996. The well-liked captain had joined the department in 1967 with experience as a Killeen police officer and Bell County sheriff's deputy. Only six years after coming to the DPS, he had earned the Ranger *cinco peso* in 1974. He worked in the Rio Grande Valley until 1985, when he gained promotion to sergeant and transferred to Company D headquarters in San Antonio. Three years later, he made captain and moved to Lubbock to command Company C. After four years on the South Plains, he came to Austin in 1992 as assistant commander under Cook. As his replacement as assistant commander, Casteel brought in Captain Gene Powell from Company E in Midland.[43]

Casteel's new boss would be former assistant director Dudley M. Thomas. Unlike Wilson, who had also chosen to retire, Thomas had spent his entire career in uniform before becoming the department's number two administrator. He had graduated from the DPS training academy in 1961, serving in the Driver License Service before moving to the Highway Patrol in 1965. By 1985 he had risen in rank to major in charge of the department's Midland region. Two years later he became chief of traffic law enforcement following Milner's ascension to director. Thomas, known for his storytelling abilities and sense of humor, held that position until 1991, when he became assistant director under Wilson.[44]

With money in the new fiscal year's budget to increase the strength of the Rangers to 105 positions plus twenty-one noncommissioned employees, Casteel began a four-tier program to fully computerize the division, connecting all Rangers to a division-wide network. In addition to that, he increased Ranger training and realigned Ranger duty stations in the Central Texas area for more efficiency.[45] He also started working to rebuild the image of the Rangers. Events that unfolded the following spring went a long way toward doing that.

Midland-based Company E captain Barry Caver had just made it home from church on April 27, 1997, when his telephone rang. Sergeant David Duncan, the Ranger stationed at Alpine in Brewster County—a political subdivision larger than some states—told the captain that a couple living in a remote development in the mountains of Jeff Davis County had been taken hostage by a group connected to a militant separatist group that called itself the Republic of Texas. As soon as Duncan hung up, Caver called a DPS pilot and asked him to get the department's Midland-based helicopter out of the hangar and ready to fly to the scene. Duncan's report had not surprised the captain. The Republic of Texas group had been getting plenty of self-generated publicity. The group's separatist rhetoric, based on the long-disproved claim that Texas had never legally been admitted to the Union, had been building toward a crisis.

After arriving at the scene, Caver succeeded late that night in talking the two men and one woman who had barged into the rural home of Joe and Margaret Ann Rowe into releasing the couple. A retired oil company pipeline technician, Rowe had suffered a minor wound in the assault on his house, and he had a heart condition.

When they released the Rowes, the camouflaged Republic of Texas "soldiers" pulled farther into the mountains to property owned by the group's most dynamic figure, Richard McLaren. Though not the ranking official in the organization, he had seniority in West Texas.

Coming only four years after the disastrous standoff with David Koresh in McLennan County, the Republic of Texas story got worldwide attention. But this time the Rangers, not the FBI, had the spotlight in the drama. With ample help from the news media, the story played out as a modern Western, Internet-age Rangers—some of them on horseback—facing late-twentieth-century separatists invoking the name of a long-dead independent republic.

Tensions built throughout the week as Captain Caver and Ranger sergeant Jess Malone of Midland continued to negotiate with McLaren. Finally, the day the DPS had determined to storm the compound and take McLaren and his followers by force, the self-styled ambassador and his fellow Republic of Texas "citizens" surrendered.[46]

"In the final analysis," Senior Captain Casteel said on July 21 in a speech at the annual convention of the Sheriff's Association of Texas, "it was not the DPS versus the Republic of Texas, not the State of Texas versus the Republic of Texas, not the New World Order versus the Republic of Texas—it was law enforcement versus a group of suspected law breakers. Some people broke the law in Jeff Davis County and they got arrested. That's all this was about."[47]

Though short-lived in comparison to the siege of adverse publicity the Rangers had endured during Cook's tenure as head of the Rangers, the Fort Davis standoff brought the Rangers extensive positive press coverage. The legislature, which had been in session during the standoff, passed congratulatory resolutions and approved a departmental budget that increased the Rangers' authorized strength to 107 effective September 1, 1997.

Nine months later, the Rangers observed their 175th birthday. In ceremonies at the Texas Ranger Hall of Fame and Museum in Waco on June 6, 1998, Governor Bush dedicated a Ranger time capsule. The thirty-six-by-twenty-four-inch steel capsule, filled with argon to preserve its contents, had been sealed in a stone-covered concrete vault next to the bronze statue of Republic of Texas–era Ranger George B. Erath on May 28. The capsule contained an assortment of memorabilia and musings offered by various active and retired twentieth-century Rangers that museum director Byron Johnson said would not be seen again until 2098.[48]

Mindful of a shorter time span—the two-year statute of limitations for civil law suits in Texas—former captain Cook filed a lawsuit in state court alleging he had been denied due process by the DPS in being forced to retire. While he did not seek reinstatement as senior captain, Cook did ask for the payment of unspecified damages.[49]

The Railroad Killer

With Cook aiming for a legal showdown with his former place of employment, a young Company A Ranger began an investigation that, as had been the case with the Fort Davis effort, would show that the Rangers could still measure up to their tradition. Andrew F. Carter Jr. had risen rapidly in rank since joining the DPS in 1989. By the fall of 1996 he had made lieutenant in the Highway Patrol, a high rank for someone his age. But on September 1, 1998, after doing well on the written examination and scoring high before a five-person interview board, Carter opted to take a pay cut to become a Ranger sergeant. To his way of thinking, his drop in rank from lieutenant to sergeant existed on paper only. He had wanted to be a Texas Ranger since shortly after his fourth birthday.

Carter had been wearing the *cinco peso* for only a few months when the police chief of one of Houston's suburban communities contacted him in early 1999 to ask for assistance with a murder case. On December 17, 1998, thirty-nine-year-old Dr. Claudia Benton had been found beaten and stabbed to death inside her fashionable West University Place home. The killer had struck her repeatedly with a bronze statuette and then stabbed her with a kitchen knife. He had then placed a plastic bag over her head and raped her. Houston police crime scene technicians lifted three good latent prints at the crime scene, and DPS crime lab personnel later found another print when they examined the victim's stolen car, which had been abandoned in San Antonio.

The Ranger submitted the prints to be run through the DPS and the FBI's automated fingerprint information system, more commonly referred to as AFIS. The computer comparison netted a hit: The prints belonged to Rafael Resendez-Ramirez, also known as Ángel Maturino

Reséndiz, a Mexican national with numerous arrests in the United States for assault, burglary, and illegal immigration. Though Carter and the University Place police had a suspect, they had no idea where he could be found. His record reflected arrests all over the United States. The young Ranger realized Resendez-Ramirez could be anywhere.

Later that spring, in Weimar, a small town in Colorado County eighty miles east of Houston, members of the United Church of Christ began arriving for their Sunday service on the morning of May 2. But the Reverend Norman "Skip" Sirnic, forty-seven, and his forty-six-year-old wife, Karen, were not at the church. When a group of congregants checked the nearby parsonage, they found the couple dead inside their residence. Both had been bludgeoned by someone wielding a sledge-hammer. Investigators later learned Mrs. Sirnic had been raped. Weimar police asked for assistance from the Rangers, as had the University Place police department.

DNA samples collected at the rural crime scene matched DNA evidence in the University Place murder. While DNA analysis maps the very building blocks of life, a different sort of linkage led to another connection between the two cases: both crime scenes lay within easy walking distance of railroad tracks. In building an extensive résumé of Resendez-Ramirez, Carter learned the suspect frequently traveled by hopping freight trains. In June, the DPS's monthly *Crime Bulletin*, a publication distributed to law enforcement agencies nationwide, featured an extensive profile of the suspect in the three Texas murders.

When a detective in Lexington, Kentucky, learned of the Texas cases, he noted numerous similarities to an unsolved murder case in his city. A young couple taking a shortcut along some railroad tracks as they walked from one party to another had been attacked by someone who killed twenty-one-year-old Christopher Maier, a University of Kentucky junior, and raped his twenty-year-old girlfriend. Beaten and left for dead, she had survived the August 29, 1997, attack. DNA analysis of biological material from the Lexington case confirmed the Kentucky officer's hunch. Resendez-Ramirez had now been linked to four murders, all within a short distance of a mainline railroad.

The killing continued. On June 4, relatives discovered seventy-three-year-old Josephine Konvicka slain inside her Fayette County residence—only three miles from where the Sirnics had lived. More significant,

Konvicka's house stood only yards from the Union Pacific tracks. The following day, police found twenty-six-year-old Noemi Dominguez, a Houston schoolteacher, beaten to death in the bedroom of her two-story fourplex. Evidence at both crime scenes pointed to Resendez-Ramirez as the killer. It also appeared that despite all the publicity given to his pre-ferred mode of travel Resendez-Ramirez still rode freight cars. A railroad track ran behind Dominguez's apartment.

Scores of local, state, and federal officers gathered in the small rail-road town of Flatonia in Fayette County on June 10, 1999, for a daylong operation. With two helicopters overhead, railroad police stopped west-bound freight trains, hoping to find Resendez-Ramirez hiding on one of the cars. The event generated considerable publicity but amounted to little more than a training exercise.

Five days later, Rangers learned that an elderly man and his daughter had been murdered in their Gorham, Illinois, residence. Eighty-year-old George Morber and daughter Carolyn Frederick, fifty-one, lived only one hundred yards from a railroad track. Again the crime looked like the work of Resendez-Ramirez.

Carter and Ranger colleague Brian Taylor, meanwhile, had inter-viewed Resendez-Ramirez's younger half sister, a U.S. citizen who lived in Albuquerque. Her pastor had met with them as well. As Carter later said, the conversations "were very personal, one-on-one discussions with family members and myself with one goal in mind . . . his surren-der." Indeed, the Ranger had joined them in prayer.[50]

As the Rangers continued their efforts to find Resendez-Ramirez be-fore he killed again, the federal First Amendment infringement lawsuit that Shepherd had filed against Cook in 1995 got tossed out by the Fifth U.S. Circuit Court of Appeals in New Orleans, albeit with some reluc-tance on the part of the court. Shepherd's petition maintained that dur-ing the interview process Cook had told interview board members to change some applicants' scores because he wanted two other women promoted instead of Shepherd, whom he allegedly compartmentalized as "too independent and . . . too opinionated." That, her attorney ar-gued, had violated her free speech right. In an opinion issued on July 6, Circuit Judge Carl E. Stewart said Cook could not have violated Shep-herd's First Amendment rights because she "concedes that she never verbally expressed" her feminist beliefs to the captain.

Still, Stewart took stern judicial notice of Cook's treatment of Shepherd. "The evidence is overwhelming that Cook acted unreasonably in deliberately rigging the selection process," the judge wrote. "Although we readily note our disdain for Cook's improper actions, we nevertheless conclude that Shepherd presented inadequate proof for her claim." The court let stand the sexual harassment suit filed by Shepherd and Steadman against the Rangers, which appeared to be heading toward a highly visible trial in Houston, the nation's fourth-largest city. The *Houston Chronicle* reported the appeals court action, but the manhunt for Resendez-Ramirez grabbed more headlines that summer.[51]

About 2:30 p.m. on Sunday, July 11, Carter and his daughter sat, focused on bobbing corks in Galveston Bay, hoping a trout would hit their shrimp, when the Ranger's cell phone rang. Resendez-Ramirez's sister, calling from New Mexico, told Carter her brother wanted to surrender. The fugitive had only three requests: a guarantee of safety in jail, permission for family visits, and a psychological evaluation. The Ranger said he would see what he could do and made for shore. Later that night, after discussing the suspect's stipulations with the district attorney's office, Carter, an FBI agent, and a U.S. marshal boarded a DPS airplane for Albuquerque. After meeting there with the sister, they drove to El Paso on Monday.

On Tuesday, July 13—Carter's thirty-second birthday—the alleged serial killer walked across from Juárez, Mexico, and surrendered to the Ranger on El Paso's Zaragosa International Bridge. But Carter had no time to celebrate his personal milestone or his more public professional achievement. The Ranger returned Resendez-Ramirez to Houston in a DPS aircraft and joined Houston detectives in getting a statement from him concerning the murder of Dr. Benton. Carter then answered questions from the news media at a crowded press conference.[52]

Rangers had been tracking down killers for generations, but that summer they undertook a new, if short-term, responsibility: providing security for a presidential candidate. Rangers began traveling out of state with Governor Bush as the Texas Republican launched his presidential campaign. Though individual Rangers had traveled outside Texas numerous times in connection with investigations or to bring prisoners back to Texas, this marked the first time they had worked outside of Texas on a regular basis since the Mexican War. Then they had been paid with federal funds. The Rangers protecting Bush on the campaign trail remained on the state payroll. To avoid attracting attention, Rangers traveling with Bush outside Texas did not wear their Western hats or double-rig gunbelts, though they did still wear boots. The use of Rangers in connection with the Bush campaign continued until Bush went under U.S. Secret Service protection following his nomination.[53]

On September 12, 1999, DPS director Thomas presented Director's Citations to Sergeant Carter and six other officers involved in the railroad killer investigation, including two other Rangers, Sergeant Taylor and Sergeant David Maxwell. "I've been in this business a long time," said Senior Captain Casteel at the award ceremony. "I know good police work when I see it . . . the efforts that all these people—not only Drew Carter but each one of these individuals—put forth in their efforts to resolve this terrible, terrible tragedy."[54]

The railroad killer case underscored both the strength of the Rangers and some of the problems they faced at the close of the twentieth century. The strong points were the Rangers' extensive training, their statewide jurisdiction, and the state-of-the-art forensic technology at their disposal. The Ranger tradition also had a crucial impact on the case. Acting quickly and decisively had been part of the Ranger culture since the days of Jack Hays. Carter had moved immediately when he got the telephone call from Resendez-Ramirez's sister, cutting short the fishing trip with his daughter and leaving for New Mexico the next morning.

But the Resendez-Ramirez case also exposed a couple of weaknesses, both connected to the same tradition that drew Carter to the Rangers and compelled him to work so hard: Law enforcement entities with venerable reputations like the Rangers and the FBI are not immune to interagency rivalries and jealousies. Even inside the DPS, jealousies existed between the Rangers and other divisions and services. While neither the Rangers nor the FBI openly discussed the issue, the Houston *Chronicle* sniffed it out shortly after Resendez-Ramirez's arrest. "Rangers locked horns with FBI over serial case: Rivalry rose over suspect's family," the newspaper reported on July 17. Though the headline made the case stronger than the text of the story, the Rangers and federal agents clearly had not worked together in perfect harmony in tracking down Resendez-Ramirez. In fact, citing two sources, one "close to the investigation" and the other being "a high-ranking Texas law enforcement official," the newspaper said the FBI had nearly blown the case by offending Resendez-Ramirez's sister. The bureau, the story continued, had aggressively tried to put Resendez-Ramirez's wife on television against her wishes and the advice of the Rangers. Of less danger to the case, but no less of an affront, the FBI had upstaged the DPS in announcing Resendez-Ramirez's arrest by Ranger Carter.

"I think it just boils down to the fact that the FBI got beat, and they can't stand it," the *Chronicle* quoted its law enforcement source, someone clearly with the Rangers. "And then the FBI struggles to understand why they are so disrespected and can't develop relationships with other agencies. They want it to be a one-way street, all for them."[55]

The Fifth U.S. Circuit Court of Appeals on December 14, 1999, upheld a lower federal district court ruling that former senior captain Cook had not been denied due process in his forced retirement. While Cook's lawsuit had cost the State of Texas nothing but time and effort on the part of several of its lawyers, the federal sexual harassment lawsuit filed by Steadman and Shepherd against the DPS proved more expensive.

The DPS quietly settled the litigation on January 20, 2000, with an agreement signed by Colonel Thomas and Steadman. The agency agreed to pay her $250,000—the maximum possible under the Texas Tort Claims Act—and granted her four weeks of administrative leave (vacation time) to be used within a year. The document stipulated that both parties to the lawsuit "acknowledge that this Agreement does not constitute any admission . . . concerning the issues in dispute . . . [and that] payment of any of the Consideration is not an admission of liability and may not be so construed."

Shepherd signed a similar settlement agreement the next day. She also received $250,000, though the DPS granted her six weeks of free vacation time—two more weeks than Steadman. The agreement still needed the approval of the state attorney general and Governor Bush, but both officials soon signed off on it.[56]

14

Entering the Twenty-first Century

The Rangers started the twenty-first century adjusting to yet another change at the top. Colonel Thomas, the DPS's ninth director, retired on February 29, 2000, after a little more than three years as head of the department. His assistant, Thomas A. Davis, Jr., thirty-six years with the agency, assumed leadership of the DPS on March 1.

Though in modern times it had not been unusual for a director to work only long enough to maximize his state retirement (which is based on an employee's three highest years of salary), for the first time ever the department gained two assistant directors. Reasoning that the DPS had grown too large for only two top administrators, the seventy-sixth legislature had funded dual assistant directors. Administrative Division Chief Frankie Waller took over as lieutenant colonel for law enforcement while David McEathron, chief of traffic law enforcement, became lieutenant colonel for support.[1]

On May 18, the investigative work coordinated by the Rangers culminated in the capital murder conviction of Ángel Maturino Reséndiz-Ramirez in the death of the Houston doctor. After the jury refused to buy his insanity defense, he requested the death penalty. Two days later, the judge sentenced him to death by lethal injection. Reséndiz-Ramirez told his attorneys not to appeal his conviction, but later changed his mind and okayed the filing of appeals in his behalf.[2]

Reséndiz-Ramirez had kept Company A extraordinarily busy the year before, but in a state with a population of more than 20 million and three of the nation's ten largest cities, none of the companies had any shortage of work. In some cases, however, Rangers did lack work space. In Waco, city officials had discussed with the DPS the need for a new Company F headquarters at Fort Fisher. The DPS had considered moving the Rangers to the agency's regional headquarters on the city's north side, but the museum wanted the Rangers to stay. According to museum director Byron Johnson, tourists visiting the museum wanted to see a "real, live Texas Ranger." Johnson continued, "Company F is more or less a living history exhibit in the building." Ranger lieutenant Clete Buckaloo, a big man even by Ranger standards, agreed. "If you step out of the office into the museum, you can almost count on being greeted by persons who come to the museum," he said. Recalling a couple from Belgium who wanted their picture taken with a Ranger, the lieutenant said, "It's part of the job, and it shows positively on the Rangers." The museum's board of directors began a campaign to raise the money it would take to renovate and expand the museum and build Company F a new headquarters. The effort gained momentum with a $100,000 contribution from the widow of a former special Ranger, but the economic slump following the September 11 terrorist attacks made the process slow going.[3]

In March 2001, during the regular session of the seventy-seventh legislature, a North Texas lawmaker introduced a bill to make the Rangers a semiautonomous state agency. Thrown in the hopper by Republican senator Chris Harris of Arlington, the measure would have pulled the Rangers from the DPS, making the person in charge of the Rangers report directly to the three-member Public Safety Commission with authority equal to the director of the DPS. Despite a separate command structure, the legislation stipulated, the Rangers still would have access to the DPS's crime lab and other support services. The bill died in the Senate's Committee on Criminal Justice.[4]

Though the effort to separate the Rangers from the DPS went nowhere, the Rangers did pick up more manpower with the passage of Senate Bill 786 and its companion in the lower chamber, House Bill

1748. The two measures created an unsolved crimes component formally called the Texas Ranger Unsolved Crimes Investigation Team effective September 1, 2001. Its only responsibility—with the exception of emergencies—would be cold cases. Based in San Antonio under the supervision of a lieutenant, the unit received funding for eight rangers.[5]

Senior Captain Casteel had testified before the Senate Committee on Criminal Justice on the proposed cold-case legislation, but he decided not to stay around for the unit's organization. After five years as commander of the Rangers, a period that saw their stabilization and the restoration of much of their prestige, the popular captain decided to retire. Hundreds of friends and colleagues showed up for barbecue, beans, potato salad, and fellowship at his August 16, 2001, farewell party in Austin, a rite of passage very much part of the DPS culture. Company B lieutenant Richard Sweeney, the Ranger who had replaced Casteel in the Rio Grande Valley in 1987, took the microphone. Noting with great formality that singing the national anthem seemed in order, the lieutenant asked everyone to stand. But when he placed his right hand over his heart, the crowd could see that he had his fist shaped in the form of a pistol. Before that had time to sink in, the public address system blared the *Lone Ranger* theme, not the work of Francis Scott Key. Many in the crowd laughed to the point of tears.[6]

"You Feel Like You Are a Part of History."

Fifty-three-year-old C. J. Havra took over as senior captain on September 1, 2001. A Vietnam veteran, Havra had been with the DPS since 1969. He was promoted to the Rangers in 1981 and spent the next nine years in Midland. In 1990 he made lieutenant, and transferred to San Antonio as second in command of Company D. When longtime captain Jack Dean retired in 1993, Havra succeeded him in the position. Asked by a San Antonio newspaper reporter about his elevation to the top job in the Rangers, Havra modestly slipped into second person: "You feel like you are a part of history."[7] A few days later, Houston-based Company A Captain Earl Pearson became assistant commander of the Rangers, the highest-ranking African American in the service's history.[8]

Few, if any, former or current Rangers would have disagreed with Havra's remark about being a part of history. The new senior captain already had on his desk an invitation to a high-dollar gala planned that fall as a fund-raiser for a new facility dedicated to the Ranger's role in Texas history. Having outgrown the Depression-era Rangers and Pioneers Museum in San Antonio, the Former Texas Rangers Association Foundation had begun planning for a larger education and research center in Kerrville, a scenic Hill Country city sixty-two miles west of San Antonio. Four hundred Ranger friends and supporters gathered at the Y.O. Ranch Resort Hotel in Kerrville on September 28, 2001, for the event, Silver Stars & Six Guns 2001. Paying $125 a person for a prime rib dinner and boot-scooting music from Cody Widner and the Sumthin' Country Band, the Ranger supporters traded on the past to help new generations learn about the state and its Rangers.

"The Texas Rangers have a reputation for doing things right, and Silver Stars and Six Guns is no exception," foundation board president and retired Ranger Joe Davis said before the gala. "Our goal is to send our friends home with enough good memories to fill their own personal museums—and a desire to come back and see us."

The planners of the celebration achieved that goal, but the attendees left with more than good memories. Before the dancing started, they had spent tens of thousands of dollars on an assortment of silent and live auction items. Davis had donated a gunbelt and holster he wore as a Ranger. Retired captain John Wood put his Ranger commission up for auction. John Aycock, who had retired only a few weeks earlier, furnished a skeet-shooting vest with padded shoulder and pockets for shotgun shells. A limited-edition longhorn hide–bound book published in 1969 to showcase a collection of Ranger photographs acquired by the late rancher Charles Schreiner III, a charter member of the foundation board, brought in $6,000. An oil painting depicting the Frontier Battalion in action fetched more than $15,000, the highest price for a single item sold.[9]

Six weeks later, Captain Jack Hays's great-great-grandson—John W. Hays—visited the Central Texas county named in his forebear's honor for the November 16, 2001, dedication of a life-size bronze statue depicting the young Ranger captain astride a charging horse, his raised right hand holding a Colt revolver. Funded by a $125,000 grant from the McCoy Foundation, the nine-feet-eight-inch-tall statue by San Marcos sculptor Jason Scull stood on a four-and-a-half-foot square limestone base in the northeast corner of the courthouse square in downtown San Marcos, thirty miles south of Austin. A local committee headed by historian Al Lowman had worked for two years to develop and erect the monument.

"It is right that Jack Hays should be honored this way in the county . . . named for him," said Charles Pascoe, district deputy grand master of the Grand Masonic Lodge of Texas. "He is the quintessential Texan."[10]

Not long before Hays decided to decamp for California in 1848, Hays County had been organized after state lawmakers voted to create a new political subdivision by removing a large tract of land from the southern end of Travis County. Hays's old friend and former Republic of Texas vice president Edward Burleson, who represented Central Texas in the state senate, introduced the bill that named the new county for the hard-fighting captain who had contributed so much to the tradition and legend of the Rangers.[11]

A deluge triggered by a slow-moving cold front dumped more than a foot of rain in some places in Central Texas the day before the dedication ceremony. A lingering threat of rain forced the speech making inside the courthouse, but those willing to brave the weather went outside for the unveiling of the statue, which had been draped in a large Texas flag. "Colonel Jack was a legend in his own time and that's very rare in mankind's history," John W. Hays said. "It makes us very proud." His son Doug Hays, the ranger captain's great-great-great-grandson, added: "I'm just trying to live up to him."[12]

The same could be said for the Texas Rangers of the twenty-first century.

"I believe the common thread from the first days of the Rangers until today is pretty much the same," Captain Havra said in 2002. "Their job one-hundred-and-eighty years ago . . . was to protect the innocent . . . citizens against the people who take advantage of the weak and defenseless. We are still doing that today. We still have that passion."[13]

Havra retired in 2004 to become chief investigator for the Bexar County District Attorney's Office in San Antonio. Promoted as his successor effective May 1, 2004, was his assistant chief, Captain Pearson, a twenty-eight-year DPS veteran who joined the Rangers in 1989. He had been promoted to lieutenant of Waco-based Company F in 1992 just in time for the complicated Branch Davidian investigation. When Pearson made captain in 1996, the department transferred him to Houston as commander of Company A. He led the Rangers until retiring on August 31, 2005.[14]

With Pearson's retirement, assistant Ranger chief Captain Ray Coffman took over as senior captain on September 12, 2005. After joining the DPS in 1976, Coffman was promoted from the Highway Patrol to the Narcotics Service, where he eventually made lieutenant. But when he applied for a Ranger opening and got the job offer, he took a pay cut to pin on the *cinco peso*. Ten years later he was promoted to Ranger lieutenant and became Company D's captain in 2001 when Havra moved to Austin.

Coffman's first partner in the Highway Patrol had been Stan Guffey, who also became a Ranger. After Guffey's line-of-duty death near Marble Falls in 1987, Coffman transferred from the Rio Grande Valley to take over his old friend's duty station at Brady. With the exception of a brief tour in Bryan–College Station, Coffman stayed in Brady until becoming a lieutenant and transferring to Austin.[15]

"I Saw Kids with Fear in Their Eyes . . ."

On February 23, 2005, Ranger Sergeant Brian Burzynski was sitting in his Fort Stockton office working on reports when he got a telephone call from a Midland man who said he volunteered his time as a math tutor at the Texas Youth Commission's all-male maximum-security juvenile correction facility at Pyote in Ward County. The man said several boys had told him of rampant sexual abuse at the facility on the part of TYC employees.

Burzynski immediately drove fifty-six miles to Pyote to begin looking into the situation. Over the next sixty days, he gathered 108 statements and collected 354 pieces of physical evidence. By July, the thirty-five-year-old Ranger felt he had solid cases against assistant superintendent Ray Brookins and principal John Paul Hernandez. Both men denied the allegation.[16]

Burzynski handed his evidence over to Ward County District Attorney Randy Reynolds for prosecution. Then, as Company E captain Barry Caver later wrote: "For almost a year and a half, Ranger Burzynski continued to gather proof while the district attorney decided what to do." Actually, as a report of the Joint Select Committee on the Operation and Management of the Texas Youth Commission later noted, "The Ward County District Attorney failed to prosecute the case, after repeated attempts by the Texas Ranger."[17]

The Ranger requested assistance from the state Attorney General's Office in November 2006, which, after some delay, eventually came. The weekly *Texas Observer* broke the story on February 23, 2007—two years to the day after Burzynski got the telephone call that began the case. When the Dallas *Morning News* and other newspapers began digging into the story it exploded into a major scandal and soon became the focus of a legislative investigation.

On March 6, Company D Ranger Lance Coleman began working with the Attorney General's Office on the TYC investigation. Two days later, a newly established TYC tip hotline took a call from an anonymous informant who reported that the superintendent of a TYC facility in San Antonio had been seen shredding records. Coleman interviewed the woman and on March 9 arrested her for tampering with evidence.[18]

The same day Coleman began his investigation of the document-shredding, Sergeant Burzynski came to Austin to testify at a hearing of the legislature's Joint Committee of the Operation and Management of the Texas Youth Commission.

"When I interviewed the victims in this case," Burzynski told the committee, "I saw kids with fear in their eyes, kids who knew they were trapped in an institution within a system that would not respond to their cries for help. Perhaps their families failed them, TYC definitely failed them. I promised each of those victims I would do everything in my power as a Texas Ranger to ensure justice would be served."

When the Ranger concluded his remarks, the members of the committee and citizens sitting in the gallery gave him a standing ovation.

"We've got one great Ranger here today," committee member Representative Jerry Madden said after listening to the sergeant. "This is why we have Texas Rangers," added Senator John Whitmire of Houston.[19]

On March 14, Company E sergeant Nick Hanna, working with the attorney general and TYC investigators, arrested a former Ron Jackson Unit guard in Brownwood for sexual assault.[20]

Near the end of the legislative session that spring, the House adopted a concurrent resolution praising Sergeant Burzynski for his efforts.[21] On September 1, Colonel Davis followed that with a Director's Citation commending Burzynski's work in the TYC investigation.

"Sergeant Burzynski's thorough investigation techniques and his determined perseverance in seeking prosecutorial action against the sexual predators responsible for this abuse undoubtedly played a significant role in a comprehensive investigation being conducted at each of the Texas Youth Commission facilities in the state," Davis said. "[His] initiative, diligence, and commitment in pursuing prosecution against high-ranking members of a state agency . . . reflects the high moral standards the public has come to admire and respect from officers of the Texas Department of Public Safety and the Texas Ranger Division."

As a result of the Ranger's work, the Texas Youth Commission got a thorough house cleaning. Its board resigned, its director retired, and other ranking employees resigned or got fired. Governor Rick Perry issued an executive order placing the agency under conservatorship and later signed into law Senate Bill 103, an act providing for a sweeping overhaul of TYC.[22]

The lawmakers who commended Sergeant Burzynski's work on the TYC case also provided funding for one of the Ranger service's larger growth spurts, increasing the force's authorized strength from 118 to 134. The additional funding allowed the division to add an additional lieutenant per company, giving each company a captain and two lieutenants. Two to four Rangers are stationed at each of the division's seven headquarters, with the rest assigned to various towns and cities in their company area. Each Ranger is responsible for two to three counties, some as many as six.

In addition, the legislature provided more funding for the Rangers' Unsolved Crime Investigative Team. The equivalent of a company, it operated through December 2007 with a captain, a lieutenant and eight rangers stationed at San Antonio. But in January 2008 the Rangers decentralized the team, with one UCIT Ranger assigned to each company. In 2007 the team cleared eight old murder cases, one dating back to 1988. The year before the team had solved four cold cases, one going back twenty-six years.

The TYC case was only one of 5,054 offenses investigated or activities handled by the Rangers in 2007. One hundred-thirty-four Rangers investigated 594 homicides, 164 armed robberies, 231 burglaries, 822 felony thefts, and 3,243 cases listed in the DPS's 2007 annual report as "other." A footnote in the Ranger division's statistical chart explained that "other" included fraud, forgery, assault, and other offenses, as well as serving warrants or subpoenas.[23]

Also in 2007, two years after taking over as senior captain, Coffman oversaw organization of the first full new Ranger company since the reorganization of the DPS in 1957, Company G. With headquarters in McAllen, the new company encompasses fifteen counties, from Brownsville to Del Rio along the Texas-Mexico border. The reorganization reduced the area of San Antonio–headquartered Company D by eleven counties while removing four counties from Midland-based Company E's territory.[24]

YEARNING FOR ZION IN TEXAS

In the spring of 2008, the Rangers became involved in a headline-grabbing case somewhat reminiscent of the Branch Davidian standoff fifteen years earlier. Once again, it involved a splinter religious group with a fortresslike house of worship standing prominently on private property. Too, the investigation necessitated a major commitment of personnel and resources as well as collection and management of a massive amount of evidence. Unlike Waco, the operation played out peacefully, if controversially.

The weekly Eldorado *Success* in Schleicher County had exposed in 2004 that a recently sold 1,700-acre ranch four miles north of town would not be a corporate hunting retreat as its buyers had claimed but the new home of the Fundamentalist Church of Jesus Christ of Latter-Day Saints (FLDS), a secretive Mormon group that continued to practice polygamy. Rangers and local officers soon saw the potential for another Branch Davidian–style incident in Texas. In fact, Ranger sergeant Brooks Long of Ozona had made several visits to the ranch and worked closely with Schleicher County Sheriff David Doran in checking for any illegal activities there, particularly what the FLDS called "spiritual marriages" of older men to underage females.

On March 29, 2008, the state Child Protective Services' San Angelo hotline received a call from a female who identified herself as "Sarah." She said she was inside the YFZ ranch, sixteen years old, pregnant, and had been sexually and physically abused by her forty-nine-year-old husband. CPS referred the matter to the Rangers, and Sergeant Long began drawing up an affidavit for a search warrant to be served at the ranch. Working with Sheriff Doran, Company E captain Caver—a veteran of the

Mount Carmel investigation and the man who led the Rangers' response to the 1997 Republic of Texas standoff in Jeff Davis County—began planning a raid.

More than two hundred state and local law enforcement officers, including thirty-five Rangers, surrounded the ranch on the afternoon of April 3. Caver and Sergeant Jess Malone, the company's trained negotiator, went through the green metal ranch gate first. Not knowing how the polygamists would react, a team of Rangers and other officers entered the property wearing body armor and carrying assault rifles. An armored vehicle from the Midland County Sheriff's Department stood by just in case. Depending on their assignment, other Rangers wore normal attire and carried only their sidearm.

Inside the ranch seemed like a movie set to some of the Rangers. All the women wore long, prairie-style dresses. The men dressed in equally plain shirts and pants. Not only did the children also look like they had just come from central casting, the Rangers soon found they knew nothing of the outside world, having never seen toys or munched cookies. The Rangers first went to the ranch's combination school and community center to parlay with FLDS elders and set up a command post. Malone explained as he had at the ranch gate that a district judge had issued a search warrant and asked for the group's cooperation. Though they had legal authority to do so, he said the Rangers did not want to break down any doors or force open any file cabinets or safes.

"We tried to treat them with respect," Malone later recalled, "but it was not reciprocated."

As soon as the Rangers had secured the ranch, a team of CPS investigators came on the property and began interviewing adult occupants and some of their children. As had been the case at Fort Davis in 1997, Caver, Malone, and most of the other personnel who had entered the ranch worked all night and well into Friday before being able to get any sleep. Later that day, CPS with assistance from the DPS and local officers began removing children from the ranch.

"There was a lot of deception," Malone said. "They would answer a question with a question. Different people gave the same names and made things confusing by moving around from house to house, sneaking through the brush. By the second day, we allowed no vehicle movement. By the third day, it was pretty much martial law as we tried to collect evidence over an area of four square miles."

When the Rangers got ready to enter the four-story temple, a group of fifty-seven men ringed it, holding hands. Their leader told Captain Caver they intended to offer "passive resistance."

"Define 'passive resistance,'" the captain said.

The man replied that the men would continue to stand around the temple but once the Rangers approached they would not physically resist. Instead, he said, they would kneel and begin praying.

"That's a damn good idea," Caver told the man.

Still concerned about an attempt at violent resistance, Caver had his own plan. The Rangers let the men stand around the temple all day long before finally approaching it later in the day. If the men had any fight in them, the West Texas heat had sucked it out of them.

Using a battering ram, the Rangers broke through the temple's massive double doors. Finally inside, they searched it floor-by-floor. No one would unlock any of the doors, leaving the Rangers no choice but to break open some seventy-five doors. Finding large vaults in the temple's bomb shelter–like basement, the lawmen had to bring in locksmiths to get them open.

Under Texas law, a search warrant is valid for three days, exclusive of the day of issue and return. When it became evident that the search of the ranch could not be completed in that time frame, the Rangers obtained an extension from the judge who had signed the original warrant.

Within four days of entering the ranch, CPS had taken more than four hundred children into protective custody of the state. The agency initially sheltered them in nearby Eldorado, but on April 6 began busing them to a temporary but more comfortable shelter at old Fort Concho in San Angelo. The Rangers filled and numbered 372 boxes of evidence including some 100,000 pages of documents found in what the FLDS called its Bishop's Records. They also seized computers containing digital information and under the search warrant, drew blood for DNA analysis.

Based on the Ranger investigation, fifty-five-year-old sect leader Warren Jeffs and four other men were indicted by a Schleicher County grand jury July 22, 2008, on charges of sexual assault on a child, a first-degree felony punishable by five to ninety-nine years or life and a $10,000 fine. A sixth person, a doctor who ran a clinic at the ranch, was indicted on three counts of failure to report child sexual abuse, a misdemeanor. Three more persons were named in sealed indictments in August with three additional persons named in sealed indictments issued by the grand jury on September 24.

By the winter of 2008, all but two of the children taken in the raid had been returned to their families but the Ranger and CPS investigation remained ongoing. A report released by the state agency on December 22 said that of 439 children removed from the YFZ ranch, 275 had been abused or neglected. Twelve girls between the ages of twelve and fifteen, the report said, had been sexually abused by entering into "spiritual marriages." Seven of the girls had children.[25]

A Major Shakeup

In the predawn hours of June 8, 2008, someone tossed a Molotov cocktail against the front door of the 1856-vintage Texas Governor's Mansion across 11th Street from the state Capitol in downtown Austin. Fire quickly swept through the two-story Greek Revival structure, severely damaging it. The only good news for state officials and taxpayers was that the mansion had been undergoing renovation before the fire and all the historic furniture, art work, and other contents had been placed into storage off-site. Too, no injuries occurred.

Mansion security and gubernatorial protection are provided by the DPS, which almost immediately became the target of legislative scrutiny over possible lapses in protecting the 152-year-old building. Indeed, an internal DPS investigation showed some of the mansion's agency-operated security cameras had not been working and that only one Highway Patrol trooper had been on guard at the mansion on the night of the fire. Looking into the possibility that the attack on the Governor's Mansion might have been in reprisal for the Ranger-led raid on the YFZ Ranch in West Texas earlier that spring, the Rangers assisted the State Fire Marshal's Office in the investigation. In the spring of 2009 the case remained open, with no arrests having been made.

Though the mansion fire did not come up, on June 24 Colonel Davis got raked over the figurative coals at a hearing before the state's Sunset Advisory Commission, a body that periodically reviews the function of all state agencies. (The Sunset review had already been scheduled before the mansion fire.) The legislative panel had been critical of the department's computer system, the operation of its vehicle inspection program, and its efforts to collect intelligence concerning possible terrorism. None of those issues involved the Rangers, but the man in the committee's crosshairs ran the whole department.

After listening to the committee's criticism, Davis countered that he felt the DPS was "operating better than I've ever seen it."

The colonel's comment seemed to take the committee off-guard. "When you say that . . . it's hard for me to see that," Representative Lois Kolkhorst from Brenham said. Referring to the management issues set forth in the Sunset Commission's May 2008 audit of the agency, Representative Ruth Jones McClendon of San Antonio said, "It seems like we have a disconnect here."

When his turn came to testify, Public Safety Commission Chairman Allan Polunsky, who like his mid-1930s predecessor, Albert Sidney Johnson, had been taking an atypical hands-on role in overseeing the department, said, "We will reform this agency and make it relevant to the twenty-first century."

While denying that he might be thinking about a new director for the department, the commission chairman said, "I expect that Colonel Davis will make the necessary changes. . . . If he is unsuccessful or unwilling to do so . . . then we will find someone else."

Only seventeen days later, on July 11, the sixty-seven-year-old Davis had the department's public information office issue a one-sentence statement to the state's news media: "After forty-three years and nine months with the Texas Department of Public Safety, I am retiring on August 31, 2008."

The five-member Public Safety Commission soon named Highway Patrol major Stan Clark, a regional commander who had been stationed at the DPS's Garland headquarters in North Texas, as interim director of the agency. In naming him, the commission passed over numerous higher-ranking administrators. That set up a wave of high-level retirements unprecedented in the seventy-eight-year history of the department.

Bypassed by the commission as Davis's replacement, Lieutenant Colonel David McEathron announced his retirement as the agency's second-in-command. Joining the lieutenant colonel in retirement were the head of the Highway Patrol, Chief Randy Ellison; the chief of the

Criminal Law Enforcement Division, Kent Mawyer; the chief of the Administrative Division, Burton Christian, and his assistant, Lester Mills; the assistant commander of the Rangers, Captain Jim Miller; and the department's longtime general counsel, Mary Ann Courter. In all, thirteen key administrators opted to take retirement.

In his swan song "Dear fellow employee" column in the department's monthly employee newsletter, Davis said all the things a top administrator always says when leaving. But there was one exception that read like a subtle response to the criticism the DPS had been getting: "I urge you to protect your integrity as strenuously as you protect yourself and the people of Texas. Your integrity is your greatest asset. Once it's gone, it's all but impossible to regain it."[26]

The Public Safety Commission had set change in motion even before Davis announced his retirement. At its June 18, 2008, meeting, the commission had voted to hire Austin-based Deloitte Consulting to undertake a study of the DPS's management and organizational structure. The $950,000 report, released October 28, proposed a sweeping reorganization of the eight-thousand-employee state agency.

"DPS is not well organized to meet the challenges it faces today," the report declared. "Law enforcement operations are fragmented across several divisions, and are hampered by bureaucratic complexity and redundancy. . . ."

The seventy-four-page report had no specific recommendation regarding the Rangers, though if its suggested new organization chart were adopted, the head of the Rangers would fall one level lower in the chain of command, reporting to a new deputy director for law enforcement rather than to the assistant director and director, as had been the case since the designation of the Rangers as a separate division of the DPS. But the suggested organizational changes would reshape the DPS more profoundly than at any other time in its history, including the 1957 reorganization.

Retired Admiral Bob Inman of Austin, former director of the Central Intelligence Agency, reviewed the report at the request of the Public Safety Commission.

"[It] separates Department of Public Safety employees into two groups," Inman said of the Deloitte plan. "One who works normal office hours with a focus on improved service to the citizens of Texas, and the other group who are on call seven days a week, twenty-four hours a day, and whose lives could be at risk, where professionalism and competency at law enforcement are mandatory."

Under the Deloitte plan, all DPS law enforcement functions would be combined under a new deputy director for law enforcement. These elements would be supervised under a new regional command structure, compared to the longtime system where each law enforcement service (Rangers, Highway Patrol, and Criminal Law Enforcement) had a different chain of command. The report also recommended a new DPS organization for intelligence-gathering and counterterrorism. The remainder of the report's suggestions involved human resource issues, improving information technology, financial processes, and customer service.

"These are broad and sweeping recommendations which will serve DPS well over the coming years," commission chairman Polunsky said of the report.

The recommendations were not universally applauded. "While nearly everyone agrees that DPS is overdue for an overhaul," the *Texas Observer* said, "some aspects of the plan raise privacy and civil liberties concerns—including a special operations group that some fear might get into the business of spying on protest groups or political enemies."

In November, the commission named a special committee to begin work on how to implement the Deloitte plan and on December 17 named an executive search firm to look for a new DPS director.[27]

The unparalleled spat of top-level retirements at the DPS continued through late fall with Captain Coffman's retirement as Ranger chief. On December 10, acting director Clark named Captain Antonio "Tony" Leal as the new senior captain, the first-ever Hispanic to lead the Rangers. At forty-four, Leal also became the youngest senior captain in the history of the service.

"It is my goal to continue to uphold the Ranger tradition, while moving ahead with the goals of the department as a whole," Leal said following his appointment.[28]

CHAOS IN MEXICO

Nearly a century after the Mexican Revolution brought death and destruction to both sides of the Rio Grande and enveloped the Texas Rangers in long-lasting controversy, a vicious drug war in Mexico raised concerns in Texas and Washington that the struggle would bleed over into Texas.

On February 17, 2009, a shoot-out in Reynosa, Mexico, a city of more than half a million residents in the state of Tamaulipas across from McAllen, Texas, claimed the lives of five suspected drug dealers and five Mexican soldiers. With apparently unrelated violent protests occurring in Monterrey and on the international bridge between Laredo and Nuevo Laredo at about the same time, the state's Emergency Operations Center at DPS headquarters in Austin went on heightened alert for twenty-four hours. The incident prompted the U.S. State Department to issue a travel alert urging U.S. citizens to exercise caution if visiting Mexico. Other nations put out similar warnings.

"Since the beginning of last year," Vice President Joe Biden said on March 11, 2009, in announcing the nomination of the nation's newest drug czar, Gil Kerlikowske, "there have been nearly seven thousand drug-related murders in Mexico. . . . Violent drug-trafficking organizations are threatening both the United States and Mexican communities."

The Border, Maritime, and Global Counterterrorism committee of the U.S. House of Representatives heard testimony on March 12, 2009, concerning the possibility that the high-stakes war between rival drug cartels and the Mexican government's effort to suppress it, a conflict that led to 6,290 drug-related homicides in that nation in 2008, and more than one thousand homicides in the first quarter of 2009, could affect Texas and other border states. Of particular concern to Texas authorities is El Paso, located across the Rio Grande from Jaurez. More than 1,800 people had been killed in that Mexican city of 1.6 million since January 2008. Some cities in the U.S., including Phoenix, also were seeing a sharp increase in kidnappings and ransom demands on the part of Mexican nationals.

"Anything you can think of that's happened in Mexico, we have to think could happen here," Steve McCraw, Governor Rick Perry's homeland security director, told the Fort Worth *Star-Telegram* in early March. McCraw, a retired FBI official, predicted the situation in Mexico would "get worse before it gets better."

The Texas Rangers are a component of a coordinated state homeland security program called Operation Border Star. Run from the DPS headquarters, the task force (supported by $107 million appropriated by the legislature in 2007 with more funds expected in 2009) also includes DPS troopers, border sheriffs and police, the U.S. Border Patrol, the U.S. Coast Guard, and other state and federal agencies.

At the federal level, the U.S. Department of Homeland Security had a contingency plan in place should cross-border violence erupt. In the worst-case scenario, which planners say could include the collapse of the Mexican government or its loss of control in certain states, U.S. troops would be dispatched to the border, officials said. Another concern was the possibility of an enormous exodus from Mexico into the U.S. in the event of a major destabilization.

Whatever happens along Texas's 1,254-mile international border, just as has been the case since 1846—when Rangers participated in the U.S. war with Mexico that assured Texas's status as the twenty-eighth state of the Union—the men and women who wear the *cinco peso* will be part of the story.

Epilogue: Burying the War Club

A student of Ranger history, Texas lawyer Shelton Smith of Wimberley, had an idea. The last fight between the Rangers and Comanches had been in 1878. One hundred and twenty-seven years later, it seemed entirely fitting that the two former antagonists bury the metaphorical war club and sign a peace treaty.

With the blessing of the Former Texas Rangers Foundation board over which he presided, Smith in the spring of 2005 began an e-mail and telephonic discussion with Wallace Coffey, chairman of the Comanche Nation. (Since the death of Chief Quanah Parker in 1911, all subsequent leaders of the Comanche Nation have held the title of chairman rather than chief.)

Coffey—great-great-great-grandson of the Comanche chief Ten Bears—liked the notion and invited Smith to the Comanche reservation north of Lawton, Oklahoma, for a powwow on June 7. Smith, in turn, asked his friend retired Ranger Joaquin Jackson of Alpine if he would join the meeting as a symbolic representative of the Rangers.

Jackson and his wife, Shirley, drove to Wichita Falls, spent the night there, and teamed up with Smith the following morning in Lawton.

The three Texans went to the Comanche tribal office, nine miles north of town, where Coffey's assistant took them to the chairman's office. Jackson noticed a framed master's diploma from Harvard hanging on his wall. Coffey had long flowing black hair and stood nearly a foot shorter than the former Ranger. Sharply dressed in a business suit, he greeted them cordially and introduced them to the tribal medicine man and elder, Thomas Blackstar. Wearing dark glasses and a baseball cap, he had little to say.

After a few pleasantries, Smith laid out his proposal: The Rangers and Comanches had never had a peace treaty. He envisioned a joint weekend fund-raising event, including a Saturday night gala highlighted with the signing of a peace document ornately inscribed on a buffalo hide. He believed the Ranger-Comanche gathering might bring in as much as $1 million, an amount the foundation and Comanches could split fifty-fifty. Too, it would generate national publicity for the foundation's efforts to build a Texas ranch education and research center as well as for the Comanche Nation.

"We could have the event in San Antonio," Smith suggested.

No, said the chairman. He knew the Comanche history as well as Smith knew the Rangers' history. His people had been betrayed in San Antonio in 1840, the result being a massacre still painful in the Comanche collective memory, the Council House fight.

"How about Austin, then?" Smith asked.

"That would be OK," Coffey said.

The Comanche chairman suggested that a delegation from the former Ranger group come to Lawton the following September to ride horses in the parade highlighting the annual Comanche Nation Fair.

Smith readily agreed.

Near noon, Coffey invited the visitors to lunch.

As they sat about to place their orders, Jackson saw a young, nicely dressed Comanche woman approaching their table. Coffey greeted the woman, a local educator, and introduced her to his guests from the Lone Star State.

"This man is a Texas Ranger," Coffey said, gesturing toward Jackson.

The six-foot-five Jackson stood and removed his big hat.

The woman with coal-black eyes looked up at the tall Texan.

"The enemy," she practically spit.

Startled, Jackson forced a smile.

"No, ma'am," he said, "not anymore."

With a withering look, the woman turned her back to him and left.

"If looks could kill, I'd be a dead man," Jackson recalled.

Despite the uncomfortable scene in the restaurant, before they parted that afternoon Coffey assured Shelton Smith that the seven-member tribal business council would consider his treaty proposal at its next regular meeting.

"A week or two later," Jackson recalled, "the chairman called Shelton and said the committee had rejected signing a treaty. He said all the women had argued against it. They said the Texas Rangers had killed too many of their ancestors."

Smith regretted the decision but did not try to fight it.

"I really believed we could have had a truly historic event and would have raised a lot of money for scholarships for young Texans and Comanches," Smith said. "Unfortunately, even after more than a hundred years, the old wounds were still too deep and raw."[1]

Notes

1. "Heroes of Old"

1. "The Heroes of Old." Dallas *Morning News,* October 5, 1900. Joseph Greaves Booth, born July 3, 1838, in Royton, England, came to Texas around 1858. He enlisted in the Rangers February 5, 1860, at San Antonio, where he had been working as a clerk, and served for seven months, until September 7, 1860. Shortly after the Civil War broke out, he joined Terry's Texas Rangers (formally known as the Eighth Texas Cavalry) on September 16, 1861, and served with the regiment through the bloody battle of Shiloh. He was discharged in May 1862 suffering from an unknown disability. A longtime drummer, or traveling salesman, Booth also was active in the United Confederate Veterans and the Traveler's Protective Association. He died in Austin on October 1, 1910, leaving a wife and four children. At the time of his death, he served on the board of managers of the state-operated Confederate Home in the capital city. The Texas Ranger Association met in Austin for the first time in 1897. In 1906, the organization began publishing an annual bulletin. The association's sixth volume, a twenty-page booklet printed in February 1907, contained a couple of articles by former captain George W. Baylor on the Apache chief Victorio, a story about Jack Hays during the Mexican War by Mrs. Moore Murdock, "National Commandant, Dames of 1846," an excerpt from Victor M. Rose's *History of Ross' Texas Confederate Brigade,* and a story about a fight Captain June Peak had with Indians in 1878.
2. Frederick Wilkins, *The Law Comes to Texas: The Texas Rangers 1870–1901* (Austin: State House Press, 1999), p. 345.
3. "Rangers to Reorganize," *Austin Daily Statesman,* May 27, 1900.

4. Wilkins, *The Law Comes to Texas*, pp. 345–346.

5. Wilkins, *The Law Comes to Texas*, p. 347.

6. Gonzales *Inquirer*, October 16, 1900.

7. Adjutant General's Department of Texas, *Report of the Adjutant General, 1899–1900*, p. 23.

8. Albert Bigelow Paine, *Captain Bill McDonald Texas Ranger: A Story of Frontier Reform* (New York: Little & Ives 1909), p. 261.

9. Adjutant General's Department of Texas, *Report of the Adjutant General, 1899–1900*, pp. 23–24; author's interview with Bob Snow, Kerrville, Texas, 1986; Henry T. Fletcher, "Violent Early Days of Big Bend Section Recalled," *Frontier Times*, May 1934, pp. 355–357.

10. Works Projects Administration, *Beaumont: A Guide to the City and Its Environs* (Houston: Anson Jones Press, n.d. [1940]), pp. 103–104.

11. "Message to Congress [*sic*]," January 10, 1901, 27th Texas Legislature, *House Journal*, pp. 23–24.

12. Paul N. Spellman, *Captain J.A. Brooks: Texas Ranger* (Denton: University of North Texas Press, 2007), pp. 125–126, 129–131.

13. Mike Cox, *Texas Ranger Tales II* (Plano: Republic of Texas Press, 1999), p. 143; General Order No. 62, July 3, 1901, cited in Wilkins, *The Law Comes to Texas*, p. 348; Adjutant General's Department of Texas, *Report of the Adjutant General, 1901–1902*, pp. 28–29.

14. The biggest legislative fight had not been over reorganizing the Rangers but over a provision in the original bills that all Rangers "give good and sufficient bond in the sum of $1,000, with not less than two sureties, conditioned for faithful performance of all duties required, said bond to be approved by the Governor and Comptroller." Supporters of that language argued that bonding would ensure that the Rangers employed reputable men, while opponents contended that the cost of the bond would make hiring difficult. The bonding requirement finally died in conference committee and the bill moved on to final passage. Spellman discusses the legislative debate over House Bill 52 in detail in *Captain J.A. Brooks*, pp. 129–131.

15. Richard J. Mertz, " 'No One Can Arrest Me': The Story of Gregorio Cortez," *Journal of South Texas* 1 (1974): pp. 1–17; J. Frank Dobie, *The Flavor of Texas* (Dallas: Dealey and Lowe, 1936), pp. 123–124. Cortez's July 7, 1913, pardon from Governor O. B. Colquitt apparently had less to do with guilt or innocence than politics and the need for intelligence on Mexican revolutionary activities. Charles H. Harris III and Louis R. Sadler in *The Texas Rangers and the Mexican Revolution* (Albuquerque: University of New Mexico Press, 2004), p. 128, assert that Cortez's pardon had been "instigated" by F. A. Chapa, one of Colquitt's top political allies and a player in much of the behind-the-scenes intrigue attendant to Texas's role in the early years of the Mexican Revolution. Chapa connected Cortez with the San Antonio office of the Bureau of Investigation and the bureau began using him as an informant.

16. Americo Paredes, *"With His Pistol in His Hand": A Border Ballad and Its Hero* (Austin: University of Texas Press, 1958), p. 198.

17. Earl Mayo, "The Texas Rangers: The Most Efficient Police Force in the World," *Frank Leslie's Popular Monthly*, October 1901, p. 525.

18. Seguin *Enterprise*, April 18, 1902, cited in Paredes, *"With His Pistol in His Hand,"* p. 31.

19. William Warren Sterling, *Trails and Trials of a Texas Ranger* (Norman: University of Oklahoma Press, 1969 reprint of 1959 ed.), p. 323.

20. Adjutant General's Department of Texas, *Report of the Adjutant General, 1901–1902*, p. 34; "Report of Captain J.A. Brooks, Commanding Company A, Ranger Force," *Report of the Adjutant General, 1903–1904*, p. 153; "Ramon Cerda Killed," Brownsville *Daily Herald*, May 17, 1902; "Cowardly Assassination," Brownsville Daily Herald, September 10, 1902; Stan Redding, "Storied Rangers Modern, Mobile, but Still Retain Spirit of Old West," Houston *Chronicle*, February 4, 1962. De la Cerda had not been the first member of his family to die violently. Six years before, a Brownsville policeman shot and killed de la Cerda's father. A year before Ranger Baker killed de la Cerda, his older brother Arturo, twenty-five, died of an accidental gunshot wound.

21. Mary Margaret Amberson, James A. McAllen, and Margaret H. McAllen, *I Would Rather Sleep in Texas: A History of the Lower Rio Grande Valley and the People of the Santa Anita Land Grant* (Austin: Texas State Historical Association, 2002), p. 444.

22. Sterling, *Trails and Trials of a Texas Ranger*, p. 325; for more on Ranger A. Y. Baker, see Sterling, pp. 134–141; Catherine G. Baker, "The Man of the Hour," *Junior Historian* 26, no. 1 (September 1965): pp. 13–16, 27–29. Just one day shy of a year before the killing of Ranger Roebuck, an event precipitated by Ranger efforts to suppress cattle rustling, the 28th Judicial District Grand Jury issued a report praising Captain Brooks and his men. Decrying severe depredations by cattle thieves, the report went on to ". . . hereby earnestly recommend that the present force of State rangers in this county be increased to the strength of a company, with headquarters at the county seat." Brownsville *Daily Herald*, September 10, 1901.

23. Adjutant General's Departmnet of Texas, *Report of the Adjutant General, 1901–1902*, p. 30.

24. Congress passed a new Militia Act in 1903, combining all state militia units into a National Guard with both state and federal responsibilities. Valentine J. Belfiglio, *Honor, Pride, Duty: A History of the Texas State Guard* (Austin: Eakin Press, 1995), p. 52.

25. Works Projects Administration, *Beaumont*, p. 113.

26. Judith Walker Linsley and Ellen Walker Rienstra, *Beaumont: A Chronicle of Promise* (Woodland Hills, Cal.: Windsor Publications, 1982), p. 83.

27. Sterling, *Trails and Trials of a Texas Ranger*, p. 327.

28. Paul N. Spellman, *Spindletop Boom Days* (College Station: Texas A&M Press, 2001), p. 203.

29. J. A. Brooks to General John A. Hulen, January 24, 1904, Adjutant General's Records.

30. Brooks to Hulen, February 9, 1904, and Hulen to Brooks, February 13, 1904, Adjutant General's Records. Bates proved to be the last survivor of Brooks's Company A. For more on his career see M. Frank Sweeny, "Sole Surviving Member of Co. A Texas Rangers, Winfred Bates Once Killed Mexican Colonel," Kerrville *Times*, December 29, 1954.

31. Sterling, *Trails and Trials of a Texas Ranger*, pp. 330–331.

32. Sterling, *Trails and Trials of a Texas Ranger*, p. 331.

33. Adjutant General's Department of Texas, *Report of the Adjutant General, 1903–1904*, p. 164. Led by Adjutant General John A. Hulen, a contingent of Rangers took control of Hempstead on April 25, 1905, to prevent further violence following a courthouse square "dry" rally the night before that erupted into a gun battle, leaving four men dead. One of the victims was U.S. congressman John M. Pinckney. "The killings are the direct result of a Prohibition movement in Waller County which was begun some years ago, and the feeling has been intense," the Associated Press reported in a dispatch published nationwide. A local option issue having recently been approved by the electorate, the meeting had been called to prepare a petition to the governor requesting that Rangers be sent to the county to enforce the new law. "Texas Rangers Keep Peace at Hempstead," Los Angeles *Times*, April 26, 1905.

34. Frank W. Johnson. *A History of Texas and Texans*. Ed. Eugene C. Barker, with the assistance of Ernest William Winkler. (Chicago and New York: American Historical Society, 1916), vol. 1, p. 520.

35. Adjutant General's Department of Texas, *Report of the Adjutant General, 1906*, pp. 32–41.

36. John D. Weaver, *The Brownsville Raid* (College Station: Texas A&M University Press, 1992, reprint of 1970 edition), p. 86. William Neal witnessed the incident and gives his version of it in "The Shooting Up of Brownsville, Texas, 1906" in *Century of Conflict, 1821–1913*, (Waco: Texian Press, 1966), pp. 135–147. While not mentioning the role of Captain McDonald, Neal's recollection captures the tension between local residents and the black soldiers.

37. The so-called Brownsville Affair remained virtually forgotten until 1972, when President Richard M. Nixon reversed Theodore Roosevelt's order and changed the discharges of the black troops to honorable.

38. Robert M. Utley, *Lone Star Justice* New York: Oxford University Press, 2002, p. 281.

39. Mike Cox, *Texas Ranger Tales: Stories That Need Telling* (Plano: Republic of Texas Press, 1997) pp. 299–301.

40. Gary D. Hall, *Murder & Malice: Crimes of Passion from Victoria County, Texas 1891–1913* (Austin: Nortex Press, 2006), pp. 145–163; Harold J. Weiss, Jr. "The Texas Rangers and Captain Bill McDonald in General—and the Conditt Murder Case in Particular," *South Texas Studies* (Victoria: Victoria College Press, 1998), pp. 52–70; Paine, *Captain Bill McDonald Texas Ranger*, p. 312.

41. Victoria *Advocate*, April 3, 1907, and June 29, 1908.

42. Adjutant General's Department of Texas, *Report of the Adjutant General, 1906*, p. 30.

43. Austin *Statesman*, July 14, 1906; "Increased Force of State Rangers Is Called For," San Antonio *Daily Express*, August 29, 1906.

44. Adjutant General's Department of Texas, *Report of the Adjutant General, 1906*, p. 30.

45. San Antonio *Daily Express*, August 29, 1906.

46. Weaver, *The Brownsville Raid*, p. 87.

47. Sterling, *Trails and Trials of a Texas Ranger*, pp. 353–358.

48. Adjutant General's Department of Texas, *Report of the Adjutant General, 1906*, p. 31.

49. Paul N. Spellman, *Captain John H. Rogers, Texas Ranger* (Denton: University of North Texas Press, 2003), pp. 136–137; Harry Van Demark, "Religion and Bullets: Two Factors Which Have Figured Prominently in the Making of a Famous Texas Ranger," *Texas Monthly* 3, no. 2 (March 1929): pp. 349–351.

50. San Antonio *Daily Express*, undated clipping, W. J. McDonald Scrapbook, Former Texas Rangers Association Collection. Ranger enlistment records show a private Thurlow W. Weed served in Sieker's company, but he had not been a captain as the photo caption implied.

51. Texas State Historical Association *The New Handbook of Texas* (Austin: Texas State Historical Association), 1995, vol. 4, pp. 1002–1003.

52. "Abolish the Rangers," Houston *Chronicle*, undated clipping, W. J. McDonald Scrapbook, Former Texas Rangers Association Collection.

53. "Ranger Shot by Attorney at Groveton," San Antonio *Daily Express*, April 27, 1907; Sterling, *Trails and Trials of a Texas Ranger*, p. 360.

54. "Bill M'Donald in Literature," Houston *Post*, undated clipping, W. J. McDonald Scrapbook, Former Texas Rangers Association Collection.

55. Adjutant General's Department of Texas, *Biennial Report of the Adjutant General, 1908*, pp. 14–15.

56. Katie Daffan, *Texas Hero Stories: An Historical Reader for the Grades* (Boston: Benj. H. Sanborn., 1908), pp. 91–92.

57. Adjutant General's Department of Texas, *Biennial Report of the Adjutant General, 1908*, p. 15. Homer White's younger brother, Sam Houston White, served as Hamilton County sheriff from 1934 to 1945, rounding out his law enforcement career as a Ranger. Throughout his state career, Houston White wore the

two Colt revolvers his brother carried when gunned down in Parker County. Stationed at Sonora, White mentored rookie Ranger Arthur Hill following his appointment on September 1, 1947. The DPS had stationed Hill at Alpine in the Big Bend. S. E. Spinks, *Law on the Last Frontier: Texas Ranger Arthur Hill* (Lubbock: Texas Tech University Press, 2007), p. 51.

58. Daffan, *Texas Hero Stories*, p. 92.

59. "Captain M'Donald Subject of a Book," undated newspaper clipping, W. J. McDonald Scrapbook, Former Texas Rangers Association Collection.

60. Paine, *Captain Bill McDonald Texas Ranger*, p. 220.

61. Paine, *Captain Bill McDonald Texas Ranger*, p. 79.

62. "Outlaws Wish Texas to Disband Rangers," Los Angeles *Times*, January 10, 1909.

63. *The New Handbook of Texas*, vol. 1, p. 452.

64. William MacLeod Raine, *A Texas Ranger* (New York: G. W. Dillingham 1911), p. 42.

65. Cox, *Texas Ranger Tales II*, p. 249.

66. For one Ranger's experiences during the early 1900s, see Verdon R. Adams, *Tom White: The Life of a Lawman* (El Paso: Texas Western Press, 1972), pp. 14–24. Based primarily on former Ranger White's oral recollections, the book is not footnoted and has no bibliography, but the chapter on White's Ranger service contains several interesting incidents.

2. *Los Rinches*

1. Frank N. Samponaro and Paul J. Vanderwood, *War Scare on the Rio Grande: Robert Runyon's Photographs of the Border Conflict, 1913–1916* (Austin: Texas State Historical Association, 1992), pp. 77–78. *Rinche* is a derisive Mexican colloquial term for Ranger.

2. Samponaro and Vanderwood, *War Scare on the Rio Grande*, pp. 77–78. Most estimates put the Mexican Revolution's death toll at one million.

3. Don M. Coerver and Linda B. Hall, *Texas and the Mexican Revolution: A Study in State and National Border Policy, 1910–1920* (San Antonio: Trinity University Press, 1984), p. 21. In a campaign speech at Big Sandy in East Texas, O. B. Colquitt called the Rangers "the secret police force of the governor." Referring to an incident of Ranger heavy-handedness in Amarillo, the candidate said if he had been governor, "he would have fired the Rangers into the middle of the gulf of Mexico." Harris and Sadler, *The Texas Rangers and the Mexican Revolution* p. 61, citing Austin *Statesman*, July 7, 1910.

4. W. Dirk Raat, *Revoltosos: Mexico's Rebels in the United States, 1903–1923* (College Station: Texas A&M University Press, 1981), p. 208.

5. "U.S. Consulate Is Attacked," Eagle Pass *News-Guide*, November 12, 1910. For a concise summary of the early days of the Mexican Revolution, see Gerald G.

Raun, "The Madero Revolution," *Journal of Big Bend Studies* (Alpine: Center for Big Bend Studies, Sul Ross State University, 2006), pp. 85–120.

6. Eagle Pass *News-Guide*, November 19, 1910; William D. Carrigan and Clive Webb, "The Lynching of Persons of Mexican Origin or Descent in the United States, 1848 to 1928," *Journal of Social History* 37, no. 2 (Winter 2003): pp. 411–438. Gerald Raun, "Seventeen Days in November: The Lynching of Antonio Rodriguez and American-Mexican Relations, November 3–19, 1910." *Journal of Big Bend Studies*, Vol. 7, 1995, pp. 157-179. Unknown to the staff of the Eagle Pass newspaper, the very next day after dismissing the "disturbances" in Mexico and right across the river from their office in Ciudad Porfirio Díaz (now Piedras Negras), Madero pronounced the Mexican election null and void and said he was taking over as provisional president. Earl H. Elam, "The Madero Revolution and the Bloody Bend," *Journal of Big Bend Studies* Vol. 13, 2001, p. 167.

7. Cecilia Thompson, *History of Marfa and Presidio County, Texas, 1535–1946*, vol. 2 (Austin: Nortex Press, 1985), p. 77.

8. Eagle Pass *News-Guide*, December 10, 1910.

9. Marfa *New Era*, December 17, 1910; Harris and Sadler, *Texas Rangers and the Mexican Revolution*, p. 55.

10. Eagle Pass *News-Guide*, December 17, 1910. The Middleton, New York, newspaper's comments on the Rangers likely had been stimulated by an editorial in that morning's New York *Times*. The November 28, 1910, *Times* editorial, headlined "The Texas Rangers," referred to the recent unrest on the border and observed: "Perhaps Texas . . . will conquer its disposition to abolish the Rangers. . . . Let the Texas Rangers be preserved for the good of all of us. While they exist Texas will not permit the Mexicans to whip us." Harris and Sadler, *The Texas Rangers and the Mexican Revolution*, p. 54.

11. Thompson, *History of Marfa and Presidio County, Texas*, vol. 2, p. 80.

12. Record of Proclamations, Texas Secretary of State, 1911, pp. 113–115.

13. *The New Handbook of Texas*, vol. 3, p. 803. In addition to his National Guard service, Hutchings had been on the staffs of Governors Sul Ross and James Hogg. In 1910, during the gubernatorial campaign, Hutchings had served as secretary of the Travis County Colquitt Club. Harris and Sadler, *The Texas Rangers and the Mexican Revolution*, p. 67.

14. Lindsay Carter, "The Texas Rangers: Interesting Facts About Our Greatest Body of Fighting Men," *The Texas Magazine* 3, no. 4 (February 1911): p. 27.

15. Hughes to Hutchings, May 9, 1911, Texas State Archives, as cited in Robert M. Utley, *Lone Star Lawmen: The Second Century of the Texas Rangers* (Oxford: Oxford University Press, 2007), p. 12. David Dorado Romo covers the Battle of Juárez in detail in his *Ringside Seat to a Revolution: An Underground Cultural History of El Paso and Juarez, 1893–1923* (El Paso: Cinco Puntos Press, 2005), pp. 82, 86–106.

16. *The New Handbook of Texas*, vol. 4, pp. 686–688.

17. Coerver and Hall, *Texas and the Mexican Revolution*, p. 28; *Biennial Report of the Adjutant General, 1911–1912*. Eventually, the U.S. Treasury Department deposited $9,639.41 into the state comptroller's Ranger fund.

18. Adjutant General's Department of Texas, *Biennial Report of the Adjutant General, 1911–1912*, p. 8. The newly constituted force consisted of forty-two men organized into four companies. Austin-based Company D had only one man, Captain William Smith, an Australian who had served in Theodore Roosevelt's Rough Riders. Harris and Sadler, *The Texas Rangers and the Mexican Revolution*, pp. 76–77.

19. Utley, *Lone Star Lawmen*, p. 10. As Utley notes, the federal funding lasted only four months, but Fox stayed on the payroll. For more on Fox see Al Ritter and Chick Davis, "Captain Monroe Fox and the Incident at Porvenir," *Oklahoma State Trooper*, Winter 1996, pp. 35–41.

20. Adjutant General's Department of Texas, *Biennial Report of the Adjutant General, 1911–1912*. Hutchings's standards were published as General Order 5, Headquarters Ranger Force, Adjutant General's Office, October 2, 1911.

21. *The New Handbook of Texas*, vol. 4, pp. 686–688.

22. Harris and Sadler, *The Texas Rangers and the Mexican Revolution*, pp. 90–92, 98–99; Jack Martin, *Border Boss: Captain John R. Hughes, Texas Ranger* (Austin: Statehouse Press, 1990 reprint of 1942 edition), pp. 196–199.

23. Utley, *Lone Star Lawmen*, p. 15, citing Private C. R. Moore to Adjutant General, May 21, 1912, Texas State Archives, and U.S. Army Lieutenant Clarence A. Daugherty's endorsement to Moore's report, June 1, 1912, Walter Prescott Webb Collection, Center for American History, University of Texas at Austin.

24. Utley, *Lone Star Lawmen*, p. 16, citing telegram, Hughes to Adjutant General, January 30, 1913, Texas State Archives, and Moore to Adjutant General, February 5, 1913, Texas State Archives; "Shoot Straight If Necessary," Dallas *Morning News*, January 31, 1913.

25. Coerver and Hall, *Texas and the Mexican Revolution*, p. 57.

26. Harris and Sadler, *The Texas Rangers and the Mexican Revolution*, p. 115. Despite his bluster, prior to Election Day Colquitt had to divert most of the border Rangers to prevent politically motivated violence. Utley, *Lone Star Lawmen*, p. 14, citing Colquitt to Hutchings, October 28, 29, and November 1, 1912, Texas State Archives.

27. Cox, *Texas Ranger Tales*, pp. 120–121.

28. San Antonio *Express*, July 29, 1913.

29. Coerver and Hall, *Texas and the Mexican Revolution*, pp. 64–65.

30. Walter Prescott Webb, *The Texas Rangers: A Century of Frontier Defense* (Boston: Houghton Mifflin 1935), p. 490. Another version of the incident has Vergara crossing after having sought help from Webb County sheriff Amador Sanchez, a Colquitt supporter with connections in Mexico. In this scenario, the

Laredo lawman supposedly told Vergara he would talk with Mexican authorities to see what could be done about Vergara's missing livestock. Soon the sheriff reported to Vergara that he had it worked out so that he could go to Hidalgo and reclaim his horses, the implication being that Sanchez had participated in a setup.

31. Austin *Daily Statesman*, February 26–27, 1914.
32. San Antonio *Express*, December 10, 1914.
33. Coerver and Hall, *Texas and the Mexican Revolution*, pp. 65–74.
34. "Texas Rangers 'Invade' Mexico and Recover Vergara's Body," Austin *Statesman*, March 9, 1914; Austin *Statesman*, March 10, 11, 1914.
35. Austin *Statesman*, March 13, 1914.
36. Austin *Statesman*, March 13, 1914.
37. Dallas *Morning News*, March 11, 12, 1914; Austin *Statesman*, March 11, 1914.
38. Laredo *Times*, March 18, 1914.
39. Based on U.S. military records and Colquitt's correspondence, Harris and Sadler make a convincing case in *Texas Rangers and the Mexican Revolution* (pp. 169–170) that Colquitt plotted behind the scenes with Adjutant General Hutchings to have Vergara's killers kidnapped and returned to Texas for trial. The volatile scheme failed when the Army found out about it and took steps to prevent it. Publicly, Colquitt offered a $2,500 reward for delivery of the Vergara suspects.
40. "The Texas Rangers, Fearless Men," Los Angeles *Times*, June 29, 1914.
41. Webb, *The Texas Rangers*, p. 495. Webb covers the Vergara incident pp. 486–495; Harris and Saddler, *Texas Rangers and the Mexican Revolution*, relate the story pp. 165–171. Webb infers that Captain Sanders really did recover Vergara's body and only offered his clarification so that Colquitt could placate Washington. Harris and Saddler conclude that Colquitt knew all along that Vergara's body had not been recovered by the Rangers, but capitalized on the news media's inference to make political points.

3. *Los Sediciosos*

1. For more on the Plan of San Diego, see Alan Gerlach, "Conditions Along the Border—1915: The Plan de San Diego," *New Mexico Historical Review* 43 (July 1968): pp. 195–212; James A. Sandos, *Rebellion in the Borderlands: Anarchism and the Plan of San Diego, 1904–1923* (Norman: University of Oklahoma Press, 1992); and L. H. Warburton, "The Plan de San Diego: Background and Selected Documents," *Journal of South Texas* 12, no. 1 (1999): pp. 125–155. Harris and Sadler, based on FBI records not opened until 1977 and not seriously scrutinized by scholars for more than two decades after they became available, believe Ramos had been an agent of the Carranza government, not Huerta's regime. "Documents in the Federal Bureau of Investigation archive on the Mexican

Revolution definitively deposit the Plan at the feet of the *carrancistas*," they write. Harris and Sadler, *The Texas Rangers in the Mexican Revolution*, pp. 220–221. In addition to Ramos, who had the misfortune of being caught with a copy of the plan, Agustin Garza, a Duval County schoolteacher; San Benito rancher Aniceto Pizana, an active supporter of revolution since 1904; Luis de la Rosa (who led the Norias raiders); and Jacobo Villarreal were deeply involved in executing the plan. Harris and Sadler, (p. 483) cite a military report that flatly asserts Villarreal, a known Carranza official, wrote the plan. Later in their book (pp. 212–213), Harris and Saddler write that speculation as to the plan's authorship includes the *carrancistas*, the Germans, the *huertistas*, the *magonistas*, the Germans, and even former U.S. Marshal and later Ranger captain W. M. Hanson. Another suspect they name is radical journalist Francisco Alvarez Tostado. The document almost certainly gained inspiration from the anarchist *cronicas* of Ricardo Flores Magon (1873–1922) and the newspaper he and his brother published, *Regeneracion*. Long opposed to Porfirio Díaz, Flores Magon also did not like American business interests in Mexico (mining and ranch ownership, primarily) or the discriminatory treatment most Mexican-Americans received. As Harris and Saddler conclude, "No one knows for certain who wrote the Plan de San Diego." For an overview of Flores Magon, see Ignacio Lopez-Calvo, "The Spanish-Language Cronica in Los Angeles: Francisco P. Ramirez and Ricardo Flores Magon," *Journal of Spanish Language Media* 1 (Denton: Center for Spanish Language Media, University of North Texas, 2008): pp. 125–136.

2. Cox, *Texas Ranger Tales II*, pp. 148–161; Emilio Zamora, Cynthia Orozco, and Rodolfo Rocha, eds., *Mexican Americans in Texas History: Selected Essays* (College Station: Texas A&M University Press, 2000), pp. 103–119.

3. Cox, *Texas Ranger Tales*, p. 134.

4. "Plots Against United States," Austin *Statesman*, February 3, 1915.

5. Austin *American*, March 6, 1915; "Ten Additional Rangers," Dallas *Morning News*, March 27, 1915.

6. Samponaro and Vanderwood, *War Scare on the Rio Grande*, p. 75.

7. Adjutant General's Department of Texas, *Biennial Report of the Adjutant General, 1917*, p. 11; Cox, *Texas Ranger Tales*, pp. 141–145; "Details of Ranger's Death," Dallas *Morning News*, May 29, 1915. Tony Cano and Ann Sochat, *Bandido: The True Story of Chico Cano, the Last Western Bandit* (Canutillo, Tex.: Reata Publishing, 1997), passim. Born in 1887 on a remote ranch in the mountains of Chihuahua, Mexico, Chico Cano became the Big Bend's most infamous bandit. Western novelist Elmer Kelton of San Angelo, Texas, summarized him this way: "To his many enemies he was a bandit. To those he called friend, he was a hero. . . . Tough, resourceful, mercurial in temperament, he was a walking contradiction. His loyalties were easily changeable and always for sale. . . . His intimate knowledge of the Big Bend country on both sides of the river and his network of friends always allowed him to escape." Neither the

Rangers, the U.S. Customs Service, the military, nor enemies on his side of the river ever caught up with Cano. Though by all rights he should have died with his boots on, cancer claimed him at the age of fifty-six on August 28, 1943, in Cedillos, Mexico. He is buried in that village's cemetery in a grave no longer marked, only a few miles south of the Rio Grande.

8. Thompson, *History of Marfa and Presidio County, Texas*, vol. 2, p. 117.

9. Pat Goodrich, *Captain Ransom, Texas Ranger: An American Hero (1874–1918)* (Nappanee, Ind.: Evangel Publishing House, 2007), p. 136.

10. Utley, *Lone Star Lawmen*, p. 28, citing Testimony of E. A. Sterling, February 13, 1919, *Proceedings of the Joint Committee of the Senate and House in the Investigation of the Texas Ranger Force*, 1919, pp. 1502–1503.

11. Harris and Sadler, *The Texas Rangers and the Mexican Revolution*, pp. 250–252, pp. 255–258. Forty-four when appointed by Governor Ferguson, Ransom had served in the Spanish-American War and during the Philippine Insurrection. He had been in law enforcement since 1902, starting as a sheriff's deputy in Fort Bend County. He served two nonconsecutive enlistments in the Rangers but achieved most of his reputation as a special Houston police detective and later as the department's controversial chief.

12. "Mexicans Hear Weird Tales," Los Angeles *Times*, August 17, 1915; Harris and Sadler, *The Texas Rangers and the Mexican Revolution*, p. 272.

13. Goodrich, *Captain Ransom, Texas Ranger*, p. 140.

14. Samponaro and Vanderwood, *War Scare on the Rio Grande*, pp. 73–98; Scout Report of Capt. H. L. Ransom, G. D., for August 1915, Texas State Archives.

15. "Ranger Force Is Increased," Dallas *Morning News*, August 8, 1915.

16. Benjamin Heber Johnson, *Revolution in Texas: How a Forgotten Rebellion and Its Bloody Suppression Turned Mexicans into Texans* (New Haven: Yale University Press, 2003), pp. 91–92; Glenn Harding and Cindy Lee, *Rails to the Rio* (Raymondville, Tex.: privately published, 2003), pp. 51–52; Don Graham, *Kings of Texas: The 150-Year Saga of an American Ranching Empire* (New York: John Wiley and Sons, 2003), pp. 201–204; "Four Mexicans Slain in Attack at Norias," Dallas *Morning News*, August 10, 1915; "Sixty Mexican Outlaws Attacked 15 Americans but Were Driven Off," Austin *Statesman*, August 9, 1915. The Austin daily played the Norias fight as its banner story. The intensity of the news coverage in the aftermath of the raid dropped off after August 17, when a devastating hurricane struck Galveston, killing some two hundred people.

17. Harris and Sadler, *The Texas Rangers and the Mexican Revolution*, pp. 263–267. The Norias attack led to one of the more famous and widely distributed Ranger photographs, one of a series of postcards sold by Valley photographer Robert Runyon, who took numerous grisly Mexican Revolution images south of the Rio Grande as well. His staged images from Norias showed Captain Fox with King Ranch employee Tom Tate and another man astride their horses, ropes attached to three of the dead raiders. Near the three lay another dead

man, identified only as a bandit. Tape-recorded in Kerrville by the author in 1986, retired state game warden Bob Snow (1898–1987), who grew up in Willacy County, said his older brother Luke had been among those playing poker at the Norias headquarters when the raiders struck. Luke Snow had taken part in the firefight, using his .30-30 Winchester. Bob Snow said he went to the ranch the following day, arriving in time to see the slain Mexicans being buried. He said one of the Rangers asked if he would like to say a few words over the mass grave. Snow refused, saying they had tried to kill his brother. Finally, Snow related, a Ranger stepped up and offered: "Dust to dust, if the——don't kill you, the Rangers must." The missing word was in Spanish and cannot be distinguished clearly enough for translation. The possible fill-in-the-blank choices include *soldiers, federales, hueristas, cabrones* (a catchall epithet), or perhaps a slang word for a sexually transmitted disease. Those four men buried that day were among an estimated one hundred suspected bandits, Mexican Nationals, or Mexican-Americans killed by Rangers or other lawmen between August 1915 and August 1916. *Investigation of Mexican Affairs*, vol. 1, p. 1,265, cited in Amberson and McAllen, *I Would Rather Sleep in Texas*, p. 490. Over the years, contemporary fatality estimates have been revised upward, ranging from a realistic three hundred to an unlikely five thousand. Zamora, Orozco, and Rocha, eds., *Mexican Americans in Texas History: Selected Essays*, p. 116. Newspaper coverage of bandit raids and Ranger responses relied heavily on hearsay, rumor, and speculation. As the Austin *Statesman* noted on August 12, 1915, concerning a skirmish that followed the Norias raid, "It is not known whether soldiers, county officers or Rangers were in the fight. Officers have adopted a policy of refusing to give details of fights in which they were concerned."

18. Harris and Sadler, *The Texas Rangers and the Mexican Revolution*, p. 266–267; Samponaro and Vanderwood, *War Scare on the Rio Grande*, p. 88; Austin *Statesman*, August 14, 1915.

19. Brownsville *Daily Herald*, October 19, 20, and 21, 1915; Dallas *Morning News*, October 20, 1915; Frank Cushman Pierce, *Texas' Last Frontier: A Brief History of the Lower Rio Grande Valley* (Menasha, Wis.: George Banta Publishing Company, 1917), pp. 96–97; Brian Robertson, *Wild Horse Desert: The Heritage of South Texas* (Edinburg, Tex.: New Santander Press, 1985), pp. 257–258; Harris and Sadler, *The Texas Rangers and the Mexican Revolution*, pp. 290–292. For a readable if not always accurate account of the Olmito attack, see Sterling, *Trails and Trials of a Texas Ranger*, pp. 42–43. The man who went from Ranger private to adjutant general had a mixed view of Ransom. While noting that the controversial captain had a soft side, Sterling recalled a night he spent listening to Ransom and an army officer exchange stories about their service during the Philippine Insurrection. "The tales they told about executing Filipinos made the Bandit War look like a minor purge," Sterling wrote (p. 47). The two Olmito

attack suspects saved by Sheriff Vann from execution by Ransom were later found to be innocent. Utley, *Lone Star Lawmen*, pp. 42–43. Not all the Olmito suspects encountered by Rangers ended up dead. One of Ransom's men, Ranger Raymond Bellamy, included this entry in his scouting report: "Nov. 6, 1915- Arrested Laura Lopez for train wrecking on Oct. 18, took him to Brownsville Jail." Adjutant General's Correspondence, Texas State Archives. Whether Lopez was convicted in connection with the attack remains unclear.

20. Utley, *Lone Star Lawmen*, p. 43, citing Ferguson to Funston, November 10, 1915, and Hutchings to Ferguson, November 19, 1915, Texas State Archives.

21. Cox, *Texas Ranger Tales II*, p. 156. Back east, having read newspaper stories about contemporary Ranger activity on the border, writer Frank Fowler fictionally resurrected the career of Frontier Battalion captain June Peak and placed him in twentieth-century service along the border in *The Bronco Rider Boys with the Texas Rangers*, a gee-whiz adventure novel for boys. When Donald Mackay and Billie Winkle, two of the three principal characters, encounter the captain and his Rangers in Mexico, one of them asks Peak what he is doing " 'this side of the Rio Grande?' 'Well, I declare,' responded Captain Peak, looking around at his men with a twinkle in his eye, 'we must have crossed the river without seeing it.' " Fowler, p. 21.

22. Coerver and Hall, *Texas and the Mexican Revolution*, p. 93.

23. Willeford, Glenn, "¡Mueran Los Gringos!," *Dirty Cop? The Rise and Fall of a Texas Sheriff: Memoir and Essays*, (Alpine, TX: Johnson's Ranch and Trading Post Press, 2007), pp. 178–188; Coerver and Hall, *Texas and the Mexican Revolution*, p. 95; Amberson and McAllen, *I Would Rather Sleep in Texas*, p. 488.

24. A thorough overview of the Glenn Spring raid is in Ron C. Tyler, *The Big Bend: A History of the Last Frontier* (College Station: Texas A&M Press, 1996), pp. 162–174. Texas newspapers covered the raid, but due to the remoteness of the scene, stories varied in accuracy. One participant told his story in "Two Missing Americans Reach Marathon Safely," Dallas *Morning News*, May 10, 1917. Utley, *Lone Star Lawmen* (pp. 54–55), notes that Captain Fox did not reach Glenn Spring until four days after the raid. With U.S. soldiers already in pursuit of the bandits, he and his men stayed in Texas.

25. Coerver and Hall, *Texas and the Mexican Revolution*, p. 99.

26. Coerver and Hall, *Texas and the Mexican Revolution*, p. 95; Adjutant General's Department of Texas, *Report of the Adjutant General, 1915–1916*, pp. 3, 11. The Ranger force was increased several times during 1915 and 1916, only to be reduced to four officers and thirty-six privates when tensions eased. These temporary increases cost $25,755.64 during the biennium.

27. Tracy Hammond Lewis, *Along the Rio Grande* (New York: Lewis Publishing Company, 1916), p. 176.

28. Paredes, *"With His Pistol in His Hand,"* p. 24. Paredes discusses at length the Ranger legend and makes his case for the intense animosity many South

Texas Hispanics harbored for the Rangers in the early twentieth century, pp. 23–32.

29. Lewis, *Along the Rio Grande*, p. 177.

30. Lewis, *Along the Rio Grande*, pp. 178–180.

31. Born November 22, 1880, in San Saba, George W. "Buck" Connor listed his occupation as stockman when he enlisted in the Rangers at El Paso on May 1, 1916. Already gray-headed at thirty-six, he stood only five feet four and a half inches. His papers at the Texas State Archives show he resigned from Captain Henry Ransom's Company D on May 31 after only a month's service. A writer of Western fiction and a movie actor, Connor appeared in eighty-five films from 1912 to 1941. He died in Quartzsite, Arizona, on February 4, 1947, at sixty-six.

32. Robert V. Haynes, *A Night of Violence: The Houston Riot of 1917* (Baton Rouge: Louisiana State University Press, 1976), p. 183; Kenneth E. Hendrickson, Jr., *Chief Executives of Texas: From Stephen F. Austin to John B. Connally, Jr.* (College Station: Texas A&M University Press, 1995), p. 158.

33. *The New Handbook of Texas*, vol. 3, p. 462; Julian Samora, Joe Bernal, and Albert Pena, *Gunpowder Justice: A Reassessment of the Texas Rangers* (Notre Dame: University of Notre Dame Press, 1979), pp. 41–42.

34. Thompson, *History of Marfa and Presidio County, Texas*, vol. 2, pp. 144–148, 194; Glenn Justice, *Revolution on the Rio Grande: Mexican Raids and Army Pursuits, 1916–1919* (El Paso: Texas Western Press, 1992), pp. 1–33; Smithers, W. D. "The Long Rio Grande," *True West*, July–August 1963, pp. 26–28. "Of all the atrocities that had been committed in other raids, none aroused the people in the Big Bend as did the brutal murder of Mickey [Welch]," Smithers wrote. Later noted for his photography and historical writing, Smithers (1895–1981) first came to the Big Bend as a civilian muleskinner for the military during the bandit troubles. He knew the Brites and many of those involved in the aftermath of the raid.

35. Webb, *The Texas Rangers*, pp. 495–497; "Exciting Career of Captain K. F. Cunningham," *Texas Ranger* 6, no. 2, April 1938, p. 82; Harris and Sadler, *The Texas Rangers and the Mexican Revolution*, pp. 337–339. Harris and Sadler point out that Cunningham, a former prison farm warden, rode into Mexico without official permission. "Have corralled bunch of Indio Ranch goats across Rio Grande river," the captain wired Austin. "Think we can recover stolen property if you will grant permission to cross river. Answer." The reply from Austin contained no ambiguity: "Cannot give you authority to cross river." The army did have authority to cross the river, so nothing ever came of the fact that Cunningham disobeyed orders. Cunningham's brother John F. Cunningham also served in the Rangers. Another brother, Aaron W. Cunningham, held the rank of captain in the Rangers for six months in 1921.

36. Harris and Sadler, pp. 341–342. "We have already appointed about 18 more Rangers than our appropriation is going to allow us," Assistant Adjutant General Walter F. Woodul noted on January 8, 1918.

37. "Duties of Special Rangers," Adjutant General's Department, Austin, 1918.

38. Glenn Justice, *Little Known History of the Texas Big Bend: Documented Chronicles from Cabeza De Vaca to the Era of Pancho Villa* (Odessa: Rimrock Press, 2001), p. 150.

39. In addition to leader Bud Weaver, the Company B Rangers who raided Porvenir included A. C. Barker, Allen Cole, W. K. Duncan, Clint Holden, Max Newman, J. H. McCampbell, and J. B. Oliphant. As Utley notes in *Lone Star Lawmen* (p. 60), the men ranged in age from nineteen to forty-three (Weaver) and in experience as Rangers from four months to three years.

40. Robert Keil, *Bosque Bonito: Violent Times Along the Borderland During the Mexican Revolution*, edited by Elizabeth McBride, Occasional Papers no. 7 (Alpine, Tex.: Center for Big Bend Studies, Sull Ross State University, 2002), pp. 29–34.

41. A few years after the Porvenir incident, a Texas Ranger stationed in the Big Bend told newspaper reporter and pulp fiction writer Barry Scobee about a shoot-out "across the Rio Grande" during the bandit troubles. That inspired Scobee to write a short story called "Leaden Laughter" for *Adventure Magazine*. "Well, I'll say, Mister Texas Ranger . . . ," Scobee wrote in the pulp fiction piece, "You stitched that hombre—stitched him nine times from the Adam's apple to the belt buckle . . . what the hell gun did you shoot him with, Mister?" Scobee's Ranger answered, "An Army Colt's forty-five caliber," probably referring to the Colt Model 1911 semiautomatic, not the earlier Colt six-shooter. Even so, the Model 1911 held only eight rounds—not nine. Whatever handgun the Rangers who shot down the prisoners at Porvenir used, they must have had to stop and reload to "stitch" the men they killed. F. Romer, *Makers of History: A Story of the Development of the History of Our Country and the Part Played in It by the Colt* (Hartford, Conn.: Colt's Patent Fire Arms, 1926), p. 60.

42. Justice, *Little Known History of the Texas Big Bend*, pp. 148–158; Harry Warren, "The Porvenir Massacre in Presidio County, Texas, on January 28, 1918," Harry Warren Papers, Archives of the Big Bend, Sul Ross State University, Alpine, Texas; Al Ritter and Chick Davis, "Captain Monroe Fox and the Incident at Porvenir," pp. 35–41. Writer-historian Glenn Justice, former Upton County sheriff Glenn Willeford, and several others visited the abandoned village of Porvenir on April 19, 2008. The ruins of an old cotton gin stood as the only evidence of former occupation. Locating what they believed to be the site of the massacre, they found a military-issue .30-.06 rifle shell casing marked "1 F A 1909" and four spent pistol rounds, including three .45 Long Colt slugs and one copper-jacketed .45 ACP bullet. One of the revolver bullets appeared to have hit something, while the other two .45 Long Colt bullets were not deformed other than bearing lands and grooves indicating they had been fired. The semiautomatic slug also appeared to have hit something, as its nose was deformed. Visiting the site five years before, Justice found a military-issue brass

12-gauge "trench gun" shot shell of World War I vintage. E-mail, Glenn Willeford to author, April 26, 2008.

43. Harris and Sadler, *The Texas Rangers and the Mexican Revolution*, p. 355. The elder Neville buried his son, sold his ranch, moved to Marfa, and opened a café he called the Long Horn. But according to writer-historian Glenn Justice, Neville did more than cook and pour coffee. Armed with a Special Texas Ranger commission and a well-used six-gun, Neville spent many nights looking for Mexicans he suspected of taking part in the raid that claimed his son. "Neville's daughter recalled that her father kept a black book with some sixty names in it and over the years until his death in 1952, he scratched out many of the names in the book," Justice wrote. Justice, *Revolution on the Rio Grande: Mexican Raids and Army Pursuits, 1916–1917* (El Paso: Texas Western Press, 1992), pp. 54–55, citing Lois Neville Kelly to Clifford Casey, September 9, 1972, Clifford B. Casey Collection, Archives of the Big Bend, Sul Ross State University.

44. Justice, *Little Known History of the Texas Big Bend*, pp. 159–164.

45. Adjutant General's Department of Texas, *Report of the Adjutant General, 1917–1918*, p. 60.

46. Cox, *Texas Ranger Tales II*, p. 168.

47. Austin *Statesman*, July 11, 1918.

48. Official Order No. 36, Ranger Force Order Book.

49. Adjutant General's Department of Texas, *Report of the Adjutant General, 1917–1918*, pp. 11, 61–62.

50. Dallas *Morning News*, July 13, 15, and 17 and November 1, 1918.

51. A Senate committee investigating the border troubles tallied 550 American deaths from November 1910 to September 1919. A 1917 history of the Rio Grande Valley claimed: "One hundred Mexicans have been executed by the Texas Rangers and Deputy Sheriffs without process of law. Some place the figure at 300. Most of these executions, it has been asserted, were by reason of data furnished the Rangers implicating the particular Mexicans in the raids which were occurring." Pierce, *Texas' Last Frontier*, p. 114. Total damage from bandit raids was estimated at more than a half-billion dollars. Amberson, McAllen, and McAllen, *I Would Rather Sleep in Texas*, p. 492.

4. Jose Canales Takes On the Rangers

1. Adjutant General's Department of Texas, *Report of the Adjutant General, 1917–1918*, p. 63.

2. Harris and Sadler, *The Texas Rangers and the Mexican Revolution*, pp. 428–430; J. T. Canales, "Juan N. Cortina: Bandit or Patriot?" an address by J. T. Canales before the Lower Rio Grande Valley Historical Society, at San Benito, Texas, October 25, 1951; Utley, *Lone Star Lawmen*, p. 73.

3. Harris and Sadler, *The Texas Rangers and the Mexican Revolution*, pp. 430–431.

4. Utley, *Lone Star Lawmen*, pp. 71–72.

5. Even before Canales's bill went into the hopper, three other House members had put their name on a bill requiring a $2,500 bond for Rangers. "Query for Texas?" the Austin *American* asked in a headline over a two-paragraph story about the bill's filing, "Why Be a Ranger If You Have $2500." Austin *American*, January 17, 1919. Canales had already tried to impress on Governor Hobby and Adjutant General Harley that the Rangers needed gentling. Nearly a year earlier, in March 1918, Canales had met with both men, along with Captain Hanson and Francisco Chapa, to relate to them various instances of excess. After the meeting, Harley assured Canales that he would rein in the Rangers, but Canales saw no improvement. Utley, *Lone Star Lawmen*, pp. 69–70, citing Texas Ranger Force Investigation, Texas State Archives, pp. 878–879. Canales's characterization of Rangers as "men of desperate character" was made on January 13, 1919, and is contained in *Transcript of Proceedings, Joint Committee of the Senate and the House in the Investigation of the State Ranger Force*, Texas Legislature, 1919, p. 148.

6. "Hobby's Message to the People of Texas Makes Accounting of His Stewardship," Austin *American*, January 18, 1919. A year earlier, in a letter to political adviser Francisco Chapa, the governor had promised to reshape the Rangers. "The . . . old time ranger known as the 'gun man' will be eliminated under my administration, and only men who are peaceful and law abiding, and yet who are firm, will be employed in the service," Hobby wrote. Utley, *Lone Star Lawmen*, p. 69, citing Hobby to Chapa, January 5, 1918, Hobby governor's papers, 301–336, vol. 6, Texas State Archives, pp. 500–501.

7. Johnson, *Revolution in Texas*, pp. 172–173.

8. "Canales' Life Threatened by Texas Rangers Says Brownsville Legislator," Austin *American*, January 24, 1919.

9. "Canales Almost Wins Fight for Ranger Regulation but Border Opposition Appears," Austin *American*, January 28, 1919.

10. "Rangers Under House Fire Will Bring to Light Charges Filed with General Harley," Austin *American*, January 25, 1919. Actually, as Harris and Sadler point out in *The Texas Rangers and the Mexican Revolution* (p. 432), Canales would have preferred to see the Rangers abolished. In a January 17, 1919, letter to Cameron County sheriff William Vann, Canales asked the sheriff to push the Sheriff's Association of Texas to "petition the Legislature for a law requiring that the Rangers should be under the civil authorities and not to override them; or to abolish the Ranger force entirely as a menace to our democratic idea of local self government."

11. *Transcript of Proceedings, Joint Committee on the House and Senate in the Investigation of the Texas State Ranger Force*, Texas Legislature, passim.

12. Special Order No. 2A, Ranger Force Order Book; "All Texas Rangers Holding 'Specials' Get Them Revoked," Austin *American*, January 20, 1919. Several additional Ranger privates soon received notification of suspension in another round of orders. Special Orders 10 and 11, Ranger Force Order Book.

13. Special Orders No. 4A and 5, 6 and 7, January 30, 1919 Ranger Force Order Book.

14. "Harley and Canales Meet Before Committee in Plan to Investigate Rangers," Austin *American*, January 31, 1919.

15. "Ranger Hearing Gets New Phrases from Texas Border," Austin *American*, February 5, 1919.

16. Austin *American*, February 8, 1919; Dallas *Morning News*, February 8, 1919; Galveston *Daily News*, February 9, 1919; San Antonio *Express*, February 9, 1919. Cunningham had joined the Rangers on December 10, 1917. Born March 23, 1874, he was the grandson of Ranger captain James Cunningham (1816–1894), who took part in the 1865 Dove Creek fight. A Spanish-American War Veteran, K. F. Cunningham died October 31, 1937.

17. Special Order No. 9, February 7, 1919, Ranger Force Order Book.

18. Special Order No. 19, February 11, 1919 Ranger Force Order Book.

19. A note written on the bottom of Harley's letter by one Loyalty Ranger shows that not all of them had been swellheaded over having a special Ranger commission: "Inclosed [*sic*] find my com as per your request. I never carried a gun as I thot Cotulla had enough gun men already but any time I can serve you in any way command me. Yours Truly, S. [Simon] Cotulla." Harley to Cotulla, February 19, 1919 Adjutant General's Records, Texas State Archives.

20. Special Order No. 21, March 10, 1919, Ranger Force Order Book.

21. Special Order No. 22, March 10, 1919, Ranger Force Order Book.

22. Special Order No. 27, March 19, 1919, Ranger Force Order Book.

23. "Sheriff Vann Explains to Ranger Committee How to 'Ransomize,'" Austin *American*, February 8, 1919. By the time his name came up in the legislative hearing, Ransom had himself been "Ransomized." He had been shot to death in a Sweetwater hotel, killed in his nightclothes on April 1, 1918, by a stray bullet when a gunfight broke out in the hall outside his room. The fight had been between two men over family issues and had nothing to do with Ransom or the Rangers. Ranger William H. Koon quickly captured the two participants. Harris and Sadler, *The Texas Rangers in the Mexican Revolution*, p. 382; "Henry Ransom Long Known as a Gunfighter," Houston *Chronicle*, April 2, 1918.

24. Samponaro and Vanderwood, *War Scare on the Rio Grande*, p. 82; Spellman, *Captain John H. Rogers, Texas Ranger*, p. 190.

25. Utley, *Lone Star Lawmen*, pp. 81–82, citing *Journal of the House of Representatives of the Regular Session of the 36th Legislature*, pp. 535–539, and Dallas *Morning News*, February 21, 1919. After leaving the legislature, Canales went on to play an active role in the Mexican-American civil rights movement in

Texas. Canales also wrote articles, monographs, and books on a variety of subjects. He died on March 30, 1976, in Brownsville. *The New Handbook of Texas,* vol. 1, pp. 953–954. For more on Canales and the Texas Rangers, see Carlos Larralde, "J.T. Canales and the Texas Rangers," *Journal of South Texas,* 10, no. 1 (1977): pp. 38–68; and Richard Henry Ribb, "Jose Tomas Canales and the Texas Rangers: Myth, Identity and Power in South Texas, 1900–1920," Ph.D dissertation, University of Texas at Austin, 2001. Captain Hanson, who Canales believed had been a major part of the problem with the Rangers, resigned on September 4, 1919, to go to work as chief investigator for U.S. Senator Albert B. Fall's committee investigating the situation along the border. Harris and Sadler, *The Texas Rangers and the Mexican Revolution,* p. 481. Hanson's last job was serving as bailiff of the municipal court in San Antonio, where he died on February 20, 1931. Harris and Sadler, p. 493.

26. Ribb, pp. 358–365, "Rules and Regulations . . . Governing State Ranger Force of the State of Texas, compiled by the Adjutant General's Department, Austin, 1919," p. 9.

27. Llerena Friend, "W.P. Webb's Texas Rangers." *Southwestern Historical Quarterly* 74 (January 1971): pp. 293–322; William A. Owens, *Three Friends: Bedichek, Dobie, Webb* (Garden City, N.Y.: Doubleday, 1969), p. 248.

28. James A. Harley to Captain Jerry Gray, June 30, 1919, Former Texas Rangers Association Collection.

29. *Rules and Regulations Governing State Ranger Force of the State of Texas,* compiled by the Adjutant General's Department, Austin, 1919, p. 1.

30. Adjutant General's Department of Texas, *Biennial Report of the Adjutant General, 1919–1920,* p. 27.

31. Jacob F. Wolters, *Martial Law and Its Administration* (Austin: Gammel's Book Store, 1930), pp. 54-55; William Tuttle, "Violence in a 'Heathen' Land: The Longview Race Riot of 1919," *Phylon: Review of Race and Culture* 33 (1972): pp. 324–333; Harry Krenek, *The Power Vested* (Austin: Presidial Press, 1980), pp. 105–113.

32. Adjutant General's Department of Texas, *Biennial Report of the Adjutant General, 1919–1920,* p. 44.

5. "AN ASSET TO ANY LAW ABIDING COMMUNITY"

1. C. C. Sapp, "The Fiery Double Cross in Texas," *Debunker,* August 1929, p. 50.

2. Norman D. Brown, *Hood, Bonnet, and Little Brown Jug: Texas Politics, 1921–1928* (College Station: Texas A&M University Press, 1984), pp. 49–87.

3. Krenek, *The Power Vested,* pp. 5–32; Adjutant General's Department of Texas, *Biennial Report of the Adjutant General, 1919–1920,* pp. 67–81; Clifford Farrington, *Biracial Unions on Galveston's Waterfront, 1865–1925* (Austin: Texas State Historical Association, 2007), pp. 178–189. Farrington writes that none of

the shots fired in the violence preceding martial law at Galveston resulted in any injuries and maintains that Hobby acted on exaggerated reports from anti-union elements. The only death associated with the strike occurred after National Guard troops arrived, when a jumpy sentry shot and killed an officer refusing to stop his vehicle at a checkpoint. A report submitted to Adjutant General Cope on June 28, 1920, listed more than thirty-five "instances of fights, threats, violence and intimidation" associated with the strike since March 15. The findings came from a court of inquiry conducted by General Jacob F. Wolters in which forty-four witnesses testified. Galveston *Daily News*, June 29, 1920.

4. Adjutant General's Department of Texas, *Biennial Report of the Adjutant General, 1919–1920*, p. 79.

5. General and Special Orders Number 19, May 13, 1920, and Special Orders Number 20, May 20, 1920, Ranger Force Order Book.

6. Brownson Malsch, *Captain M.T. Lone Wolf Gonzaullas: The Only Texas Ranger Captain of Spanish Descent* (Austin: Shoal Creek Publishers, 1980), p. 7. On November 24, 1920, Gonzaullas and Ranger Martin Koonsman shot and wounded Frank Watkins, a grocery store operator in Ranger who sold bootleg whiskey under the counter. Watkins had been trying to escape arrest when the two Rangers shot him. Eleven days later, Eastland County sheriff S. E. Nolley charged both Rangers with aggravated assault and booked them into his jail. When Adjutant General Cope sent nine more Rangers to the boom town, the sheriff dropped the charges, saving face by claiming he had only filed the complaints to protect the two state lawmen. James Randolph Ward, "The Texas Rangers, 1919–1935: A Study in Law Enforcement," Ph.D. dissertation, Texas Christian University, 1972, pp. 46–47.

7. Krenek, *The Power Vested*, p. 27; General and Special Orders, Ranger Force Order Book; Ward, "The Texas Rangers, 1919–1935," p. 35; William D. Angel, Jr., "Controlling the Workers: The Galveston Dock Workers' Strike of 1920 and Its Impact on Labor Relations in Texas," *East Texas Historical Journal* 23, no. 2 (1985): pp. 14–27; Ralph W. Steen, *Twentieth Century Texas: An Economic and Social History.* (Austin: Steck Company, 1941), pp. 115–117. In reaction to the Galveston strike, a special session of the legislature enacted an open-port law, a measure that prohibited any interference "through the use of physical violence . . . or by intimidation" of persons "loading or unloading or transporting any commerce" in Texas. Six years later the statute, referred to more commonly as an "antistrike law" than as the open-port law, was ruled unconstitutional by the Texas Court of Criminal Appeals. "Galveston Mayor Would Keep Rangers," Dallas *Morning News*, January 6, 1921; "Ranger Captain Presented with Diamond Stick Pin," *Dallas Morning News*, December 22, 1920. Brooks, not to be confused with Captain J. A. Brooks and no relation, had been appointed captain in October 1919 and held the job through February 1921.

8. Austin *Statesman*, January 11, 20–25, and 29 and February 1, 1920; Austin *American*, January 21, 23, 25, 26, 27, 29, and 30, 1920; Ward, "The Texas Rangers,

1919–1935," pp. 28–31. The history of the Red River boundary dispute is explored in C. A. Welborn, *History of the Red River Controversy: The Western Boundary of the Louisiana Purchase* (Quanah, Tex.: Nortex Offset Publications, 1973).

9. Minnie King Benton, *Boomtown A Portrait of Burkburnett* (Quanah, Tex.: Nortex Offset Publications, 1972), pp. 23–24.

10. Diana Davids Olien and Roger M. Olien, *Oil in Texas: The Gusher Age, 1895–1945* (Austin: University of Texas Press, 2002), p. 84.

11. Ward, "The Texas Rangers, 1919–1935," p. 31, citing Stevens to Hobby, February 3, 1920, Adjutant General's Records. Hobby had appointed forty-seven-year-old Charles F. Stevens as captain on November 27, 1917. He went to the Rio Grande Valley to replace Captain Ransom, who had been transferred to Sweetwater in West Texas. In the Valley, Stevens did not get along any better with Cameron County sheriff W. T. Vann than Ransom had. Utley, *Lone Star Lawmen*, pp. 70–71. After resigning his Ranger captaincy, Stevens soon became a federal Prohibition agent and, except for a three-year stint with U.S. Customs, spent the rest of his career seizing illegal alcohol and arresting smugglers. On September 25, 1929, parties unknown ambushed Stevens and two of his men as they drove back to San Antonio after breaking up a moonshining operation in Atascosa County. The former Ranger captain died of multiple gunshot wounds later that day. Harris and Sadler, *The Texas Rangers and the Mexican Revolution*, p. 494.

12. Hendrickson, *Chief Executives of Texas*, p. 171.

13. Pat Neff, *The Battles of Peace* (Fort Worth: Bunker Press, 1925), p. 142.

14. Brown, *Hood, Bonnet, and Little Brown Jug*, p. 214. Less than a month after taking office, Neff reorganized the Rangers, disbanding Companies E and F and the emergency companies. He reconstituted Company B and appointed a new set of captains: Roy C. Nichols, assigned to command the Austin-based Headquarters Company; Jerry Gray, Company A at Presidio; Tom Hickman, Company B, Fort Worth; A. W. Cunningham, Company C, Del Rio; and W. L. Wright, Company D, Hebbronville. *Adjutant General's Report, 1921–1922*, pp. 53–54. For more on Neff and his policies and programs, see Emma Morrill Shirley, "The Administration of Pat M. Neff Governor of Texas 1921–1925," *Baylor Bulletin* 41, no. 4 (December 1938).

15. Neff, *The Battles of Peace*, pp. 37–47.

16. Adjutant General's Department of Texas, *Report of the Adjutant General, 1917–1918*, p. 62.

17. Maude T. Gilliland, *Horsebackers of the Brush Country: A Story of the Texas Rangers and the Mexican Liquor Smugglers* (Brownsville Tex.: Springman-King Company, 1968), pp. 25–26; Houston *Chronicle*, January 8, 1922; Walter Prescott Webb, "Veteran Ranger Protects Border," *The State Trooper*, September 1924, pp. 13–14; Ward, "The Texas Rangers, 1919–1935," pp. 56–57. What enabled Wright to cover so much territory was reliance on new technology: He used a heavy Ford truck instead of packhorses to transport supplies to Ranger campsites in advance.

18. T. J. Barragy, "J. Frank Dobie: Rancher and Folklorist," Texas Longhorn Breeders Association Web site, www.tlbaa.org, accessed December 21, 1999.

19. Sterling, *Trails and Trials of a Texas Ranger*, pp. 83–85.

20. Adjutant General's Department of Texas, *Annual Reports of the Adjutant General of Texas, 1921–1922*, pp. 91–92; Boyce House, *Roaring Ranger: The World's Biggest Boom* (San Antonio: Naylor Company, 1951), passim. The Ranger boom began October 21, 1917, when W. K. Gordon brought in a gusher on the J. H. McClesky farm. In a year, Ranger's population increased from one thousand to twenty-five thousand.

21. Adjutant General's Department of Texas, *Annual Reports of the Adjutant General of Texas, 1921–1922*, p. 93.

22. Brown, *Hood, Bonnet, and Little Brown Jug*, p. 60. An anti-Klan book published in 1922 said Texas "has been the scene of nearly 100 unlawful punishments by masked men." In one instance, the letters *K.K.K.* were "branded on the head of a negro who was horsewhipped on the charge of having been found in a white woman's room." On April 10, 1921, the book continued, an attorney in Houston "was whisked from a downtown street, driven to the country and tarred and feathered. The masked men then took him back to the city and threw him out of the automobile into a crowd. He was nude except for his coat of tar and feathers." *Ku Klux Klan Secrets Exposed* (Chicago: Ezra A. Cook, Publisher, 1922), pp. 69–70.

23. General and Special Orders, March 9, 1921, Ranger Force Order Book; Ward, "The Texas Rangers, 1919–1935," p. 65. Hickman, thirty-five, had joined the Rangers on June 16, 1919, became a sergeant in 1920, and made captain a year later.

24. Gray to Barton, December 27, 1921, Former Texas Rangers Association Collection.

25. Thompson, *History of Marfa and Presidio County, Texas*, vol. 2, pp. 228–229.

26. Webb, *The Texas Rangers*, pp. 526–530; Ward, "The Texas Rangers, 1919–1935," pp. 65–66. Hamer had drifted in and out of the Rangers since first enlisting under Captain J. H. Rogers in 1906, his periodic departures for other law enforcement jobs usually triggered by a chance to earn a better salary or by political realities. By April 11, 1920, when he went to work as a federal Prohibition agent based in Austin, Hamer had nearly five years' experience as a Ranger. After seventeen months on the trail of bootleggers, he rejoined the Rangers in September 1921, this time as a captain. "I hate to leave Austin," he told a friend, "but I sure will be glad to throw my leg over a horse again."

27. Boyce House, *Oil Boom* (Caldwell, Idaho: Caxton Printers, 1941), pp. 126–127.

28. Adjutant General's Department of Texas, *Annual Reports of the Adjutant General of Texas, 1921–1922*, p. 37.

29. Wolters, *Martial Law and Its Administration* pp. 81–89; Dorothy Blodgett, Terrell Blodgett, and David L. Scott, *The Land, the Law, and the Lord: The Life of Pat Neff* (Austin: Home Place Publishers, 2007), p. 14.

30. Adjutant General's Department of Texas, *Annual Reports of the Adjutant General of Texas, 1921–1922*, pp. 39–40.

31. Adjutant General's Department of Texas, *Annual Reports of the Adjutant General of Texas, 1921–1922*, pp. 39–40. For an overview of the Mexia boom see Nanine Simmons, "Booming Mexia in the Roaring '20s: 21 Pages of Living Legend and Fact!" (Waco, Tex.: Waco Times Herald, 1955).

32. Brown, *Hood, Bonnet, and Little Brown Jug*, pp. 52, 58; Ward, "The Texas Rangers, 1919–1935," p. 63.

33. Spellman, *Captain John H. Rogers, Texas Ranger*, p. 209.

34. Brown, *Hood, Bonnet, and Little Brown Jug*, p. 450; Ward, "The Texas Rangers, 1919–1935," p. 63. When Ward, historian Ben Proctor, and two others interviewed former Ranger Marvin "Red Burton" on April 7, 1968, in Mart, Texas, Burton asserted that Adjutant General Barton had been a "big shot" in the Klan. Ward also cites a 1923 letter in the Adjutant General Records alleging that Ranger sergeant J. W. McCormick was a KKK member. Given the Klan's oath of secrecy, whether those claims amount to political slander or truth may never be determined. The Rangers may not have been infested with Klan members, but management did have to weed out the occasional bad apple. Between December 1920 and April 1921, Captain Wright discharged a man for drinking confiscated liquor, and a Ranger working out of Del Rio got the boot for running his own bootlegging operation. In Longview a Ranger lost his job for arresting men without warrants, and in Lufkin a Ranger got fired for "cavorting" with a local girl and charging a substantial hotel bill to the state. Ward, pp. 85–86.

35. Adjutant General's Department of Texas, *Annual Reports of the Adjutant General of Texas, 1921–1922*, pp. 55–56; Austin *Statesman*, July 26, 1922; Ward, "The Texas Rangers, 1919–1935," p. 80. The emergency Rangers were hired under a 1920 state statute, Article 6755, Title 116, *Complete Statutes of Texas*.

36. Ward, "The Texas Rangers, 1919–1935," pp. 80–81; Jack Maguire, *Katy's Baby* (Austin: Nortex Press, 1991), pp. 66–70; Blodgett, Blodgett, and Scott, *The Land, the Law, and the Lord*, pp. 122–123. That September, Rangers became embroiled in another labor situation. John Wilkinson, president of District 21 of the United Mine Workers, filed a federal lawsuit alleging misconduct by the Rangers during a coal miners' strike at Bridgeport, in Northwest Texas. Henry Zweiful of Fort Worth, U.S. Attorney for the Western District, investigated along with state officials and termed the complaints against the Rangers "unfounded." Wilkinson continued with his suit, but it went nowhere. Roberto R. Calderon, *Mexican Coal Mining Labor in Texas and Coahuila, 1880–1930* (College Station: Texas A&M University Press, 2000), pp. 161–162; p. 167, citing *Coal Age*, November 2, 1922.

37. Adjutant General's Department of Texas, *Annual Reports of the Adjutant General of Texas, 1921–1922*, pp. 111–112; Neff, *The Battles of Peace*, p. 76.

38. Adjutant General's Department of Texas, *Annual Reports of the Adjutant General of Texas, 1921–1922*, p. 58.

39. Brown, *Hood, Bonnet, and Little Brown Jug*, p.130; Ward, "The Texas Rangers, 1919–1935," p. 89. With a mid-1922 homicide rate of 23.6 per 100,000 in population, Texas accounted for nearly 10 percent of all U.S. homicides. Prosecution also left plenty to be desired. Of twenty-one hundred reported homicides as of June 30, 1922, only 741 suspects had been indicted. Of those, only 270 were convicted. Those convictions resulted in only seven death sentences and eighteen life prison terms. Atticus Webb, *Crime: Our National Shame* (Binghamton, N.Y.: Vail-Ballou Press, 1924), pp. 16, 103, 104.

40. Ward, "The Texas Rangers, 1919–1935," pp. 98–99; San Antonio *Express*, July 25, 1924; San Antonio *Light*, July 25, 1924. Rangers based in Corpus Christi and Marshall also vigorously enforced Prohibition in those two cities. Ward, pp. 91–93. Another major focus of Ranger attention was Somervell County. Known as the "mountain moonshine rendezvous," the county was the principal supply point for Dallas, Fort Worth, Waco, and Wichita Falls. Based on information provided by an undercover operative, Rangers seized or destroyed twenty-three stills and arrested twenty-seven offenders in a series of raids in the county on August 25, 1923. Ward, pp. 103–108.

41. Webb, *The Texas Rangers*, p. 551. Webb said Neff sent thirty Rangers to San Antonio, but the Ranger roster shows only ten men, the captain making eleven. A twelfth Ranger went on the payroll in San Antonio in January 1924. Ward, "The Texas Rangers, 1919–1935," p. 100.

42. Neff, *The Battles of Peace*, p. 138.

43. Ward, "The Texas Rangers, 1919–1935," pp. 94–98.

44. Author's interview with Joe Dial, May 1, 2008, Austin, Texas. William Angelo Dial, a native of Greenville in East Texas, served in Wright's company through July 1924. He had another hitch in the Rangers from November 1, 1931, to October 31, 1933, resigning when "Ma" Ferguson got elected as governor. Following his death on June 17, 1963, in accordance with his wishes Dial was buried in the State Cemetery in Austin. His grave lies near that of legendary former Ranger William Alexander Anderson "Big Foot" Wallace, on high ground above the graves of "Ma" and "Pa" Ferguson. That way, Dial told his family, he could "keep an eye on the scoundrels."

45. Walter Prescott Webb, "Rangers Called in to Clean Up Austin," *The State Trooper*, 5 November 1924, pp. 21–22; Ward, "The Texas Rangers, 1919–1935," p. 102. In October 1923, pamphlets calling for the abolishment of the Rangers began appearing in San Antonio. This had not been the first time a Ranger got into legal difficulty in San Antonio. On December 11, 1910, a San Antonio police captain arrested Ranger captain Marvin E. Bailey, who had come to the police station on state business, for unlawfully carrying a pistol. A state district judge quickly ruled that a Ranger was a peace officer with a legal right to be armed and

ordered the captain's release from jail. Harris and Sadler, *The Texas Rangers and the Mexican Revolution*, pp. 61–62.

46. San Antonio *Express*, January 10, 1924.

47. San Antonio *Light*, January 12, 1924; Ward, "The Texas Rangers, 1919–1935," p. 102. When Taylor's case came to trial in Cuero in January 1925, the judge entered an instructed verdict of not guilty.

48. New York *Times*, November 1, 1923.

49. Brown, *Hood, Bonnet, and Little Brown Jug*, passim; Sapp, "The Fiery Double Cross in Texas," p. 55.

50. Sapp, "The Fiery Double Cross in Texas," passim.

51. "State Ranger Law Attacked," San Antonio *Express*, August 2, 1924.

52. Webb, *Crime: Our National Shame*, pp. 221–222.

53. San Antonio *Light*, August 2, 1924.

54. "Elgin to Push Fight Against Rangers," San Antonio *Light*, August 3, 1924. Though Elgin probably filed the suit at the urging of San Antonio's political machine, Rangers had raided his residence in 1923 looking for evidence of gambling. Too, his memory of Governor E. J. Davis's reign during Reconstruction also had a motivating effect. An 1871 graduate of Baylor University, Elgin commanded a Waco militia company, the Grays, during Davis's administration. After publishing a newspaper in Waco and later working to bring a deepwater port to Rockport, Elgin moved to San Antonio in 1904 and stayed there the rest of his long life, always active in politics. He died at the age of eighty-eight on September 22, 1938. San Antonio *Express*, September 23, 1938; Grace Miller White, "Captain John E. Elgin, Texian," *Frontier Times*, May 1944, pp. 337–340. As he got older, Elgin mellowed in his attitude toward the Rangers. Only a few months before he died, he gave a speech at the Ranger reunion in Coleman. After praising the effectiveness of the Frontier Battalion, he said, "From this organization the Ranger service of Texas has been continued and perpetuated and almost universally the men selected to fill the places of these gallant officers as they retired have been worthy successors." "Texas Rangers and Their Great Leaders," *Frontier Times*, August 1938, pp. 471–476.

55. Elton Cude, *The Free and Wild Dukedom of Bexar* (San Antonio: Munguia Printers, 1978), p. 218. The adjutant general's report for the 1923–1924 biennial contained no mention of the San Antonio takeover and no statistics on Ranger cases. All the publication noted was that the force had spent $111,289.52 of its fiscal 1923 appropriation of $120,970 and $105,015.41 of its $114,220.65 allocation for fiscal 1924. Adjutant General's Department of Texas, *Reports of the Adjutant General of the State of Texas, 1923–1924*, p. 75.

56. Brown, *Hood, Bonnet, and Little Brown Jug*, p. 238.

57. Ward, "The Texas Rangers, 1919–1935," p. 119, citing R. W. Aldrich to Cal Spear, December 22, 1924.

58. San Antonio *Express*, January 18, 1925.

59. "Texas Rangers Pass into History," San Antonio *Light,* January 17, 1925.

60. Walter Presott Webb, "Fight Against Texas Rangers: A Discussion of the Motives Involved in the Suit to Enjoin Continuance of the Force," *The State Trooper* 6 (July 1925): p. 18.

61. Owen P. White, "Texas Rangers Range No More," *New York Times Magazine,* February 1, 1925.

62. White, "Texas Rangers Range No More."

63. Neff, *The Battles of Peace,* pp. 138–139. During the San Antonio takeover, Rangers made 442 liquor law arrests, filing most of their cases in federal court due to the lack of local prosecution. In addition, they made thirty felony arrests and 543 misdemeanor arrests for such crimes as carrying a prohibited weapon, gaming, and theft. Webb, "Rangers Called In to Clean Up Austin," pp. 21–22.

64. Neff, *The Battles of Peace,* p. 141.

65. Ward, "The Texas Rangers, 1919–1935," pp. 123–124. As it turned out, Yancy Story's wrongdoing ran deeper than auto theft. Hickman believed Story had been pulling bank robberies. Using undercover operatives to develop more information, Hickman eventually had enough probable cause to raid the Story Ranch on August 24, 1926. Rangers and Denton County sheriff's deputies turned up enough evidence to get Story and five accomplices indicted for an array of charges, including bank robbery and murder. Utley, *Lone Star Lawmen,* p. 114.

66. Webb, *The Texas Rangers,* pp. 550–551.

67. Walter Prescott Webb, "Says Texas Rangers Are Needed Now," Dallas *Morning News,* February 18, 1925.

68. Waco *Times-Herald,* February 20, 1925.

69. Austin *Statesman,* February 21, 1925.

70. "Rangers Rebuked in Jury Report," San Antonio *Express,* February 26, 1925.

71. *Senate Journal,* 39th Legislature, Regular Session, 866–867, 1092.

72. Born in Mississippi, Fly grew up in Gonzales County. As a young man, he moved from an early interest in medicine to the law, getting his license to practice after passing an oral test of his legal knowledge. Appointed to the Fourth Court of Civil Appeals in 1893 by Governor James S. Hogg when the court was created, Fly became chief justice in 1911 and remained on the court forty-one years. His opinions filled 337 volumes of the *Southwest Reporter.* Jay Brandon, *Law and Liberty: A History of the Legal Profession in San Antonio* (Dallas: Taylor Publishing Company, 1996), pp. 47, 106–107.

73. "Rangers Win Court Fight," Austin *American,* February 26, 1925.

74. Marshall *News,* February 26, 1925.

75. Ward, "The Texas Rangers, 1919–1935," pp. 125–126. Hamer and Wright would return to the Rangers eventually, but Gray's 1925 resignation marked the end of his career as a regular Ranger. He held special Ranger commissions intermittently through January 18, 1933.

76. Austin *American*, May 21, 1925.

77. Captain Nichols, forty-nine, came to the Rangers with solid experience gained as a Houston police officer and Fort Bend County deputy. He never received the adoring media attention Captain Hickman enjoyed, but Nichols proved his mettle in dealing with East Texas bootleggers and keeping the peace in his area of operation. Working with local officers and federal agents, during the summer of 1925 Nichols and his Rangers smashed four stills, seized ten thousand quarts of whiskey, and made 142 arrests, including twenty-three still operators. On September 18, 1925, Nichols and Harrison County sheriff John C. Sanders stood off a mob encircling the courthouse in Marshall and prevented the lynching of three black men accused of killing a white man in Panola County. Utley, *Lone Star Lawmen*, p. 112, citing Ward, "The Texas Rangers, 1919–1935."

78. Ward, "The Texas Rangers, 1919–1935," pp. 126–133.

79. Dallas *Morning News*, February 17, 1926.

80. Walter P. Webb, "Texas Rangers Kept Idle," *The State Trooper* 7, no. 10 (June 1926): p. 13. Webb wrote sixteen articles for *The State Trooper* from March 1924 to July 1927.

81. Webb, "Texas Rangers Kept Idle," p. 13.

82. For more on Governor Dan Moody, see Ken Anderson, *Dan Moody: Crusader for Justice* (Georgetown, Tex.: Georgetown Press, 2008).

83. Walter P. Webb, "Rangers Solve Mystery: Murderers of Kindly Physician Are Followed, Even Across Border, and Confession Is Secured from Them," *The State Trooper* 8, no. 2 (October 1926): pp. 9–10.

84. Cox, *Texas Ranger Tales II*, pp. 180–184.

85. Walter P. Webb, "Rangers Arrest Lawmakers: Texas Representatives Taken in custody when one accepts $1,000 from opponent of measure," *The State Trooper* 8, no. 8 (April 1927): pp. 11–12. Brown, *Hood, Bonnet, and Little Brown Jug*, pp. 346–347.

86. The 1927 spring cleanup in Borger followed an October 1926 Ranger sweep led by Captain Roy Nichols, dispatched from East Texas to police the newly founded town. Teaming up with federal agents and Hutchinson County sheriff Joseph Ownbey, the Rangers made fifty arrests and closed twenty joints. Nichols had the prisoners transported to Amarillo under heavy guard and ordered all the other undesirables to get out of town or soon join their colleagues in the Potter County Jail. When Borger incorporated, newly elected mayor John R. Miller said he would organize a police force, and the Rangers left. Cox, *Texas Ranger Tales*, pp. 197–208; Utley, *Lone Star Lawmen*, pp. 116–117, citing Ward, The Texas Rangers, 1919–*1935*, and Fort Worth *Press*, October 16, 1926.

87. Adjutant General's Department of Texas, *Reports of the Adjutant General, 1927–1928*, p. 19.

88. Special Order No. 7, April 30, 1927, Ranger Force Order Book.

89. Spellman, *Captain John H. Rogers, Texas Ranger*, p. 218.

90. Walter P. Webb, "May Increase Rangers," *The State Trooper* 8, no. 10 (July 1927): pp. 13–14.

91. Webb, "May Increase Rangers."

92. "Let's Build a Monument to the Texas Ranger," *Frontier Times*, September 1927, pp. 34–37.

93. Richard R. Moore, *West Texas After the Discovery of Oil: A Modern Frontier.* (Austin: Jenkins Publishing Company, 1971), p. 39.

94. "Posse Closes in on Texas Bandits," San Antonio *Light*, December 28, 1927; "Cisco Bandits Captured Alive," San Antonio *Light*, December 30, 1927; William Whitaker, "Retired Hero Recalls Cisco's Christmas Bank Heist," Abilene *Reporter-News*, December 18, 1977; Lynn Walker, "In Cisco, Texas, Dec. 23 Proves Dangerous For Many," Wichita Falls *Times Record News*, December 22, 2007. For a fictionalized treatment of the robbery, see A.C. Greene, *The Santa Claus Bank Robbery* (New York: Alfred A. Knopf, 1972).

95. "Heroes of the Frontier," New York *Herald-Tribune*, October 16, 1927.

96. W. M. Massie, "Why We Pay for Dead Bandits," *Bunker's Monthly*, February 1928, pp. 173–180.

97. John H. Jenkins and Gordon Frost, *I'm Frank Hamer: The Life of a Texas Peace Officer*, (Austin: Pemberton Press, 1968), pp. 151–160; *Frontier Times*, November 1929, p. 54.

98. "The Hudson Pension Bill," *Frontier Times*, May 1928, pp. 334–335.

99. Adjutant General's Department of Texas, *Reports of the Adjutant General, 1927–1928*, pp. 20, 35.

100. New York *World*, March 25, 1929. Wink came into being in early 1927 following a major oil discovery on the Hendrick Ranch in remote Winkler County. The Dallas *Morning News* reported on December 4, 1927, that Wink had grown from "only a prairie" as of March 1 that year into a town of three thousand residents by November 1. Rangers first hit town in October 1927, making eighty arrests for gambling and liquor violations on October 22. According to an Associated Press dispatch, the state officers gave "undesirables" twenty-four hours to leave town. But not everyone took the Rangers up on their demand. About a month later, Rangers under Captain Wright raided two gambling joints in Wink. They arrested 102 men and confiscated card and dice tables, guns, and whiskey. Of those arrested, only one said he earned his living as a gambler. The others gave their occupations as either cooks or waiters. In February 1928 Wright's men rounded up 150 more miscreants. Rangers carried out another raid and made numerous arrests on July 14, the Associated Press quoting the county sheriff as saying the state lawmen "were not invited by him." Evidently inspired by the Ranger presence in Wink, one brazen crook thought that posing as a state lawman might net him some easy money. Around midnight on May 1, 1928, a man wearing a cowboy hat and armed with a pistol burst into the

bedroom of the wife of the out-of-town proprietor of Wink's Blackie Hotel. Announcing he was a Texas Ranger, the intruder said he was taking her to jail unless she gave him $150. The terrified woman handed over the money but the man said he needed more. After making her get dressed, the bogus Ranger walked his victim at gunpoint to a nearby store where she awakened the wife of the owner and said she needed cash to avoid arrest. After collecting that second batch of money, the phony Ranger departed. Wink officers soon arrested the man for armed robbery and transferred him to the Reeves County Jail in Pecos. "Bedroom Bandit Tears Night Attire from Woman Victim: Man Poses as Ranger; Wink Cops Jail Him," Pyote *Gazette*, May 2, 1928. In addition to keeping a wary eye out for Rangers, the gambling set in Wink could not even trust their fellow operators. In an apparent turf dispute, on August 27, 1928, two men dynamited a garage in Wink whose owners had been indicted in Pecos for operating a gambling hall. On December 22, while searching a rooming house for four men who had escaped from jail, special Ranger John Northcott had some trouble with the proprietor of the place and shot him to death. Dallas *Morning News*, October 26, 1927, November 16, 1927, February 29, 1928, July 18, 1928, August 29, 1928, and December 24, 1928. By early in 1929, as the New York *World* story indicated, Wink had finally calmed down.

101. *State Highway Department of Texas Seventh Biennial Report, September 1, 1928, to August 31, 1930* (Austin, 1930), pp. 99–101.

102. "F.P.E. [Finger Print Expert] Helps Put Man in Electric Chair," *Finger Print and Identification Magazine* 11, no. 1, (July 1929): p. 31; "Mason County Sheriff Slain," Dallas *Morning News*, March 1, 1929s "One Man Held in Killing of Mason Sheriff," Dallas *Morning News*, March 2, 1929.

103. Ken Kesselus, *Alvin Wirtz: The Senator, LBJ, and LCRA* (Austin: Eakin Press, 2001), p. 47, citing *Senate Journal*, 39th Legislature, Regular Session, pp. 325–326; Austin *American*, June 7, 1929.

104. Austin *Statesman*, June 12, 1929; Wes Petty, *Murder in the Southwest* (Lubbock: Chaparral Graphics Group, 1994), pp. 62–63.

105. Acts 1929, 41st Legislature, p. 512.

106. Adjutant General's Department of Texas, *Reports of the Adjutant General, 1928–1930*, pp. 102–111.

107. During the 1920s, Rangers battled oil-field lawlessness (in chronological order) at Burkburnett and Newton in Wichita County; Ranger and Desdemona in Eastland County; Breckenridge, Necessity, Crystal Falls, and Gunsight in Stephens County; Mexia in Limestone County; Corsicana in Navarro County; Best in Reagan County; Mirando City in Webb County; Borger in Hutchinson County; Wink in Winkler County; McCamey and Rankin in Upshur County; and Pettus in Bee County. Carl Coke Rister, *Oil: Titan of the Southwest* (Norman: University of Oklahoma Press, 1949), passim.

108. Adjutant General's Department of Texas, *Reports of the Adjutant General, 1928–1930*, pp. 51–53, 103; Walter Prescott, Webb, "They Should Be Exempt," *The State Trooper* 8, no. 10 (June 1927): p. 17.

6. CRIME OUTRIDES THE RANGERS

1. Paris *Morning News Extra*, May 9, 1930.
2. Fort Worth *Press*, May 10 and May 11, 1930; Houston *Press*, May 10, 1930.
3. Adjutant General's Department of Texas, *Reports of the Adjutant General, 1928–1930*, pp. 54–55; Krenek, *The Power Vested*, pp. 113–131; Cox, *Texas Ranger Tales II*, pp. 193–205. This account of the Sherman riot is informed by the author's interview of his grandfather L. A. Wilke (1897–1984), who covered the Sherman riot for the Fort Worth *Press* and who for a time had been inside the jail with Hamer and the other Rangers as mob members fired .22s inside, the small bullets ricocheting off the bars. Wilke later used his Speed Graffic camera to take an available light photograph of Hughes's hanging body, silhouetted by fire. The Fort Worth newspaper deemed the image too gruesome and did not publish it.
4. Cox, *Texas Ranger Tales II*, p. 202; Governor Moody declared martial law in Sherman's Precinct 1 on May 10, 1930, keeping the order in place for two weeks. Adjutant General's Department of Texas, *Reports of the Adjutant General, 1928–1930*, pp. 55–56. At issue during and for a time after the incident was whether the governor had ordered Hamer not to fire into the mob. Moody and Hamer both denied the allegation, which apparently had been a mob-spread rumor. Krenek, *The Power Vested*, pp. 121–128; Ward, "The Texas Rangers, 1919–1935," pp. 175–178; Edward Hake Phillips, "The Sherman Courthouse Riot of 1930," *East Texas Historical Journal*, Fall 1987, pp. 12–19. Only two months after the Sherman incident, Rangers had better success in protecting a threatened black prisoner. This time it happened in Wheeler County in the Panhandle. When Jesse Lee Washington was arrested for killing Mrs. Henry Vaughan of Shamrock, a mob threatened to take action. Sheriff W. K. McLemore asked the governor for assistance, and four Rangers armed with Thompson submachine guns, rifles, scatterguns, and gas grenades in addition to their sidearms left Austin for the High Plains on July 13—"Lone Wolf" Gonzaullas, Bob Goss, J. P. Huddleston, and W. H. Kirby. A combination of careful planning, subterfuge, cooperation of local officials, and a bold show of force kept the prisoner safe. Utley, *Lone Star Lawmen*, pp. 133–134, citing Amarillo *Daily News*, July 17 and July 29, 1930; *Daily News*, July 17 and July 28, 1930; Papa *Times*, July 18, 1930; Austin *Statesman*, July 15, 1930; among other sources.
5. *State Highway Department of Texas Seventh Biennial Report*, pp. 99–110.
6. *DPS Chaparral*, May–June 1957, p. 2.
7. *State Highway Department of Texas Seventh Biennial Report*, pp. 99–110.

8. *The New Handbook of Texas*, vol. 2, pp. 772–774.

9. Ross S. Sterling and Ed Kilman, *Ross Sterling, Texan: A Memoir by the Founder of Humble Oil and Refining Company*, edited and revised by Don Carleton, (Austin: University of Texas Press, 2007), pp. 131–132.

10. Kilgore *News Herald*, July 19, 1970; Ward, "The Texas Rangers, 1919–1935," pp. 188-191. The names of some of the establishments that sprang up say it all: The Black Cat, the Bloody Bucket, and the Silver Dollar flourished, as did two enclaves of vice just outside the Kilgore city limits, Little Juarez and Rat Town. A good overview of this period can be found in Terry Stembridge and Caleb Pirtle, III, *Kilgore: Echoes from Forgotten Streets* (Dallas: Dockery House Publishing, 2003), pp. 140–171.

11. "Texas Rangers May Lose Even Their Name," *Frontier Times*, January 1931, pp. 157–159.

12. Malsch, *Captain M.T. Lone Wolf Gonzaullas*, p. 105.

13. "Getting Busted in the Boom," Dallas *Morning News*, January 20, 2002.

14. Malsch, *Captain M.T. Lone Wolf Gonzaullas*, p. 105. With reinforcements from Company D, Rangers executed a "general cleanup" of Kilgore on March 2, 1931. More than five hundred "suspicious characters" were arrested inside a day. After interrogating everyone, the Rangers culled their catch to forty suspected felons, including killers and bank robbers, and ordered the rest to leave town if they knew what was good for them. Twelve houses of prostitution, three saloons, and one gambling establishment were shut down in the operation. Ward, "The Texas Rangers, 1919–1935," p. 192.

15. "High Praise Given Peace Officers for Good Law Enforcement Here," Kilgore *Daily News*, April 2, 1931.

16. James W. Robinson, *The DPS Story: History of the Development of the Department of Public Safety in Texas*. (Austin: Texas Department of Public Safety, 1974), p. 6.

17. *The New Handbook of Texas*, vol. 3, pp. 336–337.

18. Austin *American*, July 8, 1931.

19. Cox, *Texas Ranger Tales II*, pp.186–188. In its August 31, 1931, issue, *Time* devoted six paragraphs to the "Red River War," including an account of the shooting exhibition reportedly put on for reporters by Hickman and Goss. That spurred Clyde T. Ervin, chief physicist for the Peters Cartridge Company, to write *Time* that a .45 Colt single action "is not capable of shooting 20 shots at 50 feet inside a circle less than about 1¾ inches in diameter even when fired from a machine rest. . . ." The same issue, dated August 31, 1931, carried a response from Hickman saying he was puzzled that the newspapers and magazines had reported the target shooting "without making the least effort to verify it." In fact, he said, "during the entire dispute over the Red River free and toll bridges, I did not have a pistol in my hand, in fact I am such a poor marksman that I never shoot until the other fellow has shot at

me." However, the captain continued, "Ranger Bob Goss . . . can hit a playing card turned edgewise with his pistol turned upside down. He does this
about twice out of every five shots . . ."

20. "Sterling's Message," Austin *American*, July 16, 1931.

21. Austin *American*, August 17, 1931; Ward, "The Texas Rangers, 1919–1935,"
p. 198; Rister, *Oil*, pp. 315–320.

22. Sterling and Kilman, *Ross Sterling, Texan*, p. 165.

23. Krenek, *The Power Vested*, p. 156.

24. Sterling and Kilman, *Ross Sterling, Texan*, p. 165.

25. Olien and Olien, *Oil in Texas*, pp. 185–188.

26. Austin *American*, August 31, 1931.

27. Malsch, *Captain M.T. Lone Wolf Gonzaullas*, pp. 113–116.

28. "Chronological Listing of Key Events in the History of the Railroad Commission of Texas (1866–1939)," http://www.rrc.state.tx.us/history; Ward, "The Texas
Rangers, 1919–1935," pp. 201–202.

29. Robert A. Calvert and Arnoldo De Leon, *The History of Texas* (Arlington
Heights, Ill.: Harland Davidson, 1990), p. 299. Less than a week before the election, Adjutant General Sterling orchestrated one last oil-field cleanup, an action
not totally in the interest of law and order. The general instructed Rangers to
roust a "horde of floaters" who had been brought to East Texas "to help steal the
election" for Ferguson. Thirty-seven Rangers, most of the force, spread out over
Gregg County on August 21, 1932, making numerous arrests. When the governor learned of the crackdown, he ordered Sterling to stop the operation and
send the Rangers back to their regular stations. After the election, Sterling and
his Rangers in East Texas obtained what they considered valid evidence of election fraud, but the governor's legal team warned that contesting the election
would be "fraught with uncertainties." Eventually, as Sterling put it, "it became apparent that through loopholes and weaknesses in our election laws, the
Fergusons would be allowed to get away with their ill gotten gains." Sterling,
Trails and Trials of a Texas Ranger, pp. 269, 273; Ward, "The Texas Rangers,
1919–1935," pp. 205–206.

30. Sterling, *Trails and Trials of a Texas Ranger*, pp. 212–213; Austin *Statesman*,
February 7, 1935. Roberts died in Austin on February 6, 1935, and was buried in
the Texas State Cemetery.

31. Adjutant General's Department of Texas, *Reports of the Adjutant General,
1931–1932*, p. 23. Ward, "The Texas Rangers, 1919–1935" (pp. 182–183), credits General Sterling, who had attended Texas A&M University, with having
done much to professionalize the Rangers. Despite the scarcity of state funds
during the Depression, Sterling had succeeded in getting more money for
Ranger car allowances, designating every third Ranger as a "car man" responsible for providing transportation for other Rangers. When it came time to select

captains, Sterling furnished the governor a list of men he considered to have the "character, personality, experience, and ability" to do the job. This at least reduced the politics involved in Ranger appointments.

32. La Grange *Journal*, November 10, 1932; Patrick M. McConal, *Over the Wall: The Men Behind the 1934 Death House Escape* (Austin: Eakin Press, 2000), pp. 71–72.

33. Jenkins and Frost, *I'm Frank Hamer*, p. 174. Utley, *Lone Star Lawman*, (pp. 152–153), notes that appointment records indicate Ferguson, likely at the direction of her husband, made all personnel decisions in Temple as early as two months before taking office. Nearly half of the Rangers Ferguson fired soon went to work as guards or investigators for the oil companies in East Texas, including Hamer and "Lone Wolf" Gonzaullas. Utley, (p. 155).

34. Author's interview with Harrison Hamer Jr., Waco, Texas, September 23, 2000; General Order No. 2, 1933, Ranger Force Order Book.

35. Adjutant General's Department of Texas, *Report of the Adjutant General, 1933–1934*, p. 46. Other than Aldrich, the only captain named by Ferguson who had any real experience was the forty-six-year-old Vaughan, who had served under the legendary Captain John R. Hughes in 1912 and continued on the force until 1918. For more detail on Vaughan's career, see Cox, *Texas Ranger Tales*, pp. 126–128. Odneal, forty-six, had been a Ranger sergeant during Mrs. Ferguson's first term, but he had not been kept on when Governor Moody took office in 1927. The thirty-five-year-old Hammond had no law enforcement experience, and Robbins, forty-eight, had spent most of his life as a farmer, though he had spent three years as a sheriff's deputy. Utley, *Lone Star Lawmen*, pp. 153–154.

36. Joint Legislative Committee on Organization and Economy and Griffenhagen Associates, *The Government of the State of Texas* (Austin: 1933), part III, pp. 54–70.

37. Jim Harmon, *The Great Radio Heroes* (Garden City, N.Y.: Doubleday Company, 1967), pp. 195–213. Jack Deeds played the Lone Ranger for six shows, followed by George Stenius, who lasted three months before being replaced by Bruce Beemer. Beemer did the hero's voice for a few months but then Earl Graser got the job and carried the role until 1941. That year Beemer returned and starred in the show until 1954.

38. General Orders No. 3 and 4, November 1933, Ranger Force Order Book.

39. Adjutant General's Department of Texas, *Report of the Adjutant General, 1933–1934*.

40. Thompson, *A History of Marfa and Presidio County, Texas*, vol. 2, pp. 387–388.

41. General Orders No. 6, 1933, Ranger Force Order Book.

42. Discharged from the Rangers, Byars was found guilty by a Travis County district court jury on October 21. His punishment was assessed as twenty-five years in prison. Austin *American*, July 6, 1933, and October 22, 1933.

43. Sterling. *Trails and Trials of a Texas Ranger*, pp. 83–84.

44. *Frontier Times*, December 1933, p. 142.

45. Sid Underwood, *Depression Desperado: The Chronicle of Raymond Hamilton*, (Austin: Eakin Press, 1995), p. 67.

46. Underwood, *Depression Desperado*, p. 47. Though she knew quite well that Hamer was not in the Ferguson camp, the governor approved the prison director's request to hire the former captain. Lee Simmons, *Assignment Huntsville* (Austin: University of Texas Press, 1957), pp. 126–132.

47. Cox, *Texas Ranger Tales*, pp. 225–227; Two weeks after former Ranger Gault joined Hamer in the hunt for Bonnie and Clyde, another man who should have been preoccupied with the case had other things on his mind. On April 28, 1934, in poor health and with little to show for his brief career as a Ranger, Company B captain Harry Odneal stood in front of a mirror in his residence, put a pistol to his head, and pulled the trigger. Fort Worth *Star-Telegram*, April 28, 1934.

48. Webb, *Crime: Our National Shame*, p. 222.

49. Austin *Statesman*, May 24, 1934; for more on Bonnie and Clyde, John Neal Phillips, *Running With Bonnie and Clyde*, (Norman: University of Oklahoma Press 1996) and E. R. Milner, *The Life and Times of Bonnie and Clyde*, (Carbondale: Southern Illinois University Press, 1996), are useful sources. James R. Knight with Jonathan Davis, *Bonnie and Clyde: A Twenty-first Century Update* (Austin: Eakin Press, 2003) also provides a solid overview of the case. See also Mitch Roth, "Bonnie and Clyde in Texas: The End of the Texas Outlaw Tradition." *East Texas Historical Journal* Vol. 35 (1995), pp. 30–38 and Dick McMahan, *The Bucher Murder was the Turning Point for Clyde Barrow, Bonnie Parker and Raymond Hamilton*. (Dallas: Southwest Historical Publications, 2007).

50. Underwood, *Depression Desperado*, pp. 118, 121; W. R. and Mabel Draper, *The Blood-Soaked Career of Bonnie Parker: How Bandit Clyde Barrow and His Cigar-Smoking Moll Fought It Out with the Law* (Girard, Kans.: Haldeman-Julius Publications, 1946), p. 32. Hamer's success in coordinating the track down of Clyde Barrow and Bonnie Parker in 102 days had not escaped the notice of the U.S. Department of Justice, at the time vigorously hunting the nation's top desperado, John Dillinger. Adjutant General Hutchings told a reporter that the federal government was considering offering Hamer a job. Hamer said he had not been contacted by federal officials but had a ready answer when asked if he thought he could find the notorious Indiana bank robber: "Sure, I believe I could catch Dillinger if they gave me a chance." Federal agents eventually caught up with Dillinger in Chicago, with the help of the fugitive's cooperative girlfriend.

51. Karl Ashburn, "Crime in Texas," *Southwest Review* 19, no. 4 (July 1934): pp. 363–373.

52. "Crime Outrides Texas Rangers Says Magazine," El Paso *Herald-Post*, July 12, 1934. Though hampered by mediocre leadership and corruption, the Ferguson-era Rangers were not completely ineffective. In the summer of 1933, Captain Estill Hamer and Rangers Sid Kelso, Fred Holland, and Jim Shown cracked a $500,000 negotiable bond theft case that began in New York but moved to San Antonio. Working with federal agents and private detectives, Hamer developed enough evidence to file charges against three San Antonio men for receiving and concealing stolen property. The Rangers also found evidence that enabled federal agents to get theft indictments against three Missouri gangsters. In April 1934, Sergeant Joe Osoba interviewed some three hundred people in San Saba County before clearing a murder case with the arrest of four men, one of them a deputy sheriff. Ward, "The Texas Rangers, 1919–1935," pp. 218–219.

53. William Helmer with Rick Mattix, *Public Enemies: America's Criminal Past, 1919–1940* (New York: Checkmark Books, Facts on File, 1998), pp. 271–272. A thorough overview of the national war on crime in the early 1930s can be found in Claire Bond Potter, *War on Crime: Bandits, G-men, and the Politics of Mass Culture* (New Brunswick, N.J.: Rutgers University Press, 1998). See also David R. Johnson, *American Law Enforcement: A History* (Wheeling, Ill.: Forum Press, 1981).

54. Friend, "W.P. Webb's Texas Rangers," pp. 293–322; C. L. Douglas, *The Gentlemen in the White Hats: Dramatic Episodes in the History of the Texas Rangers* (Dallas: South-West Press, 1934), p. 7.

55. Ward, "The Texas Rangers, 1919–1935," p. 222.

56. Stephen W. Schuster IV, "The Modernization of the Texas Rangers, 1930–1936," M.A. thesis, Texas Christian University, 1965, p. 69, citing *Report and Recommendations of the Senate Committee Investigating Crime, 43rd Texas Legislature, 1933–1934*, pp. 63–64; San Antonio *Light*, August 10, 1934; San Antonio *Express*, August 10, 1934; Ward, "The Texas Rangers, 1919–1935," p. 223. Former captain Robbins ended up with an eight-year prison sentence.

57. Harry Benge Crozier, "Texas Rangers Need New Deal for New Order," Dallas *Morning News*, December 8, 1934.

7. "A Great Unstrapping of Six-shooter Belts . . ."

1. Ward, "The Texas Rangers, 1919–1935," p. 227; Thomas Lee Charlton, "The Texas Department of Public Safety, 1935–1957," M.A. thesis, University of Texas, 1961, p. 20.

2. Tom Hickman's Dallas *Morning News* articles were: "All-American Center Heads Indiana Police," December 10, 1934, "Texas Rangers Used as Model by Penn Force," December 11, 1934, "Road Patrols in Maryland and Delaware," December 12, 1934, "Troopers Have Rural Duties in New Jersey," December 13, 1934, "New

York Has Rigorous Test for Troopers," December 14, 1934, and "Bay State Has Two Units of State Police," December 15, 1934.

3. "Rangers Losing Reputation; Only 36 Regular Members on Force; More than 1,600 'Special' Rangers," New York *Times*, February 9, 1935, p. 9; "Texas' Once Famous Ranger Band Found to Have Degenerated," *Frontier Times*, May 1935, p. 363.

4. "The Rangers Ride Once More," Dallas *Dispatch*, June 9, 1935.

5. Schuster, "The Modernization of the Texas Rangers, 1930–1936," p. 72. The three Rangers making the cut were Quartermaster Roy Aldrich and Privates Fred Holland and Sid Kelso. Ward, "The Texas Rangers, 1919–1935," p. 228. Of the trio, Aldrich had the biggest impact on the Rangers. Though he had his detractors, he played a major coordinative role in the organization, especially in the 1920s. Aldrich had seen combat as a U.S. soldier in the Philippines and as a solider of fortune in the Boer War. He wore a sheriff's badge in Oklahoma four years and tried his hand at business before joining the Rangers in 1915. For more details on Aldrich's long state career, see Cox, *Texas Ranger Tales*, pp. 160–171.

6. Dallas *Dispatch*, June 9, 1935; Ward, "The Texas Rangers, 1919–1935," pp. 228–229. Allred promoted Sergeant Kelso to command Company A in Houston. The governor's choices for Ranger captaincies included former Archer County sheriff Fred McDaniel, Company B, Fort Worth; former Ranger J. W. McCormick, Company C, San Augustine; and South Texas rancher Will McMurrey, Company D, Hebbronville. R. C. Hawkins was appointed a captain to work with Allred in the Governor's Office.

7. Schuster, "The Modernization of the Texas Rangers, 1930–1936," p. 72. Johnson, a native of Waxahachie, attended the University of Texas and served as a state representative from Ellis County while doing so. After graduating from UT, he studied law at Yale University and also attended Cambridge University in the United Kingdom. Wounded in the Battle of Saint-Mihiel during World War I, he went on to a long career in law and in the Texas National Guard. In a 1964 interview, Johnson said Governor Allred "asked me to make a study and set up a state police force." The original Highway Patrol, he said, "was a good patrol as far as it went," but its officers could only make arrests if they saw a crime in progress. The Rangers under the adjutant general, he said, "had some fine officers," but also "deputy sheriffs or sheriffs who'd lost their jobs." Kent Biffle, "Shaping of Rangers, Patrol Took Years," Dallas *Morning News*, August 23, 1964.

8. Ward, "The Texas Rangers, 1919–1935," p. 231.

9. *Report and Recommendations of the Senate Committee Investigating Crime*, 43rd Texas Legislature, 1933–1934, Austin, 1934.

10. "Rangers Becoming Lamented Tradition," El Paso *Herald-Post*, April 3, 1935.

11. Born in Sebastian County, Arkansas, in February 1885, McCormick attended college in Fort Smith. An athletic star, after college he played as a catcher for

the St. Louis Cardinals before going into law enforcement. He began his career as city marshal of Mansfield, Arkansas, and claimed to have served as Fort Smith's police chief, though that department has no record of him as chief. One newspaper story about McCormick said he had served in the Royal Canadian Mounted Police before becoming a Ranger, but that agency has no record of anyone by his name. Records do show that McCormick joined the Rangers on March 27, 1920, at thirty-five. He left the force to become Wichita Falls' police chief on April 18, 1921. While police chief, he shot and killed Oklahoma outlaw Bud Ballew at a café and bar in downtown Wichita Falls. McCormick continued to serve intermittently as a Ranger through the 1920s. Elected sheriff of Carson County, he served from November 4, 1930, to January 1, 1935. He was appointed as Ranger captain January 16, 1935—the seventh and final time he took the Ranger oath. Later he served with the Wichita County Sheriff's Department and again with the Wichita Falls Police Department, ending his career as a juvenile officer. He died in Austin on September 19, 1962. For more on McCormick, see Glenn Shelton, *Wichita Falls: A Lady with a Past* (Wichita Falls, Tex.: Western Christian Foundation, 1978), pp. 55–61, 65–74; the dates of McCormick's Ranger service can be found in Oath of Members, Ranger Force, Texas State Archives.

12. Dallas *Morning News*, January 6, 1935; Utley, *Lone Star Lawmen*, pp. 168–170.
13. "San Augustine's Honor Visitors, Texas Rangers, to Be Feted with Dance," Dallas *Morning News*, March 22, 1935. In December, the appreciative citizenry gave Captain McCormick and his two men silver-inlaid pistols and custommade gunbelts with silver buckles.
14. Robert W. Calvert to Jack Maguire, September 27, 1985, copy in author's collection.
15. Austin *Statesman*, April 11 and April 13, 1935.
16. "Safety Department Created; Combines Rangers and Patrol," Dallas *Morning News, May 4, 1935*; Austin *Statesman*, May 3 and May 7, 1935.
17. *General and Special Laws of the State of Texas*, 44th Legislature, Regular Session, 1935, pp. 444–454.
18. San Antonio *Express*, May 15, 1935.
19. "Passing of Rangers Turns Back the Pages of History in Texas," *Christian Science Monitor*, undated clipping (1935), author's collection.
20. "The Texas Rangers Brought Law and Order," *Frontier Times*, July 1935, pp. 425–428; the other three components of the DPS headquarters structure were a Bureau of Communication, Bureau of Identification, and Bureau of Education. Ward, "The Texas Rangers, 1919–1935," pp. 232–233.
21. "Ex-Ranger Recalls Exciting Days in Old-Time El Paso," El Paso *World News*, July 14, 1935.
22. Austin *Statesman*, August 12, 1935; Texas Department of Public Safety, *Department of Public Safety Annual Report, August 10, 1935–December 1, 1936*.

23. *Sheriff's Association of Texas Magazine*, September 1935, p. 10.

24. Lufkin *Daily News*, September 28, 1938; Jack Martin, "Colonel Homer Garrison, Jr., Director of the Texas Department of Public Safety," *True Detective Mysteries*, August 1940), pp. 66–67, 116; "Col. Garrison: Man and Boy Officer of Law Enforcement," Austin *American-Statesman*, May 7, 1950; "In Memory Homer Garrison, Jr.," *Texas Defense Digest* 16, no. 5 (May 1968): p. 1. Garrison was born July 21, 1901, in East Texas at Kickapoo, a small town in Anderson County. The oldest of nine children Homer and Mattie Garrison would have, at birth he weighed ten pounds on a rusty cotton scale, and by the time he was grown he stood six feet two inches tall and weighed two hundred pounds. After an extended illness forced him to drop out of Lufkin High School during the tenth grade, Garrison worked briefly for his father, the Angelina County district clerk, and later became county surveyor. In 1920, at nineteen, Garrison began his law enforcement career as a deputy under Angelina County sheriff Art Youngblood. During a particularly muddy reelection campaign, the sheriff offered a $100 reward to anyone who could prove anything bad about his young chief deputy. No one ever collected the money.

25. Texas Department of Public Safety, *DPS Annual Report, August 10, 1935 to December 1, 1936*, p. 11; Malsch, *Captain M.T. Lone Wolf Gonzaullas*, p. 122, 125.

26. *Sheriff's Association of Texas Magazine*, September 1935, p. 21.

27. Charlton, "The Texas Department of Public Safety, 1935–1957," p. 45. Earlier that month, Phares told reporters "hard-boiled officers" had no place in the new agency. "I'm going to develop the department just like the Texas highway patrol was developed." Austin *American-Statesman*, September 8, 1935.

28. Texas Department of Public Safety, Minutes, Meeting of Public Safety Commission, October 6, 1935. Johnson remained on the commission through December 1939. He served as a colonel during World War II and went on to assume command of the Texas National Guard's Forty-ninth Armored Division. He retired as a major general in 1959. Biffle, "Shaping of Rangers, Patrol Took Years."

29. Gilbert Mers, *Working the Waterfront: The Ups and Downs of a Rebel Longshoreman* (Austin: University of Texas Press, 1988), p. 91.

30. Mers, *Working the Waterfront*, p. 99.

31. After Hickman moved to Austin as captain of Headquarters Company in May 1935, Fred McDaniel, his replacement as head of Company B, had raided the Top o' the Hill and briefly shut it down. When he became senior captain, Hickman ordered the other captains not to conduct gambling raids without his permission. The Top o' the Hill, meanwhile, had long since reopened and continued to do a brisk business. Utley, *Lone Star Lawmen*, p. 180.

32. Texas Department of Public Safety, Minute Number 7, November 7, 1935, placed Phares in charge of the Texas Rangers effective immediately. Less than a week later, Minute Number 13, signed by Phares and the three members of the Public Safety Commission on November 12, said Hickman was "relieved of his

duties as Senior Captain of the Texas Rangers" and "permanently removed from the personnel of the Department of Public Safety." Charlton, "The Texas Department of Public Safety, 1935–1957," pp. 54–61. Following Captain Mc-Cormick's raid, Assistant District Attorney Dawson Davis told a reporter for the Fort Worth bureau of the Dallas *Morning News* that the list of witnesses furnished by McCormick consisted of phony names. Too, the Rangers had not had a search warrant when they made the raid. "Group Arrested in Ranger Raid Are Turned Loose," Dallas *Morning News*, November 20, 1935.

33. Charlton, "The Texas Department of Public Safety, 1935–1957," p. 61, citing DPS Special Orders, November 12, 1935. Hickman had enough friends in the legislature to engineer a stormy but short-lived legislative investigation into his dismissal. In fact, the exercise proved far more embarrassing than helpful to the former captain. At the first hearing on December 3, held in Fort Worth at the Texas Hotel, Hickman succeeded in getting his side of the story, including the details of his distinguished career, on the record: he charged that politics still plagued Texas law enforcement, adding that he and Louis Phares did not get along and Phares intended to "smother the Rangers." The three-member committee met again in San Antonio on December 13, the hearing preceded by a scuffle involving Senior Captain McCormick and Bexar County sheriff's deputy (and former Ranger) Frank Matthews. McCormick told reporters that he had hit Matthews in the face because the deputy made disparaging remarks about Governor Allred. Public Safety Commission Chairman Johnson, and Ed Clark, Allred's secretary, testified that morning about Hickman's dismissal. During an afternoon session, Bexar County sheriff Albert West Jr. and others went on record with complaints about the antigambling activity of the Rangers in San Antonio. But back in Austin the following day, Allred got in the figurative last lick when he interrupted a conference between the three committee members at the Capitol. Demanding a court reporter to take down his testimony, the governor made a long statement—occasionally slapping his hand down on the table where he sat—setting forth the reasons Hickman had been fired, stating for the record that in a private meeting with the captain he had told him, "To be frank with you, Tom, you have been inexcusably negligent. . . . and to be most charitable . . . you have laid down on this job . . ." The governor went on to offer a list of thirteen reasons Hickman had been discharged. Essentially the captain had been resting on his laurels, spending a lot of time attending rodeos while doing little work for the state. The committee held no further meetings and issued no report, and Hickman stayed fired. The state's major newspapers had a field day covering the two scheduled and one ad hoc committee meetings. "Law Enforcing Declared Not Out of Politics," Dallas *Morning News*, December 4, 1935; "Tom Hickman Gave Raid Tip, Says Governor," Dallas *Morning News*, December 15, 1935.

34. "S-men Put Damper on Gambling in Houston," Austin *American*, December 30, 1935.

35. "Rangers Hunt Cattle Rustlers As S-men War on Gambling," Austin *American-Statesman*, December 31, 1935.

36. "Drive on Gaming Houses Promised," Austin *American-Statesman*, January 11, 1936.

37. "Big-Shot Gaming on the Run in Texas, McCormick Avers," Austin *American-Statesman*, January 15, 1936. McCormick clearly saw himself as Allred's bulldog. The following spring, for instance, "solely upon my own authority" McCormick arrested the publisher of a Jacksonville-based political publication calling for Allred's impeachment and seized three thousand copies of the newspaper. Allred denied any knowledge of the matter. The Associated Press quoted McCormick as saying, "I told them [he had also detained several newsboys] I would not have any such literature distributed about any prominent man." "Papers Attacking Governor Seized by Texas Rangers," Dallas *Morning News*, April 28, 1937.

38. New York *Herald-Tribune*, November 2, 1935; New York *Times*, November 16, 1935.

39. *Frontier Times*, March 1936, pp. 291–292.

40. Webb, "The Texas Rangers, 1919–1935," p. 567. Aside from his unabashed Ranger partisanship, Webb's concern over the future of the Rangers may have come from a literal reading of the law creating the DPS. The act provided only that Rangers "aid in the execution of the laws" and "make arrests and . . . execute all process in criminal cases in any county in the State." That wording left the Public Safety Commission considerable leeway. Ward, "The Texas Rangers, 1919–1935," pp. 236–237.

41. Austin *American-Statesman*, October 9, 1936.

42. "Johnson, West Swap Hot Words," Austin *American-Statesman*, April 10, 1936.

43. "Chief Praises Ranger Force, Organization Far from Being on Way Out, Carmichael Says," El Paso *Times*, May 21, 1936.

44. *Sheriff's Association of Texas Magazine*, July–August 1936, p. 8.

45. *Frontier Times*, May 1936, p. 292. The act creating the DPS called for only three Ranger companies, a headquarters unit and two mounted companies. The Public Safety Commission got around that by invoking language in the law that gave it authority to organize the Rangers as it saw fit to "meet extraordinary conditions." Accordingly, the commission stuck to the traditional organization of a headquarters company and five field companies. The next session of the legislature, March 7, 1936, amended the 1935 act to formalize that the Rangers would consist of "six captains, one headquarters sergeant and such numbers of privates as may be authorized by the Legislature." Ward, "The Texas Rangers, 1919–1935," pp. 235–236.

46. Kenneth B. Ragsdale, *Centennial '36: The Year America Discovered Texas* (College Station: Texas A&M University Press, 1987), p. 230; "Go to Town on

'Rangers,'" *Box Office*, September 5, 1936, p. 33; "Ranger Quarters at Fair Approved for WPA Project," Dallas *Morning News*, February 20, 1936; "Logs Arrive, Work Started at Fair on Rangers' Quarters," Dallas *Morning News*, March 7, 1936; "Ranger Building to Serve Force after Fair Ends," Dallas *Morning News*, November 26, 1936. The Rangers continued to use the log building until 1958, when they moved into more modern quarters. The DPS Driver License office remained in the Fair Park building until the spring of 1963. "Public Safety Department Plans Move About May 1," Dallas *Morning News*, April 7, 1958; "DPS License Service to Quit Park Building," Dallas *Morning News*, May 2, 1963.

47. Jim Griffin, "Texas Rangers Magazine," Pulp Rack, http://www.pulprack.com/arch/000029.html, accessed January 14, 2003. *Texas Rangers* magazine made its appearance in October 1936 and continued through 206 issues until February 1958. The Jim Hatfield stories were credited to Jackson Cole, a Better Publications house name. At least twelve authors wrote as Cole. A. Leslie Scott, who wrote fifty-five Jim Hatfield stories, created the Hatfield character. *Texas Highways*, July 1999, p. 3.

48. *Sheriff's Association of Texas Magazine*, July–August 1936, p. 5.

49. "Texas Ranger Chief Shifted," El Paso *Times*, July 31, 1936; Texas Department of Public safety, Minutes, Meeting of the Public Safety Commission, July 23, 1936.

50. Necah Stewart Furman, *Walter Prescott Webb: His Life and Impact* (Albuquerque: University of New Mexico Press, 1976), p. 117.

51. Dallas *Morning News*, August 24, 1936.

52. Texas Department of Public Safety, *DPS Annual Report, August 10, 1935 to December 1, 1936*, p. 3.

53. Mona D. Sizer, *Texas Justice Bought and Paid For* (Plano: Republic of Texas Press, 2001), pp. 1–65. "We don't seem to be able to get anywhere with it [the Blanton case]," Captain Bill McMurrey wrote Col. H. H. Carmichael on February 19, 1937. "Everything we get just peters out. . . . The District Attorney . . . just finished a Grand Jury investigation. . . . He told [Ranger Joe H.] Bridge that He [sic] didn't have a suggestion to make at present, and that it looked like we had done about as good a job under the circumstances as could have been done, and it looked like we would have to wait and see if some one wouldn't get interested in the Reward money and tell something and give us a break." Joe H. Bridge, Jr., *The Life and Times of Joe H. Bridge, Texas Ranger 1936–1956* (Lampasas, Tex.: Privately published, 2005), p. 124. The Blanton disappearance was not the Rangers' only frustrating case during the early years of the DPS. On March 31, 1938, a truck driver found the bodies of two women in a roadside park near Van Horn in Culberson County. Identified as Mrs. Weston G. Frome of Berkeley, California, and her daughter, Nancy, the women had been shot in the head. The twenty-two-year-old daughter also had been tortured with cigar

or cigarette burns. Neither of the women had been raped, and none of their property seemed to be missing. The fact that the spare tire on their vehicle had been ripped open led Rangers to speculate the two had been mistaken for narcotics smugglers and killed by someone looking for their drugs, but that was never substantiated. Ranger Pete Crawford and other investigators questioned more than fifteen hundred persons in the case. Despite a $10,000 reward, no charges were ever filed in the double murders. Charlton, "The Texas Department of Public Safety, 1935–1957," pp. 100–102.

54. Texas Department of Public Safety, *DPS Annual Report, August 10, 1935 to December 1, 1936*, pp. 3, 15.

55. Malsch, *Captain M.T. Lone Wolf Gonzaullas*, p. 138.

56. Gonzaullas to The Texas Company, June 24, 1938, author's collection.

57. Caddo Cameron, *It's Hell to Be a Ranger* (New York: Sun Dial Press, 1937). Cameron's first novel, originally published as a series in *Short Stories* (May 10 and May 25, 1936), was *Rangers Is Powerful Hard to Kill*, "a rip-snorting story of the West proving that brains and guts sure pull like hell in double harness." A prolific Western writer, Cameron (1888–?) was the pseudonym of Charles Mather Beeler, an Oklahoma native.

58. Robert G. Goss, Private, Texas Rangers Co. A, Weekly reports, March 13, and March 20, 1937, Goss Papers, Nita Stewart Haley Memorial Library, Midland, Texas; Captain H. B. Purvis, Texas Rangers, Co. A, "Report of the Investigation of the Murder of the Sheriff of Marion, Co. J.A. Brown," Goss Papers; "Assassin Fires Buckshot Blast Through Window," Marshall *News-Messenger*, March 11, 1937. www.usgennet.org/usa/tx/topic/Cemeteries/Executed/Deathrow.html. Charlie Brooks, convicted of Sheriff Brown's murder, was assessed the death penalty and electrocuted at the state prison in Huntsville on May 31, 1938.

59. Goss Papers.

60. H. H. Carmichael as told to Westmoreland Gray, "We Rangers: Lawmen of the Frontier, 1937 Model," *Best Action Western Stories*, September 1937, pp. 104–105, as cited in Utley, *Lone Star Lawman*, p. 189.

61. El Paso *Times*, November 15, 1937. The marker commemorating Captain Frank Jones is located at a roadside park in El Paso County two miles west of Ysleta off U.S. 80. In 1936–37, the captain's grave lay several hundred feet away in what was then an alfalfa field. Removing his remains and reburying them at the new marker was discussed, but the record is unclear as to whether it ever happened. Candice DuCoin of Round Rock, Texas, a descendant of Jones, discusses the issue in her book on Jones and other relatives who served as Rangers or sheriffs, *Lawmen on the Texas Frontier: Rangers and Sheriffs* (Round Rock, TX: Riata Books, 2007), pp. 133–137. Included in her account is a photograph of four old Rangers visiting the monument on May 12, 1938. The photograph is credited to the Western History Collections, University of Oklahoma, which holds a copy, but for posterity's sake it should be noted that the picture was

taken by this author's late grandfather, L. A. Wilke, who at the time was manager of El Paso's Gateway Club, a Chamber of Commerce-like organization dedicated to increasing tourism in the area.

62. Austin *American-Statesman*, April 2, 1938; Charlton, "The Texas Department of Public Safety, 1935–1957," p. 94. Phares and his son went on to establish the L. G. Phares Detective Agency, later renamed the L. G. Phares Protective System. The firm grew into one of the largest burglar alarm companies in the Southwest. The former DPS director died in Austin May 15, 1957, at the age of seventy-seven. *DPS Chaparral*, May–June 1957, p. 2.

63. Austin *American-Statesman*, September 25, 1938; Charlton, "The Texas Department of Public Safety, 1935–1957," pp. 96–97; Lufkin *Daily News*, September 28, 1938; Bridge, *The Life and Times of Joe H. Bridge, Texas Ranger 1936–1956*, p. 105; Austin *American-Statesman*, May 7, 1950. That Christmas, the department's officers chipped in to buy the new director the gold, diamond-studded badge that had been worn by his late predecessor. Carmichael's widow at first would not sell the badge, but she changed her mind after learning it was intended for Garrison. He sent a letter to all the patrolmen and Rangers thanking them for the gift, using the opportunity to put his philosophy down in writing. "The heights to which we can rise are altogether dependent upon our efforts," he declared in the undated letter. "The stepping stones on which we will ascend will be formed by a continuation of the fine spirit of cooperation with each other and the knowledge that OUR work—yours in the field, and mine confined to the four walls of this office—has made us all really ONE, the Department of Public Safety." Garrison soon picked his second-in-command. Ranger captain S. O. Hamm, who had headed Company B since the previous November, became assistant director on October 9, 1938. He had fought with the Thirty-sixth Infantry Division during the world war and served as a Dallas police officer and later as a Ranger before joining the Highway Department's License and Weight Division in 1927. Three years later, he helped train the first fifty Highway Patrol recruits. He had been a Highway Patrol captain in Abilene before his transfer to the Rangers in 1937. "Faces of the Month," *Texas Parade*, November 1938, p. 18. Hamm served as assistant director until December 20, 1939, when at his request, for health reasons, he took a pay cut and returned to the Rangers as captain of Company D. He resigned from the department effective June 30, 1943. Texas Department of Public Safety, Minutes, Public Safety Commission Meeting, Austin, Texas, June 30, 1943.

64. Hendrickson, *Chief Executives of Texas*, p. 198.

65. Charlton, "The Texas Department of Public Safety, 1935–1957," pp. 103–104; Texas Department of Public Safety, Minutes, Public Safety Commission Meeting, July 13, 1939. Commission members spent much of their time discussing "retrenchments" brought about by Governor O'Daniel's budget cutting. The panel approved the wording of a statement to be issued to DPS employees and the press.

66. Texas Department of Public Safety, *DPS Annual Report, Fiscal Year Ending August 31, 1939*, p. 3; Bridge, *The Life and Times of Joe H. Bridge, Texas Ranger 1936–1956*, pp. 103–104. The department did more than tally numbers. Well ahead of the private sector, the DPS had begun using a two-page "Efficiency Report" to evaluate its law enforcement personnel. Each year, a Ranger's captain had to fill out the report for each of his men. Ratings included Unsatisfactory, Satisfactory, and Excellent.

67. Texas Department of Public Safety, Minutes, Public Safety Commission Meeting, July 13, 1939.

8. "The Name of the Texas Rangers Has Been Carried to the Battlefields of the World"

1. Roy Aldrich stayed with the Rangers until October 31, 1947, when he retired at the age of seventy-eight, one of the first ninety state employees in the newly created state retirement system. He lived another seven years, dying in Austin on January 29, 1955. For more details on Aldrich's long career, see Cox, *Texas Rangers Tales*, pp. 160–171, and Virginia Duncan, "The Life of Captain Roy W. Aldrich," M.A. thesis, Sul Ross State Teachers College, 1942.

2. "Ex–Texas Ranger Gets Valor Award," Dallas *Morning News*, December 14, 1940.

3. Texas Department of Public Safety, *Department of Public Safety Biennial Report*, 1938–1940, pp. 42–43. As equipment became available, the DPS had begun installing radio transmitters at its offices across the state. On July 6, 1941, the Dallas *Morning News* published a photograph of the radio equipment recently installed at the Rangers' log cabin headquarters at Fair Park. With donated parts and a cost to the state of only $8, the new radio "could fit into a desk drawer" and "broadcasts to a roving squad car stationed on a state highway fifteen miles away."

4. Jenkins and Frost, *I'm Frank Hamer*, p. 269; "Former Ranger Urged for Post," Austin *American-Statesman*, March 11, 1951. After Pearl Harbor, Hamer also sought a special Ranger commission from the Public Safety Commission, but on December 20, 1941, the DPS's policy-setting body turned him down for reasons not specified in the panel's minutes. Hamer's two sons, Frank Jr. and Billy, joined the Marines, but only one of them survived the war. Billy Hamer died at Iwo Jima in 1945, a blow from which the former captain never fully recovered. Hamer occasionally did some security work after the war but retired in 1949 and moved from Houston to Austin. On March 11, 1951, the Austin *American-Statesman* carried an International News Service story that "reports are being circulated in Houston and other cities that a number of persons would like to see Captain Frank Hamer, whose career as a law enforcement officer wrote a colorful chapter in Texas history, back in harness again in state law enforcement." Specifically, the article con-

tinued, "it is said that they want Governor Allan Shivers to appoint the former Texas Ranger to the State Public Safety Commission." The six-paragraph story went on to say that unnamed Hamer boosters felt he could "revitalize the Ranger force to cope with the spread of organized crime and potential espionage and sabotage." Nothing came of the idea. Hamer died in Austin on July 10, 1955, at seventy-one and is buried in Memorial Park Cemetery.

5. Texas Department of Public Safety, *Department of Public Safety Biennial Report*, 1938–1940, p. 25.

6. Paredes, *"With His Pistol in His Hand,"* pp. 5–6, 9.

7. Hendrickson, *Chief Executives of Texas*, p. 199.

8. "O'Daniel Can't Boss Rangers, Mann Rules / Governor Must Use Moral Suasion to Enforce Laws," Dallas *Morning News*, September 7, 1940; "Mann Decides O'Daniel Can Boss Rangers," Dallas *Morning News*, September 18, 1940; R. S. Carver, "Ranger Control Said to Rest in Governor," Dallas *Morning News*, September 29, 1940.

9. "Old Glory Still Clings to the Texas Ranger," Alamo *News*, March 20, 1941; Bridge, *The Life and Times of Joe H. Bridge, Texas Ranger 1936–1956*, p. 95. Ranger Joe H. Bridge, then stationed in Del Rio and later at Harlingen in South Texas, traveled 12,639 miles during a fourteen-week period in 1940, averaging more than nine hundred miles a month in his state car, Number 42.

10. "World-Noted Crime Fighters Learn to Use Modern Police Science, but They're Still Same Sort of Men Who Cleaned Up Frontier," Austin *American-Statesman*, May 25, 1941.

11. "W. Lee Asks Rangers Under Adjutant General," Austin *American-Statesman*, May 29, 1941.

12. Hugh Williamson, Associated Press, "Texas Rangers Start Drive on New Type of Cattle Rustlers," August 22, 1941.

13. "Texas Rangers Still Fighting Rustlers in the Southwest," Uvalde *Leader-News*, June 19, 1942.

14. "Texas Rangers Still Fighting Rustlers in the Southwest." In addition to cattle rustling, the Rangers still pursued the occasional horse thief. Ranger Joe H. Bridge and Cattle Inspector R. B. Hale crossed into Mexico in June 1943 on the trail of a Mexican man suspected of stealing six good horses from the Tom East Ranch in Jim Hogg County. Bridge and the other officer located the man and had him arrested by Mexican authorities. The man then agreed to lead the officers to the horses, a journey that covered two thousand miles across two Mexican states. When the Ranger and cattle inspector brought the horses back into Texas, an article in the Corpus Christi *Caller* claimed that they were the first stolen horses known to have been legally returned to Texas from Mexico. Evelyn Edwards, "Horse Thievery Enters New Era: Ranger Recovers Ranch's Mounts," Corpus Christi *Caller*, undated clipping published in Bridge, *The Life and Times of Joe H. Bridge, Texas Ranger 1936–1956*, p. 56.

15. "Texas Rangers Still Fighting Rustlers in the Southwest."

16. Felix McKnight, "Texas Ranger Still Scourge of Outlaws," Dallas *Morning News*, September 10, 1941; "Old Ranger Sees New Tricks," Dallas *Morning News*, September 11, 1941; and "ID Bureau Vital to Crime Control," Dallas *Morning News*, September 11, 1941.

17. "Capt. Lone Wolf Gonzales [*sic*] Tells About Advancement [of] Texas Stalwart Rangers," Waxahachie *Light*, September 4, 1941.

18. Tex Holt, *Texas Terror* (New York: Gateway Books, 1941); Texas Department of Public Safety, Minutes, Public Safety Commission Meeting, October 25, 1941, Austin, Texas.

19. Valentine J. Belfiglio, *Honor, Pride, Duty*, pp. 59–60. House Bill 45, signed into law on February 10, 1941, authorized the Texas Defense Guard. Within a year, the guard had 17,497 officers and enlisted men. The forty-eighth legislature changed its name to the Texas State Guard in 1943.

20. Houston *Post*, January 16, 1942.

21. "If Texas Is Invaded," Wichita Falls *Times*, June 19, 1942.

22. "44 Aliens Taken with Gunpowder, Harbor Maps," Dallas *Morning News*, February 28, 1942.

23. *DPS News*, July 1942, p. 7.

24. "Address by Governor on Civilian Defense Plans," n.p., January 1, 1942.

25. "Texas' War Effort Is in High Gear," Fort Worth *Star-Telegram*, March 25, 1942.

26. George Sessions Perry, *Texas a World in Itself* (New York: Whittlesey House, 1942), p. 6.

27. Perry, *Texas*, p. 6.

28. Halsell, *Ranger*, p. 38.

29. "French Think Texas Rangers Are After 'Em," Dallas *Morning News*, August 20, 1942; "Now You Know: The Dieppe Raid," *Texas Ranger Dispatch Magazine*, no. 2 (Winter 2000).

30. *DPS News*, September 1942, p. 5.

31. *DPS News*, September 1942, p. 1.

32. *DPS News*, October 1942, p. 8.

33. *DPS News*, December 1942, p. 21; "Junior Texas Rangers: Scrap Scouts," San Antonio *Express*, September 30, 1942.

34. *DPS News*, n.d. [1942].

35. "Picturesque Texas Rangers Ride the Big Bend Country in Search of Alien Hide-Outs," San Angelo *Standard-Times*, March 20, 1942. Captain Gully Cowsert of Junction, Best's successor as Company E commander, continued until his retirement in 1958 to periodically scout the river for smugglers and cattle thieves with his men. One Ranger who made many of those weeks-long scouts, Arthur Hill, came to question their effectiveness. Criminals learned to look for Ranger camps and successfully avoided most Ranger patrols, he said.

"I think ol' Cap just liked to camp," Hill later remarked. Spinks, *The Last Frontier*, pp. 46–47.

36. *DPS News*, December 1942, p. 16.

37. *DPS News*, December 1942, p. 15.

38. Texas Department of Public Safety, *Progress Report, Texas Department of Public Safety, 1942–1944*, pp. 14–19. Fred Hickman (no relation to Tom Hickman) had been one of the original license and weight inspectors hired by the Highway Department in 1927. He had prior experience as a policeman, deputy sheriff, and Ranger. After creation of the DPS, he had worked his way up in rank, becoming chief of the Highway Patrol following Phares's ouster. The Public Safety Commission appointed Hickman assistant director on January 4, 1940.

39. *DPS News*, December 1942, p. 1.

40. Malsch, *Lone Wolf*, pp. 145–148; "Texas Officers Slay Escaped Killer Lacy," Dallas *Morning News*, January 27, 1943.

41. *DPS News*, March–April 1943, p. 7.

42. James S. Olson and Sharon Phair, "The Anatomy of a Race Riot: Beaumont, Texas, 1943," *Texana*, 11, no. 1 (1973): pp. 64–72.

43. "Ranger Captains Plan Against War-Bred Crimes," San Antonio *Express*, August 6, 1943.

44. Texas Department of Public Safety, *Progress Report, Texas Department of Public Safety, 1942–1944*, pp. 9, 13.

45. Texas Department of Public Safety, *Progress Report, Texas Department of Public Safety, 1942–1944*, p. 95.

46. Dallas *Morning News*, January 30, 1945; Austin *American-Statesman*, May 17, 1945.

47. J. Marvin Hunter, "Texas Rangers Are Still Active," *Frontier Times*, July 1945, pp. 294–298.

48. *Texas Week*, 1, no. 10 (October 12, 1946): p. 4.

49. Cox, *Texas Ranger Tales*, pp. 246–265.

50. "Valenta vs. Purvis," *Texas Week* 1, 15 (November 16, 1946); p. 8.

51. "Big Starts," *Texas Week* 1, 26 (January 25, 1947): p. 7; "Gamblers' Plot to Move into Dallas Smashed," Dallas *Morning News*, December 19, 1946.

52. James M. Day, *Captain Clint Peoples: Texas Ranger* (Waco, Tex.: Texian Press, 1980), p. 73.

53. James W. Robinson, *The DPS Story: History of the Development of the Department of Public Safety in Texas* (Austin: Department of Public Safety, 1974), pp. 23–25; Hugh W. Stephens, *The Texas City Disaster, 1947* (Austin: University of Texas Press, 1997), p. 100.

54. Cox, *Texas Ranger Tales*, pp. 134–135.

55. Texas Department of Public Safety, *Texas Department of Public Safety Biennial Report 1947–48*, p. 8, shows Ranger strength at forty-five men, plus six

captains. Considering Texas's vast size, that gave the people of the state one Ranger for every 5,941 square miles or, calculated another way, one Ranger for every 142,000 Texans. Standing orders held: "Each Ranger will stay in his district and will be held responsible for the ranger work in that district." Rangers were not to leave their assigned area without permission of their captain, "except in case of an extreme emergency and such emergency will be explained in your weekly report." Further, Rangers were to work closely with county sheriffs, their district attorney, and local officers "as often as possible as your cooperation with the local officers and with one another is essential." Bridge, *The Life and Times of Joe H. Bridge, Texas Ranger 1936–1956*, p. 112.

56. Spinks, *Law on the Last Frontier*, pp. 44–45. Hill's boss was Company E captain Gully Cowsert. *Sheep and Goat Raiser Magazine*'s July 1948 issue said of the West Texas Rangers: "Captain Cowsert's company is composed of ex-cowpunchers reared in the livestock country, not the drug store cowboy type with fancy Palomino horses and lots of fancy silver buckles, but regular ducking jacket cowhands who know how to sleep on the ground and eat around the chuck wagon."

57. Texas Department of Public Safety, *Texas Department of Public Safety Biennial Report 1947–48*, p. 8

58. Texas Department of Public Safety, *Texas Department of Public Safety Biennial Report 1947–48*, p. 3.

59. Garrison to Keach, September 3, 1949, author's collection.

60. Keach to Garrison, August 31, 1948, author's collection.

61. Garrison to Keach, November 15, 1948, author's collection.

62. Garrison to Keach, March 18, 1949, author's collection.

63. Garrison to Martin, March 18, 1949, author's collection. Despite Garrison's optimism that the Rangers would get to the bottom of the Texarkana case, they never did. Gonzaullas and his successors followed hundreds of leads, but no charges were ever filed. Cox, *Texas Ranger Tales*, pp. 246–265.

64. Garrison to Keach, April 6, 1949, author's collection.

65. Keach to Garrison, April 28, 1949, author's collection.

66. Garrison to Keach, May 6, 1949, author's collection.

67. Garrison to Keach, July 21, 1949, author's collection. After agreeing to cooperate fully on the proposed Ranger movie, the colonel wrote: "We realize the public relations and educational value that such a production would have for the Texas Rangers and law enforcement generally. . . ."

68. Lynn Ashby, "When the Mafia Didn't Come Here," *Houston Post*, January 10, 1990.

69. Douglas V. Meed, *Texas Ranger Johnny Klevenhagen* (Plano: Republic of Texas Press, 2000), pp. 84–85, 88; Michael Dorman, *King of the Courtroom: Percy Foreman for the Defense* (New York: Dell Books, 1969), pp. 207–211; "Jury Will Hear Story of Carlino Admitted Killing," Dallas *Morning News*, October 31, 1950.

70. As early as 1919, Ranger captain Charles F. Stevens, freshly returned from a scout into Mexico across from El Paso in which an army airplane had kept the military apprised of his position, wrote headquarters in Austin: "If the Ranger Force would have an aero-plane or two, they would be of great service to the Ranger Force." Harris and Sadler, *The Texas Rangers and the Mexican Revolution*, p. 475. Shortly after the creation of the DPS, working with U.S. Customs and Border Patrol agents, Rangers Pete Crawford and Levi Duncan on April 29, 1936, searched the Big Bend by air and horseback, looking for smugglers. The two Rangers flew in a U.S. Coast Guard plane. "Hedge-hopping over peaks and into narrow canyons," the Associated Press reported, "Rangers spot smugglers from the air, drop instructions to Rangers mounted on horseback and circle around to direct the search."A "radio broadcasting unit" in the Ranger camp "summons planes from San Antonio." El Paso *Times*, April 30, 1936.

71. Jim Boutwell, "Notes on Early DPS Aviation," n.d. (ca. 1983), copy in author's collection.

72. Roger W. Benedict, "Texas Rangers Keep Horses but Now Fight Labor, Race Troubles," *Wall Street Journal*, October 15, 1959.

73. Texas Department of Public Safety, *Texas Department of Public Safety Biennial Report 1947–48*, p. 3.

9. Garrison's Rangers

1. Garrison to Keach, August 26, 1950, author's collection.

2. "Radio and Television," New York *Times*, April 18, 1950.

3. Garrison to Keach, July 19, 1950, author's collection.

4. Keach to Garrison, June 22, 1950, author's collection.

5. Dennis Holder, "One Riot, One Ranger: The Legendary Career of Texas' Toughest Ranger, Capt. Jay Banks," *Family Weekly*, June 30, 1985, pp. 11–12.

6. Holder, "One Riot, One Ranger"; "Cohen Hits Wichita Falls and the Law Greets Him," Dallas *Morning News*, August 31, 1950; "Cohen Gits from State of Arrest," Dallas *Morning News*, September 1, 1950. A wiseguy literally and figuratively, Mickey Cohen told reporters, "The next time I come to Texas I'm going to try to get a passport. I don't know why there is all this fuss over me." A target of the 1950 U.S. Senate Kefauver Commission's investigation into organized crime, not long after his Texas visit Cohen got convicted of income tax evasion and spent four years in federal prison. In 1961 he went back to prison on another tax evasion conviction. One of America's best-known gangsters, he died of cancer in Los Angeles July 29, 1976.

7. Los Angeles *Mirror*, October 17, 1950.

8. Garrison to Keach, May 29, 1950, author's collection.

9. Garrison to Keach, June 5, 1950, author's collection.

10. Garrison to Keach, October 24, 1950, author's collection.

11. Garrison to Keach, February 7, 1951, author's collection.

12. Keach to Garrison, January 4, 1951, author's collection.

13. *Texas Rangers*, 41, no. 2 (January 1951): p. 9.

14. Don E. Carleton, *Red Scare* (Austin: Texas Monthly Press, 1985), pp. 96–97, 100.

15. Dan Murph, *Texas Giant: The Life of Price Daniel* (Austin: Eakin Press, 2000), pp. 90–91.

16. Garrison to Keach, June 25, 1951, author's collection.

17. Robert Stephens, "Manuel Trazazas Gonzaullas," *Texas Ranger Dispatch Magazine*, issue 7 (Summer 2002).

18. Malsch, *"Lone Wolf" Gonzaullas, Texas Ranger*, introduction to new edition by Harold J. Weiss, xii–xiii; Weiss included Gonzaullas among what he considered the "Big Four" captains of the first half of the twentieth century, the other three being Hamer, Hickman, and Wright. These men, in Weiss's view, should be remembered as the workhorse successors of the group W. W. "Bill" Sterling called the Four Great Captains, J. A. Brooks, John R. Hughes, W. J. "Bill" McDonald, and John H. Rogers.

19. Lee McGiffin, *Ten Tall Texans: Tales of the Texas Rangers* (New York: Lee and Shepard Company, 1956), pp. 217–218.

20. *Newsweek* 38 (August 6, 1951): p. 54.

21. Garrison to Jack Chertok, August 17, 1951, author's collection.

22. Dallas *Morning News*, July 7, 1951.

23. Dallas *Morning News*, July 13, 1951.

24. "Home Bombing Charges Filed Against 2 Men," Dallas *Morning News*, July 24, 1951; "Suspect Tells Officers of Part in Bomb Plot," Dallas *Morning News*, July 25, 1951; Austin *American-Statesman*, July 26, 1951.

25. Susie Mills, *Legend in Bronze: The Biography of Jay Banks* (Dallas: Ussery Printing Company, 1982), pp. 59–75.

26. Garrison to Keach, September 19, 1951, author's collection.

27. Garrison to Keach, November 11, 1951, author's collection.

28. San Angelo *Standard-Times*, March 1, March 2, 1952; "Kern, Ranger Beat Up Foreman; Carlino Free," Houston *Post*, March 1, 1952; "Kern Plants 20-Year Punch on Foreman," Houston *Chronicle*, March 1, 1952; "Court Slugfest Called Outrage," Houston *Post*, March 2, 1952; "Foreman Row Echoes as Far as Austin," Houston *Chronicle*, March 2, 1952.

29. Texas Department of Public Safety, *Department of Public Safety Biennial Report Fiscal Years 1951–1952*, pp. 12–13.

30. Terry Salomonson, *The Western Logs* (Howell, Minn.: n.p., 1998), pp. 115–121.

31. Allen, *The Real Book about the Texas Rangers*, pp. 187–188.

32. Aldridge to Garrison, December 5, 1952, author's collection.

33. Aldridge to Garrison, December 5, 1952, author's collection.

34. *The Law Creating the Department of Public Safety*, DPS Publication PI-30, January 1978, pp. 15–17.

35. Joe Austell small interviews with author, Austin, Texas, May 14, 1974, and March 9, 1977.

36. "Out to Get the Rangers," *Newsweek* 45 (March 21, 1955): p. 30.

37. Hart Stillwell, "Farewell Peacemaker," *True West*, Winter 1953, p. 15.

38. John E. Clark, *The Fall of the Duke of Duval: A Prosecutor's Journal* (Austin: Eakin Press, 1995), passim; Bridge, *The Life and Times of Joe H. Bridge, Texas Ranger 1936–1956*, pp. 73–79; Don Hinga, "Turbulent Times Vanish and Duval Like Fiesta Now as Rangers Take Over," Corpus Christi *Caller*, May 25, 1952. On May 7, 1952, Captain Allee sent Rangers Joe H. Bridge and Charlie Miller to San Diego to keep the peace during an election campaign. The two Rangers spent most of their time sitting outside the 79th District Court grand jury room as jurors heard evidence on allegations of voter intimidation by the Parr machine. When the grand jury recessed without returning any indictments, the Rangers kept a watchful eye on the courthouse from an apartment across the street, where they stayed until after the July 26 election.

39. Gladwyn Hill, "Pistols, Rangers, Indictments Mix in Old-Time Texas Political Row," New York *Times*, February 5, 1954.

40. "Parrs, Rangers Trade Punches," Austin *American-Statesman*, January 20, 1954.

41. "Rumors Say Rangers Face Charges in Brawl," Austin *American-Statesman*, January 19, 1954; Bridge, *The Life and Times of Joe H. Bridge, Texas Ranger 1936–1956*, pp. 80–91. Ranger Bridge summarized the incident in his weekly report: "Capt. Allee gave me a warrant for George Parr and told me and Ranger Russell to go to San Diego, contact Archer Parr . . . and get George and bring him to Alice. We left Alice at 10:00 A.M. [Arrived] San Diego 10:30 A.M. Went to Sheriff's office where Office Deputy called Sheriff Parr and told him we were there and waited to see him. The Office Deputy told us Sheriff Parr would be there in a few minutes. We waited some half or three quarters of an hour and Sheriff Parr did not come. I ask [sic] one of the Deputies to go see what happened. He returned in about five minutes and said Sheriff Parr had loaded George Parr in his car and gone to Alice. Ranger Russell and I returned to Alice where Sheriff Parr got smart with me and we had a little fracas. Col. Garrison is informed [and] has all information. . . ."

42. Dallas *Morning News*, January 26, 1954.

43. Clark, *The Fall of the Duke of Duval*, p. 74.

44. Rusk *Cherokeean*, April 16, 1955.

45. Ben H. Proctor, *One Riot: Episodes of the Texas Rangers in the 20th Century* (Austin: Eakin Press, 1991), pp. 95–101.

46. Texas Department of Public Safety, *Texas Department of Public Safety Biennial Report 1955–1956*, p. 19, has a photograph of a Ranger talking on a field radio while standing next to the newly purchased armored vehicle. John L. Davis, *The Texas Rangers: Images and Incidents* (San Antonio: University of Texas Institute of Texan Cultures, 1991), p. 103; Herbert Molloy Mason, Jr., *The Texas*

Rangers (New York: Meredith Press, 1967), pp. 144–145. The vehicle had a "three-way" shortwave radio and siren.

47. Tim Brooks and Earle Marsh, *The Complete Directory to Prime Time Network TV Shows, 1946–Present* (New York: Ballantine Books, 1985), pp. 824–825.

48. Davis, *The Texas Rangers*, p. 95, 97.

49. DPS *Chaparral*, January–February, 1956, p. 6.

50. DPS *Chaparral*, January–February, 1957, p. 14.

51. McGiffin, *Ten Tall Texans: Tales of the Texas Rangers*, p. 12.

52. DPS *Chaparral*, May–June 1956, p. 20.

53. DPS *Chaparral*, June–August 1956.

54. Meed, *Texas Ranger Johnny Klevenhagen*, pp. 187–197.

55. Robert W. Stephens, *Bullets and Buckshot* (Dallas: privately printed, 2002), p. 322.

56. Linda Jay Puckett, *Cast a Long Shadow: A Casebook of the Law Enforcement Career of Texas Ranger Captain E.J. (Jay) Banks* (Dallas: Ussery Printing, 1984), p. 94; Robyn Duff Lading, *Desegregating Texas Schools: Eisenhower, Shivers and the Crisis at Mansfield High* (Austin: University of Texas Press, 1996), pp. 94–114; Ricky F. Dobbs, *Yellow Dogs and Republicans: Allan Shivers and Texas Two-Party Politics* (College Station: Texas A&M University Press, 2005), pp. 137–140. Five years after the incident, Texas writer and liberal Democrat J. Frank Dobie put the Mansfield affair into perspective: "A few years ago Governor. . . . Shivers sent the Texas Rangers to uphold a mob opposing the Supreme Court's decision on desegregation of public schools. Everybody remembers the old Texas Ranger story of one [Ranger] to one mob. This was probably the first time in the history of the state that the chief executive dispatched armed forces not to quell a mob but to uphold it." San Antonio *Light*, January 7, 1962. That the mayor and others left town for the Labor Day weekend is contained in Lading, p. 98, citing John Howard Griffin and Theodore Freeman, *Mansfield, Texas: A Report of the Crisis Situation Resulting from Efforts to Desegregate the School System* (New York: Anti-Defamation League of B'nai B'rith), 1957, p. 5 and George Norris Green, *The Establishment in Texas Politics: The Primitive Years, 1938–1957* (Westport, Conn: Greenwood Press, 1979), p. 189.

57. "The Arkansas Traveler," *Arkansas Gazette*, September 13, 1956.

58. DPS *Chaparral*, November–December 1956, p. 11.

59. Karl Detzer, "Texas Rangers Still Ride the Trail," *Reader's Digest*, September 1957, pp. 140–141.

60. Clint Peoples later gave historian James Day his take on Hickman's dismissal. Peoples said Hickman believed that Sergeant Sid Kelso, a Ferguson-era Ranger, had tipped Top o' Hill Terrace owner Fred Browning about the planned gambling raid. Kelso eventually was "released from the service." In the late 1940s, after Peoples made Ranger, he arrested Kelso for running a gambling operation in Austin. Day, *Captain Clint Peoples, Texas Ranger*, p. 69.

61. Fort Worth *Star-Telegram*, April 30, May 1, 1957; Fort Worth *Press*, April 30, May 1, 1957; Dallas *Morning News*, May 1, 1957; Ann Arnold, *Gamblers and Gangsters: Fort Worth's Jacksboro Highway in the 1940s & 1950s* (Austin: Eakin Press, 1998), pp. 155–161; Puckett, *Cast a Long Shadow*, pp. 110–122; Spinks, *Law on the Last Frontier*, pp. 131–138. Spinks's account, based on interviews with Ranger participant Arthur Hill and records he kept after his retirement, is the best overview of the Norris shooting.

62. Will Wilson, "Shutting Down 'Sin City,'" chapter one from unpublished Will Wilson memoir, edited by Betty Wilke Cox, March 13, 2002, draft, author's collection; James P. Simpson and Geoffrey Leavenworth, *Flak Bait* (Waco, Tex.: Eakin Press, 2007), "Galveston and the Rackets," pp. 99–126; Steven Long, "Shutdown: June 10, 1957, the Day the Wheels Stopped Turning," *In Between Magazine* (Galveston), May 1982, pp. 11–15; Meed, *Texas Ranger Johnny Klevenhagen*, pp. 206–207; Frank E. Chalfant, *Galveston: Island of Chance* (Houston: Treasures of Nostalgia, 1997), pp. 22–47, 59–68, is the best source for information on the Maceo empire and the history of the storied Balinese Room, which was destroyed by Hurricane Ike on September 13, 2008; Gary Cartwright, *Galveston: A History of the Island* (New York: Atheneum, 1991), pp. 249–261. Utley, *Lone Star Lawmen* (p. 219), points out that even after the 1957 cleanup, two Rangers had to be detailed to sit around other Galveston clubs to scare off gambling-minded customers. That practice continued through 1960.

63. Detzer, "Texas Rangers Still Ride the Trail," pp. 139–142.

64. Klevenhagen suffered a heart attack while attending a football game on November 15, 1958, and died eleven days later in a Houston hospital. Meed, *Texas Ranger Johnny Klevenhagen*, pp. 218–220.

65. Texas Research League report; Day, *Captain Clint Peoples, Texas Ranger*, p. 123.

66. Day, *Captain Clint Peoples, Texas Ranger*, p. 123.

67. Paredes, *"With His Pistol in His Hand,"* pp. 23–24.

68. Paredes, *"With His Pistol in His Hand,"* pp. 24–25, 32. The life and work of Americo Paredes has been explored in Jose R. Lopez Morin, *The Legacy of Americo Paredes* (College Station: Texas A&M University Press, 2006), and Ramon Saldivar, *The Borderlands of Culture: Americo Paredes and the Transnational Imaginary* (Durham, N.C.: Duke University Press, 2006). For more on corridos, see James Nicolopulous, "Another Fifty Years of the *Corrido*: A Reassessment," *Aztlan: A Journal of Chicano Studies* 22, no. 1 (Spring 1997), UCLA Chicano Studies Research Center, accessed at http://sincronia.cuesh.udg.mx/nicolopulos.html.

69. "West Still Wild and Wooly, Facts on Teamsters Reveal," Washington *Evening Star*, November 18, 1958.

70. Zeno Smith Scrapbook, Nita Stewart Haley Memorial Library, Midland, Texas. "Accused Teamster Sits Tight As Probers Hear Recordings," Dallas *Morning News*, November 19, 1958.

71. Ed Gooding and Robert Nieman, *Ed Gooding: Soldier, Texas Ranger* (Longview, Tex.: Ranger Publishing, 2001), pp. 147–151.

72. Sterling, *Trails and Trials of a Texas Ranger*, pp. xi–xii.

73. Sterling, *Trails and Trials of a Texas Ranger*, p. 524.

74. Austin *American-Statesman*, April 27, 1960.

10. FEET OF CLAY

1. Alice Hutson, *From Chalk to Bronze: A Biography of Waldine Tauch* (Austin: Shoal Creek Publishers, 1978), pp. 134–139.

2. "Ranger Quits After Fuss with DPS," Austin *American-Statesman*, March 3, 1960; "Garrison Says Ranger Dismissed from Post," Austin *American-Statesman* March 4, 1960. The same day Garrison said Banks had been dismissed, one of the captain's men, Fort Worth–based Ranger W. J. Wimberly, quit in support of Banks. Banks at first flatly denied he had been ordered by Garrison to shut down the Tarrant County gambling operation, but on March 7 Texas newspapers carried a wire story that stated Banks had decided not to pursue the matter. "Too many conflicting statements and conjectures have already been made," he said. "Only personal hurt and damage to our state can result from the continuance of this. . . . I have . . . requested that no other Rangers make any move or any further statement in my behalf." "Ex-Ranger Urges Full Support for Successor," Austin *American-Statesman*, March 7, 1960. Not long after he left the Rangers, the city of Big Spring hired Banks as police chief. He later worked with collaborators to produce two books on his colorful career. He died August 3, 1987. "E.J. Banks, Former Texas Ranger and Model for Love Field Statue," Fort Worth *Star-Telegram*, August 8, 1987.

3. "They're Still Catching Rustlers in Texas," *Family Weekly*, October 9, 1960.

4. Houston *Post*, February 26, 1961. Hickman completed his six-year term on the Public Safety Commission on December 31, 1962. Twenty-eight days later he died of heart failure.

5. Dallas *Times-Herald*, May 1, 1961.

6. Texas Department of Public Safety, *Texas Department of Public Safety Biennial Report 1961–1962*, p. 24; DPS Public Information Office news release, October 8, 1961.

7. Author's interview with Joaquin Jackson, November 16, 2002, Alpine, Texas.

8. Dick McAlpin, "Bank Bandit–Kidnap Suspect Caught," Beaumont *Enterprise*, January 18, 1962.

9. Jack Maguire, "Texas Ranger Personalities," n.d., unpublished notes from Jack Maguire Papers, copy in author's collection.

10. Kyle Thompson, "The Legendary Ranger: More Fact than Fiction," Dallas *Morning News*, October 13, 1963.

11. Glenn Elliott, with Robert Nieman, *Glenn Elliott: A Ranger's Ranger* (Waco, Tex.: Texian Press, 1999), pp. 88–90.

12. *Biennial Report of Attorney General Will Wilson*, Austin, December 14, 1962, pp. 42–43; Texas Department of Public Safety, *Texas Department of Public Safety Biennial Report 1961–1962*, p. 26.

13. Dallas *Morning News*, June 6, 1962.

14. "Rangers Adopt New Badge," DPS *Chaparral*, Fall 1962, pp. 16–17; "Texas Rangers Now Wear New Badges," *Texas Public Employee*, November 1962, p. 11, cited in Cox, *Texas Ranger Tales*, p 274; "New Badge Adopted for Texas Rangers," *Texas Lawman* 31, no. 8 (November 1962) p. 6.

15. Stan Redding, "Today's Ranger: Same Breed as 1861 'Half Savage,'" Houston *Chronicle*, February 10, 1963.

16. Joseph Chadwick, *The Texas Rangers: A Concise History of the Most Colorful Law Enforcement Group in the Frontier West* (New York: Monarch Books, 1963), p. 140.

17. Samora, Bernal, and Pena, *Gunpowder Justice*, pp. 106–107.

18. Armando Navarro, *The Cristal Experiment: A Chicano Struggle for Community Control* (Madison: University of Wisconsin Press, 1998), p. 32.

19. Navarro, *The Cristal Experiment*, p. 37.

20. San Antonio *Express*, April 30, 1963; San Antonio *Light*, April 30, 1963.

21. San Antonio *Express*, May 7, 1963.

22. San Antonio *Express*, May 9, 1963; "Shock Waves from Popeye Land," *Texas Observer*, May 16, 1963.

23. Navarro, *The Cristal Experiment*, p. 39. The most complete account of the 1963 Crystal City election and its aftermath is in Samora, Bernal, and Pena, *Gunpowder Justice*, pp. 89–125. For an overview of the 1962–1963 Crystal City events and subsequent developments, see John Staples Shockley, *Chicano Revolt in a Texas Town* (Notre Dame: University of Notre Dame Press, 1974).

24. Elliott, *Glenn Elliott: A Ranger's Ranger.* When President Kennedy and Governor Connally were shot, Dr. G. Tom Shires, chief of surgical services at Dallas's Parkland Hospital, was in Galveston giving a talk to the Western Surgical Association. Ordered to find the doctor and get him back to Dallas so he could operate on the wounded Connally, a Company A Ranger pulled Shires out of the meeting and put him on a plane to Dallas. Shires arrived at Parkland just as the president's body was being wheeled out and quickly scrubbed for the operation on the badly wounded governor. Connally recovered, serving two more terms as governor. "Dr. G. Tom Shires Dead at 81," Los Angeles *Times*, November 1, 2007. p. 91.

25. Thomas E. Turner, "Waco CC Offer Accepted by DPS," Dallas *Morning News*, April 16, 1964.

26. James M. Day, *One Man's Dream: Fort Fisher and the Texas Ranger Hall of Fame* (Waco, Tex.: Texian Press, 1976), pp. 7, 9, 11.

27. Wade Everett, *Texas Ranger*, (New York: Ballantine Books, 1964), p. 23. Wade Everett was a pseudonym used by two longtime Western fiction writers, Wade Everett Cook (1921–1964) and Giles A. Lutz (1910–1982.)

28. Douglas Freelander, "The Texas Rangers 62-Man Force Still Has a Big Job," Houston *Post*, August 16, 1964.

29. "All Rangers End Training Session," Houston *Post*, November 15, 1964.

30. "Suiting Up the Rangers," *Dupont Magazine*, November–December 1964, pp. 9–11. Not all the Rangers liked their quasi uniforms, which some began to refer to as "Garrison Suits." Each Ranger's ensemble included a regular suit coat, a short coat, and two pairs of trousers. Retired captain Grady Sessums recalled that the sleeves on one of his coats ran too long, while the sleeves on the other did not extend long enough. The Ranger service did not reorder the suits, which the men who had them used until they wore out. Never warmly embraced by the rank-in-file Rangers, the suits had virtually disappeared by the mid-1970s. Author's interviews with Grady Sessums, Pecos, Texas, September 6, 2008, and Kerrville, Texas, September 20, 2008.

31. Dorothy Lillard, "They Haven't Slipped Away: Texas Rangers Show Gain," Dallas *Morning News*, September 27, 1965.

32. Samora, Bernal, and Pena, *Gunpowder Justice*, p. 132.

33. Gooding and Nieman, *Ed Gooding*, pp. 191–194.

34. Samora, Bernal, and Pena, *Gunpowder Justice*, pp. 132–134, citing *Medrano v. Allee* 347 F. Supp. 605 (1972), 612.

35. "Texas Ranger Museum Planned for DPS," *Texas Lawman*, October 1966, p. 6.

36. *Texas Lawman*, October 1966, p. 23.

37. "Ranger Talks to Rights Panel," San Antonio *Express*, December 15, 1968.

38. Samora, Bernal, and Pena, *Gunpowder Justice*, pp. 141–142.

39. Kemper Diehl, "Clergyman Charges Texas Rangers Too Rough," San Antonio *Express-News*, May 28, 1967.

40. Samora, Bernal, and Pena, *Gunpowder Justice*, p. 148.

41. "Conversations with the Captain," *Texas Observer*, June 9, 1967, p. 23.

42. Ben H. Proctor, "The Modern Texas Rangers: A Law-Enforcement Dilemma in the Rio Grande Valley," papers of the seventh annual conference of the Western History Association, San Francisco, California, October 12–14, 1967.

43. Samora, Bernal, and Pena, *Gunpowder Justice*, p. 153.

44. "Trouble in the Melon Patch," *Newsweek*, 69 June 19, 1967, pp. 38–39. Retired Ranger Joaquin Jackson, by 2008 the only surviving Ranger participant in the controversy, offers his perspective on the strike in *One Ranger Returns* (Austin: University of Texas Press, 2008), pp. 1–18.

45. Samora, Bernal, and Pena, *Gunpowder Justice*, pp. 154–156.

46. Dennis Farney, "The Texas Rangers/Lawmen Get Their Man, but Their Tactics Are Currently Under Fire," *Wall Street Journal* 47, no. 232 (December 3, 1967).

47. Carlos R. Soltero, "Miranda v. Arizona (1966) and the rights of the criminally accused," *Latinos and American Law: Landmark Supreme Court Cases.* (Austin: University of Texas Press, 2006), pp. 61–74.

48. Day, *Captain Clint Peoples, Texas Ranger*, p. 148; "Tribute Paid Col. Garrison," Houston *Post*, May 10, 1966.

49. Texas Department of Public Safety, *DPS 1967–1968 Biennial Report*, p. 7; "Texas Ranger Activity 1967 Calendar Year," undated DPS memorandum.

50. *Courtesy Service Protection: The Texas Department of Public Safety's Sixtieth Anniversary*, historical text by Dr. Mitchel Roth, edited by Mike Cox, Laureen Chernow, and Sherri Deatherage Green. (Dallas: Taylor Publishing Company, 1995), p. 63.

51. "Austin Burial Set Thursday for Col. Homer Garrison Jr.," Dallas *Morning News*, May 8, 1968.

52. Author's interview with Joaquin Jackson, November 16, 2002, Alpine, Texas.

53. *Courtesy Service Protection: The Texas Department of Public Safety's Sixtieth Anniversary*, p. 65.

54. Sterlin Holmesly, *HemisFair '68 and the Transformation of San Antonio* (San Antonio: Maverick Publishing Company, 2003), pp. 7–12.

55. San Antonio *Express-News*, December 15, 1968.

56. Day, *Captain Clint Peoples, Texas Ranger*, p. 156.

57. "Ranger Captain Denies 'Brutality,'" Austin *American-Statesman*, December 15, 1968.

58. Elliott, *Glenn Elliott: A Ranger's Ranger*, pp.103–113. For the Rangers, the long strike in Dangerfield amounted to round two of the same fight. Nine years earlier, beginning on September 21, 1957, a wildcat strike shut down the Lone Star Steel plant, which employed thirty-five hundred workers in Cass and Morris counties. Though many of the strikers soon went back to work, the company fired those who refused to return to the job and hired scabs to replace them. That triggered what one newspaper called "unbridled chaos," including four non-injury bombings targeting property, four shotgun blasts directed at the residences of nonunion workers or their vehicles, several beatings, and other acts of intimidation. Rangers manned roadblocks, patrolled the plant and adjacent areas, and made several arrests, but the situation remained tense and tied up a lot of DPS manpower until the strike ended after forty-three days. Spinks, *Law on the Last Frontier*, pp. 141–149.

59. Day, *Captain Clint Peoples, Texas Ranger*, p. 149.

60. Larry McMurtry, *In a Narrow Grave* (Austin: Encino Press, 1968), pp. 39–40.

61. Author's interview with Joaquin Jackson, November 16, 2002, Alpine, Texas; San Antonio *Express*, April 4, 1969.

62. Elliott, *Glenn Elliott: A Ranger's Ranger*, p. 112.

63. Robinson, *The DPS Story*, pp. 37–38.

64. "Remarks by Colonel Wilson E. Speir/Director, Texas Department of Public Safety/Banquet to Honor Retiring Texas Rangers/Waco, Texas/7:30 p.m. Thursday, July 24, 1968," copy in author's collection.

65. Nicholas C. Chriss, "First Mexican-American Joins Forces with Texas Rangers," Los Angeles *Times*, September 9, 1969. In "Ranger Allee gets Secret Weapon," n.d., n.p., an article in an obviously pro–Raza Unida, anti-Ranger publication, an anonymous author wrote: "A former Mexican-American, Arturo Rodriquez, has joined the notorious union- and minority-hating South Texas Ranger company headed by Capt. A.Y. Allee. . . . For a cop, being named to the Texas Rangers might be considered a promotion but for a Mexican American it must be degrading since his own people have suffered long and greatly at the hand of Allee and his mob. Mexican-American union organizers and union members have been beaten and threatened by Texas Rangers. Rodriquez will be a traitor to his people if he carries on the tradition of the Texas Rangers." Rodriquez was the first Hispanic Ranger since the organization of the DPS, but he was far from the first Hispanic Ranger. A check of Ranger muster records by a researcher for the Texas Ranger Hall of Fame and Museum in Waco found fifty Hispanic surnames recorded between 1838 and 1874. http://www.texasranger .org/Library/Hispanic_&_Indian_Rangers.htm. First stationed in Crystal City, on January 1, 1971, Rodriquez was transferred to San Antonio. He worked there until July 7, 1974, when he resigned to join the federal Drug Enforcement Agency. In a memorandum submitted to Captain John M. Wood on June 21, 1974, Rodriquez wrote: "The Texas Rangers have meant to me the apex of my law enforcement career and I shall cherish that memory for as long as I live. I never dreamed as a boy that I would become one of the famed and historic Texas Rangers. . . . I regret the necessity of leaving, but with the high cost of living . . . I feel that I have to look after my family and I could not make myself pass up this new opportunity."

66. Paul Allen, "Terrell Sheriff Says Ranger Choices Weren't Proper." San Angelo *Standard-Times*, September 21, 1969. Ten days before Cooksey's comments made headlines, the San Antonio *Express* published a sarcastic letter from a woman with a Hispanic surname: "The article about the appointment of Arturo Rodriguez to the esteemed Texas Rangers reports that Ranger Allee said the reason for waiting 50 years to appoint a Mexican-American was that 'he never had had a qualified candidate before.' This statement filled me with such awe and respect for Ranger Rodriguez that I felt compelled to leave my ironing board and issue an instant call to the people of San Antonio to join with me in finding suitable tribute to this remarkable man. When one considers the number of Mexican-Americans who have lived in Texas in 50 years and then considers that Ranger Rodriguez is the first of these to qualify as a Texas Ranger, the significance. . . . is overwhelming! He must be trustworthy, loyal, helpful, friendly, courteous, kind, obedient, cheerful, thrifty, brave, clean and reverent to

a degree that few of us have ever witnessed in a fellow human being!" The writer went on to suggest that it might not be wise to expose "this paragon to the rigors and dangers of Rangering?" Perhaps, she went on, "it would be more appropriate for we citizens, to show our unbounded appreciation, to have Ranger Rodriguez dedicated as a permanent exhibit in the Institute of Texan Cultures." " 'Salute' to New Ranger," San Antonio *Express*, September 11, 1969.

67. "Lawmen Standing in Line to Become Texas Rangers," Dallas *Times-Herald*, September 21, 1969; " 'Ranger Mystique' 500 Seek Jobs in Larger Force" Dallas *Morning News*, September 21, 1969.

68. Colonel Speir swore in eleven more Rangers on October 1, increasing the service from sixty-two men to a newly authorized strength of seventy-three Rangers. Five hundred men had applied for the available positions. Rangers now earned $8,916 a year plus a $500 annual clothing allowance. In addition, the title of senior captain was reintroduced into the Ranger organizational chart on November 1. Waco-based Captain Peoples, a Ranger since December 1946, gained promotion to the new position, assuming supervisory responsibility for the entire service. Day, *Captain Clint Peoples*, pp. 154–155.

11. "Do the Needful"

1. Bill Cunningham, "Retiring Ranger Capt. Allee: 'No Regrets Whatsoever,' " San Antonio *Express-News*, September 13, 1970. For more on Allee and his family, see Dorothy Abbott McCoy, *It's a Good Thing for Texas* (McAllen, Tex.: Steve Alden Publishing Company, 1981), pp. 1–19. Two years after his retirement, Allee made news again by scuffling with someone at a grocery store in Carrizo Springs. Ranger Art Rodriguez wrote his former captain on June 30, 1972, expressing his support. Allee responded with a letter of appreciation two days later. "There is more to this besides what you read in the paper," Allee wrote. "They are trying to spread their politics over here in Dimmitt Co., too, so we will have to wait and see what happens." A. Y. Allee to Art Rodriguez, July 2, 1972, copy in author's collection. "The whole country was changing," Rodriguez later recalled, "and bless his heart, Cap [Allee] tried to change. But he was from the old school and he didn't know how to." Mike Cochran, Associated Press, "First Hispanic Ranger Rose to the Challenge," San Antonio *Express*, March 10, 1996.

2. Tom Tiede, "Some Won't Miss Allee," San Antonio *Express*, September 9, 1970.

3. John Kifner, "Texas Ranger Not a Hero to All," New York *Times*, March 23, 1970.

4. "Allee Ill Prepared for Advice to Abolish Texas Rangers," Corpus Christi *Caller-Times*, March 24, 1970.

5. Author's interview with Clint Peoples, June 20, 1972, Austin, Texas.

6. Daryl James, editor, *No Apologies: Texas Radicals Celebrate the '60.* (Austin: Eakin Press, 1992), p. 163; Austin *American-Statesman*, May 5–8, 1970.

7. James, *No Apologies*, p. 31.

8. Austin *American-Statesman*, May 23, 1971; author's interview with Grady Sessums, September 5, 2008, Pecos, Texas. Sessums, a native of Sweetwater, promoted from the Highway Patrol into the Rangers in 1969 and was stationed at Del Rio on the Texas-Mexico border. When he made sergeant on July 1, 1975, he got transferred to Company A in Houston, later being named captain. He retired in 1982. Sessums said "just do the needful" had been Captain Jim Riddell's standard enjoiner to his men, four words well summarizing the Ranger ethos.

9. Author's interview with Sessums.

10. Author's interview with Al Mitchell, September 5–6, 2008, Pecos, Texas.

11. Gooding and Nieman, *Ed Gooding*, p. 216.

12. Procter, *Just One Riot*, p. 17; Day, *Captain Clint Peoples, Texas Ranger*, p. 156. In addition to having to score high on a test and do well in a face-to-face job interview, only people who had "high morals and good self-control" would be selected by Peoples to be Rangers. Rangers also had to be "compatible."

13. United States Commission on Civil Rights, *A Report of the Texas Advisory Committee to the United States Commission on Civil Rights*, Washington, D.C., February 1970.

14. Richard Finegan, "Texas Rangers Now All White-Hat Guys," San Antonio *News*, October 30, 1970.

15. Day, *Captain Clint Peoples, Texas Ranger*, pp. 157–158.

16. "Gov. Smith Okays Ranger Celebration," Austin *American-Statesman*, June 8, 1971; Day, *Captain Clint Peoples, Texas Ranger*, p. 158.

17. Evan Moore, "Desperado of 1930s Is Slain: Family at Bedford Kidnapped," Fort Worth *Star-Telegram*, October 14, 1971; Clint Peoples to J. C. Ray, October 14, 1971, copy in author's collection. Though hailed as a hero for his role in the Walters case, Arnold took a forced retirement as of November 30, 1983. A report by his captain dated March 5, 1984, noted: "Unsatisfactory performance complaint lodged against Ranger T.E. Arnold carried into this period and was resolved by his retirement. . . ." Utley, *Lone Star Lawmen*, p. 268, citing Capt. G. W. Burks to Senior Capt. W. D. Wilson, "Company B Status Report September 1, 1983 through February 29,1984," March 5, 1984, Texas State Archives.

18. Samora, Bernal, and Pena, *Gunpowder Justice*, pp. 154–155.

19. "Sissy Would Disarm Rangers," Dallas *Morning News*, March 27, 1972; "Sissy vs. the Rangers," Dallas *Morning News*, March 29, 1972; "Texas Rangers 1, Sissy Farenthold 1," Dallas *Morning News*, April 5, 1972; Day, *Captain Clint Peoples, Texas Ranger*, p. 156. Farenthold's great-great-uncle had been a frontier-era Ranger. Art Wiese, "Should We Abolish the Rangers?" Houston *Post*, August 20, 1972. Years later, in working with University of Texas historian Dr. Don Carleton on writing his memoir, Governor Briscoe recalled, "I was most appreciative of Mrs. Farenthold's remark about abolishing the Texas Rangers, because I knew that most Texans admire them and cherish their legacy as much

as I do. She handed me a wonderful issue to use against her." Dolph Briscoe as told to Don Carleton, *Dolph Briscoe: My Life in Texas Ranching and Politics* (Austin: Center for American History, University of Texas at Austin, 2008), pp. 183–184.

20. "NBC Takes Close Look at Activities of Texas Rangers," El Paso *Herald-Post,* May 20, 1972.

21. Preston McGraw, "The Texas Rangers Today: More Helicopters than Horses," Houston *Chronicle,* September 10, 1972.

22. Day, *Captain Clint Peoples, Texas Ranger,* p. 171.

23. Peoples to L. A. Wilke, August 1, 1974, author's collection.

24. Cactus Pryor, "Texas Rangers," KTBC Radio, Austin, Texas, January 1973, copy of script in author's collection.

25. "The Texas Rangers' 150th Anniversary," undated news release, author's collection.

26. Peoples to Speir, June 11, 1973, copy in author's collection.

27. The seventy-three-year-old Texas-born actor also made a quip about Zsa Zsa Gabor and bra burning. Someone complained that his remarks had "undignified" the celebration, there being ladies present. In addition, Wills, who had paid his own air fare and volunteered his time at the affair, was not happy about being presented a plaque to deliver to the absent Slim Pickens. "I had met this man [actor Pickens] on several occasions but I didn't know his address, and I was supposed to deliver this plaque," Wills wrote in a long, rambling letter to Governor Briscoe nine days after the event. Clearly feeling unappreciated, the actor said he was resigning his commission as an honorary Texas Ranger and would be mailing his plaque back to Colonel Speir. Wills to Briscoe, August 13, 1973, copy in author's collection.

28. "Sod Broken at Waco for Shrine to 150-Year-Old State Rangers," Austin *American-Statesman,* August 5, 1973; Day, *Captain Clint Peoples, Texas Ranger,* pp.158–160.

29. *Rolling Stone,* September 27, 1973. Flippo referred to three of Texas's biggest news stories of the early 1970s: the Sharpstown Scandal, a complicated stock fraud case that ended the political careers of Texas House Speaker Gus Mutscher, Lieutenant Governor Ben Barnes, and Governor Preston Smith; the August 1, 1973, forced closure of a longtime La Grange brothel called the Chicken Ranch, a move instigated by Governor Dolph Briscoe and Attorney General John Hill; and serial killer Dean Corll (1939–1973), who along with David Brooks and Elmer Wayne Henley was believed complicit in the homosexual murders of twenty-seven boys in Houston. Corll's crimes came to light after Henley shot and killed him on August 8, 1973. The most complete overview of Sharpstown is found in Sam Kinch Jr. and Ben Proctor, *Texas Under a Cloud: Story of the Texas Stock Fraud Scandal* (Austin: Jenkins Publishing Company, 1973). The best overview of the Chicken Ranch saga is Jan Hutson,

The Chicken Ranch: The True Story of the Best Little Whorehouse in Texas
(San Jose, Cl.: Authors Choice Press, 1980). For more on Corll, see Jack Olsen,
The Man with the Candy: The Story of the Houston Mass Murders (New York:
Simon and Schuster, 1974).

30. "Clint Peoples Investigation," DPS Case Files, Texas Ranger Service 10–22,
     1998/097-II, Texas State Archives, containing "Investigative Assignment re
     Donald 'Red' Barry," Criminal Law Enforcement Chief J. M. Ray to Colonel
     Wilson E. Speir, November 21, 1973; Day, Captain Clint Peoples, Texas Ranger,
     p. 162.

31. Allee v. Medrano, 416 U.S. 802 (1974); Samora, Bernal, and Pena, Gunpowder
     Justice, pp. 155–156.

32. Wilson McKinney, Fred Carrasco: The Heroin Merchant (Austin: Heidelberg
     Publishers, 1975), pp. 236–237.

33. Proctor, Just One Riot, pp. 102–140.

34. Proctor, Just One Riot, p. 135; William T. Harper, Eleven Days in Hell: The
     1974 Carrasco Prison Siege at Huntsville, Texas (Denton: University of North
     Texas Press, 2004), pp. 288–289.

35. Harper, Eleven Days in Hell, pp. 288–291; Dallas Times-Herald, August 5,
     1974.

36. First convicted of capital murder in 1975, Cuevas after three trials was executed
     by lethal injection on May 23, 1991. Based on the Ranger investigation, trusty
     Lawrence James Hall was convicted in 1984 of smuggling into prison the
     weapons Carrasco used. Already in for life, Hall received another life sentence.
     He died in prison of natural causes on April 6, 1993. Harper, Eleven Days in
     Hell, pp. 298–300.

37. Huntsville Item, August 4, 1974. One of the hostages, Aline House, wrote
     of her experiences in The Carrasco Tragedy: Eleven Days of Terror in the
     Huntsville Prison (Waco, Tex.: Texian Press, 1976).

38. Clark, The Fall of the Duke of Duval, passim.

39. Dudley Lynch, The Duke of Duval: The Life & Times of George B. Parr (Waco,
     Tex.: Texian Press, 1976) p. 133.

40. Clark, The Fall of the Duke of Duval, pp. 323–324.

41. Author's interview with Ray Martinez, September 23, 2003, Kerrville, Texas.

42. Clark, The Fall of the Duke of Duval, p. 327.

43. "Two Men and One Ranger," Austin American-Statesman, June 16, 1971.

44. Texas Department of Public Safety, Texas Department of Public Safety Biennial
     Report 1976–1977, p. 9.

45. "Hall to Honor Rangers," Austin American-Statesman, February 1, 1976.

46. "Rootin' Tootin' Ranger Days Recalled at Hall of Fame Dedication in Waco,"
     Austin American-Statesman, February 8, 1976.

47. "Arrest of Texas Ranger Bob Elder of Company A," John M. Wood, Captain,
     Texas Rangers, Company D, to W. D. Wilson, Senior Ranger Captain, September

1, 1976, copy in author's collection; Nicholas C. Chriss, Los Angeles *Times*, "Racial Slurs Cost Texas Ranger Job," Austin *American-Statesman*, October 3, 1976; Stan Redding, "The Technicality is Overlooked As a 'Ranger's Ranger' Is Buried," Houston *Chronicle*, November 4, 1976.

48. "Jury Convicts Hayes of Aggravated Assault," Dallas *Morning News*, July 9, 1976. A San Angelo jury on July 8, 1976, convicted former Castroville city marshal Frank Hayes of aggravated assault in the September 14, 1975, shotgun killing of Richard Morales, a man Hayes and a Medina County sheriff's deputy had arrested on a theft warrant. Hayes and the deputy took the prisoner alone to a remote area of Medina County where the city marshal then told the deputy to leave. No one saw Morales again in the county. After Rangers began an investigation into the case, Morales's body was found in a shallow grave near Carthage in East Texas, four hundred miles from Castroville.

49. Saralee Tiede, " 'New' Texas Rangers Gain Prestige, Support," Dallas *Times-Herald*, October 17, 1977.

50. Joe Pouncy and Kathleen Hast, "Two Charged in Ranger's Murder," Dallas *Morning News*, February 22, 1978; "Slain Ranger Now Part of Law Enforcement Legend," Dallas *Morning News*, February 22, 1978; "Texas Ranger Killed in Narcotics Raid," *DPS Chaparral* 20, no. 4 (April 1978): pp. 1, 4–5; Gary Cartwright, "The Death of a Ranger," *Texas Monthly*, August 1978, pp. 99–105, 165–177. Gregory Ott, sentenced to life in prison for killing the Ranger, won parole from the Texas Department of Criminal Justice on May 25, 2004, after twenty-six years and three months behind bars. Pam Easton, Associated Press, "Man Who Killed Ranger Out of Jail After 26 Years," Austin *American-Statesman*, May 26, 2004.

51. "DPS Internal Affairs Section Formed," *DPS Chaparral*, October 1978.

52. Utley, *Lone Star Lawmen*, pp. 278–280, citing "Summary of Ranger Participation in Judge John Wood Murder Case," Senior Captain W. D. Wilson to Colonel James B. Adams, April 13, 1982. The best overview of the case is Gary Cartwright's *Dirty Dealing: Drug Smuggling on the Mexican Border and the Assassination of a Federal Judge, An American Parable* (New York: Atheneum, 1984). Later developments in the case are covered in "Joseph Chagra, 50, Lawyer Linked to Assassination, Dies," New York *Times*, December 15, 1996, El Paso *Times*, July 25, 2008, December 31, 2003, and "Jimmy Chagra, implicated in conspiracy to kill federal judge in San Antonio, dead at 63," Associated Press, July 26, 2008; and "Woody Harrelson's dad dies in prison," Associated Press, March 21, 2007.

53. Nancy Baker Jones and Ruthe Winegarten, *Capitol Women: Texas Female Legislators, 1923–1999* (Austin: University of Texas Press, 2000), p. 192.

54. Robert Heard, *The Miracle of the Killer Bees: 12 Senators Who Changed Texas Politics* (Austin: Honey Hill Publishing Company, 1981), pp. 13, 27, 36–37, 52–56.

55. Clay Robison, " 'Killer Bees' Say Democrats Did 'the Right Thing,' " Houston *Chronicle*, May 13, 2003; recollection of George Strong, www.political.com/analysis-arc/0246.html, accessed September 26, 2003; Carolyn Barta, *Bill Clements: Texian to his Toenails* (Austin: Eakin Press, 1996), p. 226.

56. Gooding and Nieman, *Ed Gooding*, p. 253.

12. "RANGER SPEED"

1. Dendy's son, thirty-four-year-old DPS narcotics investigator Kirby Wayne Dendy, gained promotion to Texas Ranger on May 1, 1987. The younger Dendy was assigned to Company B and stationed in Fort Worth, while his father was a member of Waco-based Company F. Kirby Dendy promoted to lieutenant on August 1, 1992, and transferred to Midland. A little more than three years later, he made captain and went to Waco. Dendy's promotion to the Rangers marked the fourth time in modern Ranger history that a son had followed his father into the Rangers, another tradition that would continue. As of 2008, the father-son Ranger list contained six pairs: Hardy B. and L. H. Purvis, A. Y. and A. Y. Allee Jr., Bennie and Glenn Krueger, Buster and Jeff Collins, Jack and Kyle Dean, and Bob and Randy Prince. The elder Hardy, Allee, Dean, and Prince all retired as captains. "Information for the News Media," Texas Department of Public Safety, May 18, 1987; "21st Century Shining Star: Captain Kirby Dendy Company F, Waco," *Texas Ranger Dispatch Magazine*, issue 10 (Spring 2003).

2. David Lindsey and Tupper Hull, "Kidnapped Girl Rescued in Shoot-out: Five Suspects Arrested After 100-mph Chase," Dallas *Times-Herald*, January 14, 1985; David Lindsey, "Everyday Hero: Ranger Dodges Bullets to Rescue Teen," Dallas *Times-Herald*, January 14, 1985; Karen Potter and Cindy Rugeley, "Alvarado Girl Freed After Fight," Fort Worth *Star-Telegram*, January 14, 1985; Preston Lerner, "Gunsmoke Obscures Story of Rescue," Fort Worth *Star-Telegram*, January 16, 1985; author's interview with Bob Mitchell, Waco, Texas, March 28, 2003. Though five persons were charged in the kidnapping, prosecutors said their leader was James Wesley Foote, thirty-four, who had addresses in both Arlington and Alvarado. Twenty-seven-year-old Michael Lynn Mills of Dallas was described as Foote's prime accomplice. Both men received life sentences in 249th State District Court for aggravated kidnapping on March 28, 1985. But Foote soon caused trouble again. On July 4, 1985, having been transferred from prison back to Johnson County for questioning in connection with another case, Foote escaped during an outside exercise period. Ranger Eddie Almond assisted in his recapture seven days later. Cindy Rugeley, "2 Kidnappers in McNeil Case Get Life Terms," Fort Worth *Star-Telegram*, March 29, 1985; *Texas Lawman*, August 1985: p. 33.

3. Mike Cochran, Associated Press, "Texas Rangers Gallop into '80s," Fort Worth *Star-Telegram*, June 16, 1985.

4. Author's interview with Mitchell.

5. Carolyn Barta, *Bill Clements: Texian to His Toenails* (Austin: Eakin Press, 1996), p. 263.

6. "1 Career, 1 Ranger," Dallas *Morning News*, January 13, 1985. Internal Ranger folklore has it that Wilson, knowing his lung cancer would kill him sooner or later, entrusted one of his captains with a whiskey bottle Wilson had partially filled with his urine. Should he should die before Peoples, Wilson requested, please pour the contents of the bottle on his former boss's grave after Peoples's death. The tale further holds that the captain, though respectfully allowing for some time to pass after Peoples's June 22, 1992, death in a traffic crash, eventually complied with Wilson's request.

7. Terry Donahue, "Yankee Wears Ranger Badge," San Antonio *Express-News*, January 15, 1984; Gordon Dillow, "The Lone Ranger: There's Only One Texas Ranger Who Isn't from Texas. And Would You Believe He's a Cop from New York?" *Philip Morris Magazine*, July–August 1985, pp. 10–13. While Steele got media attention as a Yankee Texas Ranger, he was not the first modern Ranger to come to the force from an out-of-state law enforcement agency. That distinction belonged to Al Mitchell, a longtime New Mexico State Police investigator then assigned to Hobbs, New Mexico, drafted by Company E captain Jim Riddell in 1970. Mitchell worked as a DPS narcotics agent in Lubbock until a Ranger slot opened in Midland. He served as a Ranger for eight years, spending much of his time working oil-field crime. Author's interview with Al Mitchell, Pecos, Texas, September 5–6, 2008.

8. Gordon Dillow, "Modern Texas Rangers Feel Weight of Tradition," San Antonio *Light*, June 21, 1981. Earlier that year, the Dallas *Morning News* published a four-part series on the Rangers by staff writers Bill Deener and Earl Golz. Senior Captain Wilson's quote about horses was in the first installment, "Rangers' Legend Left in a Cloud of Dust," published January 25, 1981.

9. Dillow, "Modern Texas Rangers Feel Weight of Tradition."

10. Henry Tatum, "Ranger's New Motto: Have Gun, Will Travel," Dallas *Morning News*, August 15, 1980.

11. Dallas *Morning News*, September 21, 1981; Texas Department of Public Safety, *Annual Report 1981*, p. 14.

12. "Witnesses Find Ranger Hypnotic," San Antonio *Express*, July 29, 1983.

13. Lieutenant Harold Couch to Awards Committee, Nomination for Medal of Valor Award, Department of Public Safety Interoffice Memorandum, May 23, 1983; Maurice Beckham to James B. Adams, Awards Review Board Recommendation, July 1, 1983; Texas Department of Public Safety, *Texas Department of Public Safety 1984 Annual Report*, p. 12; http://www.texasranger.org/today/medalhonor.htm.

14. Mike Cox, *The Confessions of Henry Lee Lucas* (New York: Pocket Books, 1990), passim.

15. Author's interview with Bob Prince.

16. Cox, *The Confessions of Henry Lee Lucas*, pp. 185, 301.

17. *Courtesy Service Protection: The Texas Department of Public Safety's Sixtieth Anniversary*, pp. 72–73.

18. Cox, *The Confessions of Henry Lee Lucas*, pp. 231–232.

19. Texas Department of Public Safety, "Information for the Press," November 30, 1984; Rob Meckel, "Texas Rangers' Incoming Chief Outdoes Dream: Close Calls in 17 years with Legendary Lawmen," Houston *Post*, December 16, 1984. Born in Orange County in 1935, Block graduated from the DPS training academy in 1958 and worked as a Highway Patrol trooper in Humble and Beaumont before being promoted to Texas Ranger in 1967. His first station was Brownwood. In 1974 he made sergeant and was transferred to San Antonio. Seven years later he was named captain and moved to Austin as assistant senior captain.

20. Dallas *Times-Herald*, April 14, and April 15 1985.

21. Cox, *The Confessions of Henry Lee Lucas*, pp. 239–242.

22. Cox, *The Confessions of Henry Lee Lucas*, pp. 243–244.

23. Prince to Block, April 24, 1985, copy in author's collection.

24. Cox, *The Confessions of Henry Lee Lucas*, pp. 255–259. The Texas Department of Corrections became the Texas Department of Criminal Justice in 1989.

25. Mark Busby, *Larry McMurtry and the West: An Ambivalent Relationship* (Denton: University of North Texas Press, 1995), pp. 178–200; Clay Reynolds, ed., *Taking Stock: A Larry McMurtry Casebook* (Dallas: Southern Methodist University Press, 1989), pp. 327–334.

26. *Fifty Years for Texas: 50th Anniversary Celebration of the Department of Public Safety, Program, Menu, History, Active and Retired D.P.S. Employees.* Texas: Department of Public Safety, Austin, 1985.

27. Cochran, "Texas Rangers Gallop into '80s."

28. Bill Hendricks, "Overtime Ruling Forcing Rangers to Cut Services," San Antonio *Express-News*, August 27, 1985; The Oyez Project, *Garcia v. San Antonio Metropolitan Transit Authority*, 469 U.S. 528 (1985), available at http://www.oyez.org/oyez/resource/case/133, accessed February 21, 2004.

29. Lt. H. D. Cleckler Jr. to James B. Adams, Director, December 9, 1985, copy of memorandum in author's collection.

30. "Lucas Report Questions Confessions," *The Mattox Administration 1983–1990: Texas Attorney General: The People's Lawyer*, Austin, 1990, p. 43.

31. Cox, *The Confessions of Henry Lee Lucas*, p. 300.

32. "HBG: Rangers, CAF Can Hold Any Attack," San Antonio *Express-News*, March 14, 1986.

33. Released in 1987, the 104-minute film received moderately favorable reviews. "This over-the-top, ultra-macho modern Western," one reviewer wrote, "looks heavily influenced by Peckinpah's 'The Wild Bunch,' and doesn't rise very much above its genre, despite a very hard-bitten hero and a malevolently attractive villain." Nolte, with coaching from Ranger Joaquin Jackson, played Ranger Jack Benteen. His chief antagonist, Cash Bailey, was played by Powers Boothe. Rip

Torn was cast as the local sheriff and Ranger Benteen's friend. Benteen's more intimate friend, Sarita Cisneros, was portrayed by Maria Conchita Alonso. http://www.allwatchers.com/topics/info_17191.asp. *TV Guide* gave the film three out of five stars, calling it "worthy of watching." http://www.txguide.com/movies/database/showmovie.asp?MI=16149. Laredo-based Ranger Doyle Holdridge met with colleague Jackson and Nolte in Uvalde to further add to the actor's sense of what real Rangers were like.

34. Patti Muck, "Counties in a Huff over Rangers' Birthplace," Houston *Chronicle*, April 13, 1986.

35. "Lone Ranger Is Riding High, Pistols in Hand," Houston *Chronicle*, January 15, 1987; John Makeig, "Pawned .45s Hotter'n a Pistol: You Don't Swipe Guns off the Ol' Lone Ranger, Star Says," Houston *Chronicle*, April 28, 1987; John Makeig, "Lone Ranger Thief Gets Cleanup Duty," Houston *Chronicle*, September 7, 1988. A jury sentenced Edward Louis Young III of Missouri City, a man with no prior convictions, to ten years' probation after finding him guilty of stealing Moore's pistols. In pronouncing sentence, as a condition of probation, state district judge Ted Poe assessed Young one month in the county jail and a $5,000 fine plus $500 in restitution to the man who had purchased the guns. The judge also required that Young perform six hundred hours of community service by shoveling manure from the Houston Police Department's Mounted Patrol stables.

36. Texas Department of Public Safety, Report of Investigation, CAPITAL MURDER-F-87-015.

37. "'Then Here's to the Texas Ranger . . .' Eulogy for Texas Ranger Stanley Keith Guffey Nov. 28, 1948–Jan. 22, 1987. Delivered by Col. James B. Adams Director Texas Department of Public Safety and Chief of the Texas Rangers. Brady, Texas Jan. 26, 1987" (Austin: Texas Department of Public Safety, 1987). The Public Safety Commission later presented Aycock a Medal of Valor for his role in the case, also posthumously awarding the medal to Guffey.

38. *Courtesy Service Protection: The Texas Department of Public Safety's Sixtieth Anniversary*, pp. 75–76; "State Legislator Calls for Program to Help Black Lawmen Advance," Dallas *Morning News*, July 18, 1987.

39. Only the State Cemetery in Austin has more Ranger graves than this little-known rural cemetery, which some historians believe could contain as many as twelve additional Ranger graves. Among the more notable Rangers buried there, in addition to Sowell (1847–1921), are Neal Coldwell (1844–1925), who served in the Frontier Battalion from 1874 to 1883 as both captain and quartermaster, and Nelson Orcelus Reynolds (1846–1922), a Ranger from 1874 to 1879 noted for settling feuds and protecting outlaw John Wesley Hardin following his arrest and return to Texas. Speech by Senior Captain H. R. Block, August 22, 1987, copy in author's collection; Mike Bowlin, "Marker Ceremony to Honor Rangers," Kerrville *Daily Times*, August 21, 1987; Gary Martin, "Texas Rangers

Honor 32 Dead During Graveside Celebration," San Antonio *Express-News*, August 23, 1987. On October 23, 1999, the Former Texas Rangers Association held another memorial service at the cemetery, having placed at each grave a metal cross with a Ranger star in its center.

40. Lynn Ashby, "Even a Business Card Packs a Punch," Houston *Post*, March 10, 1989.

41. *Courtesy Service Protection: The Texas Department of Public Safety's Sixtieth Anniversary*, pp. 77–78; "Black Lawman to Join Texas Rangers," Associated Press, July 30, 1988.

42. Vernon M. Stehling to Leo E. Gossett, July 17, 1987.

43. Associated Press, "Black Lawman to Join Texas Rangers," July 30, 1988.

44. A. Phillips Brooks, "Ranger Candidate Perseveres, Dreams," Austin *American-Statesman*, January 16, 1988.

45. Peggy Fikac, Associated Press, "First Black Texas Ranger Wants Out of the Limelight," Houston *Chronicle*, December 11, 1988.

46. Production of the $20 million adaptation of McMurtry's novel began east of Austin on March 17, 1988, and concluded in New Mexico July 2 that year. A month after its airing, the advertising revenue generated by the series was estimated at $30 million. A "prequel" already was being discussed. When it aired, the miniseries did not delight every viewer. Retired Ranger Lewis Rigler said, "I first became acquainted with the Texas Rangers in 1921. Through the years I have known very well Tom Hickman, Manny Gault, Frank Hamer, Jay Banks, Alfred Allee, M. T. (Lone Wolf) Gonzaullas, Clint Peoples . . . and Johnny Klevenhagen. None of those mentioned would be proud to claim *Lonesome Dove*. . . . I never heard of a Ranger captain paying a prostitute for her favors." Ed Bark, "The Miniseries Writes a New Page in TV excellence," Dallas *Morning News*, February 5, 1989; Kent Biffle, " 'Dove' Still Ruffling a Lot of Feathers," Dallas *Morning News*, February 19, 1989; Bill Carter, "The Bucks Keep Rolling In for 'Lonesome Dove,' " Dallas *Morning News*, March 7, 1989; Allan C. Kimball, "There's Plenty of Parallels Between 'Dove' and 'Wind,' " Houston *Post*, February 4, 1989; Art Chapman, " 'Lonesome Dove': The Revered Novel Comes to TV Tonight and a Previewing Shows That It Surpasses All Expectations," Fort Worth *Star-Telegram*, February 5, 1989; Louis B. Parks, "Home on the Range with Lonesome Dove," Houston *Chronicle*, February 7, 1989.

47. Cox, *The Confessions of Henry Lee Lucas*, p. 298.

48. Kevin Merida, "Bush Talks Texas During Remarks in State Capitol," Dallas *Morning News*, April 28, 1989.

13. "Last Bastion of the Good-Old-Boy System . . ."

1. "Bush Never Learned Maxim of Texas Rangers," San Antonio *Express-News*, November 4, 1990.

2. Texas Government Code, Section 411.021. Composition. Amended by Acts 1993, 73rd Legislature; Texas Department of Public Safety, *Texas Department of Public Safety Annual Report, 1992,* p. 11.

3. "Texas Department of Public Safety Information for the News Media," July 1, 1992; Mike Cochran, Associated Press, "Former Ranger Says Chief Created Schism in Agency," Dallas *Morning News,* December 4, 1995. Cochran wrote: "Capt. Cook created ill feelings throughout the DPS for a clever political maneuver that moved the Rangers from under the supervisory wing of Criminal Law Enforcement. By legislative mandate, the agency became a fourth major division of the DPS, headed by Capt. Cook."

4. Mike Cochran, Associated Press, "Top Ranger Takes Aim at Detractors," San Antonio *Express-News,* August 13, 1995.

5. Christy Hoppe, "'A Wall of Brotherhood,'" Dallas *Morning News,* June 19, 1995; Robert Draper, "The Twilight of the Texas Rangers: A Proud, Hidebound Institution Confronts a World of High-Tech Law Enforcement and Political Correctness," *Texas Monthly,* February 1994, pp. 111–112.

6. Dallas *Morning News,* October 22, 1992.

7. Hoppe, "'A Wall of Brotherhood.'" The DPS Internal Affairs report into Steadman's treatment as a Ranger quoted Madiera: "We needed to get it done [recruit women and minorities], or we would have minorities forced upon us that we didn't want, so we needed to get the people we wanted. Explicitly, I was told we need to find females."

8. "DNA Basics," Texas Department of Public Safety Public Information Office, April 2003; "CODIS (Combined DNA Index System)," Texas Department of Public Safety Public Information Office, April 2003. The DPS Crime Lab began accepting DNA samples on January 1, 1994, and made its first DNA match to a previously unknown suspect in August 1998. By September 30, 2002, with more than 133,500 profiled DNA samples in its CODIS database, the department's crime lab had matched submitted DNA samples to 968 offenders in its database. An additional fifty offender profiles had been matched to the national CODIS database. *Annual Report, 1993, Texas Department of Public Safety,* p. 41.

9. Mike Cox, *Stand-Off in Texas: "Just Call Me a Spokesman for DPS . . ."* (Austin: Eakin Press, 1998), pp. 48–70; author's interview with Bob Prince, September 22, 2008. A UT graduate student, Jody Ginn of Austin, Texas, finally brought to light that Koresh had offered to surrender to the Rangers in a research paper titled "Texas Rangers Historical Footage Research," prepared for Professor Caroline Frick, Ph.D., University of Texas at Austin, Summer 2008. Ginn wrote: "It has long been rumored in Texas law enforcement circles that David Koresh had agreed to . . . surrender to the Texas Rangers and that the FBI refused [to] cooperative with that plan. . . . However, www.footage.net documents a segment available from CNN Image Source of the 1995 [congressional] hearings during which Koresh's attorney, Dick DeGuerin, testified in

detail to his negotiations with the then-Chief of the Rangers (Maurice Cook), to Koresh's agreement to the plan, and to the FBI's unwillingness to go along with it." Additional insight into the Branch-Davidian siege can be found in Stuart A. Wright, editor, *Armageddon in Waco: Critical Perspectives on the Branch Davidian Conflict*, Chicago: University of Chicago Press, 1995; Sergeant George L. Turner to Senior Captain Bruce Casteel, "Branch Davidian Evidence," June 30, 1999; Sergeant Joey D. Gordon to Casteel, "Review of Evidence Related to the Branch Davidian Investigation," September 10, 1999 and Gordon to Casteel, "Branch Davidian Report #2," February 16, 2000, Texas Department of Public Safety; and John C. Danforth, *Final Report to the Deputy Attorney General concerning the 1993 Confrontation at the Mt. Carmel Complex, Waco, Texas*, Washington, D.C., November 8, 2000.

10. "Fort Worth Rumored to Be Site of CBS Prime-time Drama," Austin *American-Statesman*, June 27, 1992; "Chuck Norris Punches Up a CBS Action Show," *USA Today*, September 2, 1992; Lucius Lomax, "They Don't Make 'Rangers' like Walker Anymore: The Last Texas Ranger," Austin *Chronicle*, October 26, 2001; <http://www.sonypictures.com/tv/shows/walker/about.html.

11. Stuart Eskenazl, "Women Officers Prove They're Right as Rangers," Austin *American-Statesman*, August 4, 1993. Both women got their silver stars on August 3, 1993, during promotional ceremonies at the DPS training academy auditorium. Also promoted to the Rangers was Richard Lindsey Shing, a former Highway Patrol sergeant who was the first Asian-American Ranger.

12. Jack Cowan, "Rangers Casualties in the Gender War," n.p., June 27, 1993.

13. Eskenazl, "Women Officers Prove They're Right as Rangers." Earlier that year, the seventy-third legislature amended the Texas Government Code, Section 411.0221, Qualifications, adding this subsection: "(b) The Texas Rangers is an equal employment opportunity employer; all personnel decisions shall be made without regard to race, color, sex, national origin, or religion."

14. Draper, "The Myth of the Texas Rangers," pp. 76–82, 107–108, 110, 112–113, 118.

15. Donnis Baggett, "Texas Still Needs Its Rangers," Dallas *Morning News*, January 30, 1994.

16. Associated Press, "State Trooper Says Ex-Ranger in Tears After Retreat," San Antonio *Express-News*, July 6, 1995, p. 8B.

17. "Ex-Ranger Says Colleagues Belittled Her as Too Ladylike," San Antonio *Express-News*, May 27, 1995; Hoppe, "'A Wall of Brotherhood.'"

18. Vivienne Heines, "A Ranger in Spirit, Not Name: Female Officer Says No to Legendary Unit," Corpus Christi *Caller-Times*, July 24, 1994. Senior Captain Cook later said he recalled only three other persons ever turning down a chance to be a Ranger.

19. Dallas *Morning News*, July 13, 1995.

20. "Ex-Ranger Says Colleagues Belittled Her as Too Ladylike."

21. Christy Hoppe, "2 Rangers Suspended in '94 Case: Racial, Sexual Slurs Against Officer Alleged," Dallas *Morning News,* July 13, 1995; Chip Brown, Associated Press, "Two Rangers Disciplined Last Year for Slurs," Austin *American-Statesman,* July 13, 1995.

22. "Second Woman Hits Rangers with Civil Rights Complaint," San Antonio *Express-News,* May 24, 1995.

23. Chip Brown, "Commissioner Defends Rangers on Harassment," Austin *American-Statesman,* May 24, 1995.

24. "Texas Rangers Face Probe into '94 Outing," Austin *American-Statesman,* July 11, 1995.

25. "Ex-Ranger Says Colleagues Belittled Her as Too Ladylike."

26. Associated Press, June 4, 1995.

27. Chip Brown, Associated Press, "Richards Says Rangers, Women Must Come to an Understanding," Austin *American-Statesman,* June 15, 1995.

28. Hoppe, "'A Wall of Brotherhood.'"

29. Stefanie Scott, "Woman Found 'Incompatible' as Ranger," San Antonio *Express-News,* July 12, 1995.

30. Janet Wilson, "Rangers Show That Boys Will Still Be Boys," Austin *American-Statesman,* July 12, 1995.

31. Christy, "2 Rangers Suspended in '94 case."

32. Associated Press, "Records Show 2 Rangers Disciplined in Slurs Probe," San Antonio *Express-News,* July 13, 1995.

33. Brown, "Two Rangers Disciplined Last Year for Slurs."

34. "Bush Defends Rangers Amid Allegations of Discrimination," Austin *American-Statesman,* July 14, 1995.

35. "Grand Jury Indicts Texas Ranger After Gun Pulled on Trooper," San Antonio *Express-News,* July 15, 1995. The felony aggravated assault charge against Sergeant Hilton later was reduced to deadly conduct, a misdemeanor. Tried before visiting Harris County Court-at-Law Judge Loretta Muldrow in September 1997, the Ranger was acquitted. Hilton was re-instated to duty in October 1997 and awarded back pay. Hilton later transferred to Company F, and as of November 2008 was stationed in Temple. "Suspended Ranger Cleared of Wrongdoing," Associated Press, December 15, 1997.

36. Clay Robison, "New Attitude Needed by Proud Rangers," Houston *Chronicle,* July 16, 1995.

37. Dave McNeely, "Honor in Initiation Rites Appears Hollow at Best," Austin *American-Statesman,* July 16, 1995.

38. *Cheryl Steadman; et al. v. the Texas Rangers; et al.,* No. 97-20862, Appeals from the United States District Court for the Southern District of Texas.

39. Cochran, "Former Ranger Says Chief Created Schism in Agency."

40. "Texas Rangers Chief to Retire at Age 52," Austin *American-Statesman,* February 8, 1996.

41. "Cook Got 'Ultimatum' to Retire, Sources Say," Houston *Chronicle*, February 9, 1996.

42. Associated Press, "Court Grants Summary Judgment for AP, Houston Chronicle in Libel Suit," May 12, 2000. The 1st District Court of Appeals in Houston granted summary judgment in favor of the defendants May 11, 2000, effectively ending Cook's quest for damages.

43. "Former Commander of the Texas Rangers Elected President of F.T.R.A.," *Former Texas Ranger Straight Talk*, Kerrville, Texas, August 2003, pp. 1, 5; Texas Department of Public Safety, *Texas Department of Public Safety Annual Report, 1996*, p. 9.

44. *Courtesy Service Protection: The Texas Department of Public Safety's Sixtieth Anniversary*, p. 83.

45. Texas Department of Public Safety, *Texas Department of Public Safety Annual Report, 1996*, pp. 9–10.

46. Cox, *Stand-Off in Texas*, passim.

47. Cox, *Stand-Off in Texas*, p. 247.

48. Mike Cox, "Texas Rangers: From Horses to Helicopters," *Texas Almanac 2000–2001* (Dallas: Belo Communications, 2001), pp. 23–28.

49. Associated Press, "Court Grants Summary Judgment for AP, Houston Chronicle in Libel Suit," May 12, 2000.

50. "Rafael Resendez-Ramirez," *Crime Bulletin*, Texas Department of Public Safety, June 18, 1999, pp. 1–2; "The Faces of a Fugitive," *Newsweek*, July 5, 1999, pp. 20–23; Valerie Kalfrin, "The Makings of a Suspected Killer: The 23-Year Criminal History of Rafael Resendez-Ramirez," http://www.apboline.com/serialkiller/ramirez/chronology.html, accessed July 14, 1999.

51. Polly Ross Hughes, "Rangers Dodge Bullet: Appellate Panel Rejects Free-Speech Case, but Famed Agency Still Facing Sex-Bias Suit," Houston *Chronicle*, July 8, 1998. Shepherd's attorney appealed to the United States Supreme Court, but on January 18, 2000, the high court, without comment, refused to reverse the Fifth Circuit. Laurie Asseo, Associated Press, "Would-be Texas Ranger Loses Supreme Court Appeal," January 18, 2000; *Cheryl Steadman; et al. v. the Texas Rangers; et al.*, No. 97-20862, Appeals from the United States District Court for the Southern District of Texas.

52. David Galloway, " 'Railway Killer' Suspect in Custody," Houston *Chronicle*, July 14, 1999; Bruce Tomaso, "Rail Killing Suspect Surrenders," Dallas *Morning News*, July 14, 1999; Lisa Sandberg and Jaime Castillo, "Resendez-Ramirez Gives Up," San Antonio *Express-News*, July 14, 1999; Michael Janofsky, "Fugitive Suspected of Committing at Least Eight Murders Is Arrested," New York *Times*, July 14, 1999. Being able to talk with people, either to establish and maintain a good working relationship with other law enforcement agencies and prosecutors, to glean information from witnesses during an investigation, or to gain a confession from a recalcitrant suspect is considered an essential Ranger

skill, something that often sets them apart from other officers. In his forth-coming (2009) memoir, *Working the Border*, retired Ranger Doyle Holdridge, who spent his entire Ranger career stationed at Laredo, wrote that he believed a Ranger's ability to successfully interview people is one of the key factors be-hind the force's modern reputation. Retired Ranger Morgan Miller, whose long-time duty station was Victoria, recalled hearing what one of his predecessors used to tell suspects before he started talking to them, long prior to the Miranda rights requirement. "Son," the Ranger would say, "I have found that the truth lies in one of two places in a man. It's either in his heart or his ass. If it's in your heart, I'll talk it out of you. If it's in your ass, I'll kick it out of you." Author's interview with Miller, November 1, 2007. A story that may be apocryphal con-cerns a defendant who was asked by his lawyer if the Ranger who had testified against him had beaten him to extract his confession. "No," the defendant said, "but he sure sweet-talked the hell out of me." In his memoir, Holdridge noted three other things that make a Ranger: training, paying attention to detail, and a strong work ethic. "I really don't know what it is that makes Rangers work the way they do," he wrote. "I have worked for years with other agencies and I have noticed that when they got tired, or it was the end of their shift, they would put the case on hold and go home. The Rangers that I knew never paid much attention to the clock."

53. DPS *Chaparral*, October 2000, p. 2. Lieutenant Michael Escalante, head of the DPS's Governor Protective Detail, earned a Director's Citation for his role in coordinating the department's handling of Bush's security during the presiden-tial nomination campaign. Also recognized was Sergeant Alan Trevino, the pro-tective team leader who assisted in the logistical work. Though the department's newsletter made no mention of the Ranger involvement, it noted that the lieu-tenant had "supervised the largest detail contingent in history."

54. "Cops Who Nailed Drifter Are Hailed," San Antonio *Express*, September 13, 1999.

55. Houston *Chronicle*, July 16, 1999.

56. "Settlement and Indemnity Agreement and Release . . . Between Cheryl Stead-man and the Texas Department of Public Safety and the Texas Rangers," January 20, 2000, and "Settlement and Indemnity Agreement and Release . . . Between Lisa Shepherd . . . ," January 21, 2000, in Cause Number H-05-5700 in the United States District Court for the Southern District of Texas, Houston Division. By 2003, the Rangers still had only two women, Sergeants Marrie Garcia and Christina Nix. By race, the 116 Rangers were 81 percent white, 12 percent His-panic, 4 percent black, and 2 percent Asian or American Indian. For a more de-tailed analysis, see Tony Plohetski, "Rangers: 94 White Men and 22 Others: 180 Years After Agency Was Formed, Diversity Eludes Force," Austin *American-Statesman*, March 30, 2003. As of March 2009, the Rangers included three women, Sergeants Melba L. Molina, Company G, Laredo; Laura Simmons,

Company B, Greenville; and Wende Wakeman, Company A, Conroe. Sergeants Garcia and Nix were retired.

14. Entering the Twenty-first Century

1. DPS *Chaparral* (March 2000), p. 1.
2. C. Bryson Hull, "Houston Jury Convicts Killer, Who Asks for Death Sentence," *Austin American-Statesman*, May 19, 2000.
3. "Keeping the Rangers at the Fort: Campaign to Build Headquarters Gets Start," Waco *Tribune-Herald*, March 27, 2000.
4. Senate Research Center, S.B. 1088, 77th Legislature (Regular Session), Bill Analysis, March 26, 2001.
5. "Texas Rangers Today," http://www.texasranger.org/today/unsolvedCrimes .htm; "Justice Delayed Is Justice Denied," Texas Ranger briefing paper presented to Senate Committee on Criminal Justice, Austin: 2000. Texas law enforcement agencies had reported 23,300 homicides since 1987, but only 71 percent had been cleared. That left 6,738 murders unsolved. "Since there is no statute of limitations on the offense of murder, the state has the moral and statutory obligation to pursue these [unsolved] cases to a successful resolution or until no other leads are viable," the report said. After organizing in 2001, by the end of 2002, the Ranger Unsolved Crimes Investigation Team had reopened forty-two old cases, one of them dating back to 1953. Three of the investigations led to arrests. Of those, two homicides were made through DNA evidence while the third case was solved when a ranger obtained a third-party confession. *Texas Department of Public Safety Annual Report 2002*, p. 20.
6. "Senior Ranger Captain Bruce Casteel Retires to Floresville," Floresville *Chronicle-Journal*, August 23, 2001.
7. Bill Hendricks, "S. A. Man Chosen to Lead Texas Rangers: Officer Started Fighting Crime as a Trooper in 1969," San Antonio *Express-News*, August 31, 2001.
8. "DPS Announces New Texas Rangers Assistant Chief," Information for the News Media, Texas Department of Public Safety Public Information Office, September 10, 2001. A 1975 graduate of the DPS Training Academy, Pearson had been a ranger since 1989. Initially stationed at Brenham, he moved to Company F in Waco after promoting to lieutenant in 1992. Four years later, he made captain and assumed command of Company A in Houston. Following the retirement of Havra, Colonel Davis named Pearson as Senior Ranger Captain on April 23, 2004. "DPS names new chief of the Texas Rangers," DPS Information for the News Media, April 23, 2004.
9. Former Texas Rangers Foundation Board Papers, author's collection. By July 1, 2003, the foundation had raised enough money to purchase fifteen acres of land on State Highway 173 in Kerrville, a location just across the road from the National Center for American Western Art, as the future site of the $6 million,

15,840 square foot Texas Rangers History and Education Center. The board also had a set of drawings and preliminary plans from San Antonio architect Chris Carson. To be placed outside the museum, the association envisioned a Ranger Ring of Honor, a stone wall surrounding a twenty-five-foot diameter stone star. Raymond, Jeff, "Texas Rangers to Build Educational Center," Kerrville *Daily Times*, July 3, 2003; "What Makes a Legend?" Former Texas Rangers Foundation, Kerrville: 2003, pp. 8–15. The Foundation staged its eighth annual gala in Kerrville on September 20, 2008 and planned a groundbreaking for the new facility in 2009.

10. Mary Elizabeth Davis, "Jack Hays the Texas Ranger: Local Citizens Dedicate Statue to County's Namesake," Wimberley *View*, November 24, 2001.

11. Z. T. Fulmore, *The History And Geography Of Texas As Told In County Names* (Austin: The Steck Company, 1935 reprint of 1915 edition), pp. 217–219. Of Texas's 254 counties, forty-nine are named in honor of a Ranger, though some of the men gained renown for other reasons as well. Seven of those forty-nine counties were named for Rangers who served with Captain Hays. Sloan Rodgers to author, December 29, 2003.

12. Davis, "Jack Hays the Texas Ranger: Local Citizens Dedicate Statue to County's Namesake."

13. Art Chapman and Peyton D. Woodson, "Meet the New Texas Rangers: A Breed Apart," Fort Worth *Star-Telegram*, October 27, 2002. The journalists interviewed rookie Ranger sergeant A. P. Davidson, who said, "I would rather be a Texas Ranger than the president of the United States. I couldn't want for any more. I really couldn't." The same year Davidson pinned on the *cinco peso* for the first time, to commemorate the Rangers' 180th birthday National Aeronautics and Space Administration astronaut Paul Lockhart took a silver Ranger badge with him on the space shuttle *Endeavor*'s June 5–June 19 mission.

14. "DPS Names New Chief of the Texas Rangers," Information for the News Media, Texas Department of Public Safety, April 23, 2004.

15. "DPS Announces New Texas Ranger Chief, Assistant Chief," Information for the News Media, Texas Department of Public Safety, September 12, 2005.

16. An army veteran who had served for six months as an Odom County sheriff's deputy and later spent four years as a detective for the Hereford Police Department, Burzynski graduated from the DPS training academy in 2000 as a Highway Patrol trooper. After four years at Dimmitt, on October 1, 2004, he was promoted to Ranger sergeant. His new station would be Fort Stockton, replacing a Ranger who had retired. By 2006, a year after Burzynski began his investigation into the TYC sexual abuse allegations, he achieved the Texas Commission on Law Enforcement Standards and Education's master peace officer certification marking completion of 4,000 hours of law enforcement training. Author's interview with Brian Burzynski, September 15, 2008. The Ranger was promoted to lieutenant in the latter part of 2008 and was transferred to Company C in Amarillo.

17. *Joint Select Committee on the Operation and Management of the Texas Youth Commission: Preliminary Report of Initial Findings and Recommendations*, 80th Texas Legislature (2007), p. 1.

18. Texas Department of Public Safety, *Texas Department of Public Safety Annual Report, 2007*, p. 26.

19. "Ranger Keeps Promise to Kids," Houston *Chronicle*, March 9, 2007; "Lawmakers Lambaste TYC Board for Failing to Act," Dallas *Morning News*, March 8, 2007.

20. Texas Department of Public Safety, *Texas Department of Public Safety Annual Report, 2007*, p. 28.

21. HCR 235, 80th Legislature, Texas Legislative Reference Library.

22. The criminal cases against the two former TYC employees accused of sexually abusing juveniles at the Pyote facility were expected to go to trial in 2009.

22. Texas Department of Public Safety, *Texas Department of Public Safety Annual Report, 2007*, pp. 26–32; *Agency Strategic Plan, Fiscal Years 2009–2013*, p. 84.

23. Texas Department of Public Safety, *Texas Department of Public Safety Annual Report 2007*, p. 22.

24. *Texas Ranger Dispatch* (Spring 2008), p. 21.

25. Author's interview with Ranger Sgt. Jess Malone, Aug. 6, 2008, Midland, Texas; e-mail, Barry Caver to author, July 22, 2008; "Eldorado Investigation: A Report from the Texas Department of Family and Protective Services," Austin: Texas Department of Family and Protective Services, December 22, 2008; "CPS final report: Most Children from FLDS Ranch were Abused or Neglected," Austin *American-Statesman*, December 24, 2008.

26. Austin *American-Statesman*, June 25, 2008; Clay Robinson, "Leadership Exodus Offers Opportunity to Rebuild DPS," Houston Chronicle, September 15, 2008; *DPS Chaparral*, September 2008, p. 1.

27. "DPS Receives Deloitte Management and Organizational Structure Study," Texas Department of Public Safety Information for the News Media, n.d. (October 28, 2008); "Texas Department of Public Safety Management and Organizational Structure Study," Austin: Deloitte Consulting, October 28, 2008; "Overhaul of DPS moves forward," Austin *American-Statesman*, November 15, 2008; "New Eye on Texas," *Texas Observer*, November 28, 2008.

28. "New Texas Ranger Chief Makes History," Texas Department of Public Safety Information for the News Media, December 18, 2008. Born in Sugar Land and raised in Fort Bend County, Leal joined the DPS as a Highway Patrol trooper in June 1984. He worked in Stafford and Rosenberg before making sergeant and transferring to San Antonio. In 1994 he was promoted to Ranger. Eight years later he made lieutenant and was assigned to Austin. In 2005, he was promoted to captain of Company A in Houston where he had remained until assuming overall command of the Rangers. Captain L. C. Wilson was named assistant Ranger chief on February 1, 2009.

29. "Feds Plan 'Surge' if Mexico Drug War Spills Over," Associated Press, January 10, 2008; "U.S. Rattled as Mexico Drug War Bleeds over Border," Reuters, March 1, 2009; "Texas Makes Emergency Plans in Case Violence Spills Over from Mexico," Fort Worth *Star-Telegram*, March 8, 2009; "Homeland Security Plans for Violence on U.S. Border," Associated Press, March 12, 2009; "Violent Spillover from Mexico is Focus of House Hearing," Cable News Network, March 12, 2009.

Epilogue: Burying the War Club

1. Author's interview with Joaquin Jackson, September 6, 2008, Pecos, Texas; author's interview with Shelton Smith, September 15, 2008. The Rangers did not defeat the Comanches single-handedly. As T. R. Fehrenbach in his *Comanches: The Destruction of a People* (New York: Alfred A. Knopf, 1974), and other authors have pointed out, it took a lot of help from the U.S. Army.

Bibliography

Government Documents

Adjutant General's Department of Texas. Annual and Biennial Reports, 1900–1934.

Barton, Thomas D. *State Ranger and Martial Law Activities of the National Guard of Texas, 1921 and 1922.* Austin: Von Boeckmann-Jones, 1923.

"Chronological Listing of Key Events in the History of the Railroad Commission of Texas (1866–1939)," http://www.rrc.state.tx.us/history.

Danforth John C., *Final Report to the Deputy Attorney General Concerning the 1993 Confrontation at the Mt. Carmel Complex, Waco, Texas*, Washington, D.C., November 8, 2000.

DPS Chaparral. Austin: Texas Department of Public Safety.

DPS News. Austin: Texas Department of Public Safety.

"Eldorado Investigation." Austin: Texas Department of Family and Protective Services. December 22, 2008.

Fifty Years For Texas: 50th Anniversary Celebration of the Department of Public Safety, Program, Menu, History, Active and Retired D.P.S. Employees. Austin: Texas Department of Public Safety, 1985.

General and Special Laws of the State of Texas. 44th Legislature, Regular Session, 1935.

Hearings Before the Committee on Invalid Pensions . . . on H.R. 7899 a Bill Extending the Provisions of Pension Laws Relating to Indian War Veterans to Members of Companies E and F, Frontier Battalion, Texas Rangers . . . Washington, D.C., 1940.

Joint Legislative Committee on Organization and Economy and Griffenhagen Associates. *The Government of the State of Texas.* Austin, 1933.

"Justice Delayed Is Justice Denied." Texas Ranger briefing paper presented to Senate Committee on Criminal Justice, Austin, 2000.

"Lucas Report Questions Confessions." *The Mattox Administration 1983–1990: Texas Attorney General: The People's Lawyer,* Austin, 1990.

Ranger Force Order Book. Texas Ranger Division, Texas Department of Public Safety.

Report and Recommendations of the Senate Committee Investigating Crime. 43rd Texas Legislature, 1933–1934. Austin: 1934.

Report on the Brownsville Affray. Message from the President . . . a Report from the Secretary of War, Together with Several Documents, Including a Letter of General Nettleton, and Memoranda as to Precedents for the Summary Discharge or Mustering Out Of Regiments or Companies. Senate Document 155, December 1906. Part II, Additional Testimony Relating to the Brownsville Affray. January 1907. Washington, D.C., 1907.

Robinson, James W. *The DPS Story: History of the Development of the Department of Public Safety in Texas.* Austin: Texas Department of Public Safety, 1974.

State Highway Department of Texas Seventh Biennial Report, September 1, 1928, to August 31, 1930. Austin, 1930.

Texas Department of Public Safety. Biennial and Annual Reports, 1935–2008.

———. *Management and Organizational Structure Study.* Austin: Deloitte Consulting, October 28, 2008.

———. Minutes of the Public Safety Commission, 1935–1942.

The Texas Department of Public Safety, Its Services and Organization: A Report . . . to the Texas Public Safety Commission As Adopted by the Commission Sept. 1, 1957. Austin: Texas Research League, 1957.

United States Commission on Civil Rights. *A Report of the Texas Advisory Committee to the United States Commission on Civil Rights.* Washington, D.C., February 1970.

United States District Court for the Southern District of Texas. *Cheryl Steadman; et al. v. the Texas Rangers; et al., No. 97–20862,* Appeals from the United States District Court for the Southern District of Texas.

[Wilson, Will.] *Biennial Report of Attorney General Will Wilson.* Austin, December 14, 1962.

Unpublished Material

Aldrich, Roy W. Papers. Archives of the Big Bend, Sul Ross State University, Alpine, Texas.

Boutwell, Jim. "Notes on Early DPS Aviation." N.d. (circa 1983). Copy in author's collection.

Favor, Bob. "My Rangering Days." 2004. Author's collection.

Goss, Robert G. Papers. Nita Stewart Haley Memorial Library, Midland, Texas.

Hamer, Harrison F. "Ancestors and Descendants of Franklin Augustus Hamer and Lou Emma Frances." 2000. Author's collection.

Hickman, Paul. "Life Story of Captain Tom R. Hickman." 1983. Author's collection.

Holdridge, Doyle. "Working the Border." 2008. Unpublished manuscript. Author's collection.

Madison, Virginia. Papers. Author's Collection.

Maguire, Jack. "Texas Ranger Personalities." N.d., unpublished notes from Jack Maguire Papers, author's collection.

Peoples, Clint. Papers. Dallas Public Library.

Rodriguez, Arturo. "The Tejano Ranger." Author's collection.

Smith, Zeno. Papers. Nita Stewart Haley Memorial Library, Midland, Texas.

Warren, Harry. "The Porvenir Massacre in Presidio County, Texas, on January 28, 1918." Harry Warren Papers. Archives of the Big Bend, Sul Ross State University, Alpine, Texas.

Wilke, L. A. Papers. Author's collection.

Wilson, Will. "Shutting Down 'Sin City,'" chapter one, Wilson Wilson Memoir, March 13, 2002 draft, edited by Betty Wilke Cox. Author's collection.

Books

Adams, Verdon R. *Tom White: The Life of a Lawman.* El Paso: Texas Western Press, 1972.

Albers, E. G., Jr. *The Life and Reflections of a Texas Ranger.* Waco, Tex.: Texian Press, 1998.

Allen, Ruth. *The Great Southwest Strike.* University of Texas Publications 4214. Austin: University of Texas Press, 1942.

Amberson, Mary Margaret, James A. McAllen, and Margaret H. McAllen. *I Would Rather Sleep in Texas: A History of the Lower Rio Grande Valley and the People of the Santa Anita Land Grant.* Austin: Texas State Historical Association, 2002.

Anderson, Ken. *Dan Moody: Crusader for Justice.* Georgetown, Tex.: Georgetown Press, 2008.

Arnold, Ann. *Gamblers and Gangsters: Fort Worth's Jacksboro Highway in the 1940s & 1950s.* Austin: Eakin Press, 1998.

Barta, Carolyn. *Bill Clements: Texian to His Toenails.* Austin: Eakin Press, 1996.

Baugh, Virgil E. *A Pair of Texas Rangers: Bill McDonald and John Hughes.* Washington, D.C.: The Westerners, 1970.

Belfiglio, Valentine J. *Honor, Pride, Duty: A History of the Texas State Guard.* Austin: Eakin Press, 1995.

Benton, Minnie King. *Boomtown: A Portrait of Burkburnett.* Quanah, Tex.: Nortex Offset Publications, 1972.

Blodgett, Dorothy, Terrell Blodgett, and David L. Scott. *The Land, the Law, and the Lord: The Life of Pat Neff*. Austin: Home Place Publishers, 2007.

Brandon, Jay. *Law and Liberty: A History of the Legal Profession in San Antonio*. Dallas: Taylor Publishing Company, 1996.

Bridge, Joe H., Jr. *The Life and Times of Joe H. Bridge, Texas Ranger 1936–1956*. Lampasas, Tex.: Privately published, 2005.

Briscoe, Dolph, as told to Don Carleton. *Dolph Briscoe: My Life in Texas Ranching and Politics*. Austin: Center for American History, University of Texas at Austin, 2008.

Brooks, Tim, and Earle Marsh. *The Complete Directory to Prime Time Network TV Shows, 1946–Present*. New York: Ballantine Books, 1985.

Brown, Norman D. *Hood, Bonnet, and Little Brown Jug: Texas Politics, 1921–1928*. College Station: Texas A&M University Press, 1984.

Busby, Mark. *Larry McMurtry and the West: An Ambivalent Relationship*. Denton: University of North Texas Press, 1995.

Calderon, Roberto R. *Mexican Coal Mining Labor in Texas and Coahuila, 1880–1930*. College Station: Texas A&M University Press, 2000.

Calvert, Robert A., and Arnoldo De Leon. *The History of Texas*. Arlington Heights, Ill.: Harland Davidson, 1990.

Cano, Tony, and Ann Sochat. *Bandido: The True Story of Chico Cano, the Last Western Bandit*. Canutillo, Tex.: Reata Publishing, 1997.

Carleton, Don E. *Red Scare*. Austin: Texas Monthly Press, 1985.

Cartwright, Gary. *Galveston: A History of the Island*. New York: Atheneum, 1991.

Castleman, Harvey N. *The Texas Rangers, the Story of an Organization That Is Unique, like Nothing Else in America*. Girard, Kans.: Haldeman-Julius Publications, 1944.

Chadwick, Joseph. *The Texas Rangers: A Concise History of the Most Colorful Law Enforcement Group in the Frontier West*. New York: Monarch Books, 1963.

Chalfant, Frank E. *Galveston: Island of Chance*. Houston: Treasures of Nostalgia, 1997.

Clark, John E. *The Fall of the Duke of Duval: A Prosecutor's Journal*. Austin: Eakin Press, 1995.

Coerver, Don M., and Linda B. Hall. *Texas and the Mexican Revolution: A Study in State and National Border Policy, 1910–1920*. San Antonio: Trinity University Press, 1984.

Courtesy Service Protection: The Texas Department of Public Safety's Sixtieth Anniversary. Historical text by Dr. Mitchel Roth, edited by Mike Cox, Laureen Chernow, and Sherri Deatherage Green. Dallas: Taylor Publishing Company, 1995.

Cox, Mike. *The Confessions of Henry Lee Lucas*. New York: Pocket Books, 1990.

———. *Stand-Off in Texas: "Just Call Me a Spokesman for DPS . . . "* Austin: Eakin Press, 1998.

———. *The Texas Rangers: Wearing the Cinco Peso, 1831–1900*. New York: Forge, 2008.

———. *Texas Ranger Tales: Stories That Need Telling*. Plano: Republic of Texas Press, 1997.

———. *Texas Ranger Tales II*. Plano: Republic of Texas Press, 1999.

Cude, Elton. *The Free and Wild Dukedom of Bexar*. San Antonio: Munguia Printers, 1978.

Davis, John L. *The Texas Rangers: Images and Incidents*. San Antonio: University of Texas Institute of Texan Cultures, 1991.

Day, James M. *Captain Clint Peoples, Texas Ranger: Fifty Years a Lawman*. Waco, Tex.: Texian Press, 1980.

———. "One Man's Dream: Fort Fisher and the Texas Ranger Hall of Fame." Waco, Tex.: Texian Press, 1976.

De Leon, Arnoldo. *They Called Them Greasers*. Austin: University of Texas Press, 1983.

Desmond, H. A. *Texas Knights of the Hill Country: Story of the Texas Rangers*. Kerrville, Tex.: Herring Printing, 1976.

Dobbs, Ricky F. *Yellow Dogs and Republicans: Allan Shivers and Texas Two-Party Politics*. College Station: Texas A&M University Press, 2005.

Dobie, J. Frank. *The Flavor of Texas*. Dallas: Dealey and Lowe, 1936.

Dorman, Michael. *King of the Courtroom: Percy Foreman for the Defense*. New York: Dell Books, 1969.

Douglas, C. L. *The Gentlemen in the White Hats: Dramatic Episodes in the History of the Texas Rangers*. Dallas: South-West Press, 1934.

Draper, W. R. and Mabel. *The Blood-Soaked Career of Bonnie Parker: How Bandit Clyde Barrow and His Cigar-Smoking Moll Fought It Out with the Law*. Girard, Kans.: Haldeman-Julius Publications, 1946.

Dykes, Jeff. *Rangers All: A Catalog and Check List*. College Park, Md.: Jeff Dykes Western Books, 1968.

DuCoin, Candice. *Lawmen on the Texas Frontier: Rangers and Sheriffs*. Round Rock, Tex.: Riata Books, 2007.

Elliott, Glenn, with Robert Nieman. *Glenn Elliott: A Ranger's Ranger*. Waco, Tex.: Texian Press, 1999.

———. *Glenn Elliott: Still a Ranger's Ranger*. Longview, Tex.: Ranger Publishing, 2002.

Farrington, Clifford. *Biracial Unions on Galveston's Waterfront, 1865–1925*. Austin: Texas State Historical Association, 2007.

Fortune, Jan I. *Fugitives: The Story of Clyde Barrow and Bonnie Parker*. Dallas: The Ranger Press, 1934.

Friends of the Moody Texas Ranger Library. *The Texas Ranger Annual*. 3 vols. Waco, 1982–1984.

Furman, Necah Stewart. *Walter Prescott Webb: His Life and Impact*. Albuquerque: University of New Mexico Press, 1976.

Gillett, James B. *Six Years with the Texas Rangers, 1875 to 1881*. Austin: Von-Boeckmann Jones, 1921.

———. New Haven: Yale University Press, 1925. Edited, with an introduction by M. M. Quaife.

Gilliland, Maude T. *Horsebackers of the Brush Country: A Story of the Texas Rangers and the Mexican Liquor Smugglers*. Brownsville, Tex.: Springman-King Company, 1968.

———. *Rincon (Remote Dwelling Place): A Story of Life on a South Texas Ranch at the Turn of the Century*. Brownsville, Tex.: Springman-King Company, 1964.

———. *Wilson County Texas Rangers 1837–1977*. Brownsville, Tex.: Springman-King Company, 1977.

Gooding, Ed, and Robert Nieman. *Ed Gooding: Soldier, Texas Ranger*. Longview, Tex.: Ranger Publishing, 2001.

Goodrich, Pat. *Captain Ransom, Texas Ranger: An American Hero (1874–1918)*. Nappanee, Id.: Evangel Publishing House, 2007.

Graham, Don. *Kings of Texas: The 150-Year Saga of an American Ranching Empire*. New York: John Wiley and Sons, 2003.

Gutierrez, Jose Angel. *The Making of a Chicano Militant: Lessons from Cristal*. Madison: University of Wisconsin Press, 1998.

Hall, Gary D. *Murder & Malice: Crimes of Passion from Victoria County, Texas 1891–1913*. Austin: Nortex Press, 2006.

Harding, Glenn, and Cindy Lee. *Rails to the Rio*. Raymondville, Tex.: Privately published, 2003.

Harmon, Jim. *The Great Radio Heroes*. Garden City, N.Y.: Doubleday Company, 1967.

Harper, William T. *Eleven Days in Hell: The 1974 Carrasco Prison Siege at Huntsville, Texas*. Denton: University of North Texas Press, 2004.

Harris, Charles H. III, and Louis R. Sadler. *The Texas Rangers and the Mexican Revolution*. Albuquerque: University of New Mexico Press, 2004.

Hausenfluke, Gene. *Texas Ranger Sesquicentennial Anniversary, 1823–1973*. Fort Worth: Heritage Publications, 1973.

Haynes, Robert V. *A Night of Violence: The Houston Riot of 1917*. Baton Rouge: Louisiana State University Press, 1976.

Heard, Robert. *The Miracle of the Killer Bees: 12 Senators Who Changed Texas Politics*. Austin: Honey Hill Publishing Company, 1981.

Helmer, William, with Rick Mattix. *Public Enemies: America's Criminal Past, 1919–1940*. New York: Checkmark Books, Facts on File, 1998.

Hendrickson, Kenneth E., Jr. *Chief Executives of Texas: From Stephen F. Austin to John B. Connally, Jr.* College Station: Texas A&M University Press, 1995.

Henry, Will. *The Texas Rangers*. New York: Random House, 1957.

Holmesly, Sterlin. *HemisFair '68 and the Transformation of San Antonio*. San Antonio: Maverick Publishing Company, 2003.

Horton, David M., and Ryan Kellus Turner. *Lone Star Justice: A Comprehensive Overview of the Texas Criminal, Justice System*. Austin: Eakin Press, 1999.

House, Aline. *The Carrasco Tragedy: Eleven Days of Terror in the Huntsville Prison*. Waco, Tex.: Texian Press, 1976.

House, Boyce. *Roaring Ranger: The World's Biggest Boom*. San Antonio: Naylor Company, 1951.

Hutson, Alice. *From Chalk to Bronze: A Biography of Waldine Tauch*. Austin: Shoal Creek Publishers, 1978.

Ingmire, Frances Terry. *Texas Ranger Service Records, 1847–1900*. St. Louis: privately printed, 1982.

Jackson, H. Joaquin, and David Marion Wilkinson. *One Ranger: A Memoir*. Austin: University of Texas Press, 2005.

——— with James L. Haley. *One Ranger Returns*. Austin: University of Texas Press, 2008.

James, Daryl, editor. *No Apologies: Texas Radicals Celebrate the '60s*. Austin: Eakin Press, 1992.

Jenkins, John H. and Gordon H. Frost, *I'm Frank Hamer: The Life of a Texas Peace Officer*. Austin: Pemberton Press, 1968.

Johnson, Benjamin Heber. *Revolution in Texas: How a Forgotten Rebellion and Its Bloody Suppression Turned Mexicans into Texans*. New Haven: Yale University Press, 2003.

Johnson, David R. *American Law Enforcement: A History*. Wheeling, Ill.: Forum Press, 1981.

Johnson, Frank W. *A History of Texas and Texans*. Ed. Eugene C. Barker with the assistance of Ernest William Winkler. Chicago and New York: American Historical Society, 1916.

Jones, Nancy Baker, and Ruthe Winegarten. *Capitol Women: Texas Female Legislators, 1923–1999*. Austin: University of Texas Press, 2000.

Justice, Glenn. *Little Known History of the Texas Big Bend: Documented Chronicles from Cabeza De Vaca to the Era of Pancho Villa*. Odessa: Rimrock Press, 2001.

———. *Revolution on the Rio Grande: Mexican Raids and Army Pursuits, 1916–1917*. El Paso: Texas Western Press, 1992.

Keating, Bern. *An Illustrated History of the Texas Rangers*. New York: Rand McNally, 1975.

Keil, Robert. *Bosque Bonito: Violent Times Along the Borderland During the Mexican Revolution!* edited by Elizabeth McBride. Alpine, Tex.: Sul Ross State University, 2002.

Kesselus, Ken. *Alvin Wirtz: The Senator, LBJ, and LCRA*. Austin: Eakin Press, 2001.

Kilgore, D. E. *A Ranger Legacy: 150 Years of Service to Texas*. Austin: Madrona Press, 1973.

Knight, James R., with Jonathan Davis. *Bonnie and Clyde: A Twenty-first Century Update*. Austin: Eakin Press, 2003.

Knowles, Thomas W. *They Rode for the Lone Star: The Saga of the Texas Rangers.* Dallas: Taylor Publishing Company, 1999.

Krenek, Harry. *The Power Vested.* Austin: Presidial Press, 1980.

Ku Klux Klan Secrets Exposed. Chicago: Ezra A. Cook, Publisher, 1922.

Lading, Robyn Duff. *Desegregating Texas Schools: Eisenhower, Shivers and the Crisis at Mansfield High.* Austin: University of Texas Press, 1996.

Lauterbach, Stewart, and Christina Stopka, compilers. *Ranger Songs and Verse: A Collection for the 175th Anniversary Gala of the Texas Rangers.* Waco: Texas Ranger Hall of Fame and Museum, 1998.

Leiker, James N. *Racial Borders: Black Soldiers Along the Rio Grande.* College Station: Texas A&M University Press, 2002.

Lewis, Tracy Hammond. *Along the Rio Grande.* New York: Lewis Publishing Company, 1916.

Linsley, Judith Walker, and Ellen Walker Rienstra. *Beaumont: A Chronicle of Promise.* Woodland Hills, Cal.: Windsor Publications, 1982.

Luttrell, Ida Harbison. *The Road to Randado: The Life Story of Former Texas Ranger Pell Harbison and His Pioneer Ancestors.* Spring, Tex.: Panther Creek Press, 2004.

Lynch, Dudley. *The Duke of Duval: The Life & Times of George B. Parr.* Waco, Tex.: Texian Press, 1976.

McConal, Patrick M. *Over the Wall: The Men Behind the 1934 Death House Escape.* Austin: Eakin Press, 2000.

McCoy, Dorothy Abbott. *It's a Good Thing for Texas.* McAllen, Tex.: Steve Alden Publishing Company, 1981.

McGiffin, Lee. *Ten Tall Texans: Tales of the Texas Rangers.* New York: Lee and Shepard Company, 1956.

McKinney, Wilson. *Fred Carrasco: The Heroin Merchant.* Austin: Heidelberg Publishers, 1975.

McMahan, Dick. *The Bucher Murder was the Turning Point for Clyde Barrow, Bonnie Parker and Raymond Hamilton.* Dallas: Southwestern Historical Publications, 2007.

Maguire, Jack. *Katy's Baby.* Austin: Nortex Press, 1991.

Maltby, Jeff. *Captain Jeff, or Frontier Life in Texas with the Texas Rangers.* Colorado, Tex.: Whipkey Printing Company, 1906. Facsimile reprint. Waco, Tex.: Texian Press, 1967.

Malsch, Brownson. *Captain M.T. Lone Wolf Gonzaullas: The Only Texas Ranger Captain of Spanish Descent.* Austin: Shoal Creek Publishers, 1980.

Martin, Jack. *Border Boss: Captain John R. Hughes, Texas Ranger.* San Antonio: Naylor Company, 1990 reprint of 1942 edition.

Martinez, Ramiro. *They Call Me Ranger Ray: From the UT Tower Sniper to Corruption in South Texas.* Austin: Rio Bravo Publishing, 2005.

Mason, Herbert Malloy, Jr. *The Texas Rangers.* New York: Meredith Press, 1967.

Meed, Douglas V. *Texas Ranger Johnny Klevenhagen*. Plano: Republic of Texas Press, 2000.

Mills, Susie. *Legend in Bronze: The Biography of Jay Banks*. Dallas: Ussery Printing Company, 1982.

Milner, E.R. *The Life and Times of Bonnie and Clyde*. Carbondale: Southern Illinois University Press, 1996.

Moore, Richard R. *West Texas After the Discovery of Oil: A Modern Frontier*. Austin: Jenkins Publishing Company, 1971.

Morin, Jose R. Lopez. *The Legacy of Americo Paredes*. College Station: Texas A&M University Press, 2006.

Murph, Dan. *Texas Giant: The Life of Price Daniel*. Austin: Eakin Press, 2000.

Navarro, Armando. *The Cristal Experiment: A Chicano Struggle for Community Control*. Madison: University of Wisconsin Press, 1998.

Neff, Pat. *The Battles of Peace*. Fort Worth: Bunker Press, 1925.

Olien, Diana Davids, and Roger M. Olien. *Oil in Texas: The Gusher Age, 1895–1945*. Austin: University of Texas Press, 2002.

Owens, William A. *Three Friends: Bedichek, Dobie, Webb*. Garden City, N.Y.: Doubleday, 1969.

Paine, Albert Bigelow. *Captain Bill McDonald Texas Ranger: A Story of Frontier Reform*. New York: Little & Ives, 1909.

Paredes, Americo. *"With His Pistol in His Hand": A Border Ballad and Its Hero*. Austin: University of Texas Press, 1958.

Patterson. C. L. *Atascosa County, Texas—a Progressive and Diversified Agricultural and Livestock Haven*. Pleasanton, Tex.: 1938.

Perry, George Sessions. *Texas a World In Itself*. New York: Whittlesey House, 1942.

Petty, Wes. *Murder in the Southwest*. Lubbock: Chaparral Graphics Group, 1994.

Peyton, Green. *For God and Texas: The Life of P.B. Hill*. New York: Whittlesey House, 1947.

Phillips, John Neal. *Running With Bonnie and Clyde: The Ten Fast Years of Ralph Fults*. Norman: University of Oklahoma Press, 1996.

Pierce, Frank Cushman. *Texas' Last Frontier: A Brief History of the Lower Rio Grande Valley*. Menasha, Ws.: George Banta Publishing Company, 1917.

Potter, Claire Bond. *War on Crime: Bandits, G-men, and the Politics of Mass Culture*. New Brunswick, N.J.: Rutgers University Press, 1998.

Prassel, Frank Richard. *The Western Peace Officer: A Legacy of Law and Order*. Norman: University of Oklahoma Press, 1972.

Procter, Ben H. *Just One Riot: Episodes of the Texas Rangers in the 20th Century*. Austin: Eakin Press, 1991.

Puckett, Linda Jay. *Cast a Long Shadow: A Casebook of the Law Enforcement Career of Texas Ranger Captain E.J. (Jay) Banks* Dallas: Ussery Printing, 1984.

Raat, W. Dirk. *Revoltosos: Mexico's Rebels in the United States, 1903–1923*. College Station: Texas A&M University Press, 1981.

Ragsdale, Kenneth B. *Centennial '36: The Year America Discovered Texas*. College Station: Texas A&M University Press, 1987.

Rayburn, John C. and Virginia Kemp Rayburn. *Century of Conflict, 1821–1913*. Waco: Texian Press, 1966.

Reynolds, Clay, ed. *Taking Stock: A Larry McMurtry Casebook*. Dallas: Southern Methodist University Press, 1989.

Rigler, Lewis C., and Judyth Wagner Rigler. *In the Line of Duty: Reflections of a Texas Ranger Private*. Houston: Larksdale, 1984.

Rister, Carl Coke. *Oil: Titan of the Southwest*. Norman: University of Oklahoma Press, 1949.

Robertson, Brian. *Wild Horse Desert: The Heritage of South Texas*. Edinburg, Tex.: New Santander Press, 1985.

Romer, F. *Makers of History: A Story of the Development of the History of Our Country and the Part Played in It by the Colt*. Hartford, Conn.: Colt's Patent Fire Arms, 1926.

Romo, David Dorado. *Ringside Seat to a Revolution: An Underground Cultural History of El Paso and Juarez, 1893–1923*. El Paso: Cinco Puntos Press, 2005

Saldivar, Ramon. *The Borderlands of Culture: Americo Paredes and the Transnational Imaginary*. Durham, N.C.: Duke University Press, 2006.

Salomonson, Terry. *The Western Logs*. Howell, Minn.: n.p., 1998.

Samora, Julian, Joe Bernal, and Albert Pena. *Gunpowder Justice: A Reassessment of the Texas Rangers*. Notre Dame: University of Notre Dame Press, 1979.

Samponaro, Frank N., and Paul J. Vanderwood. *War Scare on the Rio Grande: Robert Runyon's Photographs of the Border Conflict, 1913–1916*. Austin: Texas State Historical Association, 1992.

Sandos, James A. *Rebellion in the Borderlands: Anarchism and the Plan of San Diego, 1904–1923*. Norman: University of Oklahoma Press, 1992.

Schreiner III, Charles, ed. *A Pictorial History of the Texas Rangers*. Mountain Home: YO Ranch, 1969.

Shelton, Glenn. *Wichita Falls: A Lady with a Past*. Wichita Falls, Tex.: Western Christian Foundation, 1978.

Shockley, John Staples. *Chicano Revolt in a Texas Town*. Notre Dame: University of Notre Dame Press, 1974.

Simmons, Lee. *Assignment Huntsville*. Austin: University of Texas Press, 1957.

Simmons, Nanine. *Booming Mexia in the Roaring '20s: 21 Pages of Living Legend and Fact!* Waco, Tex.: Waco Times Herald, 1955.

Simpson, James P., and Geoffrey Leavenworth. *Flak Bait*. Waco, Tex.: Eakin Press, 2007.

Sizer, Mona D. *Texas Justice Bought and Paid For*. Plano: Republic of Texas Press, 2001.

Spellman, Paul N. *Captain J.A. Brooks, Texas Ranger*. Denton: University of North Texas Press, 2007.

———. *Captain John H. Rogers, Texas Ranger.* Denton: University of North Texas Press, 2003.

———. *Spindletop Boom Days.* College Station: Texas A&M Press, 2001.

Spinks, S. E. *Law on the Last Frontier: Texas Ranger Arthur Hill.* Lubbock: Texas Tech University Press, 2007.

Steen, Ralph W. *Twentieth Century Texas: An Economic and Social History.* Austin: Steck Company, 1941.

Stembridge, Terry, and Caleb Pirtle III. *Kilgore: Echoes From Forgotten Streets.* Dallas: Dockery House Publishing, 2003.

Stephens, Hugh W. *The Texas City Disaster, 1947.* Austin: University of Texas Press, 1997.

Stephens, Robert M. *Bullets and Buckshot.* Dallas: Privately printed, 2002.

———. *Lone Wolf: The Story of Texas Ranger Captain M.T. Gonzaullas.* Privately printed, n.d.

———. *Texas Ranger Sketches.* Privately printed, 1972.

———. *The Texas Rangers, an American Legend.* Rogers, Ark.: Daisy Manufacturing, 1973.

Sterling, Ross S. and Ed Kilman, edited and revised by Don Carleton. *Ross Sterling, Texan: A Memoir by the Founder of Humble Oil and Refining Company.* Austin: University of Texas Press, 2007.

Sterling, William Warren. *Trails and Trials of a Texas Ranger.* Norman: University of Oklahoma Press, 1969 reprint of 1959 ed.

Stout, Joseph A., Jr. *Border Conflict: Villistas, Carrancistas, and the Punitive Expedition, 1915–1920.* Fort Worth: Texas Christian University Press, 1999.

Sullivan, W. John L. *Twelve Years in the Saddle for Law and Order on the Frontiers of Texas.* Austin: Von Boeckmann-Jones, 1909.

Texas Research League. *The Texas Department of Public Safety: Its Services and Organization.* Austin: 1957.

Texas State Historical Association. *The New Handbook of Texas.* 6 vols. Austin: Texas State Historical Association, 1995.

Thomas, Lowell. *This Side of Hell: Dan Edwards, Adventurer.* New York: Doubleday, Doran, 1932.

Thompson, Cecilia. *History of Marfa and Presidio County, Texas, 1535–1946.* 2 vols. Austin: Nortex Press, 1985.

Toepperwein, Herman. *Texas Rangers.* San Antonio: Hall of Texas History, 1968.

Tyler, Ron C. *The Big Bend: A History of the Last Frontier.* College Station: Texas A&M Press, 1996.

Underwood, Sid. *Depression Desperado: The Chronicle of Raymond Hamilton.* Austin: Eakin Press, 1995.

Utley, Robert M. *Lone Star Lawmen: The Second Century of the Texas Rangers.* New York: Oxford University Press, 2007.

Warnock, Roland A. as told to Kirby F. Warnock. *A Texas Cowboy*. Dallas: Trans Pecos Productions, 1992.

Weaver, John D. *The Brownsville Raid*. College Station: Texas A&M University Press, 1992, reprint of 1970 edition.

Webb, Atticus. *Crime: Our National Shame*. Binghamton, N.Y.: Vail-Ballou Press, 1924.

Webb, Walter Prescott. *The Texas Rangers: A Century of Frontier Defense*. Boston: Haughton Mifflin, 1935.

Welborn, C. A. *History of the Red River Controversy: The Western Boundary of the Louisiana Purchase*. Quanah, Tex.: Nortex Offset Publications, 1973.

Wilkins, Frederick. *The Law Comes to Texas: The Texas Rangers 1870–1901*. Austin: State House Press, 1999.

Willeford, Glenn. *Dirty Cop? The Rise and Fall of a Texas Sheriff: Memoir and Essays*. Alpine and Ciudad Chihuahua: Johnson's Trading Post Press, 2007.

Wolters, Jacob F. *Martial Law and Its Administration*. Austin: Gammel's Book Store, 1930.

Works Projects Administration. *Beaumont: A Guide to the City and Its Environs*. Houston: Anson Jones Press, n.d. (1940).

Zamora, Emilio, Cynthia Orozco, and Rodolfo Rocha, eds. *Mexican Americans in Texas History: Selected Essays*. Austin: Texas State Historical Association, 2000.

Articles

Angel, William D., Jr. "Controlling the Workers: The Galveston Dock Workers' Strike of 1920 and Its Impact on Labor Relations in Texas." *East Texas Historical Journal* 23, no. 2 (1985): pp. 14–27.

Ashburn, Karl. "Crime in Texas." *Southwest Review* 19, no. 4 (July 1934): pp. 363–373.

Baker, Catherine G. "The Man of the Hour." *The Junior Historian* 26, no. 1 (September 1965): pp. 13–16, 27–29.

Banks, Jimmy. "Rangers in the Sky." *Texas Parade*, September 1958, pp. 53–56.

———. "The Texas Rangers," *Saga*, September 1967, pp. 34–36, 62–67.

"The Border Sheriff Now Speaks for Himself." *Frontier Times*, May 1931, pp. 360–368.

Boyle, Robert D. "Chaos in the East Texas Oil Field." *Southwestern Historical Quarterly* (January 1966): pp. 340–352.

Carrigan, William D., and Clive Webb. "The Lynching of Persons of Mexican Origin or Descent in the United States, 1848 to 1928." *Journal of Social History* Volume 37, no. 2 (Winter 2003): pp. 411–438.

Carter, Lindsay. "The Texas Rangers: Interesting Facts About Our Greatest Body of Fighting Men." *The Texas Magazine* 3, no. 4 (February 1911).

Cartwright, Gary. "The Death of a Ranger." *Texas Monthly*, August 1978.

Circelli, Jerry. "Texas Rangers." *Western Horseman*, September 2005.

Coffey, Jim. "Will Wright: Rangers and Prohibition." *Texas Ranger Dispatch*, Summer 2006.

Colloff, Pamela. "Law of the Land." *Texas Monthly*, April 2007, pp. 114–121, 208, 210, 212, 214, 216, 218, 220, 222, 224.

Cox, Mike. "Texas Rangers: From Horses to Helicopters." *Texas Almanac 2000–2001*, (Dallas: Belo Communications, 2001), pp. 23–28.

Crockett, Norman. "Crime on the Petroleum Frontier: Borger, Texas, in the Late 1920s." *Panhandle-Plains Historical Review* 64 (1991): pp. 53–56.

Cunningham, Joe. "The Fabulous Fifty." *The Cattleman*, November 1952, pp. 29–32, 50.

Davidge, Sarah Ellen. "Texas Rangers Were Rough and Ready Fighters." *Frontier Times*, November 1935.

Davis, Roy. "Texas Rangers Today." *Western Horseman*, August 1964, pp. 48–50.

Detzer, Karl W. "Texas Rangers Still Ride the Trail." *Reader's Digest*, September 1957, pp. 139–142.

Dillow, Gordon, "The Lone Ranger: There's Only One Texas Ranger Who Isn't from Texas. And Would You Believe He's a Cop from New York?" *Philip Morris Magazine*, July–August 1985.

Draper, Robert. "The Myth of the Texas Rangers." *Texas Monthly*, February 1994.

Dunkle, Glen. "The Texas Rangers From Horseback To Automobile." *Virginia Trooper*, March 1965, pp. 13–15.

Elam, Earl H., "The Madero Revolution and the Bloody Bend." *Journal of Big Bend Studies* 13 (2001): p. 167.

"Exciting Career of Captain K. F. Cunningham." *Texas Rangers* 6, no. 2, April 1938, p. 82.

"Faces of the Month." *Texas Parade*, November 1938, p. 18.

Fidler, Paul E. "A State Police Force for Texas." *Texas Municipalities* Vol. 22 March 1935.

Fletcher, Henry T. "Violent Early Days of Big Bend Section Recalled," *Frontier Times*, May 1934, pp. 355–357.

"Former Commander of the Texas Rangers Elected President of F.T.R.A." *Former Texas Ranger Straight Talk*, Kerrville, Texas, August 2003, p. 1, 5.

"F.P.E. [Finger Print Expert] Helps Put Man in Electric Chair." *Finger Print and Identification Magazine* 11, no. 1 (July 1929): p. 31.

Friend, Llerena. "W.P. Webb's Texas Rangers." *Southwestern Historical Quarterly*. 74 (January 1971): pp. 293–323.

Gerlach, Alan. "Conditions Along the Border—1915: The Plan de San Diego." *New Mexico Historical Review* 43 (July 1968): pp. 195–212.

Glassman, Don. "The Modern Rangers: The True Story of Today's Texas Lawmen." *Texas Rangers* 34, no. 4 (June 1949).

Graybill, Andrew R. "Rural Police and the Defense of the Cattleman's Empire in Texas and Alberta, 1875–1900." *Agricultural History* 79, no. 3 (Summer 2005): pp. 253–280.

Green, Hartwell. "Texas Rangers: There's a Glorious Frontier Legend Behind Them—and a Rugged Road Ahead." *Holiday*, November 1948, pp. 114–115, 133/137.

Griffin, Jim. "Texas Rangers Magazine." Pulp Rack, http://www.pulprack.com/arch/000029.html, accessed January 14, 2003.

Haley, J. Evetts. "Texas Ranger." *The Shamrock*, Fall 1963 pp. 3–6, 13.

"History of the Department of Public Safety." *Texas DPSOA Monthly Special 50th Anniversary Issue*, August 1985.

Holder, Dennis. "One Riot, One Ranger: The Legendary Career of Texas' Toughest Ranger, Capt. Jay Banks." *Family Weekly*, June 30, 1985, pp. 11–12.

"Hudson Pension Bill, The." *Frontier Times*, May 1928, pp. 334–335.

Hunter, J. Marvin. "Texas Rangers Are Still Active." *Frontier Times*, July 1945, pp. 294–298.

"In Memory Homer Garrison, Jr." *Texas Defense Digest* 16, no. 5 (May 1968): p. 1.

Kelley, Dayton. "Ranger Hall of Fame." *FBI Bulletin*, Spring 1976, pp. 16–23.

Lawrence, Sharon Orleans. "Law and Order in the Texas Lake Country: The Texas Rangers." *Texas Lake Country*. July-December 2001, pp. 10–11.

"Let's Build a Monument to the Texas Ranger." *Frontier Times*, September 1927, pp. 34–37.

Long, Steven. "Shutdown: June 10, 1957, the Day the Wheels Stopped Turning." *In Between Magazine* (Galveston), May 1982, pp. 11–15.

Lopez-Calvo, Ignacio. "The Spanish-Language Cronica in Los Angeles: Francisco P. Ramirez and Ricardo Flores Magon." *Journal of Spanish Language Media*, (Denton: Center for Spanish Language Media, University of North Texas, 2008): pp. 125–136.

Martin, George. "Vengeance of a Phantom." *Texas Parade*, October 1953, pp. 31–32.

Martin, Jack. "Colonel Homer Garrison, Jr., Director of the Texas Department of Public Safety." *True Detective Mysteries*, August 1940, pp. 66–67, 116.

Massie, W. M. "Why We Pay for Dead Bandits." *Bunker's Monthly*, February 1928, pp. 173–180.

Means, Joyce E. "Joe Sitter Versus Chico Cano: What Really Happened." *West Texas Historical Association Year Book* 72 (1996): pp. 86–104.

Meed, Douglas V. "Daggers on the Gallows: The Revenge of Texas Ranger Captain Boss Hughes." *True West* 46 (May 1999): pp. 44–49.

Mertz, Richard J. " 'No One Can Arrest Me': The Story of Gregorio Cortez." *Journal of South Texas* 1 (1974): pp. 1–17.

Miller, Burt. "Texas Rangers: The Texas Devils." *Guns & Ammo Guide to Guns of the Gunfighters*, 1975, pp. 154–162, 214, 220.

Nicolopulous, James. "Another Fifty Years of the *Corrido:* A Reassessment." *Aztlan: A Journal of Chicano Studies* 22, no. 1 (Spring 1997), UCLA Chicano Studies Research Center.

"Now You Know: The Dieppe Raid." *Texas Ranger Dispatch*, no. 2 (Winter 2000).

Olson, James S., and Sharon Phair. "The Anatomy of a Race Riot: Beaumont, Texas, 1943." *Texana* 11, no. 1 (1973): pp. 64–72.

"Out to Get the Rangers." *Newsweek* 45 (March 21, 1955): p. 30.

Parsons, Chuck. "The Border Boss: John R. Hughes." *Texas Ranger Dispatch*, no. 10 (Summer 2003).

Pattie, James. "A. Y. Allee: The Man and the Legend." *Texas Parade*, July 1971.

Phillips, Edward Hake. "The Sherman Courthouse Riot of 1930." *East Texas Historical Journal*, Fall 1987, pp. 12–19.

"Rangers Adopt New Badge." *DPS Chaparral*, Fall 1962, pp. 16–17.

Raun, Gerald G. "The Madero Revolution." *Journal of Big Bend Studies* (Alpine: Center for Big Bend Studies, Sul Ross State University, 2006), pp. 85–120.

———. "Seventeen Days in November: The Lynching of Antonio Rodriguez and American-Mexican Relations, November 3–19, 1910." *Journal of Big Bend Studies* 7 (1995): pp. 157–179.

"Red River War." *Time*, August 3, 1931.

Redding, Stan. "Storied Rangers Modern, Mobile, but Still Retain Spirit of Old West," Houston *Chronicle*, February 4, 1962.

———. "Tall in the Saddle for 150 Years." *State Journal of Peace Officers*, May 1973.

———. "Top Gun of the Texas Rangers." *True Detective Magazine*, February 1963.

———. "What Is a Ranger?" *Houston Chronicle Texas Magazine*, February 9, 1969.

Rhinehart, Marilyn D. " 'Underground Patriots': Thurber Coal Miners and the Struggle for Individual Freedom, 1888–1903." *Southwestern Historical Quarterly* 92 (April 1989): pp. 509–542.

Ritter, Al, and Chick Davis. "Captain Monroe Fox and the Incident at Porvenir." *Oklahoma State Trooper*, Winter 1996, pp. 35–41.

Rogers, Erma. "Roosevelt in Texas." *The Junior Historian*, November 1958, p. 29.

Roth, Mitch. "Bonnie and Clyde in Texas: The End of the Texas Outlaw Tradition." *East Texas Historical Journal* 35 (1995): pp. 30–38.

Sapp, C. C. "The Fiery Double Cross in Texas." *The Debunker*, August 1929, p. 50.

Schmelke, Gino L. "The Texas Rangers: The Pride Continues." *The Thin Blue Line* 1, no. 11 (1987): pp. 4–6.

Schroeder, Eric G. "True Tales of the Texas Rangers." Newspaper Enterprise Association, December 23, 1928.

Schuster, Stephen W. "The Modernization of the Texas Rangers: 1933–1936." *West Texas Historical Association Year Book* 43 (1967): pp. 65–79.

Sherman, Jean Dale. "A Century with the Texas Rangers." *The Cattleman* 23, no. 17 (1937).

Shoemaker, Kyle W. "How Mexia Was Made a Clean City." *Owenwood Magazine*, 1 May 1922.

Silva, Lee. "Interview with a Texas Ranger: 70 Years Later—a Texas Ranger Tells It Like It Was." *Guns & Ammo Guns of the Gunfighters*, 1974.

Smithers, W. D. "The Long Rio Grande." *True West*. July–August 1963, pp. 26–28.

Steely, Jim. "Legend of the Texas Rangers." *Texas Highways*, May 1984, pp. 39–45.

Stephens, Robert. "Manuel Trazazas Gonzaullas." *Texas Ranger Dispatch Magazine*, issue 7 (Summer 2002).

Stillwell, Hart. "Farewell Peacemaker." *True West*, Winter 1953, p. 15.

"Suiting Up the Rangers." *Dupont Magazine*, November–December 1964.

[Texas Department of Public Safety Officers Association]. "In Memory . . . a Tribute to Texas Ranger Stan Guffey." *Texas DPSOA Monthly*, March 1987, pp. 37, 39, 41, 43, 45.

"Texas' Once Famous Ranger Band Found to Have Degenerated." *Frontier Times*, May 1935, p. 363.

"The Texas Ranger As He Is." *Leslie's Illustrated Weekly Newspaper*, April 16, 1914.

Texas Ranger Dispatch. 1–20 (2000-2008). www.texasranger.org

"Texas Ranger Monument." *Texas Parade*, May 1954, pp. 17–18.

"Texas Ranger Museum Planned for DPS." *Texas Lawman*, October 1966, p. 6.

"Texas Rangers." *True West* (July 2002), pp. 18–19, 21–25.

"Texas Rangers and Their Great Leaders." *Frontier Times*, August 1938, pp. 471–476.

"The Texas Rangers Brought Law and Order." *Frontier Times*, July 1935, pp. 425–428.

"Texas Rangers May Lose Even Their Name." *Frontier Times*, January 1931, pp. 157–159.

"Texas Rangers Now Wear New Badges." *Texas Public Employee*, November 1962, p. 11.

"Texas Rangers Riding Highways and Byways: Century-Old Force Is Conducting Intensified Campaign to Prevent Livestock Theft." *The Cattleman* 28, no. 6 (November 1941): p. 31.

"They're Still Catching Rustlers in Texas." *Family Weekly*, October 9, 1960.

"Tom Hickman's Shooting." *Time*, August 31, 1931.

"Trouble in the Melon Patch." *Newsweek*, 69 June 19, 1967, pp. 38–39.

Tuttle, William. "Violence in a 'Heathen' Land: The Longview Race Riot of 1919." *Phylon: Review of Race and Culture* 33 (1972): pp. 324–333.

Van Demark, Harry. "Religion and Bullets: Two Factors Which Have Figured Prominently in the Making of a Famous Texas Ranger." *Texas Monthly* 3, no. 2 (March 1929): pp. 349–351.

Virgines, George E. "Heraldry of the Texas Rangers." *Password* 37, no. 2 (Summer 1992): pp. 83–88.

Warburton, L. H. "The Plan de San Diego: Background and Selected Documents." *Journal of South Texas* 12, no. 1 (1999): pp. 125–155.

Ward, James R. "Establishing Law and Order in the Oil Fields: The 1924 Ranger Raids in Navarro County, Texas." *Texana* 8 (1970): pp. 38–46.

Webb, Walter Prescott. "Fight Against Texas Rangers: A Discussion of the Motives Involved in the Suit to Enjoin Continuance of the Force." *The State Trooper* 6 (July 1925).

———. "Lawless Town Gets Ranger Justice: Cleanup of Law Breakers is Object Lesson of Need of Strong State Force." *The State Trooper* 5 (April 1924).

———. "Lone Ranger Gets Bandits: Texas Officer Secures Surrender of Gang Which Robbed Banks and Shot Up Town." *The State Trooper* 7 (March 1926).

———. "May Increase Rangers." *The State Trooper* 8, no. 10 (July 1927): pp. 13–14.

———. "Oil Town Cleaned Up: Texas Rangers Summoned to Restore Order When Local Officials Could Not Enforce Law." *The State Trooper* 8 (December 1926).

———. "Rangers Arrest Lawmakers: Texas Representatives Taken in Custody When One Accepts $1,000 from Opponent of Measure." *The State Trooper* 8, no. 8 (April 1927): pp. 11–12.

———. "Rangers Called in to Clean Up Austin." *The State Trooper*, 5 November 1924, pp. 21–22.

———. "Rangers Reorganized: Governor of Texas Appoints Captains to Replace Men Appointed in Ferguson Regime." *The State Trooper* 8 (July 1927).

———. "Rangers Solve Mystery: Murderers of Kindly Physician Are Followed, Even Across Border, and Confession Is Secured from Them." *The State Trooper*, vol. 8, no. 2, (October 1926): pp. 9–10.

———. "Texas Ranger Case Important: Statement of Law Involved in Use of Force to Preserve State's Authority Is Comprehensive." *The State Trooper* 6 (August 1925).

———. "Texas Rangers in Eclipse: Present State Administration Has Discredited Force by Policy of Interference with Its Duties." *The State Trooper* 7 (January 1926).

———. "Texas Rangers Kept Idle." *The State Trooper* 7, no. 10 (June 1926): p. 13.

———. "Texas Rangers of Today: A Description of the Oldest Police Force in America." *The State Trooper* 5 (March 1924).

———. "Texas Rangers Quell Trouble: Outbreaks of Lawlessness Require Treatment in Firm Fashion by Lone Star State Police Force." *The State Trooper* 5 (August 1924).

———. "They Should Be Exempt." *The State Trooper* 8, no. 10 (June 1927): p. 17.

———. "Veteran Ranger Protects Border: Captain Wright Who Enforces the Law in the Big Bend Region Is a Pupil of Famous Rangers." *The State Trooper* 5 (September 1924).

Weiss, Harold J., Jr. "The Texas Rangers and Captain Bill McDonald in General—and the Condic Murder Case in Particular." *South Texas Studies* (Victoria College Press, 1998), pp. 52–70.

————. "Organized Constabularies: The Texas Rangers and the Early State Police Movement in the American Southwest." *Journal of the West.* Vol. XXXIV, No. 1, January 1995, pp. 27–33.

White, Grace Miller. "Captain John E. Elgin, Texian." *Frontier Times*, May 1944, pp. 337–340.

White, Owen P. "Texas Rangers Range No More." *New York Times Magazine*, February 1, 1925.

Wilke, L. A. "Texas Ranger: That Certain Kind of Man." *Texas Parade*, November 1973.

Wilhite, George. "175 Years of Lone Star Justice." *Cowboys&Country*, Winter 1998, pp. 56–61.

"Wrangling the Rangers." *Farm and Ranch*. April 1, 1937, pp. 18–19, 50.

Zastrow, Steve. "Texas Rangers: Tall Men, Tall Tales." *Corpus Christi Magazine*, February 1984, pp. 55–56, 107.

Theses and Dissertations

Charlton, Thomas Lee. "The Texas Department of Public Safety, 1935–1957." M.A. thesis, University of Texas, 1961.

Duncan, Virginia. "The Life of Captain Roy W. Aldrich." M.A. thesis, Sul Ross State Teachers College, 1942.

Fielder, Betty B. "Price Daniel, Texas and Segregation." M.A. thesis, Lamar University, 1997.

Leal, Ray Robert. "The 1966–67 South Texas Farm Workers Strike." Ph.D. dissertation, Indiana University, 1983.

McClung, John B. "Texas Rangers along the Rio Grande." Ph.D. dissertation, Texas Christian University, 1981.

Ribb, Richard Henry. "Jose Tomas Canales and the Texas Rangers: Myth, Identity and Power in South Texas, 1900–1920." Ph.D. dissertation, University of Texas at Austin, 2001.

Schuster, Stephen W., IV. "The Modernization of the Texas Rangers, 1930–1936." M.A. thesis, Texas Christian University, 1965.

Shirley, Emma Morrill. "The Administration of Pat M. Neff, Governor of Texas 1921–1925." M.A. thesis, University of Texas at Austin, 1938, published in *Baylor Bulletin* 41, no. 4 (December 1938).

Ward, James Randolph. "The Texas Rangers, 1919–1935: A Study in Law Enforcement." Ph.D. dissertation, Texas Christian University, 1972.

Weiss, Harold J., Jr. " 'Yours to Command': Captain William J. 'Bill' McDonald and the Panhandle Rangers of Texas." Ph.D dissertation, Indiana University, 1982.

Newspapers

Amarillo *Daily News*	Kilgore *News Herald*
Austin *American-Statesman*	La Grange *Journal*
Beaumont *Enterprise*	Laredo *Times*
Brownsville *Herald*	Los Angeles *Times*
Coleman County *Chronicle*	Lufkin *Daily News*
Corpus Christi *Caller-Times*	Marshall *News*
Dallas *Dispatch*	New York *Times*
Dallas *Morning News*	Paris *Morning News*
Dallas *Times-Herald*	Pecos *Enterprise*
Eagle Pass *News-Guide*	Rusk *Cherokeean*
El Paso *Herald-Post*	San Angelo *Standard-Times*
El Paso *Times*	San Antonio *Express*
El Paso *World News*	San Antonio *Light*
Fort Worth *Press*	San Antonio *News*
Fort Worth *Star-Telegram*	Victoria *Advocate*
Galveston *Daily News*	Waco *Times-Herald*
Gonzales *Inquirer*	Waco *Tribune-Herald*
Houston *Chronicle*	Wichita Falls *Times*
Houston *Post*	

Index